International and Comparative Mediation

Global Trends in Dispute Resolution

VOLUME 4

Series Editor:
Nadja Alexander

Gardens are tranquil spaces to think and reflect;
to plant seeds of ideas and watch them grow;
to discover different varieties
carried over from other landscapes;
to explore new paths; and
to harvest solutions.

Global Trends in Dispute Resolution offers readers a garden rich in ideas and insights into contemporary dispute resolution principles, processes, and practices. The series leads the way in first-class debate and analysis of dispute resolution trends across our rapidly globalizing world. More particularly, it analyzes dispute resolution developments in various geographical regions around the world and in relation to diverse transnational practice areas. These practice areas include not only well-established legal categories such as intellectual property, construction, and resources law, but also emerging dispute resolution developments ranging from dispute systems design to cross-border mediation in private and public law.

With a particular focus on new initiatives and ADR practices, the *Global Trends in Dispute Resolution* series aims to provide practitioners, scholars, policy-makers, and 'pracademics' (that elusive yet rapidly emerging category of practical academics and academically-oriented practitioners – you know who you are) with the resources both to cultivate the dispute resolution gardens of the world and to explore new paths within and beyond them.

KLUWER LAW INTERNATIONAL

International and Comparative Mediation

Legal Perspectives

By
Nadja Alexander

Wolters Kluwer
Law & Business

AUSTIN BOSTON CHICAGO NEW YORK THE NETHERLANDS

ISBN 9789041132246

Published by:
Kluwer Law International
P.O. Box 316
2400 AH Alphen aan den Rijn
The Netherlands

Sold and distributed in North, Central and South America by:
Aspen Publishers, Inc.
7201 McKinney Circle
Frederick, MD 21704
United States of America

Sold and distributed in all other countries by:
Turpin Distribution Services Ltd
Stratton Business Park
Pegasus Drive
Biggleswade
Bedfordshire SG18 8TQ
United Kingdom

Printed in the United Kingdom on acid-free paper

The cover for this book was prepared with the assistance of Matt Raimondo.

To the girl from Rathdowne St

– Lynette Nixon –

Table of Contents

List of Tables and Diagrams

Preface

This book was originally conceived as a general treatise on the principles and practice of cross-border mediation with one chapter to be devoted to legal issues. However as I started to write, I soon discovered a paucity of literature on the legal issues relevant to mediation at the international and comparative level. And so the single chapter grew into a book of its own.

During the unfolding of this book, there have been considerable developments in the international and comparative mediation field. The adoption of cross-border legal instruments on mediation such as the European Union Directive on Certain Aspects of Mediation in Civil and Commercial Matters (2008) and the UNCITRAL Model Law on International Commercial Conciliation (2002) have generated a spate of regulatory activity in the field, providing invaluable raw material for the book. Many scholars have made contributions to the literature since I began writing and the book has benefited from their collective wisdom. There have also been important developments in international mediation practice. Mediation usage is on the rise both as an independent process and one incorporated into multi-tiered dispute resolution procedures. Dispute resolution organisations are increasingly operating across borders and offer international mediation services and precedents in the form of mediation clauses, agreements, codes of conduct and rules. In relation to quality assurance, the International Mediation Institute has made significant inroads in relation to the establishment of international standards for mediator accreditation and mediation practice. Finally mediation has become an integral component of many international law reform projects designed to assist transitional democracies and fragile states develop the know-how and systems to manage their disputes more effectively and thereby contribute towards economic and political stability.

Given the breathtaking pace of mediation developments around the world, this book has focused its attention on three cross-border legal instruments and six national jurisdictions – three countries from the common law tradition (Australian, England and the United States) and three from the civil law tradition (Austria, France and Germany). However examples from other countries are also found throughout the book.

The 'internationality' of this book goes beyond its subject-matter. The following pages have been written in four continents – I did not make it to Antarctica – over a number of years, in trains, cafes, libraries, airports, offices, hair dressing salons, restaurants, living rooms, mediation rooms, waiting rooms and hospitals. Thanks go to many people from all around the world who offered the time they had and without whom this book would not have been possible.

For research assistance with various parts of the book, I am grateful to Mizzi Walker (Germany), Caitlin Goss (England/Australia), Vasudha Sathanapally (Australia), Ninja Antonia Farle (Germany), Patricia Metzlar (Australia), Lindsey Santerre (Canada), Sebastian Himstedt (Germany) and Josh Underhill (Australia). Austrian commentator, Gernot Koren, provided invaluable assistance on the Austrian law in the early chapters of the book. Kathrin Wolf (Germany/Australia) sustained an unflagging motivation and commitment in relation to the civil law research and to ensuring that sufficient attention was devoted to Austria and Germany comparable to their common law cousins. Thanks go to the versatile Alex Ivett (Australia) who has been a great researcher, proof-reader and indexer. I keep reminding myself that writing is rewriting, and here my deep appreciation goes to Tammy White (Australia) who has continued to patiently update the manuscript and format the entire book. Thank you to my lovely friend, and fellow author, Libbie Escolme-Schmidt (Australia/England) for knowing that champagne solves all the problems of the world, albeit temporarily.

At Kluwer Law International, Eleanor Taylor (England) and Vincent Verschoor (Netherlands) have shepherded the development of this book as part of the series *Global Trends in Dispute Resolution* and I am grateful for their commitment to publishing quality scholarship.

A number of people have read and provided valuable feedback on the manuscript. Professor Lars Kirchoff of the Europa-Universitat Viadrina in Germany, Professor George Fox of Murdoch University in Australia and Deborah MacFarlane of Victoria University in Australia have cast their expert eyes over earlier drafts and I have incorporated their wisdom in the final version. I am particularly indebted to Professor Laurence Boulle of the University of the Witwatersrand in South Africa for his thoughtful and intelligent comments on the manuscript, his editorial talent and for reminding me that perfection is the enemy of the good.

Finally to my wonderful global family – Jules, JJ, Mushi, Mon, Saskia, Frog and Ray – for not complaining if I was not always 'present', for supporting me in a myriad of ways and for remembering to periodically enquire about the progress of the book.

Every effort has been made to incorporate the most up to date statements of law from around the world. However mediation law is driving in the fast lane and accelerating. I would appreciate hearing from readers who notice any inaccuracies in this regard.

International and Comparative Mediation – Legal Perspectives is the fourth volume in the *Global Trends in Dispute Resolution* book series. It can be cited as GTDR4.

Nadja Alexander Johannesburg, October 2009

List of Abbreviations*

AAA	American Arbitration Association
ABA	American Bar Association
ACDC	Australian Commercial Disputes Centre
ADNDRC	Asian Domain Name Dispute Resolution Centre
ADR	Alternative Dispute Resolution
AIJA	Australasian Institute of Judicial Administration
ALI	American Law Institute
BGB	Bürgerliches Gesetzbuch (German Civil Code)
BGH	Bundesgerichtshof (German Federal Court)
BRAO	Bundesrechtsanwaltsordnung (German National Lawyers' Rules)
Brussels I Regulation	Council Regulation (EC) No 44/2001 of 22 December 2000 on jurisdiction and the recognition and enforcement of judgments in civil and commercial matters
C pr civ	Code de procédure civile (French Civil Procedure Code)
CCBE	Council of the Bars and Law Societies of the European Union
CCR	Center for Conflict Resolution (United States)
CEDR	Centre for Effective Dispute Resolution (England)
CIDRA	Chicago International Dispute Resolution Association (United States)
CISG	United Nations Convention on Contracts for the International Sale of Goods (1980) also referred to as the UN Convention on the International Sale of Goods
CLOUT	Case Law on UNCITRAL Texts
CMAP	Centre de Médiation et d'Arbitrage de Paris
CMC	Civil Mediation Council (England)

* The abbreviations in this list appear in the book more than once.

Cour d'appel de Versailles	Versailles Court of Appeal
Cour d'appel de Paris	Paris Court of Appeal
CPR	International Institute for Conflict Prevention and Resolution
CPR	Civil Procedure Rules (1998) (England)
CRCICA	Cairo Regional Center for International Commercial Arbitration
Draft Guide to Enactment	Draft Guide to Enactment and Use of the UNCITRAL Model Law on International Commercial Conciliation (2002)
ECC-Net	European Consumers Network
ECJ	European Court of Justice
EGBGB	Einführungsgesetz zum Bürgerlichen Gesetzbuch (Introductory Law to the German Civil Code)
EGZPO	Gesetz betreffend die Einführung der Zivilprozessordnung (Introductory Law to the German Code of Civil Procedure)
The European Directive on Mediation	The European Union Directive on Certain Aspects of Mediation in Civil and Commercial Matters (2008)
FAA	Federal Arbitration Act (1925) (United States)
FIAS	Foreign Investment Advisory Service
FRCP	Federal Rules of Civil Procedure (1938) (United States)
GG	Grundgesetz (German Constitution)
Guide to Enactment	Guide to Enactment and Use of the UNCITRAL Model Law on International Commercial Conciliation (2002)
Hague Child Abduction Convention	The Hague Convention of 25 October 1980 on the Civil Aspects of International Child Abduction
Hague Child Protection Convention	The Hague Convention of 19 October 1996 on Jurisdiction, Applicable Law, Recognition, Enforcement and Co-operation in respect of Parental Responsibility and Measures for the Protection of Children

Hague Adult Protection Convention	The Hague Convention of 13 January 2000 on the International Protection of Adults
Hague Choice of Court Convention	The Hague Convention of 30 June 2005 on Choice of Court Agreements
HKIAC	Hong Kong International Arbitration Centre
HREOC	Human Rights and Equal Opportunity Commission (Australia)
IAMA	Institute of Arbitrators and Mediators (Australia)
ICANN	Internet Corporation for Assigned Names and Numbers
ICC	International Chamber of Commerce (Paris)
ICDR	International Centre for Dispute Resolution (the United States)
IMI	International Mediation Institute (The Hague)
INTA	International Trademark Association (New York)
JDR	Judicial Dispute Resolution
LCIA	London Court of International Arbitration
LEADR	Association of Dispute Resolvers (Australia)
MAMIF	Mission d'aide à la médiation internationale pour les familles
MEDAL	International Mediation Services Alliance
MFBE	Médiation familiale binationale en Europe (France)
MLICA	UNCITRAL Model Law on International Commercial Arbitration (1985), also referred to as the UNCITRAL Model Law on Arbitration
MLICC	UNCITRAL Model Law on International Commercial Conciliation (2002), also referred to as the UNCITRAL Model Law on Conciliation
MDR	Multi-tiered Dispute Resolution
NADRAC	National Alternative Dispute Resolution Advisory Council (Australia)
NAF	National Arbitration Forum (United States)
NAFTA	North American Free Trade Agreement
New York Convention	New York Convention on the Recognition and Enforcement of Foreign Arbitral Awards 1958

NCCUSL	National Conference of Commissioners for Uniform State Laws (United States)
NMI	Netherlands Mediation Institute
ODR Services	Online Dispute Resolution Services
OGH	Oberster Gerichtshof (Austrian Supreme Court)
OLG	Oberlandesgericht Rostock (Superior Regional Court of Rostock, Germany)
OECD	Organisation for Economic Co-operation and Development
PCA	Permanent Court of Arbitration
RMAB	Recognised Mediator Accreditation Body (Australia)
Rome I	Commission Regulation (EC) N° 593/2008 of 17 June 2008 on the Law Applicable to Contractual Obligations (Rome I)
Rome II	Commission Regulation (EC) N° 864/2007 of 11 July 2007 on the Law Applicable to Non-Contractual Obligations (Rome II) OJ L199, July 2007
SEAM	Senior executive appraisal mediation
StPO	Strafprozessordnung (Austrian Criminal Procedure Code)
StPO	Strafprozessordnung (German Criminal Procedure Code)
UAR	UNCITRAL Arbitration Rules (1976)
UCR	UNCITRAL Conciliation Rules (1980)
UMA	Uniform Mediation Act (2001) (United States)
UNCITRAL	United Nations Commission on International Trade Law
UNCTAD	United Nations Conference on Trade and Development
UNIDROIT	International Institute for the Unification of Private Law
VCAT	Victorian Civil and Administrative Tribunal
WIPO	World Intellectual Property Organisation
WTO	World Trade Organisation
ZivMediatG	Zivilrechts-Mediations-Gesetz 2001 (Austrian Law on Mediation in Civil Cases)

ZivMediat-AV	Zivilrechts-Mediations-Ausbildungsverordnung 2004 (Austrian Mediation Training Regulations)
ZPO	Zivilprozessordnung (German Code of Civil Procedure)
ZPO-E	Zivilprozessordnung ZPO-Entwurf (Draft Law on Civil Procedure) (Switzerland)

About the Author

Nadja Alexander[*] is Professor of Law at City University Hong Kong, Adjunct Professor of Law at Murdoch University in Australia, and Honorary Research Fellow at University of the Witwatersrand in South Africa. She has extensive experience as a mediation practitioner, trainer, author and consultant in Australia, Europe, the United States and the Asia/Pacific region. Her books are published internationally and her work has appeared in the English, German and Russian languages.

Professor Alexander is a multi award winning teacher (1994, 1995, 1996 *Queensland* and 1997 *Australia*) and has been named one of Australia's top five law academics by Business Woman Magazine.

Her mediation practice extends to commercial, organisational and intercultural disputes and a range of legal-political issues. Professor Alexander is engaged in the design of mediation policy and legislation in various countries and is a member of the Standards Commission of the International Mediation Institute, the National Alternative Dispute Resolution Advisory Council in Australia (NADRAC), the ADR Committee of the Law Council of Australia and the Expert Advisory Committee on Mediation to the German Federal Government. She is a special consultant on international and comparative mediation to the Dispute Resolution Centre at Bond University Australia. Her conflict resolution work with communities in post-conflict regions continues to be the most challenging and inspiring part of her job. She can be contacted at nadjaalexander@mac.com.

[*] BA, LLB (*Hons*) *Qld*, Dip Internat Studies *Vienna*, LLM (*summa cum laude*), Dr jur (*summa cum laude*) *Tübingen*.

Chapter 1
International and Comparative Mediation: Definitions and Developments

1. Overview

Mediation is one of the fastest growing forms of dispute resolution in the world. The implementation of mediation systems and practices throughout the world demonstrates the attractiveness of the process to different cultural traditions and legal jurisdictions. Mediation is an integral part of many court programs in developed countries around the world. It also forms a central part of judicial reform projects in developing countries and transitional democracies. It is the primary form of dispute resolution in countless private and public industry sectors and has contributed to the expansion of community services worldwide.

At first glance the benefits of mediation over determinative dispute resolution mechanisms such as arbitration and litigation are easy to identify. Mediation is said to offer better time and cost efficiencies than determinative processes. It is an informal and flexible process, which can be tailored to accommodate the cultural, structural and commercial differences that may emerge in international dispute resolution. Privacy and confidentiality are more assured than they are in most litigation procedures. Mediators are trained to take a client-centred approach to dispute resolution, which focuses on interests and relationships and encourages party autonomy. However mediation is not without its risks and limitations – especially in international settings.

The main shortcomings of mediation in the international domain relate to its lack of finality and its uncertainty in relation to enforceability issues. While there are international legal frameworks for arbitration practice incorporating foreign recognition and enforceability of arbitral awards, they do not exist in relation to mediation. The rapid growth of international mediation practice has not been matched by appropriate international regulation, although some efforts are being made in this regard.

The risks and opportunities associated with international mediation point to its primary paradox – the ubiquitous tension between diversity and consistency.[1] On one hand, there is a desire to experiment and develop mediation as a flexible process able to accommodate the relationship needs of all stakeholders in a world in which geo-political borders have decreasing

1 An analysis of the diversity–consistency tension is found in NADRAC (National Alternative Dispute Resolution Advisory Council), *A Framework for Standards* (Canberra: Attorney-General's Department 2001) chapter 2 and recommendation 1 at 71.

importance. On the other hand, there is a push to provide users of mediation with consistency, predictability and quality in procedures and outcomes.

2. Exploring Mediation through Selected Jurisdictions and Legal Instruments

The following chapters describe and analyse how the diversity–consistency tension is being managed in relation to mediation of disputes both within and across national boundaries. While the book draws on examples from around the world, it bases its examination of mediation law and practice primarily on three common law jurisdictions, the United States, Australia and England[2] and three civil law jurisdictions, Austria, Germany and France. These jurisdictions have been selected as a basis for comparing mediation in two legal traditions, civil law and common law, with their different mediation experiences.

Australia and the United States represent two of the leading mediation jurisdictions and have generated a significant amount of mediation-related case law. These court decisions are of particular interest as they form an integral part of the law of mediation in these countries. England is a major European jurisdiction of the common law tradition which has been slower to embrace mediation than its common law cousins, Australia and the United States. Although a common law country, its mediation experience is intermingled with that of the civil law member states of the European Union.

In civil law Europe there has been an expansion of legislation and legal literature dealing with mediation but few reported cases. This is in part due to the absence of a strong doctrine of precedent in civil law jurisprudence and it also reflects the limited extent of mediation practice in those jurisdictions. In France, for example, the number of disputes going to mediation in civil matters represents less than two per cent of the courts' overall caseload.[3]

Austria, France and Germany have been selected for specific focus in this book for the following reasons. Austria was the first country in the world to adopt a relatively comprehensive mediation statute and valuable insights can be gained from examining the implications of this law for mediation practice. Germany and France are two major civil law jurisdictions with their own legal cultures and they are dealing with the implementation requirements of the European Directive on Mediation in different ways.[4] The Directive requires

2 English law applies in England and Wales, therefore technically the jurisdiction referred to encompasses both entities.

3 J-P Bonafé-Schmitt (translation by D Macfarlane) 'Global Trends in Mediation: Training and Accreditation in France' (2009) 11 *ADR Bulletin* 47.

4 Directive 2008/52/EC on Certain Aspects of Mediation in Civil and Commercial Matters, proposal as adopted by the European Parliament and the Council of the

member states of the European Union to regulate aspects of mediation and is set to have a major influence on the mediation landscape in Europe.

In addition to the Directive this book will examine two other cross-border legal instruments, namely the United Nations Commission on International Trade Law (UNCITRAL) Model Law on International Commercial Conciliation (2002) (MLICC) and the Uniform Mediation Act (2001) (UMA) in the United States. These three legal instruments will be introduced in terms of their relevance and purpose in the next chapter which deals with law and mediation.

This book is not intended to provide an exhaustive worldwide account of developments in international and comparative mediation regulation. Rather it provides an insight into emerging international trends and the diversity of mediation regulation applicable to international disputes with reference predominantly, but not exclusively, to the selected jurisdictions and cross-border legal instruments.

Before a legal analysis can be commenced, an introduction of the subject matter is required. Chapter 1 offers an introduction to the main themes of the book and defines important terms. It distinguishes mediation from other dispute resolution processes and traces the development of international mediation from historical and institutional perspectives.

3. TRAVEL TROUBLES AND OTHER STORIES

It can be difficult to understand disputes on a purely theoretical basis. For this reason a number of hypothetical situations are given below to provide concrete examples of the types of problems that may arise. References to international dispute resolution frequently conjure up images of sophisticated business professionals, multinational corporations, complex structural relationships, enormous amounts of money and glamorous locations such as London, Paris and New York. The *Travel Troubles* case lives up to the image. It is a complex international dispute involving several multinational corporate parties and large amounts of money.

Felixtours Australia Pty Ltd (Felixtours) is a leading supplier of wholesale Australian holiday packages. It is one of 12 subsidiaries of My Way Worldwide Inc. (My Way), a Washington-based multinational enterprise. The

European Union on 21 May 2008, L 136/3, 24.05.2008. For a comparison of the French Code de procédure civile (Civil Procedure Code) and the German Bürgerliches Gesetzbuch (German Civil Code) see S Grundman and M Schauer (eds), *The Architecture of European Codes and Contract Law* (Alphen aan den Rijn: Kluwer Law International 2006) at 712. For a comparison of the French and German Legal systems, see P Cruz, *Comparative Law in a Changing World* (3rd ed, New York: Routledge-Cavendish 2007) chapter 2.

global financial market collapse has profoundly affected the market for overseas tourism. This has led to a very difficult year for Felixtours.

Customers have cancelled flights because of financial and currency volatility. While experts predict that the decline in tourism will last no more than 18 months in Australia, the short-term fallout has been catastrophic for many industry operators including Felixtours. Felixtours had pre-purchased large volumes of hotel accommodation, charter flights and associated services. It has sought to maintain its contractual obligations to the hotels and airline charter companies but has fallen heavily into debt because of difficulties in meeting many retailers' invoices and in receiving payments from its own debtors.

Felixtours has continued to follow the international business model of My Way in terms of customer relationship management. However Felixtours feels that the My Way business model is becoming increasingly inappropriate for the Asia-Pacific Region. One particularly contentious aspect of the My Way model is that any debtors with payments outstanding for more than 45 days are automatically issued with a letter of demand enclosing draft court proceedings to recover monies outstanding to the My Way Group.

Felixtours has temporarily secured a large overdraft with an Australian bank but is looking to My Way for financial support in order to continue operating. If financial support is not forthcoming, Felixtours will be forced to cease further payments to its suppliers, then to commence action against its retailers for breach of their contractual obligations.

Felixtours is concerned that if it issues legal proceedings retailers will be reluctant to continue doing business with My Way altogether. This would cause immeasurable damage to business relationships, which have been stable and profitable during the previous 20 years. The Australian company is also concerned about taking legal proceedings against the foreign retailers, as the contracts establishing their business relationships are partly oral, partly written and in recent years supplemented by emails. Preliminary advice from Felixtours' lawyers suggests that litigation could be protracted and expensive and that the enforcement of court judgments in countries such as Denmark, Saudi Arabia and even certain provinces and states of Canada and the United States may not be possible.

While many disputes reflect the level of complexity and sophistication of the *Travel Troubles* case, it would be misleading to treat them as representative of the types of cases seeking international dispute resolution services. The following stories represent an emerging and significant new wave of global disputants. The stories illustrate different types of disputes that cross national borders and they, along with high end commercial cases, will be used to illustrate various points made in this chapter.

Logos in Cyberspace: Simon is a musician and in his spare time designs logos for independent local music bands. He works from a room in his home in a small town in Australia. Recently his designs have caught the attention of a young up-and-coming Slovenian band, *The Gothic Bimbos*. In an email to Simon *The Gothic Bimbos* explain that they are impressed with his work and want to engage Simon to design a logo for them. Excited at the prospect of working with a European band, Simon quickly agrees in a return email. He begins work and within a fortnight of late nights, multiple drafts and frequent cyber-chatting with *the Gothic Bimbos* he completes the design. *The Gothic Bimbos* decide they do not like the design and will not pay for the work. Simon has never engaged the services of a lawyer in his life and has never seen the inside of a courthouse. Yet he has now encountered his first international commercial dispute.

Global Rice: Artaban is a paramount chief from Tikopia in the Solomon Islands. He lives in a village with no running water, a two-way radio, which his village shares with a number of other villages and a generator that provides electricity to the community hall and church. Several years ago his provincial government representative approached him about a Malaysian company wanting to set up a rice farm in an area that includes the land to which Artaban's tribe holds communal title. According to the government representative, this venture promised significant economic benefits to the region and specifically to the tribe. Artaban signed the agreement on behalf of his tribe. Unfortunately the rice farm did not bring the expected benefits and profits to the tribe have not been near what was promised. Furthermore unemployment has increased in the area, as has infighting among members of the tribe with land grabs being made by certain individuals. More land has been cleared than was needed for rice farming and some of the farmed land is no longer in use for rice production. However no efforts have been made to restore any of this land to a pre-contractual state according to Artaban's understanding of the terms of the agreement. Artaban has been advised to seek compensation from the Malaysian investor for breach of contract and also for misleading and deceptive conduct in relation to statements about expected profits. Artaban does not really understand what this means, yet he finds himself engaged in his first international dispute involving issues of investment, business, the environment and land and resources law, not to mention public policy.

Simon and Artaban do not consider themselves to be international dealmakers. Yet they are part of a growing number of people, working from suburban homes to remote Pacific villages, who find themselves involved in complex international legal transactions. The increasing accessibility of the internet and the corresponding growth of small businesses engaging in cross-border transactions has contributed to a significantly higher volume of international transactions and dramatically changed the nature of contemporary business. Political and legal changes in some parts of the world have provided traditional peoples with a degree of self-determination which, in turn, has given them a voice in making decisions about their future, in particular in relation to how the resources attached to their land and seabed areas are used and by whom.

The *Global Rice* scenario shows how difficult it can be to define disputes according to one legal category. Business disputes involving elements of different areas of law such as contract, investment, company, copyright, domain name, energy, resources and construction are not uncommon.

Online memories: This story takes us to France, where Francesca has financed her law studies through performance work as an oriental dancer. Now a corporate lawyer, she decides it is time to move on from the dance hobby that had served her so well and to sell her 30 extravagant and decorative costumes. She puts them on e-bay for auction. After a rush of bids on the site, all Francesca's costumes are sold, money is transferred and the costumes are posted to the expectant purchasers. Francesca's favourite costume is purchased by a dancer from Latvia, who, upon receiving the costume, complains that it is excessively worn and damaged and is therefore not acceptable. She demands her money back. Flexible and inexpensive dispute resolution options are called for in this situation.

Global family: Consider the case of Joe and Marie, refugees from Bosnia who together with their small child, Anton, start a new life in the United States. On an extended trip back home with their son, Marie falls in love with the Chilean Ambassador to Bosnia. She leaves her husband and she and Anton move in with her new partner, the Ambassador, who is about to begin his next term of office in Germany. Joe is beside himself and uncertain about how to reach his son. Joe's lawyer mentions something about international child abduction and the Hague Convention.

Accordingly the image of international dispute resolution requires updating to include the new faces of global business – the Simons and the Artabans. In addition the Francescas, Joes and Maries of the world are playing an increasingly significant role in dispute resolution practice as consumer disputes and inter-family conflicts claim their space on the international stage. Sometimes the international aspect to a dispute is not foreseen. This may the case in online transactions in which the geography of buyers and sellers is not revealed and in family disputes where one party unexpectedly moves to another jurisdiction. International dispute resolution mechanisms must be sufficiently flexible to cope with the increasingly diverse attributes and needs of disputants in multi-state contexts where the borders of the global community are fluid.

While the focus of this book is on the use of mediation in international disputes, mediation also has transactional applications, sometimes known as deal mediation or project management mediation. Transactional mediation is used in negotiations, where the parties are negotiating a long-term commitment such as starting a business or a public–private partnership together. While the mediator is responsible for maintaining the process and assisting the parties to develop appropriate negotiating strategies, the parties themselves can concentrate on the business and other substantive aspects of the transactions, in addition to building their relationship with one another. Transactional mediators keep the parties on track and ensure that all participants feel they have had a fair hearing and all agenda items are adequately addressed.[5]

The high profile Vienna airport mediation is a useful example of multi-party transactional mediation involving private and public sector parties, transborder issues and an international mediation team. The mediation was initiated by the board of the airport operating company, Flughafen Wien AG, as a forum for discussing and negotiating its extension plans – especially the planned construction of a third runway – with the main parties affected by them.[6]

Another form of transactional mediation is partnering – a collaborative contracting process which operates as a form of conflict prevention and risk management in long-term projects.[7] The parties commit to work together in good faith throughout the life of the project. This may involve participation in communication and conflict management workshops early in the life of the project. At the first sign of potential conflict the parties typically agree to meet off-site with a mediator to discuss a strategy for dealing with the issue before it escalates.[8]

Similarly alliancing draws on transactional negotiation and mediation and dispute system design principles. It involves pooling resources and ideas and developing a working climate of trust and collaboration that pre-empts disputes and makes dispute resolution clauses redundant. Like partnering it is suitable for long-term projects: the establishment costs are high, the time investment is substantial and the effectiveness of alliance boards and integrated development teams increases with the length of the project. Alliancing has enjoyed particular success in the oil and gas industry in the United States.[9]

5 See S Peppet, 'Contract Formation in Imperfect Markets: Should we use Mediators in Deals?' (2004) 19 *Ohio State Journal of Dispute Resolution* 285 and R Buckley, 'The Applicability of Mediation Skills to the Creation of Contracts' (1992) 3 *Alternative Dispute Resolution Journal* 227.

6 H Zillessen, 'The Transformative Effect of Mediation in the Public Arena' (2004) 7 *ADR Bulletin* 82.

7 See E Carroll and K Mackie, *International Mediation – The Art of Business Diplomacy* (2nd ed, Alphen aan den Rijn and West Sussex: Kluwer Law International and Tottel Publishing 2006) at 145–148 and D Johnson 'Partnering in Government Contracts: the Ultimate in Dispute Resolution' (1990) 1 *World Arbitration and Mediation Report* 141.

8 See for example M McIlwrath and R Calabresi, '"Just Winning" is not a Business Goal: An Approach to Selling Managers on the Concept of Mediation in International Commercial Disputes' (2007) 4 *Transnational Dispute Management* 1 and K Boeckstiegel, 'Mediation/Alternative Dispute Resolution in Oil, Gas and Energy Transactions: Superior to Arbitration/Litigation from a Commercial and Management Perspective' (2004) 11 *Transnational Dispute Management* 1.

9 See N Rubins and F Deringer, 'Dispute Management in the Oil, Gas and Energy Industries' (2004) 11 *Transnational Dispute Management* 2 and H Dundas, 'Dispute

4. Defining Basic Terms

> Define your terms, you will permit me again to say, or we shall never understand one another…[10]
>
> Voltaire 1764

It is useful to establish some definitions at the start. The search for a common language is one of the major challenges in international dispute resolution. Clients and their legal advisers are required to understand the type of process into which they are entering when they agree to mediation or other dispute resolution process. Their understanding of the meaning of terms used in this context will affect their choice of process, selection of service-providers and manner of preparation. However the flexibility and adaptability of mediation – a feature which makes the process attractive to many disputants – is a contributive cause of definitional differences. Moreover in an age of globalisation, the distinctions between public and private law, between national and foreign actors and between domestic and international law have become increasingly difficult to define. As a result the use of terminology is varied and can be confusing.

4.1 (Alternative) Dispute Resolution

ADR is the internationally recognised acronym for alternative dispute resolution.[11] A commonly held view is that ADR refers to a range of dispute resolution processes that provide an alternative to litigation through the courts.[12]

Resolution in the Oil and Gas Industry: An Oilman's Perspective' (2004) 11 *Transnational Dispute Management* 3.

10 F Voltaire, *Dictionnaire Philosophique* (Geneva: Gabriel Grasset 1764).

11 Compare other versions of the acronym ADR: for example the International Chamber of Commerce (ICC) ADR Rules refer to 'amicable dispute resolution' and other commentators refer to 'appropriate dispute resolution' or 'additional dispute resolution'. On ADR terminology see G Tillet, 'Terminology in dispute resolution: A review of issues and literature' (2004) 15 *Australasian Dispute Resolution Journal* 178, NADRAC, *ADR Terminology: A Discussion Paper* (Canberra: Attorney-General's Department 2002) available at www.nadrac.gov.au and L Street, 'The Language of Dispute Resolution' (1992) 66 *Australian Law Journal* 194.

12 See D Yarn (ed), *Dictionary of Conflict Resolution* (California: Jossey-Bass 1999) at 17, H Burgess and G Burgess, *Encyclopaedia of Conflict Resolution* (Santa Barbara: ABC-CLIO 1997) at 8, E Martin, *A Dictionary of Law* (Oxford: Oxford University Press 1997) at 23, B Heussen, 'Die Organisation von Mediationsverhandlungen' in F Haft and K von Schlieffen (eds), *Handbuch Mediation* (2nd ed, München: C H Beck, 2009) 407 at 424 and T Sourdin, *Alternative Dispute Resolution* (3rd ed, Australia: Thomson Lawbook Co 2008) chapter 1. For commentary and criticism of this trend, see H Astor and C Chinkin, *Dispute Resolution in Australia* (Sydney: Butterworths

Baruch Bush challenges the ADR/litigation dichotomy as misleading for a number of reasons. First, much ADR occurs in, or in the context of, courts rather than separate from them, and a growing number of court procedures involve elements of ADR processes. It can therefore be difficult to separate the courts from ADR. Moreover, the ADR/litigation distinction masks the great variety of different ADR processes that exist, some of which – arbitration, for example – have more in common with court adjudication than with mediation. Gathering all ADR processes under one umbrella, as a contrast to court adjudication, suggests that they all share common values, which is not the case.[13]

Some writers distinguish ADR from arbitration on the basis that ADR involves consensual resolution, and arbitration results in a decision imposed upon the parties. Further, arbitration was a well recognised and widely used process in legal and commercial practice well before modern ADR developed its worldwide momentum.[14] According to this view, the emergence of ADR represented a movement away from expert-driven adjudicative and legalistic processes such as arbitration towards facilitative dispute resolution, driven by the principles of party autonomy, confidentiality and consent.

Given these inconsistencies in use of the term ADR, a number of writers prefer the umbrella term *dispute resolution* to describe the field within which they operate.[15] Dispute resolution processes include arbitration and court adjudication, as well as mediation and all other processes that aim to settle, resolve, transform, determine, manage or otherwise deal with disputes. This concept removes the dilemma of what is and what is not *alternative* by including all processes within its reach. It encourages a focus on individual processes, rather than lumping together ADR processes with markedly different characteristics.

In this book the term *dispute resolution* will be used in preference to ADR. Individual dispute resolution processes can be classified according to the dynamic of how and by whom decisions are made. The resulting categories are called determinative, advisory and facilitative dispute resolution.[16]

2002) at 76–81 and L Boulle and M Nesic, *Mediation: Principles, Process, Practice* (London: Butterworths 2001) at 30–33 and 87.

13 R Baruch Bush, 'Defining Quality in Dispute Resolution: Taxonomies and Anti-Taxonomies of Quality Arguments' (1989) 66 *Denver Law Review* 335 at 343.

14 R Charlton, *Dispute Resolution Guidebook* (Sydney: Law Book Co 2000) at 3.

15 See for example L Boulle, *Mediation: Principles, Process, Practice* (2nd ed, Sydney: Lexis Nexis 2005) chapter 1.

16 See NADRAC, *What is ADR?* (Canberra: Attorney-General's Department 2008) located at www.nadrac.gov.au. For a list of dispute resolution processes with definitions see NADRAC (2002), above note 11 at the same web site. On the use of the determinative process and final offer arbitration in international disputes, see D Plant, *We Must Talk Because We Can: Mediating International Intellectual Property Disputes* (Paris: International Chamber of Commerce 2008) at 107–108.

Determinative Processes involve an independent dispute resolution practitioner imposing a decision on the parties with respect to the outcome of their dispute. Determinative processes include judicial and tribunal adjudication, arbitration and private judging. *Advisory processes* allow the dispute resolution practitioner to make suggestions or formal recommendations regarding the merits of the case and as to an appropriate outcome for the dispute, which are not binding on the parties. All parties must accept and agree to the settlement recommendations of the dispute resolution practitioner before the outcome becomes binding upon them. Advisory processes include neutral evaluation and conciliation. *Facilitative processes* refer to consensus-based processes in which the dispute resolution practitioner facilitates a negotiation or communication between disputing parties with a view to assisting them make decisions about how to deal with their dispute. Facilitative processes typically follow a procedure, which includes identification and exploration of issues, generation of options and bargaining towards an agreement. Mediation is an example of a facilitative process.

Beyond this triadic taxonomy, parties can blend or combine aspects of facilitative, advisory and determinative processes to create a hybrid process or multi-tiered procedure that best suits their needs. Med–arb, a combination of mediation and arbitration, is a classic example of a hybrid process. The med–arb process may take a number of forms. Most often it involves mediation followed by arbitration on those issues which were not resolved by mediation. Alternatively, parties may agree to mediate certain issues in dispute and arbitrate others.

Conversely arb–med is an example of a hybrid process, which begins with a determinative element and then moves to a facilitative mode to explore the possibility of agreement between the parties. Usually an arbitral decision is made but not communicated to the parties and will only be communicated in the form of an award if the ensuing mediation does not result in agreement. However in some forms of arb–med, the arbitrator's decision will be communicated without an award being issued directly after the arbitration phase. Knowing their default position, the parties then have an opportunity to reach a resolution on terms more favourable to both of them.

Mediation windows are an increasingly common feature in arbitration proceedings where a window may be opened in the course of the proceedings to attempt to resolve the dispute through mediation. As long as the mediation window is open, the arbitration procedure is suspended.[17] Alternatively

[17] On mediation windows see K Berger, 'Integration of Mediation Elements into Arbitration: 'Hybrid' Procedures and 'Intuitive' Mediation by International Arbitrators' (2003) 19 *Arbitration International* 3, L Cao, 'Combining Conciliation and Arbitration in China: Overview and Latest Developments' (2006) *International Arbitration Law Review* at 89 et seq, I Yang, 'Med–arb in Mainland China: a bold Chinese invention or a recipe for disaster?' (2008) Session II *International*

mediation windows may open alongside the arbitration, where different representatives are available for each process. *Centre de Médiation et d'Arbitrage de Paris* (CMAP) in France has developed a specific hybrid procedure called *med-arb simultanés* according to which an arbitration process runs simultaneously with, and independently from, a mediation process. Generally the parties set a time frame for the completion of the mediation. If the mediation does not result in a mediated settlement then the arbitration will result in an award binding on the parties eight days after the mediation deadline has expired. During the parallel processes, the mediator and arbitrator are not able to communicate with each other about the case. However at the end of each day or during breaks, the parties may consult with their legal representatives in each process in relation to the progress that has been made. *Med-arb simultanés* aims to do away with the concerns associated with the same dispute resolution professional/s acting as mediator and arbitrator. At the same time it offers clients the finality of an arbitral award should the mediation not result in settlement.[18]

Another blended process is mini-trial or SEAM (senior executive appraisal mediation). This hybrid process is primarily used in disputes between organisations. It typically involves a combination of formal submissions to a panel of senior executives of the disputing organisations followed by mediation.[19]

Fact-finding methods may also be incorporated into dispute resolution processes. Fact-finding processes such as expert determination investigate, elucidate and determine facts such as the valuation of business stock. They can make useful contributions towards settlement in mediation.

Parties can agree to mix dispute resolution processes in virtually any way they wish to meet their needs. On organisation and industry levels, this approach is called dispute systems design.[20] Here the focus is on the design of procedures and systems to capture and manage grievances, complaints, disputes

Arbitration Conference Proceedings 1–3 and the 2009 Report of the CEDR (Centre for Effective Dispute Resolution) Commission on Settlement in International Arbitration at 3 and 10–17, available at www.cedr.com.

18 See the CMAP website at www.cmap.fr.

19 On SEAM, see I Hanger, 'Senior Executive Appraisal Mediation' (2000) 3 *ADR Bulletin* 45. On mini-trial see C Chatterjee and A Lefcovitch, *Alternative Dispute Resolution: A Practical Guide* (London: Routledge 2008) chapter 8, H Brown and A Marriott QC, *ADR Principles and Practice* (2nd ed, London: Sweet and Maxwell Limited 1999) 16–38, J Henry, 'ADR and Construction Disputes: The Mini-Trial' (1988) 2 *Journal of Performance of Constructed Facilities* 13, AAA Resolution Services, *Mini-Trial: Involving Senior Management* (New York: American Arbitration Association 2005) located at www.adr.org, and J Risse and C Wagner, 'Mediation im Wirtschaftsrecht' in F Haft and K von Schlieffen (eds), *Handbuch Mediation* (2nd ed, München: C H Beck, 2009) at 580–584.

20 See generally C Costantino and C Merchant, *Designing Conflict Management Systems* (San Francisco: Jossey-Bass Publishers 1996).

and other manifestations of conflict. In terms of design principles, initial interventions typically begin with flexible, interest-based processes, before moving to advisory processes and ultimately rights-based determinative processes. The rationale behind the increasingly interventionist approach is founded on the greater efficiency of moving people from facilitative processes to more formalised determinative ones, than in the opposite sequence. Generally speaking, once disputants are focussed on a highly structured rights-based process with minimal self-determination, it is difficult to move away from their fixed positions. Moreover it is widely believed that parties are more likely to participate in a process if encouraged to do so from the start as opposed to much later.

4.2 Mediation

There are many models of mediation practice. They vary according to factors such as the parties' goals for the mediation, the types of mediator intervention and the nature of the interaction between the parties. The parties' goals in mediation will vary from case to case. For some parties cost and time efficient settlement is their primary aim. For others who are contemplating a continuing commercial relationship, the need to make strategic and long-term business decisions will be a priority. In other situations where personal or professional relationships have broken down, the goal of mediation might be reconciliation among the parties. Throughout its text the UMA implicitly recognises the mediation objectives of service delivery, access to justice, party autonomy and self-determination. These objectives are served by different mediator approaches. Mediator interventions can be described as directive or elicitive or in terms of the extent to which mediators focus on the content as distinct from the process. Yet another factor differentiating mediation models relates to the nature of the interaction between the parties. In mediation parties may interact with each other as hard bargainers or as problem-solvers, or they may engage in a dialogue to explore the issues between them. Recognised mediation models include *facilitative* mediation, *wise counsel* mediation, *settlement* mediation, *expert advisory* mediation, *transformative* mediation and *tradition-based* mediation, each with differing objectives, procedures and value assumptions.[21]

In the quotation at the start of this section, Voltaire highlights the importance of definitions for understanding. He also suggests that those who define the meaning of words do more than set the meaning, they construct reality.[22] These factors apply to mediation. The various ways in which mediation has been defined by scholars, policy-makers, legislatures, courts and dispute

[21] See N Alexander, 'The Mediation Metamodel: Understanding Practice' (2008) 26 *Conflict Resolution Quarterly* 97.

[22] Voltaire (1764), above note 10.

resolution organisations has influenced its practice. Conceptual definitions of mediation draw upon the objectives and values of the process without reference to its actual practice. They can be found in the policy documents of community mediation centres. They frequently attempt to identify the underlying philosophy of mediation and set theoretical parameters, objectives and criteria for conducting the process. In many cases the detailed mediation policies of the mediation centres shape their practice. Centres such as the Mediation Centre Frankfurt–Oder in Germany, the Dispute Resolution Branch at the Departments of Justice in various Australian states and similar centres in the United States - have become known for a distinctive model of mediation practice, sometimes referred to as the facilitative model.[23] A legislative illustration of a conceptual definition of mediation can be found in Article 1(1) of the Austrian Law on Mediation in Civil Cases 2001, which refers to the principles of neutrality, voluntariness, systematic communication methods and self-determination. The definition also refers to the specialist qualifications required of mediators[24]. The National Alternative Dispute Resolution Advisory Council (NADRAC) in Australia emphasises in its definition the process skills of mediators. The definition makes clear that mediation is neither a determinative nor an advisory process, but falls short of describing the process as facilitative. The UMA definition of mediation refers to,

> a process in which a mediator facilitates communication and negotiation between parties to assist them in reaching a voluntary agreement regarding their dispute.

The Reporters' Working Notes explain that the definition has been framed to exclude determinative processes, as well as interventions such as counselling. However the definition remains broad and seems to include negotiation-based processes where the mediator plays an advisory role.[25]

Conversely there is also evidence that definitions of mediation have been influenced by practice, making them more descriptive than conceptual in nature. Early exponents of action-based mediation theory are Kressel and Pruitt,

[23] Information about the Mediationsstelle in Frankfurt–Oder in Germany can be found at www.mediationsstelle-ffo.de. Information about the Dispute Resolution Branch in Queensland is available at www.justice.qld.gov.au. In the United States see, for example, The Center for Conflict Resolution (CCR) at www.ccrchicago.org.

[24] See the Zivilrechts-Mediations-Gesetz 2001 (ZivMediatG). For an analysis of the Austrian definition of mediation see M Roth and D Gherdane, 'Mediation in Österreich – Zivilrechts-Mediations-Gesetz: Rechtlicher Rahmen und Praktische Erfahrungen' in K Hopt and F Steffek (eds), *Mediation – Rechtstatsachen, Rechtsvergleich, Regelungen* (Tübingen: Mohr Siebeck 2008) 103 at 108–112.

[25] See Reporter's Notes to the UMA in National Conference of Commissioners on Uniform State Laws, *Uniform Mediation Act with Prefatory Note and Comments* (Chicago: NCCUSL 2001). See also the discussion on conciliation below in the section entitled, 'A word on terminology'.

who used an inductive approach to develop their research on, and theories of, mediation from practice.[26] Della Noce presents the view that where mediation values are not prescribed in conceptual definitions, the way mediation is practised is a result of the worldviews and personal theories of mediators themselves. She argues that differences in mediation practice do matter and that the values that in fact underpin practice must be recognised by policy makers.[27] Descriptive definitions attempt to describe what occurs in practice and provide structures for thinking about and analysing practice.

Descriptive definitions of mediation are often found in general legislation on mediation and court-annexed mediation statutes. The MLICC offers a descriptive definition of conciliation (here the term is used interchangeably with mediation), which recognises the diversity in mediation practice and is formulated in such a way as to extend to most mediation models and even to other dispute resolution processes such as neutral evaluation.[28] It simply describes conciliation as a process whereby parties request a third person to assist them in their attempts to reach an amicable settlement of their dispute. Similarly the definitions of mediation in the European Directive on Mediation (Article 3(a) and (b)) and the French Civil Procedure Code (Article 131-1 Code de procédure civile, C pr civ) are characterised by very general wording and without reference to particular values. As with the MLICC definition, these definitions encompass a range of dispute resolution models.

A lack of specific and meaningful definitions in mediation regulation may not only reflect but also encourage diverse mediation practices ranging from interest-based and relational approaches to settlement and advisory models of mediation.[29] In some cases it may be helpful to look behind the words of the legislation to the objectives of the regulatory scheme to identify mediation values and intended approaches. However clear mediation values and principles are not always articulated in policy documents.

26 See K Kressel et al, *Mediation Research: The Process and Effectiveness of Third-Party Intervention* (San Francisco: Jossey-Bass Publishers 1989) and L Sinclair and W Stuart, 'Reciprocal-Influence Mediation Model: A Guide for Practice and Research' (2007) 25 *Conflict Resolution Quarterly* 185 at 186–188. The latter publication summarises the work of other theorists who have drawn on practice.

27 D Della Noce, R Baruch Bush and J Folger, 'Clarifying the theoretical Underpinnings of Mediation: Implications for Policy and Practice' (2002) 3 *Pepperdine Dispute Resolution Law Journal* 39 and D Della Noce, 'Mediation Policy: Theory Matters' (Mediate.com 1999) available at www.mediate.com.

28 UNCITRAL MLICC (2002) Art. 3(1) defines conciliation.

29 On different mediation practice models see M Alberstein, 'Forms of Mediation and Law: Cultures of Dispute Resolution' (2007) 22 *Ohio State Journal on Dispute Resolution* 321, N Antaki, 'Cultural Diversity and ADR Practices in the World' in J Goldsmith, A Ingen-Housz and G Pointon (eds), *ADR in Business* (Alphen aan den Rijn: Kluwer Law International 2006) at 1 and Alexander (2008), above note 21 at 97.

The chapters that follow analyse the relationship between mediation regulation and international practice. In particular they examine how mediation is defined, encouraged and managed through regulation. Both conceptual and descriptive definitions of mediation will be used as the context requires.

For the purposes of this book mediation is conceptually defined as an assisted decision-making process, which typically – but not invariably – takes the form of a facilitated negotiation or dialogue.[30] The mediator assists parties to make decisions about the issues in dispute between them and about appropriate norms for the regulation of future relationships. Generally mediation is based on principles such as party autonomy, client-centredness and choice, confidentiality and a focus on interests and needs rather than rights and positions. The process is voluntary in so far as parties are not required to make any decisions or to reach agreement. In so far as decisions are made, they are said to reflect the parties' choices and priorities. This conceptual definition corresponds to the facilitative model of mediation. As indicated earlier however, there are variations to the process represented by different models of mediation. Accordingly this book's descriptive definition of mediation views mediation as a decision-making process supported by an independent third party. It is sufficiently broad to embrace different mediation practices.

4.3 A Word on Terminology

The terms *mediation*, *conciliation* and *arbitration* are sometimes used interchangeably and are sometimes also confused, particularly with the increasing use of hybrid processes such as med–arb.[31] Astor and Chinkin highlight the fact that confusion is due, in part, to different cultural understandings of the three processes.[32] Illustrating this point, Carbonneau

30 Australian National Mediator Accreditation Standards, s 2 of the Practice Standards (2007) at www.mediationworld.net.

31 See Antaki (2006), above note 29 at 3 and E Ginkel, 'The UNCITRAL Model Law on International Commercial Conciliation: A Critical Appraisal' (2004) 21 *The Journal of International Arbitration* 1 at footnote 3. Schneider suggests that the term *mediation* is more frequently used in the United States and the term *conciliation* elsewhere, while recognising the usage of both terms in England: M Schneider, 'Combining Arbitration with Conciliation' (2003) 1 *International Oil, Gas and Energy Dispute Management Journal* 20. See comments on the terminological confusion by C Baylis, 'Reviewing Statutory Models Of Mediation/Conciliation In New Zealand: Three Conclusions – Part 1' (1999) 38 *Victoria University of Wellington Law Review*. Finally there are some court decisions where the terms are used interchangeably: see, for example, the Australian case of *Hooper Bailie Associated Ltd v Natcon Group Pty Ltd* (1992) 28 NSWLR 194 at 203–206 and the French Supreme Court decision, Cass 2 d civil chamber 16.06.1993.

32 Astor and Chinkin (2002), above note 12 at 93. The authors refer to Asian jurisdictions where the arbitrator is expected to assist the parties to settle the dispute

points out that in Japan '[a]rbitration often takes the form of and becomes, mediation.'[33] Yang points out that in the People's Republic of China the same Chinese word, *tiaojie*, is used to refer to mediation and conciliation and that the terms are therefore interchangeable.[34]

Leading academic literature in many regions of the world considers conciliation as a more directive and interventionist process than facilitative mediation, which has been defined earlier. On this view, a conciliator may move beyond the process-focused role of a mediator and provide advice to the parties regarding the substantive issues in dispute, the legal merits of the situation and an appropriate outcome for the dispute, even going so far as to suggest terms of settlement.[35] Underpinning this understanding of conciliation is the notion that the conciliator is required to be an expert on the subject matter of the dispute as well as the process of conciliation. Other commentators suggest the opposite – mediation is the advisory process and conciliation the facilitative one – demonstrating the flexibility of terminology in this area.[36]

The debates of the Working Group on the MLICC highlight the different views on terminology.[37] Ultimately the Working Group opted for the term *conciliation* and gave it a broad definition, an umbrella term for non-

at all stages of the arbitration process, using her decision-making authority only as a last resort.

33 T Carbonneau, *The Law and Practice of Arbitration* (New York: Juris Publishing 2004) at 51.

34 Yang (2008), above note 17 at footnote 1.

35 On Australian literature, see Astor and Chinkin (2002), above note 12 at 86, Boulle (2005), above note 15 chapter 3 at 100. See also the references to statutory conciliation in the Australian literature, referring to conciliation that occurs within the framework of a specific statute such as the Australian Federal anti-discrimination legislation. On American literature, see D Weckstein, 'In Praise of Party Empowerment – and of Mediator Activism' (1997) 33 *Williamette Law Review* 501 at 514 and L Weir, 'Conciliation as a Mechanism for the Resolution of International Economic and Business Disputes' (1991) 14 *Fordham International Law Journal* 578 at 584. On the difference between the role of 'Schlichter' (conciliator) and 'Mediator' in the German literature, see S Breidenbach, *Mediation* (Köln: Verlag Dr. Otto Schmidt 1995) at 4 and G Bierbrauer, J Falke and K Koch, 'Konflikt und Konfliktbeilegung. Eine interdisziplinare Studie uber Rechtsgrundlage und Funktion der Schiedsmanninstitution' in G Bierbrauer, J Falke, B Giese, K Koch and H Rodingen, *Zugang zum Recht* (Bielefeld: Gieseking 1978) at 141.

36 See Street (1992) above note 11 and I Brownlie, 'The Peaceful Settlement of International Disputes in Practice' (1995) 7 *Pace International Law Review* 257 at 262–263 and A Prujiner, 'Recent Developments in Mediation in Canada' in N Alexander (ed), *Global Trends in Mediation* (2nd ed, Alphen aan den Rijn: Kluwer Law International 2006) at 83–84.

37 See UN Doc. A/CN.9/485 at paragraph 107–109 and UN Doc. A/CN.9/487 at paragraph 104.

determinative dispute resolution including mediation and conciliation.[38] A generic definition of conciliation is consistent with Pel's and others' definitions of mediation as a specific method of conciliation.[39] According to Pel, the more advisory and settlement-oriented models of mediation, described earlier in this chapter, technically fall into the category of conciliation, whereas the facilitative, transformative and wise counsel models are better described as mediation.

This book uses the term *mediation* in a broad sense, except when referring to laws which use the term *conciliation,* such as the MLICC.

4.4 Law

Notions of law differ. Glenn points out that law may attach to a particular territory (for example, a country in a civil or common law jurisdiction) or it may be personal, attaching to people of a certain religion (for example, shari'a law) or tribe (for example, chthonic or customary law in indigenous societies throughout the world). It may attach to both people and territory, for example in socialist countries where movement beyond the jurisdiction is substantially restricted.

Sources of law are varied and include case law, legislation, international customary law, *lex mercatoria*, notions of natural law and religious law and chthonic understandings of 'shared information on how to live a life'.[40] A western secular democracy with a positivist law tradition, for example, looks primarily to its democratically elected parliament to authorise and legitimise law. Many of the laws referred to in this book are parliamentary laws, for example the Austrian Law on Mediation in Civil Cases 2001.[41] Talmudic law and Islamic law are based on a pyramid of sources and ultimately on divine authority.[42] The word of God as revealed to Moses and contained in the first five books of the Hebrew Bible, or the Old Testament, provides the final divine

[38] See, for example, the Report of the Secretary-General on Conciliation of International Trade Disputes UN Doc. A/CN.9/167 (1979) at 4.

[39] See M Pel, *Referral to Mediation* (The Hague: Sdu Uitgevers 2008) at 19 and P Couvrat and G Giudicelli-Delage, *Conciliation et médiation, JurisClasseur Procédure civile* (Paris: JurisClasseur 2003) Fasc 160.

[40] H Glenn, *Legal Traditions of the World* (2nd ed, Oxford: OUP 2004) at 65. Glenn questions whether customary or chthonic traditions can be said to have sources of law. An explanation of *lex mercatoria* is provided below in the discussion on international commercial arbitration.

[41] See the Zivilrechts-Mediations-Gesetz 2001 (ZivMediatG) and Zivilrechts-Mediations-Ausbildungsverordnung 2004 (ZivMediat-AV) BGBl I N° 29/2003, referred to in this book as the Austrian Law on Mediation in Civil Cases 2001 and the Austrian Mediation Training Regulations 2004 respectively.

[42] See Glenn (2004), above note 40 at 92 et seq in relation to Talmudic law and at 170 et seq in relation to Islamic law.

authority for Talmudic law. Islamic law derives its ultimate legitimacy from the Koran, which contains the word of Allah, or God, revealed to the Prophet Muhammad. Bunter writes that,

> [i]n their search for an authentic cultural and religious polity the Arabs may be increasingly turning to the Shar'ia as the main source of legislation. This is explicit in the constitution of the Islamic Republic of Iran and also in the particular laws that frame the workings of the petroleum sector in that country.

By way of example he explains how different forms of agreement have emerged to comply with the Islamic law prohibition on *riba*, that is the paying or receiving of interest.[43] Examples of other types of law such as case law, international customary law and *lex mercatoria* appear throughout the book.

Factors such as the role of law in society and how law is interpreted and applied, and by whom, influence the real meaning of a law in a given legal jurisdiction. Here *thick* notions of law and terms such as *legal culture* and *tradition* are useful. These ideas move one away from Eurocentric notions of law in an attempt to embrace a more inclusive perspective. Glenn illustrates the point when he explains that western traditions of civil and common law involve a degree of bivalent (true/false) logic in identifying and applying laws, standards and precedents consistently to different cases in order to ensure fairness, equity and justice. Eastern traditions such as Hinduism, Confucianism and Buddhism embrace a multivalent logic which doubts the certainty of positivist categories and more easily tolerates multiple and even inconsistent truths than bivalent approaches.[44]

Accordingly reliance on positivist criteria for defining and comparing laws may disregard some valuable perspectives. Mallat refers to the influence of the French Napoleonic Code on codification of law in the Middle East, beginning with the *Majalla* in the Ottoman Empire (1869–76) and extending to contemporary nation-states in the region. He points out that the continuing significance of Islamic tradition has contributed to major differences in how these codified laws are interpreted and applied in comparison with European applications.[45] Similarly although Turkey took over the Swiss Civil Code, the Turkish and Swiss private law systems remain very different today.[46]

43 M Bunter, 'The Islamic (Shar'ia) Law and Petroleum Developments in the Countries of North Africa and the Arabian Gulf' (2004) 1 *Transnational Dispute Management Journal* 1 at 3 and 20.

44 Glenn (2004), above note 40 at 350–353.

45 C Mallat, 'Comparative Law and the Islamic (Middle Eastern) Legal Culture' in M Reimann and R Zimmermann (eds), *The Oxford Handbook of Comparative Law* (Oxford: Oxford University Press 2006) at 629.

46 J Smits, 'Comparative Law and Its Influence on National Legal Systems' in M Reimann and R Zimmermann (eds), *The Oxford Handbook of Comparative Law* (Oxford: Oxford University Press 2006) at 537.

Interaction among different legal traditions creates opportunities for reciprocal influences and can lead to legal co-existence, co-option and blending of ideas about law. In first nation-states, chthonic or indigenous law – which is interwoven with morality, religion, social rules and etiquette – may co-exist with western institutions and law or be co-opted into formal institutions.[47] Co-option is an attempt to formally apply indigenous law, or at least a hybrid version of it. Examples of such co-option include the use of mediation in the National Native Title Tribunal (NNTT) in Australia and restorative justice through sentencing tribunals such as Koori and Nunga courts in Australia and circle sentencing in Australia and Canada.[48] Much debate surrounds the ability of western institutions, which have been established according to western positivist traditions, to incorporate the thick layers of meaning embedded in chthonic laws. Initiatives to document chthonic law also raise questions about how much meaning is likely to be lost in the process.[49]

Just as it can increase understanding among systems of law, the interaction of different legal traditions can lead to confrontation. While the laws of most nation-states are largely territorial, personal laws such as the shar'ia law are growing in significance as populations become more mobile and the influence of Islam expands.[50] To a large extent, territorial and personal laws co-exist with one another. However, in their search for formal recognition, different notions of law have clashed as illustrated by the rejection of proposals to establish a shar'ia law tribunal in Canadian provinces in 2005.[51]

In the *Global Rice* scenario introduced earlier different understandings of law are likely to emerge in relation to notions of land use and ownership and

47 For a detailed explanation of chthonic traditions, see Glenn (2004), above note 40 at 60–91.

48 On the NNTT and its mediative role see www.nntt.gov.au and *Franks v Western Australia* [2006] FCA 1811. On sentencing circles in Australia see D Dick, 'Circle Sentencing of Aboriginal Offenders' (Paper presented at the Sentencing: Principles, Perspectives and Possibilities Conference, Canberra, 10–12 February 2006). For the use of sentencing circles in Canada see *R v Moses* (1992) 71 CCC (3d) 347 (Yukon Territorial Court).

49 See T Bennett, 'Comparative Law and African Customary Law' in M Reimann and R Zimmermann (eds), *The Oxford Handbook of Comparative Law* (Oxford: Oxford University Press 2006) at 642 et seq in relation to the formalisation of African customary law.

50 Mallat (2006), above note 45 at 634, 638–9. J Hussein, 'Islam's Shariah and Australian law' (2006) *The Brisbane Institute* available at www.brisinst.org.au. Hussein states that 'In Australia, Muslim migrants bring the Shariah with them as their personal law; and in only a very few instances does it come into conflict with Australian law.'

51 BBC News, 'Sharia law move quashed in Canada' (2005) at www.bbc.co.uk. Compare the interaction of Sharia'a law with the English common law in the United Kingdom at www.independent.co.uk and www.bbc.co.uk.

contractual obligations. In addition the rights and obligations of groups or individuals within the tribe may differ depending on whether one is reading the formal law in isolation or within a chthonic context. As an illustration, the rights and obligations of customary chiefs may, in certain circumstances, clash with those set out in the investment agreement. Contract partners, recognised by formal law, may not have the same rights to enter into agreements under customary law. In these and similar circumstances the gap between the practices of positive law and legal tradition, between what a law says and what it means and between law-making and compliance can be significant. In these situations the value of the western concept of rule of law is significantly diminished and the potential for mediation is accentuated.

Since the common law's inception in England, common law jurisdictions have been noted for high levels of tolerance of outsider legal traditions, especially where they are operating at a local level.[52] The significant amount of dispositive (or default) law in western legal traditions – whether common or civil law systems – permits private parties to contract in concepts and principles from other legal systems. Typically this occurs through international contractual arrangements. To illustrate the point, one might consider a dispute resolution clause signed in Bahrain as part of a commercial banking contract by parties from Switzerland, France and Saudi Arabia. The clause stipulates that the substantive law of the United Arab Emirates is to apply to the resolution of any dispute arising out of the contract and that mediation is to be employed as the initial dispute resolution process. The place of mediation is London. This scenario shows the potential interaction of different legal regimes in relation to a future dispute, which could require authoritative resolution in one or other jurisdiction.

Yet another way to think about law is in terms of regulation, which can derive from the state, self-management and the market place. Law as regulation is examined in the next chapter. In this book law is defined broadly and encompasses the various notions of law, legal tradition and regulation referred to in this section and the chapter that follows.

4.5 National, Cross-Border, International and Transnational

Economic and social globalisation has created new and sometimes contradictory notions of space, location and jurisdiction. This complex reality is reflected in the breadth and diversity of terms used to designate different aspects of social intercourse, trade, dispute resolution and other activities across nation-states, political boundaries and geographical borders – international, transnational, cross-border, supra-national and so on. Mediation and other forms of dispute resolution have contributed to this complexity by being in some situations

[52] Glenn (2004), above note 40 at 222 et seq.

closely bounded by place and space and in others freeing themselves from these constraints. Here a brief outline is provided of how key terms are used and understood in this book.

The term *national* refers to geo-political entities and the concepts associated with the nation-state – sovereignty, law-making and citizenship. Thus national law denotes the normative statements emanating from parliaments, courts, tribunals and executive authorities of the nation-state.

The term *cross-border* is used to refer to activities which traverse one or more geo-political boundary, whether between nation-states or within them. Thus a business transaction or dispute between entities in states A and B, or in sub-national provinces C and A, is cross-border in nature.[53] The United Nations Convention on Contracts for the International Sale of Goods (CISG) is a cross-border treaty operating among different nation-states, and the UMA is a cross-border instrument that aims to unify the regulation of certain aspects of mediation across interstate borders within the United States. The term cross-border is used in a generic sense in this book. More nuanced meanings are provided by the terms international and transnational.

Traditionally the term *international* referred to activities, laws and disputes that occurred among different nation-states, in recognition of their boundaries, jurisdiction and sovereignty. It has been used extensively by organisations and commentators in relation to political, economic and social relations, which are built on the notion of the nation-state as a defining element of the relationships concerned. International law and international relations are reflections of this traditional conception. The sources of international law are custom, which is consistent state practice developed over time, and treaties whose legitimacy derives from the participating states. However its modern usage sometimes stretches the concept of international to include non-state entities such as international organisations, trading corporations and even individuals[54] and this elasticity is reflected in the use of the term in this book.

Whereas the terms international and cross-border highlight the significance of geo-political borders and nation-states, terms such as *transnational* and *transborder* imply their insignificance to a greater or lesser degree. These terms refer to activities which straddle geo-political borders, but are wholly or in part independent from those borders and the concept of the

[53] See, for example, the use of this term in a European Union context: European Commission, *Justice and Home Affairs: Glossary* at www.ec.europa.eu.

[54] See J Starke and I Shearer, *Starke's International Law* (London: Butterworths 1994) at 61 and F Vicuna, 'Individuals and Non-State Entities before International Courts and Tribunals' (2001) 5 *Max Planck Yearbook of United Nations Law* 53.

nation-state. They emphasise the blurring of legal, economic and geographic boundaries, denoting degrees of *borderless* activity.[55]

Transnational law is broad in scope as it sources are not only those in traditional international law (custom and treaties) and domestic law (legislation, executive regulation, court decisions) but also the decisions and policies of industry bodies, corporations, community organisations and the modern *lex mercatoria* developed through avenues such as the decisions of private arbitrators. This plurality of sources makes transnational law at times difficult to identify and coordinate.

The terms *transnational* and *transborder* are used where appropriate to emphasise different aspects of the globalised and integrated world and have less official connotations than *international* and *cross-border*. In relation to citizenship the term *transborder* is used to refer to individuals or corporations living or existing beyond the borders of one nation-state, for example persons with multiple nationalities of different states.[56] In relation to the internet it is used to indicate its disassociation from many political, legal, cultural and physical boundaries and constraints.

In the context of globalisation the choice of terminology highlights the fuzziness and potential unsuitability of traditional legal categories. It also emphasises the changing role of geo-political borders as they compete with socio-economic, cultural, ethnic and other boundaries for recognition. A cross-border transaction or dispute may involve the law of different national legal systems, or international economic law, or transnational law, or a combination thereof. The rapid growth of mediation and other alternative forms of dispute resolution around the world has both been a response to the indeterminacy of traditional boundaries and a contributing factor to the reduced significance of geographic borders in terms of dispute resolution activities. Conversely there is an increasing importance attached to borders in relation to regulatory issues such as the confidentiality of mediation processes and admissibility of statements made in mediation in subsequent arbitral or legal proceedings. Finally as regards matters of enforceability, mediation is mainly reliant on national legal systems, whether in individual business transactions or international trade disputes.

[55] On this point in the context of international education see J Knight, 'Updating the Definition of Internationalization' (2003) *Centre for International Higher Education: Boston College* at www.bc.edu.

[56] N Schiller, 'Transborder Citizenship: an outcome of legal pluralism within international social fields' in F Benda-Beckmann, K Benda-Beckmann and A Griffiths (eds), *Mobile People, Mobile Law: Expanding Legal Relations in a Contracting World* (London: Ashgate 2005) at 27.

4.6 International Comparative Approaches

There is no court system to deal with international disputes between private non-state actors or commercial disputes involving state actors. Therefore reference must first be made to national courts and the international co-operation that exists among them. The exploration of different notions of law earlier in the chapter highlights the utility of comparative approaches to law for understanding how legal processes and agreements operate across cultures, borders and other boundaries.[57] Disentangling the multiple layers of law in identifying the applicable law, who will enforce legal remedies and how enforcement will occur, is a vital component of the comparative lawyer's role.[58]

In an age of information overload encouraged by contemporary globalisation processes, comparative law provides a way of following the movement and interaction of legal traditions around the world.[59] It also provides a way to track the extension of legal traditions beyond nation-states as international legal norms develop.[60] Finally comparative insights can extend perspectives of law and contribute to a more particularised understanding of one's own legal framework.[61] Comparative law methods are employed in a range of activities including:

- the classification of laws according to legal systems such as civil law, common law, Islamic law, socialist law and others;[62]
- the structuring of knowledge about, and translation of, laws of different jurisdictions; [63]
- attempts to harmonise or unify laws of different jurisdictions and the interpretation of those laws;[64] and

57 J Griffiths, 'What is Legal Pluralism?' (1986) 24 *Journal of Legal Pluralism and Unofficial Law* 1.

58 M Reimann, 'Comparative Law and Private International Law' in M Reimann and R Zimmermann (eds), *The Oxford Handbook of Comparative Law* (Oxford: Oxford University Press 2006) 1363 at 1393–1395.

59 Glenn (2004) above note 40 at 163.

60 Glenn (2004) above note 40 at 52.

61 V Curran, 'Comparative Law and Language' in M Reimann and R Zimmerman (eds), *The Oxford Handbook of Comparative Law* (Oxford: Oxford University Press 2006) 675 at 697.

62 The two major works in this field are: R David and J Brierley, *Major Legal Systems in the World Today* (3rd ed, London: Stevens Publishing 1985) and K Zweigert and H Kötz, *Einführung in die Rechtsvergleichung* (3rd ed, Tübingen: Mohr Siebeck 1996). For a critique of this approach see P Glenn, 'Legal Families and Legal Traditions' in M Reimann and R Zimmermann (eds), *The Oxford Handbook of Comparative Law* (Oxford: Oxford University Press 2006) at 422 et seq.

63 On the translation of laws as much more than a linguistic exercise see Curran (2006), above note 61 at 696.

– law reform and legal transplant initiatives.

Comparative law scholarship grew out of the positivist Eurocentric civil law tradition. It emerged in the 19th century as a complement to the rise of nation-states and the nationalisation of law in Europe to become the primary methodology used in private international law.[65] Thus comparison of national laws and exchange of information came to form the basis of international dispute resolution.

More recent comparative law approaches display dissatisfaction with the narrowness of positivist legal theory. Legal pluralism, for example, provides a framework for comparison and analysis of the parallel and often contradictory regulations of social, economic and political organisation that exist in most contemporary legal systems. These regulations are based on different types of legitimisation: international law, state law, religious law, chthonic law and forms of self-regulation. Wherever more than one normative order operates within a discrete group, there is plurality of law.[66]

Glenn, drawing on a wide understanding of law referred to above, proposes a casuistic comparative method which encompasses the notion of tradition as a source of law and as a comparative method – on a case by case and an issue by issue basis. Here tradition is defined as an evolving tub of information that is constantly being exchanged, developed, refined and changed between generations. However communication does not only occur vertically between generations within one tradition; it also occurs horizontally among different traditions. Traditions-based approaches embrace the dynamic character of law and create space for the co-existence and reconciliation of diverse notions of dispute resolution. They acknowledge chthonic practices and norms as well as contemporary local and global developments in dispute resolution and open possibilities about how the role of mediation can be understood, harnessed and implemented in a globalising world.[67]

64 Council Regulation (EC) N° 44/2001 of 22 December 2000 on Jurisdiction and the Recognition and Enforcement of Judgments in Civil and Commercial Matters. The case law of the European Court of Justice (ECJ) in relation to the Brussels Regulation I illustrates the use of comparative law to develop a 'transborder' interpretation of this international convention: see Reimann (2006), above note 58 at 1388.

65 J Gordley, 'Comparative Law and Legal History' in M Reimann and R Zimmermann (eds), *The Oxford Handbook of Comparative Law* (Oxford: Oxford University Press 2006) at 759.

66 On legal pluralism, see Griffiths (1986), above note 57. See also G Sarfaty, 'International Norm Diffusion in the Pimicikamak Cree Nation: A Model of Legal Mediation' (2007) 48 *Harvard International Law Journal* 443 at 446 et seq.

67 See Glenn (2004), above note 40 at 350 et seq. On the application of mediation to international disputes involving different concepts of law, see Sarfaty (2007), above note 66.

Consistent with the inclusive definition of law elucidated earlier, a traditions-based approach will underpin the comparisons of international mediation law in this book. The following chapters will take into account a variety of jurisdictional policies and practices focussing on the countries and cross-border legal instruments identified earlier.

5. Distinguishing Mediation from other Dispute Resolution Processes

Mediation can occur in close connection with arbitration and other processes. There is an increasing tendency to combine mediation with other dispute resolution processes through the device of multi-tiered dispute resolution (MDR) clauses. As litigation about MDR clauses has demonstrated, it is not always a straightforward matter to draw a line between where one dispute resolution process ends and another begins.[68] In this section mediation is distinguished from three other dispute resolution processes: negotiation, judicial settlement and arbitration.

5.1 Mediation and Negotiation

As explained earlier, mediation and negotiation are closely related processes and mediation can be described as facilitated negotiation. Despite their similarities, mediation and negotiation can be distinguished from each other in three ways.

1. In mediation, a third party enters the negotiations to assist the parties move through the negotiation process, while leaving the outcome of the negotiations ultimately up to them; in negotiation there is no independent dispute resolution practitioner assisting the parties to move towards their outcome.
2. The phases of a mediation process are generally more structured and explicit than those of a negotiation.
3. Courts in a number of jurisdictions including Australia, the US, the UK, Sweden and France have held that agreements to mediate can be enforceable where the process is set out with sufficient certainty, whereas agreements to negotiate generally are not enforceable.[69]

[68] See, for example, the *Channel Tunnel Group Ltd v Balfour Beatty Construction Ltd* [1993] AC 334. Here the court had to decide whether or not an MDR clause could be defined as an arbitration clause for the purposes of identifying the applicable legislation.

[69] For more detail on this point, see Chapter 4.

5.2 Mediation and Judicial Settlement

Judges in many parts of the world are required by law to attempt to settle a matter before hearing the case. This feature of the judicial system has a long tradition in many Asian legal systems, such as China, where litigation has always been a last resort and settlement preferred. It also is a hallmark of the judicial function in many civil law jurisdictions.[70] Traditionally no formal legal requirement for judges to attempt to settle matters before them has existed in common law jurisdictions, although civil reform is increasingly incorporating the notion of judicial settlement or encouragement to settle in different ways.[71] Despite some controversy and confusion about the relationship between mediation and judicial settlement, the distinction has been recognised by a number of legal instruments including the European Directive on Mediation[72] and the UMA.[73]

There have been a few studies on the practice of judicial settlement and the procedures involved. They indicate that judicial attempts to encourage parties to settle tend to be activist, interventionist and legalistic.[74] The procedure rarely follows any particular mediation style and traditionally there are no separate and private sessions between judge and each party. Research indicates that practice tends to be more directive than facilitative and fairly legalistic in character.[75]

70 In Germany the relevant section of the Code of Civil Procedure (Zivilprozessordnung ZPO) is § 278.

71 For example, the Woolf Report in England: Woolf, *Final Report to the Lord Chancellor on the Civil Justice System in England and Wales* (London: HMSO 1996). In Australia the Less Adversarial Trial (LAT) is a significant part of reform in family law jurisdictions, see www.familycourt.gov.au.

72 See the European Directive on Mediation, which clearly distinguishes between judicial settlement and mediation, discussed in Chapter 3.

73 The UMA is available at www.nccusl.org.

74 See M Galanter and M Cahill, '"Most Cases Settle": Judicial Promotion and Regulation of Settlements' (1993–1994) 46 *Stanford Law Review* 1339 et seq, J Resnik, 'Managerial Judges' (1982–1983) 96 *Harvard Law Review* 374, J Wall Jr, L Schiller and R Ebert, 'Should Judges Grease the Slow Wheels of Justice? A Survey on the Effectiveness of Judicial Mediary Techniques' (1984–1985) 8 *American Journal of Trial Advocacy* 83 at 95 et seq and D Warwel, *Gerichtsnahe Mediation: Empirische Untersuchung der Verhaltens- und Vorgehensweisen von Richtermediatoren in Gerichtsnahen Mediationsverfahren* (Dr W Hopf: Berlin 2007) at 124–133.

75 See R Greger, *Abschlussbericht zum Forschungsprojekt – Aussergerichtliche Streitbeilegung in Bayern* (Friedrich-Alexander-Universität Erlangen-Nűrnberg 2004) at 13, D Treuer, 'Impressionen über den gerichtlichen Vergleich' in W Gottwald and F Haft (eds), *Verhandeln und Vergleichen als juristische Fertigkeiten* (Tübingen: Attempto 1993) at 116, H Rottleuthner, 'Alternativen im gerichtlichen Verfahren' in E Blankenburg, W Gottwald and D Strempel (eds), *Alternativen in der Ziviljustiz:*

The judicial settlement function can also be distinguished from mediation by the fact that the same judge will hear the case following an unsuccessful attempt to settle. Where judges attempt to conduct facilitative mediation with private sessions resulting in non-agreement, adjudicating the same matter may pose an ethical dilemma and role conflict,[76] issues considered in Chapter 3. It is for this reason that private sessions are generally not conducted with the parties where judges resort to conducting mediation.

Yet another difference between mediation and judicial settlement lies in the fact that in many legal systems the judicial settlement function must be consistent with the overall objective of the judicial role, namely to find a legal outcome for the disputants. This feature of judicial settlement is illustrated in Chapter 3. The mediation process is not restricted in this way. Parties are rather encouraged to seek creative solutions based on their needs and interests rather than a strict application of legal principles.

5.3 Mediation and Arbitration

As described earlier in this chapter, mediation is a facilitative process, which focuses on parties' commercial, financial, social and personal interests, without excluding their rights and which promotes the principles of confidentiality and party autonomy in decision-making. Conversely arbitration is a rights-based determinative process in which the parties agree to be bound by the decision of an arbitrator or arbitral panel. The decision is issued in the form of an arbitral award. In international commercial arbitration decisions are generally based on principles of international business law known as *lex mercatoria* and notions of equity.[77]

In his comparison Lewinski identifies neutrality and confidentiality[78] as the core ethical principles of both mediation and arbitration.[79] Mediation and

Berichte, Analysen, Perspektiven (Köln: Bundesanzeiger 1982) at 145 and R Rogowski, 'Die aktive Rolle des Richters im Prozessvergleich: Überblick über die rechtssoziologische Forschung zur vermittelnden Rolle des Zivilrichters in der Bundesrepublik Deutschland' in E Blankenburg, W Gottwald and D Strempel (eds), *Alternativen in der Ziviljustiz: Berichte, Analysen, Perspektiven* (Köln: Bundesanzeiger 1982) at 171.

76 W Gottwald and D Treuer, *Vergleichspraxis: Tips für Richter und Anwälte* (Stuttgart: Boorberg 1991).

77 See the section entitled 'Arbitration in International Dispute Resolution' later in this chapter.

78 For a different view on confidentiality in arbitration see the Australian High Court decision of *Esso Australia Resources Ltd v Plowman* (1995) 183 CLR 10. In relation to mediation, note that the requirement for confidentiality is not universal, see Chapter 6.

79 K Lewinski, 'Professional Ethics in Alternative Dispute Resolution' (2004) 3 *Journal of International Dispute Resolution* 15.

arbitration are normally processes in which the parties can select the arbitrator or mediator, the venue and the timing of the process. However although they do share a number of features that distinguish them from court processes, mediation and arbitration are fundamentally different in other respects.

Arbitration has been practised much longer than mediation and courts are more familiar with it than mediation. It is easier to delineate arbitration processes, their commencement and termination, and various stages, compared with the more flexible and party-centred process of mediation. Therefore compliance issues are more easily determined in the case of the former.

Both international and domestic arbitration usually have the benefit of regulation by a comprehensive statutory framework;[80] mediation, especially if it has an international element, is less likely to be supported by specific legislation in relation to its validity, interpretation and enforcement. Although arbitral awards are final and binding on the parties, they are subject to review by courts on procedural and in some cases substantive aspects of the arbitral award. The nature of judicial review is usually limited by statute and varies in nature and extent from jurisdiction to jurisdiction.

Mediated outcomes, by contrast, are the result of agreements between disputing parties. In so far as they take the form of legally binding contracts, they are, in the absence of legislation to the contrary, subject to the same principles of review and enforcement as general contracts. As explained previously, arbitration and mediation often converge in the form of hybrid or multi-tiered processes. Interesting questions arise as to the legal status of MDR clauses and specifically whether, in part or in their totality, they fall within the scope of relevant arbitration legislation.[81] As with judicial settlement discussed in the previous section, ethical challenges may emerge when facilitative and determinative processes meet. These are discussed in Chapter 3.

Numerous legal questions that arise in the context of arbitration also arise with respect to mediation. These include the enforceability of dispute resolution clauses and outcomes, questions relating to the impartiality of the dispute resolution practitioner, admissibility of evidence in subsequent proceedings and suspension of litigation limitation periods. However the differences between the determinative process of arbitration and the facilitative process of mediation demand a differentiated analysis of the issues. Accordingly lawyers must be careful not to place mediation issues in the same legal basket as arbitration issues. While insights can be drawn from domestic and international arbitration legislation and case law, mediation must be treated as an independent development if is to remain a real alternative to both litigation and arbitration.

80 Arbitration is generally regulated by domestic statute. In relation to international disputes, the UNCITRAL Model Law on International Commercial Arbitration (1985) (MLICA) forms the basis of most modern regulations on arbitration.

81 See the *Channel Tunnel Group Ltd v Balfour Beatty Construction Ltd* [1993] AC 334, above note 68.

Table 1
Comparing Dispute Resolution Processes

Table 1 highlights the main features of the dispute resolution processes: negotiation, mediation, judicial settlement and arbitration.

Process Feature	Negotiation	Mediation	Judicial Settlement	Arbitration
Who participates?	Parties, legal or other professional representatives (optional), other stakeholders with parties' consent.	Parties, legal or other professional representatives (optional), mediator, other stakeholders with parties' consent.	Parties, judge, legal or other professional representatives (depends on practice of court).	Parties, legal or other professional representatives (optional), arbitrator, witnesses, experts.
Who decides outcome?	Parties reach agreement on some or all of the issues.	Parties reach agreement on some or all of the issues with the assistance of the mediator.	Parties reach agreement on the issues in dispute with the assistance and guidance of the judge.	Arbitrator determines questions of law and fact and makes an award.

Process Feature	Negotiation	Mediation	Judicial Settlement	Arbitration
Role and selection of dispute resolution practitioner	There is no independent dispute resolution professional. Parties may engage professional advisers and advocates to assist them in negotiations.	The role is generally facilitative and may contain advisory elements. Specifically a mediator encourages candour, highlights common and competing party interests, sets agenda for discussion, assists parties explore options for settlement, encourages concessions, assists parties to reach and document agreement. Mediator/s are selected by parties, or if they cannot agree, by a nominated authority such as president of the mediation organisation.	The role tends to be directive and advisory, although individual judges may have more facilitative approaches to settlement. Parties are allocated a judge by the court and cannot select their preferred judge.	The role is determinative. Specifically, the arbitrator listens to party submissions on rights and entitlements, receives evidence, calls witnesses, makes decisions, issues award binding on the parties. Arbitrator/s selected by parties according to agreed procedure. For panels of three, a typical selection procedure involves each party choosing one arbitrator from their own jurisdiction and agreeing on a third from another (neutral) jurisdiction.

Process Feature	Negotiation	Mediation	Judicial Settlement	Arbitration
Format of Proceedings	Parties discuss issues in dispute between them. They may set an agenda to help structure discussions. No formal documentation of process unless parties wish to do so.	The process is flexible and usually consists of parties participating in a series of joint and separate meetings with the mediator. Generally the process is structured by the mediator in accordance with applicable laws, rules and standards. Mediation may be administered on an *ad hoc* basis or institutionally. No formal documentation of process. In some jurisdictions mediators' notes are destroyed as a matter of practice.	The process is structured by the judge in accordance with applicable rules and practice directions. Generally private sessions are not permitted and no formal record is kept of the settlement discussions. However, a public record of the formal aspects of the proceedings may be made available in some jurisdictions.	Generally the process consists of written submissions, supplemented by oral arguments made by the parties' representatives. Documentary evidence may be used and witnesses may be called. The arbitrator may not meet with the parties separately. Arbitration may be administered on an *ad hoc* basis or institutionally. Process is formally documented.
Level of Formality	Can range from informal to formal discussions.	Can range from informal to formal discussions.	Generally more formal than mediation.	Generally more formal than mediation.

Process Feature	Negotiation	Mediation	Judicial Settlement	Arbitration
Levels of privacy and confidentiality	Private forum. Negotiations are usually on confidential and *without prejudice* basis.	Private forum. Generally conducted on a confidential and without prejudice basis but could have public elements.	Public forum if conducted in court room. Private forum if conducted in judge's chambers but proceedings on the record. Limits on confidentiality.	Private forum. Generally conducted on a confidential basis.* * For a different view see the *Esso* case, above note 78.
Criteria relevant to decision-making	Criteria may include a combination of needs and interests relevant to the parties and their respective legal rights.	Criteria may include a combination of needs and interests relevant to the parties and their respective legal rights.	Legal rights and obligations play a stronger role than in mediation and negotiation. Criteria may also include interests relevant to the parties, depending on judge's approach to settlement.	Nominated national law/s, *lex mercatoria*, equity and public policy.

Process Feature	Negotiation	Mediation	Judicial Settlement	Arbitration
Nature of outcome	Mutually acceptable agreement on all or some of the issues in dispute. If no agreement, parties walk away from the process.	Mutually acceptable agreement on all or some of the issues in dispute. If no agreement, parties walk away from the process or it is determined by court or tribunal.	Mutually acceptable agreement on the issues in dispute. If no agreement, the dispute is subject to judicial determination.	Binding decision in the form of an award. Sometimes decision is supported by reasoned opinion; other times not.
Legal consequences of outcome	Where agreements take the form of a binding contract, the general law of contract applies. Attempts to set aside the agreement and breach of agreement issues will therefore be subject to the principles of contract law. Note: in some jurisdictions settlement negotiations resulting in agreement may be subject to different laws.	Where agreements take the form of a binding contract, the general law of contract applies – unless specific provisions relating to mediated agreements apply. In the absence of specific provisions to the contrary, attempts to set aside the agreement and breach of agreement issues will be subject to the principles of contract law.	Judicial settlement agreements are generally subject to statutory provisions, which make the settlement binding and enforceable. Such agreements may enjoy a higher level of enforceability compared to general contract, such as that of a court order. Appeal on limited grounds only.	The award is binding on the parties and legally enforceable. Appeal on limited grounds only.

Process Feature	Negotiation	Mediation	Judicial Settlement	Arbitration
International recognition of outcome	May be difficult. Subject to laws of jurisdiction where recognition is sought.	May be difficult. Subject to laws of jurisdiction where recognition is sought.	*Prima facie* subject to laws of jurisdiction where recognition is sought. Possible recognition as court judgment through bilateral and multilateral arrangements such as the Choice of Court Convention 2005 and the Brussels I Regulation.	International recognition through various international conventions, especially the New York Convention on the Recognition and Enforcement of Foreign Arbitral Awards 1958.

Process Feature	Negotiation	Mediation	Judicial Settlement	Arbitration
Time frame for process	Set by parties and their professional advisers. In court-referred settlement negotiations, time frames may be set by the court.	In *ad hoc* mediations, time frames are set by parties and their professional advisers in consultation with the mediator. In institutional mediations, guidelines for time frames may be indicated by organisational guidelines. Where mediation has been initiated as part of a dispute resolution clause, the clause may set time frames. In court-referred mediation, time frames may be set by the court.	Research shows that judicial settlement processes are relatively short compared to other dispute resolution process. Maximum time: circa 2 to 3 hours.	In *ad hoc* arbitrations; time frames are set by the arbitrator or arbitration panel in consultation with the parties and their professional advisers. In institutional arbitrations guidelines for time frames may be indicated by organisational guidelines. Where arbitration has been initiated as part of a dispute resolution clause, the clause may set timeframes. In court-referred arbitration time frames may be set by the court.

Process Feature	Negotiation	Mediation	Judicial Settlement	Arbitration
Costs involved in process (apart from incidental expenses)	Fees for professional advisers, eg lawyers in preparing and participating in the negotiations.	Fees for professional advisers, mediator/s, institution administering the mediation, experts consulted in the course of the mediation. *Note:* With the exception of the costs of one's own professional advisers, these costs are generally divided as agreed between the parties.	Fees for professional advisers, eg lawyers in preparing and participating in the settlement process and court costs.	Fees for professional advisers, arbitrator/s, institution administering the arbitration (eg ICC), experts consulted in the course of the arbitration, witnesses, and potentially the cost of the other side's legal expenses if case is lost.

Process Feature	Negotiation	Mediation	Judicial Settlement	Arbitration
Circumstances where dispute resolution form is appropriate	Continuance of a good relationship is important. Parties have the legal and real capacity to engage in negotiations. Parties have authority to settle. Parties seeking remedy that court cannot order. Parties require a forum to encourage clarification and a better understanding of the issues. Need for speedy resolution. Confidentiality desirable. Costs of other dispute resolution processes such as arbitration and litigation outweighs value of dispute.	Continuance of a good relationship is important. Parties have reached an impasse. Parties' level of hostility makes negotiation difficult and the presence of the mediator enables them to save face. Parties seeking remedy that court cannot order. Parties require a forum to encourage clarification and better understanding of the issues. Need for speedy resolution. Confidentiality desirable. Costs of other dispute resolution processes such as arbitration and litigation outweighs value of dispute.	Parties are in litigation process. Have prepared for, or previously engaged in negotiation or mediation. Parties' level of hostility makes negotiation difficult and the presence of the judge enables them to save face and move forward. Possibility of resolution before trial completed. High level of enforceability of outcome desirable. Privacy and confidentiality not essential.	Facilitative and advisory dispute resolution processes unsuitable or exhausted. Privacy desirable. Confidentiality not essential. Finality of binding decision desirable. High level of enforceability of outcome desirable.

Process Feature	Negotiation	Mediation	Judicial Settlement	Arbitration
Circumstances where procedure is inappropriate	Remedy sought is required urgently and must come from court eg injunction. Extreme power imbalance between parties and/or their representatives, eg at least one party feels unable to negotiate on a level playing field with the other. Parties refuse to move from positions. Repeat player party (eg insurance company) is seeking a precedent/ ruling. Delay may result in forfeiture of legal rights. Issues of public importance may require precedent from courts.	Remedy sought is required urgently and must come from court eg injunction. Mediator unable to address issues of power imbalance between parties. Mediator unable to assist the parties resolve deadlock. Repeat player party (eg insurance company) is seeking a precedent/ ruling. Delay may result in forfeiture of legal rights. Issues of public importance may require precedent from courts.	Parties seek solution based on interests, not rights-based criteria. Relationship is of paramount importance to parties.	Dispute is suitable for facilitative or advisory processes. Parties seek solution on non-legal basis. Relationship is of paramount importance to parties.

6. ARBITRATION IN INTERNATIONAL DISPUTE RESOLUTION

The original manifestation of international private justice was arbitration. It provided opportunities to reduce the complexity, formality and cost of international litigation, thus making it a potentially attractive forum for disputants. While international arbitration is still a significant dispute resolution mechanism for international private disputes,[82] other processes such as mediation are growing in popularity. As a sign of the times many arbitrators offer mediation services in addition to arbitration. This section provides an overview of international arbitration followed by an explanation for the growing significance of international mediation in the 21st century.

International arbitration can be conducted either institutionally or *ad hoc*. In institutional arbitration parties refer the administration of the arbitration proceedings to an international arbitration organisation such as the International Chamber of Commerce (ICC). These organisations typically possess and utilise a standard set of rules and procedures, such as the ICC Rules on International Arbitration or the UNCITRAL Arbitration Rules (1976) (UAR), and have access to an extensive panel of experienced and professional arbitrators. In an *ad hoc* arbitration, parties are responsible for setting up the arbitral tribunal to administer the proceedings and hear the dispute.[83] There is a greater capacity to customise the substantive and procedural rules of the arbitration to suit their particular dispute, although the parties will often make use of institutional rules.

Arbitration's substantive flexibility is found in the ability of the arbitration panel to base its decision on norms other than national law. The *lex mercatoria* is a body of universal principles reflecting international business practices and trade usage.[84] Through decision-making based on the *lex mercatoria* arbitrators contribute to an international common law of commercial contracts and business transactions.[85] Carbonneau refers to this as the 'structuring of a de facto international legal system and the development of a world law of commerce.'[86]

The flexibility of arbitration is also found in the application of the principles of amiable composition and *ex aequo et bono*. The principles promote

82 See G Lagerberg and L Mistelis, *International Arbitration: Corporate Attitudes and Practices 2008* (PWC: London 2008), available at www.pwc.co.uk.

83 G Kwatra, *Arbitration and alternative dispute resolution: How to settle international business disputes* (New Delhi: Indian Council of Arbitration, United Nations Conference on Trade and Development (UNCTAD) and World Trade Organisation (WTO) 2005) at 37.

84 R Goode, 'Usage and its Reception in International Commercial Law' (1997) 46 *International and Comparative Law Quarterly* 1.

85 Carbonneau (2004), above note 33 at 45.

86 T Carbonneau, *Cases and Materials on the Law and Practice of Arbitration* (New York: Juris Publishing 2002) at 337.

the idea that the decision-making of an arbitrator need not be limited to the strict application of the law. While derived from separate traditions, the concepts have similar meanings according to jurisdiction.[87] Yu explains that the term *ex aequo et bono* refers to standards of morality, fairness and law that operate in a sphere of justice higher than positive law and may include an arbitrator's own sense of justice. Amiable composition embraces similar notions but refers to a process which aims at achieving an equitable result while operating within the framework of natural justice, judicial procedure and public policy. Reference is made to the *amiable compositeur* as one who brings principles of equity into the arbitral decision-making process.[88]

Another significant feature of international commercial arbitration is its high level of enforceability. Arbitral awards are enforceable in many domestic courts by virtue of the New York Convention on Arbitral Awards. In a survey conducted by Bühring-Uhle about the perceived advantages of arbitration for continental European and US lawyers, the existence of an enforcement mechanism rated as one of arbitration's strong advantages, second only to its perceived neutrality.[89] Interestingly for American lawyers, enforceability was most relevant, while for German lawyers neutrality was most important.

The initial *raison d'être* for the use of arbitration in cross-border disputes was to have an internationally acceptable, efficient and effective method of resolving disputes. In comparison to international litigation, research shows that international commercial arbitration still enjoys relatively high levels of usage, effectiveness and satisfaction with the system among participants.[90] At the same time there is growing sentiment that arbitration no longer serves the needs of an increasingly diverse pool of disputants as effectively as it did in decades past. US-style litigation has had a significant impact on late 20th century Eurocentric practices of international commercial arbitration through the

87 H Yu, 'Amiable Composition – A Learning Curve' (2000) 17 *Journal of International Arbitration* 79 at 82 with further references.

88 This principle, derived from civil law, is often enshrined in arbitration legislation. As an example see s 22(2) Commercial Arbitration Act 1984 (NSW). See also M Pryles, 'The Arbitrator as Amiable Compositeur' (1988) 7 *The Arbitrator* 70 and Yu (2000), above note 87 at 79–98. Mayer refers to Aristotle's view that 'the arbitrator aims at achieving equity, the judge at applying the law', P Mayer, 'Reflections on the International Arbitrator's Duty to Apply the Law' (2001) 17 *Arbitration International* 235 at 325.

89 C Bühring-Uhle, L Kirchhoff and G Scherer *Arbitration and Mediation in International Business* (2nd ed, Alphen aan den Rijn: Kluwer Law International 2006) at 108–109 and C Bühring-Uhle, G Scherer and L Kirchhoff, 'The Arbitrator as Mediator: Some Empirical Insights' (2003) 20 *Journal of International Arbitration* 81–88. See also the findings of the PWC international arbitration survey: Lagerberg and Mistelis (2008) above note 82.

90 See the results of the PWC (Price Waterhouse Coopers) survey of corporate users attitudes to international arbitration: Lagerberg and Mistelis (2008) above note 82.

increased involvement of American lawyers and the processes of globalisation. The increasing legalisation of the process, for example, the introduction of discovery-like procedures, has imbued arbitration with many of the disadvantages of litigation it sought to avoid. Interestingly, this Americanisation of international arbitration was not immediately accompanied by an increased number of US-related disputes. This was largely due to the fact that until the 1980s United States law enabled parties to avoid arbitration clauses for matters involving anti-trust and securities issues.[91] Therefore, these categories of disputes in the United States, whether of a national or international character, were managed through the US courts or, in relation to smaller matters, through arbitration by the American Arbitration Association (AAA).

An analysis of the cost of international commercial arbitration shows that approximately two per cent of the total expenditure for an international commercial arbitration relates to administration of the procedure, 16 per cent covers the fees and costs of the arbitrators and 82 per cent is spent on the fees and costs associated with legal advisers and parties preparing and presenting the case.[92] Today most arbitration costs are consumed by the litigious and adversarial nature of arbitration advocacy.

Despite these onerous cost and time implications for arbitration, the absence of appellate review still means that arbitration may be more efficient than litigation. However there will be many exceptions to this generalisation. Rubino Sammartano evaluates the attitudinal shift towards arbitration since the mid 1940s, citing a transition from ‘a time when parties placed their disputes confidently in the hands of a highly respected arbitrator without any formality, accepting in advance any decision he made and promptly performing in accordance with it’,[93] to an environment in which arbitration has become increasingly complex and more frequently challenged.[94]

91 Y Dezalay and B Garth, *Dealing in Virtue: International Commercial Arbitration and the Construction of a Transnational Legal Order* (Chicago: University of Chicago Press 1996) at 156 et seq.

92 J Zamora, ‘Reducing Time and Costs on International Arbitration’ in *Modern Law for Global Commerce: Congress to celebrate the 40th annual session of UNCITRAL* (Vienna: UNCITRAL 2007) available at www.uncitral.org. See also Kwatra (2005), above note 83 at 51, who states that most of the costs in an international dispute consist of lawyers’ fees. In November 2008, the Federal Attorney-General of Australia announced a review of the legislation applicable to international arbitration. The aim of the revision is to make Australia a more attractive location for international disputants engaged in arbitration by reducing the delay and expense associated with it: R McClelland, ‘Simply resolving disputes’ paper presented at the *International Commercial Arbitration Conference, Making it Work for Business* (Sydney: 2008).

93 M Rubino-Sammartano, *International Arbitration Law* (Deventer: Kluwer Law and Taxation Publishers 1990) at 514.

94 Rubino-Sammartano (1990), above note 93.

Historically arbitration and judicial determination have, in legal terms, been strongly connected. Courts have exercised a supervisory function over arbitration through the principle of *lex loci arbitri* (the law of the place of the arbitration). This overseeing function has taken the form of judicial review on the merits and/or the arbitral procedure, according to jurisdiction. Civil law jurisdictions historically supported the development of a non-political arbitration regime by adopting a non-interventionist approach on matters of merit.[95] In the common law the *case stated* procedure operated in English law between 1854[96] and 1979 and was replicated in legislation throughout the Commonwealth. This procedure allowed the arbitral panel or either of the parties to refer a legal question or a case to the court for a review on the merits. Referral to a court could occur either during the conduct of the arbitration or at the enforcement stage of proceedings. In certain situations a court was empowered to direct an arbitrator to 'state a legal question' before it for judicial determination.[97] The *case stated* procedure was abolished in 1979 by virtue of the English Arbitration Act 1979 and replaced with a limited appeal on points of law to the High Court. US law continues to permit courts to review arbitral rulings on the merits, although, as Carbonneau points out, there is no general policy mandate that originally prompted or continues to justify this approach.[98] It appears to be the outcome of a piecemeal development of arbitration law in that country.

Similar considerations pertain to national courts' role in international disputes dealt with through arbitration. For example a number of common law jurisdictions traditionally have been reluctant to release final substantive decision-making power to international arbitration panels. However this approach is changing. In the United States, for example, the federal judicial policy has reduced the judicial role in supervising the conduct of international arbitration, thereby minimising the potential interference with arbitral awards. In English law parties to an international arbitration are able to contract out of the limited appeal on points of law in certain circumstances causing courts to forfeit their substantive decision-making power. In civil law jurisdictions the *anational* approach to arbitration, referred above, has generally been extended to international disputes with courts maintaining their non-interventionist approach on matters of merit.

Parties desiring to resolve their dispute through international arbitration will hesitate before choosing as the place of arbitration a jurisdiction that

95 On this issue, see J Lew, L Mistelis and S Kröll, *Comparative International Commercial Arbitration* (The Hague: Kluwer Law International 2003) at 85–6. On the theory of *anational* arbitration, see Carbonneau (2004), above note 33 at 47.

96 The Common Law Procedure Act 1854, s 5.

97 See, for example, the description of the case stated procedure described in W Park, 'The Lex Loci Arbitri and International Commercial Arbitration' (1983) 32 *International and Comparative Law Quarterly* 21 at 22.

98 Carbonneau (2004), above note 33 at 43 et seq.

actively promotes merit reviews of arbitral decisions. Where national courts have wide powers to review arbitration awards on the merits, there are likely to be more challenges to arbitral awards by disgruntled disputants prepared to run the risk of a less favourable outcome from a court. This affects the attractiveness of arbitration as an efficient and effective dispute resolution process.

Conversely, judicial review of international arbitration procedures may be desirable as it can address issues such as arbitrator bias and breaches of natural justice (or due process as it is called in some jurisdictions). Unlike judicial review on the merits, the limited nature of procedural review provides arbitrators the latitude for the continued development of the *lex mercatoria*.

The modern trend led by the UNCITRAL Model Law on International Commercial Arbitration (1985) (MLICA) is to limit judicial review to elements of procedure, including procedural fairness. Jurisdictions with modern international arbitration statutes typically support the development of international arbitration and *lex mercatoria* by permitting limited procedural review of arbitral awards only. Generally these statutes do not permit review on the merits. Jurisdictions with such a policy include France, Spain, Portugal, Italy, Australia, England and a growing number of Central and South American countries. Jurisdictions, which allow no substantive or procedural review at all include Switzerland and Belgium.[99]

Judicial procedural review of arbitration can be described as a double-edged sword, reflecting the continuing tension between the public and private justice systems. Its proponents argue that procedural review imbues the arbitration process with a sense of legitimacy and provides participants with an assurance that review is possible in certain situations – such as if proceedings have been conducted with a manifest lack of procedural fairness. Other commentators argue that the modern trend towards judicial review on limited procedural matters is insufficient as, in the words of Scheuerman, 'it remains a system of dispute resolution in which confidentiality (and even secrecy) is far-reaching and recourse to clear legal rules (or precedent) remains relatively limited'.[100] Opponents of judicial review argue that collateral or post-award litigation simply provides scope for delaying tactics and defeats the intention of arbitration to provide finality. Furthermore practice is not consistent from state to state. As Theofrastous observes, '[t]he debate is decades old – should parties

99 For an international overview of national arbitration laws, see Carbonneau (2004), above note 33 at 47 et seq.

100 W Scheuerman, 'Global Law in Our High Speed Economy' (2002) *43rd Annual International Studies Association Convention, New Orleans.* Available at www.isanet.org.

engaged in binding alternative dispute resolution be free to unfetter themselves from the legal norms of any particular state?'[101]

As regards international dispute resolution, cross-border arbitration, regardless of the merits of the arguments about judicial review, operates 'in the shadow of the law' with the consequence that arbitrators are becoming increasingly reluctant to decide matters *ex aequo et bono* or as *amiable compositeur*. The set of criteria upon which arbitrators are able to base their decisions is becoming ever narrower and increasingly legal.[102] Mayer observes that 'amiable composition [...] has become the exception and arbitration statutes treat it as such, sometimes even ignoring it.'[103] Commentators advising on the drafting of international agreements typically warn readers of the undesirability of empowering an arbitrator to act as *amiable compositeur* or decide the dispute *ex aequo et bono*.[104]

In short, international commercial arbitration has retreated from the civil law model which has dominated for so long. It has also been a catalyst for a move away from the *lex mercatoria* and the role of the arbitrator as *amiable compositeur* towards legalisation in the form of technically detailed arbitration clauses with a high level of specificity regarding forum and applicable law. In addition to the possibility of judicial review, litigation about the interpretation of arbitration clauses in relation to forum and applicable law is not unusual in international arbitration cases.

A further aspect of the international commercial arbitration regime, frequently glossed over by commentators, is the monopoly of Western industrialised countries over the process. UNCITRAL's mandate to actively consider the interests and needs of developing countries[105] can only extend to the development of policy, legal texts and the like. The implementation of the work of UNCITRAL and similar bodies, however, reflects the political and economic interests of the powerful. While there has been a power struggle between civil and common law interests, the stakeholders representing these interests – elite law firms, senior members of the judiciary and the bar, transnational businesses based in western industrialised countries (often with

101 T Theofrastous, 'International Commercial Arbitration in Europe: Subsidiarity and Supremacy in Light of the De-Localization Debate' (1999) 31 *Case Western Reserve Journal of International Law* 455 at 459.

102 See J Waincymer, *WTO Litigation: Procedural Aspects of Formal Dispute Settlement* (London: Cameron May 2002) at 67.

103 See Mayer (2001), above note 88 at 325.

104 See P Friedland, *Arbitration Clauses for International Contracts* (New York: Juris Publishing 2000) at chapter 11(2).

105 General Assembly resolution 2205 (XXI) of 17 December 1966, which established the Commission on International Trade Law and set forth its mandate, provides that 'The Commission shall bear in mind the interests of all peoples and particularly those of developing countries, in the extensive development of international trade.'

significant investments in developing countries) and their respective governments – have collaborated in closing the door to the interests and participation of other legal systems and their arbitrators. For example, despite efforts by various Arab arbitration groups to break into the international arbitration network,[106] Cairo and other Middle Eastern centres remain at the periphery of international arbitration practice. This outsider status has not changed despite the following factors: Egyptian arbitration law reflects the most modern arbitration law reform based on the UNCITRAL Model Law on Arbitration; the practice of the Cairo Regional Center for International Commercial Arbitration (CRCICA) is characterised by the application of the UNCITRAL Arbitration Rules by highly educated and experienced arbitrators; and Cairo is located strategically between the global North and South – the industrialised and developing worlds. Yet attempts to develop international arbitration mechanisms that reflect political, cultural and social norms within the Middle East have not been very successful. It seems that to enter the game of international arbitration, the new kids on the block must first prove themselves by conforming to existing norms of practice such as European choice of law clauses or, insofar as it is still applied, the Eurocentric *lex mercatoria*. By applying the *lex mercatoria* in arbitrations conducted in developing countries, arbitrators can avoid applying the local law, trade usage and practice, while purporting to apply universal principles of commercial practice. Dezalay and Garth point out the paradox of promoting an Islamic Arbitration Center in Cairo by emphasising its ability to conform to Western practices.[107]

Yet another challenge to international arbitration is found in the difficulties facing disputants in a globalising environment in which the role of geo–political borders continues to be challenged. Globalisation aims to increase freedom of movement for goods, services and capital,[108] which in turn creates new challenges in terms of sovereignty. For example, public policy and other issues once within the realm of nation-states are now the legitimate or claimed concern and responsibility of a range of national and transnational actors. The *Global Rice* case involving Artaban and the Malaysian rice field investors described earlier highlights the complexities of dealing with disputes which cross boundaries, not only of nation-states, but of tribes, literacy levels, wealth and notions of law, property and public policy. The case represents vast cultural

[106] For example, the Euro–Arab Chamber of Commerce and the Arab Association of International Arbitration.

[107] See Dezalay and Garth (1996), above note 91 at 243. For a different view, see L Trakman, 'Legal Traditions' and International Commercial Arbitration' (2007) 17 *American Review of International Arbitration* 1.

[108] Note the impact that regional identities such as the European Union have had on freedom of movement. While increasing freedoms within their zone of influence, regional borders become harder to cross than ever before. See L Boulle, *The Law of Globalisation* (Gold Coast: Bond University Press 2008) at 4.

differences among parties in terms of business practices and ways of life. How well equipped is the system of international arbitration to deal with these challenges?

Returning to the international *Travel Troubles* case introduced earlier in the chapter, the following short analysis highlights the risks and opportunities of international arbitration. In this case arbitration offers Felixtours various advantages over litigation:

– Parties can select an institutional or *ad hoc* approach. Either way, and subject to choice of law and related principles, they have greater control over issues such as:

  a. who determines the outcome of the dispute/s;
  b. where the arbitration will take place; and
  c. the law or principles to be applied.

– Arbitral awards are binding. For Felixtours this means that the process ensures finality to the dispute. The New York Convention on Arbitral Awards offers Felixtours some assurance in terms of enforceability of foreign awards, in so far as the other disputant parties are subject to the Convention through their national jurisdictions. While the Hague Choice of Court Convention exists in relation to the recognition of court decisions it has fewer signatories than the New York convention and most have yet to ratify the Convention.
– Arbitration is a well-established and recognised dispute resolution process in the international business arena.

The increased institutionalisation and legalisation of international arbitration presents the following risks for Felixtours:

– Arbitration and enforcement processes are likely to be accompanied by lengthy delays and corresponding expense. Arbitration may also be accompanied by collateral national litigation regarding the interpretation of arbitration clauses.
– Despite the finality of an arbitral award, the potential for judicial review of the award, for example for bias on the part of the arbitrator, may create further uncertainty.
– The preservation of the long-standing business relationships among the various Felixtours groups and their business partners will not play a significant role in arbitration.
– Communication between parties to the arbitration is likely to be strained as each party focuses on gathering information to strengthen their case and weaken that of the others. The longer the arbitration and

> enforcement processes take, the more likely it is that business relationships will suffer permanent damage.

While the ideal of international commercial arbitration may have been fast and cost-effective justice based on the universal commercial principles of *lex mercatoria*, the reality can be lengthy, expensive, formal and legally technical arbitration,[109] accompanied by parallel collateral national litigation.[110] The framework for dispute resolution based on the notion of the supreme and sovereign nation state and the rule of law, while not obsolete, is no longer adequate.[111] To the extent that international arbitration is dependent on national laws and infrastructure as its basis for decision-making and execution of awards, it may lack the flexibility to meet the challenges of emerging transnationality and globalisation. International arbitration falls short of a transnational character where awards can be vacated on grounds of national law or public policy.[112]

Moreover, references to *international* and *universal* principles and practices in the arbitration context really refer to principles and practices established and protectively nurtured by European and American arbitration experts. Despite attempts by outsiders to break into the inner circle of international arbitration, the mainstream of international commercial arbitration has never become truly international. Current trends towards standardisation and legalisation may minimise opportunities for the incorporation of flexible and culturally-based practices such as the prohibition of interest (*riba*) under Islamic law.[113]

[109] See comments by J Najar, the senior counsel of General Electric's commercial finance business for Europe, the Middle East and Africa in 'Call for much simpler international arbitration' (2008) *Australian Financial Review*. See also Dezalay and Garth (1996), above note 91 at 54.

[110] C Bühring-Uhle et al (2006), above note 89 at 148.

[111] On the necessity of law and specifically the positive correlation between quality commercial and financial laws and economic advancement in eastern and central Europe see G Sanders, 'Multilateral organizations and technical legal assistance: Learning from Experience' (2007) *Modern Law for Global Commerce: Congress to celebrate the 40th annual session for UNCITRAL: Studies, Proposals and Backgrounds Papers* at 37.

[112] These procedures are discussed in detail in Chapter 2. Note Watt's comment on the diminishing role of national public policy in the enforcement of arbitral awards: H Watt, 'Globalization and Comparative Law' in M Reimann and R Zimmermann (eds), *The Oxford Handbook of Comparative Law* (Oxford: Oxford University Press 2006) at 601.

[113] See M El-Gamal, *Islamic Finance: Law, Economics and Practice* (Cambridge: Cambridge University Press 2006) at 49 et seq and N Majeed, 'Good Faith and Due Process: Lessons from the Shari'ah' (2004) 20 *Arbitration International* 97 at 98–99.

These developments have both undermined the attractiveness of the arbitration process and heralded the entrance of mediation and other forms of dispute resolution on the international scene.

7. MEDIATION IN INTERNATIONAL DISPUTE RESOLUTION

Co-existing with the world of international arbitration, there is, as Charny points out, an extensive array of 'extra-legal forces that help maintain the functioning of markets'[114] – that is, a large number of legally unenforceable arrangements in business transactions, that are enforced not through judicial or arbitral proceedings, but by means of non-legal sanctions.[115] He suggests that '[l]egal intervention may disrupt a delicate social equilibrium'.[116] From this perspective there will always be a need to resolve disputes on the basis of factors other than law.

Whether disputes involve high or low monetary stakes, or whether they are classified as consumer, commercial or family disputes, mediation and other facilitative and advisory dispute resolution processes allow legal and extra-legal considerations to be considered simultaneously; terms of settlement need not focus solely on a restricted range of legal remedies. Mediation processes are sufficiently flexible to accommodate a range of stakeholders (not all of whom might have legal standing) in ways the formality of arbitration and litigation would not normally allow. In the *Global Rice* dispute introduced previously, certain interested and affected parties, such as government representatives and those making land grabs, may not have legal standing. If all affected parties are not invited to the table, the potential for reaching a sustainable settlement of the dispute can be compromised. The facilitative nature of mediation supports an inclusive approach to problem-solving and can be advantageous in these types of situations.

Mediation therefore has cross-cultural appeal. Its informality and flexibility imbue the process with the potential to accommodate cultural sensitivities and differences in a manner not possible in formal arbitration proceedings. Rights-based determinative forms of dispute resolution such as litigation and arbitration do not allow for exploration of the cultural differences that may have led to the dispute. Rather the jurisdiction's dominant culture, procedures and decision-makers will apply. The flexibility of mediation, coupled with the ability to design one's own variations of the process, allows

114 D Charny, 'Nonlegal Sanctions in Commercial Relations' (1990) 104 *Harvard Law Review* 374 at 376.

115 His examples include the heavy reliance on (legally unenforceable) agreements in principle, oral promises and policies.

116 See Charny (1990), above note 114 at 388.

skilled conflict management practitioners to move between cultures, explore differences and create a forum culturally acceptable to a variety of participants with a view to agreeing on appropriate norms for the regulation of future relationships.[117]

Mediation is considered to be cost-effective, in particular in comparison with arbitration.[118] The Singapore Mediation Centre's mediation fee table provides an illustration of fees for international mediation in Table 2. In November 2008 the Centre had mediated S$1.7 billion worth of disputes.

Table 2
Singapore Mediation Centre Mediation Fees

Quantum of Claim	Mediation Fee
Up to S$100 000 (Singapore dollars)	S$900 per party per day
Above S$100 000 up to S$250 000	S$1 200 per party per day
Above S$250 000 up to S$500 000	S$1 800 per party per day
Above S$500 000 up to S$1 000 000	S$2 200 per party per day
Above S$1 000 000 up to S$2 500 000	S$2 600 per party per day
Above S$2 500 000 up to S$5 000 000	S$2 800 per party per day
Above S$5 000 000	S$2 900 per party per day plus pro-rata portion of 0.05 per cent of the quantum above S$5 000 000

In another illustration Carroll and Mackie provide the following cost comparison of arbitration and mediation in an international commercial dispute.

117 For a model on cross-cultural business negotiation factors, see J Salacuse, *Making Global Deals* (New York: Times Books 1992) at 70.

118 For studies indicating quantitative advantages of mediation over litigation see U Froschauer and M Lüger, 'Empirische Forschung im Kontext von Mediation' (2009) 1 *Perspektive Mediation* at 8 and L Krainer, 'Wenn Forschung in die Praxis interveniert… – Begleitforschung Flughafen Wien-Schwechat' (2009) 1 *Perspektive Mediation* at 28, T Stipanowich, 'ADR and the 'Vanishing Trial': The Growth and Impact of 'Alternative Dispute Resolution' (2004) 1 *Journal of Empirical Legal Studies* at 843–912. For a different view, see the following major US research: J Kakalik et al, *An Evaluation of Mediation and Neutral Early Evaluation under the Civil Justice Reform Act* (California: RAND 1996). Also see W Brazil, 'Court ADR 25 Years after Pound: Have we Found a Better Way?' (2002) 18 *Ohio State Journal on Dispute Resolution* 93 at 101 and R Ingleby, *In the Ball Park: Alternative Dispute Resolution and the Courts* (Melbourne: Australian Institute of Judicial Administration 1991).

Table 3
Cost Comparison of Mediation and Arbitration[119]

	Mediation	Arbitration
Amount at issue	US$20 000 000	US$20 000 000
Time to reach result	2–6 months	24–36 months
Management time	100 hours	700 hours
Cost of mediator/arbitrator panel	US$17 000	US$350 000 – US$750 000
Legal costs	US$90 000	US$400 000 – US$600 000
Result	Agreed commercial solution	Binding award

The case illustrates some of the qualitative and quantitative features of mediation in comparison with arbitration.[120] The data in the table is taken from a case in which the clients chose to mediate. Therefore the arbitration costs are estimated, calculated on the same hourly rate as the mediators. Figures will vary according to jurisdiction. Carroll and Mackie explain that by opting for mediation, the parties in this case remained in control of decision-making and, under the guidance of the mediators, were able to see the limitations of a purely legal solution to the case. Further, had the matter not settled, the investment in mediation could still have yielded positive results such as isolating the issues in dispute and engaging parties in dialogue as a step towards restoring their business relationship. In addition the low cost of mediation relative to arbitration means that the ability to finance arbitration or litigation is not usually thwarted by mediation; in fact the work done in mediations that do not settle may save time for preparation of other proceedings. With less time spent managing the disputes, commercial parties not only save transactions costs but are able to refocus on their respective businesses. In terms of enforcement, it is widely believed in mediation circles that parties will be more likely to comply with an agreement they themselves have made than with a decision imposed upon them such as an arbitral award or a court ruling. However the evidence is mixed on this point.[121]

119 Table 3 and an explanation of the calculations can be found in Carroll and Mackie (2006), above note 7 at 69–70.

120 For empirical research on the differences between mediation and arbitration see, for example, S Goldberg and J Brett, 'Disputants' Perspectives on the Differences Between Mediation and Arbitration' (1990) 6 *Negotiation Journal* 249.

121 See Stipanowich (2004), above note 118 at 843–912. See also C McEwan and R Maiman, 'Mediation in Small Claims Court: Consensual Processes and Outcomes' in

The enforceability of mediation agreements varies according to the legal status of the mediated outcome and the extent to which it is recognised by local courts. This variability across jurisdictions, and consequent legal uncertainty, is viewed by many as a major limitation of international mediation. Conversely court recognition and enforcement of foreign arbitral awards has been greatly facilitated by the New York Convention on Arbitral Awards, although enforcement is not without considerable cost and time investment.

8. Mediation – Historical and Contemporary Perspectives

Antaki distinguishes between two primary world traditions in mediation, namely intuitive or informal mediation, on one hand and cognitive, scientific or western on the other.[122] While the former continues to be practised in Arab and Muslim countries, much of Asia, the Pacific and Africa, the latter approach, western mediation, emerged in the United States and according to the author is spreading worldwide.[123] Antaki goes on to consider the development of mediation and similar processes throughout history from chthonic traditional societies to nation-states and modern justice systems. He also explores how mediation models vary according to whether they are serving a communitarian social structure or a mainly individualistic one.

Historical references to mediation and conciliation can be found in literature on ancient civilisations and traditional community-based societies without formal political and legal systems. In Roman law mediators were known by a number of names including *internuncius*, *medium*, *intercessor*, *philantropus*, *interpolator*, *conciliator*, *interlocutor* and finally mediator.

Many traditional indigenous societies in Australia,[124] New Zealand,[125] Asia,[126] the Pacific,[127] the Americas[128] and Africa[129] feature a network of strong

K Kressel et al (eds), *Mediation Research: The Process and Effectiveness of Third Party Interventions* (San Francisco: Jossey-Bass Publishers 1989) at 53, C McEwen and R Maiman, 'Mediation in Small Claims Court: Achieving Compliance Through Consent' (1981) 18 *Law and Society Review* at 11 and K Mack, *Court Referral to ADR: Criteria and Research* (Canberra: AIJA (Australasian Institute of Judicial Administration) and NADRAC 2003) at 28.

122 See Antaki (2006), above note 29.

123 See Antaki (2006), above note 29 at 5.

124 On indigenous Australia see L Behrendt, *Aboriginal Dispute Resolution* (Sydney: Federation Press 1995) at 16 and V Böge, 'Traditionale Methoden der Konfliktbearbeitung: Möglichkeiten und Grenzen' (2008) 3 *Perspektive Mediation* 116.

125 See, for example, I MacDuff, 'What you do with *Taniwha* at the table?' (2003) *Negotiation Journal* 195.

kinship ties throughout the community, which lends itself to a communitarian approach to conflict resolution and healing where the best interests of the community rather than the individual remain paramount. Mediation practised in Asian socialist systems such as China draws on both Confucian traditions and simultaneously reinforces contemporary political ideals. In China mediations are conducted by community and district leaders and frequently involve public dimensions. In various religious communities mediation continues to be practised with a religious elder acting as mediator in promoting religious values and ideals.[130]

In many of these communities, elders still play the roles of mediator, advisor and judge. These roles were not clearly defined or compartmentalised in the way they are today.[131] Antaki writes,

> Islam recognises mediation (wasata), conciliation (tawfik, solh), reconciliation (islah) and arbitration (tahkim), but it is clear from the verses quoted that the different forms overlap and are sometimes mixed, which is typical of that time. This characteristic is still very much alive today everywhere in countries with a communitarian culture.[132]

Anthropological studies on legal systems reveal many processes, previously assumed to be strictly formalistic in nature, to be in reality complex systems involving mediation and other forms of dispute resolution. Research has shown, for example, that the Icelandic Althing previously thought to be 'the oldest

[126] See, for example, B Goh, *Negotiating with the Chinese* (England: Dartmouth Publishing 1996), S Lubman (ed), *China's Legal Reforms* (Oxford: Oxford University Press 1996) at 1286, A Black, 'Alternative Dispute Resolution in Brunei-Darussalam: the Blending of Imported and Traditional Processes' (2001) 13 *Bond Law Review* 305.

[127] See, for example, T Flucher, 'Ho `o pono pono: Wie die Polynesier die Harmonie wiederherstellen' (2008) 3 *Perspektive Mediation* 154.

[128] See for example, C Barie, 'Justitia zieht sich den Schleier von den Augen: Spuren des indigenen Gewohnheitsrechts in Bolivien' (2008) 3 *Perspektive Mediation* 148.

[129] See, for example, N Shucker, 'The Role of Law in Development and Investment in Sub-Saharan Africa' (1999) 30 *Law and Policy in International Business* 667, S Steixner, 'Traditionelle Paarkonfliktregelung in Burkina Faso: Von der Konfliktprävention bis zum Versöhnungsritual' (2008) 3 *Perspektive Mediation* 124, H Mayer and C Boness, 'Mediations und Versöhnungskonzepte im Südlichen Africa' (2008) 3 *Perspektive Mediation* 130 and N Tshibangu, 'Eine Richtschnur entlang der Beziehungsnähte zwischen Individuen und Gemeinschaft' (2008) 3 *Perspektive Mediation* 142.

[130] See for example Tshibangu (2008), above note 129 and Flucher (2008), above note 127.

[131] See Antaki (2006), above note 29.

[132] See Antaki (2006), above note 29 at 13.

continuing parliament' in the world was more akin to a multi-door courthouse for resolving disputes through negotiation, mediation and arbitration.[133]

The scientific mediation movement began with community and court-based initiatives in the 1970s in the United States, in the 1980s in Australia, Canada and New Zealand and in the late 1980s and early 1990s in continental Europe. It is tempting to suggest that the primary reason behind the surge in the scientific ADR movement, particularly in common law jurisdictions, was the inordinate delay and escalating costs of resolving disputes through national court systems. Much has been made of the cost-saving advantages of mediation in business disputes. Media headlines such as, 'Mediation saves millions', highlight the potential for mediation to resolve complex and high value disputes in a matter of days and weeks rather than months and years.[134]

However, while the inefficiencies of the justice system in many countries provided the push to put mediation on the politico–legal map, contemporary mediation offers more than quantitative advantages of time and money. Empirical research indicates high party satisfaction rates with the mediation process.[135] The rise of mediation reflects the need to address the

[133] See, for example, the revision of the understanding of the Icelandic Althing by H Thorláksson, 'The Icelandic Commonwealth Period: Building a New Society' in W Fitzhugh and E Ward (eds), *Vikings: The North Atlantic Saga* (Washington DC/New York: Smithsonian Books 2000) 175, referred to in J Nafziger, 'Comparative Dispute Resolution: A New Look' (2002) 10 *Willamette Journal of International Law and Dispute Resolution* 11 at 14.

[134] See L Hattam, 'Mediation saves millions' (2004) *Herald Sun.*

[135] For research that indicates a higher level of party satisfaction with the mediation process compared with litigation see NADRAC, *ADR Research: A Resource Paper* (2004) available at www.nadrac.gov.au at 34, M Robertson, 'The Stamp of Statistical Approval' (2004) 7 *ADR Bulletin* 12. In Germany see K Zenk, R Strobel, J Hupfeld; and A Böttger *Gerichtsnahe Mediation in Niedersachsen – Die Evaluation eines Modellversuchs* (Baden-Baden: Nomos 2007) at 130 and G Spindler, *Gerichtsnahe Mediation in Niedersachsen – eine juristisch-ökonomishe Analyse* (Göttingen: Universitätsverlag Göttingen 2006) at paras 582 et seq, 591 et seq and 618. For a summary of empirical research in Germany, which confirms both qualitative and quantative advantages in relation to court-related mediation, see J von Bargen, *Gerichtsinterne Mediation*, Veröffentlichungen zum Verfahrensrecht N° 57 (Tübingen: Mohr Siebeck 2008) and W Gottwald, 'Gerichtsnahe Mediation' in F Haft and K von Schlieffen (eds) *Handbuch Mediation* (2nd ed, München: C H Beck 2009) § 39 at 981 et seq. For an analysis of how party satisfaction varies according to mediator style, see P McDermott and R Obar, 'What's Going On in Mediation: An Empirical Analysis of the Influence of a Mediator's Style on Party Satisfaction and Monetary Benefit' (2004) 9 *Harvard Negotiation Law Review* 75. Compare the findings of McAdoo and Welsh that while parties may report satisfaction with mediation, lawyers and judges appear to be less convinced of its success in achieving substantive, procedural and efficient justice: B McAdoo and N Welsh, 'Look Before You Leap and Keep on Looking: Lessons From the Institutionalization of Court-

alienating effects of formal law on civil society and the resulting loss of social cohesion.[136] Here mediation is seen as a means to shift the responsibility for dispute resolution back to local communities and to the people involved in the dispute. Other factors contributing to the worldwide interest in mediation include socio–cultural changes such as the decline of the culturally homogenous nation-state, the increasing pluralisation of societal value systems and the changing face of the (international) business community to include traditional owners of resources, e-traders, more women and small entrepreneurs.[137] One of the vignettes at the start of this chapter, *Logos in Cyberspace*, tells the story of Simon, a young music and design entrepreneur who is in dispute with a group of musicians in Slovenia. In many ways Simon is representative of a new globalising world order. He connects to a borderless world through internet technology. He works primarily from home, so his overheads are low and he earns what he needs. Simon does business with people of his own generation who have similar musical and artistic tastes, irrespective of national culture and ethnicity. He cannot begin to imagine how difficult such interactions would have been for someone in his situation throughout most of the twentieth century. For Simon mediation is an attractive option: he can talk through his differences with the Bimbos from Slovenia, there are creative problem-solving options such as adjusting the design and mediation is affordable for Simon, especially if he can participate in the process online.

In addition parenting disputes increasingly cross national borders as the story of Joe and Marie – introduced earlier – illustrates. Here mediation offers a more personal and culturally-adaptable conflict resolution process than litigation, one which is generally more suited to achieving innovative and practical solutions that are in the interests of the children.

As a form of private justice, mediation sits well with the ongoing privatisation of previously state-owned services such as health, utilities and railways. Industry groups have embraced mediation and other forms of dispute resolution as a means to reduce the cost of consumer dispute resolution, enhance confidentiality of internal processes and decrease the external influence of courts over the outcomes of disputes between businesses and their customers.

Connected Mediation' (2004–2005) 5 *Nevada Law Journal* 399 at 399–432, J Shack, *Bibliographic Summary of Cost, Pace and Satisfaction Studies of Court-Related Mediation Programs*, (2003) Center for Analysis of Alternative Dispute Resolution Systems 862 available at www.caadrs.org/studies/MedStudyBiblio.htm and M Delaney and T Wright, *Plaintiff's Satisfaction with Dispute Resolution Processes: Trial, Arbitration, Pre-trial conference and Mediation* (Sydney: Justice Research Centre 1997).

136 See Glenn (2004), above note 40 at 137–138.

137 See N Alexander, 'Global Trends in Mediation: Riding the Third Wave' in N Alexander (ed), *Global Trends in Mediation* (2nd ed, Alphen aan den Rijn: Kluwer Law International 2006) at 6–7.

Finally the regionalisation and globalisation of trade and law through groupings such as the European Union, North American Free Trade Agreement (NAFTA), World Trade Organisation (WTO) and various bodies of the United Nation such as UNCITRAL highlight the potential for mediation of international disputes. In this context the influence of the elite international law firm, the interests of which increasingly span law, business and politics, has led to further support for the flexibility, efficiency and confidentiality offered by mediation.

9. The Institutionalisation of Mediation

The institutionalisation of mediation and ADR can be described in two phases: an initial phase involving national mediation organisations and a second phase represented by international collaborative initiatives. The first phase began in the 1980s as organisations such as the International Institute for Conflict Prevention and Resolution (CPR) and JAMS Endispute in the United States, LEADR[138] and the Institute of Arbitrators and Mediators (IAMA) in Australia and CEDR (Centre for Effective Dispute Resolution) Solve in the United Kingdom, promoted and formalised a range of dispute resolution processes from mediation to arbitration. At the same time, the public justice system began offering dispute resolution services annexed to the court in a bid to reduce delays in getting cases to trial and the costs of resolving disputes generally, providing litigants with a range of dispute processing options.[139] While settlement rates in court-referred mediation vary greatly, they are usually said to be more than 50 per cent and figures of 80 to 90 per cent are not uncommon. In the Philippines, for example, some 20 000 cases were referred to mediation under court programs in 2004. Of the 7600 which completed the process 82

[138] LEADR is an Association of Dispute Resolvers.

[139] Empirical research to date has delivered mixed results on the question of whether court-related ADR, in particular, mediation does in fact reduce time and costs involved in dispute resolution. See for example the inconclusive results of the RAND report, J Kakalik et al, 'Just, Speedy and Inexpensive? An Evaluation of Judicial Case Management under the Civil Justice Reform Act' (1997) 17 *Alabama Law Review* at 38. However, see the results of a significant study in Ontario, which demonstrated that the use of ADR resulted in improvements in court-based dispute resolution in terms of time, costs and outcomes, R Hann and C Baar, *Evaluation of the Ontario Mandatory Mediation Program (Rule 24.1): Final Report – The First 23 Months* (Alberta: Queen's Printer 2001). In relation to France see Deckert on empirical studies showing reductions in time for mediation compared to court processes, K Deckert, 'Mediation in Frankreich – Rechtlicher Rahmen und praktische Erfahrungen' in K Hopt and F Steffek (eds), *Mediation – Rechtstatsachen, Rechtsvergleich, Regelungen* (Tübingen: Mohr Siebeck 2008) 183 at 251.

percent were settled.[140] The Singapore Mediation Centre reports a settlement rate of 73.9 per cent overall and 66.15 per cent for court-referred matters.[141] Statistics from other countries and regions in 2008 show similar results.[142]

During this initial phase, mediation began redefining business dispute resolution in many jurisdictions across the globe – its biggest impact being on the formal justice systems of western industrialised nations. However, the international market for business dispute resolution remained focused on arbitration, with American lawyers encouraged by the decision in the watershed Mitsubishi case in which the US Supreme Court for the first time upheld contractual commitments to engage in arbitration and other dispute resolution processes in international commercial settings.[143]

The mid to late 1990s signalled the beginning of the second phase of the institutionalisation of mediation during which domestic trends began to extend to cross-border dispute management. International commercial arbitration institutions – such as the ICC in Paris and the LCIA in London – and national ADR organisations – such as ACDC in Sydney, ADR Center in Rome, CEDR in London, CPR in New York and JAMS in California[144] – began to develop their cross-border mediation services and facilities.[145] The first transatlantic alliance of ADR organisations, the Mediation Services Alliance (MEDAL), was founded in 2005.[146] In 2009 JAMS in the United States and ADR Center in Italy announced an agreement to form the JAMS International

[140] R Würtz, Chief of USAID, in a speech available at www.philippines.usaid.gov. For statistics from other jurisdictions see Stipanowich (2004), above note 118 at 843–912. See also L Bingham et al, 'Dispute Resolution and the Vanishing Trial: Comparing Federal Government Litigation and ADR Outcomes' *3rd Annual Conference on Empirical Legal Studies Papers* available at www.ssrn.com. McEwan and Maiman (1989), above note 121 at 53. NSW Law Reform Commission, *Research Report 12: Mediation and Community Justice Centres: An Empirical Study* (Sydney: NSWLR 2004).

[141] L Onn, 'Institutionalised Commercial Mediation in Singapore' (2008) Session I *International Arbitration Conference Proceedings* 2–12.

[142] For example, on the Balkans see G Van Der Burght, 'Mediation in the Balkans: Promising Developments' (2008) 74 *Arbitration* 167.

[143] See *Mitsubishi Motors Corp v Soler Chysler-Plymouth, Inc* 473 US 614 (1985).

[144] ICC is the International Chamber of Commerce, LCIA the London Court of International Arbitration, ACDC the Australian Commercial Disputes Centre, CEDR the Centre for Effective Dispute Resolution and CPR the International Institute for Conflict Prevention and Resolution.

[145] For the mediation and conciliation rules of selected organisations that offer cross-border mediation see Appendix B.

[146] International News, 'JAMS and CEDR Announce Strategic Alliance' (2005) 16 *World Arbitration and Mediation Report* 178. The members of MEDAL are listed in the Comparative Rules table in Appendix B.

ADR Center to provide mediation and arbitration of cross-border disputes and training services worldwide.

In addition, organisations that offer international mediation services in specialised fields include the World Intellectual Property Organisation (WIPO) for intellectual property disputes[147] and the International Ice Hockey Federation in relation to its own sporting disputes.[148] E-commerce and e-conflict have contributed to a proliferation of online dispute resolution services (ODR) across borders. ODR service-providers for the Internet Corporation for Assigned Names and Numbers (ICANN)'s[149] Uniform Domain Name Dispute Resolution policy include WIPO, Asian Domain Name Dispute Resolution Centre (ADNDRC),[150] and the National Arbitration Forum (NAF)[151] based in the United States. Other prominent international online mediation service-providers include the Claim Room and Square Trade. The largest on-line auction house in the world, E-Bay, offers dissatisfied customers ODR services, including mediation. This is likely to be Francesca's first port of call in her E-Bay dispute with the Latvian purchaser, described earlier.

European Union policy has specifically addressed international mediation in consumer disputes. In 2005 the European Union established the European Consumers Network (ECC-Net) to inform customers of their rights and assist in the resolution of cross-border complaints and disputes. ECC-Net receives complaints from consumers and, where necessary, directs complainants to the dispute resolution database they maintain.[152] In addition FIN-Net has been established as an EU cooperation network between national out-of-court dispute settlement bodies for financial services. The European Commission issued Recommendations in 1998 and 2001 reinforcing its support for the use of mediation in international consumer disputes.[153]

In relation to family disputes, there are numerous cross-border regulatory instruments. The Hague Conference on Private International Law has produced three relevant Conventions. The first is the Hague Child Protection Convention of 1996 which promotes the use of mediation with respect to matters

[147] World Intellectual Property Organisation (WIPO) has an Arbitration and Mediation Centre, see www.wipo.int.

[148] I Blackshaw, *Mediating Sports Disputes: National and International Perspectives* (The Hague: TMC Asser Press 2002) at 170.

[149] Internet Corporation for Assigned Names and Numbers at www.icann.org.

[150] Asian Domain Name Dispute Resolution Centre (ADNDRC) at www.adndrc.org.

[151] National Arbitration Forum (NAF) at www.domains.adrforum.com.

[152] Available at www.ec.europa.eu.

[153] Recommendation on the principles applicable to the bodies responsible for out-of-court settlement of consumer disputes (98/257/EC) 30 March 1998. Recommendation on the principles for out-of-court bodies involved in the consensual resolution of consumer disputes (C(2001) 1016) 4 April 2001.

that fall under the Convention[154] (Article 31). The Hague Adult Protection Convention[155] is a sister Convention reflecting much of the 1996 Hague Convention in the context of vulnerable adults. Finally the Hague Child Abduction Convention[156] also makes provision for mediation.

In the European Union, Council Regulations, Directives and Recommendations have been adopted that address cross-border family mediation, reinforcing support for mediation in family disputes.[157] Numerous organisations, projects and working groups have been established to facilitate and mediate disputes involving alleged international child abduction, usually by one of the child's parents. These include Reunite (UK),[158] MAMIF (France),[159] and MFBE (Germany/France),[160] and the US–German Bilateral International Parental Abduction Working Group, which is engaged in a US–German mediation pilot. In terms of training and research, the European Forum for Family Mediation Training and Research, MFBE, is a significant cross-border institution.

In 2007 the Permanent Bureau of the Hague Conference on Private International Law released a feasibility study on cross-border mediation in family matters. The study examines the development of international family mediation practice and concludes with some suggestions for future work in the field including greater international cooperation and communication about available mediators, mediation services and national laws on family mediation. Finally the study suggests that the Hague Conference continue to work towards uniform or harmonised standards in relation to mediator approval and practice and laws regulating mediation, specifically those relating to incentives and

[154] The Hague Convention of 19 October 1996 on Jurisdiction, Applicable Law, Recognition, Enforcement and Co-operation in respect of Parental Responsibility and Measures for the Protection of Children.

[155] The Hague Convention of 13 January 2000 on the International Protection of Adults.

[156] The Hague Convention of 25 October 1980 on the Civil Aspects of International Child Abduction.

[157] See the Regulation Concerning Jurisdiction and the Recognition and Enforcement of Judgments in Matrimonial Matters and the Matters of Parental Responsibility (N° 2201/2003) adopted 27 November 2003, the Directive to improve access to justice in cross-border disputes by establishing minimum common rules relating to legal aid for such disputes (Directive 2002/8/EC) adopted 27 January 2003. Recommendation on Family Mediation and equality of sexes (Recommendation 1639 (2003)) adopted 21 June 2004, Recommendation on Family Mediation (Recommendation (98)1) adopted 21 January 1998.

[158] See www.reunite.org.

[159] MAMIF stands for *Mission d'aide à la médiation internationale pour les familles.* See the MAMIF website at www.enlevement-parental.justice.gouv.fr.

[160] MFBE stands for *Médiation familiale binationale en Europe*, available at www.mfbe.eu.

requirements to mediate, confidentiality and the international recognition and enforceability of mediated agreements.[161]

Returning to the *Global Family* story introduced earlier, Joe is not much interested in the details of the Hague Convention on Child Abduction. Rather he is worried about his child's welfare and how he will be able see him if Anton accompanies his mother to Germany. Mediation has the potential to provide a forum in which he and Marie can talk together to create an arrangement that works for them and Anton and also addresses the needs of Marie's new partner. The US–German mediation project or one of the other organisations referred to earlier might be a useful starting point.

As is the case with international arbitration, international mediation may be *ad hoc* or institutional. The growing number of organisations offering mediation services and rules may encourage an increased use of institutional mediation at an international level. However there will also be more opportunities for parties to shop around and select suitable mediators, rules, venues and related services for acceptable prices.

In relation to international disputes, research indicates that mediation is more likely to be integrated into arbitration and negotiation processes than conducted as a separate process. According to one international survey, settlements may occur prior to arbitral awards being issued however they are more likely to take place after an arbitral award has been issued in order to reduce enforcement costs.[162] Another survey indicates that the extent to which mediation and informal settlement attempts take place in international arbitration varies according to legal culture. The researchers write that,

> [i]n line with German judicial tradition, German practitioners favour informal mediation attempts by the arbitrator(s), whereas non-American Common Law practitioners seem to have the most "progressive" attitude toward mediation windows using separate mediators.[163]

Thus resistance to the use of mediation as a dispute resolution process independent of arbitration seems to stem from lack of information about the process and the absence of international legal frameworks to support mediation and other non-determinative processes. The survey further indicated that civil lawyers, who generally had less experience with mediation and other forms of

161 See Hague Convention of Private International Law, *Feasibility Study On Cross-Border Mediation In Family Matters* (General Affairs and Policy 2007) at 21–28.

162 According to a survey of corporate users of international arbitration, settlements are reached without an arbitral award in 25 per cent of cases. In a further 7 per cent of cases settlement is reached with the support of a consent award. 40 per cent of corporate counsel surveyed indicated that they had negotiated settlements after the arbitral award was rendered: Lagerberg and Mistelis (2008) above note 82.

163 See Bühring-Uhle et al (2006), above note 89 at 128.

non-determinative dispute resolution in their respective domestic legal arenas compared with common law lawyers, felt that there was no need for international commercial mediation. American lawyers were more positive about mediation in an international commercial setting. The findings suggest that exposure to mediation in national jurisdictions influences the preparedness of lawyers to engage in mediation on an international level.[164]

10. MEDIATION STORIES

This introductory chapter has shown that mediation has different stories. It is in part the story of how western legal systems have responded to increasing complexity, non-affordability, inaccessibility and anonymity of litigation. Initially described as an alternative to court, mediation is increasingly becoming an integrated or interrelated part of many legal systems, thereby extending western concepts of justice, law and dispute resolution. In the 21st century mediation is at the forefront of contemporary social and legal development and is finding a place in both physical dispute resolution forums and worldwide electronic-based communities.[165]

Other stories go back to the wisdom of traditional mediation-like practices as the inspiration for contemporary mediation. As a dispute resolution forum, mediation-like processes have enjoyed relevance in traditional societies based on collective ideals of sustainability. They continue to play a role in communitarian structures such as indigenous communities, religious institutions and socialist regimes. In this story mediation is offered as one strategy to fill the gap between thin positivist law and thick notions of law and lore, tradition and culture typical of chthonic practices. Mediation is described as an interdisciplinary movement developing within and around positivist law.

Finally there are those who see mediation as a significant tradition in its own right, moving across legal systems and influencing, and being influenced by, major traditions of law, society and culture. In this story contemporary mediation emerges out of the continuous exchange of ideas and cross-fertilisation that occurs among legal traditions. Mediation has the ability to draw upon internationally shared values of dispute resolution as evidenced by regulatory instruments such as the MLICC. At the same time national regulatory policy ensures a continuing role for domestic law in international mediation practice. The next chapter explores the concept of private international law in relation to mediation and establishes a framework for understanding regulatory issues.

164 See Bühring-Uhle et al (2006), above note 89 at 112.

165 See, for example, B Pappas, 'Online Court: Online Dispute Resolution and the Future of Small Claims' (2008) *UCLA Journal of Law and Technology* 2.

Chapter 2
Law in the Mediation Equation

Good laws lead to the making of better ones; bad ones bring about worse.[1]
Jean Jacque Rousseau

1. Overview

Litigation in connection with mediation is on the rise.[2] As mediation practice continues to grow, US research indicates an increase in the number of cases dealing with aspects of mediation, particularly in the state courts of Texas, California and Florida.[3] Similar trends are evident in Australia and other common law countries, although the volume of litigation varies considerably in each jurisdiction. While there is generally less litigation to do with mediation in civil law countries, it too is increasing with the growth of mediation. To the extent that the case law development of mediation is a function of the willingness of participants to litigate about mediation, a philosophical paradox emerges. Coben and Thompson call the phenomenon of litigating in relation to a process designed to avoid litigation *disputing irony*. It encapsulates the theme of this chapter and raises the question: What's law got to do with it?

Chapter 2 highlights the relationship between law and mediation in an international and comparative context. Case law, legislation, practice directions, codes of conduct, standards and other regulatory instruments on mediation

1 J Rousseau (G Cole translation), *On the Social Contract* (New York: Dover Thrift Books 2003) at 64.

2 Relative to the increasing number of mediations taking place in jurisdictions such as Australia and the United States, however, litigation in connection with mediation remains minimal.

3 J Coben and P Thompson, 'Disputing Irony: A Systematic Look at Litigation About Mediation' (2006) 11 *Harvard Negotiation Law Review* 43 at 51–55. In the period 1999–2003 the authors calculated that there were 1223 reported judicial decisions in the United States involving significant mediation issues. 873 were appellate decisions, 290 federal trial and 60 were state trial decisions. Since that time the number of cases involving mediation issues has continued to increase, particularly in the federal courts, as reported in J Coben and P Thompson, 'Mediation Litigation Trends: 1999–2007' (2007) 1 *World Arbitration and Mediation Review* 395 at 398. These figures do not include the majority of trial decisions about mediation issues that contain no reported opinion; nor does it contain the many judicial decisions that merely mention mediation without deciding a significant mediation issue. Finally litigation matters about mediation that did not reach a hearing are not reflected in these statistics. It is important to bear in mind that there are many more disputes involving legal questions on mediation that are not subject to judicial opinion.

determine how mediation is understood and applied by a range of actors including referring bodies such as courts, dispute resolution organisations, mediators and professional advisors and by the parties themselves. The broad and inclusive definition of law from Chapter 1 is retained here and the context provides specific nuances to the meaning of law.

As indicated previously, in adopting a comparative and international approach to the law of mediation this book focuses primarily on three cross-border legal instruments and six jurisdictions. The jurisdictions – Australia, Austria, England, France, Germany and the United States – have been introduced in Chapter 1. The cross-border legal instruments that will be introduced in the pages that follow are the European Union Directive on Certain Aspects of Mediation in Civil and Commercial Matters (2008), the UNCITRAL Model Law on International Commercial Conciliation (2002) (MLICC) and the Uniform Mediation Act (2001) (UMA) in the United States.

A significant part of this chapter is devoted to the mediation mix – a systematic approach to thinking about and analysing the law relating to mediation. The mediation mix draws upon regulatory theory and the relationship between law and mediation in different countries, highlighting the complexity of the issues surrounding mediation regulation at local, national and international levels. First, four international regulatory trends in mediation are introduced: the market-contract, self-regulatory, formal framework and formal legislative approaches. Against this background specific aspects of the regulatory provisions on mediation are examined. The mediation mix is the resulting framework and it brings form and content together. It also offers a language for comparing regulatory approaches to mediation. The mediation mix asks the question: what aspects of mediation can and should be regulated and how? The mediation mix is useful for analysing regulation trends in a given jurisdiction, for comparing trends in different jurisdictions, countries and regions and for planning regulation policy. Finally it shows how different types of regulation can respond to tensions thrown up by the diversity–consistency debate.[4]

The chapter begins with a consideration of private international law and how it relates to cross-border mediation. This is followed by the mediation mix which identifies the types of legal issues in mediation that may be subject to private international law principles.

2. PRIVATE INTERNATIONAL LAW AND MEDIATION

Parties to an international dispute may find themselves at mediation in one of a number of ways. Typical paths to mediation include court referrals, civil procedure laws that require mediation before a court action is filed, dispute

[4] On the diversity–consistency debate see the discussion in this chapter.

resolution clauses and post-dispute agreements to mediate.[5] In all situations, interesting questions of procedural and substantive law may arise. The branch of law known as private international law or conflict of laws is potentially applicable here.

As explained below, each country has its own body of private international law. However, the chapters that follow do not examine the private international law relating to mediation in specific jurisdictions. Rather they identify and explore trends in the development of the law relevant to international mediation, from the perspectives of different legal jurisdictions and in the light of selected international legal instruments. An understanding of basic principles of private international law serves as a useful basis for the international and comparative analyses in Chapters 3 to 9.

2.1 Definition and Objectives of Private International Law

Private international law refers to the domestic law of a country that deals with how it manages disputes containing a foreign element. These are disputes between non-state actors, or involving states acting as private transactors, that cross state borders. Such disputes are variously described as cross-border and international. There is nothing international about the laws themselves; they take the form of national legislation and case law.[6] In some countries with a federal structure, such as Australia, private international law also applies to disputes with an interstate element. In these examples *interstate* equates to *foreign* for the purposes of private international law. Germany also has a federal structure and while the rules of private international law do not apply directly, they provide a reference point for decision-making when interstate conflicts of law issues arise.[7]

The primary objectives of private international law are threefold. First, it aims to enhance international co-operation and recognition of, and respect for, foreign jurisdictions and law by providing a set of practical rules in appropriate cases. A second goal is to achieve consistency, predictability and certainty in the private international law of different jurisdictions and the legal and socio-economic consequences of its application. Finally private international law aims

5 Pre-mediation issues are dealt with in Chapters 3 and 4.

6 D McClean and K Beevers, *The Conflict of Laws* (6th ed, London: Sweet and Maxwell 2005) at 4 and M Reimann, 'Comparative Law and Private International law' in M Reimann and R Zimmermann (eds), *The Oxford Handbook of Comparative Law* (Oxford: Oxford University Press 2006) at 1364.

7 See J Kropholler, *Internationales Privatrecht* (Tübingen: Mohr Siebeck 2006) at 206. Kropholler explains that in relation to disputes between different states, Germany applies rules which follow the private international law rules. See the Introductory Law to the German Civil Code, §§ 3 N° 1 and 236 (Einführungsgesetz zum Bürgerlichen Gesetzbuch).

to achieve particular justice on a case-by-case basis, namely to give legal effect to the intention of parties in their dealings with one another.[8]

Private international law primarily deals with issues of jurisdiction, choice of law and forum and the recognition and enforcement of foreign judgments. Mortensen explains these factors as follows.[9] Jurisdictional issues deal with the question of whether the local court (forum) has the power to hear and decide the matter or whether the case has sufficient connection with another state to warrant the local court restraining or limiting its own power. Forum clauses indicate the parties' choice of court or jurisdiction in relation to disputes arising out of a contract. Choice of law refers to the law to be applied by the court which has jurisdiction. Choice of law clauses are vehicles for parties to choose the law they wish to apply to identified disputes. They are also referred to as proper law clauses. The following proper law clause is taken from the International Mediation Institute's (IMI) Professional Conduct Assessment Process:

> This Professional Conduct Assessment Process will be exclusively governed by the law of any applicable mediation agreement between the parties, but in the absence of such agreement will be governed by the law of the place where the IMI Certified Mediator who is the subject of the complaint maintains his or her principal place of business ("the Governing Law").[10]

Issues relating to recognition and enforcement of foreign judgments occur where judgment has been rendered in another state and recognition or enforcement is sought in the local court. Subject to international agreements to the contrary,[11] domestic courts are not required to recognise or enforce judgments of foreign courts. When parties select a specific legal system for dispute resolution, they risk a judgment from that national court being unenforceable in other territories, for example in the country where the other party resides or their business is located.

2.2 The Role of Contract in Private International Law

Contract can be used to manage and reduce the risks associated with disputes that cross national borders. These risks include:

8 R Mortensen, *Private International Law in Australia* (Sydney: LexisNexis Butterworths 2006) at 17–22.

9 See Mortensen (2006), above note 8 at 3.

10 See IMI website, www.imimediation.org/code_professional_conduct-.html.

11 See the section on International and Other Cross-border Legal Instruments later in this chapter.

- excessive costs and delay associated with determining jurisdictional issues before the substantive matters can be heard; [12]
- the unpredictability of law and forum and its impact on the subject matter of the dispute;
- lack of clarity about preferred language and potential multilingual confusion; and
- the impact of unexpected economic changes and currency fluctuations.

The dispute resolution clause is an ideal vehicle to manage private international law issues in relation to mediation. Most professionally drafted international dispute resolution clauses include a choice of law sub-clause and a forum selection sub-clause.[13] Choices of forum and law encourage the export of legal and other services beyond borders and offer opportunities for increased access to justice where parties are able to negotiate their own dispute resolution terms. Drawing on freedom of contract principles, courts increasingly give effect to correctly drafted dispute resolution clauses.[14]

Within a forum selection clause parties can designate a court in a particular jurisdiction or a specific dispute resolution process such as arbitration or mediation. Where parties select a forum but no law, it is no more than an indication that the law of the selected forum is to apply. Forums may be selected for reasons – such as interpersonal networks and familiarity with own courts – that have little to do with the nature and content of their laws.[15] For example a contractor in country A supplying a manufacturer for the first time in country B might prefer to deal with the law of its own legal system with which it is familiar, even though enforcement might be sought in country B. Where parties have only inserted a forum selection clause into their contract, the choice of law question is left to the court of the forum to decide. Therefore the distinction

[12] On different approaches to financing litigation see J Zekoll, 'Comparative Civil Procedure' in M Reimann and R Zimmermann (eds), *The Oxford Handbook of Comparative Law* (Oxford: Oxford University Press 2006) at 1356–7.

[13] See the following decisions of The United States Supreme Court in relation to forum selection: in an international context *The Bremen v Zapata Offshore Co*, 407 US 1 (1972) and in a domestic setting *Carnival Cruise Lines, Inc v Shute*, 499 US 585 (1991). The Court has recognised the validity of such clauses, upholding them in both cases and has strongly endorsed their use. See also *Vimar Seguros y Reaseguros SA v M/V Sky Reefer* 515 US 528 (1995) which involved an arbitration clause and which has been applied by a number of District courts to choice of court clauses.

[14] The elements of legally enforceable dispute resolution clauses are considered in Chapter 4.

[15] J Smits, 'Diversity of Contract Law and the European International Market' in J Smits (ed), *The Need for a European Contract Law: Empirical and Legal Perspectives* (Groningen: Europa Law Publishing 2005) at 171.

between these two types of clause is important for parties and their legal representatives.

Despite the advantages associated with the increased certainty and predictability that well-drafted choice of law and forum clauses bring, there are limits to contractual freedom in this regard. Forum shopping provides a practical illustration. The practice of *shopping* for a jurisdiction with substantive and procedural rules favourable to one's case, such as higher damages awards from the plaintiff's perspective, can increase the cost and time-frame for resolving a dispute and the uncertainty surrounding applicable law. The doctrine of *forum non conveniens,* or inappropriate forum, allows courts to decline jurisdiction on the basis that the choice of forum is an attempt to avoid the operation of a relevant mandatory law or because there is a more appropriate forum, such as a court in another jurisdiction.[16] In addition the freedom of choice of forum may be limited by consumer protection legislation,[17] evidence of duress in the selection of the law and other factors.

Inconsistencies can also arise in the way courts around the world interpret and apply laws. This situation presents itself in the case of the various national public policy exceptions to the enforcement of international commercial arbitral awards.[18] By analogy such policy exceptions are likely to impact the enforceability of mediated settlement agreements.[19] Parties can never be completely certain about the jurisdiction in which a legal claim will ultimately be made, the policies of that court in relation to mediation and how the court will deal with a dispute resolution clause.

The following eight categories of law may be relevant to the mediation of international disputes and may need to be taken into account when drafting clauses:

1. the law governing the parties' capacity to agree to a dispute resolution clause and enter into an agreement to mediate;
2. the law governing the dispute resolution clause;

16 See C Bühring-Uhle, L Kirchhoff and G Scherer *Arbitration and Mediation in International Business* (2nd ed, Alphen aan den Rijn: Kluwer Law International 2006) at 14.

17 Council Regulation (EC) N° 44/2001 of 22 December 2000 on Jurisdiction and the Recognition and Enforcement of Judgments in Civil and Commercial Matters. See, for example, Articles 17 and 23(5) Brussels 1 Regulation.

18 On the challenges of the diversity of public policy exceptions and attempts to harmonise them, see C Abraham, 'How to Promote a Uniform Interpretation of Public Policy?' in *Modern Law for Global Commerce: Congress to celebrate the 40th annual session of UNCITRAL* (Vienna: UNCITRAL 2007) available at www.uncitral.org.

19 On the enforceability of mediated agreements as regulated by the UNCITRAL Model Law on International Commercial Conciliation (2002), see Chapter 9.

3. the law governing the agreement to mediate;
4. the law governing the mediation process and the conduct of the mediator, the legal representatives and other participants in the mediation;
5. the laws of the jurisdictions in which the mediated outcome (for example, agreement, deed, consent award) is sought to be recognised and enforced, or set aside;
6. the law of the jurisdictions in which competing judicial or arbitral proceedings are initiated;[20]
7. the law applicable to the subject-matter of the mediation;[21] and
8. the law of the jurisdiction in which provisional remedies or judicial assistance with the gathering of evidence or witnesses is sought.

2.3 The Principles of Private International Law

The two main theories underpinning private international law are *substantivism* and *selectivism*. Substantivism proposes the establishment of one set of universally acceptable substantive and procedural rules for cross-border cases. In selectivism the paramount principle is party autonomy manifested through choice of legal forum and choice of law principles. The private international law of most national jurisdictions is based on selectivism.[22]

Savigny's seminal 1880 *Treatise on the Conflict of Laws*[23] developed and documented choice of law rules with a view to their recognition and application in all countries. Savigny argued that only through uniform application of choice of law principles could consistent approaches in international litigation be achieved in the jurisprudence of national courts. However despite these efforts, differences in jurisdictional approaches to selectivism continue to contribute to its unpredictability and increase the likelihood of clashes among private international laws.

Different European and American approaches to choice of law illustrate this point. European choice of law principles highlight the concept of *conflicts justice*, that is choosing the seat of law with the better claim, irrespective of substantive content of the law. Here a rule-oriented, multilateral approach based on pre-determined neutral criteria, such as domicile and *situs*, is preferred. By

20 See Bühring-Uhle et al (2006), above note 16 at 58 on the limits of 'delocalisation' with respect to international commercial arbitration.

21 In relation to arbitration, Bühring-Uhle et al (2006) point out that the law applicable to the substance of the dispute need not be a national law as parties may agree that the dispute be determined according to the principles of international commercial or trade law (*lex meratoria*), above note 16 at 44.

22 See Reimann (2006), above note 6 at 1374–1375.

23 F von Savigny (W Guthrie Translation), *A Treatise on the Conflict of Laws* (2nd ed, London: Stevens and Sons 1880).

way of example, the UNCITRAL Model Law on Arbitration (1985) (MLICA) defines arbitration as 'international' according to *inter alia* the location of the places of business of the parties.[24] The term *internationality* is further expanded to disputes in which the place of arbitration, the place of contract performance and the place of subject-matter of the dispute is located outside the state in which the parties have their place of businesses, and to disputes where the parties have entered into an express agreement 'that the subject-matter of the arbitration agreement relates to more than one country'.[25]

Conversely the American approach aims to select the law that will better achieve a just result as between the parties (*material justice*). Here there is scope for local courts to take into account the content of the law and its underlying policies. The US-led trend is to frame private international laws as general guidelines accompanied by broadly defined and even subjective criteria, providing the decision-maker with much more latitude than in the traditional European approach. Such an approach is consistent with the concept of *interest analysis* espoused by American legal theorist Brainerd Currie.[26] Interest analyses effectively permit courts to favour the interests and policies of their own jurisdictions over those of foreign jurisdictions.[27] This unilateral approach contrasts with the multilateralism of the Europeans, who attempt to apply a more objective, and therefore arguably internationally acceptable, test.

Another layer of complexity is added to private international law by its sheer diversity in terms of the different forms, nature and scope of conflicts legislation throughout the world.[28] The increasing movement of people around the globe and the compression of space through time, primarily through the speed of global communications, have intensified contacts among legal systems. Rather than reducing the need for conflicts legislation, accelerating economic globalisation has encouraged many countries to update their legislation on international dispute resolution. Reimann summarises the different approaches to regulation of private international law in national legal systems:

> In most cases such legislation either updates or supersedes older (usually more fragmentary) statutes (as in Germany, Japan and Liechtenstein), in a few others it codifies choice-of-law rules for the first time (as in Belgium, […] the United Kingdom, or Oregon). Some statutes encompass private international law as a whole, that is, including jurisdiction, judgments recognition and perhaps other topics (as in Italy, Switzerland, or Slovenia); other focus just on choice of law (as

24 See Article 1(3) MLICA.

25 See Article 1(3) MLICA. For a discussion on the term *internationality* see the Report of the United Nations Commission on International Trade Law on the work of its eighteenth session (Vienna: 3–21 June 1985) (A/40/17) at 8.

26 B Currie, *Selected Essays on the Conflict of Laws* (Durham NC: Duke University Press 1963) at 183.

27 See Mortensen (2006), above note 8 at 14.

28 See Reimann (2006), above note 6 at 1363, 1379.

> in Austria, the Netherlands or Quebec). Some are integrated into larger (civil or procedural) codes (as in Bulgaria, Louisiana, or Russia); many are free-standing acts (as in Poland, Turkey or Venezuela)[...][29]

Even the task of locating the applicable conflicts rules in a particular jurisdiction can be challenging. As a response to these substantive and procedural complexities, the European Union has begun the transition from national to regional (European) private international law rules in relation to contractual and non-contractual obligations. The Rome I and II Regulations (2009) [30] provide a uniform set of rules and one court, the European Court of Justice (ECJ), to interpret and enforce them. This development will significantly simplify conflicts legislation in European Union member-states, despite the exceptions in Rome II that will see numerous areas continue to be regulated at the national level.

2.4 Choice of Law in Practice

The ability to select the applicable law in international transactions allows well-resourced parties to choose a law tailored to their specific needs. It also permits powerful international actors to pursue standardisation through the same choice of law clause in all contracts. In a survey of 175 businesses across Europe, two thirds considered the ability to make a choice of law from different legal systems to be an advantage.[31]

While gathering information and making the choice of law increases transaction costs, these costs become less over time where the law of the same jurisdiction is repeatedly selected. However each time one party succeeds in putting their standard preferred choice of law into the contract, the other may have a less preferred choice and have to bear associated transaction costs. For some – perhaps the one-third minority in the business survey referred to earlier – the international harmonisation of positive law rules may create more costs than it reduces. For this reason it can be useful to distinguish between choice of law in a standardised legal environment, on one hand, and on the other, selecting law on a contract-by-contract basis.

29 See Reimann (2006), above note 6 at 1379.

30 See Regulation (EC) N° 593/2008 of the European Parliament and of the Council of 17 June 2008 on the law applicable to contractual obligations (Rome I) and Regulation (EC) N° 864/2007 of the European Parliament and of the Council of 11 July 2007 on the law applicable to non-contractual obligations (Rome II).

31 G Wagner, 'Transaction costs, choice of law and uniform contract law' in *Modern Law for Global Commerce: Congress to celebrate the 40th annual session for UNCITRAL: Studies, Proposals and Backgrounds Papers* (Vienna: UNCITRAL 2007) at 21.

As indicated previously, developments in globalisation and regionalisation and factors such as interpersonal connections, business relationships, trust and culture exert a much greater influence over the decision of whether businesses will engage in international trade than questions of applicable law. In Smits' words, the role of informal incentives such as 'habits, traditions, "networks" and other informal norms' may be much more influential than formal norms and harmonisation policies.[32] This view is consistent with research suggesting that countries with similar legal systems engage in greater amounts of trade with one another, than countries with different legal systems.[33] There are likely to be more informal connections among people from similar legal cultures.

Other factors that are said to influence the choice of law in favour of a particular jurisdiction include the quality of the judiciary, the expertise of the courts in particular types of international disputes, the absence of corruption, the presence of witnesses in the selected jurisdiction and the efficiency and cost-effectiveness of litigation.[34]

In order to enhance the effectiveness of mediation, it is important for parties drafting dispute resolution clauses to select a jurisdiction with developed and suitable mediation laws that support not only the mediation process but also the outcomes of mediation. However, when signing a contract containing a mediation clause, parties are usually not thinking about disputes which may arise in the future; they may not even be sure in which jurisdiction a future mediation might take place. Accordingly the mediation-friendliness of jurisdictions is seldom a primary factor weighing on the minds of parties when entering into their contractual arrangements.[35]

32 See Smits (2005), above note 15 at 171.

33 See A Turrini and T van Ypersele, *Legal Costs as Barriers to Trade*, CEPR Discussion Paper N° 5751 (London: Centre for Economic Policy Research 2006) and F den Butter and R Mosch, *Trade, Trust and Transaction Costs* (Tinbergen Institute Working Paper No. 2003–082/3 2003). On the controversial nature of empirical research in this area see H Wagner, 'Costs of legal uncertainty. Is harmonisation of law a good solution?' in *Modern Law for Global Commerce: Congress to celebrate the 40th annual session for UNCITRAL: Studies, Proposals and Backgrounds Papers* (Vienna: UNCITRAL 2007) at 31–32.

34 See generally A Bell, *Forum Shopping and Venue in International Litigation* (Oxford: Oxford University Press 2003).

35 On this point see H Eidenmüller, 'A Legal Framework for National and International Mediation Proceedings' (2002) 12 *IDR-Beilage* 14 at 18.

3. International and Other Cross-border Legal Instruments

As a response to the challenges implicit in the conflicts that emerge among domestic laws, international legal groups and intergovernmental organisations continue to work towards the harmonisation and unification of law initiatives through international conventions, treaties, regulations, directives, model laws and rules and declarations. These legal instruments constitute an increasingly significant source of international mediation law. This section introduces the types of legal instruments relevant to cross-border mediation.

International conventions are binding on signatory states; however they are not necessarily effective domestically unless and until they are incorporated into the domestic law of the relevant state. A monist approach to this issue takes the view that both international and domestic laws are naturally integrated. Therefore once a country has signed an international agreement, the terms of the agreement are automatically binding and effective on a domestic level. Countries with monist approaches include the Netherlands, Germany, France and the United States. In contrast a dualist approach, followed by many Commonwealth countries such as the United Kingdom and Australia, views international and domestic legal systems as distinct. For international laws to have effect in dualist jurisdictions, they must be implemented through legislation passed by domestic legislature.[36]

International conventions dealing with the recognition and enforcement of decisions of judicial, arbitral or similar bodies among signatory states include:

- the Hague Convention on Choice of Court[37] and Brussels Regulation I[38] in relation to court decisions; and
- the 1958 New York Convention in relation to arbitral awards.[39]

These conventions may be relevant to mediation in two ways.[40] First, court decisions about aspects of mediation such as enforceability of mediated

[36] In Australia, this was confirmed by the High Court in *Bradley v Commonwealth* (1973) 128 CLR 557.

[37] See the Hague Convention on Private International Law 20th Session (2005) available at www.hcch.net.

[38] The Brussels (1968) and Lugano Conventions (1988) now encapsulated in Brussels I Regulation cited in note 17.

[39] The New York Convention on the Recognition and Enforcement of Foreign Arbitral Awards 1958. The Convention was initiated by the ICC and sponsored by the United Nations. In March 2009, 144 nations had acceded to or ratified it.

[40] See T Wiwen-Nilsson, 'Conciliation: Enforcement of settlement agreements' in *Modern Law for Global Commerce: Congress to celebrate the 40th annual session of UNCITRAL* (Vienna: UNCITRAL 2007) available at www.uncitral.org.

settlements and confidentiality are covered by the Convention. In addition it is conceivable that mediated settlements insofar as they are adopted into arbitral awards, or take the form of judgements or consent orders, would be covered under the Convention.[41]

The New York Convention does not expressly address the issue of awards on agreed terms, however Wiwen-Nilsson argues that the majority view endorses the application of the Convention to settlement awards. This topic is considered further in Chapter 7.

Although the Brussels and Hague Conventions deal with a similar subject-matter, the scope of each Convention differs considerably. Signed by 64 countries, the Hague Choice of Court Convention deals with commercial agreements in which the parties identify their choice of court. The original goal of the Hague Judgment Project was to achieve a truly supra-regional, international convention on jurisdiction and judgment recognition. Although it extends to a large number of countries – subject to ratification – it is limited in terms of the content it covers. Judgments in relation to the following matters are excluded from the Convention's operation on the basis that they may interfere with national public policy or are matters of peculiar local regulation: wills, insolvency, personal injury, competition matters, intellectual property and disputes about rights *in rem* in relation to immovable property.

In contrast the Brussels Convention operates on a regional EU level only and therefore is geographically more limited than the Hague Convention. However it deals with jurisdiction and judgement recognition issues in virtually all civil and commercial matters. Its scope is therefore wider than the Hague Convention. Importantly the Brussels Convention has been replaced by EC Council Regulation 44/2001 (Brussels Regulation 1).

Regulations of the European Union are self-executing legislative instruments and do not require any implementing measures. They are *prima facie* directly applicable in all member countries. Therefore the provisions of the Regulation are interpreted and enforced in a uniform manner by the European Court of Justice. The case law of the Court in relation to Brussels Regulation I provides an illustration of the use of the comparative law method to develop an internationally uniform interpretation of its terms.[42] The Court in its determination of cases uses a comparative approach, drawing on and comparing, case law from different member-states.[43] Accordingly the decisions and interpretations of the European Court of Justice draw from the jurisprudence of multiple jurisdictions and contribute to a uniform interpretation and application

41 See L Boulle, 'Making Litigation Attractive Internationally' (2006) 8 *ADR Bulletin* 81 at 82.

42 See the Brussels I Regulation, cited in note 17.

43 See Reimann (2006) above note 6 at 1388. See also Zekoll (2006) above note 12 at 1340–41. Zekoll provides further examples of initiatives towards the Europeanisation of procedural rules applicable to cross-border disputes.

of the Regulation in member-states. Conversely they also influence the development of domestic laws of member-states and thereby encourage their harmonisation. The reconciliation of different European common and civil laws at a regional level, the so-called Europeanisation of law, has been cited as evidence for a rising acceptance of a jurisprudence of tolerance.[44] At a national level, the legal comparativist, Glenn, refers to a new role for courts in mediating between local law and regional European legal instruments in an attempt to balance local needs and global goals.[45]

Directives are legislative acts of the European Union, which require member-states to achieve a particular result without dictating the means of achieving it.[46] Member-states are normally granted considerable flexibility in relation to the type of regulatory instruments they select and the exact rules they adopt.[47] As a result differences in specific national rules may emerge within the framework of EU directives. However, as issues relating to directives fall within the jurisdiction of the ECJ, member-states will have less individual influence over private international law so that risks associated with diverse national approaches will be reduced. The European Directive on Mediation regulates aspects of cross-border mediation such as confidentiality throughout the 27 member-states of the European Union. The Directive requires member-states to implement its terms and amend inconsistent regulations within three years, that is, by October 2011.[48]

Another type of legal instrument is the Model Law. The UNCITRAL Model Law on Conciliation provides a model for the regulation of mediation in international commercial matters. As a model law, it has no legal force until

[44] See F Snyder, *The Europeanisation of Law: The Legal Effects of European Integration* (Oxford: Hart Publishing 2000) and J Ziller, *The Europeanisation of Law: From the Enlargement of the Areas of European Law to a Transformation of the Law of the Member States (L'Européisation Du Droit: De L'Élargissement Des Champs Du Droit De L'Union Européenne À Une Transformation Des Droits Des États Membres)* (EUI Working Paper LAW No. 2006/19 2006) available at www.ssrn.com.

[45] See H Glenn, *Legal Traditions of the World* (2nd ed, Oxford: Oxford University Press 2004) at 257.

[46] Article 249 Treaty Establishing the European Economic Community, opened for signature 25 March 1957, 298 UNTS 11, Article 249 (entered into force 1 January 1958), also known as the Treaty of Rome. Although binding on states and not individuals, in exceptional cases where the terms of a directive are unconditional and sufficiently certain it can have 'direct effect'. See European Court of Justice Decision, Van Duyn, 4 December 1974.

[47] See generally P Craig and G de Burca, *EU Law: Text, Cases and Materials* (Oxford: Oxford University Press 2003).

[48] See the Directive 2008/52/EC on Certain Aspects of Mediation in Civil and Commercial Matters, proposal as adopted by the European Parliament and the Council of the European Union on 21 May 2008, L 136/3, 24.05.2008.

enacted as a law of a nation-state. It is the first legislative text that offers an international legal framework for mediation and is dealt with extensively in Chapters 8 and 9.

The Uniform Mediation Act is a model law introduced in the United States to reduce the complexity in the multiple variations of mediation regulation in state jurisdictions. It deals primarily with cross-border mediation within the United States – in other words inter-state mediation. In relation to international disputes, however, the UMA adopts the UNCITRAL Model Law thereby encouraging US participation in the international framework of the United Nations.

Other private law-making projects include the American Law Institute's (ALI) Judgment Recognition Initiative.[49] The Institute has also collaborated with UNIDROIT (International Institute for the Unification of Private Law) in the ALI/UNIDROIT Project to produce *The Principles of International Civil Procedure*.[50] These are a set of international procedural principles and rules that countries may choose to adopt for adjudication of disputes arising from international transactions. The Project is an attempt to establish an international system for litigation and was inspired by the model of the Federal Rules of Civil Procedure in the United States.

The next section establishes a conceptual framework for the law of mediation.[51] It draws on examples from around the world including cross-border legal instruments on mediation.

4. Diversity–Consistency and the Art of Regulation

Mediation is a highly flexible and adaptable process – a factor which can create challenges for regulators. Despite many policy debates on the suitability of regulating mediation,[52] policy and law-makers have managed to promulgate

49 See www.ali.org.

50 See *The Principles of International Civil Procedure*, available at www.ali.org.

51 Parts of the rest of this chapter are drawn from N Alexander, 'Mediation and the Art of Regulation' (2008) 8 (1) *QUT Law and Justice Journal* 1, with kind permission from the publishers.

52 See, for example, the debate within the Japanese ADR Study Committee on whether regulation by legislation was consistent with the essence of ADR. This Committee was established to consider and make recommendations on the development of ADR in Japan: see A Yamada, 'The Impact of ADR Law of 2004: Liberalisation or Legalisation?' in *Session III: Conference Proceedings of the International Arbitration Conference: Mediation, Arbitration and Recent Developments* (Taipei: 2008) at 2–16. See also the debates of the UNCITRAL Working Group on Conciliation, *Report of the Working Group on Arbitration on the work of its thirty-fifth session* (Vienna: 2003) Document N° A/CN.9/506 at 6 available at

thousands of laws, codes and standards on the significant yet elusive subject of mediation.[53] There are many forces at play in the regulation of contemporary mediation practice. They reflect a rapidly growing marketplace moving in different and sometimes contradictory, directions. Press has identified six trends in mediation practice:

1. institutionalisation (co-option of mediation into court programs, government agencies and business and community organisations);
2. regulation (codes, standards, rules and legislation);
3. legalisation (case law on aspects of mediation);
4. innovation (experimentation with court-annexed mediation models);
5. internationalisation (international mediator accreditation); and
6. co-ordination (for example among legislatures in relation to 'model' laws and among mediation organisations).[54]

Regulation has been, and continues to be, one of the most controversial topics in the development of mediation from a life skill to an occupation and finally to a profession. In considering approaches to regulating mediation, it is useful to begin with the theme that has continued to define and dominate discussions, debates and developments in relation to ADR around the world: the diversity–consistency dilemma.[55]

The diversity–consistency dilemma refers to the tensions between two motivations: to embrace, on one hand, diversity in practice through flexibility and innovation, and the pressure, on the other, to establish consistent and reliable measures of quality in mediation practice through regulation.[56] The debate begins with the issue of definitional consistency and the risks of excluding certain mediation practices in the search for uniformity;[57] it extends to

www.uncitral.org and see the debates leading up to the enactment of the Uniform Mediation Act 2001: The United States National Conference of Commissioners on Uniform State Laws, *Uniform Mediation Act* (Colorado: 1999) at 5–6.

53 In 2009 a Lexis keyword search of the term mediation in United States legislation *alone* results in more than 3000 hits. This figure does not include codes, case law, practice directions and other standards.

54 S Press, 'International Trends in Dispute Resolution' (2000) 3 *ADR Bulletin* at 21.

55 See NADRAC, *A Framework for Standards* (Canberra: Attorney-General's Department 2001) at 4 and 70–71, in particular recommendation 1.

56 See NADRAC (2001), above note 55.

57 On concerns that standardisation will have negative effects on Australian indigenous mediation, see H Bishop, *Influences Impacting on Aboriginal ADR Processes in the Context of Social and Cultural Perspectives* (Perth: Submission to NADRAC 2000). On similar concerns regarding the interests of family mediators and their clients see NADRAC, *Fairness and Justice in Alternative Dispute Resolution: Discussion paper* (Canberra: Attorney-General's Department 1997). On advantages and disadvantages of ADR standards see NADRAC, *The Development of Standards for ADR:*

concerns that rule consistency may stifle the growth of mediation, inhibit its opportunities for innovative development and lead it down the highly legalised path that arbitration has travelled.[58]

Diversity–consistency tensions reflect a multiplicity of interests relating to consumers, practitioners, service-providers and governments. For consumers, by way of example, there is a demand for a flexible and responsive process which accommodates their needs and which offers quality and accountability in its delivery. In a professional field as new as mediation, many consumers remain uninformed about quality and unable to judge mediator qualifications and performance. Consumer confusion is exacerbated by the diversity of mediation practice, spanning transformative, negotiation-based and advisory models.[59] Protecting consumers from incompetent and unconscionable practices demands mediator accountability which, in turn, requires some level of transparency and disclosure in relation to mediation processes combined with appropriate practice and approval standards. However competing concerns for protecting the integrity of the process through strong confidentiality provisions can reduce mediator accountability. Finally the question of accountability raises the issue of the obligations of mediation service providers to inform clients about the nature of the dispute resolution process they are entering and the qualification and skills of their mediators.

This book argues that it is a question neither of diversity at the expense of consistency nor flexibility over form. Rather decisions need to be made about which aspects of mediation are most usefully standardised and which are best served by more flexible arrangements.

Discussion Paper (Canberra: Attorney-General's Department 2000), chapter 4. For an examination of intercultural differences in mediation, see C-H Mayer and C Boness, *Interkulturelle Mediation und Konfliktberatung* (Berlin: Waxman 2004).

58 For debates about rule consistency see T Altobelli 'New South Wales ADR Legislation: The Need for Greater Consistency and Co-ordination' (1997) 8 *Australian Dispute Resolution Journal* at 200, T Altobelli, 'Mediation in the nineties: The Promise of the Future' (2000) 4 *Macarthur Law Review* at 106 and R Carroll, 'Trends in Mediation Legislation: 'All for One and One for All' or 'One at All'?' (2002) 30 *University of Western Australia Law Review* 167 at 195 et seq. See also comments in relation to the adoption of the Uniform Mediation Act 2001 in the United States, for example, R Benjamin, 'The Uniform Mediation Act: A Trojan Horse?' (2001) and the 'Uniform Mediation Act Working Reporter's Notes', both available at www.mediate.com.

59 The Australian National Mediator Standards make specific provision for advisory mediation. See ss 2(6) and (7) of the Practice Standards available at www.mediationworld.net.

4.1 You Cannot Not Regulate

Regulation is often associated with statutory intervention. This represents an outcome-focussed and now outdated view based on 'simplistic and mechanistic models of economic rationalism, legalism and government control'.[60] Traditional distinctions between public and private, and between regulated and deregulated, can be confusing as regulatory frameworks increasingly comprise different layers. Contemporary theories of regulation have shifted their focus from outcomes to process and from government rule-making to the broader context of institutions and interest groups engaged in the process of decision-making. Regulation in the 21st century increasingly embraces pluralist thinking and views regulation as a system – or a web – comprising various stakeholders, democratic processes and a range of regulatory instruments and interactions.[61] As shown in the previous chapter, pluralistic approaches to law move beyond positivist understandings of legality to embrace non-state, non-legislative and less formalistic methods of regulating society.[62]

Regulation by the market is often thought of as involving the absence of law or the result of deregulation by the state. However deregulated spaces are not empty. They involve the reduction, removal or absence of one kind of regulation only, such as legislation. Where the market dominates, the laws of supply and demand have a regulatory effect. In addition so-called deregulated spaces may be filled with other forms of regulation such as well-established business or professional practices, industry or professional codes of conduct and complaints and disciplinary mechanisms.

In this light the debate about whether or not to regulate mediation is misinformed. Regulation has always occurred and it cannot be – and could not have been – avoided. A more useful question is how to regulate appropriately in the light of the different approaches to regulation.

4.2 Four Approaches to the Regulation of Mediation

There are many potential forms of mediation regulation. They include regulation by the market, private contractual instruments, self-regulation through standards, benchmarks and professional ethics, domestic legislation, judicial decisions, executive and administrative pronouncements, international legal instruments

60 J Braithwaite, 'Responsive Regulation for Australia' in P Grabosky and J Braithwaite (eds) *Business Regulation and Australia's Future* (Canberra: Australian Institute of Criminology 1993) at 97.

61 See C Parker, C Scott, N Lacey and J Braithwaite (eds), *Regulating Law* (Oxford: *Oxford* University Press 2004) especially the following chapters: H Collins, 'Regulating Contract Law' at 29, C Scott, 'Regulating Constitutions' at 227 and J Braithwaite and C Parker, 'Conclusion' at 270 et seq.

62 See Glenn (2004), above note 45 at chapters 3, 9 and 10.

and customary law. Regulatory forms do not operate in isolation but are bundled together in various ways depending on factors such as government policy, legal tradition and local culture. From a global perspective, the various forms of mediation regulation can be categorised in four primary approaches:

1. market-contract regulation;
2. self-regulation;
3. formal regulatory framework; and
4. formal legislative regulation.

These approaches do not represent an evolutionary or developmental model of regulatory approaches to mediation. Rather they represent a scale of increasing institutionalisation and formalism. Each approach will be discussed in turn.

4.2.1 Market-Contract Regulation

As the term suggests, the market-contract approach to mediation is based on free market and contract law concepts and derives from values such as freedom of the individual, choice and competition and commitment to contractual undertakings. In this approach parties can engage in any kind of arrangement for the provision of mediation services in terms of the laws of supply and demand and subject to the legal niceties of private contract.

Market principles assume that consumers have access to information in order to make informed choices. In the context of mediation this would entail that parties are educated about what expectations they can have of mediators and different mediation processes and that they have the ability to differentiate between good and poor quality mediation. Supply and demand are functions of individual decisions of producers and consumers within a given market. Collectively these decisions determine the allocation of resources, production levels and consumer patterns without state intervention. In other words, according to market principles, the laws of supply and demand would determine the price and quality of goods and services related to mediation. The market relies only on minimalist legal infrastructure such as the enforcement of the rules of contract and property law.

Private contracting is both an expression of party autonomy and a form of self-regulation. Here parties choose the parameters for their relationship and interaction by means of private contractual arrangements. Typical contractual arrangements in relation to mediation include:

- dispute resolution clauses in commercial or other contracts which trigger mediation processes;

- agreements to mediate, which contain the rights and obligations of contracting parties in the mediation and the nature of the process they have agreed to enter;
- confidentiality agreements with non-party participants in the mediation; and
- mediated settlements.

While relying on court application of the law for ultimate enforcement, private contracting gives legal form to the ideals of party autonomy and individual responsibility. It gives parties the opportunity to self-regulate on a mutualised basis to create their own terms for engaging in mediation. In transactions in which the stakes are high for the parties, contractual provisions tailor-made to suit their particular needs can be a valuable investment of time and money. In the case of repeat transactions with the same party, these costs are reduced. Conversely in low stakes matters standard contracts usually regulate the parties' mediation relationship. In addition to terms specified in the contract, contract terms may be incorporated by reference. References to institutional mediation practice standards, model clauses and other precedents are common.[63]

Market principles and private contracting combine to make up the market-contract approach. Regulatory instruments of the market-contract approach include the ability of a court or mediation body to remove a mediator from their mediator panel for misconduct. Here the power of the court or mediation body to withdraw referral opportunities from mediators is likely to influence mediator behaviour. The potential of repeat deals, reputation power and individualised arrangements available though private contracting are powerful regulatory mechanisms in this approach, encouraging quality and consistency in practice.[64] The benefits of the market-contract approach can be summed up with the terms autonomy, flexibility and individual responsibility. Where consumers have access to accurate information about mediators their reputations will influence the choice of mediator and those with poor track records will gradually be pushed from the market.[65] To use Darwinian language it may be described as *survival of the fittest*.[66]

[63] For standard clauses and institutional rules on cross-border mediation, see Appendices A and B.

[64] D Charney, 'Non-legal Sanctions in Commercial Relationships' (1990) 104 *Harvard Law Review* 375 at 392–394.

[65] On the search for quality meditors in France see K Deckert, 'Mediation in Frankreich – Rechtlicher Rahmen und praktische Erfahrungen' in K Hopt and F Steffek (eds), *Mediation – Rechtstatsachen, Rechtsvergleich, Regelungen* (Tübingen: Mohr Siebeck 2008) 183 at 214.

[66] See D Quammen (ed), *Charles Darwin on the Origin of the Species: The Illustrated Edition* (London: Sterling 2008).

The risks of the market-contract approach lie in the imperfections of the market and the realities concerning access to information. People do not always act rationally. Not all market participants have access to relevant information, and even if they do, they may not use the information rationally. Structural barriers such as wealth and education make choice more illusory than real in some situations. It has been suggested that the very low number of complaints about mediation service-providers[67] supports a market-contract approach to mediation.[68] However the absence of consumer complaints by no means equates with consumer satisfaction. Not only must consumers be sufficiently informed and educated about mediation to assess its quality, they also need access to feedback mechanisms to express their views. Australian research indicates that 'vulnerable consumers', that is those who live in low socio-economic geographical regions or rural areas, are more likely to experience difficulty in accessing dispute resolution and complaint schemes than those from advantaged demographic backgrounds.[69]

Moreover the use of standard contracts by major organisations and other repeat players distorts the notion of freedom of contract, in that bargaining power is rarely equal in the consumer context. In order to address and prevent issues of market dominance by organisations and individuals, legal mechanisms to respond to market failure or other circumstances requiring redress are also present.[70] Consumer protection provisions, which may be implied by law, provide a useful illustration. According to the European Community Directive on Unfair Contract Terms, dispute resolution clauses in consumer contracts signed *before* the dispute arose are unenforceable. However agreements to engage in a dispute resolution process such as mediation *after* the dispute has arisen may be enforceable. In other words consumers cannot bind themselves to delay or forfeit their right to a court hearing by virtue of a mediation clause in a standard consumer contract – a clause with respect to which they may not have had any real choice and of which they may not have been made aware.[71] Where

67 On complaints statistics in relation to ADR see, for example, NADRAC (2001), above note 55 at 2.76.

68 See, for example, submission of the Law Council of Australia in 2004 to NADRAC in relation to the establishment of *National Mediator Approval Standards*, available at www.lawcouncil.asn.au.

69 See T Sourdin, 'An Alternative for Whom? Access to ADR Processes' (2007) *NADRAC Research Forum* available at www.nadrac.gov.au.

70 See L Boulle, *The Law of Globalisation* (Gold Coast: BUP 2008), chapter 2.

71 EC Unfair Contract Terms Directive 93/13/EEC OJ L95, 21 April 1993, 29–34. Note that Statutory Instrument 1999 N° 2083 The Unfair Terms in Consumer Contracts Regulations 1999 makes no reference to ADR but in Schedule 2(q) it declares arbitration not covered by legal provisions to be unfair if there is no opportunity to review the decision in the courts.

an agreement to mediate is made after the dispute arose, the *prima facie* assumption is that consumers are aware of the process choice they are making.

Finally the power of the courts in relation to contracts cannot be underestimated. Courts are increasingly required to decide upon the precise meaning of bargains that parties have put together. This may leave considerable scope for interpretation in relation to non-specific, implied or otherwise incorporated contractual terms. As an illustration, the incorporation of general terms such as *good faith* and *reasonable* allow for a certain amount of subjective interpretation in relation to the performance of the contract. Such terms also reflect the inability of legal terminology to define acceptable behaviour in relation to a process with the flexibility of mediation. Ultimately the meaning of these terms depends on a variety of factors, including the mix of negotiating cultures and legal traditions involved in the transaction. In some jurisdictions the term good faith could potentially invalidate a contract and in others courts are quite comfortable with its connotations.[72] Thus the limits of party autonomy become apparent with the recognition of the extent to which courts can effectively write terms into commercial contracts. In their role as judicial decision-makers, courts can easily find themselves trying to balance competing interests of government and public policy, on one hand, and private parties, on the other. As the following chapters show litigation about mediation has contributed to significant bodies of case law on diverse aspects of the system.[73]

4.2.2 Self-Regulation

Here self-regulatory approaches refer to collective, community and industry-led regulatory initiatives. *Self-regulation* can take the form of codes, standards, benchmarks and similar instruments established by private or public bodies, or a combination of both. Examples of private bodies include dispute resolution organisations, private training institutions, chambers of commerce, and professional associations of lawyers, counsellors and other professions. Public bodies such as government agencies, legislative bodies, courts, tribunals, publicly-sponsored dispute resolution centres and public education and training institutions are regularly involved in the establishment of approval and practice standards for mediators. Industry-led mediation initiatives such as the Australian National Mediator Accreditation System rely on input from both public and private bodies. Individual self-regulation through private contract has been discussed earlier in relation to the market-contract approach.

Self-regulatory approaches refer to community and industry-based initiatives embracing collaborative, consultative and reflective processes, as

72 On the term *good faith* in mediation clauses and agreements to mediate, see Chapter 4.

73 See Coben and Thompson (2006), above note 3 at 43.

distinct from top down policy regulation. Self-regulatory approaches embody reflexive and responsive theories of regulation. *Responsiveness* refers to collaboration between government and the group or collective being regulated. *Reflexion* builds upon the notion of responsiveness and highlights the opportunity for actors to identify issues, reflect upon them and negotiate their own solutions.[74]

In the development of mediation practice around the world self-regulatory instruments have played, and continue to play, a significant role. Self-regulatory mediator approval and practice standards, for example, enjoy the support of a growing number of governments.[75] In the Netherlands the mediator standards of one organisation, NMI, effectively operate as national standards in the mediation marketplace.[76] NMI provides an independent quality assurance system through accreditation and independent personal certification in conformity with the European Standard EN 45013. In England the Civil Mediation Council (CMC) is an industry body formed in 2006, which comprises representatives of mediation providers and the Ministry of Constitutional Affairs. It has been responsible for the development of a national pilot accreditation scheme for mediators. In the United States the Texas Credentialing Association is an industry initiative that aims to cover all mediation credentialing in the state and has broad consultation with mediators, trainers and users in the state of Texas.[77] The German Federal Ministry of Justice has indicated the desirability of an industry-driven self-regulatory approach to mediator standards.[78]

74 On reflexivity and responsiveness see J Black, 'Decentralising Regulation: Understanding the Role of Regulation and Self-Regulation in a "Post-Regulatory" World' (2001) 54 *Current Legal Problems* 103 at 127. On reflexive regulation, see D Hess, 'Social Reporting: A Reflexive Law Approach to Corporate Social Responsiveness' (1999) 25 *Journal of Corporate Law* at 41. Collins defines reflexive regulation as regulation which seeks to achieve the cooperation and collaboration of those subject to regulation, see H Collins, *Regulating Contracts* (Oxford: Oxford University Press 1999).

75 See *Soft Law and the Consumer Interest* (Bruxelles: European Consumer Law Group 2001), available at www.ec.europa.eu. The Dutch Minster of Justice in a letter to the House of Representatives described his reticence at regulating mediation, available at http://english.justitie.nl. Further the European Commission has advocated self-regulation of mediation, see CEDR News, 'Proposed mediation directive adopted by European Commission' available at www.cedr.com.

76 On the Netherlands Mediation Institute (NMI), see www.nmi-mediation.nl.

77 See American Bar Association (ABA) Section of Dispute Resolution Task Force on Credentialing, 'Report on Mediator Credentialing and Quality Assurance' (2002) at 28, available at www.abanet.org.

78 See comments by G Nettersheim at the *Jahrestreffen der Freunde des Max Planck Instituts für ausländisches und internationals Privatrecht* (Hamburg, 13 June 2009) and L Graf-Schlicker at the *13th Mediations-Kongress (*Berlin, April 2009).

The Australian National Mediator Accreditation System (2008) is a notable illustration of national self-regulation on an industry basis. National mediator approval and practice standards came into operation on 1 January 2008, with a transitional period until 1 January 2010. During this time the National Mediator Accreditation Committee (NMAC), comprising representatives of identified interest groups, will negotiate the details for implementing the Standards and establishing a permanent National Mediator Standards Body (NMSB). These negotiations are being assisted and facilitated by the National Alternative Dispute Resolution Advisory Council (NADRAC), a state nominated body. The System, which includes national mediator approval and practice standards, is the result of years of informal and formal consultation and collaboration. In terms of the System, mediators wishing to be accredited to the national standard must comply with training and assessment standards and join a recognised mediator accreditation body (RMAB). At the time of writing RMABs are self-recognising bodies, reinforcing the self-regulatory aspects of the System. Practice and compliance issues within the System are dealt with by dialogue and consultation among members of the NMAC. In so far as courts, tribunals, government departments and other mediator users require by formal regulation that mediators meet the national standards, a mixed model begins to emerge, embracing both reflexive and formalistic regulatory approaches.

In the absence of a supra-national government and judiciary, self-regulation is the preferred method for regulating international mediation. The private self-regulatory mediator accreditation initiative of the IMI is a case in point.[79]

Self-regulatory standards can also be found in organisations that offer mediation such as professional associations and commercial providers of mediation services. In France civil mediation practice is largely regulated by the self-regulatory codes of conduct, accreditation requirements and other standards of mediation organisations, industry groups and numerous other public and private bodies.[80] In many jurisdictions mediator approval and/or mediation practice standards have been developed on a sector-by-sector basis by court programs, employer bodies of mediators, industry bodies and other service providers.[81] While sector-specific self-regulation remains in force, general minimum standards in relation to all forms of mediation have emerged as the preferred self-regulatory form in jurisdictions such as the Netherlands and Australia.

79 See www.imimediation.org.

80 For examples of these self-regulatory developments see Deckert (2008), above note 65 at 191–192.

81 See, for example, mediation developments in Germany, the United States, Canada, Denmark, Australia, England and Wales, Scotland, Italy, Switzerland, South Africa and France described in N Alexander (ed), *Global Trends in Mediation* (2nd ed, Alphen aan den Rijn: Kluwer Law International 2006).

Self-regulatory instruments also extend to model mediation clauses and to established practices of co-mediation, supervision, mediation intake and preparation and mediation client surveys. Courts and tribunals may rely on the self-regulatory instruments when interpreting contracts incorporating them. This has occurred in a number of cases in relation to the enforceability of mediation clauses in Australia and the United States.[82]

Corporate and government pledges to use ADR and avoid litigation are a growing form of self-regulation. Prominent examples from around the world include the UK Government Pledge 2001,[83] the Viadrina Declaration 2008 which records German and Polish judicial support for mediation in cross-border family and child kidnapping disputes, the CPR ADR Pledge signed by more than 5500 American companies and law firms,[84] the International Trademark Association (INTA) ADR Pledge,[85] the Individual and Corporate Pledges of the Mediation First Community in Hong Kong,[86] and the Euro-Mediterranean Charter on Appropriate Dispute Resolution 2007, signed by the Arab Union of Lawyers, the Egyptian Bar Association, the Council of the Bars and Law Societies of the European Union (CCBE) and the Union of Turkish Bars.[87]

As a matter of best practice self-regulatory models should include consumer awareness, education initiatives and an effective feedback and management strategy to deal with complaints.[88] It is vital to develop mechanisms for ongoing development of soft regulation to respond to the evolution and maturation of the field, such as issues relating to infrastructure and co-ordination of mediation services. In Australia, as discussed earlier, a topical illustration of such a mechanism is the transition process (2008–2010) to implement the Australian National Mediator Standards (2008) and to establish a peak body (NMSB) on accreditation issues. The Australian Standards are said to be *living documents* and review processes have been put in place.[89]

The perceived benefits of self-regulation are numerous. Participants in the regulatory process are experts with an intimate and sensitive knowledge of the needs and interests of the regulated group and its various constituents. Self-regulation promotes innovation and choice in terms of the selection of the self-regulatory mix and is generally more flexible, adaptable and responsive than

82 On this point and for case references see Chapter 4.

83 The 2007 report from the Department for Constitutional Affairs on the Effectiveness of the Pledge is available at www.justice.gov.uk.

84 On the CPR ADR pledge, see www.cpradr.org.

85 On the INTA ADR pledge, see www.inta.org.

86 See www.mediate.com.hk.

87 Informally called the Rome Declaration, the *Euro-Mediterranean Charter* is available at www.adrmeda.org.

88 See earlier comments in relation to research on consumer access to ADR.

89 T Sourdin, 'Australian National Mediator Accreditation System – Report on Project' (2007) at 11 available at www.nadrac.gov.au.

formal regulatory forms. There is room to experiment, to collect feedback from disputants, courts, service providers and other interest groups and to adjust regulation in accordance with that feedback. It is said to achieve a greater degree of buy-in from industry members as they have the opportunity to participate in decision-making on regulation issues. The legitimacy of, and conformity with, the regulation are also enhanced through the participatory nature of self-regulatory approaches. Self-regulation is also associated with reduced costs in relation to information collection, reduced monitoring and enforcement and less formality. Many of the costs of regulation are absorbed by the industry itself in self-regulation models.[90] Successful self-regulatory models also remove the need for the introduction of comprehensive legislation in a given industry. Alternatively, as Zalar suggests, self-regulatory pilots and programs provide tried and tested models upon which legislatures can build.[91]

The primary risks associated with self-regulatory approaches relate to resource levels in terms of available knowledge, capacity and motivation. Effective responsive and reflexive processes require sustained buy-in and input by key interest groups, communities and governments. Where levels of industry and expert input wane, self-regulatory structures lose their efficacy and more government-directed involvement may be justified. In addition self-regulatory schemes may be susceptible to domination by specific individuals and groups not representative of broader industry and consumer interests.

4.2.3 Formal Regulatory Framework

As with the self-regulatory approach, the formal framework approach is based on reflexive and responsive theories of regulation. Formal parameters or guidelines are established within which the mediation community can self-regulate various aspects of mediation. As such the formal framework approach represents a meeting of descending and ascending regulatory approaches. It is also referred to as co-regulation.

The framework usually takes the form of legislative or executive instruments such as international conventions, directives, legislation and model laws. It establishes formal and legally recognised parameters within which softer forms of regulation such as voluntary self-regulation can fill in the regulatory

[90] Consider, for example, the proposed resourcing of the self-regulatory Australian mediation standards through a combination of fees from RMABs (Registered Mediation Approval Bodies) and funding from government sources: Sourdin (2007), above note 89 at 38.

[91] A Zalar, *Towards Primary Dispute Resolution Systems: Global Trends in Civil and Family Mediation: An Overview of Best Practice in Europe* (The Hague: Conflicthuntering 2006).

details. The European Directive on Mediation[92] illustrates this approach well. It defines mediation, thereby establishing its scope and goes on to identify the aspects of mediation that require regulation by EU member-states. The recitals clearly recognise different forms of regulation of mediation including self-regulation (recital 14), specifically referring to the European Code of Conduct for Mediators and market-based solutions (recital 17). Recital 16 encourages member-states to ensure that appropriate quality control mechanisms for mediation services are in place. Article 4 of the Directive requires member-states to encourage mediators and mediation organisations to adhere to voluntary codes of conduct and other quality control mechanisms.

Formal framework approaches can accommodate diverse interest groups while still pursuing common policies. They are most effective where a single body, such as the European Court of Justice, has the power to interpret and enforce regulatory issues as they arise. Uniform interpretation of framework provisions enhances the robustness of the framework itself. Conversely the absence of uniform, or at least harmonised, interpretation and application of regulatory issues in a framework approach serves to dilute the strength of a shared framework.

In France a National Consultative Council on Family Mediation was established by decree in 2001.[93] It was given a specific mandate to establish a State Diploma of Family Mediation, a code of practice for family mediators and a national public information program. Effectively the formal decree provided a framework and the Council filled in the details. The formal framework was developed after consultation in the mediation community, and the decree came about as the result of the Sassier Report which canvassed the views of over 80 representatives of groups interested in family mediation. The French government was also instrumental in creating a framework for social mediation with the adoption of a Charter of Social Mediation in 2001.[94]

Another illustration of the formal framework approach is the ADR Law of 2004 in Japan, which came into effect in 2007.[95] The Act has the stated

[92] Directive 2008/52/EC on Certain Aspects of Mediation in Civil and Commercial Matters, above note 48.

[93] National Consultative Council on Family Mediation (8 October 2001) (*Arrêté portant création du Conseil national consultatif de la médiation familiale*).

[94] See Guide DIV–CNFPT, *La médiation sociale. Une démarche de proximité au service de la cohésion sociale et de la tranquillité publique* (Social médiation : A step towards social cohesion and public order) (Paris: Repères 2004) available at www.ville.gouv.fr/IMG/pdf/mediation-sociale_cle28fd48.pdf.

[95] An Act on Promotion of Use of Alternative Dispute Resolution (Act N° 151 of 2004). See also H Baum and E Schwittek, 'Mediation in Japan – Entwicklung und Praxis der aussergerichtlichen Streitbeilegung' in K Hopt and F Steffek (eds), *Mediation – Rechtstatsachen, Rechtsvergleich, Regelungen* (Tübingen: Mohr Siebeck 2008) 483 at 501–502.

purpose of providing a legislative framework for ADR in Japan. In particular the Law aims to promote the use of mediation and ADR through efficiency and quality assurance measures. Among others things, the Law provides clarity on how ADR impacts on litigation limitation periods. It also establishes a certification system for ADR organisations.

While model laws typically aim to achieve mirror legislative enactment in target jurisdictions (a formal legislative approach), these instruments may also be effective as guidelines or frameworks for local regulators and interest groups. In Australia it has been suggested that a national model law dealing with evidentiary privilege and other rights and obligations of participants in mediation could effectively support the harmonising of local policy and law-making initiatives by offering guidelines for desirable regulatory outcomes.[96] In other words the Model Law could act as a reform guide to regulatory policy. This approach may be attractive for countries able to maintain a manageable overview of their regulatory initiatives in mediation such as Australia. However countries with significantly larger populations, higher number of sub-national jurisdictions and numerous pieces of local and state legislation, such as the United States, are likely to find a national framework approach for all aspects of mediation unattainable. Here formal legislative approaches may be considered a more attractive option.

4.2.4 Formal Legislative Regulation

As the term implies, formal legislative regulation relies primarily on legislation supported by formal institutions, such as the executive and judiciary, to regulate mediation. The formal legislative approach, arguably a manifestation of traditional Eurocentric civil law thinking, focuses on positive notions of law and sits well with the concept of an *active* state. According to Damaska active states tend to adopt paternalistic, welfare-oriented and interventionist approaches in relation to their citizens.[97] They select policies based on the premise that they know what is good for civil society. To this end a systemised body of legal norms and policies defines what is appropriate and just according to state interests and values. Formal legislative strategies on mediation represent a strong endorsement of mediation by the state and contribute towards its recognition as a legitimate dispute resolution practice and profession. French commentator Bonafé-Schmitt identifies the omnipresent role of the French state as a defining characteristic of the regulation of mediation in France. He writes,

> This can be seen not only in the development of court-based mediation but also, for example, in the area of employment with the creation of new jobs associated with

96 See Carroll (2002), above note 58 at 207.

97 M Damaska, *The Faces of Justice and State Authority: A Comparative Approach to the Legal Process* (New Haven: Yale University Press 1986) at 73–88.

community liaison such as those carried out by the so-called Agents Locaux de Médiation Sociale (literally, local agents of social mediation).[98]

The Austrian Law on Mediation in Civil Cases 2001 and Training Regulations 2004 evidences a dominant formal legislative approach to the regulation of the approval and practice of mediators in civil matters. Specific legislation focussing on areas such as neighbourhood, family, victim-offender and other categories of mediation practice have also been enacted in Austria.[99] Following Austria's lead, the Slovak Republic introduced comprehensive mediation legislation in 2004 and other European states are following suit.[100] Zalar points out that the majority of transitional European democracies passed statutory mediation laws as a first step in developing mediation practice and culture. He refers to Croatia, Montenegro, Serbia, Macedonia, Slovakia, Malta and Bosnia as examples.[101]

Formal legislative approaches aim to clarify current arrangements, set goals of practice consistency, establish certainty on legal issues and provide consumer protection. The Uniform Mediation Act in the United States is an example of a formal legislative approach in relation to the confidentiality aspects of mediation. At the time of drafting the UMA, mediation was regulated in more than 2500 statutes, a major factor contributing to the confusion that surrounds choice of law in domestic cross-border disputes.[102] In terms of the implementation of UMA provisions, the repeal or retention of current state statutory provisions is left largely to individual states. Such an approach aims to encourage adoption of the UMA in as many states as possible by allowing their laws to remain intact except insofar as states wish to amend to achieve uniformity with the UMA. However the success or otherwise of the UMA is the subject of considerable debate.[103]

[98] See J-P Bonafé-Schmitt (translation by D Macfarlane), 'Global Trends in Mediation: Training and Accreditation in France' (2009) 11 *ADR Bulletin* 47.

[99] On Austrian mediation legislation see S Ferz and E Filler, *Mediation: Gesetzestexte und Kommentar* (Vienna: WUV 2003) and M Roth and D Gherdane, 'Mediation in Österreich – Zivilrechts-Mediations-Gesetz: Rechtlicher Rahmen und praktische Erfahrung' in K Hopt and F Steffek (eds), *Mediation – Rechtstatsachen, Rechtsvergleich, Regelungen* (Tübingen: Mohr Siebeck 2008) 105 at 112 et seq.

[100] Slovakian Act of 25 June 2004 on Mediation and Amendment of Certain Acts.

[101] See Zalar (2006), above note 91.

[102] See above note 53, which suggests that the figure has grown to more than 3000.

[103] See, for example, the International Academy of Mediators opposition to the UMA, available at www.mediate.com. See also W Fagan and B Shannon, 'A Potential Threat to Texas ADR' (2002) 65 *Texas Bar Journal* at 27.

Many transitional democracies show a preference for centralised and comprehensive formal legislative regulation of mediation.[104] Countries who are eager to attract investment, and enter bi- and multilateral political and economic arrangements, are motivated to demonstrate to the rest of the world legal systems that are democratic, dispute resolution friendly and modern. Here formal, documented laws are more readily recognised internationally than softer forms of regulation.

However there are limitations to legislative approaches in the mediation context. A significant issue relates to the impact of legislation on the mediation process itself. When mediation processes are formalised in written law, they are potentially transformed.[105] There is a shift from everyday vernacular to legal terminology. There may even be a change in language as well as terminology. In many countries the language of the courts remains that of former colonial powers. So, for example, in Timor Leste the language of the courts remains Portuguese while the primary language of the population is Tetum. Finally, through law mediation is transformed from a living understanding of values and processes into a structured set of rules and principles. Whereas mediation may have been immediately available and accessible to all, its legalisation creates boundaries and determines who is in the club and who is not. Legalisation potentially transforms mediation from a life skill into a closed profession.

Legislative mechanisms, therefore, are limited in their capacity to deal with non-legal perspectives and high levels of generality, complexity, unpredictability and innovation. It is difficult to be rigidly exacting and sweepingly general at the same time. This goes some way to explaining the widespread use of sector-specific mediation legislation in common law countries such as Australia, the United States and England. These jurisdictions have deliberately chosen not to enact comprehensive national mediation legislation.[106] A focus on specific contexts, sectors and industries allows for tailor-made legislative solutions.

Furthermore, while delegation of discretion is possible as part of the legislative process, it typically falls to state-funded regulatory agencies operating in accordance with government-approved policies. Therefore, the benefits of the direct industry expertise entertained in self-regulatory schemes may be lost in the legal layers of the legislative process. Processes of statutory regulation are philosophically antithetical to the values mediation is seeking to

[104] On mediation legislation in Eastern Europe, R Morek, 'Waiting for the Directive: Recent Developments in Civil and Commercial Mediation Law in Central and Eastern Europe: Selected Issues' (Vienna: European Mediation Conference 2007).

[105] See T Bennett, 'Comparative Law and African Customary Law' in M Reimann and R Zimmermann (eds), *The Oxford Handbook of Comparative Law* (Oxford: Oxford University Press 2006) at 671.

[106] For a sampling of Australian sector-specific legislation on mediation, see the Australian section on www.mediationworld.net.

support, namely party autonomy and participation in democratic decision-making processes. Accordingly, compliance motivation is a risk in such regulatory approaches.[107]

Finally the judiciary can play a significant role in the interpretation of legislation, particularly in common law jurisdictions, where the terms *judicial lawmakers* and *judicial creativity* were invented.[108] In the course of exercising their judicial function, courts may fill gaps in the law left by legislators and lend clarity and case-specific meaning to imprecise terms such as good faith in the context of participation in mediation. Depending on one's view, this contribution of the courts can serve to add flexibility to the otherwise rigid nature of legislation or it can lead to less predictability in the application of the law. Over time, however, judicial precedents develop around statutes to give them meaning and some degree of certainty for case application.

4.3 Four Regulatory Approaches in Practice: A Multi-Layered Approach

The four approaches to mediation regulation are not mutually exclusive. In their review of mediation trends around the world, Hopt and Steffek reflect on the unusually high number of regulatory actors – courts, parliaments, executives, private mediation organisations and so on – representing different groups playing their part in regulating mediation.[109] Virtually all jurisdictions have aspects of at least two of the regulatory approaches defined earlier and jurisdictions with extensive mediation experience are likely to show evidence of all four approaches.

Mediation in Anglo-American jurisdictions generally has followed a mixed regulatory approach with significant legislative, self-regulatory and market elements. In the United States the regulation of mediation is characterised by significant legislation on a sector-by-sector basis and court rules on mediation or dispute resolution in virtually every court of the country, in addition to self-regulation on a sector or organisational basis. Such an approach supports diversity in mediation practice on a sector-by-sector basis, while striving for uniformity within the relevant sector. The UMA is an attempt to encourage uniformity in states' laws in relation to limited aspects of mediation such as confidentiality. For high-end commercial disputes where

107 See Black (2001), above note 74 at 106.

108 See M Cappelletti, 'The Law Making Power of the Judge and its Limits: A Comparative Analysis' (1981) 8 *Monash University Law Review* at 15 and D Dyzenhaus and M Taggart, 'Reasoned Decisions and Legal Theory' in D Edlin (ed), *Common Law Theory* (New York: Cambridge University Press 2007) at 146.

109 See K Hopt and F Steffek, 'Mediation – Rechtsvergleich, Regelungsmodelle, Grundsatzprobleme' in K Hopt and F Steffek (eds), *Mediation – Rechtstatsachen, Rechtsvergleich, Regelungen* (Tübingen: Mohr Siebeck 2008) 3 at 89–90.

parties choose to tailor dispute resolution to suit their particular needs, the market-contract approach is thriving.

The Australian experience has some strong parallels. A formal legislative approach is evident in the hundreds of statutes that regulate mediation, mainly on a sector-by-sector basis.[110] The regulation of family dispute resolution is an example of a sector-specific legislative approach.[111] As indicated previously, while formal framework legislation does not play a major role, at least one author has suggested the use of a Model Law with a framework function. The introduction of national mediator approval and mediation practice standards in 2008 signalled the emergence of a national self-regulatory approach to minimum level approval and practice regulations.[112] Importantly, the voluntary and minimalist nature of the national self-regulatory initiative continues to encourage diversity over and above the minimum standard. It does not prevent mediators from operating outside the standards, leaving it to the market to make decisions about which mediators to engage: mediators approved to the national minimum standards or mediators without the nationally recognised accreditation. In other words there remains scope for the market-contract approach to develop. The virtual absence of litigation against mediators suggests that mediation is low risk practice. Relative to the amount of practice, there are few cases against mediators and those that have arisen have influenced practice in a constructive manner.[113] Therefore the current regulatory approach is likely to continue.

On the European continent there is a discernable trend towards a formal legislative approach, particularly in Eastern and Central Europe. This approach has been boosted by the adoption of the European Directive on Mediation. Where there are gaps in the formal legislative approach, opportunities for other regulatory forms such as self-regulation and market-contract approaches emerge.[114] Two civil law jurisdictions with well-developed self-regulatory practices operating before the introduction of broad national legislation to regulate mediation are Slovenia and the Netherlands.[115]

110 For an overview of the Australian regulatory experience, see L Boulle, *Mediation: Principles Process Practice* (Sydney: LexisNexis 2005) at 284 et seq.

111 In Australia the Family Dispute Resolution Practitioners Accreditation System is regulated under the Family Law Act 1975 (Cth) and the Family Law Regulations 1984 (Cth).

112 See the Australian National Mediator Accreditation System Standards, available at www.mediationworld.net.

113 See, for example, the specific disclosure requirements for mediators who adopt an advisory model: Australian National Mediator Approval Standards, ss 2(4) and 5(4) and Australian National Mediator Practice Standards, s 2(7).

114 For an illustration of this phenomenon in relation to the Austrian Law on Mediation, see the section entitled The Mediation Mix later in this chapter.

115 See Zalar (2006), above note 91.

Contemporary best practice models recommend a combination of private and public mechanisms in regulated markets with a high level of responsiveness to needs, interests and changes. Experts further suggest that reflexive and responsive processes – often associated with self-regulatory approaches and even formal framework approaches – encourage performance *beyond compliance*.[116] In other words, participation in determining regulatory measures does more than enhance awareness, understanding and compliance – it supports aspirations to achieve best practice in the regulated market.

The Organisation for Economic Co-operation and Development (OECD) *Guiding Principles for Regulatory Quality and Performance* provides a useful policy illustration. Adopted by the OECD Council in 2005, it endorses a regulation mix which promotes 'innovation though market incentives and goal-based approaches' and is compatible with 'competition, trade investment-facilitating principles at domestic and international levels.'[117] These principles echo those of legal reform projects which promote mediation as a dispute management mechanism that provides benefits for trade and investment and economic growth and stability.[118] They are also reflective of the principles of interest-based mediation itself.

The art of regulation lies in the ability to turn the tensions of the diversity–consistency debate into appropriate regulatory form. It requires a sophisticated understanding of the possibilities that regulatory mechanisms offer and what they mean for the future of mediation practice. In relation to mediation the question that needs to be asked is, what aspects of mediation are to be regulated and how. This part of the chapter has dealt with the *how* question and introduced four general approaches to the regulation of mediation. The next part deals with the *what* question. It introduces a classification method to describe the various aspects of mediation that may be subject to different regulatory approaches.

116 N Gunningham, P Grabosky and D Sinclair, *Smart Regulation* (Oxford: Clarendon Press 1998) at 391.

117 *The Guiding Principles for Regulatory Performance and Quality* (OECD 2005) is available at www.oecd.org.

118 For an example of such a reform project see *Facilitating Trade and Investment in the Mediterranean Region*, a project sponsored by the European Union, at www.adrmeda.org and FIAS (Foreign Investment Advisory Service). The project highlights the role of mediation in justice reform to improve the investment climate for both domestic and foreign investors and thereby maximise poverty reduction.

5. ANALYSING THE CONTENT OF MEDIATION REGULATION

There are many ways to describe and classify the content of mediation regulation. Each method offers a different insight into the characteristics and objectives of the regulatory instrument in question. The various categories of mediation regulation described here are not exhaustive. Neither are they exclusive. Rather they highlight the complexity and plurality of mediation as an object of regulation. Consistent with the approach taken throughout the book, the term *law* is understood in a broad sense and in the following section is used interchangeably with the term *regulation.*

5.1 The Law of Mediation and the Law in Mediation

One classification method favoured among German writers distinguishes between the law *of* mediation and law *in* mediation.[119] Law *in* mediation refers to laws relevant to the substance of the dispute being mediated. Here parties and their legal advisers may, in mediation, refer to strict legal rules or they may seek to rely on the principles underlying certain laws to guide their deliberations. Legal representatives often use law to support their arguments in mediation. Law sets the parameters for both settlement outcomes and walk-away alternatives in the event that the parties do not reach an agreement. It can also provide an objective benchmark for possible solutions and thereby influence the content and terms of mediated agreements. Conversely parties may knowingly deviate from relevant law and elect to base their decisions on other criteria such as business and personal interests.

In the story of Joe and Marie outlined in Chapter 1, the dispute relates to parenting issues across borders. Relevant laws in the mediation might include the Hague Convention on the Civil Aspects of International Child Abduction in addition to the applicable family law. The implications of taxation law for mediated settlements further illustrate the significance of law in mediation. In the Australian case of *Tapoohi*[120] a party sought to have the mediated agreement set aside on the basis that her lawyers did not advise her of the international taxation implications of the settlement. In other words, the argument centred on the role of law *in* mediation, or rather the absence of it on this issue.

Another example of law in mediation is found in statutory conciliation taking place within a legislative framework. Here expert advisory mediation is

[119] See C Duve, H Eidenmüller and A Hacke, *Mediation in der Wirtschaft* (Köln Dr Otto Schmidt Verlag 2003) at 88–90 and N Alexander, J Ade and C Olbrisch, *Mediation, Mediation, Schlichtung, Verhandlungsmanagement* (Münster: Alpmann Schmidt 2005) at 120–180.

[120] *Tapoohi v Lewenberg and Ors* [2003] VSC 379 and see the references to this case in Chapters 3 and 7.

usually employed.[121] The substantive terms of conciliated agreements between the parties must fall within the parameters of relevant legislation. In relation to the Australian Human Rights and Equal Opportunity Commission (HREOC), Raymond and Georgalis comment that,

> in facilitating the conciliation process, HREOC officers are seen to have a legitimate role to intervene to ensure a fair process for both parties, to provide information on a range of possible settlement options and to ensure any agreement does not contravene the interest and purpose of the legislation.[122]

Statutory conciliation operates in areas where there is a perceived need to balance the principle of party autonomy in mediation with the accountability of the state in relation to the protection of disempowered parties. In addition to human rights and anti-discrimination, statutory conciliation can found in areas such as health care, consumer law and workplace law.[123]

The law *of* mediation (also called mediation law) refers to the legislation, case law, contractual terms and other legally binding standards that constitute the legal framework for mediation. Mediation laws extend to any laws that directly or indirectly regulate aspects of the mediation process or outcome. In this context an Australian commentator refers to 'law applying incidentally to mediation.'[124] She provides examples from the law of evidence and the law of trade practices that go to issues of confidentiality in mediation and enforceability of mediated agreements.

Issues frequently the subject of mediation law include the confidentiality of the process and the enforceability of mediation clauses,

[121] On expert advisory mediation see Chapter 1 and N Alexander, 'The Mediation Meta Model: Understanding Practice' (2008) 26 *Conflict Resolution Quarterly* 97 at 107.

[122] T Raymond and S Georgalis, 'Dispute Resolution in the Changing Shadow of the Law: A Study of the Parties' View on the Conciliation Process in Federal and Anti-discrimination Law' (2003) 6 *ADR Bulletin* at 31. In relation to workplace matters, see South African Labour Relations Act 66 of 1995 discussed in M Paleker, 'Mediation in South Africa: Here But Not all There' in N Alexander, *Global Trends in Mediation* (2nd ed, Alphen aan den Rijn: Kluwer Law International 2006) at 355–360.

[123] For illustrations from the United States, see s 1164 California Labor Code in relation to workplace disputes and Revised Code of Washington (RCW) 7.70.100 in relation to health care.

[124] See Carroll (2002), above note 58 at 175. Here Carroll considers Australian laws which incidentally impact on mediation. The Evidence Act 1995 (Cth) s 131, for example, refers to the prima facie inadmissibility in federal court proceedings of evidence of settlement negotiations; Part V of the Trade Practices Act 1974 (Cth) deals with the law of contract and negligence for corporations. Compare the Californian Evidence Code, which contains specific mediation provisions in ss 1115–1128.

agreements to mediate and mediated settlements. Mediation model laws such as the UNCITRAL Model Law on Conciliation and the UMA in the United States provide model precedents for respective legislatures to follow. There are thousands of laws, court rules and institutional standards in the United States alone, and a rapidly growing number in other countries of the world, that contribute to the law of mediation. The differentiation between the law *in*, and the law *of*, mediation is useful because it assists in understanding the relationship between the legal system and the mediation process. The rest of the chapter, and indeed the book, focuses on the law of mediation, which can be differentiated according to whether it regulates issues internal to the process or the interface between the legal system and mediation. Distinctions can also be made between default and mandatory laws.

5.2 A Functional Approach to Mediation Law: Triggering, Procedural, Standard-Setting and Beneficial Laws

One way to understand the law of mediation is to characterise mediation laws in terms of their functions. They may facilitate access to mediation and trigger the mediation process (triggering laws), deal with the mediation process (procedural laws), enhance and support the recognition and practice of mediators by establishing standards for mediation (standard-setting provisions), or protect and benefit mediators or consumers by setting out their rights and obligations (beneficial mediation laws).[125]

Triggering laws can initiate the mediation process in a number of different ways. The most common of these include:

– Mandatory information sessions about mediation, sometimes including assessment of suitability for mediation (usually found in family mediation programs).[126]

[125] For other classifications of mediation laws see: *Mediation Discussion Paper* (Canberra: Attorney-General's Department 1994) which distinguishes procedural and regulatory mediation laws. A third category, beneficial, is added by Carroll in Carroll (2002), above note 58 et seq 167. See also D Clapshaw and S Freeman-Greene. 'Do we need a mediation Act? Part 1' (2003) 6 *ADR Bulletin* 61 at 65.

[126] Illustrations of this approach can be found in France in Article 255 of the Civil Procedure Code (Code de procédure civile, C pr civ) and in Part III of the Family Law Act 1996 (UK) especially s 29. In Austria legislation has been introduced requiring attendance at mediation information sessions in family disputes: see the changes to the Law on Marriage and the Civil Procedure Code (Familienrechts-Änderungsgesetzes 2009 – FamRÄG 2009) in which mediation is canvassed as a possible option as part of mandatory legal advice sessions. Finally Article 5 of the European Directive on Mediation recognises the right of national courts to invite parties to attend information sessions on the use of mediation.

- Mandatory consideration of mediation or ADR, according to which lawyers are required to consult with their clients and consider the use of mediation or other ADR forms in civil cases and in some jurisdictions report to the court on the outcome of such consideration.[127] Financial sanctions may apply for failure to comply with these requirements.[128]
- Referrals to mediation with all parties' consent.[129]
- Referrals to mediation at the request of at least one of the parties.[130]
- Mandatory referral to mediation at the discretion of a referring body irrespective of the parties' wishes.[131]
- Pre-filing mediation, according to which prospective litigants cannot file a claim in court until they have attempted mediation.[132]

127 See, for example, the mandatory consideration ADR rule in Minnesota: Minnesota General Rules of Practice 114. The operation of the rule is explained in B McAdoo and N Welsh, 'Look Before You Leap and Keep on Looking: Lessons From the Institutionalization of Court-Connected Mediation' (2004–2005) 5 *Nevada Law Journal* 399 at 407–408. In England see Practice Direction to the Pre-action Protocols 4.7 and the Civil Procedure Rules (UK) r 1.4 and the case of *Halsey v Milton Keynes General NHS Trust* and *Steel v Joy and Halliday* [2004] EWCA Civ 576.

128 In England see, for example, Civil Procedure Rules (UK) r 44.3 providing that, in imposing costs orders, courts 'must have regard to all the circumstances, including (a) the conduct of all the parties' before and during the proceedings and especially in relation to pre-action protocols.

129 Illustrations of this approach can be found in France in Article 131-1 C pr civ, in Germany § 278 V 2 Code of Civil Procedure and in Australia in the Federal Court Rules (Amendment) 1991 N° 461, r 4(1).

130 Illustrations of this approach can be found in the United States s 44.102(2)(a) Florida Statutes 2008, Title V, Ch 44 and in the Farm Debt mediation legislation in Australia, Canada and the United States.

131 Illustrations of this approach can be found in Australia and the United States. In Australia see T Sourdin, 'Mediation in Australia: Impacts on Litigation' in N Alexander, *Global Trends in Mediation* (2nd ed, Alphen aan den Rijn: Kluwer Law International 2006) 37 at 51–61. Examples include s 24A Victoria Supreme Court Act 1986. In the United States, see K Kovach, 'Mediation in the United States: Issues Ripe for Regulation' in N Alexander, *Global Trends in Mediation* (2nd ed, Alphen aan den Rijn: Kluwer Law International 2006) at 396–397. Examples include r 3.871 California Rules of Court – Civil Rules in relation to disputes not over USD50 000, r 16 Ohio Rules of Civil Procedure, § 44.102, § 44.108 and in relation to appellate mediation § 44.1011(2)(a), Title V, Ch 44, Florida Statutes 2008 and § 154.021 and § 154.022 Texas Civil Practice and Remedies Code. In Delaware all appeals from the Delaware Bankruptcy Court to the Federal District Court must first go to mediation: Procedure to Govern Mediation, July 23, 2004, authorised by the Chief Judge of the United States District Court for the District of Delaware.

132 Illustrations of this approach can be found in Germany in § 15a of the Introductory Law to the Code of Civil Procedure (Gesetz betreffend die Einführung der Zivilprozessordnung, EGZPO) and the Bavarian Conciliation Law (Bayerisches

In some jurisdictions multiple triggering mechanisms may be present. In Queensland, Australia, for example, where a mandatory referral model exists, it is also possible for litigating parties to obtain a consent order for mediation.[133] In Florida mediation may be mandated by the court; alternatively referral to mediation may be made upon the application of one party.[134] Article 1(1) of the European Directive on Mediation[135] specifies its objective as being, *inter alia*, to 'facilitate access to alternative dispute resolution'. Article 5 sets out different mediation triggering mechanisms that member-states may consider in their regulation policy, including court information sessions on mediation and voluntary and mandatory referrals.

There are also financial incentives that function as indirect triggers for mediation. Various forms of incentive, including cost sanctions imposed against parties who unreasonably refuse to participate in mediation and legal aid and other government subsidies for mediation, are found in various forms in England, Australia and the United States.[136] In another variation, the Slovenian Bar Association has increased lawyers' fees for mediated settlements by 50 per cent. This is not only a motivation for lawyers to use mediation but also for them to encourage settlement.

Procedural laws manage aspects of the mediation process such as commencement, termination and mediation protocols and the selection and appointment of mediators. Examples can be found in Articles 4, 5, 7 and 11 of the MLICC. In addition the mediation rules of dispute resolution organisations, bar associations and other professional bodies typically deal with procedure. Insofar as they are incorporated into private contracts and therefore bind parties, these rules are illustrative of procedural laws.[137] A global review of mediation

Schlichtungsgesetz). In Australia see s 60I(8) Family Law Act 1975 (see also www.ag.gov.au) for an example of pre-filing mediation.

133 For example, s 102 of the Supreme Court of Queensland Act 1991 (Qld) and r 320 of the Uniform Civil Procedure Rules 1999 allow the court to refer the party to mediation where a party asks court for an Order; the form for a Consent Order for ADR is Form 24.

134 See above notes 130 and 131 for references to the relevant sections of the Florida Statute.

135 See the European Directive on Mediation cited above in note 48.

136 See the following chapters in K Hopt and F Steffek (eds), *Mediation – Rechtstatsachen, Rechtsvergleich, Regelungen* (Tübingen: Mohr Siebeck 2008): J Scherpe and B Vollers, 'Mediation in England – Rechtlicher Rahmen und praktische Erfahrungen ' 259 at 266–272, R Kulms, 'Alternative Streitbeilegung durch Mediation in den USA' 403 at 422–425, 433 and 441–443, U Magnus, 'Mediation in Australien' 569 at 576.

137 See the Comparative Table of International Mediation Rules in Appendix B for more illustrations of procedural rules.

regulatory practice has shown that most jurisdictions prefer to use non-legislative regulatory forms in relation to internal process issues.[138]

Standard-setting regulations address issues such as qualifications, competency standards for, and certification or registration of, mediators. Standard-setting provisions can be prohibitive in the sense that they forbid those who do not meet the standards from offering mediation services. This is analogous to provisions relating to the practice of professional services such as law and medicine. More typically standard-setting provisions offer mediators a regulatory system within which to operate, provided they meet the required standards. The Australian National Mediator Approval Standards (2008) reflects this approach. Mediators who demonstrate that they meet the standard may operate under the National Mediator Accreditation System. Those who do not meet the standard may still call themselves mediators but do not offer the quality assurance that national accreditation promises. Nationally accredited mediators are subject to the Standards, which, according to Article 1(1),

> govern the relationship of mediators with the participants in the mediation, their professional colleagues, courts and the general public so that all will benefit from high standards of practice in mediation.

Article 1(2) goes on to explain that the Practice Standards specify practice and competency standards for mediators and provide information about what is to be expected from mediators and the mediation process. A similar approach is taken by the IMI and ADR Institute of Canada Inc.[139]

Regulation about mediation standards frequently assumes a self-regulatory form with mediation providers or industry groups setting their own requirements for recognition and quality. This is the case in France, Germany, England, the United States and other countries where different mediation standards co-exist in the absence of a uniform standard.

Family mediation is one area that is likely to have stricter and more formal regulatory control than mediation generally. In addition to the Hague Convention and EU provisions relating to family mediation outlined in Chapter 1, a number of countries including Australia, Austria and France have formal standards set out by legislation in relation to recognition of family mediators.[140]

138 See F Steffek, 'Mediation in Europa und der Welt' (2009) 1 *Zeitschrift für Konfliktmanagement* 21 at 23.

139 See the IMI Code of Professional Conduct, above note 10.

140 In Australia the Family Dispute Resolution Practitioners Accreditation System is regulated under the Family Law Act 1975 (Cth) and the Family Law Regulations 1984 (Cth). In France, see the Law of 26 May 2004 Relating to Family Mediation and Decree No. 2003–1166 of 2 December 2003 (Décret portant création du diplôme d'Etat de médiateur familial), which established the State Diploma in Family Mediation and the Order of 12 February 2004 relating to the Degree of State Family

Standard-setting provisions can also take the form of recommendations. The European Code of Conduct for Mediators is a useful regional example of standard-setting regulations that are advisory in nature. As indicated earlier Article 4 of the European Directive on Mediation requires member-states to adopt standards to ensure the quality of mediation and reference is made to the European Code of Conduct in recital 17 of the Directive. In the United States the ABA's Section on Dispute Resolution offers mediators and organisations providing mediation services Model Standards of Conduct for Mediators.[141]

Typically mediators who meet the required standards and mediate within a legislative system or contractual framework offered by the standard-setting body will have the benefit of provisions setting out their rights and protections. These are called beneficial laws and are explained below. Mediators falling outside the standard-setting regulation will not have the benefit of these rights and protections.

Beneficial mediation laws set out rights and obligations of those involved in the mediation, thereby protecting the integrity of the mediation process and benefiting its participants. Examples of these are legislative provisions and common law principles relating to matters of confidentiality, such as confidential information, without prejudice privilege, legal professional privilege and – where it is recognised – mediation privilege.[142] In addition provisions relating to disclosure requirements and to mediator liability fall into the category of beneficial mediation laws.[143] The UMA primarily deals with beneficial laws relating to confidentiality and privilege. Articles 6, 7 and 8 of the European Directive on Mediation contain beneficial laws on enforceability of mediated settlements, admissibility of evidence and the operation of limitation periods. The UNCITRAL Model Law on Conciliation also addresses these issues in Articles 10, 13, 14 and in the optional Article X.[144]

This discussion shows that regulatory instruments may contain different types of mediation provisions. For example, the extensive Slovakian Law on Mediation[145] contains (1) triggering provisions establishing courts as (non-exclusive) referral agents for mediation, (2) procedural provisions about

Mediator (Arrêté relative au diplôme d'Etat de médiateur familial), which deals with training and certification issues. In Austria see the Marriage Law Reform (Eherechts-Änderungsgesetz 1999, BGBl I 125/1999) and Children's Law Reform (Kindschaftsrechts-Änderungsgesetz 2001, BGBl I 135/2000). On the reform proposals for the Family Law Act 1996 (UK), which have largely not been implemented see Scherpe and Vollers (2008) above note 134 at 306–314.

141 The Model Standards are available at www.abanet.org.

142 On the law of confidentiality in mediation, see Chapter 6.

143 On the duties of participants in mediation and mediator liability see Chapter 5.

144 Article X on limitation periods is found in the footnote to Article 4 of the MLICC.

145 Slovakian Act of 25 June 2004 on Mediation and Amendment of Certain Acts, above note 100.

commencement and termination of mediation, (3) standard-setting laws for mediator qualifications and approval and (4) beneficial laws relating to mediation clauses and contracts, confidentiality, evidential matters and the legal effect of mediated settlements.

The Austrian Law on Mediation is an example of legislation which contains standard-setting (mediator qualification standards) and beneficial laws (provisions relating to confidentiality, evidence and suspension of court proceedings). Unlike the Slovakian law, it does not provide a path to mediation for parties (trigger) or address process issues such as commencement and termination (procedure). For this reason, it has been described as a law for mediators and not one for the mediation process.[146]

The MLICC contains mainly procedural and beneficial provisions, leaving mediation triggers and quality control to nation-states. The European Directive on Mediation requires member-states to regulate with respect to triggering, standard-setting and beneficial laws. Little attention is given to procedural issues in the Directive.

5.3 Laws Regulating the Interface Between Mediation and Legal System

Mediation laws, which regulate the interface between mediation and other proceedings, can be distinguished from those which focus solely on procedural aspects of mediation. The distinction highlights the role of mediation in the legal system and the fact that mediation does not and cannot exist in a legal vacuum. Interface laws are laws that:

- manage the interface between the mediation process and other proceedings such as arbitration and litigation;
- regulate issues such as the admissibility of information from the mediation as evidence in subsequent proceedings;
- determine the enforceability of mediated settlements in the legal system; or
- suspend litigation limitation periods for making legal claims.

There is considerable overlap between interface provisions and beneficial provisions. This occurs because rights and obligations – contained in beneficial laws – frequently have an impact upon other proceedings such as discovery and subsequent arbitral and judicial proceedings.

[146] E Filler, *Expertenrunde zum Stand der Gesetzgebung Mediation in Europa*, a joint initiative of Berliner Anwaltsverein (BAV) and the Internationale Vereinigung für Konfliktmanagement und Mediation (IVKM) eV, Berlin, 19 October 2007.

The following articles of the European Directive on Mediation can be categorised as interface provisions: Article 3 to the extent that it draws the boundaries between judicial settlement and judicial mediation, Article 6 on enforceability of mediated settlements, Article 7 on admissibility of evidence and Article 8 on limitation periods. The following articles of the MLICC also provide examples of interface provisions: Article 10 on admissibility of evidence, Article 12 on mediators as arbitrators, Articles 13 and 14 on enforceability of agreements to mediate and mediated settlements and the optional Article X on limitation periods.

The interface–procedural distinction is significant in terms of identifying issues that are suitable for legislative regulation and those more usefully dealt with through other regulatory methods. In general, legislation better serves regulatory objectives relating to what happens when mediation processes interface with the legal system. Here legislation is able to promote certainty and consistency in relation to other legal procedures in so far as they may come into contact with mediation. Other forms of regulation such as self-regulation and market-contract approaches may be suitable when dealing with issues specific to the mediation process itself. Here law and policy makers can draw upon the mediation principle of party autonomy to permit parties to tailor mediation processes to suit their needs.

Finally distinguishing interface from procedural regulations is useful in determining whether or mediation rules should be mandatory or of a default nature. This point is addressed later in the context of regulation design.

5.4 Default and Mandatory Laws

Mediation laws can be differentiated in terms of whether they operate as default or mandatory provisions.[147] Default rules support the notion of party autonomy and operate only in the absence of express agreement to the contrary by the parties. Many dispute resolution arrangements are regulated through a combination of contract and dispositive law.

The UMA and the MLICC provide illustrations of default laws. The UMA in the United States provides default beneficial rules relating to issues of admissibility of material from mediation as evidence in subsequent proceedings. Section 4(c) UMA permits parties to opt out of the provisions relating to privilege provided certain writing and notice requirements are satisfied. French commentators take the view that the provisions of the Civil Procedure Code relating to mediation are default in nature, thereby permitting parties to contract out of them.[148] The UNCITRAL Model Law on Conciliation is an example of a

[147] See H Eidenmüller, 'A Legal Framework for National and International Mediation Proceedings' (2002) 12 *Journal of International Dispute Resolution Beilage* 14 at 15.

[148] See Article 131-1 C pr civ et seq, Decree N° 96-652 of 22 July 1996, Article 2, Official Journal of 23 July 1996) and the following commentators referred to in

default model law. Here parties can enter into contractual arrangements that displace the application of the entire law. However, once parties opt into the law, most provisions remain as default in nature and only two provisions are mandatory.[149]

Mandatory rules apply irrespective of arrangements to the contrary. In other words, parties cannot contract out of mandatory rules as they can with respect to default rules. Article 6(3) MLICC, which enshrines the principle of fair treatment in mediation, operates as a mandatory rule in the Model Law. Encapsulating notions of procedural fairness and impartiality, this provision was considered by the drafters of the Model Law to be so fundamental as to override the other primary tenet of mediation, party autonomy.

5.5 The Scope of Mediation Laws: General, Sector-Specific and Integrated

Finally mediation laws can be categorised according to their target audience, namely whether they are general, sector-specific or integrated.[150] General mediation laws extend to all mediation and/or mediators in a given jurisdiction. Here mediation is accorded a high level of regulatory recognition as a dispute resolution practice. While there is no country that has national general mediation law that covers all areas of mediation practice and all aspects of mediation in those areas, there are a number of examples that move in this direction.[151] In 2001 Austria was the first country to enact a national mediation law in civil matters, moving towards a general law. However as the title of the legislation suggests, the scope of the law extends to civil matters only[152] and criminal matters are excluded.[153] The legislation recognises mediation as a profession in

Deckert (2008) above note 65 at 187: C Jarrosson 'Modes alternatifs de règlement des conflits' (1998) *Procèdures* in 161 at 163, G Pluyette 'Principes et applications récentes des décrets des 22 juillet et 13 décembre 1996 sur la conciliation et la médiation judiciaires' (1997) *Rev arbitrage* 505 and J Timsit, 'La médiation: une alternative à la justice, et non une justice alternative' *Gaz Pal* 14–15.11.2001 1773 at 1774.

149 See Articles 2 and 6(3) MLICC (2002).

150 See, for example, two New Zealand authors who distinguish between uniform or general laws and context-specific laws: Clapshaw and Freeman-Greene (2003), above note 125 at 61 and D Clapshaw and S Freeman-Greene. 'Do we need a mediation Act? Part 2' (2003) 6 *ADR Bulletin* 5 at 95. The reference here is to Part 2 at 99. See also Carroll who distinguishes between uniform, mediation-specific and context-specific mediation laws: Carroll (2002), above note 58 at 175 et seq.

151 For a similar view see Hopt and Steffek (2008), above note 109 at 57.

152 See the comments of Hopt and Steffek (2008) in relation to the scope of the Austrian law, above note 109 at 18.

153 Restorative justice processes in criminal matters called *aussergerichtlicher Tatausgleich* (ATA) are covered under different regulations: see Ferz and Filler

its own right and is targeted at mediators. The Laws on Mediation in Bosnia,[154] Slovakia[155] and Macedonia[156] are also examples of comprehensive mediation laws of national application. Japan's framework ADR Law in 2004 has a national scope, although there are also other laws dealing with aspects of mediation.[157] Finally the Philippine Alternative Dispute Resolution Act of 2004 deals not only with mediation but with all forms of facilitative and advisory dispute resolution as well as arbitration. In relation to mediation it covers voluntary mediation, both ad hoc and institutional. Court-annexed mediation is subject to more specific legislation and certain other matters including labour disputes are excluded from the application of the general law (s 7).[158]

The UMA and the European Directive on Mediation are legal instruments which have broad potential application. In its definition of mediation, the UMA distinguishes collective bargaining situations, peer mediation and judicial settlement and excludes them from the application of the Act. The Directive applies to mediation of cross-border disputes in civil and commercial matters. However recital 8 in the preamble to the Directive states that nothing should prevent member-states from applying such provisions to internal mediation processes. Throughout this book references to laws of general application include references to laws with a wider application than sector-specific laws.

Sector-specific regulation refers to laws dedicated to mediation in a specific industry, court, mediation program, area of law or other defined context. A cross-border illustration of sector-specific mediation regulation is the European Directive on Insurance Mediation.[159] Farm debt legislation in Australia, the United States and Canada provides an example of national regulation of this type, requiring mediation before foreclosure on farms can be executed. Here the legislatures have responded to the needs of their respective farming sectors in the form of opportunities to renegotiate terms and conditions with banks though mediation.[160] Similarly the Watertight Homes Resolution

(2003), above note 99 at 173–214. Although translated into English as victim-offender mediation, the German term *Mediation* does not appear in the Austrian terminology. *Ausgleich* refers to balance in a restorative justice sense.

154 The Law on Mediation Procedure of 29 June 2004. Article 1 states '[t]his law governs the mediation procedure on the territory of Bosnia and Herzegovina.'

155 Slovakian Act of 25 June 2004 on Mediation and Amendment of Certain Acts.

156 Mediation Law of Macedonia of 1 November 2008.

157 An Act on Promotion of Use of Alternative Dispute Resolution (Act N° 151 of 2004).

158 See ss 2 and 7 Alternative Dispute Resolution Act, 2004 (Republic Act N° 9285) in the Philippines.

159 Directive 2002/92/EC on Insurance Mediation, see www.ec.europa.eu and www.eur-lex.europa.eu.

160 In Canada see Farm Debt Mediation Act, SC 1997, c 21. In Australia see the Farm Debt Mediation Act (NSW) 1994.

Service Act 2002 in New Zealand was created as a response to a crisis in the local building industry.

Other examples of sector-specific mediation laws include those setting up community justice and mediation centres in Australia,[161] Singapore[162] and Sri Lanka.[163] Stand-alone court-annexed mediation rules and legislation fall into the category of sector-specific regulation. Illustrations include, from Germany, the Bavarian Conciliation Law[164] which deals with mandatory conciliation of certain Magistrates Courts cases, from the United States, the Alabama Rules of Appellate Mediation, from Australia, the Supreme Court Practice Direction N° 4 2002 (Qld) and Supreme Court Practice Note N° 118 2001 (NSW).

Integrated mediation laws are similar to sector-specific laws in that they focus on a particular topic or sector but differ in that they are not stand-alone laws. Integrated laws are incorporated into regulatory instruments dealing with a particular topic. In the United States the Californian Evidence Code (ss 1115–1128) contains provisions relating to admissibility of evidence of what occurred in mediation. Here mediation provisions are integrated into the laws of evidence and are therefore described as integrated mediation laws. Other legal provisions about mediation can be found in the Californian Code of Civil Procedure, thereby providing further examples of integrated mediation laws. An example of an integrated mediation law on a federal level is the Individuals With Disabilities Education Act 1990 (IDEA) in the United States. The statute governs the provision of funding for the education of students with disabilities and provides a guide for the Department of Education in relation to disputes involving such students. Mediation features strongly in the legislation as the dispute resolution process of choice.

Court-annexed mediation legislation is commonly integrated into the legislation of a relevant court. Illustrations include the Alberta Provincial Court Act 2000 and regulations under the Act, the Small Claims Tribunal Act 1985 of Singapore, the California Family Code ss 3160–3188 in the United States and the Federal Court of Australia Act 1976 (Cth) and Family Law Act 1975 (Cth) in Australia. In Germany § 278V(2) of the Code of Civil Procedure (ZPO) provides for judicial referral to ADR. Similarly in France and England provisions for court-referred mediation are integrated into the general civil procedural law.[165]

Other illustrations of integrated mediation laws include the Native Title Act 1993 (Cth) in Australia, which deals with a range of matters including

161 For example, the Community Justice Centres Act 1983 (NSW) in Australia.

162 For example, the Community Mediation Centre Act 1998 in Singapore.

163 N Alexander, 'Von der Mediation im Gemeinwesen zur Wirtschaftsmediation' (2007) 2 *Perspektive Mediation* at 84.

164 Bayerisches Schlichtungsgesetz (BaySchlG) (2000), GVBl N° 11/2000 (268–272).

165 In England see the Civil Procedure Rules and in France see Articles 21, 131, 1071, 1108 of the C pr civ.

mediation related to native title claims by Aboriginal Australians and Torres Strait Islanders. Similarly in New Zealand the Treaty of Waitangi Act 1975 deals with claims made against the New Zealand government for breaches of the Treaty of Waitangi and mediation is one of many topics addressed within the legislation.

The tripartite classification of general, sector-specific and integrated mediation regulation reveals different practices in common law and civil jurisdictions. An emphasis on sector-specific and integrated laws is characteristic of most countries in the common law tradition. It reflects a reactive, decentralised and piecemeal approach to regulation and a tradition of experimentation and trial and error consistent with the development of the common law itself. While countries with civil law traditions have also passed a limited number of sector-specific and integrated laws mainly related to court-referred mediation, there has been a trend to enact more generally applicable and centralised laws. This pattern is consistent with the more interventionist and paternalistic active state model[166] and leaves a small window open for experimentation. The European Directive on Mediation is likely to further encourage this trend towards comprehensive general legislation among member-states.

5.6 Using the Classifications as a Design Tool for Regulation

The above classifications of mediation regulation can be employed as a tool in making strategic choices about regulation design. This section outlines a series of design questions for those making decisions about the content of law and policy in relation to mediation. As has been the case throughout this chapter, the terms *regulation* and *law* are used in a broad sense and can refer to any of the four regulatory approaches introduced earlier. The design process is summarised in Diagram 1.

[166] On the active state, see Damaska (1986), above note 97 and the discussion earlier in this chapter.

Diagram 1
Strategic Choices about Content in Mediation Regulation Design

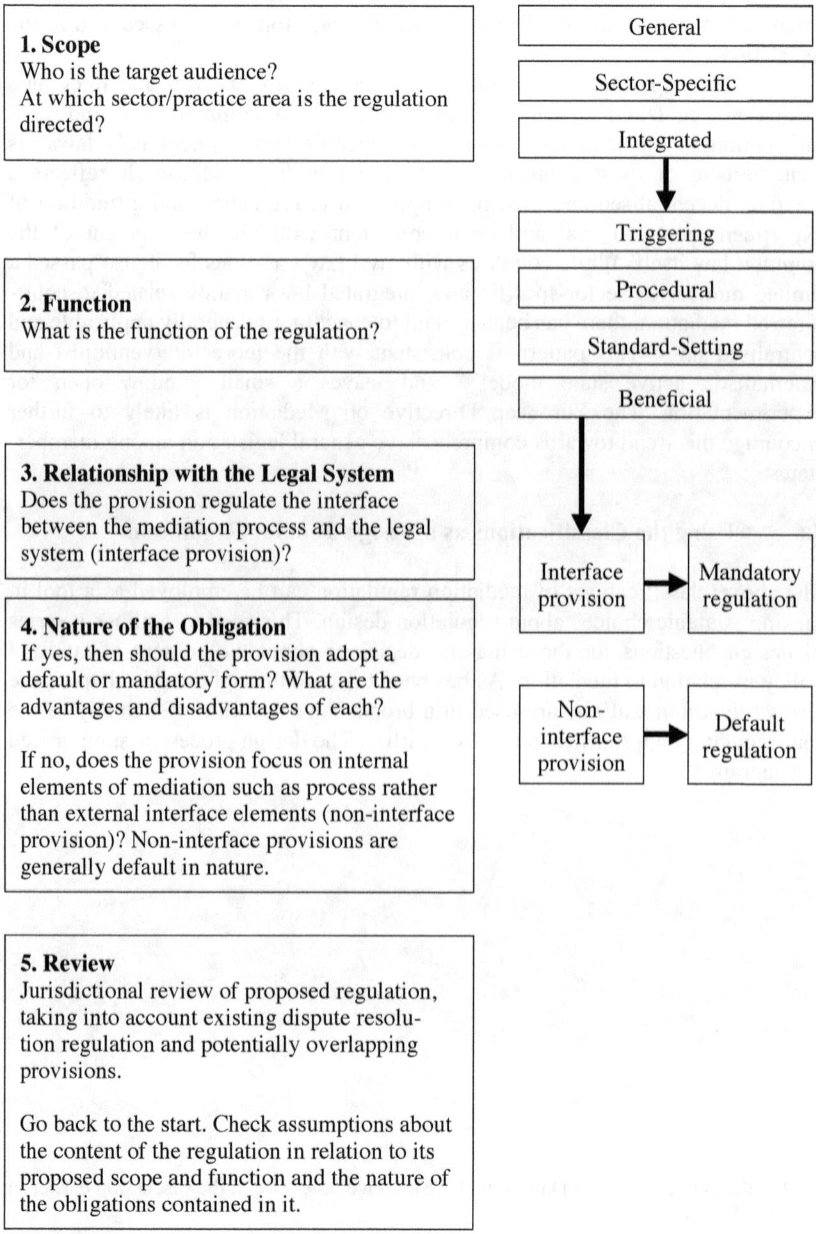

The threshold design question relates to determination of the target audience. Is the proposed regulation to extend to all mediators and mediations or is it to be restricted to a particular sector? The types of provisions that could conceivably be suitable for general application may include those relating to suspension of limitation periods and admissibility of evidence in subsequent proceedings, in other words, interface provisions.[167] Where regulation is limited to interface provisions in a particular substantive area, such as evidential provisions, it may be useful to consider whether it may more effectively enjoy general application through integrated legislation such as s 1119 Californian Evidence Code. Certain aspects of mediator disclosure may be suitable for general regulation such as disclosure to the parties; however, others such as disclosure to third parties may require differentiated regulation, for example, as between commercial and family matters.[168] Finally minimum standards may be suitable for general application, whereas aspirational and best practice standards are likely to differ across sectors, for example, as between family, commercial, community and international trade mediation practice.

The appropriateness of general as opposed to sector-specific and integrated regulation depends on a number of factors. General mediation laws usually result in broadly-worded provisions with many exceptions and scope for deviation, such as the frequently found 'unless parties agree to the contrary'. Such provisions may be difficult to apply uniformly across all sectors, causing inconsistency in the application of the law. The risk of subordinating the diversity and flexibility of mediation through precisely-worded general legislation is greater than through differentiated types of regulation. It is for this very reason that it is difficult to find examples of general mediation laws drafted with mandatory specific language.

Conversely sector-specific and integrated laws are able to accommodate precise language which responds to specific needs. There are many aspects of mediation that may need to be regulated differently according to their context. These include approaches to confidentiality, mediator accountability and enforceability of mediated settlements. Confidentiality needs may vary according to culture and levels of public interest. Many confidentiality rules provide a public policy exception, though this can be subject to varying interpretations. The mediation of inter-governmental disputes and environmental conflicts, where there is significant public interest, may require higher levels of transparency than the mediation of commercial litigation matters. In the mediation of Australian native title claims confidentiality provisions have to be more flexible due to cultural expectations. The drafters of the UNCITRAL Model Law on Conciliation recognised this challenge, and Articles 9 and 10 on

[167] By way of example, the law of confidentiality and privilege as it applies to mediation is the focus of the general mediation law, UMA.

[168] Carroll (2002), above note 58 at 206.

confidentiality take the form of default provisions, with broad exceptions to the rule against admissibility of mediation evidence in Article 10(3).

Mediator accountability can also be dealt with in different ways. In court-annexed, government and statutory contexts the issue of accountability is frequently addressed through mediator immunity provisions,[169] whereas private commercial mediators rarely enjoy such protection. While there are calls for uniform regulation of enforcement of international mediated settlements, it remains one of the most difficult areas to regulate. The diversity in content of mediated settlements means that different forms of documentation and enforcement – such as contract, arbitral award, court order and summary judgment – are appropriate for different kinds of disputes while certain other mediated outcomes may not lend themselves to a legally binding form.[170] Neighbourhood disputes and interpersonal and workplace issues are illustrative here. Such disputes can easily contain a cross-border or international element where parties live in border regions, where interpersonal disputes occur in cyberspace chat rooms or where a Canadian customer makes a complaint about a call centre employee in India. Here agreements to behave in a certain way, to apologise, or to maintain a united front to outsiders despite differences may not always be capable of legal form and enforcement. Sometimes parties will prefer to document their agreement as a memorandum of understanding rather than create a legally binding instrument. The complexity of developing acceptable uniform rules for mediated settlements and other aspects of mediation is evident. In a telling example, Article 14 of the UNCITRAL Model Law on Conciliation dealt with the dilemma by simply *not* dealing with it. The provision stipulates that a mediated settlement is 'binding and enforceable' and then requires the enacting state to specify provisions governing such enforcement. Ironically Article 14 of the Model Law, when enacted in different states, will effectively create numerous state-specific provisions instead of the uniformity which is UNCITRAL's mandate to develop.

Lack of specificity and clarity is not the only risk associated with mediation laws. In relation to the scope of mediation laws, Baylis laments the absence of detail and as a consequence, transparency. She argues for greater use of sector-specific and integrated regulation to provide specificity and clarity in relation to the interpretation and application of mediation regulation.[171] The more general the legislation is in its scope, the more likely that it will overlap with other regulatory instruments which primarily or incidentally regulate

169 See, for example, § 44.107 in the United States: Florida 2008 Statutes, Title V, Ch 44, in Australia: s 113 Queensland Supreme Court Act 1991, s 53C Federal Court of Australia Act 1976 and s 9 Victorian Civil and Administrative Tribunal (VCAT) Code of Conduct.

170 See, for example, s 31(3) Dispute Resolution Centres Act 1990 (Qld) Australia.

171 C Baylis and R Carroll, 'Power in ADR: Power Issues in Mediation' (2005) 7 *ADR Bulletin* at 133–138.

mediation. This can have serious consequences, especially in relation to standard-setting and beneficial provisions. Carroll illustrates the point well in the context of s 27(3) of the Commercial Arbitration Act 1984 (NSW), which makes provisions for arbitrators to mediate and s 51 of the same Act providing for arbitrator immunity except in cases of fraud. If the Australian federal legislature were to pass a general mediation law, the following two issues would arise:

- Would arbitrators still be acting as arbitrators when mediating, or would they fall under the provisions of the proposed general mediation law?
- Would s 51 immunity apply to mediating arbitrators or would they be subject to general mediation provisions relating to mediator accountability?[172]

This suggests the need for lawmakers to review existing legislation with a view to determining how proposed mediation laws will interact with the regulation of other dispute resolution processes.

In situations where a non-general law is proposed then consideration must be given to whether a stand-alone, sector-specific or an integrated form is appropriate. While stand-alone regulations may raise the profile of mediation, they also contribute to a piecemeal proliferation of statutes and a corresponding reduction in the transparency of regulation overall. Integrated laws expand existing laws and therefore do not contribute to statute proliferation. However mediation provisions in integrated laws necessarily operate within the existing structures of those statutes – a factor likely to influence how mediation is practised.

Once the target coverage of the regulation has been established, its content must be considered. Here reference is made to the classification system of triggering, procedural, standard-setting and beneficial regulation. The following comments and questions provide a guide for regulation designers:

- Is the aim of the regulation to trigger the use of mediation and if so, how? Here policy questions arise relating to the nature of the gatekeeper role and the extent to which parties have discretion as to their participation in mediation.[173]

[172] See the submission of the Law Society of Western Australia in relation to the NADRAC Issues Paper on Alternative Dispute Resolution in the Civil Justice System. Point A5(a) suggests amendments to arbitration legislation to 'confer greater immunities on arbitrators who endeavour to resolve disputes by mediation or conciliation'.

[173] On court referral to mediation see Chapter 3. On the duties of parties to participate in mediation, see Chapter 5.

- Are any process aspects of mediation to be covered under the regulation? If so, which elements of the mediation process will be covered by the proposed regulation and which elements will be left to other forms of regulation? What is the rationale for this choice?
- Are standards to be set for mediators or in relation to the mediation process? Standards for mediators can relate to approval, authentication, accreditation, qualification and certification. Standards for the conduct of mediation are generally referred to as practice standards or codes of conduct. Standards may also be set for service-provider organisations.[174]
- Questions about rights and obligations of participants in the mediation process are regulated in beneficial laws. Here tensions surrounding the following issues can be addressed: confidentiality, suspension of limitation periods, accountability of mediators and other participants in the process, and enforceability of mediated settlements and agreements to mediate.

In the diversity–consistency debate the principle of party autonomy is reflected in parties' ability to help shape the process and determine its outcome. Therefore rules dealing with procedural aspects of mediation often take the form of default rules so that the parties can opt out of them. In this manner diversity of practice is encouraged. Conversely, where regulatory provisions provide an interface between mediation and the legal system (interface provisions), there is an argument that they should take the form of mandatory rather than default regulation. In relation to the MLICC, commentators such as Eidenmüller and Ginkel express their disappointment that UNCITRAL did not use the opportunity of the Model Law to set an international benchmark for mediation. They argue that mandatory provisions, in particular around issues such as admissibility of evidence and enforceability of mediated agreements (interface and beneficial laws), are likely to increase confidence in the use of mediation – especially in international contexts where conflicts of laws issues could arise.[175] Instead the Model Law appears accommodating of variations in national laws and practice, thereby supporting the continuation of different practices in international mediation.

Once the above questions and issues have been considered, it is important to return to the first question and to review the suitability of the regulation design for the target audience. Proposals for a general mediation law

[174] See, for example, s 3(5) Australian National Mediator Approval Standards, which sets out the required characteristics of RMABs available at www.mediationworld.net.

[175] See, for example, E van Ginkel, 'The UNCITRAL Model Law on International Commercial Conciliation: A Critical Appraisal' (2004) 21 *Journal of International Arbitration* 1 at 7–10. See also the discussion of private international law earlier in this chapter.

may need to be reconsidered where detailed and precise legislative regulation on multiple aspects of mediation is envisaged. Conversely, where minimum standards in relation to one aspect of mediation are being introduced in a specific sector, consideration might be given to the question of a wider application of the regulation. The achievement of a lowest common denominator for mediator accreditation in Australia is a case in point.

The above discussion has examined the content of mediation regulation. The final section of the chapter builds on this analysis and reintroduces the four regulatory approaches to mediation outlined previously. The resulting regulatory model is called the mediation mix.

6. THE MEDIATION MIX: BRINGING FORM AND CONTENT TOGETHER

The mediation mix is a model that brings together issues of (1) regulatory form, explained through the four regulatory approaches to mediation and (2) regulatory content, analysed through a series of descriptive classification schemas. The mediation mix provides a conceptual map to assist law- and policy-makers navigate the labyrinth of regulatory issues in mediation. It is represented in Diagram 2.

Diagram 2
The Mediation Mix

<table>
<tr><th colspan="3" rowspan="2">Mediation Mix</th><th colspan="4">Regulatory Forms</th></tr>
<tr><th>Market-contract approach</th><th>Self-regulatory approach</th><th>Formal frame-work approach</th><th>Formal legislative approach</th></tr>
<tr><td rowspan="11">Content</td><td rowspan="3">Scope</td><td>1. General</td><td></td><td></td><td></td><td></td></tr>
<tr><td>2. Sector-specific</td><td></td><td></td><td></td><td></td></tr>
<tr><td>3. Integrated</td><td></td><td></td><td></td><td></td></tr>
<tr><td rowspan="4">Function</td><td>1. Triggering</td><td></td><td></td><td></td><td></td></tr>
<tr><td>2. Procedural</td><td></td><td></td><td></td><td></td></tr>
<tr><td>3. Standard-setting</td><td></td><td></td><td></td><td></td></tr>
<tr><td>4. Beneficial</td><td></td><td></td><td></td><td></td></tr>
<tr><td rowspan="2">Relation-ship with legal system</td><td>1. Interface</td><td></td><td></td><td></td><td></td></tr>
<tr><td>2. Non-interface</td><td></td><td></td><td></td><td></td></tr>
<tr><td rowspan="2">Nature of obligation</td><td>1. Mandatory</td><td></td><td></td><td></td><td></td></tr>
<tr><td>2. Default</td><td></td><td></td><td></td><td></td></tr>
</table>

Despite the visual simplicity of the diagram, this chapter has shown that the complexity of the issues surrounding mediation regulation precludes a checklist approach. It is not a simple matter of placing ticks in boxes. Rather the mediation mix offers both a language and a method for planning, designing, tracking and comparing which aspects of mediation are regulated (regulatory content) and how (regulatory form). In particular it highlights how different layers of regulation can address tensions thrown up by the diversity–consistency debate.

Consider the following illustration. A national regulatory policy intended to encourage party autonomy in mediation without jeopardising legal certainty or dispute resolution quality may choose the following mediation mix. Legal certainty and predictability needs can be addressed by a formal legislative approach using mandatory regulation of beneficial provisions, especially those that interface with the legal system, for example admissibility of evidence in subsequent proceedings, limitation periods and enforceability issues. Approval and accreditation of mediators requires an approach which balances the need to accommodate diverse mediation practices with the need for consumer clarity about what to expect from mediators. European research indicates that quality standards for mediation processes and mediators should be primarily the responsibility of the service providers themselves, with a supervisory role by government.[176] Accordingly formal framework and self-regulatory approaches are appropriate here. Self-regulatory and marketplace-contract approaches in relation to procedural and practice issues recognise party autonomy and encourage experimentation on a sector by sector basis on matters that are internal to mediation process. To the extent that these types of issues are subject to legislation, the use of default laws allowing parties to agree to do things differently would acknowledge the principle of party autonomy while, at the same time, setting a policy standard. Finally, legislatively backed triggering provisions can be useful to encourage the uptake of mediation in a jurisdiction or even in a specific sector.

The mediation mix is a tool for jurisdictions around the world in the process of developing policy for mediation regulation. Within the framework approach of the European Directive on Mediation, there is scope for member-states to make use of the mediation mix to determine the specific details of their national approach. As indicated previously the mediation mix can also be used to analyse regulation trends in a given jurisdiction and to compare trends in different jurisdictions, countries and regions. For example, the MLICC envisages a formal legislative approach by nation-states. It is a sector-specific law applying only to commercial disputes, although the definition of

[176] A De Roo and R Jagtenberg, *De praktijk van mediation in ons omringende landen; een vergelijkendonderzoek* (English translation: *The Practice of Mediation in Neighboring Countries: A Comparative Research*) (The Hague: Wetenschappelijk Onderzoek- en Documentatiecentrum WODC 2003).

commercial is broad. The MLICC contains mainly beneficial provisions and a limited number of provisions that set standards for the conduct of the mediation process. It does not concern itself with mediator qualifications (standards) or the issue of how parties get to mediation (trigger). Finally the MLICC is a default law in the sense that parties can contract out of it. In fact they can also contract in to the Law, even if their dispute technically falls outside its scope. As indicated previously once parties have accepted the entire Law as such there is still much room for the expression of party autonomy through private contractual instruments as only two of the Law's provisions are mandatory. As indicated earlier this aspect of the MLICC has been criticised by a number of commentators, who argue that the default nature of provisions dealing with the interface between the mediation process and the legal system defeats the very purpose of an international law on mediation, namely to increase legal certainty surrounding these issues.

Like the MLICC, the UMA is a model law and as such it represents the formal legislative approach. In terms of content, it claims general application and on this point is wider that the MLICC, which is restricted to commercial disputes only. However, in terms of the aspects of mediation to which the UMA applies, it is much narrower than the MLICC. The primary focus of the UMA is on issues of insider/court confidentiality[177] and disclosure. These provisions can be described as beneficial and interface laws. The drafters of the UMA considered insider/court confidentiality the single most important point in terms of uniformity and legal certainty. Other aspects of mediation regulation are left to the individual states, mediation organisations and the market.

As the case of Austria shows, a jurisdiction may take a general formal legislative approach in relation to standards and beneficial aspects of mediation, while at the same time allowing a market-contract approach to deal with the question of how to get to mediation.[178] In addition to the statute law on mediation in Austria, a variety of self-regulatory initiatives to mobilise mediation have emerged throughout the country. In various courts, mediation organisations conduct information sessions to increase consumer awareness about the availability of mediation and encourage disputants to utilise mediation services. Furthermore ethical standards for mediators, which build on the European Code of Conduct for Mediators, have been developed by a national umbrella organisation of mediation organisations in Austria[179] – an illustration of a collective self-regulatory approach.

The practicalities of selecting an appropriate mix of regulatory instruments for an emerging mediation profession and implementing them are challenging tasks. Two New Zealand commentators emphasise how difficult it is

[177] Insider/court confidentiality refers to the admissibility of mediation evidence in subsequent court or tribunal proceedings, see Chapter 6.

[178] See an earlier discussion in this chapter on the Austrian Law on Mediation.

[179] The ethical standards are available at www.netzwerk-mediation.at.

find a formula that accommodates the different philosophical approaches to regulatory mediation. They point out that courts in different jurisdictions around the world are grappling with these dilemmas and suggest that this is at least partly,

> due to the relative immaturity of mediation as a profession and the somewhat unnatural and conflicting principles that underline the differences between ADR and mediation processes (consensual and subjective) and adversarial litigation processes (imposed and ostensibly objective).[180]

In a dynamic and developing professional field, participative regulatory processes with the ability to review and adapt the mediation mix to changing circumstances are vital.[181] For these reasons a multi-layered approach to regulation in mediation is advocated – a combination of market-contract, framework, legislative and self-regulatory models, with strong responsive and reflexive review mechanisms in place.[182]

7. CLOSE

This chapter has explored the nature of the relationship between law and mediation. It has highlighted the significant role that law plays in mediation especially in relation to international and other cross-border disputes. It has also provided a structure for designing, analysing and evaluating mediation laws.

The following five chapters explore legal issues in mediation from an international comparative perspective. However they are structured chronologically rather than according to the mediation mix. International mediation is very much a developing field attracting interest from diverse areas such as law, arbitration, international business, domestic mediation and many others. In terms of presenting issues to such a wide audience with varying levels of experience in, and knowledge of, mediation, a chronological structure offers two advantages: it is relatively straightforward and less complex than the mediation mix. It encourages readers – especially those familiar with the mediation process – to progress through mediation from beginning to end and consider the legal issues that may arise at each stage.

180 See Clapshaw and Freeman-Greene (2003), above note 150 at 97.

181 On the risks of over-legalisation in relation to the introduction of general legislation in the form of the UMA see R Benjamin 'The Uniform Mediation Act: A Trojan Horse?' (2001) at www.mediate.com.

182 In support of such an approach see Black (2001), above note 74 at 103 and NADRAC (2001) above note 55 and Clapshaw and Freeman-Greene (2003), above note 150 at 100.

Chapter 3
Pre-Mediation I: Selection and Referral

1. INTRODUCTION

There are many paths that lead to mediation. It may be triggered by a dispute resolution clause in a commercial contract. Promotional material may encourage disputants to approach mediation service centres. Disputants may be referred to mediation by professional advisers such as lawyers and counsellors, or by courts. In a growing number of jurisdictions there are legislative provisions requiring parties to mediate before being able to file a court claim. In some cultures mediators themselves, having heard about a conflict, may seek out the disputants. Once mediation has been selected as the process to be used, trustmark programs, in which users of mediation can comment upon, and sometimes rate, mediators and mediation, may steer disputants to particular service providers rather than to others. The variety of mechanisms that encourage or trigger the use of mediation reflects the multiple opportunities for mediation and law to intersect before parties are even seated at the mediation table. This chapter considers two interrelated issues that may arise prior to mediation, namely mediator selection and referral to mediation.

2. CHOOSING A DISPUTE RESOLUTION PROFESSIONAL: QUALITIES AND QUALIFICATIONS

Parties do not always get to choose their own mediator. In some institutionalised contexts such as judicial mediation, court-referred mediation and government-sponsored mediation programs, parties may have limited or no influence in relation to who mediates their dispute. Here mediator selection typically falls to the service-provider or referral body as is the case in court-referred and judicial mediation in Germany, and some court and tribunal mediation systems in Australia and the United States. However in user-pay court-referral systems, available in many common countries and some civil law jurisdictions, parties generally are free to agree on a mediator or mediators of their choice. In some countries a combination of these two approaches is used. In France, for example, once the parties have agreed to mediation, the judge selects a mediator with the parties' agreement. Alternatively if the parties select a mediator of their own accord, the judge must agree to the choice of mediator.[1] The parties must share

[1] See Articles 131-1, 131-4 and 131-6 of the Civil Procedural Code (Code de procédure civile C pr civ and Decree N° 96–652 of 22 July 1996, Article 2, Official

the costs of the mediation; however these are regulated by statute and strictly monitored by the court.[2]

Selecting a mediator may not seem to be a task fraught with regulatory issues. However important legal consequences can flow from the selection of a particular mediator, such as the nature and extent of mediator liability, the scope of confidentiality and the level of enforceability attaching to mediated settlements. This section shows that in the absence of an internationally recognised system for mediator recognition, a minefield of potential legal risks awaits clients, lawyers and mediators. Chapter 2 introduced readers to a range of regulatory mechanisms including standard-setting instruments that deal with mediator recognition and performance. Here recognition extends to various standards of formal approval of persons to practise as mediators. It includes registration, certification, qualifications, accreditation, credentialing, licensing and other recognition procedures.

2.1 Implications of Mediator Selection

Where parties have a say as to who will mediate their dispute, their selection can be based on any number of considerations. Factors such as personal qualities, professional qualifications, experience, personal references and the anticipated style of mediation can weigh in their decision. Descriptors such as wise, trustworthy, non-judgmental, fair, patient, respected and knowledgeable are frequently regarded as desirable mediator characteristics.[3] The diversity of mediation practice offers parties wide choice in terms of dispute resolution practitioner and process model.[4] However it can also lead to misunderstandings about the nature of the process into which parties are entering.

Mediator selection is often aligned with choice of mediation institution and sometimes with choice of law. Frequently a mediation clause will include institutional rules, which extend to the choice of mediator from the named institution. However as indicated in Chapter 1, inconsistency in mediation definitions and practice may lead to confusion and inconsistencies in terms of

Journal of 23 July 1996) and K Deckert, 'Mediation in Frankreich – Rechtlicher Rahmen und praktische Erfahrungen' in K Hopt and F Steffek (eds), *Mediation – Rechtstatsachen, Rechtsvergleich, Regelungen* (Tübingen: Mohr Siebeck 2008) 183 at 192–193.

2 See Article 131-6 (2) C pr civ and Deckert (2008), above note 1 at 201.

3 See D Bowling and D Hoffman (eds), *Bringing Peace into the Room* (San Francisco: Jossey-Bass 2003) especially chapter 10 and H Landerkin and A Pirie, 'What's the Issue? Judicial Dispute Resolution in Canada' (2004) 22 *Law in Context Special Issue* 25.

4 See the discussion on the controversy surrounding different mediator lists and choice of mediator in France in Deckert (2008) above note 1 at 214–215.

quality assurance.[5] In addition provisions in mediator codes of conduct may clash with expectations of mediators. Examples are provided by r 20 of the Chicago International Dispute Resolution Association (CIDRA) Mediation Rules, which states that the mediator is not to provide legal advice[6] and the Australian Standards to the same effect.[7] In addition the JAMS International ADR Center Mediation Agreement provides terms to the effect that the mediator is not acting as an attorney or providing legal advice on behalf of any party.[8] However in some situations high status and well-respected mediators with legal expertise relevant to the case are likely to be selected for their ability to advise parties and their lawyers on the law, facts or evidence rather than for their skills in facilitating interest-based negotiation.[9] From a cultural perspective Irani explains that Arabic cultures expect mediators to have 'all the answers and solutions.'[10] Moreover it is acceptable for mediators to 'apply pressure to help bring about agreement.'[11]

The Australian case of *Tapoohi v Lewenberg*[12] illustrates the potential for adverse legal consequences for mediators and lawyers in circumstances in which mediators move beyond a facilitative role. In this case it was alleged that directive behaviours of the mediator, such as predicting solutions, making statements which interfered with the self-determination of the parties and advising parties on enforceability issues, amounted to a breach of the mediator's duty of care to the parties. An interlocutory application by the mediator to dismiss the case against him was rejected on the basis that there was legally a case to answer. The claim against the mediator was subsequently settled. The

5 See the definitional discussion on mediation in Chapter 1.

6 Article 20: 'There is no attorney/client relationship between the mediator and any party and the mediator does not provide legal advice. The parties recognize that in the process of reaching agreement they may choose to waive or forgo a claim or defense and that they may consult an attorney if they have any questions about their legal rights.'

7 The Australian National Mediator Standards: Practice Standards provide that mediators can provide neither legal advice nor assistance of a counselling nature. However advice may be provided in blended processes if certain conditions are met: see ss 3(4)(g)(i) and 10(3) and (5) of the Standards.

8 See clause 1 of the Mediation Agreement in Appendix A.

9 On this point see M Silveira, 'Impartiality v Substantive Neutrality: Is the Mediator Authorized to Provide Legal Advice' (2007) 62 *Dispute Resolution Journal* 26.

10 G Irani, 'Islamic Mediation Techniques for Middle East Conflicts' (1999) 3 *Middle East Review of International Affairs* 4.

11 J Murray, 'The Cairo Stories: Some Reflections on Conflict Resolution in Egypt' (1997) 13 *Negotiation Journal* 53–54. For an overview of literature on mediation in the cultures of the Middle East, see H Abramson, 'Selecting Mediators and Representing Clients in Cross-Cultural Disputes' (2006) 7 *Cardozo Journal of Conflict Resolution* 253 at 265–269.

12 *Tapoohi v Lewenberg* (N° 2) [2003] VSC 2, 410.

decision sent Australian mediators scurrying to check their codes of conduct, contracts and applicable statutes to ensure that their behaviour was in line with regulatory expectations about mediator qualifications.

Conversely there are regulatory instruments that specifically permit mediators to make recommendations on the merits of the case and on possible options and terms for settlement. These include Article 6(4) of the UNCITRAL Model Law on International Commercial Conciliation (2002) (MLICC), Article 7(4) of the UNCITRAL Conciliation Rules (1980) (UCA), r 7(d) of the American Arbitration Association (AAA) International Dispute Resolution Procedures 2008, and Article 67(4) of the Indian Arbitration and Conciliation Act 1996. Here advisory models of mediation are accommodated. However this can also cause problems. In the American case of *In re Marriage of Davis*[13] the court addressed the question of whether the appointment of a special master as mediator was improper because the parties expected that the appointed person would *not* – in accordance with the principles of facilitative mediation – impose settlements or express an opinion as to the merits of the case. It is therefore important to be aware of the scope of the mediator's power. Lack of clarity about the functions of mediators and the objectives of the process may leave mediators and legal representatives open to complaints and, potentially, legal action.

In mediator selection it is important to consider the extent of mediator accountability and liability. There have been instances in a number of jurisdictions in which legal actions by dissatisfied parties to set aside mediated agreements have involved mediators and legal representatives.[14] In court-related, government and statutory contexts the issue of accountability is often addressed through mediator immunity provisions,[15] whereas commercial mediators operating privately rarely enjoy such protection and have at most a contractual indemnity.

The *Tapoohi* case referred to previously highlights the impact of the regulatory framework on the issue of accountability. Due to an apparent oversight in filing court documentation the mediator in this case was not operating under the court's statutory framework as he could, or should, have been, but rather as a private mediator. As a result, when served with a third party notice for contribution in an action against one of the legal representatives, he

[13] *In the Marriage of Loyal A and Jennifer Ives Davis* Cal Ct App (1st App Dis Div 2, Unreported) 30.11.2006.

[14] For examples of this point in addition to the *Tapoohi* case, see Chapter 7. The accountability of mediators and legal representatives is considered in Chapter 5.

[15] See the following Australian example: s 113 Supreme Court of Queensland Act 1991 (Qld). Similarly s 35 of the Dispute Resolution Centres Act 1990 (Qld) establishes a government-based community mediation service, where mediators are granted immunity.

was not able to take advantage of the statutory immunity that otherwise would have extended to him.[16]

2.2 Selecting Multi-tiered Dispute Resolution (MDR) Practitioners

Practical and economic interests are prompting a greater use of MDR practitioners in international dispute resolution. The promise of a negotiated solution with time and cost savings, combined with the finality of a determinative process like arbitration, is proving increasingly attractive for parties. The juxtaposition of facilitative processes such as mediation and determinative processes such as arbitration in MDR systems raises issues pertaining to the selection of dispute resolution practitioners. As explained in Chapter 1, a controversial point relates to the appointment of the same practitioner to conduct the various MDR phases, for example mediation and arbitration, in the same dispute.

At first glance the benefits of the same practitioner approach appear to include cost advantages, time efficiency and flexibility in moving from one process to the next. However research in the area of international arbitration indicates that European jurisdictions may be more comfortable with the notion of arbitrators making settlement and mediative interventions than their Anglo-American counterparts.[17]

There are also concerns about the integrity of the mediation process in same practitioner MDR situations. The concerns focus on the extent to which principles of mediation, such as party autonomy and a focus on interests, are compromised when one practitioner acts as both mediator and arbitrator. The risk of negative impacts on the integrity of the mediation is exacerbated when the MDR practitioner's skill lies more in arbitration than in mediation.[18]

16 M Shirley and T Cockburn, 'When Will a Mediator Operating Outside the Protection of Statutory Immunity be Liable in Negligence?' (2005) 32 *The University of Western Australia Law Review* 83.

17 See C Bühring-Uhle, L Kirchhoff and G Scherer, *Arbitration and Mediation in International Business: Procedures for Effective Conflict Management* (Alphen aan den Rijn: Kluwer Law International 2006) and the *Draft Report of the CEDR Commission on Settlement in International Arbitration* (2009) at 3, available at www.cedr.com. In France see the *med–arb simultanés* procedure developed by CMAP, which involves parallel mediation and arbitration processes with different dispute resolution practitioners: www.cmap.fr.

18 See A Jolles, 'Consequences of Multi-Tier Arbitration Clauses: Issues of Enforcement' (2006) 72 *Arbitration* 329 and J File, 'United States: Multi-Step Dispute Resolution Clauses' (2007) 3 *Mediation Committee Newsletter of the International Bar Association* 33. See also the comments of J Fisher in *Acorn Farms Ltd v Schnuriger* [2003] 3 NZLR 121, 128–129 as to the inherent differences between the roles of mediators and arbitrators.

MDR practitioners are frequently selected on the basis of their arbitration, rather than their mediation, expertise. There are various reasons for this, including:

- the fact that lawyers and commercial parties are more familiar with arbitration than mediation;
- the limited number of MDR practitioners who are equally skilled and qualified in mediation and arbitration; and
- the fact that there appear to be more arbitrators offering MDR services than mediators.

The last-mentioned factor is supported structurally by the trend in arbitration legislation to permit and even encourage arbitrators to integrate mediative skills into their practice. This point is discussed below in relation to procedural fairness.

Finally legal issues such as procedural fairness and bias become acutely relevant in MDR contexts as the American decision of *Bowden v Weickert*[19] illustrates. In this case an arbitrator was found to have exceeded his authority because he based his arbitral decision on confidential information received during the mediation. The information fell within the relevant mediation confidentiality provisions[20] and the actions of the arbitrator were found to constitute a breach.[21] As a result the arbitral award was set aside.

Natural justice principles imply that arbitrators cannot rely on confidential information received earlier within an MDR process as a basis for decision-making in a subsequent determinative role. That does not, however, necessarily mean that private sessions cannot be conducted at all, although less legal clarity surrounds this point.[22] Some scholars argue that it is impossible for MDR practitioners not to be influenced by what they have heard in confidential circumstances when making decisions. Therefore mediators who conduct private sessions (also known as caucus in some jurisdictions) cannot subsequently act as

19 *Bowden v Weickert* N° S–02–017, 2003 WL 21419175 at *7 (Ohio App 6 Dist June 20, 2003) and discussed in J Coben and P Thompson, 'Disputing Irony: A Systematic Look at Litigation about Mediation' (2006) 11 *Harvard Negotiation Law Review* 99 at 100–101. The authors comment that '[t]he same concerns about mishandling of confidential information make dual service as a mediator and guardian *ad litem* problematic.' They refer to the relevant US cases at 101, footnote 265.

20 Ohio Rev Code Ann § 2317.023.

21 For an American case in which the court approved and even encouraged sharing of information across different dispute resolution processes – settlement discussions, arbitration and court processes, see *Kamaunu v Kaaea* 57 P3d 428 (Haw 2002).

22 The legal dilemma is similar to that facing judge–mediators, which is discussed later in this chapter.

arbitrators in the same matter and make a binding decision on the case.[23] Others, however, point to the fact that judges, lawyers and other professionals are regularly required to separate information and evidence that is admissible from that which is not admissible for the purposes of decision-making. They argue that the ability to separate different types of information for decision-making is both a skill and an ethical requirement of many professions and it should be extended to MDR practitioners.[24]

Legislative approaches to the issue vary. A number of mediation statutes contain default provisions that do not permit mediators to act as arbitrators in the same matter after a mediation has terminated. As explained in Chapter 2, default laws support party autonomy by permitting parties to make different arrangements should they so wish.[25] It is prudent to put any such arrangements in writing to prevent potential claims of bias and breach of procedural fairness after the event.

There is a different trend in modern arbitration laws, namely to provide for mediation windows or other settlement opportunities within the framework of arbitration. Arbitration statutes and procedural rules that explicitly envisage that the same person may conduct arbitration proceedings as well as facilitate settlement discussions or mediation can be found many jurisdictions including Australia, England, Germany, Hong Kong, Singapore, India, Taiwan and Japan.[26] Section 27(2) of the Commercial Arbitration Act 1984 (NSW), and the

23 H Eidenmüller, *Vertrags- und Verfahrensrecht der Wirtschaftsmediation* (Köln: Dr Otto Schmidt 2001) at 50–51. For a similar view see also Bühring-Uhle et al (2006), above note 17 at 248–250 and G Horvarth, 'Schiedsgerichtsbarkeit und Mediation – Ein glückliches Paar?' 6 *SchiedsVZ* 292 at 299.

24 See *Enterprise Leasing Co v Jones* 789 So 2d 964 (Fla 2001) 967–968 in which the Florida Supreme Court held that a judge in a jury trial was not subject to automatic disqualification on the basis that he was told confidential mediation information (including the nature of certain offers) by plaintiff's counsel. The Court commented at 967–968, '[w]e can see no compelling reason to treat a trial court's knowledge of inadmissible information in the mediation context any differently from the other situations presented every day where judges are asked to set aside their personal knowledge and rule based on the evidence presented by the parties at the trial or hearing.'

25 See, for example, Article 19 of the UNCITRAL Conciliation Rules read in conjunction with Article 12 of the UNCITRAL Model Law on Conciliation. See also Article 7(3) of the International Chamber of Commerce (ICC) ADR Rules (2001).

26 See s 27 of the Commercial Arbitration Act 1984 (NSW), s 51 of the English Arbitration Act (1996), § 1053 of the German Code of Civil Procedure (ZPO), ss 2A(2) and 2B of the Hong Kong Arbitration Ordinance 1996, ss 16–17 of the Singapore International Arbitration Act 1995, s 30 of the Indian Arbitration and Conciliation Act 1996, Articles 44 and 45 of the Taiwanese Arbitration Act, and s 38(4) of the Japanese Arbitration Act (2003). In England see the 2009 Draft Report of the CEDR Commission on Settlement in International Arbitration, which considers the opportunities and risks involved in arbitrators engaging in mediation and other

mirror legislation in other Australian states,[27] suggests that the holding of private sessions during a mediation window, of itself, will not amount to a breach of the rules of natural justice. However combined with other factors – such as relying on confidential information to make a determination – a breach may still be established. Such a provision does not attempt to do away with the principles of procedural fairness; rather it seeks to recognise variations in dispute resolution processes and to honour party autonomy. In any event, MDR practitioners must remain vigilant about how they use information revealed to them in private sessions and parties may wish to clarify in contractual form their understanding of the use and implications of private sessions held during mediation windows.

2.3 Mediator Recognition

Despite significant moves towards the professionalisation of mediation, mediator recognition standards remain far from uniform in most countries. In the Netherlands alone the Netherlands Mediation Institute offers more than 13 accreditation programs, which differ in length, cost, threshold standards for entry and course content. In this diverse landscape, there are powerful initiatives to establish international recognition of mediator recognition and standards.

International business leaders such as Erik Pfeiffer, Chairman of the Board of Paranova Gruppen in Copenhagen and Wolf von Kumberg (Legal Director, Assistant General Counsel, Northrop Grumman Corporation) have publicly endorsed the development of a pool of internationally recognised mediators who carry with them a trust mark of skill and experience and the backing of reputable organisations.[28] The International Mediation Institute (IMI) is one such initiative. Founded in 2007 with financial support from three mediation organisations in the Netherlands, the United States and Singapore respectively, IMI has consulted, and continues to consult, widely with mediators, mediation users, mediation service providers and organisations, government representatives and others who have a stake in the global

settlement attempts and has established draft rules in relation to the practice: available at www.cedr.com.

27 Commercial Arbitration Act 1986 (ACT), Commercial Arbitration Act 1984 (NSW), Commercial Arbitration Act (NT), Commercial Arbitration Act 1990 (QLD), Commercial Arbitration Act 1986 (SA), Commercial Arbitration Act 1986 (Tas), Commercial Arbitration Act 1985 (WA), Commercial Arbitration Act 1984 (Vic). In Australia arbitration is regulated at the state level and all states and territories have revised their arbitration laws since 1984, enacting uniform Commercial Arbitration Acts. The Commercial Arbitration Act 1984 first took effect in Victoria on 1 April 1985 and in NSW on 1 May 1985. It was thereafter introduced in the territories and the other states. See S Hepburn, 'Natural Justice and Commercial Arbitration' (1993) 21 *The Arbitrator* 133 at 136.

28 See comments by international business leaders at www.imimediation.org.

development of mediation. At the time of writing, IMI has developed a competency certification scheme (IMI Certification Scheme) and is finalising its standards for training and assessment. The organisation intends to operate with the support of selected national mediation organisations around the world to certify international mediators.[29]

Until such time as international recognition initiatives are operating on a worldwide basis, however, selecting mediators on the basis of their qualities and qualifications remains a challenging task. It is therefore prudent to ask potential mediators for evidence of their approval status and for an explanation of their mediation training and experience. Many mediators will be subject to disclosure requirements about their experience and qualifications in any event.[30]

The following guidelines, based on a tripartite classification of mediator approval standards, will assist parties and their legal representatives to make informed choices about international mediators and their qualifications.[31] Issues surrounding mediator approval and recognition can be considered in terms of:

1. threshold/ eligibility requirements;
2. approval standards themselves; and
3. requirements for maintaining the standards.

2.3.1 *Threshold Requirements for Mediator Approval*

Mediator approval standards may contain threshold requirements that play a gatekeeping function determining eligibility and suitability for mediator approval. Examples of mediator threshold requirements include generalist or specialist education, work experience,[32] age,[33] character and other personal attributes such as communication abilities and conflict management style.[34]

29 For more information on IMI, see www.imimediation.org.

30 In relation to disclosure requirements, see for example, s 1.3 IMI Code of Professional Conduct. Section 9 of the Uniform Mediation Act (2001) states, 'At the request of a mediation party, an individual who is requested to serve as a mediator shall disclose the mediator's qualification to mediate a dispute.'

31 This classification has been used by C Pou, 'Assuring Excellence, Or Merely Reassuring? Policy And Practice In Promoting Mediator Quality' (2005) *Journal of Dispute Resolution* 303.

32 In France commercial mediation organisation CMAP requires its mediators to have at least 10 years experience in a relevant professional field such as law, business or finance. See www.cmap.fr.

33 Pursuant to § 9(1) N° 1 of the Austrian Law on Mediation in Civil Cases 2001 (ZivMediatG) mediators must be at least 28 years of age.

34 Singapore Mediation Centre neutrals are only accredited once they are assessed to have the 'appropriate temperament'.

A number of European countries including France and Austria do not permit persons with a criminal record to become qualified as mediators.[35] Other jurisdictions such as Australia, Canada and the United States insert a 'good character' or similar requirement. This effectively means that those with a criminal record are not automatically excluded and that eligibility to qualify as a mediator is determined on a case-by-case basis in relation to the 'good character' criterion.[36]

In France entry requirements into the State Diploma in Family Mediation in France include a post-baccalaureate study of two to three years in one of a number of substantive areas.[37] Setting threshold standards on the basis of education and degree requirements reflects the idea that mediation quality flows from a particular educational track or professional status. This view is not endorsed by the *Report on Mediator Credentialing and Quality Assurance* in the United States[38] and mediation communities in the United States, Canada, England and Australia have largely – but not completely – displayed preference for other approaches to the issue. Civil law jurisdictions in Europe are more likely to embrace the tertiary entry-level requirement, although this is by no means a standard approach. An illustration of specialist – as distinct from general – educational requirements can be found in those programs that require mediators to be qualified lawyers.[39] Organisations that represent lawyers, such as law societies and bar associations, typically allow only lawyers to be recognised as mediators under their schemes. Pre-training appraisal using psychologically-based questionnaires, such as the Myers–Briggs Type Indicator, is an example of threshold testing, which purports to assess applicants' prima facie suitability to be professional mediators.

35 In France, see Article 131-5 C pr civ relating to court-based conciliation and mediation. In Austria see § 11(2) ZivMediatG. Germany is likely to follow this civil law trend.

36 For example the ADR Institute Canada, Inc requires its mediators to be of good standing, Principles Criteria Protocol for the designation Chartered Mediator, 'VI. Membership.' See the section on criteria at: www.adrcanada.ca/education/mediator.html. The Australian National Mediator Approval Standards s 3 require that potential mediators demonstrate that they are of 'good character'.

37 See the Law of 26 May 2004 Relating to Family Mediation and Decree N° 2003–1166 of 2 December 2003 and comment by J-P Bonafé-Schmitt (translation by D Macfarlane), 'Global Trends in Mediation: Training and Accreditation in France' (2009) 11 *ADR Bulletin* 47 at 48.

38 See American Bar Association (ABA) Section of Dispute Resolution, Task Force on Credentialing, *Report on Mediator Credentialing and Quality Assurance* (Oct 2002) at 24–25 available at www.abanet.org/dispute/taksforce_report_2003.pdf.

39 See, for example, the District Court of Columbia mediation program for civil court matters at www.mediationworks.com/medcert3/staterequirements.htm and the conciliation program in the small claims courts in Bavaria, Germany: Article 8(1) of the Bavarian Conciliation Law (BaySchlG).

Threshold requirements in mediator accreditation systems provide useful indicators of a mediator's professional and personal background and they may also suggest the model of mediation likely to be used.

2.3.2 Attaining Mediator Approval

In terms of the requirements to attain mediator approval standards, would-be mediators may be required to undertake training, skills assessment and/or supervised or co-mediations. The duration and content of training varies according to sector, industry and jurisdictions. In jurisdictions such as Austria and Australia recognition of prior learning permits mediator candidates to obtain credit toward training requirements from previous training and work experience.[40] Conversely from July 2009 IMI mediator certification cannot be obtained through prior recognition of experience and candidates must comply with certification requirements including an assessed mediation role-play.[41]

Mediator training can be general or subject-specific. When seeking a mediator, the choice between a specialist- and a generalist-accredited mediator may have implications in terms of mediator duties and accountability. Mediators specialising in a substantive area may have more onerous responsibilities towards parties than generalist mediators. Family mediator approval systems, for example, often require training specific to the family context and the needs of children and their codes of conduct reflect this.[42] Contrary to the generalist Anglo-American trend, there is a European tendency towards specialist accreditation in a range of fields beyond family mediation including business mediation, environmental mediation, workplace mediation, intercultural mediation and many others.[43] On the international level, IMI seems to have adopted a more generalist approach in its Certification Scheme, although it does offer a more advanced certification for intercultural mediation. The European Code of Conduct for Mediators is also generalist in nature.

40 See § 5 of the Austrian Training Regulations of 2001 (ZivMediat-AV) and ss 4 and 5 of the Australian National Mediator Standards: Approval Standards (2007).

41 See www.imimediation.org.

42 See, for example, recommendation N° R (98)1 on Family Mediation in Europe (Council of Europe 1998) and European Charter for Training in Family Mediation for Separation and Divorce (1992). In the United States see the American Bar Association Task Force on Credentialing Mediators (2002), above note 38, especially the references to family mediator credentialing, and the Academy of Family Mediators, Standards of Practice for Family and Divorce Mediation at www.mediate.com//articles/afmstds.cfm. In Canada the ADR Institute of Canada requires specialised competencies in specific mediation fields such as family mediation. In Australia nationally recognised specialist family mediator accreditation is available in addition to general mediator accreditation: see Family regulation available at www.aifs.gov.au/familypathways.

43 See, for example, the case of France: Bonafé-Schmitt (2009), above note 37.

Despite the trend towards national and international accreditation standards, there remain many areas of practice where there are no set requirements for mediators to attain a required standard. Mediator recognition is left to the discretion of an authorised body to determine on a case-by-case basis. Numerous court mediation schemes follow this model. In France, for example, Article 131-5 of the French Civil Procedure Code requires, *inter alia*, that mediators must establish their qualifications in the relevant area of dispute to the satisfaction of the court.[44]

From a client's perspective, the more minimalist the mediator training and education requirements, the more importance will be attached to threshold and maintenance requirements when choosing a suitable mediator.

2.3.3 *Maintaining the Approval Standard*

Once mediators have attained the required standard and been approved, they must maintain the standard in order to retain their recognition as a professional mediator. Mediators failing to maintain their practice standards will find themselves open to complaints and possible removal from mediator lists. Standards maintenance takes different forms including continuing professional development, such as the Austrian requirement of 50 hours every five years.[45] Other requirements for standards maintenance include clinical experience, supervision,[46] skills audits, adherence to codes of conduct,[47] acquisition of professional liability insurance[48] and payment of fees and charges.

ADR Canada requires its Chartered Mediators to complete a renewal pledge every three years.[49] The Austrian mediation law registers mediators for an initial period of five years. After four years registered mediators are invited to extend their registration for another 10 years, provided they have complied with continuing professional development requirements.[50] In the Netherlands the main mediation organisation, NMI, conducts random sampling to verify that mediators have complied with their obligations to maintain their standard.[51]

44 Article 131-5 C pr civ relating to court-based conciliation and mediation. See Bonafé-Schmitt (2009), above note 37.

45 § 20 ZivMediatG in Austria.

46 See, for example, s 6(1)(b)(ii) Australian National Mediator Standards: Approval Standards (2007).

47 See, for example, s 5(7) Australian National Mediator Standards: Practice Standards (2007).

48 See, for example, s 3(1)(c) Australian National Mediator Standards: Practice Standards (2007) in Australia and § 19 ZivMediatG in Austria.

49 ADR Institute Canada, Principles Criteria Protocol for the designation of Chartered Mediators, Article VII at www.adrcanada.ca.

50 See § 13 ZivMediatG.

51 See www.nmi-mediation.nl.

Feedback and complaints mechanisms also support the maintenance of quality standards.[52] IMI requires mediators to adhere to the IMI Code of Professional Conduct or another code of conduct. Users of mediation services who believe the appropriate standards have not been met may activate the IMI Professional Conduct Assessment Process.[53]

3. JUDGES AS MEDIATORS

> From the conventional perspective of most modern legal cultures, judicial mediation is a contradiction in terms. Judges are supposed to judge (not mediate), to apply law (not interests), to evaluate (not facilitate), to order (not accommodate) and to decide (not settle).[54]

3.1 Historical View

Historically legal systems around the world have used a combination of facilitative, advisory and determinative dispute resolution approaches. In a comprehensive analysis of the Anglo-Saxon history of dispute resolution, Sanchez argues that the Anglo-Saxon legal system under the Christian medieval influence increasingly used a range of ADR processes not dissimilar to those used today, namely negotiation, conciliation and arbitration. As an illustration she points to the popular use of mediation after a determinative process had been completed – a form of arb–med by judges.[55] In 1666 Alexandre de la Roche argued for the introduction of formal court-annexed mediation and arbitration schemes in France.[56] In China and other Asian jurisdictions judges traditionally applied a combination of mediation, conciliation and adjudication in the resolution of disputes.[57] Such multi-process judicial approaches appear to have declined in the eighteenth century – at least in western industrialised countries – with the emergence of the nation-state and the rise of European ideas such as the rule of law and separation of powers.

52 See, for example, the complaints mechanism requirements in ss 3(1)(d) and 3(5)(c) Australian National Mediator Standards: Approval Standards (2007).

53 See www.imimediation.org.

54 D Spencer and M Brogan, *Mediation Law and Practice* (Melbourne: Cambridge University Press 2007) at 391.

55 See V Sanchez, 'Towards a History of ADR: The Dispute Processing Continuum in Anglo-Saxon England and Today' (1996) 11 *Ohio State Journal on Dispute Resolution* 1 at 3–5, 11–12, 30–32.

56 D Roebuck, *The Charitable Arbitrator: How to Mediate and Arbitrate in Louis XIV's France* (Oxford: Holo Books The Arbitration Press 2002).

57 P Huang, 'Court Mediation in China: Past and Present' (2006) 32 *Modern China* 275 at 288–308.

The resulting emphasis on the adjudicative role of courts pushed non-determinative processes into the background. In terms of the resolution of litigation matters, however, settlement conferences continue to have the biggest impact with between 70 and 95 per cent of litigation matters settling 'on the steps of the courthouse'.[58]

3.2 Contemporary View

Contemporary interest in judicial mediation is part of a wider development of civil and judicial reform characterised by an increase in judicial control over civil trials in both common law and civil law jurisdictions.[59] According to the legal comparativist, Cappelletti, judges from diverse legal traditions are being entrusted with more discretion and creativity in judicial decision-making as law, economics and politics become harder to distinguish from each other and new areas of law continue to emerge.[60] In England the Woolf and Jackson Reports made the case for courts to play an active role in providing information about and encouraging mediation and other forms of ADR.[61] Judicial mediation and other non-determinative judicial processes are redefining the traditional concept of judges as disinterested decision-makers. These processes are referred to collectively as judicial dispute resolution (JDR).

The view that judges make suitable mediators due to their experience in the traditional judicial settlement role has significantly shaped legal and cultural attitudes in favour of judicial mediation in much of the civil law world including Germany and Scandinavia.[62] Moreover the concept of the court as a one-stop shop for all dispute resolution needs sits well with the interventionist attitudes and practices representative of Damaska's active states as explained in the

58 See, for example, M Galanter, 'The Vanishing Trial: An Examination of Trials and Related Matters in Federal and State Courts' (2004) 1 *Journal of Empirical Studies* 459 at 489 and D Spencer, 'The Vanishing Trial Phenomenon' (2005) 43 *Law Society Journal* 58 at 59.

59 See A Zuckerman, 'Justice in Crisis: Comparative Dimensions of Civil Procedure' in A Zuckerman (ed), *Civil Justice in Crisis: Comparative Perspectives of Civil Procedure* (Oxford: Oxford University Press 1999) at 47–48.

60 M Cappelletti, *The Judicial Process in Comparative Perspective* (Oxford: Clarendon Press 1989) at 16 and 56.

61 Lord Woolf, 'Access to Justice – Chapter 18' (1995) *Interim Report to the Lord Chancellor on the Civil Justice System in England and Wales* 136 at para 4 (see also the Final Report) and Lord Justice Jackson, *Civil Litigation Costs Review: Preliminary Report* (London: Judiciary of England and Wales 2009).

62 On judicial mediation in Germany see J von Bargen, *Gerichtsinterne Mediation*, Veröffentlichungen zum Verfahrensrecht N° 57 (Tübingen: Mohr Siebeck 2008) and in Sweden see B Lindell, 'Mediation In Sweden' (2004) 7 *ADR Bulletin* 85.

previous chapter.[63] At the same time, there remain critical voices monitoring judicial mediation developments in Europe and elsewhere.[64]

In common law jurisdictions, access to justice initiatives have paved the way for innovations in case management such as:

- facilitative judging where judges integrate mediative skills into their judging role;
- hot-tubbing in which expert witnesses present their evidence concurrently and are subject to questions from one another and from the judge (also called concurrent evidence); and
- judicial mediation.

There are signs of interest in and a growing practice of judicial mediation in common law jurisdictions such as the United States, Australia, New Zealand and the common law Canadian provinces.[65] Judicial Codes of Conduct expressly

[63] See M Damaska, *The Faces of Justice and State Authority: A Comparative Approach to the Legal Process* (New Haven: Yale University Press 1986) 73–88.

[64] See, for example, T Allen, *Implementing the EU Directive on Mediation: A Draft Consultation Paper* (London: 2009). At the time of writing, the paper was in draft form. Available from CEDR library at www.cedr.com.

[65] See, for example, reports on the limited practice of judicial mediation in some Australian courts: M Schmidt, 'Successful Experiment in Judicial Mediation' (2006) 18 *Judicial Officers Bulletin* 71, M Sidis, 'Judicial Mediation in the District Court' (2006) 18 *Judicial Officers Bulletin* 75, D Spencer, 'Judicial Mediators: Is the Time Right? – Part I' (2006) 17 *Australasian Dispute Resolution Journal* 130 and D Spencer, Judicial Mediators: Is the Time Right? – Part II (2006) 17 *Australasian Dispute Resolution Journal* 189. See also the *Declaration of Principles on Court-Annexed Mediation* adopted by the Chief Justices Council in Australia which recommends that mediators should normally be court officers For a discussion on the principles, see Chief Justice JJ Spigelman AC, Speech delivered at the LEADR Dinner, (Sydney, 9 November 2000), at www.lawlink.nsw.gov.au/lawlink/supreme_court/ll_sc.nsf/pages/SCO_speech_spigelman_091100, and the Australian Institute of Judicial Administration (AIJA) *Guide to Judicial Conduct* (2002) at 19. On Canada see L Otis and E Reiter, 'Mediation by Judges: A New Phenomenon in the Transformation of Justice' (2006) 6 *Pepperdine Dispute Resolution Law Journal* 351. On New Zealand see D Spiller (ed), *Dispute Resolution in New Zealand* (2nd ed, South Melbourne: Oxford University Press 2007) at 241, E France, D Gendall and C Doherty, *Judicial Settlement Conferences Statement Of Issues And Recommendations* (New Zealand: 2005) and the District Court Rules (New Zealand) r 434. On England see The Technology and Construction Court at www.hmcourts-service.gov.uk/infoabout/tcc/index.htm. On the US see P Robinson, 'Adding Judicial Mediation to the Debate about Judges Attempting to Settle Cases Assigned to Them for Trial' (2006) 2 *Journal of Dispute Resolution* 335.

recognise the role of judge as mediator.[66] Research in the United States, Canada and New Zealand indicates that most litigation lawyers welcome judicial involvement in settlement conferences and view it as positive and helpful to the resolution of disputes.[67] The case law on JDR is primarily from the United States and Australia and there are limited reported cases on this topic in other jurisdictions.

3.3 JDR Models

There are four primary judicial dispute resolution models in practice, all of which engage the mediation process or mediative techniques to some extent:

1. judicial settlement;
2. judicial mediation;
3. judicial moderation; and
4. facilitative judging.

As explained in Chapter 1, terminology in the expanding field of dispute resolution is not always consistent. When judges participate in mediation training, it is not always clear how they will use the skills learned – unless their court already has an established JDR program. Anecdotal evidence from civil and common law jurisdictions suggests that there is considerable diversity in the ways judges conduct mediations and settlement conferences – even within the same court.

The JDR taxonomy presented in this section looks not to the labels of particular JDR programs. Rather it refers to what judges actually do and classifies their practices accordingly. Illustrations of this approach to categorising JDR practices are found both in the literature[68] and in practice.

The classification of JDR models is more than an academic exercise. It can have legal consequences for parties, as the following cases demonstrate. The first two cases considered endorse the approach of looking behind process

66 See, for example, Canon 3 ABA Model Code of Judicial Conduct (2007) in the US and s 4.7 Guidelines to Judicial Conduct endorsed by the Council of Chief Justices of Australia.

67 In the United States see W Brazil, 'Settling Civil Cases: What Lawyers Want From Judges' (1984) 23 *Judges Journal* 15 and W Brazil, 'Settling Civil Cases: Where Attorneys Disagree About Judicial Roles' (1984) 23 *Judges Journal* 20. In Canada see J Epp, 'The Role of the Judiciary in the Settlement of Civil Actions: A Survey of Vancouver Lawyers' (1996) 15 *Windsor Yearbook of Access Justice* 82. In New Zealand see K Saville-Smith and R Fraser, 'Alternative Dispute Resolution: General Civil Cases' (2004) available at www.courts.govt.nz/pubs/reports/2004/adr/index.html.

68 See Robinson (2006), above note 65, especially at 337.

labels[69] and all three highlight the legal significance of the distinctions among different forms of JDR.

In the case of *Estate of Skalka v Skalka* the Indiana Court of Appeal held that a judge, who used the term *mediator* to refer to his role before going ahead to hear and determine the case, was not necessarily engaging in the process of mediation. In this case the court found that the judge was exercising a settlement function – as distinct from mediation – and that his actions were therefore not in breach of the court's ADR rules. In another case, *Doe 1 v Superior Court,* concerning the applicability of mediation confidentiality rules to the dispute resolution process in question, the court held that the process was mediation rather than a settlement conference, despite the fact that it had been previously referred to using both terms. As a result, the confidentiality provisions applicable to mediation did apply and the party seeking to present information of what occurred at the mediation was prevented from doing so.[70]

In the *Foxgate* case,[71] the Californian Supreme Court had to determine the admissibility of a report by a retired judge–mediator in support of a motion for sanctions against a party for allegedly sabotaging the mediation. The Court suggested that the legal outcome of the case would have varied depending on whether the process was classified as a mediation to which the rules of confidentiality would apply, a judicial settlement conference in which the judge would have the power to sanction a party, or a proceeding by a special master, in which the master would be required to report to the court. In this case the judge was not a sitting judge and therefore could not conduct a settlement conference and he had not been appointed as a special master.[72] In addition the parties in the case seemed to agree that the process was mediation. The court held that the process undertaken was mediation and went on to warn parties to make their intentions very clear if they preferred a judicial settlement conference with its more limited scope for confidentiality than mediation.

These three cases also illustrate the emergence of JDR *rule shopping*, namely litigation about the classification of JDR processes in order to attract the most favourable legislation and rules to one's case.

3.3.1 Judicial Settlement

Pre-trial settlement conferences between lawyers have long been a regular feature of both common law and civil law jurisdictions. However the role of the judge as facilitator of settlements, while well established as a pre-trial

69 For a different judicial approach, which appears to pay greater attention to the process label, see the *Travelers Causality* case, below note 97.

70 See *Estate of Skalka v Skalka* 751 NE 2d 769 (Ind Ct App 2001) and *Doe 1 v Superior Court* (2005) 132 Cal App 4th 1160.

71 See *Foxgate Homeowners Ass'n v Bramalea California Inc* 25 P3d 1117 (Cal 2001).

72 See the *Foxgate* case, above note 71 at 1124–1128.

requirement in many civil law countries, is a more recent development in most common law jurisdictions.

Many civil law judges are required by law to attempt to settle a matter before hearing the case.[73] In 2007 the German Constitutional Court endorsed the court practice of attempting settlement of disputes before trial resulting in a judicial decision.[74] The judicial settlement function occurs in court and is conducted by the judge who will also hear the matter if no settlement is reached – that is, the trial judge.[75] Thus the same judge plays a role in both consensus-based and determinative processes in relation to the same matter. Applicable procedures and interventions are left to the relevant judge. Judicial settlement attempts can range from, on one hand, simply asking the question of the parties as to whether or not they want to settle in order to satisfy procedural requirements to, on the other hand, facilitating negotiations which have a lot more in common with interest-based mediation. However as indicated in Chapter 1, judicial settlement practice is largely directive, legalistic and short in duration,[76] although there is increasingly variation in this regard.[77]

Although a common practice in many jurisdictions, the dual role of facilitating settlement and acting as a trial judge may raise concerns about procedural fairness depending on how the settlement attempt is conducted.[78] Although by no means the general practice in judicial settlement, there are examples of judicial settlement conferences which allow each party a private audience with the trial judge. Such a practice may inhibit the ability of the other party to respond to all submissions made against it. While this may be acceptable in a mediation context where the parties make their own decisions, it potentially jeopardises the right to fair hearing in a process that may ultimately be determinative. There may be concerns about the ability of judges to banish all that was heard from their minds and to focus only on the legally relevant points

73 See, for example, the requirement in Germany for judges to attempt a settlement before deciding the case before them: § 278 of the Code of Civil Procedure (ZPO). Where no oral hearing is conducted (§ 279 ZPO), a combination of various provisions of the ZPO enables judges to arrange for parties to meet with them a view to exploring settlement (see §§ 118 I, 278 II, III, 492 III ZPO). See Bargen (2008), above note 62 at 65–66. See also a similar requirement in Slovenia in the Civil Procedure Act, Official Gazette N° 26/99 as amended.

74 Bundesverfassungsgericht decision of 14th February 2007: 1 BvR 1351/01.

75 See N Alexander, W Gottwald and T Trenczek, 'Mediation in Germany: The Long and Winding Road', in N Alexander (ed), *Global Trends in Mediation* (2nd ed, Alphen aan den Rijn: Kluwer Law International 2006) at 250.

76 See, for example, R Greger, 'Justizreform – und nun?' (2002) 57 *Juristenzeitung* 1020 at 1027.

77 See M Galanter, '"A Settlement Judge, Not a Trial Judge:" Judicial Mediation in the United States' (1985) 12 *Journal of Law and Society* 1 at 4–7.

78 For an examination of the different views that have emerged in the American literature on this topic, see Robinson (2006), above note 65 at 338–341.

in order to make a decision correct in law. Despite the arguments to counter this view, the perception of potential bias may remain.[79] Further where the hearing judge holds private meetings as part of a settlement attempt, the parties – knowing the same person may soon decide their case – may be reluctant to engage in the full and frank discussion so integral to the mediation process. Accordingly in most jurisdictions judicial settlement processes do not involve private sessions.[80]

As the cases referred to previously show,[81] judicial settlement may not be subject to the same rules of confidentiality applicable to mediation. The relevant rules of court are likely to have specific provisions relating to judicial settlement and generally these contain confidentiality provisions.[82] The scope of confidentiality, however, may be curtailed by regulatory features such as judicial sanctioning powers and reporting requirements.

In Chapter 1 reference is made to the view that the judicial settlement role must be exercised consistently with the overall objective of the judicial role. An illustration of this feature of judicial settlement can be found in the German Constitution (Article 20 III read in combination with Article 92), which states that the judicial role as exercised through the courts is bound by law and justice. Therefore, even while exercising their settlement function, German judges are required to lead parties towards a solution consistent with the relevant legal norms. This is not regarded as mediation – a process designed to encourage parties to explore creative solutions based on interests and needs rather than legal principles alone.[83] However where the interests and needs of the parties are aligned with the law, it is open for settlement judges to pursue interest-based solutions consistent with the relevant law.

Common law jurisdictions such as the United States, Australia, Canada and New Zealand have introduced judicial settlement as part of wider programs

79 Hogan reminds readers that '[j]udges are frequently called upon to compartmentalize their thoughts by separate rulings without defending claims to partiality.' M Hogan, 'Judicial Settlement Conferences: Empowering the Parties to Decide Through Negotiation' (1991) 27 *Willamette Law Journal* 429. See also Brunet's argument that judicial decision-making is an evolving process that can benefit from signals from the bench in interim litigation phases: E Brunet, 'Judicial Mediation and Signaling' (2003) 3 *Nevada Law Journal* 232 and Robinson (2006), above note 65 at 354.

80 For a contrasting practice, see the account of one judicial settlement attempt in the United States where the judge shuttled between parties during a break in the trial in Galanter (1985), above note 77 at 5–6.

81 See the cases of *Estate of Skalka v Skalka*, *Doe 1* and *Foxgate* referred to above at notes 70 and 71.

82 See, for example, Cal Ct Rules 3(f)(4), which states that all settlement conferences are confidential.

83 This rationale has received judicial endorsement by the Australian High Court in *R v Watson; Ex parte Armstrong* (1976) 136 CLR 248, 257–258.

of case management and civil reform.[84] Unlike the civil law tradition, which generally mandates a judicial settlement attempt before a hearing, most common law reforms encompass a discretionary judicial settlement model. In other words, judges may use judicial settlement in a given case, but are not required to do so by law.

The evolutionary interpretation of the American Federal Rule of Civil Procedure (FRCP) r 16 allowing pre-trial conferences provides an illuminating illustration of the change in views on judicial settlement practice in the United States since the late 19th century.[85] Commentators such as Galanter and Robinson point to a history of contrasting views on the topic.[86] According to the dominant view in the mid-20th century the aim of pre-trial conferences was to prepare the case for trial. Settlement was considered a potential by-product of the Rule, not a legitimate objective. With the advent of mediation and other alternatives to litigation, this view changed markedly. Galanter writes that the 1983 amendment to r 16 to expressly include settlement as one of the topics that could be addressed at a pre-trial conference brought the Rule into alignment with the thinking and practices of the time.[87]

Research from the United States and other common law jurisdictions suggests that judicial settlement is on the rise. Most judges report that they engage in varieties of judicial settlement on a weekly basis.[88] Judicial settlement is more likely to occur in jury trials and in situations where the judge doubts the settlement ability of the lawyers or has a high view of his or her own negotiation skills.[89]

3.3.2 *Judicial Mediation*

According to Galanter, the perceived benefits of judicial mediation compared to adjudication relate to process qualities, its normative character, its impact on lawyers' negotiating style and the experiences and perceptions of parties. As a

84 In Canada see Epp (1996), above note 67 and in New Zealand see Land and Resources Tribunal, *Practice Direction N° 4* (2003), Hearing Procedures – Expert Evidence – "Hot Tubbing".

85 US case law identifies the inherent authority of the court and the FRCP r16 as the source of authority for federal court judges to conduct settlement conferences in their own trials: see D Floyd, 'Can The Judge Do That? – The Need for a Clearer Judicial Role in Settlement' (1994) 26 *Arizona State Law Journal* 45.

86 See Robinson (2006), above note 65 at 337–339 and Galanter (1985), above note 77 at 1–2.

87 See Galanter (1985) above note 77 at 2 and 7.

88 See the study conducted by Robinson (2006) in relation to Californian judges, above note 65 at 345. The findings in Robinson's study suggest an increase in judicial settlement practice compared with earlier research referred to in Galanter (1985), above note 77 at 7–8.

89 See Galanter (1985) above note 77 at 7–8.

process judicial mediation is said to enhance party satisfaction, encourage parties to seek mutually beneficial outcomes, increase compliance with those outcomes and result in time and cost savings. Compared with non-judicial mediation, judicial mediation is seen to have greater normative character, as its outcomes are likely to be based on legal authority and to insulate parties from a free-ranging discussion of non-legal factors. Further lawyers may be more likely to engage in cooperative and collaborative negotiation in the presence of a judge. As a result of these factors, parties may experience the process as less stressful and more considerate of relationship and interpersonal issues. They may therefore be more satisfied with judicial mediation compared to judicial adjudication.[90]

Judicial mediation has been implemented successfully in Quebec where it is an integral part of the civil justice system. Cases are mediated by judges after the parties file a joint request for mediation. The case is then referred to another judge who acts as judicial mediator. Should the case not settle, the judicial mediator is excluded from participating in the further adjudication of the matter and the case returns to the original trial judge.[91] All documents that are part of the mediation remain with the judicial mediator and are destroyed after the procedure. A strict separation of roles of judges between their function as judges and their function as judicial mediators is enforced.[92]

As noted previously the scope of confidentiality in judicial mediation may differ from that applicable to judicial settlements. Subject to specific provisions for judicial mediation, general mediation provisions on confidentiality will be applicable.[93] In this context Robinson points out the potential for gaps in the applicable law on confidentiality where the definitions of judicial mediation are unclear.[94]

Judicially mediated settlements usually take the form of either a summary judgment, or an order of the court, which entails that they are legally final and binding. By way of example, in Quebec judicially mediated agreements at appellate level are as conclusive as any other judgment of the

90 See Galanter (1985) above note 77 at 11–12. Galanter also considers wider systemic effects – not just those related to the case at hand, at 12. See also Robinson's examination of the experiences in some Californian courts where judges reported that litigants preferred judicial mediators to private court-external mediators: Robinson (2006), above note 65 at 351.

91 On the fine line between judicial settlement and judicial mediation, see Robinson (2006), above note 65 at 353–4.

92 See J Alfini, 'Risk of Coercion Too Great: Judges Should Not Mediate Cases Assigned to Them for Trial' (1999) *Dispute Resolution Magazine* at 11, F Sander, 'A Friendly Amendment' (1999) *Dispute Resolution Magazine* at 11 and L Otis and E Reiter, 'Judicial Mediation in Quebec' in N Alexander (ed), *Global Trends in Mediation* (2nd ed, Alphen aan den Rijn: Kluwer Law International 2006) at 112.

93 See the *Foxgate* case, above note 71.

94 See Robinson (2006), above note 65 at 378–379.

court. Similar arrangements pertaining to judicial mediation, in which trial or appellate judges refer cases to other judges for mediation, have been introduced in Germany and to a lesser extent in the United States, Australia and England.[95]

Despite early confusion about the difference between judicial settlement and judicial mediation, the distinction seems be recognised in a regulatory sense. Two cross-border legal instruments – the European Directive on Mediation (recital 12, Article 3) and the Uniform Mediation Act (2001) (UMA) in the United States (s 3(b)(3)) – acknowledge the practice of judicial mediation and distinguish it from judicial settlement on the basis that in judicial mediation, the mediating judge cannot be one and the same person as the trial judge.[96] However other definitions of JDR processes vary and in practice the distinction is not always clear as the American cases cited previously show.[97] Finally a US study suggests that while judges use similar techniques in judicial settlement and judicial mediation processes, the latter process has the potential to be more interest- and relationship-focused.[98]

Judicial mediation also differs in practice from non-judicial facilitative mediation. Although judicial mediators cannot impose a binding decision or compromise judicial authority by expressing legal opinions, or in any way alter the future progress of a hearing should the mediation fail, they are still judges of the court and carry the respect, dignity and gravity that the position entails.[99]

95 For a succinct overview of all recent German judicial mediation programs, see Bargen (2008), above note 62 at 70–114 On the program in Lower Saxony in Germany see G Spindler, *Gerichtsnahe Mediation in Niedersachsen: Eine juristisch-rechtsökonomische Analyse* (Göttingen: Universitätsverlag 2006) at 6. In the United States see Robinson (2006), above note 65 at 355, in Canada see Landerkin and Pirie (2004), above note 3 at 25 and Otis and Reiter (2006), above note 92.

96 For an analysis of this approach to distinguishing judicial mediation from judicial settlement and case management conferences, see Robinson (2006), above note 65 at 379–380.

97 See the cases cited in notes 70–71 above. See also *Travelers Casualty and Surety Co v Superior Court,* 24 Cal Rptr 3d 751 (Cal Ct App 2005) where the Court appeared to go to great lengths to define the judicial dispute resolution process as a mediation rather than a settlement conference. Consequently the court held the settlement judge had exceeded his authority as a mediator and the outcome of the mediation was set aside.

98 See Robinson (2006), above note 65 at 375–378 and 380–381. In light of the similarity of JDR processes, especially judicial settlement and judicial mediation, and the difficulty in distinguishing between them, Robinson argues for the development of one set of standards for judges facilitating or encouraging settlement.

99 See Alexander, Gottwald and Trenczek (2006), above note 75 at 111. On judge–mediators in Germany R Greger, 'Justiz und Mediation – Entwicklungslinien nach Abschluss der Modellprojekte' (2007) 45 *Neue Juristische Wochenschrift* 3259. See also the discussion on coercion below.

A study in the United States compared the practices of sitting judges who mediate with retired judge–mediators. It concluded that private, retired judges acting as mediators offered more time in mediating disputes than sitting judges who mediated. In addition they were able to focus on goals such as reconciliation of the parties' interests and party autonomy. In contrast judges in the public court system were constrained by time limitations and were therefore more likely to adopt a settlement approach than one which took the time to explore parties underlying interests.[100] Similarly research findings in Germany indicate that judicial mediation distinguishes itself from other forms of mediation by its settlement focus, restricted time frame and directive nature.[101]

3.3.3 Judicial Moderation

In the German state of Bavaria the settlement function of civil judges has been expanded to provide facilitative services that resemble mediation in many ways. As part of a pilot project, trial judges referred suitable cases to judicial moderators (*Güterichter*). After assessing the suitability of the case for judicial moderation, the judicial moderator contacted the parties and offered to moderate their dispute. If the parties agreed the case was officially referred to the judicial moderator. If the moderation resulted in settlement the judicial moderator drew up a binding agreement. Otherwise the case was returned to the original trial judge and no further settlement attempts would be initiated.[102] The pilot project was positively evaluated and continues to operate in Bavaria.

Judicial moderation is known by a number of labels including *conferencing* and the term JDR itself. It comprises a wider range of techniques than is encountered in judicial settlement and facilitative mediation. These include investigative, directive, advisory, managerial, settlement and facilitative interventions. Judicial moderators are not restricted to one process or set of rules; they choose their intervention on the basis of what they perceive to be the needs of the parties. Commenting on a program in Canadian city of Calgary, Judge Flatters describes judicial moderation in relation to mediation and judicial settlement:

> Because a judge may use, borrow, or adapt some mediation techniques does not make this mediation. The difference is the framework in which the judge addresses

[100] S Burns, 'The Name of the Game is Movement: Concession Seeking in Judicial Mediation of Large Money Damages Cases' (1998) 15 *Mediation Quarterly* 359 at 363.

[101] D Warwel, *Gerichtsnahe Mediation: Empirische Untersuchung der Verhaltens- und Vorgehensweisen von Richtermediatoren in Gerichtsnahen Mediationsverfahren* (Berlin: Lit Verlag 2007) at 124–133.

[102] R Greger, *Abschlussbericht zur Evaluation des Modellversuchs Güterichter* (Erlangen: Friedrich-Alexander-Universität Erlangen-Nürnberg 2007) at 5.

> and meets the need for an impartial, nonbinding, and evaluative judicial opinion. Nevertheless, it does share with mediation an approach that is less binary and preserves, where appropriate, ongoing or long-term relationships; it permits a party to participate in a process where the discussion is framed by interests, needs, and outcomes; and the parties have control over decision making.' To this extent, it is a blend of predictive settlement (what a court would do) and problem-solving techniques (not predictive of what a court would do) in a judicially facilitated and directed negotiation framework with the judge giving a nonbinding evaluation and opinion.[103]

It is clear from this description that judicial moderation does not constitute a single analytical model but a diverse set of interventions. Other examples of judicial moderation are found in various courts and tribunals in Canada and Australia. They are known by various names including settlement conferencing and JDR,[104] although in tribunals the practice is conducted by tribunal members, who are not judges in the strict legal sense.[105] In a number of the Canadian and Australian examples – and contrary to the German program described earlier – the same judge or tribunal member conducting the judicial moderation may go on to hear and decide the case should it not settle. However if a party objects, then the matter is referred to a different person for subsequent hearing and determination.[106]

In terms of preparation for the judicial moderation role, German judges receive training in communication, negotiation and conflict management and participate in group reflections and exchanges with judicial moderators and mediators from other programs. Findings from previous projects indicate that judicial moderation has enjoyed high levels of acceptance among disputing parties and that consensual settlements are possible in the majority of referred cases. In addition knowledge and skills in negotiation, mediation and communication management have been found to be vital for effective judicial moderation.[107]

103 N Flatters, 'Family/Child Judicial Dispute Resolution (JDR) – An Overview of One Canadian Court's Settlement Conference Approach to the Pre-trial Resolution of Family and Child Welfare/Protection Matters' (2003) 41 *Family Court Review* 182 at 184.

104 See a description of some of these programs in D Zutter 'Incorporating ADR in Canadian Civil Litigation' (2001) 13 *Bond Law Review* 445 at 452–455.

105 Here *tribunals* refer to the court-like institutions in common law jurisdictions, in which cases are presided over by members rather than judges. The laws relating to the judiciary and its institutions do not per se apply to tribunals, thereby permitting them greater procedural flexibility. *Conferencing* refers to a range of dispute resolution techniques used in the tribunals to assist the parties to reach settlement.

106 See s 34F Administrative Appeals Tribunal Act 1975 (Cth) in Australia. See also Zutter (2001), above note 104 at 454–455.

107 Greger (2007), above note 102 at 129.

3.3.4 Facilitative Judging

Echoing the findings of the judicial moderation project in Germany, communication and facilitation skills have been found to be highly desirable for other aspects of judicial work, including decision-making and traditional adjudication processes. The conscious integration of these skills into judicial tasks is called facilitative judging.[108] It has also been labelled mediative adjudication.[109] As with judicial settlement, there is no separation of judicial roles in facilitative judging.

Facilitative judging models have a long history in China and other Asian jurisdictions.[110] They are also found increasingly in Australia and the United States as an extension of civil justice and mediation reforms. Facilitative processes can aid judges in hearing expert evidence and in facilitating complex multi-party cases. Processes such as concurrent evidence are being used more frequently in jurisdictions which allow for the adversarial presentation of evidence, to encourage experts to give evidence jointly and to question one another. Facilitative techniques such as active listening can help calm down anxious witnesses or parties and can increase their perception of procedural justice. Emotional intelligence and communication skills can help judges convey their decisions in a sensitive and appropriate manner, which, in turn, may increase the acceptance of and compliance with, their decisions by the parties.[111]

Other examples of facilitative judging models of adjudication have integrated elements of indigenous dispute resolution such as those found in *Murri courts*[112] and *circle sentencing*[113] in Australia. In the United States there are *tribal courts* that possess civil and criminal jurisdiction over reservation areas thus providing an alternative to formal courts.[114] Problem-solving courts are another example of facilitative judging.[115]

108 See T Sourdin, 'Facilitative Judging' in T Sourdin (ed), *Alternative Dispute Resolution and the Courts: Law in Context* (Australia: The Federation Press 2004) 64 at 65–66.

109 See Huang (2006), above note 57 at 276.

110 On the history of this practice in China, see Huang (2006), above note 57 at 275–314.

111 See Sourdin (2004), above note 108 at 78, M King 'Therapeutic Jurisprudence, Leadership and the Role of Appeal Courts' (2008) 30 *Australian Bar Review* 201, E Cheeseman 'Hot Tubbing: Concurrent Expert Evidence' (2006/2007) *Bar News* 54 and Land and Resources Tribunal (2003), above note 84.

112 See www.courts.qld.gov.au/1694.htm.

113 See www.creativespirits.info/aboriginalculture/law/circle-sentencing.html.

114 Available at www.ncsconline.org/wc/courtopics/overview.asp?topic=TribCt. For a list of tribal courts see www.tribal-institute.org/lists/justice.htm.

115 See M King 'What Can Mainstream Courts Learn From Problem-Solving Courts?' (2007) 32 *Alternative Law Journal* 91.

3.4 JDR and the Law

The expansion of the judicial role to embrace mediation in practice assumes, but by no means confirms, its legal validity. Concerns in this area centre on the compatibility of mediation with the judicial function in terms of constitutional and human rights principles and the impact of judicial mediation on procedural fairness, independence and impartiality issues. In addition rights, privileges and obligations attaching to judicial mediators may differ from those of other mediators. Parties contemplating judicial mediation should be made aware of these differences and the legal risks attached to JDR compared to non-judicial dispute resolution.

3.4.1 The Judicial Function

There is much debate about the compatibility of mediation with the judicial function. While understandings of the judicial function will vary according to legal tradition and jurisdiction, it is generally accepted that judicial power is to be exercised independently and impartially in a manner consistent with procedural fairness and constitutional requirements.[116]

The separation of powers doctrine ensures that judicial functions are kept separate from, and do not overlap with, executive and legislative tasks. However interpretation of the doctrine is not uniform, a factor which may affect the scope of the judicial function and its relation to mediation. Historically the European civil law approach endorsed a strict separation of powers doctrine characterised by a weak judiciary confined to the application of law through adjudication and an unchecked legislature and executive. This view appears to be giving way to a US-style interpretation of the doctrine, namely that separation of powers supports the maintenance of a system of checks and balances among the three arms of government – an approach which is said to encourage strong legislative, executive and judicial powers.[117] The latter view is consistent with an evolving and adaptive role of the judiciary. Cappelletti argues that the aim of the modern state is to ensure that the legal and political system, and its rights, benefits and protections, are effectively accessible to all. Accessibility, particularly in times of political and social change, demands that the judicial role has the ability to expand in scope and responsibility. Echoing this approach, Canadian commentator and judge, Landerkin, views settlement and mediation as falling within the overriding aims of the court and considers that judges can have roles beyond traditional adversarial expectations.[118] However it is imperative that judicial mediation does not overlap with the

[116] See, for example, F Wheeler, 'Due Process, Judicial Power and Chapter III in the new High Court' (2004) 32 *Federal Law Review* 205.

[117] See Cappelletti (1989), above note 60 at 23.

[118] See Landerkin and Pirie (2004), above note 3.

legislative or executive functions and that judges mediate without influence from the legislature and the executive. Effectively this means that judges who mediate must have no political discretion and are required to conduct mediations according to principles of procedural fairness and impartiality, which have been referred to previously.[119]

In some jurisdictions public confidence in the judicial role is seen as an essential part of doing justice. In Australia, for example, the High Court has recognised the principle of procedural fairness as implicit in chapter III of the Constitution and has developed an overarching test of 'public confidence in the independence of the judiciary' as part of this. Here justice must not only be done, it must be seen to be done. According to this principle the practice of judicial mediation must not undermine public confidence in judicial independence.[120] It is conceivable that this may occur in situations where judges move between handing down judgments and mediating cases. Tucker warns that, in so far as judicial mediation threatens public confidence in the impartiality of the courts, it could be declared *ultra vires* under chapter III of the Australian Constitution.[121] The concern about potential loss of public confidence in the judiciary may not be as strong in civil law jurisdictions such as Germany where judicial settlement has long been a mandatory function of judges. German commentators and jurisprudence have adopted the view that judicial mediation is an aspect of the judicial power as envisaged under the German Constitution.[122] Nonetheless it remains a contentious issue, particularly in light of the deliberations to establish national standards for mediators.[123] Generally speaking, public confidence in the judicial role is less likely to suffer where the role of judicial mediator is full-time and separate from that of trial judge.

While the debate continues about the extent to which mediation can be considered a judicial function, some commentators avoid the dilemma by arguing that judges change hats when they mediate and in that capacity do not purport to exercise the judicial function. Rather they suggest that, when

119 See Spencer (2006) Part I, above note 65 at 138.

120 See *Bruce v Coles and others* (1998) 45 NSWLR 163 at 166 per Spigelman CJ citing *Kable v DPP (NSW)* (1996) 138 ALR 577. See also Australian Institute of Judicial Administration, *Guide to Judicial Conduct* (2002) at 3, 4 and 19.

121 P Tucker, 'Judges as Mediators: A Chapter III Prohibition?' (2000) 11 *Australasian Dispute Resolution Journal* 84 at 87–90.

122 See Bargen (2008), above note 62 at 162–190, who concludes that judicial mediation falls within the scope of judicial power as envisaged by Article 92 of the German Constitution (Grundgesetz GG). R Zöller and R Greger also reach this conclusion in their commentary to the ZPO (commentary to § 278 ZPO, N° 5). Finally the Superior Regional Court (Oberlandesgericht OLG) Rostock reached the same result: OLG Rostock 3U 37/06 18.09.2006 reported in (2007) *Neue Justiz* at 76.

123 L Graf-Schlicker, 'Die EU-Richtlinie zur Mediation – zum Stand der Umsetzung' Vortrag der Leiterin der Abteilung Rechtspflege im Bundesministerium der Justiz (Berlin: 13th Mediations-Kongress 2009) 1 at 11–12.

mediating, judges exercise an extra-judicial or a non-judicial function. The notion of mediation as an extra-judicial function is legally acknowledged in a number of jurisdictions. The Slovakian Law on Mediation § 2(1) defines mediation as 'extra-judicial action in which the parties settle a dispute, arising from or concerning their contract or other legal relationship, through a mediator.'[124]

Assuming that mediation is an extra-judicial function, a question arises as to the effect of legislation that confers discretion on judges permitting them to act in a non-judicial manner. On one view, the requirement that judges act judicially is constitutionally based and therefore legislative attempts permitting judicial mediation may be unconstitutional. In Australia the *Boilermakers* case made it clear that judges exercising the judicial power of the Commonwealth cannot carry out non-judicial functions.[125] The exercise of non-judicial powers is possible only in limited circumstances, including where the non-judicial function is incidental to the exercise of judicial power,[126] and where the function is exercised in the judges' personal capacity under the doctrine of *personae designatae.*[127]

Australian commentators Moore and Tucker endorse the view that mediation is an extra-judicial function. On this basis Tucker contends that judges could be appointed as mediators only under the doctrine of *personae designatae.*[128] Implicit in the conferring of non-judicial powers on judges – in this case the power to mediate – is arguably a requirement that extra-judicial power be exercised in a manner compatible with the exercise of judicial power.[129] On this view the onus is placed on judges to maintain judicial standards and act in accordance with their constitutional role.[130]

124 See § 7(1) of the 25 June 2004 on the Slovakian Act of 25 June 2004 on Mediation and Amendment of Certain Acts.

125 See *R v Kirby; Ex parte Boilermakers' Society of Australia* (1956) 94 CLR 254.

126 *R v Kirby* above note 125. See also *Cominos v Cominos* (1972) 127 CLR 588. In this matter, the High Court was concerned with a challenge to provisions in the Commonwealth's Matrimonial Causes Act 1959. The provisions conferred upon state supreme courts the power to make maintenance orders and orders affecting property rights. The orders were made as ancillary orders in relation to the principal relief sought. The High Court found that the power to make such orders was incidental to the exercise of judicial power.

127 *Drake v Minister for Immigration and Ethnic Affairs* (1979) 24 ALR 577. This principle was subsequently approved by cases such as *Hilton v Wells* (1985) 157 CLR 57 and *Grollo v Palmer* (1995) 184 CLR 348.

128 Tucker (2000), above note 121 and M Moore, 'Judges as mediators: A Chapter III prohibition or accommodation?' (2003) 14 *Australasian Dispute Resolution Journal* 188.

129 In support of this view see the Australian High Court cases *Grollo v Palmer* (1995) 184 CLR 348, 364–5, *Wilson v Min for Aboriginal and Torres Straight Islander*

Moore concludes that, provided procedural safeguards can be put in place, the roles of judicial mediator and judge are compatible.[131] However Tucker sees the potential undermining of public confidence in the judiciary, referred to earlier in this chapter, as a reason to find the practice of judicial mediation ultimately unconstitutional.

In some jurisdictions mediation is conducted by non-judicial court officers.[132] In the case of *Harris v Caladine* the Australian High Court held that non-judicial power can be delegated to non-judicial officers such as registrars, provided their powers and functions remain reviewable by judges of the court.[133] This position supports the widespread practice of court-based mediation by non-judicial officers and employees. However the power to delegate the mediation function to non-judicial mediators may have limitations. By way of example, in the American case of *Martin v Martin*,[134] it was held to be an improper delegation of judicial authority to empower a mediator to establish a visitation schedule as this was considered an exclusive judicial function.

3.4.2 Procedural Fairness, Bias and Coercion

Regardless of whether judicial mediation is viewed as a judicial or non-judicial function, the tensions involved in the dual roles of mediator and trial judge remain and continue to fuel discussion.[135] When judges mediate the procedural integrity of both mediation and the court system is potentially undermined in a number of ways.

There is a traditional contention that judicial mediation should apply standards of procedural fairness to effectively separate the court's adjudicative and facilitative functions. In adjudicative proceedings the rules of procedural fairness encompass the principle that parties have a chance to give evidence and respond to allegations and submissions made in relation to the dispute (*audi alteram partem*) and that judges are neutral and impartial (*nemo iudex in sua*

Affairs (1996) 189 CLR 1 and *O'Donoghue v Ireland*; *Zentai v Republic of Hungary*, *Williams v USA* (2008) 234 CLR 599.

130 See the judgments of the Australian High Court in *R v Watson; Ex parte Armstrong* (1976) 136 CLR 248, 257–258. See also Articles 20 III and 92 of the German Constitution (Grundgesetz, GG), referred to earlier in the context of judicial settlement, which states that the judicial role is bound by law and justice.

131 Safeguards such as procedural fairness are discussed below.

132 See, for example, the Federal Court of Australia: Federal Court of Australia Regulations (Amendment) 1997 N° 249.

133 See *Harris v Caladine* (1991) 172 CLR 84.

134 See *Martin v Martin* 734 So 2d 1133 (Fla Dist Ct App 1999).

135 See, for example, Moore (2003), above note 128, Spencer (2006) Part I, above note 65 at 138 and Robinson (2006), above note 65 at 335.

causa).[136] In some traditions procedural fairness also requires that outcomes are reasonable and rational in the light of the circumstances and that reasons are provided to explain and justify them. All these rights are potentially challenged, in the traditional view, by judicial mediation. Another source of challenge is in relation to access to justice, which is dealt with later in this chapter.

In the Australian case of *Queensland v JL Holdings*,[137] case management procedures effectively prevented applicants from raising an arguable defence and therefore precluded the determination of the issue between the parties. On appeal the decision of the trial judge was reversed. The appeal court stated that while case management procedures are useful, they should not prevail over the injustice of precluding applicants from raising an arguable defence, thus preventing the determination of an issue between the parties. Where in the ordinary course of proceedings the exercise of JDR effectively interferes with a party's right to be heard and submit evidence in relation to a claim or allegation, it may amount to a breach of procedural fairness and form the basis of judicial review. This view accords with canon 2, r 2.6 of the ABA Model Rules of Judicial Conduct (2007) in the United States. However a 2009 decision of the High Court of Australia has cast doubt on the reasoning in the *Holdings* case with Court highlighting the need to balance individual litigant rights with broader judicial and public policy as follows:[138]

> In the past it has been left largely to the parties to prepare for trial and to seek the court's assistance as required. Those times are long gone. The allocation of power, between litigants and the courts arises from tradition and from principle and policy. It is recognised by the courts that the resolution of disputes serves the public as a whole, not merely the parties to the proceedings.

Nevertheless the perception of judicial coercion is a legitimate concern for the credibility of dispute resolution procedures conducted by judges. Sir Laurence Street is mindful of the fact that judges wield significant influence within court systems and sometimes beyond them. He highlights the risks associated with parties feeling 'a sense of coercion and hence of disenchantment with the mediated outcome that can reflect adversely on the court.'[139] Frank Sander has echoed similar sentiments amid concerns that his multi-door courthouse concept had been misinterpreted.[140] In court situations concern is also expressed that the

136 On this principle in Australia see *Wilson v Minister for Aboriginal and Torres Strait Islander Affairs* (1996) 189 CLR 1 at 15.

137 See *State of Queensland v JL Holdings Pty Ltd* (1997) 189 CLR 146 at 154.

138 See *Aon Risk Services Australia Limited v Australian National University* [2009] HCA 27 (5 August 2009). See also the references to distributive justice and Zuckerman's work at notes 59 and 233.

139 See L Street, 'Mediation and the Judicial Institution' (1997) 71 *Australian Law Journal* 794 at 795–6.

140 Sander (1999), above note 92 at 11.

fundamental mediation principle of party autonomy can be weakened[141] and Resnik contemplates the difficulty of reviewing judicial behaviour in mediation. Factors such as judicial immunity may serve to protect judicial mediators from allegations of duress or coercion.[142]

These issues can be addressed in different ways. In *Panitch v Panitch*[143] an American court cautioned judges in relation to their degree of intervention in encouraging settlement, suggesting that in particular situations it would be appropriate to refer the case to another judge to avoid perceptions of bias arising. In another case, an interesting illustration of alleged judicial impropriety involved a judge who sat on the Board of Directors of a non-profit mediation organisation. The ethics committee of the local judiciary determined that the fact that the judge held a directorship in an organisation offering mediation services would inappropriately influence litigants' decisions about whether or not to mediate. However this decision was reversed on appeal. The appeal court commented that this factor was insignificant compared to the ability of the same judge to refer the matter to mediation even without the parties' consent.[144]

Robinson summarises the diverse approaches within the United States as follows:

> The Connecticut Supreme Court has ruled that "[w]hen a judge engages in a pre-trial settlement discussion in a court case, he should automatically disqualify himself from presiding in the case in order to eliminate any appearance of impropriety."[145] The Montana Supreme Court requires the disqualification of a judge who will be the trier of fact if that judge participates in unsuccessful pre-trial settlement negotiations and is so requested to do so by one of the parties.[146] In contrast, the case law in Hawaii and California establishes that trial judges need not recuse themselves, even in bench trials, simply because they conduct settlement conferences in cases assigned to them for trial.[147]

In an attempt to circumvent procedural fairness and bias issues, many judicial mediation models either avoid private mediation sessions or refer mediation to a judge other than the trial judge or to a non-judicial court official. This practice is found in countries such as Germany, Australia and the United States, although it

141 See J Resnik, 'Managerial Judges' (1982–1983) 96 *Harvard Law Review* 374.

142 On this point, see Street (1997), above note 139 at 795–6. The legal implications of coercive mediator behaviour are addressed in Chapters 5 and 7.

143 *Panitch v Panitch* 770 A 2d 1237 (NJ Super Ct App Div 2001) especially at 1242.

144 See *Shake v Ethics Committee of the Kentucky Judiciary* 122 SW 3d 577 at 583–4 (Ky 2003).

145 See *Timm v Timm* 487 A2d 191 (Conn 1985) 193.

146 See *Shields v Thunem* 716 P2d 217 (Mont 1985) 218–219.

147 See, for example, *Moran v Guerreiro* 37 P 3d 603 (Haw 2001) 621–23.

is not the exclusive practice.[148] Spigelman CJ suggests a clear separation of the mediating and adjudicating roles and advocates initiatives to educate the public about different processes that judges can conduct including judicial mediation.[149]

However, even in these circumstances, apprehensions of bias and concerns about fairness may arise in relation to informal communications among judges and court employees as the Australian case of *Ruffles v Chilman* demonstrates. Here a trial judge upon hearing the plaintiff's evidence made a referral to mediation. The registrar, while mediating the matter, commented that the trial judge was not convinced on the strength of the plaintiff's evidence. The matter did not settle and was returned to the original trial judge. A new trial was ordered on the basis of reasonable apprehension of bias on the part of the plaintiff.[150]

In another Australian case[151] a trial judge had acted as mediator on a different matter between similar parties nine years earlier. As regards the facts of the case the judge stated that he believed this was a totally separate matter, he had no memory of the previous mediation and he had destroyed his notes and therefore no conflict of interest or potential for bias existed. However upon application by the party involved in the earlier mediation, his Honour made the following points:

- When a judge mediates he sheds his judicial mantle and acts contrary to the principle of justice that a judge should not hear representations from one party without also the presence of the other.
- Where a judge has access to parties in private meetings, a reasonable person might believe that the judge–mediator learned of information which might affect the exercise of his discretion.
- The reason judges disqualify themselves in such cases is the requirement to maintain public confidence in the administration of

[148] An exception to this principle is found in Canon 2 of the ABA Model Code of Judicial Conduct (2007) available at www.abanet.org/cpr/mcjc/toc.html. It states that judges must obtain the consent of the parties before utilising ex parte communications in attempts to facilitate settlement. However the exception is curtailed by the requirement for judges to remain cautious about private comments that might be construed to interfere with a fair trial. See also the American case of *Schauf v Schauf* 107 P3d 1237 (Kan Ct App 2005) where the Court indicated its disapproval of the dual appointment of the same person as special master and mediator in a partnership dispute. At the same time the court found no judicial error given the absence of a timely objection by the parties and therefore denied the review.

[149] See Spigelman (2000), above note 65.

[150] See *Ruffles v Chilman* [1999] WASCA 112.

[151] *The Duke Group Ltd (In Liq) v Alamain Investments Ltd and Ors* [2003] SASC 272.

> justice and they should weigh the issue of public confidence with the duty not to accede too readily to claims of bias.

In this case Debelle J disqualified himself on the basis that the integrity of the mediation process, and the court's role in promoting mediation, meant that any suggested breach of confidentiality and subsequent influence over the judge necessitated the judge standing aside.

However there are limits to the perception of bias. A number of American cases demonstrate that it is *prima facie* appropriate for a judge who has previously acted as mediator in a particular case to be required subsequently as a judge to preside over the enforceability of the settlement reached at the mediation. In the case of *Zhu v Countrywide Realty Co Inc*,[152] for example, the court refused to set aside a settlement agreement and saw no impropriety in the fact that a magistrate judge who had facilitated the settlement agreement between the parties subsequently heard an application to enforce the same settlement in a judicial capacity and did so. Particularly in circumstances where the fact that parties have reached settlement is on public court record, US courts appear unlikely to prevent judges who have mediated or otherwise facilitated the settlement from making a judicial order compelling the parties to execute settlement.[153]

Finally the issue of waiver of procedural fairness requires consideration. Here the issue is whether an individual can waive the requirement of procedural fairness in relation to judicial mediation. To the extent that such waivers may affect public confidence in the judicial system, there is a strong argument against their use.[154] In the United States, for example, judges are prohibited from accepting a waiver of disqualification from parties in relation to judicial bias.[155]

3.4.3 Desirability of Judges as Mediators in an International Context

Lawyers and their clients must weigh up the risks and opportunities associated with JDR and its various models. This section has shown that the distinctions among different JDR models can be significant for parties in terms of applicable laws that can effectively determine issues relating to the validity and

152 *Zhu v Countrywide Realty Co Inc* 66 F App'x 840 (10th Cir 2003).

153 See also the following cases: *DeMers v Lee* N° 44348–8–I 2000 WL 264022 (Wash Ct App 2000) and *Renkoph v Rems Inc* 40 F App'x 126 (6th Cir 2002). For an analysis of this case law see Coben and Thompson (2006), above note 19 at 102–3.

154 E Campbell, 'Waiver of judicial disqualification for bias or apprehended bias – a constitutional issue' (1999) 2 *Constitutional Law and Policy Review* 41.

155 See 28 USCA s 455(e) (United States Code Annotated, Title 28, Judiciary And Judicial Procedure, Part I Organization Of Courts, Chapter 21 General Provisions Applicable To Courts And Judges).

enforceability of mediated outcomes, accountability, confidentiality, bias and other issues. Moreover judicially mediated settlements may be attractive in terms of costs and international enforceability, especially in light of Brussels I Regulation and the Hague Choice of Court Convention.[156]

4. COURT REFERRAL

Court referral to mediation includes any process by which disputants are directed to mediation by a court or tribunal. Mediation court referral schemes may be regulated by statute, civil procedure rules, practice directions or judicial precedent, or can simply be informally managed by the court or tribunal.

It is important for those involved in international mediation to understand the circumstances in which their dispute may be referred to mediation and the legal impact of court-referred mediation in a given jurisdiction. These factors may affect, *inter alia,* selection of dispute resolution clauses and choice of law clauses. In the absence of a uniform approach to court-referred mediation, this section sets out a systematic method for examining court-referred mediation across jurisdictions and evaluating its legal implications for mediation participants.

4.1 Background and Development

In the contemporary dispute resolution era reform proposals heralding the introduction of mediation in connection with courts include the Danish Ministry of Justice reform proposals (2001),[157] the Lord Woolf reforms to civil procedure in the United Kingdom (1999),[158] the Coulon report in France,[159] the Dutch *More Ways to Justice ADR Policy Letter* (2000–2002),[160] reform proposals by

156 On these two legal instruments, see Chapter 2.

157 V Vindeloev, 'Mediation in Danish Law: In Retrospect and Perspective' in N Alexander (ed), *Global Trends in Mediation* (2nd ed, Alphen aan den Rijn: Kluwer Law International 2006) at 123–138.

158 Lord Woolf, *Access to Justice – Interim Report to the Lord Chancellor on the Civil Justice System in England and Wales* (1995) and www.dca.gov.uk/civil/final/index.htm. See also H Genn, *Court-Based ADR Initiatives for Non-Family Civil Disputes: Commercial Court and Court of Appeal* (London: Lord Chancellor's Department Research Secretariat 2002).

159 J Coulon, *Réflexions et propositions sur la procédure civile, Rapport au garde des Sceaux* (Paris: Ministre de la Justice 1997).

160 *Meer wegen naar het recht Beleidsbrief ADR 2000*–2002 (The Hague: Ministry of Justice 2002). For other European illustrations see A De Roo, 'Report on the Various Means of Alternative Dispute Resolution: Mediation, Conciliation, Arbitration' (Strasbourg: Council of Europe SEM/ADR 8E 1999).

the Polish Civil Law Codification Commission at the Ministry of Justice, the South African Law Commission's report on ADR (1997), the Australian Law Reform Commission's report on access to justice and civil litigation reform[161] and the European Union Green Paper on Alternative Dispute Resolution in Civil and Commercial Law 2002. In 2008 the Chief Justice of Hong Kong spoke of government policy and pilot schemes to promote the use of mediation.[162]

Prominent illustrations of legal amendments introducing court-referred mediation include the Civil Justice Reform Act (1990) in the United States,[163] the various amendments to court rules throughout Australia in the 1990s,[164] German civil procedure law reforms between 1999 and 2001,[165] the amendments to Slovenian court legislation and rules to establish its special program to tackle the case backlog at the Ljubljana District Court in Slovenia in 2000,[166] and the cautious civil procedure amendments in South Africa.[167] In England the Civil Procedure Act 1997 and the Civil Procedure Rules were the culmination of steady pressure toward ADR and mediation and provide scope for referral to mediation.[168] The European Directive on Mediation is encouraging a new wave of regulation on mediation which will include court referral.[169]

Comparing court-based mediation referral schemes is notoriously difficult due to the challenge of sorting though the countless structural,

161 Australian Law Reform Commission, *Review of the Adversarial System of Litigation,* Issues Paper 25 June 1998.

162 Speech of the Chief Justice at the Ceremonial Opening of the Legal Year 2008.

163 R Birke and L Teitz, 'US Mediation in the Twenty-first Century: The Path that brought America to Uniform Laws and Mediation in Cyberspace' in N Alexander (ed), *Global Trends in Mediation* (Cologne: Otto Schmidt 2003) at 374 et seq.

164 See, for example, the Supreme Court of Queensland Act 1991 (Qld), Uniform Civil Procedure Rules 1999 (Qld), Supreme Court (General Procedure) Rules 1996 (Vic), Magistrates Court Act 1991 (SA), District Court Act 1991 (SA) and the Law and Justice Legislation Amendment Act 1997 (Cth), amending the Federal Court of Australia Act 1976 (Cth).

165 See § 15a of the Introductory Law to the Code of Civil Procedure (EGZPO) and § 278V(2) of the Code of Civil Procedure (ZPO).

166 Special program to tackle the case backlog at the Ljubljana District Court, dated 11 December 2000 (Su 9/2000), as amended. The special program draws its legal authority from Article 62 of the Courts Act and Article 171 of the Court Rules as an implementing regulation: Courts Act, Ur l RS, N° 19/94 and 17/95, as amended. See also A Zalar, 'Managing Judicial Change Through Mediation – Part 1' (2004) 6 *ADR Bulletin* 156.

167 See the Short Process Court and Mediation in Certain Civil Cases Act 103 of 1991 and High Court Rule 37. See also South African Law Reform Commission, *Alternate Dispute Resolution Issues* (1997) Paper 8, Project 94.

168 See for example Civil Procedure Rules 1.4, 3.1 and 26.4.

169 See the Directive 2008/52/EC on Certain Aspects of Mediation in Civil and Commercial Matters, proposal as adopted by the European Parliament and the Council of the European Union on 21 May 2008, L 136/3, 24.05.2008.

substantive and procedural variations. The ability of courts in common law jurisdictions to change their court rules, in contrast to the legislative monopoly over court rules in most civil law countries, has enabled those courts to integrate mediation into the litigation process on a court-by-court basis. This has provided scope for enormous variety in common law court referral schemes. In civil law contexts there has been some experimentation insofar as it has been permitted by legislation.[170] The source of courts' powers to refer to mediation may also vary according to jurisdiction and have structural implications in relation to factors such as timing and party consent. A further complexity in comparing court mediation schemes arises in relation to the role of tribunals in common law jurisdictions. Tribunals have been described earlier as court-like institutions presided over by members rather than judges. The proliferation of common law tribunals has, at least in part, been a response to an increase in sector-specific regulation which arguably has led to a corresponding acceleration in the number of legal disputes. Tribunals possess greater procedural flexibility than courts as they are not bound by the strict rules that attach to the court system. As a result many tribunals have adopted less adversarial processes featuring greater control of the process by the presiding member and other elements typical of civil law courts. It is not uncommon for presiding tribunal members to 'mediate' or otherwise attempt to settle cases, adopting one of the four JDR models referred to earlier. In addition – and as will be shown later in this chapter – many tribunals have mediation schemes, which feature referral models more commonly found in civil law than common law courts.

4.2 A Systematic Approach to Referral

A systematic approach to mediation referral comprises two primary elements, the referral framework and the referral procedure. The referral framework provides the legal, structural and cultural context within which mediation referrals occur. The referral procedure refers to the manner in which referrals occur. Here factors such as referral discretion, criteria and method are relevant.

4.2.1 The Referral Framework

The following factors are relevant to establishing a referral framework for mediation:

1. who decides whether or not the dispute will be mediated;
2. who selects the mediator;
3. who pays for the mediation;
4. the qualifications and qualities of the mediator;

[170] See, for example, the experimentation clause in Germany, § 15a EGZPO.

5. accountability of the mediator;
6. time available for mediation;
7. the mediation venue;
8. the scope of the mediation;
9. timing of intervention;
10. how mediation is triggered;
11. sanctions for non-attendance and non-participation;
12. legal status of mediated settlements;
13. reporting requirements of mediators; and
14. litigation limitation periods.

There are two main approaches to referral frameworks, the justice approach and the market approach. The first seven of the factors listed above are indicative of whether the justice or market approach is applied. These factors are discussed in the following paragraphs. The remaining factors, while compatible with both approaches, vary in how they are applied in different courts and jurisdictions. They are considered subsequent to the first group.

The justice approach to establishing a referral framework is characterised by mediators selected and appointed by the court from a pool of nominated mediators within the court – judges, registrars or other court employees – and the mediations tend to be conducted in the court precinct. In terms of qualifications, court mediators usually have a legal qualification and a variable degree of mediation training. They often carry immunity from suit. Mediators external to the court can also be deployed in the justice model; they are generally paid a standard fee by the courts or the relevant government justice department. In most cases parties are not charged an additional full fee to cover the costs of the mediation. Given resource restrictions in many courts, mediators may be required or expected to mediate within set time limits, such as one to three hours per mediation. This type of referral framework reflects an attitude that mediation is an integral part of the overall justice system and therefore legitimately part of the dispute resolution service offered by courts. The justice approach can be found in JDR programs generally, where judges and registrars mediate. It is, however, also the dominant approach in programs using external as well as internal mediators in German and Slovenian courts. It is a favoured approach for many Australian tribunals[171] and is also found to some extent in England, the United States and other jurisdictions.

The market approach, by contrast, is based on a user-pays philosophy. Mediation is seen as an extra-judicial dispute resolution service, which the courts are prepared to *manage* but not conduct. Users of mediation are generally

[171] See, for example, Administrative Appeals Tribunal, *ADR Guidelines* (Canberra 2006). For an explanation of the meaning of tribunal in this context, see above note 105.

able to select a mediator themselves and to negotiate fees, charges and, generally, the time-frame for the mediation. Mediators are external to the court and the mediation generally takes place away from the court premises. Mediator fees and associated costs are usually split between the parties. Overall mediator accountability can be higher in market frameworks than in justice frameworks, although mediator immunity is a feature of some user-pays schemes. The qualifications of mediators vary according to jurisdiction and tend to reflect emerging national standards.[172] The market approach is found in courts in Australia, England, the United States and Austria. The approach adopted by the civil courts in France appears to be a combination of the justice and market approaches. While disputes are referred to external mediation providers, the court may recommend a mediator to the parties. In addition fees charged by mediators are regulated by law and the referring judge plays a central role in approving fees and other charges associated with mediation.[173]

As regards the second group of factors relevant to the referral framework, the following general comments can be made, some of which are amplified in subsequent chapters.

The scope of the mediation. Here the question arises as to whether the issues that can be addressed in the mediation are in any way influenced by the scope of the dispute as defined in court pleadings.[174] In France the Civil Procedure Code provides that a court-referred mediation may deal with the entirety of the dispute or only part of it.[175] However in many jurisdictions a mediation may deal with any matters relevant for resolution, regardless of whether they are identified in the pleadings.

Timing of intervention. Mediation referral can take place from an early pre-filing stage to any time during court proceedings. In pre-filing mediation schemes parties must produce a certificate indicating that they have attempted mediation before they are able to file a court claim. Pre-filing schemes emphasise early intervention before claims have been filed and discovery processes have begun.[176] It is widely believed – although the evidence on this

[172] On the trend towards national mediator standards, see Chapter 2.

[173] See Decker (2008) above note 1 at 201, 211–213 and 251. See also Articles 131-6(2), (3) and 13 of the French Civil Procedure Code (C pr civ) and Articles 22(2) and (3) of the Law of 8 February 1995 (Loi N° 95-125 du 8 février 1995).

[174] In the context of arb–med, see M Schneider, 'Combining Arbitration with Conciliation' (2004) 1 *Transnational Dispute Management* 1.

[175] Article 131-2 C pr civ.

[176] For examples of pre-filing mediation schemes, see in Australia, Retail Tenancies Amendment Act 1995 (Vic) and in Germany § 15a EGZPO. In England see the Practice Direction to the Pre-action Protocols 4.7 and the Civil Procedure Rules (UK) r 1.4, which requires parties to consider attempting mediation and ADR before proceeding with litigation.

point is mixed[177] – that mediation intervention earlier rather than later in a dispute results in better outcomes for the parties. In the English case of *Bradford v James*, for example, Mummery LJ made the following comments:

> An attempt at mediation should be made right at the beginning of the dispute and certainly well before things turn nasty and become expensive. By the time neighbours get to court it is often too late for court-based ADR and mediation schemes to have much impact. Litigation hardens attitudes. Costs become an additional aggravating issue. Almost by its own momentum the case that cried out for compromise moves onwards and upwards to a conclusion that is disastrous for one of the parties, possibly for both.[178]

Other referral schemes allow referral to mediation at any time before, or even during, the hearing. In certain cases, for example, it may be better to schedule mediation after discovery.[179] Under the French Civil Procedure Code mediation can be initiated at any time during proceedings in courts other than the Supreme Court (*Cour de Cassation*).[180] Article 128 of the Code specifies that it is the judge's prerogative to identify the most advantageous time and place for a conciliation attempt, in the absence of any mandatory provisions in relation thereto.

An increasing number of researchers[181] and courts[182] contend that timing is relevant to mediation. However research fails to link a particular timing of mediation with party satisfaction or prospects of settlement.[183] One of the reasons for this is the difficulty of isolating the timing of a mediation intervention from other contextual factors such as the *ripeness* of the dispute for mediation or another form of dispute resolution.[184] In other words, where a dispute is inappropriately referred to mediation, its chances of settlement will be low irrespective of its timing in relation to court procedures.

[177] See the discussion below.

[178] See *Bradford v James* [2008] EWCA Civ 837 at para 1. See also *Burchell v Bullard* [2005] Build LR 330 at para 50.

[179] See *ACCC v Lux* [2001] FCA 600.

[180] See Article 131-2 C pr civ. See also L Buchman, 'Mediation and the Law: Case Law and other Aspects of French Law' (2005) 1 *IBA Mediation Newsletter* 23.

[181] See Greger (2007) above note 102 at 115 and R Peters and D Mastin, 'To Mediate or Not To Mediate: That Is the Question' (2007) 62 *Dispute Resolution Journal* 14.

[182] See comments by the court in *Nigel Witham Ltd v Smith and Anor* (N° 2) [2008] EWHC 12 that 'the "critical moment" to mediate was missed by both sides, and blame should not be placed on the Defendant for an oversight by both parties'.

[183] See M Pel, *Referral to Mediation: A Practical Guide for an Effective Mediation Proposal* (The Hague: Sdu Uitgevers 2008) at 168–169.

[184] On ripeness see H Astor and C Chinkin, *Dispute Resolution in Australia* (Sydney: Butterworths 2002) at 280.

At the same time it has been shown that early mediation intervention can increase chances of settlement, although it is not a predictor of settlement.[185] Greger notes that the promise of slow, long, complex and therefore expensive litigation timeframes heightens parties' motivation to attempt mediation in order to save face, extricate themselves from litigation and move on with their lives. These factors must be balanced against the likelihood of delay if the matter does not settle at mediation.

How mediation is triggered. As previously explained triggers can be indirect (such as financial sanctions for non-participation in mediation)[186] or direct (such as official referrals to mediation). Referrals to mediation can be made with both parties' consent (so-called voluntary) or without both parties' consent (so-called mandatory), depending on jurisdiction.

Distinctions between voluntary and mandatory participation in mediation, while useful, are insufficient. Factors that influence the decision whether or not to mediate are various. So-called mandatory mediation schemes, for example, vary according to whether the court has discretion to mandate mediation or is required to send all or certain cases to mediation as a pre-trial or pre-appellate requirement.[187] Where there is a discretion to mandate mediation, a referring body *prima facie* has discretion to refer the matter to mediation, irrespective of the parties' views on the matter. However the nature of the referral framework can affect the level of influence exerted upon parties to attend mediation. Sometimes such referral schemes are triggered at the request of one of the parties. Soft mandatory schemes refer to discretionary schemes, in which, as a matter of practice, a referring body only exercises its discretion to refer where it considers the parties are likely to participate in good faith and the matter is likely to settle at mediation. The case of *Oriental Carpet Department Store Pty Ltd v Supacenta Pty Ltd*[188] is a useful illustration of this practice. Here the relevant legislation (Retail Leases Act 1994) provided for referral to mediation unless the Registrar was satisfied that that the matter was unlikely to be resolved at mediation. The court held that the attitude of the parties was a

185 See Greger (2007), above note 102 at 113–117.

186 For example, the pre-action protocols in England. Financial sanctions are considered in Chapter 7.

187 See, for example, court referral procedures in the US states of Florida (§ 44.102 Florida Statutes) and Texas (Chapter 13, Local Rules of Civil Procedure and Rules of decorum for the District Courts of Travis County, Texas) referred to in R Kulms, 'Alternative Streitbeilegung durch Mediation in den USA' in K Hopt and F Steffek (eds), *Mediation – Rechtstatsachen, Rechtsvergleich, Regelungen* (Tübingen: Mohr Siebeck 2008) 403 at 423–427.

188 *Oriental Carpet Department Store Pty Ltd v Supacenta Pty Ltd* [2003] NSWSC 783 (unreported Young CJ in Eq, 19 August 2003). See also *Australian Competition and Consumer Commission v Collagen Aesthetics Australia Pty Ltd* [2002] FCA 1134, where the court refused to exercise its discretion to mandate mediation in light of one party's firm objection to mediation.

relevant, but not conclusive, factor in determining if a matter was unlikely to be resolved at mediation. A similar approach can be found in some US courts.[189] Within the concept of mandatory referral therefore it is useful to differentiate between discretionary mandatory, soft mandatory and routine mandatory.

Despite the *de jure* voluntary nature of many court mediation schemes, there can be considerable *de facto* pressure on parties to attend mediation even in so-called voluntary referral schemes. Generally speaking, there is the potential of bias emerging where a trial judge's offer of mediation is refused by one of the parties without justification or explanation and the same judge goes on to hear the case. In England the Civil Procedure Rules and pre-action protocols effectively represent the 'strongest form of encouragement'[190] for parties to attempt mediation; if mediation is unreasonably refused by a party, courts have a broad discretion to impose costs orders against the refusing party.[191] In England and Australia legal aid funding may be refused if parties are not prepared to engage in available mediation and ADR services.[192] In France mediation is said to be voluntary in the sense that the parties must agree to mediate.[193] However once they have done so,[194] the court makes an order to this effect and parties are compelled to attend the mediation.[195] As indicated earlier both of the parties as well as the judge must agree on the choice of mediator.

Constitutional and philosophical objections to mediation compulsion have been widely debated.[196] In England the court in the case of *Halsey v Milton*

189 See, for example, *In re African-American Slave Descendants' Litigation* 272 F Supp 2d 755 (ND Ill 2003) where one of the parties objected to mediation and the court considered that the parties had fundamentally different views about the viability of claims before the court and *LLH v SCH* N° S–10174, 2002 WL 1943659 (Alaska Aug 21, 2002) where the history of lack of cooperation between the parties convinced the court that ordering mediation would be futile.

190 See Dyson LJ in *Halsey v Milton Keynes General NHS Trust and Steel v Joy and Halliday* [2004] EWCA Civ 576 at para 30.

191 See Civil Procedure Rules (CPR) r 1.4 and 44.3, and Practice Direction to the Pre-action Protocol, 4.2(f), (g), 4.6(e) and 4.7, and the line of cases that have interpreted these provisions: *Regina (Cowl and others) v Plymouth City Council* [2001] EWCA Civ 1935, *Dunnett v Railtrack plc* [2002] EWCA Civ 303, *Hurst v Leaming* [2002] EWHC 1051 (Ch), *Royal Bank of Canada v Secretary of State for Defence* [2003] EWHC 1479 (Ch) and *Halsey v Milton Keynes General NHS Trust and Steel v Joy and Halliday* [2004] EWCA Civ 576.

192 See H Genn et al, *Twisting Arms: court referred and court linked mediation under judicial pressure* (London: Ministry of Justice Research Series 2007) available at www. justice.gov.uk.

193 See Article 131-1 C pr civ and Deckert (2008), above note 1 at 211.

194 See Article 131-6 C pr civ.

195 See Article 131-15 C pr civ.

196 See, for example, T Naughton, 'Mediation and the land and environment court of New South Wales' (1992) 9 *Environment and Planning Law Journal* 219 at 223.

Keynes took the view that the Civil Procedure Rules could not be interpreted so as to effectively mandate mediation, for to do so would be 'an unacceptable restraint on the right of access to the court and, therefore, a violation of Article 6' of the European Convention on Human Rights (ECHR) which guarantees access to a fair hearing in a court of law.[197] This decision has been criticised by a number of commentators on the basis that parties who do not reach a settlement agreement at mediation are free to seek access to the courts to deal with their dispute.[198] In light of the uncertainty on this point clause 14 of the CEDR Mediation Agreement provides that parties' rights under the ECHR are not affected by the agreement to mediate and that if there is no settlement the parties' right to a fair trial remains.[199] Beyond Europe the International Covenant on Civil and Political Rights (ICCPR) is *prima facie* applicable to access to justice issues. As Bell J of the Victorian Supreme Court has noted,

> [a] judge has a fundamental duty to ensure a fair trial by giving due assistance to a self-represented litigant, whilst at the same time maintaining the reality and appearance of judicial neutrality. The duty is inherent in the rule of law and the judicial process. The human rights of equality before the law and access to justice specified in the International Covenant on Civil and Political Rights are relevant to its proper performance.[200]

At first glance these judicial comments appear to conflict with an emerging trend in many countries to compel parties – by direct or indirect means – to participate in mediation. A closer examination, however, suggests that it is a question of balance and proportionality. The principle of a right to a fair trial may be subject to restrictions, which are themselves proportionate and part of a legitimate aim of improving access to justice.[201]

Judicial comment supports the notion that courts have an inherent power to mandate mediation as part of their case management functions.[202] Most

197 *Halsey v Milton Keynes NHS Trust* and *Steel v Joy and Halliday* [2004] EWCA Civ 576. See also the comments of Laws J in *Ex parte Witham,* who concluded that it was not lawful to set fees at a non-affordable level in order to encourage mediation, as this would effectively diminish the right to sue in a practical sense: *R v Lord Chancellor, Ex parte Witham* [1998] QB 575 Div Ct.

198 See, for example, S Fielding, 'Mediation post-Halsey' (2004) 154 *New Law Journal* 1394, T Allen, 'A closer look at Halsey and Steel' (2004) available at www.cedr.com and 'What happens now? The impact of Halsey' (2004) available at www.cedr.com.

199 See Appendix A for the CEDR Mediation Agreement.

200 See *Tomasevic v Travaglini and Anor* [2007] VSC 337 at para 155. See also *Ragg v Magistrates' Court of Victoria* [2008] VSC 1.

201 See *Ashingdane v The United Kingdom* 28 May [1985] Series A N° 93 24–5, 57.

202 In the United States see *In re Atlantic Pipe Corp,* 304 F3d 135 (1st Cir 2002) for a discussion of the sources of judicial authority to mandate mediation. In Australia see

court referral mediation schemes that mandate mediation, however, do so within a statutory framework and the court relies on legislative authority and not inherent jurisdiction.[203] The European Directive on Mediation, while defining mediation as a voluntary process, acknowledges that member states may have laws mandating mediation. It seems, therefore, that the concept of voluntariness does not necessarily refer to attendance at mediation but to the nature of participation and decision-making within the process.

The reality is that court-referred mediation is increasingly encouraged, recommended or required. The results of empirical research in the United States show that,

> [c]ourts are inclined to order mediation on their own initiative, and will generally enforce a pre-existing obligation to participate in mediation, whether the obligation was judicially created, mandated by statute, or stipulated in the parties' pre-dispute contract.[204]

Dutch research shows that many parties would never find their way to mediation without encouragement and direction from a third party.[205] In this context Pel suggests that referrers have influential roles in the success of mediation.[206] Furthermore experience in numerous jurisdictions around the world suggests that court-referred ADR only begins to develop as a real alternative to court proceedings when it is subject to some degree of mandating.[207] There is also some evidence to support the view that as experience with mediation increases, so the need for mandating the process decreases.[208]

AWA Ltd v Daniels t/as Deloitte Haskins and Sells and Ors (1992) 10 ACLC 933 at para 13.

203 See 'Mandatory Mediation and Summary Jury Trial: Guidelines for Ensuring Fair and Effective Processes' (1989–1990) 103 *Harvard Law Review* 1086–1089. Examples of statutory authority to mandate mediation can be found in s 53A Federal Court of Australia Act 1976 (Cth) and Alternative Dispute Resolution Act of 1998 in the United States.

204 See J Coben and P Thompson, 'Mediation Litigation Trends' (2007) 1 *World Arbitration and Mediation Report* 395 at 397.

205 See Pel (2008), above note 183 at 161. Netherlands Project on Court-Connected Mediation www.mediationnaastrechtspraak.nl.

206 See Pel (2008), above note 183. Support for this view is also found in the German judgment of the OLG Rostock 26.09.2006 at II 6 and the Australian decision of *AWA Ltd v Daniels t/as Deloitte Haskins and Sells and Ors* (1992) 10 ACLC 933 at para 9.

207 See N Alexander, 'Global Trends in Mediation: Riding the Third Wave' in N Alexander (ed), *Global Trends in Mediation* (2nd ed, Alphen aan den Rijn: Kluwer Law International 2006) 1 at 25.

208 See N Alexander, '10 Verdicts in Court-related ADR' (2004) 22 *Law in Context Special Issue: Alternative Dispute Resolution and the Courts* 8.

Finally the issue of sanctions for non-attendance and non-participation in mediation is relevant. Sanctions may take the form of stays of proceedings, costs orders or penalties for contempt of court such as fines or imprisonment. This topic is addressed in Chapters 4 and 7.

Legal status of mediated settlements. Some court-referred programs confer special status on mediated settlements in terms of legal enforceability, such as making the settlement an order of the court. Others do not address this point at all, leaving the enforceability question to the general law on contract. This issue is dealt with in Chapter 7.

Reporting requirements of mediators. Reporting requirements vary from program to program. In general mediators are only required to report to the court on the attendance of the parties at mediation and on whether or not an agreement was reached between the parties. Information about what occurred in the mediation, the nature of the parties' participation in the process and details of the outcome typically remain confidential unless the parties agree otherwise. The reporting duties of mediators are discussed in Chapter 7.

Litigation limitation periods refer to the period of time, beginning when the cause of action arises, within which prospective plaintiffs can file a claim in court. Limitation periods cease to run once a claim has been filed with a relevant court. However where parties engage in mediation prior to filing – either on their own initiative or as required by a pre-filing court mediation scheme – questions about the impact of mediation on the limitation period are likely to arise. Some statutes expressly suspend the litigation limitation period during mediation, while others are silent on the point. In certain jurisdictions, parties may include provisions on the suspension of limitation periods in their agreements to mediate.[209] Limitation periods are considered in Chapter 7.

4.2.2 *The Referral Procedure*

Whenever courts are required to exercise discretion in relation to an order to mediate, issues may arise about the manner of its exercise. Where at least one party is dissatisfied with a court's intended referral decision, they may be able to object to the referral. In other circumstances it is conceivable that a party may seek to have a referral decision reviewed by a competent court.[210] It is therefore important to understand how referral decisions are made and the type of criteria applied. Referral procedure generally consists of two parts, namely:

1. criteria to be applied to the matter in order to determine whether or not a referral order should be made (referral criteria); and

[209] Agreements to mediate and mediation clauses are dealt with in Chapter 4.

[210] The potential role of judicial review in relation to pre-mediation case management decisions is discussed in Chapter 7.

2. referral method, namely how the criteria will be applied.

It is, in other words, not only a question of *what* criteria are to be applied but equally importantly *how* they are to be applied.

4.3 The Status and Nature of Referral Criteria

Referral criteria are those factors upon which a decision is made as to the suitability of a dispute for mediation. They are also referred to as choice drivers.[211] If a case is deemed to be suitable for mediation, it will normally be referred to a mediation process. If not it may be referred to another dispute resolution process such as neutral evaluation or may proceed to court hearing. Referral criteria vary in terms of their status, probity and legitimacy. Where judges exercise their discretion to refer a case to mediation, they may rely on criteria drawn from statutory law, case law, practice directions, government policy, court practice, doctrine, empirical evidence and their own experience and intuition. Despite the complexity of issues surrounding the referral of matters to mediation, many courts and other agencies do not have a policy on the nature of criteria to be considered for a referral to mediation and the relative weighting of the criteria.[212] In other words a decision as to the appropriateness or otherwise of mediation is left to the decision-making ability of the referrer. A number of court decisions have commented on the relevance of various referral criteria.[213] Spencer has compiled the following list of factors that Australian courts have considered when making referral orders for mandatory mediation:[214]

– Whether a party will be disadvantaged by a mandatory order to mediate (*ACCC v Collagen Aesthetics Australia Pty Ltd*).

211 Pel (2008), above note 183 at 159.

212 See, however the *ADR Guidelines* of the Administrative Appeals Tribunal in Australia, which set out referral criteria for a range of ADR processes including mediation, above note 171.

213 *Australian Competition and Consumer Commission v Collagen Aesthetics Australia Pty Ltd* [2002] FCA 1134.

214 See D Spencer, 'Enforcing Mediation Settlement Agreements in Australia' (2005) 16 *World Arbitration and Mediation Report* 4. References to the cases cited in this list are as follows: *Idoport Pty Ltd and Anor v National Australia Bank Ltd and 8 Ors*, *Idoport Pty Ltd and Market Holdings Pty Ltd v Donald Robert Argus*, *Idoport Pty Ltd "JMG" v National Australia Bank Ltd* [2001] NSWSC 427, *Australian Competition and Consumer Commission v Collagen Aesthetics Australia Pty Ltd* [2002] FCA 1134, *Barrett v Queensland Newspapers Pty Ltd and Brennan and Ruddiman* [1999] QDC 150 and *Hopcroft v Olsen* [1998] SASC 7009.

- Whether a mandatory order to mediate will cause delay in the time taken to resolve the dispute (*ACCC v Collagen Aesthetics Australia Pty Ltd*).
- Whether a mandatory order to mediate will cause unreasonable additional expense (*ACCC v Collagen Aesthetics Australia Pty Ltd*).
- Whether the parties are in intractable positions regarding resolution of the dispute (*ACCC v Collagen Aesthetics Australia Pty Ltd* and *Idoport v National Australia Bank*).
- The fact that even reluctant starters can benefit from a mandatory order to mediate (*Idoport v National Australia Bank* and *Barrett v Queensland Newspapers Pty Ltd*).
- Whether a mandatory order to mediate is appropriate in order to ensure a just, quick and cheap resolution of the dispute (*Idoport v National Australia Bank*).
- The fact that under some legislation parties must participate in good faith, thereby giving a mandatory order to mediate better chances of success (*Idoport v National Australia Bank* and *Waterhouse v Perkins*).
- The fact that most statutory schemes require the parties to discuss the possibility of using mediation to resolve their dispute (*Idoport v National Australia Bank*).
- The opportunity to create a co-operative environment within which to resolve disputes (*Idoport v National Australia Bank*).
- The length of time a case has been running (*Waterhouse v Perkins*).
- The length of time between discussing the possibility of mediation and the trial dates, if set (*Waterhouse v Perkins* and *Hopcroft v Olsen*).
- The estimated length of the trial (*Waterhouse v Perkins* and *Barrett v Queensland Newspapers Pty Ltd*).
- The estimate of costs accruing to both sides (*Waterhouse v Perkins* and *Barrett v Queensland Newspapers Pty Ltd*).
- Whether vindication is an outcome desired of one or more parties to the dispute (*Waterhouse v Perkins*).
- Whether mediation can provide vindication if desired by one or more of the parties to the dispute (*Waterhouse v Perkins*).
- Any offer by one party to pay the costs of mediation of the other party (*Waterhouse v Perkins* and *Barrett v Queensland Newspapers Pty Ltd*).
- The costs of mediating compared to those of litigating (*Waterhouse v Perkins*).
- The prospects of success of mediation (*Barrett v Queensland Newspapers Pty Ltd*).
- The willingness of the parties to engage in mediation (*Barrett v Queensland Newspapers Pty Ltd*).

- The risks associated with litigation (*Barrett v Queensland Newspapers Pty Ltd*).
- The opportunity to narrow issues for trial if settlement is not likely (*Hopcroft v Olsen*).
- Any rational reason for not ordering mediation (*Waterhouse v Perkins*).

These factors emphasise the importance of a rational cost-benefit analysis in relation to mediation, as well as the parties' attitudes and needs in relation to the dispute. They would also seem to cover the situation addressed in an American case, where the court declined to enforce a previous mediation order on the basis that the applicant had refused to participate in previous mediation sessions and there was no reason to consider that the applicant's attitude towards mediation had changed.[215]

In the context of non-mandatory referral, some cases have highlighted relationship factors such as the stress of litigation on the relationship and the opportunities for reconciliation that mediation can offer.[216] Importantly however, some factors, such as the length of time a case has been running, can both increase and decrease the likelihood of settlement depending on the presence and interaction of other relevant factors such as the degree of hostility between the parties and their ability to continue to fund litigation. In other words the meaning and relevance of referral criteria in practice is contextual.

In Europe there have also been some interesting cases and research findings on referral. In England the case of *Halsey* identified the following factors as relevant to referral, most of which are reflected in Spencer's list above:

- The nature of the dispute.
- The merits of the case.
- The extent to which other settlement methods have been attempted.
- Whether the costs of the mediation would be disproportionately high.
- Whether delay in setting up the mediation would be prejudicial.
- Whether the mediation had a reasonable prospect of success.[217]

In Germany, the *Güterichter* project in Bavaria found that the following referral criteria were effective in selecting cases suitable for judicial moderation: the prospect of constructive future-oriented resolution, the prospect of conflict

[215] See *Magann v Magann* 848 So 2d 496 (Fla Dist Ct App 2003).

[216] See, for example, *Higgins v Higgins* [2002] NSWSC 455, *Singh v Singh* [2002] NSWSC 852 and *Walhallow Aboriginal Corp Inc v Walhallow Local Aboriginal Land Council* [2003] NSWSC 545.

[217] *Halsey v Milton Keynes NHS Trust* and *Steel v Joy and Halliday* [2004] EWCA Civ 576 para [17]–[23].

resolution beyond the limits of the claim, the prospect of a win-win solution, the existence of an ongoing business and personal relationship between the parties, the existence of conflict with high emotional costs, and the potential of a lengthy trial.[218] Compared with the previous list, these factors focus more on the relational aspects of the dispute and the capacity for a constructive and creative solution.

In the Netherlands, the Dutch National Project on Court-Annexed Mediation found that while virtually all cases are suitable for mediation, all parties are not.[219] In other words relevant indicators and counter-indicators for the suitability of mediation revolve more around the parties than the nature of the case as Table 4 shows.

In terms of parties' attitudes, courts appear to look for preparedness to negotiate, reasonableness, good faith and a genuine willingness and motivation to resolve the issues as indicators of suitability for mediation. However as the case of *Morrow v chinadotcom*[220] shows, courts may take account of parties' attitudes to mediation, and in particular a party's objection to it, and still require them to attend mediation. Here the skill of the mediator is particularly relevant to issues of dispute dynamics – a point recognised by common law courts. Brooke LJ in *Dunnett* explains,

> Skilled mediators are now able to achieve results satisfactory to both parties in many cases, which are quite beyond the powers of lawyers and courts to achieve. This court has knowledge of cases where intense feelings have arisen, for instance in relation to clinical negligence claims. But when the parties are brought together on neutral soil with a skilled mediator to help them resolve their differences, it may very well be that the mediator is able to achieve a result by which the parties shake hands at the end and feel that they have gone away having settled the dispute on terms with which they are happy to live. A mediator may be able to provide solutions which are beyond the powers of the court to provide.[221]

[218] See Greger (2007), above note 102 at 82 and the section on judicial moderation, earlier in this chapter.

[219] B Niemeijer and M Pel, 'Court-Based Mediation in the Netherlands: Research, Evaluation and Future Expectations' (2005) 110 *Penn State Law Review* 345.

[220] *Morrow v chinadotcom* [2001] NSWSC 209.

[221] In England see *Dunnett v Railtrack plc (in railway administration)* [2002] 2 All ER 850 at para 14. See also *Morrow v chinadotcom* [2001] NSWSC 209 at 219, *Barrett v Qld Newspapers Pty Ltd and Brennan and Ruddiman* [1999] QDC 150 and *Waterhouse v Perkins* [2001] NSWSC 13.

Table 4
Mediation Referral Criteria[222]

Indicators of suitability for mediation	**Counter-indicators**
– Parties' and lawyers' willingness to negotiate.	– No negotiability whatsoever (NB this is often misjudged).
– Speed of process.	– Conflict escalated too far.
– Control of the process and the solution.	– Previous failed mediation.
– Mediation offers tailored solution.	– Precedent needed.
– Legal framework provides no final solution to problem.	– Public ruling needed.
– Imperative for commercial solution.	– Impending lapse of limitation or cancellation period.
– Process looks forward rather than backward.	– Excessive power imbalance.
– Common future interest.	– Health problems of one party that inhibit participation in mediation.[223]
– Process fatigue.	– At least one party is incapable of defending own interests.
– Preservation of relationship or careful termination of long-term relationship (family, neighbours, business relationship, partnership, lengthy contract).	– Parties with a cultural background incompatible with mediation.
– Multiple proceedings or conflicts between the same parties.	– Conflict in which only a court ruling on legal grounds can provide a solution.
– Interest in confidentiality treatment.	– Party with an interest in delaying tactics.
– Opportunity for separate discussions.	– Pure 'fishing expedition'.
– More parties involved in conflict than process parties alone.	– Participating to please the referrer.
– Resilient solution necessary.	– Mediation seen as a sign of weakness.
– Need to limit costs.	– Total inability of one party to trust the other to abide by any agreed settlement.
– Sustainable solution that will be complied with.	– Emotional need by one party to inflict harm/damage on the other.

[222] Adapted from Pel (2008), above note 183 at 159.

[223] On health issues, see the Australian case of *Sharp v the Canonical Administrators of St Monica's College Ltd* [2003] VCAT 42.

The participation of parties who have authority to settle is widely accepted as a significant influencing factor on both the likelihood of settlement and the level of satisfaction in mediation and related processes. The importance of this factor has been substantiated by empirical research.[224] In some jurisdictions, a court's power to refer parties to mediation includes a power to compel the attendance of parties with authority to settle.[225]

Intense conflict, particularly when combined with significant value differences between parties, has been shown to impact negatively on the likelihood of settlement and satisfaction.[226] Where parties are seeking vindication or revenge, there is a significant risk of abuse of the mediation process and it may not be a suitable option.[227] As an illustration s 27 of the Family Law Act 1996 (UK) requires that family mediators ensure that mediation participants are free from fear of violence or harm.[228]

224 C Bordeaux, R O'Leary and R Thornburgh, 'Control, Communication and Power: A Study of the Use of Alternative Dispute Resolution of Enforcement Actions at the US Environmental Protection Agency' (2001) 17 *Harvard Negotiation Law Review* 175, R Hann and C Baar, *Evaluation of the Ontario Mandatory Mediation Program (Rule 24.1): Executive Summary and Recommendations* (Canada: Queen's Printer 2001) and J Rosenberg and J Folberg, 'Alternative Dispute Resolution: An Empirical Analysis' (1994) 46 *Stanford Law Review* 1487.

225 See, for example, the following authorities in Australia: *Baulderstone Hornibrook v Dare Sutton Clark and Ors* [2000] SASC 159, *Barrett v Qld Newspapers Pty Ltd and Brennan and Ruddiman* [1999] QDC 150 and *Kilthistle N° 6 Pty Ltd et al v Austwide Homes Pty Ltd and Ors* [1997] FCA 1383.

226 A Bickerdike and L Littlefield, 'Divorce Adjustment and Mediation: Theoretically Grounded Process Research' (2000) 18 *Mediation Quarterly* 181–201, K Kressel and D Pruitt, *Mediation Research: The Process and Effectiveness of Third-Party Intervention* (San Francisco: Jossey-Bass Publishers 1989) 396–398, D Henderson, 'Mediation Success: An Empirical Analysis' (1996) 11 *Ohio State Journal on Dispute Resolution* 105, J Hiltrop, 'Factors Associated with Successful Labor Mediation' in K Kressel and D Pruitt (eds), *Mediation Research: The Process and Effectiveness of Third-Party Intervention* (San Francisco: Jossey-Bass Publishers 1989) and J Berkovitch and R Jackson, 'Negotiation or Mediation? An Exploration of Factors Affecting the Choice of Conflict Management in International Conflict' (2001) 17 *Negotiation Journal* 59.

227 K Cloke, 'Revenge, Forgiveness, and the Magic of Mediation' (1993) 11 *Mediation Quarterly* 67.

228 On power imbalance see the following references: J Rifkin, 'Mediation from a Feminist Perspective: Promise and Problems' (1984) 2 *Law and Inequality* 21, H Astor 'Feminist Issues in ADR' (1991) 65 *Law Institute Journal* 69, G LaFree and C Rack, 'The Effects of Participants Ethnicity and Gender on Monetary Outcomes in Mediated and Adjudicated Civil Cases' (1996) 30 *Law and Society Review* 767, A Barsky 'Mental Illness, Mental Capacity, and Negotiating Competence' (1996) 8 *Interaction* 9 and P Coy and T Hedeen 'Disabilities and Mediation Readiness in

The attitudes and role of lawyers or other advisers also play an important role in determining success and satisfaction in mediation. Settlement and satisfaction are more likely where lawyers are supportive of the process and where they negotiate co-operatively.[229] Lawyers can also contribute to balancing power disparities between parties. Where lawyers feel their own loss of control in respect to the process, settlement is less likely.[230] In addition courts have considered the need to involve other significant parties as an important reason to use mediation.[231]

Another characteristic of disputes that impacts on the dynamics of resolution relates to the resource investment required for mediation. Part of the referrer's consideration may include the question of whether or not the costs of mediation are likely to be a disproportionate diversion of resources for the parties. Where one party offers to pay for the mediation, this may alleviate the financial risk for the other.

From the perspective of public resources, however, mediation may mean significant potential savings. In the context of mediation referral, courts in many countries are increasingly invoking principles of distributive justice and proportionality. Distributive justice endorses the fair distribution of the resources of the justice system in order to maximise access for those who seek it. In addition the doctrine of proportionality operates on a case-by-case basis and requires that 'the procedure adopted for resolving a given dispute should be proportionate to the value, importance and complexity of the dispute.'[232] Zuckerman provides examples of this new philosophical development emanating from England (Civil Procedure Rules, Part 1.1), France, Portugal, Spain and Japan.[233]

In the Australian case of *Rajski*[234] a court took into account the long history of litigation between the parties and the drain it was placing on court resources in considering whether to refer the matter to mediation. The court in *Goulburn Loco Roundhouse Preservation Society v Sydney Electric Train Society*[235] also invoked the doctrine of proportionality but with a different result.

Court-Referred Cases: Developing Screening Criteria and Service Networks' (1998) 16 *Mediation Quarterly* 113.

229 See Kressel and Pruitt (1989) above note 226 at 396–398, Rosenberg and Folberg (1994) above note 224 at 1487 and R Wissler, 'Court Connected Mediation in General Civil Cases: What We Know from Empirical Research' (2002) 17 *Ohio State Journal of Dispute Resolution* 641.

230 See Bordeaux, O'Leary and Thornburgh (2001), above note 224.

231 On this point see *Savory Holdings Ltd v Royal Oak Mall Ltd* (HC Auckland, CP684/89, Smellie J).

232 See Zuckerman (1999), above note 59 at 48.

233 See previous note.

234 *Rajski and Anor v Tectran Corporation Pty Ltd and Ors* [2003] NSWSC 477.

235 *Goulburn Loco Roundhouse Preservation Society Inc v Sydney Electric Train Society Inc* (General) [2006] NSWCTTT 211.

It elected to hear the case rather than referring it to mediation. Two highly relevant factors in this case were the fact that the parties had previously engaged in unsuccessful settlement negotiations and that there was an important question of law to be determined.

Courts may also be reluctant to refer to mediation cases, which, in the court's view, require a public ruling or precedent. Such cases may include those where points of constitutional law or public policy issues require determination, cases in which there is a need to make the public aware of certain illegal practices such as consumer fraud, and cases in which there is a perceived need for public sanctioning of unacceptable behaviour. In some circumstances it may be in at least one party's interests to seek a precedent in a public ruling. Here test cases and class actions spring to mind.[236]

Complexity is an oft-cited referral criterion. However the literature is unclear on the impact of multiple or complex issues on settlement and satisfaction. In complex disputes with different technical issues relating to law and fact there is a possibility of breaking up the dispute, so that certain aspects are dealt with by mediation and others by litigation.[237] The utility of such an approach must be considered on a case-by-case basis.

While a number of writers suggest that cases in which the facts are still in dispute are unlikely to settle at mediation,[238] there is no empirical evidence to support this point. Research by Brett, Barsness and Goldberg suggests that this is not a significant factor in either the settlement rate or the level of party satisfaction with the process.[239]

Another unsubstantiated referral criterion relates to the monetary value of the dispute. Illustrations of this criterion's use can be found in numerous jurisdictions including Germany[240] and the United States.[241] However monetary value as a predictor of mediation suitability is not supported by the empirical

236 See H Brown and A Marriott QC, *ADR Principles and Practice* (2nd ed, London: Sweet and Maxwell Limited 1999) at 16–38.

237 See the New Zealand case of *Medex Holdings Ltd v Kao Liang-Shih* (N° 2) 2 NZ Conv C 191 at 335. Here the court noted that it is generally reluctant to make orders which will have the effect of splitting the proceedings, resulting in some of the issues being dealt with by arbitration and the remainder by the court.

238 See, for example, T Sourdin, *Alternative Dispute Resolution* (2nd ed, Sydney: Lawbook Co 2005) at 124–126 and 129–130.

239 J Brett, Z Barsness and S Goldberg, 'The Effectiveness of Mediation: An Independent Analysis of Cases Handled by Four Major Services Providers' (1996) 12 *Negotiation Journal* 266.

240 See § 15a EGZPO in Germany.

241 See the court referral model in Texas in relation to matters with a value of less than USD100 000, where the parties do not object to mediation and not more than three parties are involved: discussed in M Birner, *Das Multi-Door Courthouse* (Cologne: Otto Schmidt 2003) at 64.

research. There is no evidence to support the idea either that disputes with lower values or disputes with higher value are more appropriate for mediation.[242]

The substantive nature of the dispute is sometimes considered a relevant factor in determining the suitability for mediation. However as a referral criterion it is not without controversy and empirical research on this point is inconclusive.[243] In his final report on judicial mediation and conciliation in Bavarian courts, Greger notes that the types of cases most successfully settled through judicial mediation or conciliation were inheritance, family, business, neighbourhood and construction disputes. At the same time he suggests that factors typically characteristic of these cases are likely to be more reliable indicators of suitability for mediation than the legal category of the dispute.[244] These factors include the need for a solution beyond that which a court is able to grant as a remedy, the importance of ongoing personal or business relationships and the high emotional burden that can be present in these disputes.

Decisions about the appropriateness or not of mediation will also vary according to the perspective from which the matter is being considered. The court may be motivated by different factors from the parties, and the parties' motivations may also vary. For example, the court may be swayed by the need to reduce its caseload and maximise the use of limited public resources; one party may be motivated by the need for a speedy solution in a confidential forum; the other party may not be interested in mediation because it thinks it has a strong legal case, but may agree to mediate to gather information about the other side with no intention of reaching agreement. Where at least one party does not wish to mediate, it may be left to the courts to weigh up various factors to determine the suitability of the case for mediation.

As indicated previously, the application of referral criteria is contextual. An intense and protracted dispute may in some cases be ideal for mediation, especially where the parties have expended their resources and energy on the conflict and are ready to move on from the dispute. In another situation an intense and protracted conflict may indicate that parties are committed to continuing the dispute and require a decision from a judge or arbitrator to end it. Research has identified that combinations or bundles of criteria may, in certain

[242] See for example J Macfarlane, *Court-Based Mediation for Civil Cases: An Evaluation of the Ontario Court (General Division) ADR Centre* (Toronto: Queen's Printer for Ontario 1995), Rosenberg and Folberg (1994), above note 224 and D Henderson, 'Mediation Success: An Empirical Analysis' (1996) 11 *Ohio State Journal on Dispute Resolution* 105.

[243] See, for example, J Kakalik et al, *An Evaluation of Mediation and Neutral Early Evaluation under the Civil Justice Reform Act* (California: RAND 1996), Rosenberg and Folberg (1994), above note 224 and Wissler (2002), above note 229.

[244] See Greger (2007), above note 102 at 113–117.

circumstances, be better predictors of mediation suitability than a single criterion such as a substantive legal category.[245]

4.4 The Referral Method

Referral methods refer to the way in which referral criteria are applied and implemented. The main approaches to referral are outlined in this section. In referral programs where the power to mandate mediation lies within the discretion of a court, a *presumptive* approach often applies. Here all matters are referred to mediation, unless a party contests a proposed referral and is able to demonstrate to the court's satisfaction that the case is unsuitable for mediation. In Germany the Court-Annexed Mediation Program in Lower Saxony and in the United States[246] the Multi–Option Program at the Federal Court of Northern California adopt presumptive approaches. In other referral programs where the attitude of the parties plays a major role, it may be possible for any one party to choose to *opt out* of the referral without having to establish the unsuitability of the case for mediation – in effect referral is only possible with the consent of both parties. A *screening* approach identifies certain criteria, which make mediation unsuitable, such as an excessive power imbalance between parties, and uses these criteria to screen out unsuitable cases. More labour-intensive approaches involve a case-by-case evaluation of the suitability of a dispute for mediation or other dispute resolution processes based on referral criteria without any presumptions of suitability. Referred to as the *matching* approach, this method can be found in some multi-door courthouses in the United States that offer a range of dispute resolution processes such as mediation, neutral evaluation, med–arb and arbitration. [247] It is also found in the Lower Saxony program referred to earlier as a second available referral method.

In practical terms there are a number of ways in which the referral procedure may be implemented. Pel refers to oral and written elements in the referral method.[248] The criteria may be considered all at once in a written

245 See Pel (2008), above note 183, chapter 6.

246 For an examination of this program see W Gottwald, 'Gerichtsnahe Mediation' in F Haft and K von Schlieffen (eds), *Handbuch Mediation* (2nd ed, München: C H Beck 2009) 963 at 969.

247 See, for example, the Middlesex Multi-Door Courthouse in Cambridge MA and the literature on the multi-door courthouse: Birner (2003), above note 241, Sander (1999), above note 92 and E Gray, 'A Day in the Life of a Multi-Door Courthouse' (2007) 9 *Negotiation Journal* 3 at 215. See also the seminal article on the matching approach, F Sander and S Goldberg, 'Fitting the Forum to the Fuss: A User Friendly Guide to Selecting an ADR Procedure' (1994) 10 *Negotiation Journal* 49.

248 See Pel (2008), above note 183 at 171–172.

procedure.[249] In Germany, for example, a frequent approach in JDR programs involves the referring judge making a preliminary assessment based on the information supplied to the court in written form and then informally contacting a judicial moderator. If the judicial moderator, after an evaluation of the case file, considers it appropriate, the parties are contacted. In other words the court does not meet the parties to the dispute, nor their representatives, before exercising their discretion to refer the matter to mediation. Importantly, however, the referral is not mandatory and the parties may refuse to mediate. In French and Dutch courts, parties may be requested to complete a written questionnaire. This document has the dual purpose of encouraging the parties to reflect on their dispute and the utility of mediation as a dispute resolution approach and, at the same time, providing judges with material in addition to the case file, which can help them form their own view about the suitability of the case for mediation and whether or not to recommend the process to parties.[250]

Another approach is for the court to determine the question of referral in a directions hearing in the presence of the parties' legal representatives. The parties themselves usually do not attend directions hearings.[251] Yet another approach is to conduct a two or three stage process in which screening criteria are first formally applied, followed by interviews with the parties in order to make a contextual determination about the suitability of mediation. Such a procedure is found in the multi-door court-house program in Washington, where parties may complete a questionnaire about their perspectives on, and attitude to, the conflict and their interests. At a directions hearing a judge may discuss the results of the questionnaire with the parties and make a recommendation for a specific dispute resolution process, which if accepted becomes a referral order.[252]

5. CLOSE

This chapter has addressed the main selection and referral issues that may arise in international and domestic mediation. The process of professionalisation of mediation and mediators has highlighted the legal and strategic significance of informed selection of mediation professionals. In the context of court referral to mediation, Chapter 3 has addressed two of the more controversial issues

249 See, for example, Article 9 of the Bavarian Conciliation Law (BaySchlG) in Germany, which deals with a pre-filing procedure in small claims courts.

250 In relation to France see Deckert (2008), above note 1 at 196 and for the Netherlands, see www.rechtspraak.nl.

251 This is for example the case in the three-track ADR Program of the US Court District of Northern Alabama, see N Atlas and S Huber, *Alternative Dispute Resolution: The Litigator's Handbook* (Chicago: American Bar Association 2000) at 476.

252 See Birner (2003), above note 241 at 159.

internationally, namely the role of judges in mediation and mandatory referrals to mediation. The next chapter deals with situations where parties agree to go to mediation before litigation.

Chapter 4
Pre-Mediation II: Mediation Clauses and Agreements to Mediate

1. Introduction to Mediation Clauses

At the time of entering a contract parties seldom give much thought to dispute resolution clauses. Disputing is usually far from their thoughts as they focus on future business relationships and success. It often falls to professional advisers to design appropriate dispute management provisions for the future.

Where there is agreement on a dispute resolution method before a dispute has arisen, it typically takes the form of a clause in the substantive agreement between the parties. In contemporary international dispute resolution practice, arbitration clauses are increasingly making way for mediation and MDR clauses.[1] These clauses are popular in joint venture agreements, construction, commercial, financing and franchising contracts, as well as in intellectual property transactions.

Dispute resolution clauses are useful for numerous reasons. They provide parties with freedom to design conflict management processes that suit their needs and circumstances or select a standard process regulated by a mediation organisation. Conflict management design principles offer a systematic approach to the design and drafting of MDR clauses to address potential conflicts of varying complexity and intensity. Generally processes based on consensus, negotiation and mediation are preferred as initial interventions, followed by increasingly directive or evaluative mechanisms if the dispute remains unresolved.[2] Moreover when parties draft clauses they make decisions about managing disputes at a time when their relationship is positive and constructive. Post-dispute negotiations about process can be difficult and parties may view submitting to mediation at this stage as indicating weaknesses in their case.

As indicated in Chapter 1 mediation clauses can be standardised or they can be designed by the parties and their lawyers to suit their specific needs. The

1 See M Pryles, 'Multi-tiered Dispute Resolution Clauses' (2001) 18 *Journal of International Arbitration* 159–176. For examples, see the clauses in the following cases from England and Australia respectively: *Channel Tunnel Group Ltd v Balfour Beatty Construction Ltd and Others* [1993] 1 All ER 664, *State of New South Wales and ors v Banabelle Electrical Pty Ltd and ors* (2002) 54 NSWLR 503 at para 70. See also Chapters 1 and 3 on MDR processes and practitioners.

2 C Costantino and C Merchant, *Designing Conflict Management Systems* (San Fransisco: Jossey-Bass 1996).

standardised rules of institutions have several advantages. They simplify the drafting of mediation clauses and disputants are said to receive a set of rules that are tried and tested and therefore likely to be legally effective. Institutional rules typically provide that the associated dispute resolution institution administer and manage the mediation process, thereby alleviating parties and their lawyers from this burden. In addition most mediation service-providers maintain panels of qualified mediators from which the parties can choose. At the same time there may be limitations to using institutionalised rules. By their very nature they are standardised and not tailored to suit specific needs of the parties, although the variety of institutionalised rules means that parties are likely to find suitable precedents that provide a useful basis from which they can amend certain provisions. However once parties begin to invest resources in searching for suitable precedents, transaction costs increase and parties may wish to consider designing their own clause. Where the stakes are high for the parties, it may be worth the increase in transaction costs to design individual clauses, agreements to mediate and accompanying mediation procedures.

Most mediation clauses do not come before courts and their validity is never tested. In Australia the first litigation about mediation clauses revealed that the standard clauses of a number of prominent dispute resolution organisations were insufficiently certain and complete and therefore unenforceable.[3] Nonetheless the clauses had effectively supported hundreds of commercial agreements in terms of their dispute resolution choices. While they may not have been legally enforceable they carried moral and commercial force. Regardless of their legal status, mediation clauses can have educational and aspirational functions and focus parties' minds on the opportunities associated with mediation and other dispute resolution processes. The mere existence of a mediation clause in a contract can encourage compliance or result in parties engaging in some variation of dispute resolution once a dispute arises. Therefore most mediation clauses are effective, if not legally then in terms of increasing party awareness of, and compliance with, mediation values.

In jurisdictions where initiating mediation may be viewed as a sign of weakness by the other side,[4] the insertion of mediation clauses in a contract between parties whose relationship is positive may be a useful strategy to get otherwise reluctant parties to the table. Some commentators question the utility of mandating mediation through enforcement of contractual obligations to mediate. However research indicates that once at the mediation table, skilled

3 See, for example, the Australian case of *Elizabeth Bay Developments Pty Ltd v Boral Building Services Pty Ltd* [1995] 36 NSWLR 709.

4 See comments by Allen in relation to England before the Lord Woolf reforms: T Allen, *Implementing the EU Directive on Mediation: A Draft Consultation Paper* (London: 2009) at 28, available with updates at www.cedr.com. At the time of writing, the paper was in draft form.

mediators can guide even the most reluctant of parties to recognise opportunities for resolution. This phenomenon is called the mediation paradox.[5]

As in all areas of contract law, there is scope for misunderstandings and differences in relation to the legality and enforceability of mediation clauses. This chapter is not about all mediation clauses. It is only about a small number of them – those that become the subject of conflict between already disputing parties and litigation before the courts.

The UNCITRAL Model Law on Conciliation does not directly address the enforceability of mediation clauses and agreements to mediate. However it does recognise their *prima facie* validity in Article 13 of the MLICC, which deals with the accessibility of judicial and arbitral proceedings before mediation is complete. In addition, neither the European Directive on Mediation nor the Uniform Mediation Act in the United States addresses the issue of enforcement of mediation clauses.[6] Therefore in this chapter reference will be made to the law of various civil and common law jurisdictions.

2. FORMAL DISTINCTIONS AND TERMINOLOGY

Dispute resolution clauses and agreements are contractual referrals to dispute resolution. They take the form of clauses in commercial, workplace and other contracts between the parties. Alternatively they can be drafted as free-standing agreements. Generally *mediation clauses* regulate the manner in which all future disputes arising out of contracts are to be managed, but they can also deal with specific disputes only. Cross-border mediation clauses can include information about the way the mediation is to be conducted, how the mediator is to be

[5] On the mediation paradox see C McEwen and T Milburn, 'Explaining a Paradox in Mediation' (1993) 9 *Negotiation Journal* 1 at 23. Empirical evidence on mandatory and voluntary civil mediation settlement rates is inconclusive, some studies favouring the latter and some finding no difference: see C McEwen, 'Examining Mediation in Context: Toward Understanding Variations in Mediations Programs' in M Herrman (ed), *Blackwell Handbook of Mediation: Bridging Theory, Research and Practice* (Maine: Blackwell 2006) at 92. However some studies have found that mandatory settlement rates are approximately 40 per cent, while voluntary is at 70 per cent: see Task Force on Appellate Mediation, *Mandatory Mediation in the First Appellate District of the Court of Appeal: Report and Recommendations* (September 2001) and P Jacobs, 'A Recent Comparative History of Mandatory Mediation vs Voluntary Mediation in Ontario, Canada' (2005) *International Bar Association Mediation Newsletter*.

[6] See A Schmitz, 'Refreshing Contractual Analysis of ADR Agreements by Curing Bipolar Avoidance of Modern Common Law' (2004) 9 *Harvard Negotiation Law Review* 1 at 12 referring to the Uniform Mediation Act § 5(i) Annual Meeting Draft, July 23–30, 1999.

appointed, the venue, costs and fees, the state or national law to be applied, the impact of mediation on litigation limitation periods and the language to be used. Agreements to enter into a mediation process can also be concluded between parties after a dispute has arisen. Post-dispute agreements typically define the specific dispute to be mediated and may take the form of an appointment contract between mediator and parties. They are known as *agreements to mediate* or *mediation agreements* and are addressed later in the chapter. In practice mediation clauses and agreements to mediate may overlap in terms of their contents and, although they have different legal functions, are sometimes bundled together in one document. Unless otherwise indicated, the following discussion on mediation clauses is also relevant to agreements to mediate.

3. Recognition of Mediation Clauses

While there is considerable literature and case law on cross-border arbitration clauses, the law on international mediation clauses is in its formative stages. There is, however, a growing school of case law and jurisprudence on enforceability and interpretation of mediation clauses, especially in Anglo-American jurisdictions. Cases typically arise when one party initiates legal proceedings in respect of a dispute and the other seeks to prevent the proceedings on the basis of non-performance of a mediation clause.

The trend in many countries, including France, Germany, Australia, the United States and England, is to recognise and enforce mediation clauses provided certain conditions are met.[7] Deckert explains that in France mediation clauses are recognised as legally valid and *prima facie* enforceable. They are covered by contract law principles according to Article 1134 of the French Civil

7 However this was not always the case. See, for example, a number of US cases where the courts refused to enforce mediation and other non-binding dispute resolution clauses on the basis that it would be a futile exercise: *In re Estate of Ferdinand Marcos Human Rights Litigation* 94 F 3d 539 (9th Cir 1996), citing *Virginian Ry Co v System Fed'n* N° 40, 300 US 515, 550, 57 S Ct 592, 601 (1937). Other courts refused to issue what they referred to as a 'vain order' to enforce such clauses: *Lorch Inc. v Bessemer Hall Shopping Center Inc* 294 Ala 17, 310 So 2d 872 (1975) and *Livoti v Elston* 52 AD 2d 444, 384 NYS 2d 484 (App Div 1976). The breakthrough was made with *AMF Inc v Brunswick Corp* 621 F Supp 456, 462 (EDNY 1985) where an advisory dispute resolution clause was recognised and enforced. For an overview of the development of US case law on this topic see P Tochtermann, 'Agreements to Negotiate in the Transnational Context – Issues of Contract Law and Effective Dispute Resolution' (2008) *Uniform Law Review* 685 at 696–706.

Procedure Code (C pr civ) and the duties contained in them are legally binding on the parties; in other words they are imbued with *force obligatoire*.[8]

Conversely, in jurisdictions such as Austria and Hungary the existence of a mediation clause in a commercial contract does not prevent the institution of legal proceedings in relation to a dispute covered by the terms of the clause.[9] In other countries such as the Netherlands and Ireland the question of the enforceability of mediation clauses remains unclear.[10]

In the absence of statutory law to the contrary, the interpretation of dispute resolution clauses is based on the general law of contract.[11] Therefore the regular jurisdictional requirements for a legally binding contract come into play. These will vary significantly according to legal jurisdiction with, for example, issues of consideration being relevant in common law countries but not in other legal traditions. This chapter does not canvas the general law of

8 K Deckert, 'Mediation in Frankreich' in K Hopt and F Steffek (eds), *Mediation – Rechtstatsachen, Rechtsvergleich, Regelungen* (Tübingen: Mohr Siebeck 2008) at 196. Deckert refers to French literature supporting the approach including L Cadiet, 'L'Effet processuel des clauses de médiation' (2003) *RDC* 182 at 184 et seq and X Lagarde, 'L'Éfficacité des clauses de médiation ou de conciliation' (2000) *Rev arbitrage* 376 at 377. See also Cass civ 2ème, 06.07.2000, N° 98–17827 in relation to Article 1134 C pr civ and Cass (ch mixte) 14.02.2003 N° 00–19423 00–19424 where a court recognised mediation clauses for their full obligatory force and held that a 'friendly solution' must be sought before judicial intervention is actioned.

9 In relation to Austria see H Fasching (ed), *Zivilprozessrecht* (Vienna: Manz'sche 1984) at para 5. In relation to Hungary remedies for breach of mediation clauses may take other forms such as costs sanctions: see C Jessel-Holst, 'Mediation in Ungarn' in K Hopt and F Steffek (eds), *Mediation – Rechtstatsachen, Rechtsvergleich, Regelungen* (Tübingen: Mohr Siebeck 2008) at 908.

10 See F Steffek, 'Mediation in Europa und der Welt – Rechtsvergleichende Forschung zur Umsetzung der Mediationsrichtlinie' (2009) 1 *Zeitschrift für Konfliktmanagement* 21 at 22.

11 Interestingly some of the first US decisions to recognise and enforce mediation clauses did so *not* according to contract law principles but on the basis that mediation was analogous to arbitration and so could be enforced along with other process such as non-binding arbitration under the Federal Arbitration Act. See, for example, *Coburn v Grabowski* 1997 WL 309572 (Conn Super 1997), *Cecala v Moore* 982 F Supp 609 (ND Ill 1997) and *CB Richard Ellis Inc v American Environmental Waste Management* 1998 WL 903495 (EDNY 1998). However the differences between mediation and arbitration ultimately proved this approach to be unsustainable. See, for example the comments that 'arbitration and mediation are completely different processes that do not resemble each other at all' in *Lynn v General Electric Co* 2005 WL 701270 (D Kansas 2005) and the critical comments of Stipanowich in T Stipanowich, 'The Arbitration Penumbra: Arbitration Law And the Rapidly Changing Landscape Of Dispute Resolution' (2007) 8 *Nevada Law Journal* 427 and T Stipanowich, 'Contract and Conflict Management' (2001) *Wisconsin Law Review* 831 at 862–63.

contract, rather it highlights specific aspects of contract law that have been the subject of litigation and legislative activity in relation to mediation and MDR clauses. For example, mediation clauses must adhere to form and content requirements of the relevant jurisdiction. According to Slovakian law mediation clauses must be in writing.[12] In Germany there are different views on form requirements for mediation clauses,[13] however for the purposes of documentation and evidence it is recommended that they be in written form.[14]

The legal nature of mediation clauses can have significant implications for legal form requirements. It is therefore an important consideration when selecting applicable law (choice of law)[15] and is considered next.

3.1 The Legal Nature of Mediation Clauses

The legal nature of mediation clauses has more than academic significance. In many jurisdictions it can have direct relevance to available remedies as demonstrated later in the chapter. In countries with common law traditions, mediation clauses have been treated as conditions precedent to litigation.[16] In Australia, for example, a State Supreme Court has held that,

> The right to mediate is not a substantive right. It is a procedural mechanism, designed to assist in the resolution of disputes.[17]

In the United States Coben and Thompson state that courts routinely enforce mediation clauses as a condition precedent to litigation over the objection of one

[12] See § 7(1) of the 25 June 2004 on the Slovakian Act of 25 June 2004 on Mediation and Amendment of Certain Acts.

[13] On form requirements generally see J Risse and C Wagner, 'Mediation im Wirtschaftsrecht' in F Haft and K von Schlieffen (eds), *Handbuch Mediation* (2nd ed, München: C H Beck 2009) at 571, where the authors argue that binding mediation clauses must be in writing. Eidenmüller argues against the need for form requirements in H Eidenmüller, *Vertrags- und Verfahrensrecht in der Wirtschaftsmediation* (Köln: Dr Otto Schmidt 2001) at 10.

[14] I Beckmann, 'Wirtschaftmediation in der anwaltlichen Beratung-Praktischer Ratgeber für den Umgang mit Mediation' (2007) 13 *Deutsches Steuerrecht* 583. Mustertexte in R Walz, *Formularbuch Aussergerichtliche Streitbeilegung* (Köln: Dr Otto Schmidt 2006). Also C Lenz and A Müller (eds), *Business Mediation: Einigung ohne Gericht* (Landsberg/Lech: Moderne Industrie 1999) at 230 et seq.

[15] On choice of law see Chapter 2.

[16] In addition to Australia, England and the US, Canadian courts also follow this approach – see the Canadian case of *ODC Exhibit Systems Ltd v Lee* (1988) 41 BLR 286 (BCSC).

[17] See *Jones v Castle Hill RSL Club Ltd* [2005] NSWSC 1310.

of the parties.[18] In the American case of *Klinge v Bentien*[19] a court held that the failure of the plaintiff to request mediation and obtain a mediation release before filing suit in accordance with relevant farm mediation legislation, deprived the court of subject-matter jurisdiction to hear the dispute. In another US case, *DeValk Lincoln Mercury, Inc v Ford Motor Co*,[20] it was held that,

> the mediation clause here states that it is a condition precedent to any litigation...the mediation clause demands strict compliance with its requirement.

In civil law jurisdictions the approach to this issue varies. The Austrian Law on Mediation in Civil Cases[21] does not extend to enforceability of mediation clauses and reference must be made to the general law of civil procedure and contract. Roth and Gherdane explain that mediation clauses have no impact on civil procedural law and as such are not effective instruments to stay legal proceedings pending the fulfilment of the clause.[22] The Austrian approach seems to rely on a particular interpretation of the principle of party autonomy which effectively permits parties to change their minds about participation in mediation even if they have made a contractual commitment to engage in it. It is also based on a view that mediation, as a dispute resolution process external to the court

18 See J Coben and P Thompson, 'Disputing Irony: A Systematic Look at Litigation About Mediation' (2006) 11 *Harvard Negotiation Law Review* 43 at 108. See, for example, *Strawser v Langmaack* WL 1810704 (Cal App 4th Dist 2007) and *Ventre v Ventre* WL 100326 (Conn Super 2001). In the latter case the court refused to excuse plaintiff's failure to mediate and rejected outright a claim that mediation would have been a useless act, although the defendant had allegedly told the plaintiff that 'she had no desire to discuss the matter and had no intention of paying any monies due under the separation agreement.'

19 *Klinge v Bentien* 725 NW 2d 13 (Iowa State Supreme Court 2006), noted in '2006 Mediation Case Law Review – Part 1' (2007) 1 *World Arbitration and Mediation Report* 423.

20 *DeValk Lincoln Mercury, Inc v Ford Motor Co* 811 F 2d 326 (7th Cir 1987) at 335–336.

21 See Zivilrechts-Mediations-Gesetz 2001 (ZivMediatG) BGBl I N° 29/2003. For a discussion of the Austrian legal situation in commercial mediation in the light of the European Directive on Mediation see N Pitkowitz, 'Die neuen Mediationsregeln der EU – Ist Österreich noch Wegbereiter?' (2005) 2 *Zeitschrift für Schiedsverfahren* at 82 et seq. On the need for a German Mediation Act, see A Becker and C Horn, 'Notwendige Regelungen eines deutschen Mediationsgesetzes' (2006) 5 *Zeitschrift für Schiedsverfahren* 270.

22 See M Roth and D Gherdane, 'Mediation in Österreich - Zivilrechts-Mediations-Gesetz: Rechtlicher Rahmen und praktische Erfahrungen' in K Hopt and F Steffek (eds), *Mediation – Rechtstatsachen, Rechtsvergleich, Regelungen* (Tübingen: Mohr Siebeck 2008) 105 at 127–128.

system, is independent of civil court procedure and therefore must not be able to influence it.[23]

In Switzerland the Cassation Court of the canton of Zurich (*Kassationsgericht Zürich*) in a 1999 decision[24] held that mediation clauses were substantive rather than procedural in nature and that therefore the initiation of court proceedings was permitted, irrespective of the fact that one party may have breached the terms of a clause obliging the parties to engage in mediation prior to litigation.[25] The Swiss Court was not convinced that the mediation clause was a precondition to the claim itself. It held that any remedy for breach of a substantive clause would have to be considered as part of the substantive arguments before court, although in terms of remedies damages may be difficult to establish.[26] However subsequent judicial comment (*obiter dicta*) in Switzerland seems to support the view that mediation clauses are procedural in nature and therefore may be drafted as conditions precedent to litigation.[27]

The preponderant academic view in Switzerland concurs with the 1999 decision, namely that, in accordance with parties' intention, mediation clauses are substantive (*materiellrechtlich*) rather than procedural in nature. Therefore *prima facie* the clauses themselves have no direct impact on the initiation of court proceedings.[28] However such clauses may effectively trigger the law on civil procedure,[29] which in turn may influence court proceedings. In this way the Draft Law on Civil Procedure (ZPO–E) §§ 210–215[30] provides an interface

23 See Roth and Gherdane (2008), above note 22 at 127–128.

24 Cassation Court of the canton of Zurich (Kassationsgericht Zürich) 15 March 1999, published in *Zürcherische Rechtsprechung* 99 (2000) N° 29.

25 Cassation Court of the canton of Zurich, above note 24. See also H Eiholzer (ed), *Die Streitbeilegungsabrede: Ein Beitrag zu alternativen Formen der Streitbeilegung, namentlich der Mediation* (Freiburg Schweiz: Universitätsverlag Freiburg Schweiz 1998) at RN 552, 577, 673. Eiholzer supports the opinion of the court.

26 See Eiholzer (1998), above note 25 at RN 577 et seq on this point. Also N Voser, *Enforcement of Multi-tiered Dispute Resolution Clauses by National Courts and Arbitral Tribunals: The Civil Law Approach* (Durban: International Bar Association Conference 2002) at 5.

27 See Cassation Court of the canton of Zurich (Kassationsgericht Zürich) in *Zürcherische Rechtsprechung* 101 (2002) N° 21, 77–81, especially at 78. See also Swiss Federal Supreme Court (Cour de droit civil), decision of 06.06.2007, 4A_18/2007.

28 See C Kumpan and C Bauer, 'Mediation in der Schweiz' in K Hopt and F Steffek (eds), *Mediation – Rechtstatsachen, Rechtsvergleich, Regelungen* (Tübingen: Mohr Siebeck 2008) at 866 and S Gabriel, Die Haftung des Mediators im schweizerischen Rechtssystem' in H Hausherr (ed), *Abhandlungen zum schweizerischen Recht* (Bern: Stämpfli 2008) at 72 et seq.

29 See Articles 210–215 the Draft Law on Civil Procedure, Entwurf-Zivilprozessordnung ZPO-Entwurf at www.admin.ch/ch/d/ff/2006/7413.pdf.

30 The ZPO-Entwurf is the legislative draft for a Swiss Civil Procedural Law envisaged to come into force in 2010.

between mediation and the legal system.[31] Thus mediation clauses can have indirect procedural consequences without being categorised as conditions precedent to litigation.[32]

In Germany there has been academic debate about the legal nature of mediation clauses.[33] They are distinguished from arbitration clauses in the literature and court judgments.[34] Some writers have suggested that they be classified as procedural agreements within the German civil procedural law;[35] however mediation clauses typically include more than procedural arrangements. Others have mooted the possibility of such agreements being interpreted as civil code partnerships.[36] Such partnerships require a common purpose from which certain legal consequences flow, but the common purpose of a mediation clause is limited to the parties engaging in a process and the consequences that would flow from such a legal interpretation would not reflect the parties' intentions.[37] The dominant academic view in Germany classifies mediation clauses as contracts *sui generis* for the performance of a continuing obligation with an atypical subject-matter.[38] Whether or not, on this construction, parties are obliged to carry out the mediation remains controversial. Eidenmüller suggests that if one party fails to comply with a mediation clause the other can claim specific performance and oblige the non-compliant party to fulfil the terms of the clause.[39] The issue of remedies is considered later in this chapter.

German courts have not directly addressed the question of the legal nature of mediation clauses. In one decision the German Federal Court classified

31 T Pfisterer, 'Unterwegs zur Einigung mit Mediation in der schweizerischen ZPO' (2007) 22 *Schweizerische Juristen-Zeitung* at 541 et seq.

32 See the *Bericht zum Vorentwurf der Expertenkommission zur Schweizerischen Zivilprozessordunung* (June 2003) at 2, available at www.bj.admin.ch and Gabriel (2008), above note 28 at 74.

33 On mediation clauses in Germany see N Alexander, J Ade and C Olbrisch, *Mediation, Schlichtung, Verhandlungsmanagement* (Münster: Alpmann-Schmidt Verlag 2005) at 133–134, Eidenmüller (2001), above note 13 at 9 and Risse and Wagner (2009), above note 13 at 570 et seq.

34 See, for example, see the decision of the Higher Regional Court of Rostock, Oberlandesgericht Rostock 3 U 37/06 of 18.09.2006 at II 1.

35 B Hess, 'Rechtsgrundlagen der Mediation' in F Haft and K von Schlieffen (eds), *Handbuch Mediation* (2nd ed, München: C H Beck 2009) 1053 at 1062 et seq.

36 See §§ 705 et seq of the German Civil Code (Bürgerliches Gesetzbuch, BGB) and the commentary in O Palandt et al (eds), *Bürgerliches Gesetzbuch* (68th ed, Munich: Beck Juristischer Verlag 2009) at §§ 705 et seq.

37 See A Hutner, 'Die Mediationsvereinbarung-Regelungsgegenstände und vertragsrechtliche Qualifizierung' (2003) 5 *Zeitschrift für Schiedsverfahren* at 230.

38 See § 311(1) German Civil Code and Eidenmüller (2001), above note 13 at 23. On § 311 German Civil Code see Palandt et al (2009), above note 37 at § 311.

39 Eidenmüller (2001), above note 13 at 23.

mediation clauses as having a hybrid nature and falling between the procedural and substantive law classifications.[40] The court went on to explain that a mediation clause implies that litigation is to be used as a last resort and that parties temporarily waive their right to commence an action pending mediation.[41]

Finally in France the Supreme Court (*Cour de Cassation*) has held that a clause in an agreement, which binds parties to participate in a conciliation procedure prior to filing a court claim, is procedural in nature and will prevent parties from initiating proceedings until such time as the conciliation procedure is completed.[42]

Challenges also arise in relation to classifying the legal nature of MDR clauses. Courts in both common and civil law countries have upheld these clauses requiring mediation as a step prior to arbitration or other dispute resolution processes. In the United States, for example, courts have recognised contracting parties' intentions to mediate before arbitrating as a condition precedent to arbitration and the operation of the Federal Arbitration Act.[43] French courts have also commented on the relationship between mediation and arbitration in MDR clauses, the Supreme Court confirming that parties must respect their agreement to mediate and make all reasonable efforts to resolve their dispute before an arbitration clause will be activated.[44]

40 See the decision of the Bundesgerichtshof (German Federal Court) dated November 18, 1998 (VIII ZR 344/97), cons 3b. The decision is reproduced in *Neue Juristische Wochenzeitschrift* 1999, 647, *Zeitschrift für Wirtschafts- und Bankrecht* 1999, 651 and *Der Betrieb* 1999, 215. The decision confirmed the decision of the Bundesgerichtshof dated 23 November 1983 (VIII ZR 197/82) which is reproduced in *Neue Juristische Wochenzeitschrift* 1984 at 669. Voser welcomes this classification of mediation clauses by the German Federal Court: Voser (2002), above note 26 at 9.

41 Decision of the Bundesgerichtshof dated November 18, 1998 (VIII ZR 344/97) cons 3b, cited in the previous note. The decision has been upheld by the Superior Regional Court of Rostock, Oberlandesgericht Rostock 3 U 37/06 18.09.2006.

42 See Cour Cass 2ème, 06.07.2000, N° 98–17827, (2001) *Rev arbitrage* 749 et seq. See also the following decisions: Cass civ 2ème, 28.11.1985, N° 84–14382, (1996) *Rev arbitrage* 614 and Cass civ 1ère, 06.05.2003, N° 01–01291, (2003) *RDC* 182. In the latter case the French Supreme Court in an appeal from the Court of Appeal recognised the legitimacy and prima facie enforceability of mediation clauses. See also Deckert (2008), above note 8 at 196 et seq.

43 See the Federal Arbitration Act 9 USC 1 et seq. See also the following cases: *HIM Portland LLC v Devito Builders Inc* 317 F 3d 41 (1st Cir 2003) and *Kemiron Atl Inc v Aguakem Int'l Inc* 290 F 3d 1287 (11th Cir 2002). In *Kemiron* the contract specified that parties had to go to mediation before arbitration. The court held that since neither party requested mediation, the arbitration clause was not activated and the FAA did not apply. It stated that where contracting parties agree to make the commencement of arbitration dependent upon satisfaction of a condition precedent, the failure to satisfy the specified condition will preclude a party from initiating arbitration.

44 See Cass civ 1ère, 06.06.2007, N° 04–16204.

Where mediation is a condition precedent to arbitration, questions may arise as to the classification of an MDR clause. One issue relates to whether the mediation part of the clause forms part of the arbitration clause for the purposes of interpretation under an arbitration statute or alternatively whether it can be treated separately under mediation regulations. Here various factors come into play including parties' intention and conduct and the extent to which the agreement provides for a clear structure and process for the mediation as illustrated in the following case.

In the Australian case of *Hooper Bailie Associated Ltd v Natcon Group Pty Ltd*[45] contracting parties had an arbitration clause but agreed by correspondence to try to *conciliate* their dispute. They met with a mediator and reached agreement on a number of issues before adjourning, pending collation of further information. The plaintiff sought a stay of arbitration proceedings, alleging there was a legally binding agreement to mediate (either as a variation of the arbitration agreement or pursuant to estoppel), the effect of which was that the arbitration could not resume until mediation was concluded. The plaintiff further argued that it was an implied term of the agreement that the parties would take all reasonable steps to endeavour to resolve the mediation issues under the chairmanship of the mediator by discussion, consideration and agreement. The Supreme Court of New South Wales held that the parties' intention could be discerned from the correspondence and the evidence of how they had conducted the mediation until the point at which it was adjourned. The court ordered a stay of the arbitral proceedings, indirectly giving effect to the mediation agreement.

3.2 Authority of the Court or Tribunal

Closely related to deliberations about the nature of mediation clauses is the question of the source of power that grants courts jurisdiction to make orders in relation to mediation clauses and allows access to the courts to be blocked, at least temporarily.

In disputes about arbitration clauses the court's authority to stay proceedings is generally found in statute, although courts have also stayed proceedings initiated contrary to arbitration clauses by asserting their inherent jurisdiction to prevent abuse of their processes.[46] The following discussion

45 See, for example, the Australian case of *Hooper Bailie Associated Ltd v Natcon Group Pty Ltd* (1992) 28 NSWLR 194 at 209 and the New Zealand case of *Acorn Farms Ltd v Schnuriger* [2003] 3 NZLR 121.

46 In relation to England see *Roussel-Uclaf v G D Searle and Co* [1978] 1 Lloyd's Rep 225. In Australia see *Adelaide Steamship Industries Pty Ltd v Commonwealth* (1974) 10 SASR 203. Australian law courts have statutory authority to stay proceedings to enforce international arbitration clauses under the Arbitration (Foreign Awards and Agreements) Act 1974 (Cth) as amended by the International Arbitration

considers the power of courts and arbitral tribunals to make orders to stay proceedings pending compliance with MDR and mediation clauses respectively.

The question as to an arbitration tribunal's capacity to autonomously determine its own jurisdiction where the mediation phase of an MDR clause has not been fulfilled would seem to be answered in some jurisdictions by the arbitral principle of *competence-competence*, referring to a tribunal's right and duty to autonomously decide whether or not it has jurisdiction. However different approaches to the issue lend a heightened importance to the choice of jurisdiction in relation to MDR clauses.

In 2001 the Supreme Court of the canton of Zurich endorsed the application of the *competence-competence* principle to MDR clauses.[47] In this case the Court held that it was not for the appointing authority to decide whether the mediation phase had been fulfilled by the parties or not, this was the duty of the arbitral tribunal.

Similarly in France the principle of *competence-competence* has been endorsed in relation to med–arb clauses in the SIAL case.[48] In Germany Civil Procedure Rules[49] grant arbitral tribunals competence to rule on their own jurisdiction and in England arbitrators may decide their jurisdiction by virtue of the English Arbitration Act.[50] The principle of *competence-competence* has been confirmed in other jurisdictions, including the Republic of Korea,[51] Brazil[52] and Japan.[53] Here arbitral tribunals can determine whether or not breach of mediation clauses affects their jurisdiction, but they may be subject to varying degrees of judicial review.

Conversely in Panama the Supreme Court has ruled that a provision enshrining *competence-competence* was unconstitutional because it was against

(Amendment) Act 1989 (Cth). Similarly in the United States at both State and Federal levels, courts have statutory authority to enforce arbitration clauses and stay court proceedings: see for example the Florida Arbitration Code FS 682 and the Federal Arbitration Act 9 USC 1. The United Kingdom's Arbitration Act (1996) affords English courts the same power.

47 See the Cassation Court of the canton of Zurich (Kassationsgericht Zürich) in *Zürcherische Rechtsprechung* 101 (2002), N° 21 at 78.

48 See the decision of the Cass civ 1ère, 14.11.2007, N° 06–21629 (the *Sial* case). See also Articles 1466 and 1481–1491 C pr civ.

49 § 1040(1) of the German Code of Civil Procedure (Zivilprozessordnung, ZPO) states: 'The arbitral tribunal may rule on its own jurisdiction and in this connection on the existence or validity of the arbitration agreement. […]'.

50 See ss 30, 31, 32, 67 and 72 of the Arbitration Act 1996.

51 See the Korean Arbitration Act 1999.

52 See Article 8 of Federal Law N° 9.307 of 1996. This was also upheld in 2005 in *COPEL v Energética Rio Pedrinho SA and Others* (Case N° 174.874–9/02) by the Court of Appeal of the State of Paraná.

53 See Article 23, Japanese Arbitration Law (N° 138 of 2003, enforced on 1 March 2004).

due process and restricted the freedom of citizens' recourse to the courts.[54] In an MDR context, therefore, the jurisdiction to determine whether or not an arbitral tribunal has jurisdiction depending on compliance or otherwise with the mediation phase of an MDR clause lies with the courts. The application of *competence-competence* in the United States has been hesitant.[55] The principle is not contained in the Federal Arbitration Act and has been unevenly applied by the judiciary, with recent decisions affording arbitrators the authority to determine their own competence to hear disputes,[56] despite the traditional position that it was a matter for the courts to decide.[57]

In the absence of a legislative framework for mediation, common law courts have relied on their inherent jurisdiction which grants courts a discretionary power to stay proceedings.[58] The court's power to make such orders derives from both its inherent jurisdiction to prevent abuse of its process and its statutory jurisdiction to make interlocutory orders in relation to arbitration proceedings under the relevant arbitration legislation.

In the Australian case of *Hooper Bailie*[59] Giles J observed that for a party to proceed to court in the face of an enforceable agreement to follow a dispute resolution procedure may involve an abuse of process,

> ...namely, that the court makes people abide by their contracts, and, therefore, will restrain a plaintiff from bringing an action which he is doing in breach of his agreement with the defendant that any dispute between them will be otherwise determined.

In relation to MDR clauses the English *Channel Tunnel* case[60] shows how the characterisation of a clause as an arbitral or other dispute resolution agreement can influence the source of a court's authority to make orders and provide remedies. If the MDR clause can be characterised as an arbitration agreement

54 See Supreme Court of Panama award rendered December 13, 2001. The relevant section was Article 17 of Law N° 5 of 1998.

55 J Valdes, 'The Principle of Kompetenz-Kompetenz in International Commercial Arbitration' (2007) 22 *Mealey's International Arbitration Report* 1 at 4.

56 See, for example, *Howsam v Dean Witter* 537, US 79 (2002), *PacifiCare Health Systems Inc v Book* 538 US 401, (2003) 285 F 3d 971, 123 S Ct 1531 (2003) and *Green Tree Financial Corp v Bazzle* 123 S Ct 2402 (2003).

57 See, for example, *Steelworkers v Enterprise Wheel and Car Co* 363, US 593 (1960).

58 See, for example, the Australian case *Hooper Bailie Associated Ltd v Natcon Group Pty Ltd* (1992) 28 NSWLR 194 and the American case of *In re Atlantic Pipe Corp* 304 F3d 135 (1st Cir 2002). However court authority cannot be taken for granted: see Young J in *Townsend and Townsend v Coyne* (002023/95) (26 April 1995, unreported) NSWSC (Equity).

59 *Hooper Bailie Associated Ltd v Natcon Group Pty Ltd* (1992) 28 NSWLR 194.

60 See the *Channel Tunnel Group Ltd v Balfour Beatty Construction Ltd and Others* [1993] 1 All ER 664.

then the authority to stay litigation proceedings stems from the relevant arbitration statute, but another source of authority is required to stay proceeding pending compliance with a mediation clause. In *Channel Tunnel* the House of Lords concluded that, in relation to this particular MDR clause, a stay could be granted either under the Arbitration Act or the court's inherent jurisdiction. However the case highlights some potential challenges that may arise in relation to enforcement of MDR clauses.

In England the inherent jurisdiction identified in *Channel Tunnel*[61] is complemented by a general discretion to grant stays to encourage settlement between parties.[62] In the United States federal courts also have an inherent jurisdiction to stay proceedings.[63] The jurisdiction of German courts to reject actions on the basis that they are 'temporarily inadmissible' pending completion of mediation clauses[64] can be drawn from the Code of Civil Procedure[65] and the German Code on Court Constitution.[66]

Having established the question of jurisdiction, the court or tribunal must determine the validity of the clause. Numerous factors are relevant here, but their level of significance varies greatly according to jurisdiction. They are described and discussed in the following sections.

3.3 Does a Mediation Clause Oust the Jurisdiction of the Court?

Access to justice is a fundamental principle of the rule of law and is enshrined in constitutions of modern democracies throughout the world.[67] It is embodied in Article 8 of Universal Declaration of Human Rights 1948:[68]

> Everyone has the right to an effective remedy by the competent national tribunals for acts violating the fundamental rights granted him by the constitution or by law.

61 In relation to inherent jurisdiction see *Cable Plc and Wireless v IBM United Kingdom Ltd* [2002] EWHC 2059 (Comm Ct).

62 See the Civil Procedure Rules r 3.1(2)(f) and r 26.4.

63 See, for example, the Supreme Court in *Landis v North American Company* 299 US 248, 254 (1936), *Contracting Northwest, Inc v City of Fredericksburg, Iowa* 713 F2d 382 (8th Cir 1983) and *Philadelphia Housing Authority v Dore and Associates Contracting Inc* 111 F Supp 2d 633 (E D Pa 2000). At the state level see *Volmar Distributors Inc v New York Post Co* 152 FRD 36, 39 (SDNY 1993).

64 See F Friedrich, *Die Konsensvereinbarung im Zivilrecht* (Baden-Baden: Nomos 2003) at 185.

65 See Zivilprozessordnung (ZPO) and Friedrich (2003), above note 64.

66 See Gerichtsverfassungsgesetz (GVG) and Friedrich (2003), above note 64.

67 In France see Article 30 C pr civ. The French Constitutional Council has recognised access to justice and the courts as a constitutional right (Conseil Constitutionnel 2 December 1980).

68 See also the European Court of Human Rights decision in *Golder v the United Kingdom* 4451/70 [1975] ECHR 1 (21 February 1975).

Contracts which attempt to oust the jurisdiction of courts of law by, for example, substituting a different dispute resolution process for litigation *prima facie* violate the rule of law and are unlawful and void.[69] Thus a provision establishing mediation as the sole dispute resolution option to the exclusion of litigation[70] would be unenforceable, as would an agreement not to sue on a contract.[71]

The question has arisen as to whether dispute resolution clauses potentially violate s 6 of the Human Rights Act 1998 (UK) which gives effect to rights and freedoms guaranteed under the European Convention on Human Rights (ECHR). The European Court of Human Rights has not taken the opportunity to address the issue in mediation cases that have come before it.[72] However in *Halsey v Milton Keynes General NHS Trust* the English Court of Appeal took the view that courts do not have the power to, nor should they, force unwilling parties to engage in dispute resolution. The court considered that such a requirement could breach Article 6 of the ECHR. Lord Justice Dyson in delivering the court's judgment stated that,

> It is one thing to encourage the parties to agree to mediation, even to encourage them in the strongest terms. It is another to order them to do so. It seems to us that to oblige truly unwilling parties to refer their disputes to mediation would be to impose an unacceptable obstruction on their right of access to the court...we reiterate that the court's role is to encourage, not to compel.[73]

69 See *Doleman and Sons v Ossett Corporation* [1912] 3 KB 257 and *Felton v Mulligan* (1971) 124 CLR 367 at 385 per Windeyer J. See also *Brooks v Burns Philp Trustee Co Ltd* (1969) 121 CLR 432 at 452 per Windeyer J. For detailed discussion on ousting a court's jurisdiction see *Bulk Chartering and Consultants Australia Pty Ltd v T and T Metal Training Pty Ltd 'The Krasnogrosk'* (1993) 31 NSWLR 18 at 33–36 per Sheller JA.

70 See *Baulderstone Hornibrook Engineering Pty Ltd v Kayah Holdings Pty Limited* (1997) 14 BCL 277 per Heenan J.

71 See *Dobbs v National Bank of Australasia Ltd* (1935) 53 CLR 643 at 656.

72 See *Hokkanen v Finland* (Case N° 50/1993/445/524), European Court of Human Rights, [1996] 1 FLR 289, 23 September 1994 and *Elsholz v Germany* (app N° 25735/94 European Court of Human Rights (Grand Chamber) [2000] 3 FCR 385, 13 July 2000.

73 See *Halsey v Milton Keynes General NHS Trust* [2004] EWCA Civ 576. This view finds support in the Australian decision of *Allco (Steel) Queensland Ltd v Torres Strait Gold Pty Ltd* BC9002840, S Ct Qld 1990, which held that a mediation clause necessarily ousted the jurisdiction of the court, but this case is not considered good law and has not been subsequently applied (see the later case of *AWA v Daniels* (1992) 7 ACSR 436). The concern about access to justice has also been raised in relation to the use of mediation in divorce matters. See T Grillo, 'The Mediation Alternative: Process Dangers for Women' (1991) 100 *Yale Law Journal* 1545 and P Bryan, 'Killing Us Softly: Divorce Mediation and the Politics of Power' (1992) 40 *Buffalo Law Review* 441.

Conversely Mistelis argues that dispute resolution clauses are *prima facie* in conformity with the UK Human Rights Act as parties retain access to a fair and public trial for those issues on which settlement is not reached, and additionally in the form of judicial review of mediated settlements.[74] This view is supported by an increasing number of courts and commentators in various countries.[75] In France, for example, the judicial view that '[f]ailure to respect the contractual provisions requiring preliminary mediation proceedings cannot be a reason for the inadmissibility of court proceedings,'[76] appears to have given way to one in which a court will effectively declare an action to be *temporarily* inadmissible pending compliance with a mediation clause.

Thus a clause which establishes a condition precedent to litigation, so that the right to court action does not accrue until the condition is fulfilled, is not considered to oust the court's jurisdiction. This principle was established in relation to arbitration clauses in the well-known English case of *Scott v Avery*[77] and this has since been applied to mediation cases. In the Australian case of *Morrow v chinadotcom*, Barrett J explained that 'mediation clauses must operate as a pre-condition to parties' freedom to litigate rather than a purported denial of that freedom'.[78] In Banabelle's case the court emphasised the characterisation of dispute resolution clauses as a precondition to litigation, not a substitution.[79] Thus in countries such as Australia, England and the US where there are judicial and legislative policies in favour of mediation clauses, these are interpreted as condition precedents to litigation wherever possible.

However this does not mean that mediation clauses will always be interpreted as condition precedents to litigation as the following cases show. In *Halifax Financial Services v Intuitive Systems* the court agreed in principle that mediation clauses could be enforceable provided, *inter alia*, they were drafted as

74 See L Mistelis, 'ADR in England and Wales: A Successful Case of Public Private Partnership' in N Alexander (ed), *Global Trends in Mediation* (2nd ed, Alphen aan den Rijn: Kluwer Law International 2006) 137 at 163. Judicial review of mediated settlements is considered in Chapter 7.

75 In Germany see the decision of the Superior Regional Court (Oberlandesgericht) Rostock 2006 3 U 37/06 of 18.09.2006 at II 1 and the commentaries of H Musielak, *Zivilprozessordnung* (München: C H Beck, 2007) at Vorbemerkungen, Lit 5, Ann 11. In relation to France see Deckert (2008), above note 8 at 196–197.

76 See A Mourre, *ADR – International Application. Special Supplement to the ICC International Court of Arbitration Bulletin* (Paris: ICC Publication N° 640 2001) at 68, referring to Cass civ 2ème, 15.01.1992, N° 90–19097. For a different view see the comments of J Jarrosson in '*L'arbitrage et la Convention Européenne des droits de l'homme*' (1989) 1 *Rev arbitrage* 582: 'To have recourse to ADR is only a renunciation of the right to have a judge but not of the fundamental right of access to justice.'

77 *Scott v Avery* (1856) 5 HLC 811 [10 ER 1121].

78 *Morrow v chinadotcom* [2001] NSWSC 209 (28 March 2001).

79 *New South Wales v Banabelle Electrical Pty Ltd* (2002) 54 NSWLR 503 at para 37.

conditions precedent to the issue of litigation proceedings.[80] However on the facts the clause was held to have failed the test as a matter of construction with the court concluding that none of the provisions in the relevant clause was expressed to be a condition precedent to liability or to the institution of legal proceedings. *Halifax* has been criticised as being outdated and unduly traditional by expecting express and strictly-worded condition precedent language.[81] It was decided prior to the adoption of the English Civil Procedure Rules in 1998, which are supportive of mediation, so that a decision today may take a different course. The Australian case of *Baulderstone Hornibrook Engineering Pty Ltd v Kayah Holdings Pty Limited* provides an example of an MDR clause which was not couched in appropriate terms.[82] The clause was held to be an attempt to oust the jurisdiction of the court as it made the referee's decision final rather than just a condition precedent to commencement of litigation. Moreover the dispute was outside the particular field of expertise of the selected referee.

As familiarity with mediation clauses increases so does the willingness of courts to enforce them. However as indicated above the wording of the clause can be important. In determining enforceability of agreements to mediate, courts will weigh up the competing goals of holding the parties to their bargain, on one hand, and preserving the jurisdiction of the court, on the other.

3.4 Does a Mediation Clause Challenge Inalienable Rights?

In Germany and other civil law jurisdictions the non-ouster issue is discussed under the topic of inalienable rights (*unverzichtbare Rechte*) such as the constitutional guarantee of a right to a fair hearing with an impartial judge in accordance with the rules of natural justice.[83] The question as to whether mediation clauses breach this entrenched constitutional principle has been answered in the negative as they only constitute a temporary waiver of the right to take a matter before court.[84] For example, mediation clauses may specify a time-frame within which mediation may be attempted, such as 45 days, and

80 *Halifax Financial Services Ltd v Intuitive Systems Ltd* [1999] 1 All ER (Comm) 303.

81 See, for example, Mistelis (2006), above note 74 at 163.

82 *Baulderstone Hornibrook Engineering Pty Ltd v Kayah Holdings Pty Limited* (1997) 14 BCL 277 per Heenan J.

83 See, for example, Articles 19(4) and 20 of the German Constitution.

84 See Eidenmüller (2001), above note 13 at 14, H Prütting, 'Anmerkung zu BGH 23.11.1983' (1986) 99 *Zeitschrift für Zivilprozess* 90 at 96–97 critically commenting on a court decision and G Wagner, *Prozessverträge: Privatautonomie im Verfahrensrecht* (Tübingen: Mohr Siebeck 1998). See also the decisions of the German Federal Court (Bundesgerichtshof, BGH) dated November 18, 1998 (VIII ZR 344/97) and the Superior Regional Court of Rostock (Oberlandesgericht Rostock, OLG Rostock) 2006 3 U 37/06 on 18.09.2006 at II referred to in note 41.

before which a claim cannot be filed in court (*dilatorischer Klageverzicht*).[85] Importantly compliance with the mediation procedure by the parties must not make it factually impossible to comply with limitation periods for lodging a claim or other procedural time limits (*prozessualen Ausschlussfristen*),[86] but it is likely that these would be suspended.[87]

3.5 Does the Mediation Clause Survive the Termination of the Agreement?

Where mediation clauses are written into substantive contracts the question may arise as to whether a clause survives termination of the rest of the agreement. Here principles can be drawn from general contract law and the statutory law of arbitration.

Drawing on analogies with arbitration clauses,[88] common law commentators, lawyers and courts contend that the principle of severability in relation to arbitration clauses can be extended to other dispute resolution clauses.[89] In practice this means that mediation clauses are interpreted as separate agreements arising out of the main contract. They are viewed as ancillary to the primary contract and therefore stand on their own, surviving primary contracts that may have been terminated, rescinded, voided or even declared void *ab initio*.[90] As Kirby P put it,

85 See Lenz and Müller (1999), above note 14 at 234.

86 See Eidenmüller (2001), above note 13 at 14 et seq in regard to § 4 of the German Dismissal Protection Act (Kündigungsschutzgesetz) which stipulates a three-week limitation period for dismissal protections suits.

87 See Hess (2009), above note 36 at 1080. See Palandt et al (2009), above note 37 in relation to § 203 BGB (suspension of limitation periods for claims during negotiations) and § 242 BGB (good faith performance) which applies to other time limits by analogy. On litigation limitation periods see Chapter 7.

88 On the severability principle in relation to arbitration clauses see, for example, *Harbour Assurance Co (UK) Ltd v Kansa General International Insurance Co Ltd* [1993] QB 701, *Moschi v Lep Air Services Ltd* [1972] 2 All ER 398, the New Zealand High Court decision of *Yawata Ltd and Anor v Powell* (HC Wellington, AP 142–00, 4 October 2000, Penlington J) and the Australian High Court decision in *QH Tours Ltd and Sazalo Pty Ltd v Ship Design and Management (Aust) Pty Ltd and Gibbons* (1992) 105 ALR 371 at 384.

89 See R Giles, 'Severability of Dispute Resolution Clauses in Contracts' (1994) 10 *Building and Construction Law* 393 and P Mead, 'Enforceability of ADR Clauses' (1997) *The Arbitrator* 34.

90 Interesting legal questions arise in relation to a dispute resolution clause surviving a primary contract which arguably never existed. See the Australian High Court decision *QH Tours Ltd and Sazalo Pty Ltd v Ship Design and Management (Aust) Pty Ltd and Gibbons* (1992) 105 ALR 371 at 384. See also Giles (1994), above note 89 and D Spencer, 'Uncertainty and Incompleteness in Dispute Resolution Clauses' (1995) 2 *Commercial Dispute Resolution Journal* 23.

> the trend of legal authority favours the contention that, depending always upon its terms, an arbitration clause will ordinarily, unless the parties intend otherwise, be treated as separate from the main contract. It is in this way that the arbitration clause will not be affected by a challenge to the main agreement so as to deprive the arbitrator of jurisdiction to uphold that challenge.[91]

Although the issue of severability was not decided in the Australian mediation case of *Elizabeth Bay*,[92] it was accepted as common ground between the parties that although the construction management contract had come to an end in the middle of 1994 the provisions for mediation survived in the same manner as for arbitration. The Supreme Court of France has recognised the autonomy of mediation clauses based on analogies with arbitration clauses and held mediation clauses to be enforceable even if parties attack the validity of the contract.[93]

Similarly German law provides that where a contract is declared void or otherwise unenforceable it does not automatically follow that its mediation clause must meet the same fate;[94] rather the court must look to the parties' intention in relation to the clause's scope and whether it was within the realm of that intention that during mediation they would be able to challenge the validity of their contract without jeopardising the validity of the mediation clause and the mediation itself.[95] Thus mediation clauses and the contracts in which they are contained are not considered unilateral legal transactions (*einheitliches Rechtsgeschäft*) within the terms of § 139 of the German Civil Code. In other words they can be treated as legally separate even where the primary contract is found to be void. To remove any doubt on the issue some dispute resolution clauses specifically refer to the applicability of the clause to disputes relating to 'the existence, validity or termination' of the contract between the parties.[96]

91 See *Ferris and Stap v Plaister and Grey* (1994) 34 NSWLR 474 at 475.

92 See *Elizabeth Bay Developments Pty Ltd v Boral Building Services Pty Ltd* (1995) 36 NSWLR 709 715, referring to *Heyman v Darwins Ltd* [1942] AC 356, *Codelfa Construction Pty Ltd v State Rail Authority of New South Wales* (1982) 149 CLR 337.

93 See Cass civ 1ère, 08.04.2009, N° 08–10866 and Cass civ 2ème, 06.07.2000, N° 98–17827, (2000) *Rev Arbitrage* at 749 (with comments by C Jarrosson). On arbitration clauses see Cass civ 2ème, 04.04.2002, N° 00–18009, and Cass com, 09.04.2002, N° 98–16829: *Bull civ* N° 69.

94 See Palandt et al (2009), above note 37 at § 139 BGB.

95 See the decision of the Superior Regional Court of Rostock (OLG Rostock) 2006 3 U 37/06 on 18.09.2006 at II. The OLG referred to the German Federal Court's (Bundesgerichtshof, BGH) decision of 1998 in which the BGH stated that the principles applicable to arbitration agreements (*Schiedsvereinbarung*) are applicable to mediation clauses. See also Hutner (2003), above note 38 at 2.

96 See, for example, the med–arb clause of the London Court of International Arbitration (LCIA) in Appendix A.

The issue of the severability of clauses and sub-clauses may also arise in relation to MDR clauses where, for example, one dispute resolution phase contained in a sub-clause is unenforceable due to uncertainty. In this situation an extension of the severability argument for dispute resolution clauses would suggest that the sub-clause could be severed from the rest of the MDR clause. However a number of courts has considered severance inappropriate where the resulting clause would no longer accurately reflect the parties' intention in terms of how they envisaged disputes between them to be managed.[97] In the case of *Banabelle*,[98] referred to previously, the contract defined the experts as the persons agreed to between the parties, or the person nominated by the person prescribed in the Annexure. There was nobody prescribed in the Annexure. According to the court this led to uncertainty which infected the entire clause and ultimately resulted in its unenforceability.[99] In its reasoning the court explained that severance of the offending section of the clause, namely the default nomination provision, was inappropriate as the remainder, after severance, did not reflect the parties' intention. In addition the remainder would amount to an agreement to agree which, as discussed below, is not capable of independent operation and is therefore void.

3.6 Is the Dispute in Question Within the Scope of the Dispute Resolution Clause?

Disputes will be subject to mediation clauses where it is clear from the wording of the arrangement that parties intended such disputes to be covered by the clause. Therefore where terms of a clause apply only to disputes arising out of the contract between parties, the clause may not extend to disputes connected with the contract but not directly arising out of it. By way of example in the English case of *Farm Assist* (N° 2) the language of the mediation agreement was to the effect that the parties could not call the mediator as witness in any litigation or arbitration 'in relation to the dispute'.[100] The judge held that this wording, 'in relation to the dispute' referred to the original dispute and was not wide enough to cover a different dispute on the question as to whether duress had been deployed by one of the parties during the mediation.

Conversely courts in jurisdictions with active policies supporting mediation lean towards a generous interpretation of such clauses. For example the court in the Australian case of *Morrow v chinadotcom* adopted a broad

97 See, for example, *Baulderstone Hornibrook Engineering Pty Ltd v Kayah Holdings Pty Ltd* (1997) 14 BCL 277.

98 See *State of New South Wales and Ors v Banabelle Electrical Pty Ltd and Ors* (2002) 54 NSWLR 503 at para 70.

99 The requirement for certainty in mediation clauses is discussed below.

100 See *Farm Assist Limited (in liquidation) v The Secretary of State for the Environment, Food and Rural Affairs* (N° 2) [2009] EWHC 1102 (TCC).

construction of the scope of dispute resolution clauses, quoting Gleeson CJ in the arbitration case, *Francis Travel Marketing Pty Ltd v Virgin Atlantic Airways Ltd*,[101]

> When the parties to a commercial contract agree, at the time of making their contract, and before any disputes have yet arisen, to refer to arbitration any dispute or difference arising out of the agreement, their agreement should not be construed narrowly. They are unlikely to have intended that different disputes should be resolved before different tribunals, or that the appropriate tribunal should be determined by fine shades of difference in the legal character of individual issues, or by the ingenuity of lawyers in developing points of argument.

In this case the principle of broad construction as applied to arbitration clauses was applied to dispute resolution clauses generally, and on the facts of the case the dispute in question was held to be within the scope of the clause. Increasingly mediation clauses are worded broadly so that they include disputes arising out of, or in relation to, the contract.[102]

3.7 Is the Mediation Clause Sufficiently Certain and Complete?

Most jurisdictions have a general contract law requirement relating to certainty and completion. German and Swiss law, for example, states that mediation clause must contain the *essentialia negotii*, the essential elements of an agreement. The *essentialia negotii* arise out of the definition of mediation and the legal nature of mediation as a dispute resolution process.[103] In Switzerland mediation clauses must contain a party agreement that a certain dispute should, with the help of an identified third person (the mediator), be mutually (not authoritatively) settled. If one of the essential elements is missing the mediation clause is not valid due to lack of certainty and completeness. [104] In France the

[101] *Francis Travel Marketing Pty Ltd v Virgin Atlantic Airways Ltd* (1996) 39 NSWLR 160.

[102] See, for example, the mediation and MDR clauses in Appendix A.

[103] See Gabriel (2008), above note 28 at 69. The legal nature of mediation clauses has been considered previously.

[104] In relation to Switzerland see Eiholzer (1998) above note 25 at RN 283 and RN 343 et seq. In relation to Germany see Eidenmüller (2001), above note 13 at 10. Contractual requirements related to certainty and the *essentialia negotii* are found in the general German law of legal acts (Rechtsgeschäfte) to be valid, especially §§ 104 et seq of the German Civil Code and the standards contract terms in §§ 305 et seq of the German Civil Code.

Supreme Court has stated that mediation clauses must be clear, certain in themselves, complete and comprehensive.[105]

The basic common law principle relating to certainty in contract law is that an agreement must possess such a degree of definition and certainty as to enable it to be meaningfully undertaken and enforced. Not only must the contract be certain, it must also be complete. Completeness in contract requires all important parts of the transaction to be included in the contract. In other words there must be consensus on all essential terms.[106] There may be more flexibility with respect to non-essential contract terms. Depending on jurisdiction, non-essential terms that do not meet the legal requirement of certainty may be ignored, severed from the contract or completed by the court with the help of extrinsic evidence going to parties' intentions.

The New Zealand High Court case of *Fletcher Challenge*[107] is a leading authority on this point. Although it does not deal with mediation it provides useful insights for the mediation field. The case concerned negotiations for the acquisition of shares in a gas field and for the long-term supply of gas. There was an exchange of correspondence, a letter signed by the CEO agreeing to the deal, followed by a heads of agreement (HOA). The HOA contained a clause requiring parties to use all reasonable endeavours to complete a full agreement. A full agreement was not reached and the question was whether or not there was an enforceable agreement and, if so, whether it had been breached. The court stated that where a contract shows an intention to be bound the court will give effect to this, provided there is agreement on essential terms. Furthermore a contract is not necessarily incomplete if particular terms are not agreed or remain to be agreed provided the essential terms are clear. Thus parties can intend to be bound by an informal document even if a more formal agreement is contemplated. In this case the court decided that the parties' agreement was not incomplete, stating that certain terms were 'not agreed' or 'to be agreed', however they were not essential or necessary to make the contract workable and the court could supply reasonable terms if necessary.

The following discussion on how courts have applied the requirement of certainty and completeness to mediation clauses draws on a substantial body of case law in common law jurisdictions.

It is generally accepted that both agreements to agree and agreements to negotiate are too vague and uncertain in relation to essential terms to be

105 Cass (ch mixte), 14.2.2003, 00–19423 00–19424, (25.02.2003) *Gazette du Palais* 23 at 37, *Bull. Mixte* N°1 at 1 and a commentary by P Ancel and M Cottin, (2003) *Dalloz* at 1386–1391.

106 See *Vitol BV v Compagnie Europeene des Petroles* [1988] 1 Lloyd's Rep 574 at para 112 where Saville J provided for the manner in which it is to be determined whether an essential or inessential term is affected by uncertainty.

107 See *Fletcher Challenge Energy Ltd v Electrical Corporation of New Zealand Ltd* [2001] 2 NZLR 219 at paras 90 et seq, 106, 110 et seq and 116.

enforceable and such agreements are to be rendered void.[108] A distinction is made between these clauses and mediation clauses, which set out a specific dispute resolution procedure. In line with the reasoning of the Australian case *Hooper Bailie,*[109] the English decision in *Cable and Wireless Plc v IBM United Kingdom Ltd*[110] and the American case of *Lakeland Fire District,*[111] courts in common law jurisdictions are likely to hold mediation clauses capable of sufficient certainty for legal recognition.

The Australian decision of *Hooper Bailie* has been introduced previously in relation to the legal nature of mediation clauses. Here the basis of the alleged agreement to mediate was an exchange of correspondence between the parties which specified the issues to be dealt with by conciliation and the parameters and functions of the conciliation itself. A number of matters had been resolved at conciliation, which had been adjourned to enable the parties to gather further information relating to outstanding issues. Natcon sought to proceed directly to arbitration without reconvening the conciliation. Hooper Bailie sought a stay of arbitral proceedings which the Supreme Court of NSW ordered, thereby giving effect to the agreement to mediate. In his judgment Giles J referred to authorities in the United States, England and Australia and explained the nature of an obligation to mediate as follows,

> Conciliation or mediation is essentially consensual, and the opponents of enforceability contend it is futile to seek to enforce something which requires the co-operation and consent of a party when co-operation and consent can not be enforced; equally, they say that there can be no loss to the other party if for want of co-operation and consent the consensual process would have led to no result. The proponents of enforceability contend that this misconceives the objectives of

108 On the unenforceable nature of agreements to agree and agreements to negotiate, see the English case of *Courtney and Fairbairn Ltd v Tolaini Bros (Hotels) Ltd* [1975] 1 All ER 716 per Lord Denning at 718–720, confirmed by the House of Lords in *Walford v Miles* [1992] 1 All ER 453, the New Zealand case of *Wellington City Council v Body Corporate* 51702 (Wellington) [2002] NZLR 486, the Australian case of *Minister for Main Roads for Tasmania v Leighton Contractors Pty Ltd* (1985) 1 BCL 381, the decision of the Hong Kong Court of Appeal in *Engineering and Construction Co Ltd v Vigour Ltd* [2005] 1 HKC 579, the High Court of Singapore's discussion in *United Artists Singapore Theatres Pte Ltd v Parkway Properties Pte Ltd* [2003] 1 SLR 791 at para 214 and the California Court of Appeal case *Copeland v Baskin Robbins USA* (2002) 96 Cal App 4th 1251. For a different approach in relation to agreements to negotiate, compare the obiter dictum comments of Kirby P in *Coal Cliff Collieries Pty Ltd v Sijehama Pty Ltd* (1991) 24 NSWLR 1 and Lord Wright in *Hillas and Co Limited v Arcos Ltd* (1932) 147 LT 503.

109 *Hooper Bailie Associated Ltd v Natcon Group Pty Ltd* (1992) 28 NSWLR 194, 209.

110 *Cable and Wireless Plc v IBM United Kingdom Ltd* [2002] EWHC 2059 (Comm Ct) at 10.

111 *Lakeland Fire District v East Area General Contractors Inc* 16 AD 3d 417, (Sup Ct NY Appell Div 2005).

> alternative dispute resolution, saying that the most fundamental resistance to compromise can wane and turn to co-operation and consent if the dispute is removed from the adversarial procedures of the courts and exposed to procedures designed to promote compromise, in particular where a skilled conciliator or mediator is interposed between the parties. What is enforced is not co-operation and consent, but participation in a process from which co-operation and consent might come.

Accordingly the court took the view that an agreement to conciliate or mediate was not the same as an agreement to agree; nor was it to be likened to an agreement to negotiate, or to negotiate in good faith. Rather, it was an agreement to participate in a process known as conciliation or mediation which was capable of sufficient certainty for legal recognition.[112] In this case the court considered the contract provided a sufficiently clear structure for the mediation and was therefore enforceable. On this basis an order was granted for a stay of the arbitral proceedings.

Given that mediation clauses are *capable* of sufficient certainty to be enforceable, the question arises as to how mediation clauses should be drafted in order to comply with certainty requirements. Here case law provides useful examples of mistakes to avoid when drafting clauses.

Where mediation clauses are ambiguous in relation to the choice of process they have been held to be void for uncertainty and therefore unenforceable. In France, for example, courts have indicated that they are prepared to go beyond the label of the process and examine the intention of the parties and the role assigned to the third party intervenor.[113] Therefore just because a process is called arbitration does not mean that it is arbitration, especially where the third party's role is facilitative or advisory rather than determinative. Conversely where the role of a third party involves imposing on parties a binding decision, then the clause is likely to be defined as arbitration even if has been given another label such as mediation or conciliation. In one case the Paris Court of Appeal found that a clause in question was so unclear that it was valid neither as a mediation clause nor as an arbitration clause. The Supreme Court upheld the decision on appeal.[114] Similarly in Australia a clause referring parties to 'dispute resolution' was struck out for lack of certainty in

[112] See *Hooper Bailie Associated Ltd v Natcon Group Pty Ltd* (1992) 28 NSWLR 194 at 209.

[113] See the following two Court of Appeal decisions: CA Versailles (Cour d'appel de Versailles), 11.09.1998, N° de RG: 1996–1991 and CA Paris (Cour d'appel de Paris) 21.12.2000.

[114] See the decision of the Cour de Cassation: Cass civ 2ème, 16.06.1993, N° 91–15332. The clause provided for appointment of a judge as mediator to make a decision in relation to a dispute between parties, which decision they undertook to treat as a settlement by compromise.

Morrow v chinadotcom.[115]Adding to the challenges of interpretation, the distinction between dispute resolution processes is not always clear. French courts, for example, have taken the view that 'conciliation followed by settlement is a natural outcome of arbitration'.[116]

In the United States the court in *Ex Parte Mountain Heating and Cooling Inc*[117] refused to give effect to the following dispute resolution clause on the basis of uncertainty. The clause provided that the parties would 'settle the dispute by *arbitration* under the Construction Industry *Mediation* Rules of the American Arbitration Association.'[118] However in other situations where parties have used the term *mediation* in conjunction with terms such as *decision, binding* and *mandatory*, some courts have interpreted the parties' intention as being consistent with an arbitration agreement and enforced the clause as such.[119]

A mere reference to *mediation* in a dispute resolution clause may not meet the requisite standards of certainty and completeness. The Australian case of *Elizabeth Bay* provides a useful example in this regard.[120] Here the relevant clause read as follows,

> ... the parties agree to first endeavour to settle the dispute or difference by mediation administered by the Australian Commercial Disputes Centre (ACDC). [...] Each party confirms that it enters into this mediation with a commitment to attempt in good faith to negotiate towards achieving a settlement of the dispute.

The court held that the clause was insufficiently certain to be enforceable and provided the following reasoning. First, although both parties agreed that ACDC guidelines were incorporated by reference into the mediation clause, the court took the view that more precise wording expressly identifying and incorporating the guidelines was needed. Secondly, assuming the guidelines were incorporated into the agreement, they failed to set out a clear dispute resolution procedure apart from stipulating the presence of the parties and the exchange of an issues

115 See *Morrow v chinadotcom Ltd* [2001] NSWSC 209.

116 See CA Paris, 13.01.1984, (1984) *Rev arbitrage* at 530. See also E Gaillard and J Edelstein, 'Mediation in France' in T Carbonneau and J Jaeggi (eds), *Handbook on International Arbitration and ADR* (New York: JurisNet 2006) 243 at 250.

117 See *Ex Parte Mountain Heating and Cooling Inc* 867 So 2d 1112 (Ala 2003).

118 See *Ex Parte Mountain Heating and Cooling Inc* (2003), above note 117 at 1116.

119 See, for example, *High Valley Homes Inc v Fudge* N° 03–01–00726–CV, 2003 WL 1882261 (Tex App Apr 17 2003). However in other cases courts have taken the view that 'binding mediation' is not the same as arbitration and have refused to recognise the clause and stay legal proceedings pending arbitration: see *Oliver Design Group v Westside Deutscher Frauen-Verein* N° 81120, 2002 WL 31839158 (Ohio app Dec 19, 2002).

120 See *Elizabeth Bay Developments Pty Ltd v Boral Building Services Pty Ltd* (1995) 36 NSWLR 709.

statement between them. Given the flexibility and ensuing diversity of the mediation process, a mere reference to mediation in a dispute resolution clause does not provide sufficient clarity about the nature of the process into which the parties are contracting. Accordingly the agreement of the parties fell down for lack of certainty about the process to be followed. Finally the court commented that even if the guidelines were read as incorporating the agreement issued by the ACDC, the commitment to attempt in good faith to negotiate clause was too uncertain to be enforceable.

In relation to the use of good faith language in mediation clauses there has in the past been reluctance by courts in some jurisdictions such as England and Australia to recognise the validity of clauses incorporating terms such as *good faith.*[121] Conversely in jurisdictions such as Germany and France good faith obligations have long been implied into contractual arrangements. In recent years the hesitation surrounding good faith contractual obligations seems to be on the decline with courts increasingly recognising that good faith can provide a valuable mechanism for encouraging and evaluating participation in the mediation process.[122] The decision of *Aiton Australia Pty Ltd v Transfield Pty Ltd* is a case in point.[123] Here the court considered whether or not a commercial contract containing an obligation to negotiate in good faith complied with the certainty requirement:

> It is clear that a tension may exist between negotiation from a position of self-interest and the maintenance of good faith in attempting to settle disputes. However, maintenance of good faith in a negotiating process is not inconsistent with having regard to self-interest.[124]

While the clause did not fall short because of its good faith requirement, it was found to be incomplete for other reasons, namely for failing to identify a process for selecting a mediator and determining the mediator's remuneration and how the mediation costs were to be apportioned.

Thus courts have sometimes required strict adherence to contractual certainty principles. This approach has been criticised on the basis that it might encourage an overly detailed and legalistic specification of process in mediation clauses and that this might have a negative and prescriptive flow-on effect for conduct of the mediation itself.[125] However as courts in Australia, England and the United States have become more familiar with the standard features of mediation clauses, there have been indications that they may take a less

[121] The duty to participate in mediation in good faith is explored in Chapter 5.

[122] See generally K Kovach, 'Good Faith in Mediation – Requested, Recommended, or Required? A New Ethic' (1997) *South Texas Law Review* 575.

[123] See *Aiton Australia Pty Ltd v Transfield* [1999] NSWSC 996.

[124] See *Aiton Australia Pty Ltd v Transfield* [1999] NSWSC 996 at para 83.

[125] See *Aiton Australia Pty Ltd v Transfield* [1999] NSWSC 996.

formalistic approach and support contracting parties' intentions to mediate future disputes between them, provided the parties' intentions are sufficiently clear.[126]

An example of a more flexible approach to the issue of certainty is provided by the case *Computershare*[127] in which the Supreme Court of Victoria held that a clear framework within which parties were to negotiate in good faith and specified items upon which they were to negotiate such as choice of process, costs and venue provided a dispute resolution clause with sufficient specificity and certainty for it to be considered enforceable. Warren J added,

> where the parties have made a special agreement requiring them to address a path to a potential solution there is every reason for a Court to say such parties should be required to endeavour in good faith to achieve it. In these circumstances the Court does not need to see a set of rules laid out in advance by which the agreement, if any, between the parties may in fact be achieved.[128]

Recent English cases have emphasised the role of public policy in the recognition and enforcement of dispute resolution clauses. In *Cable and Wireless Plc v IBM United Kingdom Ltd*[129] Colman J stated,

> For the courts now to decline to enforce contractual references to ADR on the grounds of intrinsic uncertainty would be to fly in the face of public policy as expressed in the CPR [Civil Procedure Rules] and as reflected in the judgement of the Court of Appeal in *Dunnett v Railtrack Plc.*[130]

Contemporary approaches to dealing with certainty in mediation clauses have developed in a manner consistent with principles enunciated in *Fletcher Challenge* case discussed above. However the interpretation of potentially ambiguous dispute resolution clauses will inevitably depend on the circumstances of the case, the clarity of the parties' intention and relevant policy factors such as the encouragement out of court settlement and reduction of court case loads.

[126] In England see, for example, *Channel Tunnel Group Ltd v Balfour Beatty Construction Ltd* [1993] AC 334, in Australia see *Computershare Pty v Perpetual Registrars Ltd* [2002] VSC 212, in the United States see *High Valley Homes Inc v Fudge* N° 03–01–00726–CV, 2003 WL 1882261 (Tex App Apr 17 2003) and *HIM Portland LLC v Devito Brothers Inc* 317 F 3d 41 (1st Cir 2003). See also the comments of the Superior Court (OLG) Rostock 2006, Leitsatz 2.

[127] *Computershare Limited v Perpetual Registrars Ltd and Ors* N° 2 [2000] VSC 233.

[128] *Computershare Limited v Perpetual Registrars Ltd and Ors* N° 2 [2000] VSC 233 at para 7.

[129] *Cable and Wireless Plc v IBM United Kingdom Ltd* [2002] EWHC 2059 (Comm Ct) at 10.

[130] See *Dunnett v Railtrack* [2002] All ER (D) 314 (Feb).

3.8 Public Policy Considerations

While parties are generally free to agree on how they will resolve their disputes, numerous jurisdictions have legal policies restricting this contractual freedom in circumstances involving potential power imbalance and unconscionability. In the United States it has been said that one of the most common grounds for denying enforcement is unconscionability.[131] In the American case of *Garret v Hooters-Toledo*[132] the mediation clause in question required an employee to request mediation within ten days of a claim arising or else forfeit the claim and it stipulated that mediation was to be held in a city other than that in which the employee worked. Perhaps unsurprisingly the clause was held to be unconscionable, the court adopting the view that the clause's terms imposed 'burdens and barriers that would routinely defer former employees from vindicating their rights.'[133] In another example farm-debt mediation schemes effectively permit the farmer to elect mediation as the preferred dispute resolution process irrespective of the bank's or other creditor's attitude on the matter.[134]

Consumer disputes are often subject to specific forms of regulation. It is not uncommon in industry dispute resolution schemes with standard dispute resolution clauses for the industry party to be bound by an outcome, while the consumer party is granted a cooling-off period within which it can change its mind.[135]

In Germany the principle of party autonomy underpins the Civil Code but is limited by provisions of the Constitution and other laws designed to protect the individual and general public.[136] Friedrich discusses the extent to which §§ 305 to 310 of the German Civil Code[137] apply to mediation clauses in standard contract terms.[138] These provisions impose additional form and content

131 See L Katz, 'Getting to the Table, Kicking and Screaming: Drafting an Enforceable Mediation Provision' (2008) 26 *Alternatives* 183 at 185.

132 See *Garret v Hooters-Toledo* 295 F Supp 2d 774 (ND Ohio 2003). J Ralph, 'Unconscionable Mediation Clauses: *Garrett v Hooters-Toledo*' (2005) 10 *Harvard Negotiation Law Rev*iew 383.

133 See *Garret v Hooters-Toledo,* above note 132 at 783.

134 See ss 9, 9A and 10 of the Farm-Debt Mediation Act 1994 (NSW).

135 See, for example, the Financial Ombudsman Service – Banking and Finance, Terms of Reference 7.6–7.12 (July 2008). Where the consumer accepts the recommendation of the ombudsman within one month of it being made and the financial services provider does not, then the ombudsman can make a determinative finding against the financial services provider.

136 See Hess (2009), above note 36 at 1063. Eidenmüller (2001), above note 13 at 10.

137 See Palandt et al (2009), above note 37 at §§ 305 BGB et seq.

138 See F Friedrich, 'Schlichtungs- und Mediationsklauseln in Allgemeinen Geschäftsbedingungen' (2007) *Zeitschrift für Schiedsverfahren* 1 at 31 et seq.

requirements on clauses in consumer contracts to prevent discrimination against consumers. The author examines whether an interim waiver of action (*dilatorischer Klageverzicht*) pending fulfilment of a mediation clause can amount to an inappropriate discrimination according to § 307(1) of the German Civil Code[139] and the EC Unfair Contract Terms Directive.[140] Friedrich concludes that consumer friendly clauses which do not wish to fall foul of consumer protection legislation should offer mediation cost free for consumers and provide a three-month-time period within which the process can be concluded.[141]

In addition mediation clauses in standard contracts are subject to judicial content control (*richterliche Inhaltskontrolle*) under German law.[142] Courts will strike down clauses found to be unreasonably discriminatory against consumers (*unangemessene Benachteiligung*) in accordance with § 307 of the German Civil Code. Generally speaking the mediation process referred to in the clause must fulfil the requirements of fairness (*Fairnessanforderungen*)[143] in order to be considered non-discriminatory.

Finally mediation clauses in standard contracts must not be *unexpected* pursuant to § 305c of the German Civil Code.[144] A mediation clause is unexpected if it is unusual (objective test) and takes a consumer by surprise (subjective test).[145] Commentators suggest a link between the increasing use of, and therefore familiarity with, mediation clauses on one hand and the decreasing likelihood of such clauses being classified as unexpected on the other.[146]

3.9 Drafting Guidelines

Based on the previous examination of the recognition and legal validity of mediation clauses, the following points may be of use to those drafting clauses or searching for suitable precedents:

139 See BGB see Palandt et al (2009), above note 37 at § 307.

140 See the EC Unfair Contract Terms Directive 93/13/EEC OJ L95, 21 April 1993, 29–34 and 3(1), (3), N° 1q of the appendix. This instrument protects consumers against standard contract clauses interfering with consumers' legal rights and remedies before a court of law.

141 Friedrich suggests that mediation could be conducted in accordance with § 15a(1)(3) of the Introductory Law of the German Code of Civil Procedure (Gesetz betreffend die Einführung der Zivilprozessordnung, EGZPO). This law provides the legal framework for mediation of certain Magistrates' Court matters at no cost to litigants.

142 Richterliche Inhaltskontrolle. See Hess (2009), above note 36 at 1063 et seq.

143 See Hess (2009), above note 36 at 1063.

144 See Palandt et al (2009), above note 37 at § 305c BGB.

145 See Hess (2009), above note 36 at 1063.

146 See, for example, Hess (2009), above note 36 at 1063, referring to the increasing acceptance of mediation as a dispute resolution tool in Europe.

1. Mediation clauses must provide for mediation as a condition precedent to litigation, that is the clause must be in *Scott v Avery* form.
2. Mediation clauses must be certain and complete. This means clauses should specify procedures to initiate, establish, administer and conduct the mediation or MDR process including: [147]

   - Triggering mechanism: how and when (notice period) the mediation process is initiated.
   - Scope of mediation: the disputes to be covered by mediation.
   - Applicable procedural and substantive law.
   - Place of mediation and venue or method for selection thereof.
   - Language of the mediation.
   - Method for selection of mediator/s.
   - Method for selection of other participants in mediation such as representatives and experts.
   - Method for determination of costs, fees and other charges, and how and by whom they will be paid.
   - Description of mediation procedure.

3. Where parties agree to reach consensus on the matters identified in item 2 above, to create certainty there should be a fall-back arrangement in the event that they cannot agree.
4. Where clauses intend to incorporate mediation procedures, codes of conduct and standards from a recognised service-provider, language must be used which clearly incorporates the relevant instruments as amended from time to time.
5. Where institutional mediation rules are incorporated into a mediation clause (item 4), these should be tested against the requirements listed in items 2 and 3.

3.10 Waiver and Remedies

Where a party falls short of complying with a mediation clause the question of legal remedies may arise. Potential legal remedies are discussed in this section, namely specific performance, stay of proceedings, damages and fee and costs sanctions. The related issue of waiver introduces the topic.

3.10.1 Waiver

There may be situations where disputing parties who have signed a mediation or MDR clause wish to bypass mediation and go directly to court or arbitration.

[147] See also the checklist for agreements to mediate below.

This may occur, for example, where neither party considers mediation suitable for the particular dispute because they are seeking a precedent or benchmark to inform similar negotiations in the future. Alternatively the relationship between parties may be so acrimonious and one party so reluctant to engage in mediation that both may elect to proceed to court. In these circumstances disputing parties may agree to waive compliance with a mediation clause and once a clause has been waived it can no longer be enforced. While there are no formal requirements for waiver, it is sound practice to record it in writing should the issue later arise as to whether or not there was a waiver of the clause.

The issue of waiver in relation to mediation clauses has arisen in a number of French cases. The commercial chamber of the Supreme Court has addressed the question as to whether disputing parties can impliedly waive a mediation clause by engaging directly in litigation. The court held that parties may waive clauses by conduct provided the conduct is clear and mere failure to implement a clause is not sufficient. In the case before the court the mere fact of engaging directly in litigation did not deprive a party of its contractual right to invoke conciliation.[148] However in another case the court held that parties must act in good faith when asserting breach of a mediation clause and that a party whose procedural actions are inconsistent with an intention to make use of a mediation clause may be said to have waived the benefit of the clause and may therefore be prevented from raising its breach as an objection to legal proceedings.[149]

3.10.2 Specific Performance

Specific performance is an equitable remedy for breach of contract where the court orders a defaulting party to comply strictly with their agreed obligations.[150] Specific performance is a discretionary judicial remedy and it is traditionally available when damages are inadequate or inappropriate.[151] Specific performance has been used in disputes relating to land, as real property can be seen as unique, and also extends to personal chattels, irreplaceable artworks and intellectual property. As an illustration, the New South Wales Supreme Court has ordered specific performance for a contract for the purchase of a

148 Cass com, 28.11.1995, (1996) *Rev arbitrage* at 613 with comments by Jarrosson.

149 See Cass com, 08.06.1999, N° 96-18108, [1999] *RJDA* 1031 where the party initially participated in litigation proceedings – for example, by requesting modifications to the terms of reference of receiver in winding-up proceedings – without reference to, or attempted compliance with, the mediation clause.

150 See M Whincup, *Contract Law and Practice* (5th ed, The Hague: Kluwer Law International 2002) at 373.

151 However in the United States specific performance may be ordered whenever it is commercially equitable: see the Uniform Commercial Code 2–709, 2–716.

racehorse.[152] Specific performance may be inappropriate where parties come to the court with unclean hands or where an order of specific performance would be futile, for example where the courts would not be able to supervise and enforce the ordered performance of obligations.

Despite some instances of American courts granting orders of specific performance in relation to mediation clauses,[153] courts generally have been reluctant to grant such orders, taking the view that supervision is not possible and that in many cases it would be an exercise in futility, or a 'vain order' as suggested by early American cases referred to previously.[154] An Australian court, for example, has stated,[155]

> Equity will not order specific performance of a dispute resolution clause, notwithstanding that it may satisfy the legal requirements necessary for the court to determine that the clause is enforceable. This is because supervision of performance pursuant to the clause would be untenable.

It is difficult to see why courts would refuse in principle to make orders for specific performance of mediation obligations when, as indicated earlier, they are increasingly prepared to refer cases to mediation, even against the wishes of both parties. Moreover, as will be discussed in the next chapter, the behaviour of participants in mediation may be brought to the attention of courts in relation to costs awards.[156] These trends suggest a possible softening of courts' negative attitude towards specific performance as a remedy for non-compliance with mediation clauses.

3.10.3 Stay of Proceedings and Inadmissibility of Claim

Where a party commences legal proceedings and the other side does not waive its right to enforce a mediation clause, then the party wishing to rely on the clause may make an application to the court in which proceedings have been filed, seeking a stay of proceedings. A stay is a discretionary order of the court. In determining whether or not to grant a stay a court may take into account the validity and enforceability of the mediation clause, the practical effect of an

152 See *Borg v Howlett* (SCNSW, Young J, 24 May 1996, unreported).

153 See, for example, *Fisher v GE Medical Systems* 276 F Sup 2d 891 at 896 (MD Tenn 2003) and *Cabellero v Wikse* N° 27995, 2004 WL 858710 (Idaho 2004).

154 See above note 7 in relation to the 'vain order' reference.

155 See *State of New South Wales and 3 Ors v Banabelle Electrical Pty Limited* [2002] NSWSC 178 at para 29. See also *Hooper Bailie Associated Ltd v Natcon Group Pty Ltd* (1992) 28 NSWLR 194 at 210.

156 See also the comments of German commentator Eidenmüller who suggests that specific performance should be an available remedy. Eidenmüller (2001), above note 13 at 23.

order to stay proceedings and whether an abuse of process would occur without the order.

In light of courts' general reluctance to issue orders of specific performance, stays of proceedings have become preferred remedies for courts as a way of indirectly enforcing mediation clauses and agreements. In New Zealand, for example, a court has inherent powers to stay its own proceedings to prevent abuse of its process or where proceedings should not be allowed to continue on grounds that there is no reasonable cause of action or they are vexatious.[157] The onus is on the defendant to establish grounds for a stay. Under the English Civil Procedure Rules courts have a general discretion to stay proceedings[158] and a specific power to stay for purposes of dispute resolution where one party requests it or the court deems it appropriate.[159] In an interesting development, the growth of court mediation referral policies has encouraged the indirect enforcement of mediation clauses through stays of proceedings, even where mediation clauses are not valid. Thus where mediation clauses are found to be unenforceable, courts in some jurisdictions may still send the matter to mediation by virtue of their referral powers.

Where there is *prima facie* evidence of a consensual agreement to engage in mediation as a pre-condition to court proceedings, then in the absence of overriding considerations of public interest or private harm the stay will likely be granted. In the case of *Banabelle,* cited above,[160] the court in refusing specific performance of a mediation clause stayed its own proceedings and explained that,

> [t]he court may, however, effectively achieve enforcement of the clause by default, by ordering that proceedings commenced in respect of a dispute subject to the clause be stayed or adjourned until such time as the process referred to in the clause is completed.

While US courts regularly issue stays of proceedings to indirectly compel compliance with mediation clauses,[161] commentators refer to instances where courts have dismissed claims 'with and without prejudice'.[162] Without prejudice

157 See, for example, New Zealand High Court Rules r 477 and *Braid Motors Ltd v Scott* (2001) 15 PRNZ 508.

158 Civil Procedure Rules r 3.1(2)(f). See also Supreme Court Act (1981) s 49(3).

159 Civil Procedure Rules r 26.4.

160 *New South Wales v Banabelle Electrical Pty Ltd* [2002] NSWSC 178.

161 See, for example, *Brown v Terminix International Co* 2006 WL 181678 (SD Ala 2006).

162 See Coben and Thompson (2006), above note 18 at 109 referring to *Gray and Assocs, LLC v Ernst and Young LLP* N° 24–C–02–002963, 2003 WL 23497702 (Md Cir Ct June 11, 2003) where the court dismissed a complaint and ordered compliance with mediation–arbitration provisions of the parties' contract and also referring to *Jones v Trawick* N° 98–6352, 1999 WL 273969 (10th Cir May 5, 1999). In relation to

dismissals would appear to be similar to temporary inadmissibility as discussed below. This is similar to a stay of proceedings, but the legal claim is dismissed rather than suspended with the result that parties must file claims anew should mediation not result in full settlement of the dispute.

German courts will likely enforce dispute resolution clauses by an 'implied temporary waiver of action'.[163] As indicated previously the German Federal Court has taken the view that parties to a mediation clause temporarily waive their rights to commence actions pending mediation.[164] Commentators suggest that courts may also rely on §§ 133 and 157 of the German Civil Code,[165] which deal with intention of parties and interpretation of contracts, to achieve the same result. Here the parties' intention as interpreted from the mediation clause is to give mediation every chance of success before litigating. Thus any attempt to initiate prior or parallel litigation proceedings would be counterproductive and arguably not within the intended scope of the clause.[166]

Importantly German courts will only reject actions if a party relies on the mediation clause and raises an objection prior to the beginning of the hearing on the substance of the dispute.[167] Furthermore parties requesting the courts to dismiss an action, albeit temporarily, must come to the court in good faith. By way of example, where one party initiates legal proceedings on the basis that the other had communicated an intention not to comply with a mediation clause, the latter party cannot object to the action on the basis of non-compliance with the

without prejudice dismissal of a case the authors refer to *Mortimer v First Mount Vernon Indus. Loan Assoc* N° Civ AMD 03–1051, 2003 WL 23305155 (D Md May 19, 2003).

163 See H Eidenmüller, 'A Legal Framework for National and International Mediation Proceedings' (2002) *International Dispute Resolution Beilage* 14 at 16 and Eidenmüller (2001), above note 13 at 21 and 28–29.

164 See the decision of the Superior Regional Court of Rostock (Oberlandesgericht) Rostock 3 U 37/06 18.09.2006 at II 5 and the German Federal Court (Bundesgerichtshof) dated 18 November 1998 (VIII ZR 344/97), referred to above in notes 40 and 41 See also the decision of the Bundesgerichtshof dated 23 November 1983 (VIII ZR 197/82) reproduced in *Neue Juristische Wochenzeitschrift* 1984, 669 and the Magistrates Court (Amtsgericht, AG) Köpenick dated 27 August 2002 (16 C 43/02) reproduced in *Neue Zeitschrift für Miet-und Wohnungsrecht* 2004, 307.

165 See Palandt et al (2009), above note 37 at § 133 and § 157 German Civil Code (Bürgerliches Gesetzbuch, BGB).

166 See Eidenmüller (2001), above note 13 at 13, Eiholzer (1998) above note 25 at para 178 and Alexander, Ade and Olbrisch (2005), above note 34 at 136.

167 The German Federal Court held that by virtue of an analogy to § 1032(1) of the German Code of Civil Procedure the objection must be raised prior to the beginning of hearing on the substance of the dispute. § 1032 of the German Code of Civil Procedure deals with objections to legal proceedings based on non-compliance with arbitration agreements.

mediation clause.[168] Applications for interim relief[169] and certain pre-trial procedures[170] are not affected by a temporary waiver of the right to file a claim, subject to any contrary contractual provision.

In France there have been conflicting decisions on the issue of admissibility of litigation proceedings where there had been a breach of a mediation clause. In one case the first chamber of the Supreme Court held that non-compliance with mediation clauses rendered the initiation of court proceeding inadmissible unless the conciliation attempt was clearly destined to fail – an approach which would involve making a preliminary evaluation of the likely mediation outcome.[171] Subsequently the second chamber of the same court upheld a decision of the Paris Court of Appeal to the effect that non-compliance with a mediation clause could not render a court action inadmissible and that inadmissibility of legal proceedings was not a suitable sanction for breach of mediation clauses.[172] Yet other decisions have supported the first chamber's jurisprudence to the effect that legal actions brought in breach of mediation clauses are inadmissible.[173] As noted previously the Commercial Court has indicated that a party's behaviour and lack of good faith may affect their ability to assert breach of a mediation clause as an objection to the initiation of legal proceedings.[174]

In 2003 the mixed chamber (*chambre mixte*) of the French Supreme Court considered the previous authorities and in a significant judgment held that legal proceedings initiated in a manner inconsistent with a mediation clause are temporarily inadmissible (*non recevable*).[175] Deckert suggests that although this judgment established clarity on the availability of the remedy of inadmissibility, it remains unclear from the judgment whether a court could declare an action to

[168] See the decisions of the Regional Appeal Court Köln, dated 29.10.2002, N° 89 0 46/02, *Baurecht Zeitschrift* (2002) 1120.

[169] See Risse and Wagner (2009), above note 13 at 571. Also see F Friedrich, 'Regelungsgegenstände der Mediationsvereinbarung' (2004) *Monatsschrift fuer Deutsches Recht* 481 at 484.

[170] See § 485 of the German Code of Civil Procedure (Zivilprozessordnung, ZPO).

[171] See Cass civ 1ère, 04.01.1961 Bull civ N° 6 at 4–5. See also the findings of the Conseil d'Etat, 09.12.1991 N° 84308, Snoy, (1991) *Recueil Lebon* at 423 referred to in Gaillard and Edelstein (2006), above note 116 at 248.

[172] See Cass civ 2ème, 01.15.1992, 90–19097, (1992) *Rev arbitrage* at 646 with comments by Cohen.

[173] See, for example, Cass civ 2ème, 06.07.2000, N° 98–17827, (2001) *Rev arbitrage* 749 et seq.

[174] See Cass com, 08.06.1999, N° 96-18108 cited in above note 149.

[175] See Cass (ch mixte) 14.02.2003 N° 00–19423 00–19424, *Gazette du Palais* 23, 25.02.2003, 37. See also X Lagarde, 'Esquisse d'un regime juridique des clauses de conciliation' (2003) *Recueil des cours de l'Academie de Droit international* 189 at 194 and P Drouault-Gardrat and M Barbier, 'Mediation in France' (2007) available at www.twobirds.com/English/NEWS/ARTICLES/Pages/Mediation_in_France.aspx.

be temporarily inadmissible if neither party asserted breach of the mediation clause. According to Article 125(1) C pr civ, the court itself is not obliged to assess the procedural validity of claims before it hears a case, although it must react to applications by the parties in this regard.[176] The question remains, however, whether judges of their own volition may raise the issue of breach of a mediation clause in order to declare proceedings temporarily inadmissible, academic opinion being divided on the point.[177] Finally, as in other jurisdictions, the right of one party to apply for an interim injunction (*mesure provisoire*) remains, despite the existence of a mediation clause.[178]

Thus in Germany and France courts may reject the initiation of legal proceedings as *temporarily inadmissible* where made in breach of the terms of mediation clauses. German commentator Friedrich is critical of this approach and suggests that courts should order stays of the proceedings, in line with common law practices, rather than reject the action as temporarily inadmissible.[179] The latter approach requires litigants to file a completely new claim if mediation does not result in agreement and resolution of the claim, whereas the former merely involves suspension of the claim. He argues that a stay of proceedings is efficient in terms of time and costs[180] and could be achieved in Germany by an application of § 278V and § 251[181] of the German Code of Civil Procedure.[182]

As indicated previously the Austrian situation is different due to the broad interpretation of the notion of voluntariness and the understanding of

176 See Cadiet (2003), above note 8 at 182 and Ancel and Cottin (2003) in their commentary on the judgement in Cass (ch mixte) 14.02.2003, (2003) *D* 1386.

177 Deckert (2008), above note 8 at 198–199 refers to the conflicting academic opinions commenting on the judgment of the Supreme Court including Cadiet (2003), above note 8 at 188–189, who takes an affirmative view on the issue and Ancel and Cottin who adopt a negative view that judges cannot themselves raise the breach of a mediation clause as a ground to reject an action as temporarily inadmissible: see their commentary on the judgement in Cass (ch mixte) 14.02.2003, referred to above in note 175 at 1389–1390.

178 See Cass (ch mixte) 14.02.2003 N° 00-19423 00-19424 and the comments of Cadiet (2003), above note 8 at 186–187 and Ancel and Cottin (2003), above note 105.

179 See Friedrich (2003), above note 64 at 185.

180 See Friedrich (2003), above note 64 at 185.

181 § 278V of the German Civil Code (Bürgerliches Gesetzbuch, BGB) provides, *inter alia*, that courts may refer parties to mediation, conciliation and alternative dispute resolution generally. If the parties agree to this then § 251 of the German Civil Code applies. § 251 of the Code grants courts the power to rest proceedings upon application of the parties in circumstances where the outcome of mediation or similar processes would make this appropriate.

182 See Friedrich (2003), above note 64 at 185.

mediation as a process independent of the court system.[183] The Austrian Supreme Court reinforced the breadth of the principle of voluntariness, concluding that mediation cannot be initiated and conducted contrary to the will of one of the parties.[184] Thus even though mediation clauses are recognised by law, if one party, in breach of a clause, no longer wishes to participate in the process then there is no obstruction on their issuing proceedings. [185] Roth and Gherdene suggest that an alternative way to achieve a stay of court proceedings pending mediation is where the parties have consented to an interim waiver of action agreement.[186] This type of procedural agreement is recognised by Austrian law and could be signed at the same time as an agreement to mediate. Further, Austrian law does not permit enforcement of mediation clauses and the parties' obligations therein through the remedies of specific performance (*Erfüllungsklage*) or interlocutory injunction (*einstweilige Verfügung*).[187]

Finally in a cross-border arbitration case the European Court of Justice (ECJ) has issued a judgment which may have implications for remedies in relation to international mediation clauses. In *Allianz SpA v West Tankers Inc* [188] the ECJ ruled that the Brussels I Regulation relating to jurisdiction in civil and commercial matters[189] did *not* permit the court of one member state to make an order restraining a person from initiating legal proceedings in another member state on the basis of non-compliance with an arbitration agreement. The ECJ reasoned that the ability of a court in one EU jurisdiction to prevent the court of another from determining the applicability of Brussels I in its own jurisdiction would undermine trust among member states' legal systems upon which Brussels I is based. Thus the court concluded that Brussels I does not authorise the jurisdiction of a court of one member state to be reviewed by a court in another. This reasoning could be extended to mediation clauses with the

183 See Roth and Gherdane (2008), above note 22 at 110 et seq. See also S Ferz and E Filler, *Mediation – Gesetzestexte und Kommentar* (Wien: Universitätsverlag 2003) at 26 et seq and Pitkowitz (2005), above note 21 at 83.

184 See the decision of the Austrian Supreme Court (Oberster Gerichtshof, OGH) dated 15 July 1997 Ob 161/97a and the Austrian Law on Mediation in Civil Cases 2001 (Zivilrechts-Mediations-Gesetz, ZivMediatG) especially §§ 1(1), 16(2) and 17(1).

185 In technical terms the *vorübergehendes Prozesshindernis* (temporary impediment to an action doctrine) will not avail them.

186 On the term *interim waiver of action agreement* (*dilatorischer Klageverzicht*) see F Friedrich, 'Schlichtungs- und Mediationsklauseln in Allgemeinen Geschaeftsbedingungen' (2007) 1 *Zeitschrift für Schiedsverfahren* 31 at 34 et seq. See also Wagner (1998), above note 84 at 424 et seq.

187 See Roth and Gherdane (2008), above note 22 at 127–128. A Likar and K Kromer, 'Mediation und Recht: Das Recht in der Mediation' (2005) *Österreichisches Anwaltsblatt* 60 at 66.

188 See *Allianz SpA v West Tankers Inc* (Case C-185/07) [2009] WLR (D) 44.

189 See Council Regulation (EC) N° 44/2001 of 22 December 2000 on Jurisdiction and the Recognition and Enforcement of Judgments in Civil and Commercial Matters.

conceivable result that forum shopping would be encouraged among parties seeking to avoid their operation.

3.10.4 Damages

Another possible remedy for breach of mediation clauses is damages. Contractual damages are usually compensatory in nature and aim to put plaintiffs in the position in which they would have been had there been compliance with the clause.[190] In Germany, for example, compensatory damages (*Schadenseersatz bei Pflichtverletzung*) are assessed pursuant to the general paragraphs of the Civil Code which include damages due to delay in performance (*Verzug*), impossibility of performance (*Unmöglichkeit*) and breach of duty (*positive Forderungsverletzung*).

In relation to mediation clauses violation of a duty to participate in the process can theoretically lead to damages claims.[191] However in a practical sense a party is unlikely to succeed with such a claim because the duty to participate does not contain an obligation on parties in the mediation to settle the claim, and even if there was it would be impossible to foresee the nature or terms of settlement.[192] Therefore a claim for damages seems to be limited to recovery of expenditure incurred where the other party refused to participate in mediation, which in most cases is minimal or difficult to measure.[193] Alternatively nominal damages may be appropriate.[194]

A potential approach to this situation is the inclusion of a provision for liquidated damages in the event of breach.[195] Importantly the amount of

190 See *Robinson v Harman* [1848] 1 Exch Rep 850.

191 See H Prütting, 'Haftung' in F Haft and K von Schlieffen (eds), *Handbuch Mediation* (2nd ed, München: C H Beck 2009) 1135 at 1137. Eidenmüller (2001), above note 13 at 21 et seq. On the duty to participate see Chapter 5.

192 See Eidenmüller (2001), above note 13 at 22 and Alexander, Ade and Olbrisch (2005), above note 34 at 134 et seq.

193 See Prütting (2009), above note 191 at 1137 and Eiholzer (1998), above note 25 at RN 577 et seq. In Germany this category of damages is referred to as frustrated expenditure (*frustrierte Aufwendungen*). In France see Cadiet (2003), above note 8 at 183, X Lagarde, 'Droit processuel et modes alternatifs de règlement des litiges' (2001) *Rev arbitrage* 423 at 441 and the decision of the Cassation Court of the canton of Zurich (Kassationsgericht Zürich) 15 March 1999, published in *Zürcherische Rechtsprechung* 99 (2000) N° 29. In the United States see Katz (2008), above note 131.

194 See, for example, the English decision *Sunrock Aircraft Corporation v Scandinavian Airlines System Denmark-Norway-Sweden* [2007] EWHC Civ 882. Nominal damages were also awarded in the Australian case *Coal Cliff Collieries Pty Ltd v Sijehama Pty Ltd* (1991) 24 NSWLR 1.

195 See also Voser who suggests penalty clauses for non-compliance with dispute resolution clauses: Voser (2002), above note 26 at 5.

liquidated damages must be proportionate to the breach. In other words there must be a genuine pre-estimate of damage – a figure difficult to assess. Disproportionate liquidated damages clauses could amount to an unenforceable penalty and in such cases courts would be able to award nominal damages only.[196]

3.10.5 Costs and Fee Sanctions

Another remedy for breach of mediation clauses may be refusal to award lawyer's fees to the party prevailing in arbitration or litigation.[197] This type of sanction can operate in jurisdictions where costs and fees generally follow the case. Fees can also be part of dispute resolution contract provisions, such as those in California's standard form real estate agreement which provides that parties will mediate any dispute before beginning arbitration or litigation, and bars recovery of lawyer fees by anyone who refuses to participate in mediation. In *Frei v Davey*[198] the court enforced the standard mediation clause and denied a request for lawyer's fees, emphasising the value of mediation and rejecting an argument that lawyers' settlement efforts had fulfilled the same function.

4. AGREEMENTS TO MEDIATE

From a legal perspective agreements to mediate are arguably the most fundamental legal instruments in the practice of mediation, although many of the provisions originally found in these agreements are increasingly incorporated in legislation. Agreements to mediate establish the parameters of a mediator's authority and parties can vary or withdraw this authority at any time.

Whereas the primary purpose of mediation clauses is to trigger mediation in the event of disputes between parties, agreements to mediate aim to clarify the relationship between parties and mediators, as well as their respective rights and obligations *vis-à-vis* one another.[199] They build the foundations for the principles and parameters governing the mediation process and the

[196] See, for example, § 343 of the German Civil Code (BGB) to the effect that excessively high penalty damages may be reduced by the court. See also *Coal Cliff Collieries Pty Ltd v Sijehama Pty Ltd* (1991) 24 NSWLR 1, above note 194.

[197] See, for example, the following US cases: *Peoples Mortgage Corp v Kansas Bankers Surety Co* 62 Fed Appx 232, 2003 WL 1558588 (10th Cir 2003), and *Finderne Heights Condominium Ass'n Inc. v Rabinowitz* 390 NJ Super 154, 915 A 2d 16 (NJ App Div 2007). On costs sanctions see also Chapter 7.

[198] See *Frei v Davey* 124 Cal App 4th 1506 at 1514, 22 Cal Rptr 3d 429 at 435 (2004). For a similar result see *Lange v Schilling* N° C055471, 2008 WL 2192833 (Cal App 3d Dist).

[199] See H Nölting, *Mediatorenverträge* (Köln: Centrale für Mediation 2003) at 10.

relationship among mediation participants.[200] Signatories to agreements to mediate are typically the mediator, the parties and sometimes their representatives in the mediation process.

Agreements to mediate may, at least in part, be incorporated by reference into mediation clauses. Increasingly, however, parties and their representatives enter into a separate agreement to mediate, regardless of the details of the triggering clause. Therefore while mediation clauses and agreements to mediate have different goals their content may overlap. Agreements to mediate may set out all the terms of a mediation.[201] Where the mediation will take part under the auspices of a mediation organisation they may incorporate institutional rules and mediator codes of conduct approved by the organisation.[202] The European Directive on Mediation explicitly envisages and encourages this practice in Article 4.[203]

As indicated previously, in some jurisdictions such as the United States and Australia statutes have enacted basic requirements that agreements to mediate would normally introduce as private law, thereby minimising the legal necessity of agreements to mediate. Nevertheless such agreements are useful for several reasons. They can be tailored to suit the particular needs of parties and may prevail over default legal provisions. In addition they can fill gaps left by the laws on mediation, and are more likely to draw the attention of the signatories to their obligations and rights in relation to mediation than will a piece of legislation.

4.1 Nature of Agreements to Mediate

In general agreements to mediate must meet the requirements of contract law to be legally binding and enforceable. Generally no specific formalities are imposed in relation to the agreements.[204] However in some jurisdictions, especially those in the civil law tradition, agreements to mediate may fall into a specific category of contract. In Germany, for example, academic opinion categorises agreements to mediate (*Mediatorenvertrag)* as either contracts of service (*Dienstvertrag*) or more specifically as business agency service contracts (*Geschäftsbesorgungsdienstvertrag*). From the perspective of German law this

[200] See Deckert (2009), above note 8 at 212–213.

[201] See Appendix A for an example of an agreement to mediate.

[202] See Appendix B for institutional mediation rules appropriate for cross-border mediations.

[203] See Directive 2008/52/EC on Certain Aspects of Mediation in Civil and Commercial Matters, proposal as adopted by the European Parliament and the Council of the European Union on 21 May 2008, L 136/3, 24.05.2008 3–8.

[204] See Nölting (2003), above note 199 at 46.

means that agreements to mediate qualify as a pre-defined contract type known to the Civil Code and not as contracts *sui generis*.[205]

In Austria academic opinions vary as to the contract classification of an agreement to mediate, with most agreement surrounding what an agreement to mediate is not rather than what it is. The majority of commentators share the view that agreements to mediate cannot be defined as contracts to produce a work (*Werkvertrag*) due to the absence of an identifiable work as the central element of the contract.[206] In contrast to Germany there is consensus that an agreement to mediate is *not* a general service contract (*Dienstvertrag*) as the mediator is not subject to the substantive directions of either party but rather has an independent role.[207] Agreements to mediate appear to be a combination of different contract categories in Austria. They can be partly defined as independent service contracts (*freier Dienstvertrag*) due the independent role of the mediator and partly as treatment contracts (*Behandlungsvertrag*) such as those between doctor and patient on the basis of the confidential nature of the process.[208]

Signatories to the agreement to mediate are open to being sued if they are in breach of their obligations under the contract.[209] Where, for example, a mediator has breached a duty of disclosure or a conflict of interest emerges, it is conceivable that parties may sue the mediator for damages incurred due to the breach, such as costs in association with the mediation thus far, and seek to have the mediator removed. In cases where a mediator is also a notary, further and more specific claims may be made for breach of the terms of the agreement to mediate.[210]

In so far as the obligations of legal representatives towards their clients in the process are set out in the agreement, they will be accountable for breaches of these provisions. Similarly parties may be sued for breach of their obligations in the agreement, such as good faith participation or duties of confidentiality. As indicated earlier common law and statutory principles increasingly play a role here so that litigants may have several bases for legal actions, including breach

205 See Nölting (2003) above note 199 at 29.

206 See W Völkl and C Völkl (eds), *Handbuch der Beraterhaftung, Haftung und Haftungsvermeidung bei komplexen Dienstleistungen* (Wien: Manz 2007) at RN 958. M Lachmair, 'Neue Pflichten und Haftung für Mediatoren?' (2004) *Das Recht der Wirtschaft* 582.

207 See G Falk and G Koren (eds), *Zivilrechts-Mediations-Gesetz, Kommentar* (Wien: Verlag Österreich 2005) at § 17, RN 5.14.12.

208 Treatment contracts are derived from the legal classification of contracts to produce a work (Werkvertrag). See Roth and Gherhade (2008), above note 22 at 145–146.

209 On obligations of mediation participants, see Chapter 5.

210 See § 19 of the German National Rules for Notaries (Bundesnotarordnung, BNotO). See also Eidenmüller (2001), above note 13 at 40.

of contract. The specific duties of various mediation participants and the consequences for breach thereof are considered in Chapter 5.

4.2 Contents of Agreements to Mediate

This section outlines the types of matters that may be the subject of an agreement to mediate. In doing so it also highlights the overlap with mediation clauses which have been the main focus of this chapter. Agreements to mediate may include the following items:[211]

- The place of mediation.
- The parties to the mediation.
- Authority to settle at the mediation.
- Mediator identification, qualifications and appointment.
- The scope of the mediation.
- The conduct of the mediation including modalities of communication, documentation and recording,[212] convocation and representation of the parties.
- Professional fees of the mediator and by whom they will be paid.[213]
- Other charges in relation to the mediation, for example venue and amenities, and by whom they will be paid.
- A statement of principles of the mediation, which may include fair treatment (procedural fairness), party autonomy, speed and minimal cost principles.
- A description of the mediation process including preliminary meetings, mediation meetings and post-settlement sessions.
- Identification of commencement and termination times for the mediation.
- A time frame for the mediation.
- The legal status of settlements or other outcomes emerging from the mediation, for example whether a settlement needs to be in writing to have the force of law.
- Persons who may be present at the mediation.[214]

211 See Appendix A for examples of agreements to mediate.

212 The practice of covert digital recording of mediation has met with the disapproval of English courts, but it is not illegal. See Simon Brown LJ in *Fazil-Alizadeh v Nikbin* (25 February 1993) CAT 205.

213 It has been suggested that lawyers should consider a clause requiring parties to continue to fulfil their obligations under the agreement, including payment for services throughout the duration of the dispute: S Minnery, 'Drafting in Good Faith' (2004) *Proctor* 21 at 22.

214 Lenz and Müller (1999), above note 14 at 230.

- Roles and responsibilities of participants in the mediation including mediator(s), parties, legal or other representatives, experts, interpreters, witnesses, supporters, observers and others, relating to:
    - good faith participation;
    - disclosure requirements of mediators, lawyers and other professionals;
    - fair, impartial and ethical practice;
    - scope and application of confidentiality and privilege including admissibility of evidence;
    - managing abuse of power and power imbalance;
    - mediator accountability and liability;
    - termination of the process; and
    - reporting and documentation by mediator.
- The relationship of mediation to parallel procedures, such as the ability to file court proceedings or conduct arbitration while mediation is ongoing, and the impact of pre-filing mediation on court and other limitation periods.
- In MDR procedures, clarity in relation to the circumstances in which transition from one process phase to another occurs and how it is to proceed. This may include guidelines as to confidentiality as between process phases and the extent to which information revealed in one phase can be taken into account in another.[215]
- Inter-professional relations such as the relationship between mediators and arbitrators or judges who may deal with the dispute subsequently.

Mediation practice may vary according to how each of the above factors is managed. It is therefore important to address each of these factors in the agreement to mediate. A well-prepared agreement, which has been explained to all those taking part in the mediation, will go a long way to managing expectations about the purpose of the process and the roles and responsibilities of participants.

[215] See, for example, *US Steel Mining Co LLC v Wilson Downhole Services* N° 02:00CV1758 (2006) WL 2869535 (WD Pa Oct 5 2006) where the MDR agreement specified that mediation communications from the mediation phase, including from private sessions, could be taken into account in relation to decision-making should the matter proceed to the arbitration phase.

[illegible]

- good faith participation;
- [illegible]
- [illegible]
- [illegible]
- managing [illegible] and power imbalance;
- mediator accountability and liability;
- termination of the process; and
- reporting and documentation by mediator.

The relationship of mediation to parallel proceedings, such as the ability to file court proceedings or conduct arbitration while mediation is ongoing, and the impact of pre-filing mediation on court and other limitation periods.

In MDR procedures, clarity in relation to the circumstances in which transition from one process phase to another occurs and how it is to proceed. This may include guidelines as to confidentiality as between process phases and the extent to which information revealed in one phase can be taken into account in another.

Inter-professional relations, such as the relationship between mediators and arbitrators or judges who may deal with the dispute subsequently.

Mediation practice may vary according to how each of the above factors [illegible] expectations about the purpose of the process and the roles and responsibilities of participants.

[illegible] that mediation communications from the mediation phase [illegible] the matter proceed to the arbitration phase.

Chapter 5
Conduct of Mediators and Participants

1. Overview

Chapter 5 deals with the legal issues relating to conduct in mediation. What occurs at the mediation table can provide a basis for the potential liability of mediators and other participants in mediation long after the mediation is over. Where mediators fail to comply with relevant standards and where parties, lawyers and other participants fall short of fulfilling their obligations, legal disputes may emerge. Duties and standards for conduct in relation to mediation can be found in statutes, at common law, in codes of conduct and in agreements between the parties to the dispute, the mediator and the mediation provider.[1]

This Chapter deals with duties and standards of mediators and other participants in mediation, with the exception of specific obligations relating to confidentiality which are dealt with in Chapter 6. Liability for mediators and other participants in mediation is also examined.

2. Conduct of Mediators and other Participants in Mediation

This section examines in detail the duties and standards, with the exception of confidentiality, relating to mediators, lawyers and parties in mediation. Some general comments are also made about the required conduct of other participants in the process.

2.1 Mediator Duties

Mediators are responsible for conducting the mediation process and are subject to duties and obligations contained in legislation, court rules, codes of conduct, agreements to mediate and other instruments. The dearth of legal actions against mediators suggests that there is substantial compliance with mediator obligations and standards and that, from the perspective of disputing parties, it is a low risk activity. In the United States, Coben and Thompson note that mediator misconduct is not commonly used as a defence against enforcement of

1 See, for example, the arrangements at CMAP (Centre de Médiation et d'Arbitrage de Paris) whereby both the mediator and the parties are required to sign a declaration that they accept and abide by the ethical and mediation rules of the organisation: Article 7.2 of the CMAP Règlement de Médiation.

mediated settlements and that cases in which parties sue mediators for breach of their duty of care are rare.[2]

In some jurisdictions mediators' duties may differ according to their professional affiliations so that, for example, lawyer–mediators might be held to a different standard than counsellor–mediators.[3] However there is no uniformity on this point. In one American case the court held that a mediator who was also a lawyer should not be held accountable to the same disclosure standards as a lawyer.[4] Generally speaking mediator duties may include the duty to:

1. explain the process and its potential consequences for legal rights and remedies;
2. explain participant roles;
3. disclose qualifications and experience relevant to mediation;
4. have appropriate professional indemnity insurance;
5. advise parties to seek independent legal advice;
6. not to give legal advice;[5]
7. explain the parameters of confidentiality;
8. disclose potential conflicts of interest;
9. be impartial and conduct a fair process;
10. terminate the mediation process in certain circumstances;
11. report matters relating to abuse of children or crime;
12. document the outcome of the mediation; and
13. report to courts or other institutional bodies on certain aspects of the mediation outcome.

This section focuses on three mediator duties, namely those relating to disclosure, impartiality and termination of mediation. As indicated above, the confidentiality obligations of mediators and others are dealt with in Chapter 6. The reporting and documenting duties of mediators are examined together with other post-mediation issues in Chapter 7.

2.1.1 Duty of Disclosure

Mediator disclosure requirements are regularly found in codes of conduct and statements of ethical duties such as Article 2.1 of the European Code of

2 See J Coben and P Thompson 'Disputing Irony: A Systematic Look at Litigation About Mediation' (2006) 11 *Harvard Negotiation Law Review* 43 at 95 and 98.

3 See discussion below in relation to the regulation of mediators in Austria.

4 See *Chang's Imports Inc v Srader* 216 F Supp 2d 325 (SDNY 2002) where the court dismissed a claim against a lawyer–mediator for breach of duty of disclosure in relation to a conflict of interest.

5 See the discussion on impartiality below.

Conduct.[6] Article 4 of the European Directive on Mediation requires member states to encourage mediators and service-providers to adhere to codes of conduct, including on matters of disclosure. Disclosure obligations are also found in legislation and in model laws such as s 9 of the Uniform Mediation Act (2001) (UMA).

Duties of disclosure impose a continuing obligation on mediators to communicate to the parties potential conflicts of interest and grounds for bias in relation to the mediation process. Potential conflicts of interest may arise where the mediator has at any time prior to the mediation provided legal, counselling or other services to, or has had any social or professional relationship with, or financial interest in, any of the participants. In certain circumstances disclosure requirements may also require disclosure of mediators' qualifications and other matters related to their competency as in s 9 of the UMA. Disclosure requirements are closely related to issues of impartiality, independence, neutrality and fair treatment which are said to form the core aspects of the mediator's role.[7] Section 9(a)(1) of the UMA makes this explicit by requiring disclosure of matters that 'a reasonable individual would consider likely to affect the impartiality of the mediator.'[8] Article 2.1 of the European Code of Conduct contains similar requirements.

The disclosure requirements are designed to enhance self-determination by assisting parties to make fully-informed choices in relation to selection of their mediator, to remove doubts about the fairness of the process and the person conducting it, and finally to establish 'a visible, fundamental and familiar safeguard of public protection.'[9] If after full disclosure parties agree to continue with the mediator, the mediation may proceed, according to s 9(2)(g) of the UMA.[10] The European Code of Conduct also requires the explicit consent of the parties in this situation; in addition to a guarantee from mediators that they are 'certain of being able to carry out the mediation with full independence and neutrality in order to guarantee full impartiality' (Article 2.1).

6 In Australia see s 3 Australian National Mediator Practice Standards and s 5 Law Council of Australia's Ethical Guidelines for Mediators. In the US see Article 4 of the Michigan Supreme Court's Standards of Conduct for Mediators and s 7(d) of the Supreme Court of South Carolina Court Annexed ADR Rules and many of the Rules in the Comparative Table of International Mediation Rules in Appendix B.

7 The French Civil Procedure Code requires that court-appointed mediators guarantee their independence *vis-à-vis* the parties and the dispute thereby bringing together notions of impartiality, disinterestedness and the absence of any conflicts of interest which could impair independence: see Article 131-5.5 C pr civ.

8 See s 9(a)(1) UMA (2001).

9 See Reporter's Notes to the UMA in National Conference of Commissioners on Uniform State Laws, *Uniform Mediation Act with Prefatory Note and Comments* (Chicago: NCCUSL 2001).

10 Similar provisions can be found in Article 5 of the International Centre for Dispute Resolution (ICDR) International Mediation Rules: see Appendix B.

In their analysis of US cases alleging mediator conflict of interest or bias, Coben and Thompson found that alleged conflicts of interest were often *cured* by disclosure or knowledge.[11] In the case of *Lehrer v Zwernemann*[12] the plaintiff alleged, *inter alia,* misconduct, breach of contract and breach of duty based on non-disclosed conflicts of interest by the mediator defendant. In summarily dismissing the claim the court found that the plaintiff had constructive knowledge of the non-disclosed information concerning the mediator's relationship with the legal representatives of the other party. It also found that the plaintiff was not able to show any damage from the alleged misconduct.

Automatic disqualification may follow certain disclosures. In the American case of *Isaacson v Isaacson*[13] the court found that there was an inherent conflict between the roles of mediator and guardian *ad litem* – the latter being required to evaluate the case and make recommendations to the court – so that one person was precluded from acting in both roles. Another illustration is provided by Article 3 of the Model Standards of Conduct for Mediators in the United States which does more than mandate disclosure of 'actual and potential conflicts of interest that are reasonably known to the Mediator.'[14] It also prescribes consequences for certain conflicts of interest, providing that if a conflict places the integrity of the process in serious doubt mediators must remove themselves.

The continuing nature of the disclosure obligation means that if new circumstances requiring disclosure emerge during the course of a mediation, the mediator must comply with the duty at the first practicable opportunity. To enforce this requirement r 3.855(b) of the California Rules of Court imposes an *active* duty on a mediator to 'make reasonable efforts to keep informed about matters that reasonably could raise a question about his or her ability to conduct the proceedings impartially' and the mediator is required to disclose these matters to the parties. Inclusion of the word *reasonable* in the Californian provisions suggests an objective element to the test. Reasonableness depends on the circumstances and it 'is intended to convey the Drafter's intent to exclude inadvertent failures to disclose that would [otherwise] result in the loss of mediator privilege.'[15]

Interesting questions arise where a mediator is a partner or an associate of a legal adviser retained by either of the parties. It is generally thought that in such situations a mediator should not commence the mediation without the

11 See Coben and Thompson (2006), above note 2 at 95.

12 See *Lehrer v Zwernemann* 14 SW 3d 775.

13 See *Isaacson v Isaacson* 792 A 2d 525 (NJ Super Ct App Div 2002).

14 The Model Standards have been approved by the American Arbitration Association (AAA) and the Litigation and Dispute Resolution Sections of the American Bar Association (ABA) and the Association for Conflict Resolution.

15 See Reporter's Notes to s 9 UMA, above note 9 at 41.

fully-informed consent of all parties. In this regard clause II in the model agreement to mediate of the JAMS International ADR Center illustrates a comprehensive approach to disclosure.[16] First the clause contains an acknowledgment of disclosure having occurred in relation to potential conflicts of interest, not only by the mediator but also by parties and their lawyers. It then moves to the organisational level and explains the types of professional and business relationships that the Center has, or may have in the future, with other corporate and government entities. The Center has international dimensions with many of its mediators playing different roles as lawyers, arbitrators and mediators in commercial transacting and disputing contexts and the clause anticipates that prospective mediators may have – or have had – professional affiliations or relationships that could raise potential conflicts of interest. The clause further confirms the economic interest of each of its mediators in the financial success of the Center. Clause II concludes with two declarations: the first is that the mediator is unaware of any aspect of these relationships that would create a conflict or interfere with the mediator role; the second is an acknowledgement by the parties that these factors do not create a conflict of interest or the appearance of one.

As regards the provision of blended processes, mediators in Australia who engage in advice giving have an obligation to inform parties that they are offering a blended process which differs from mediation under the National Standards, and an obligation to obtain the parties' consent in order to proceed.[17]

In relation to mediators acting as arbitrators, and vice versa, many arbitration and mediation rules contain provisions that a dual role is only possible with the consent of the parties. These arrangements are considered in Chapter 7.

2.1.2 Duty of Impartiality

Impartiality is considered to be a fundamental principle of mediation and is found in various regulatory instruments including statutes, codes of conduct, self-regulatory standards and private contracts. The terms *neutrality* and *fair treatment* are also used in relation to this duty.[18]

Neutrality is a widely-used term, particularly in the United States where mediators are referred to as third party neutrals. However neutrality, as Vice explains, is an elusive concept:[19]

[16] For the precise wording of clause II and the model agreement, see Appendix A.

[17] See Australian National Mediator Practice Standards s 2(7).

[18] On the mediator's duty of impartiality generally, see P Tochtermann, *Die Unabhängigkeit und Unparteilichkeit des Mediators* (Tübingen: Mohr Siebeck 2008).

[19] J Vice (1997) quoted at www. beyondintractability.org/essay/neutrality ?nid=6713 on 02.07.2009.

> Neutrality is not something to be given an explicit and essential definition. Neutrality is not an essence; it is an absence. We must dance around it with enough synonyms and examples to be able to recognise when it ain't present.

Definitions of neutrality in the literature are wide-ranging.[20] Neutrality suggests that mediators should be free of bias and should set aside their opinions, feelings and agendas. In other words they should not make personal judgements about the parties and their dispute. Neutrality can embrace the idea that mediators ought to be disinterested outsiders with no prior knowledge of the dispute, no stake in the outcome and no relationship to the parties other than as mediator in their dispute. Neutrality may also incorporate notions of fair process and impartiality, namely that parties be treated equally and fairly in the process. Thus neutrality covers a lot of ground and as indicated previously can incorporate the meaning of the terms impartiality and independence. In France mediators must be able to demonstrate that they are neutral from both objective (reasonable person) and subjective (in the parties' eyes) perspectives.[21] Many regulatory provisions fall short of defining neutrality except, as Hopt and Steffek point out,[22] through notions of impartiality and independence.[23]

A number of commentators have questioned the utility of neutrality as a concept in mediation practice, arguing, *inter alia,* that the culture, values and personal biases of the human being behind the mediator make neutrality an unattainable ideal. Astor advocates values of transparency and the maximisation of party control as more useful principles than neutrality in relation to practitioners' duties.[24] Transparency highlights the need for disclosure which

[20] The various definitions in the text are drawn from the literature, especially Tochtermann (2008) above note 18, K Gibson, L Thompson and M Bazerman, 'Shortcomings of Neutrality in Mediation' (1996) 12 *Negotiation Journal* 71 and B Mayer, *Beyond Neutrality: Confronting the Crisis in Conflict Resolution* (San Francisco: Jossey-Bass Publishers 2004).

[21] See K Deckert, 'Mediation in Frankreich – Rechtlicher Rahmen und praktische Erfahrungen' in K Hopt and F Steffek (eds), *Mediation – Rechtstatsachen, Rechtsvergleich, Regelungen* (Tübingen: Mohr Siebeck 2008) 183 at 240 referring to *Cass Ass plén*, 6.11.1998, JCP 1998 II 10198.

[22] See K Hopt and F Steffek, 'Rechtsvergleich, Regelungsmodelle, Grundsatzprobleme' in K Hopt and F Steffek (eds), *Mediation-Rechtstatsachen, Rechtsvergleich, Regelungen* (Tübingen: Mohr Siebeck 2008) at 62.

[23] See, for example, Article 6 of the Mediation Rules of CMAP in France, Article 1(1) of the Mediation Rules of the Mediation Institute of the Stockholm Chamber of Commerce, Article 3(2) London Court of International Arbitration (LCIA) Mediation Procedure and Article 7(1) of the Permanent Court of Arbitration (PCA) Optional Conciliation Rules in the Comparative Table of International Mediation Rules in Appendix B.

[24] See, for example, H Astor, 'Mediator Neutrality: Making Sense of Theory and Practice' (2007) 16 *Social and Legal Studies* 22. See also Douglas who builds on Astor's work and advocates a relational, non-absolute understanding of neutrality and

allows parties to decide whether disclosed information warrants the dismissal or non-appointment of a mediator. It is consistent with the approach of some of the disclosure rules discussed previously. As a guiding principle, transparency maximises party control of the content and outcome of mediation and minimises the influence of a mediator's values, beliefs and assumptions. Accordingly it is said that transparency causes mediators to be less likely to find themselves advising parties on options for agreement and alternatives to settlement – a practice which is not without risk.[25]

Impartiality is a term used interchangeably with neutrality, but it has a stronger emphasis on mediator behaviour than neutrality. It denotes a disinterestedness, or absence of bias, in the sense of no partiality directed at either party in the conduct of the mediation process. This contrasts with the German notion of *Allparteilichkeit*, which literally means the ability to be partial to all parties rather than to one or the other.

The European Code of Conduct for Mediators distinguishes between independence and neutrality,[26] on one hand, and impartiality, on the other, whilst at the same time recognising in the final paragraph of Article 2.1 that all three concepts are connected with one another. Whereas the former concepts are linked to duties of disclosure around conflicts of interest (Article 2.1), impartiality is defined by reference to mediator behaviour (Article 2.2). The idea of impartiality is also encapsulated in Article 6(3) of the MLICC which provides that mediators must treat all parties fairly and conduct the process in a fair manner.[27] This provision focuses on the behaviour of mediators in the process and from a practitioner's point of view may be more tangible and achievable than neutrality. The European Directive on Mediation defines mediator in Article 3(b) as someone who conducts mediation in an impartial manner, thus signalling impartiality as a central aspect of the mediator's role. In contrast s 9(g) of the UMA contains a requirement of mediator impartiality that is optional. Given the significance of the duty of impartiality in most theory, policy and practice, it is worthwhile examining the reasons behind the decision to give

self-determination grounded in the relationship between mediators and parties: S Douglas, 'Neutrality in Mediation: A Study of Mediator Perceptions' (2008) 8 *QUT Law and Justice Journal* 139 at 150 et seq.

25 H Astor and C Chinkin, *Dispute Resolution in Australia* (Sydney: LexisNexis Butterworths 2002) at 153–154. On the risk of advice-giving by mediators, see the Australian case of *Tapoohi v Lewenberg* (N° 2) [2003] VSC 410 and referred to in Chapters 3 and 7.

26 On independence of the mediation practitioner see D Cooper and R Field, 'The Family Dispute Resolution of Parenting Matters in Australia: an Analysis of the Notion of an 'Independent' Practitioner' (2008) 8 *QUT Law and Justice Journal* 158.

27 UNCITRAL Model Law on International Commercial Conciliation (2002) referred to as MLICC.

this duty an optional character in the UMA.[28] According to the Reporter's Notes, the drafters of the UMA were swayed by the following factors:

- A concern in the mediation community that common human biases such as attributional distortions of judgment could be used as a basis for an argument of bias if there was a strict and mandatory duty of impartiality.
- Interventionist mediators – such as those using expert advisory and wise counsel models[29] – feared a plethora of lawsuits alleging breaches of the duty of impartiality by parties who no longer wished to be bound by their agreements. Although there have been very few findings of mediator misconduct by courts, parties dissatisfied with a mediated outcome in an attempt to vitiate it or have it set aside appear increasingly prepared to claim mediator duress, undue influence, coercion, inappropriate legal advice from the mediator and other manifestations of failure to maintain impartiality.[30]
- Despite the theoretical focus on impartiality, the UMA drafters did not regard impartiality as a universal mediator characteristic in practice. In family law disputes mediators must act in the best interests of the child and in healthcare disputes the mediator role may also contain an advocacy aspect.[31] Moreover in many non-western cultures mediators are not disinterested outsiders to the dispute – quite the opposite, they are often sought out precisely because they know the parties and are already aware of, or even somehow involved in, the dispute. As insiders they are active, interested and engaged.[32]

Section 9(g) of the UMA attempts to address these issues by allowing *fully-informed* parties to accept mediators who may fall short of a strict standard of

28 See Reporter's Notes to s 9 UMA, above note 9 at 46.

29 On mediation models see Chapter 1 and the literature referred to there.

30 In Australia see the case of *Tapoohi v Lewenberg* (N° 2) [2003] VSC 410 discussed in Chapters 3 and 7. In England see the case of *SITA v Watson Wyatt: Maxwell Batley Pt 20 Defendants* [2002] EWHC 2401/2025 (Ch) where the allegation of mediator bias was raised to justify one party's refusal to mediate. In the United States see the cases of *In re Young* 253 F 3d 926 (7th Cir 2001), *Patterson v Taylor* 969 P 2d 1106 (Wash Ct App 1999) and *Vitakis-Valchine v Valchine* 793 So 2d 1094 (Fla Dist Ct App 2001).

31 See, for example, the various state Nursing Home and Long Term Care Ombudsmen in the United States, at www.ltcombudsman.org. See also E Beaulieu, *A Guide for Nursing Home Social Workers* (New York: Springer Publishing Company 2002) at 127.

32 See P Wehr and J-P Lederach, 'Mediating Conflict in Central America' in J Bercovitch (ed), *Resolving International Conflicts: The Theory and Practice of Mediation* (Boulder: Lynne Rienner Publishers 1996).

impartiality. In relation to those states that choose to introduce s 9(g), the drafters of the UMA considered that the default nature of the provision would be balanced by the specific provisions and sanctions related to disclosure and the duty found elsewhere in s 9 to implement the principles of impartiality in its broad interpretive sense. In other words it was thought that potential risks arising from insufficient attention to impartiality would be minimised by the strict disclosure provisions. Consistent with the nature of a model law, enacting states desiring a stricter impartiality rule are free to deviate from the UMA and enact a higher standard.

Another aspect of impartiality arises in relation to the concept of *(unauthorised) practice of law*. Where mediators provide parties with legal advice or assistance in drafting terms of settlement they may be engaging in conduct that amounts to the practice of law, thereby attracting the application of rules regulating the legal profession. In these circumstances non-lawyer mediators may fall foul of laws restricting the practice of law to certified practitioners. This is referred to as the unauthorised practice of law. Furthermore lawyer–mediators may find that their legal professional duties relating to confidentiality, disclosure and reporting conflict with applicable mediator rules and codes of conduct, thereby leading to a lack of clarity in this regard.[33]

The facilitative model of mediation avoids this difficulty and is preferred by many industries, organisations and mediators.[34] As a non-interventionist model, it does not permit advice-giving by mediators and emphasises impartiality in the treatment of the parties and the conduct of the process. The UMA sidesteps this issue by inserting a provision on impartiality that is both optional and default in the sense that informed parties can waive the requirement. As explained earlier, this approach provides scope for advisory models of mediation which could still be questioned in terms of the unauthorised practice of law principle.

In Australia a different approach has been taken. The Australian National Mediator Standards prescribe a facilitative model of practice, thereby minimising the risk that mediators might be engaging in the unauthorised practice of law. However, as indicated above, where disputants request expert technical or legal advice from a mediator which the mediator agrees to provide, he or she is deemed to engage in a blended process and must demonstrate the competency and qualifications to advise in this area.[35]

[33] See, for example, ABA Section on Dispute Resolution, 'Mediation and the Unauthorised Practice of Law' (2002) *Mediate.com* at www.mediate.com/articles/abaupl.cfm.

[34] See, for example, clause 4 of the NADRAC Model Mediation Clause (referring to the Australian standards which endorse an interest-based model) and clause I of the JAMS International ADR Center Model Mediation Agreement (stating that the mediator is not an adviser). Both model documents are reproduced in Appendix A.

[35] See also Chapter 3 on this point.

2.1.3 Duty to Consider Termination of Mediation in Certain Circumstances

In order to preserve the integrity of mediation mediators may terminate the process in certain circumstances. By way of example Article 11 of the MLICC provides that mediators may terminate a mediation if they are of the view that further efforts at conciliation are no longer justified.[36] The type of situations that may lead a mediator to terminate a mediation are varied. Article 3.2 of the European Code of Conduct for Mediators identifies two such situations, namely where:

- a settlement is being reached that appears to the mediator as unenforceable or illegal; or
- the mediator considers that continuing the mediation is unlikely to result in a settlement.

More specifically, mediators may wish to terminate a mediation where they form the view that a party or its legal representative is:

- on a fishing expedition for information to damage the other side;
- just going through the motions of mediating;
- withholding information vital to decision-making;
- obstructing the conduct or progress of the mediation; or
- otherwise acting in bad faith;

and the behaviour of the offending party appears to the mediator to be irreversible. Another illustration is the situation where the mediator takes the view that child abuse, threats to human safety or other criminal activities are being planned or are ongoing within the parameters of the mediation.

[36] For similar provisions see the Comparative Table of International Mediation Rules in Appendix B, especially Article 6 LCIA Mediation Procedure, Article 15 PCA Optional Conciliation Rules, Article 11 of the Mediation Rules of the Mediation Institute of the Stockholm Chamber of Commerce, Article 15 UNCITRAL Conciliation Rules (UCR), Article 18 World Intellectual Property Organisation (WIPO) Mediation Rules, Article 12 ICDR International Mediation Rules, Article 6 International Institute for Conflict Prevention and Resolution (CPR) Procedures and Clauses Mediation Procedure. In relation to the mediator's duty to terminate in Austria, see the Government bill (Regierungsvorlage), RV 24 BlgNR XXII.GP. See also S Ferz and E Filler, Mediation – Gesetzestext und Kommentar (Wien: WUV Universitätsverlag, 2003) at § 17 RN 2.

2.2 Parties' Duties in Mediation

Mediation continues to be promoted in some contexts as a voluntary process which enhances party autonomy[37] Nevertheless disputing parties – especially those involved in pre-litigation and litigation procedures – are increasingly burdened by obligations relating to requirements either to participate in mediation or to consider it as an option. These obligations exist and are enforced primarily in common law jurisdictions as the following discussion demonstrates.

This section deals with two sets of obligations that may attach to parties in mediation: the duty to act reasonably in relation to mediation and the duty to participate in mediation in good faith. The former duty has been introduced by the Civil Procedure Rules (CPR) rules in England and is the subject of interest and debate there and in other countries including Germany and Australia; the latter is becoming increasingly integrated into legislation, court and institutional rules and agreements to mediate. There have been a number of English and Australian decisions, discussed below, in which parties succeeding at trial have not been able to recover their costs because they either unreasonably refused to participate in mediation or because the court considered their participation in mediation had not been in good faith. Parties may also be subject to other obligations in relation to the costs and fees of mediation,[38] preparation for mediation and other matters. These are usually detailed in the agreement to mediate. Finally mandatory court referrals to mediation and the obligations they impose on parties have been considered in Chapter 3 and will not be revisited here.

2.2.1 Duty to Act Reasonably In Relation To the Mediation Process

According to the CPR in England and Wales – and specifically the Practice Direction on Pre-Action Conduct – parties are required, *inter alia,* to follow a reasonable procedure to avoid litigation, which may include mediation. Breaches of these requirements could include unreasonably refusing to consider ADR as an option.[39] CPR r 3.1(5) provides that a court may order a party to pay a sum of money into court if that party has, without good reason, failed to comply with a rule, practice direction or a relevant pre-action protocol. There

[37] On party autonomy see Chapters 1 and 8.

[38] See, for example, the obligations of parties in France regarding mediation prepayment to the court in court-referred mediation. Article 131-6.2 C pr civ stipulates conditions for the deposit for the remuneration of the mediator; it must be a foreseeable payment and must indicate who pays it. Article 131-6.3 C pr civ deals with default of the deposit. See also Deckert (2008), above note 21 at 211–212.

[39] See para 4.4(3) Practice Direction on Pre-Action Conduct referred to as PDPAC, which lists unreasonably refusing to consider ADR as an example of non-compliance with the Practice Direction or relevant pre-action protocol.

has been a line of English cases interpreting these provisions.[40] The approach of the English courts was summarised in *Brown v Rice and Patel.*[41]

There is also a clear public policy now reflected in the CPR to encourage mediation as a preferred means of dispute resolution to litigation. CPR rule 1.4(1) obliges the court to further the overriding objective of enabling the court to deal with cases justly by actively managing cases. Rule 1.4(2)(e) defines "active case management" as including "encouraging the parties to use an alternative dispute resolution procedure if the court considers that appropriate and facilitating the use of such procedure". Rule 26.4(1) entitles a party, when filing the completed allocation questionnaire, to request that the proceedings be stayed while the parties try to settle the case by ADR. The encouragement of mediation by this court is also emphasised by chapter 17 of the Chancery Guide 2005.

The often-cited case of *Halsey v Milton Keynes General NHS Trust* set the parameters for the application of costs sanctions for unreasonable behaviour in relation to the mediation process. The court held that where a party – including a subsequently successful party – unreasonably delayed consenting to mediation until a very late stage so that the chances of a successful mediation were poor, they might – in exceptional cases – be subject to an adverse costs order. At the same time the court made clear that there was no presumption in favour of using mediation but there was an obligation on parties not to unreasonably refuse an invitation to mediate. In this regard the court enunciated factors relevant to a party's decision about entering ADR and these have been explored in Chapter 3.

A number of years later *Nigel Witham Ltd v Smith and Anor*[42] endorsed the principles enunciated in *Halsey.*[43] However on the facts of the *Witham* case no unreasonable delay was found. In fact it was rather the timing of the mediation that was in issue. Here the court found that the critical moment to mediate was missed by both parties and that even if mediation had been undertaken earlier, it may not have produced a different result in the

40 See, for example, *Regina (Cowl and others) v Plymouth City Council* [2001] EWCA Civ 1935, *Dunnett v Railtrack Plc* [2002] EWCA Civ 303, *Hurst v Leeming* [2002] EWHC 1051 (Ch), *Royal Bank of Canada v Secretary of State for Defence* [2003] EWHC 1479 (Ch), *Halsey v Milton Keynes General NHS Trust* and *Steel v Joy and Halliday* [2004] EWCA Civ 576 and *Nigel Witham Ltd v Smith and Anor* (N° 2) [2008] EWHC 12 (TCC).

41 See *Brown v Rice and Patel* [2007] EWHC 625 (Ch) at para 12 referring to *Halsey v Milton Keynes General NHS Trust* and *Steel v Joy and Halliday* [2004] EWCA Civ 576.

42 *Nigel Witham Ltd v Smith and Anor* (N° 2) [2008] EWHC 12 (TCC).

43 *Halsey v Milton Keynes General NHS Trust* and *Steel v Joy and Halliday* [2004] EWCA Civ 576.

circumstances. Other cases from common law jurisdictions have shown that an initial refusal to participate may be redeemed by later involvement.[44]

In Australia and the United States there was historically more focus on the role of courts in mandating ADR and less on the pre-litigation duties of parties. However in Australia a shift towards greater party responsibility in mediation is likely. At the time of writing proposals similar to the CPR are being considered as part of civil procedure reforms at state and federal levels in Australia.[45] For example the Victorian Law Reform Commission has proposed Standards of Conduct for Parties to Disputes according to which pre-action protocols could be introduced for the purpose of setting out codes of sensible conduct which disputants are expected to follow when there is a prospect of litigation.[46] Similarly the ADR Blueprint in New South Wales contains a number of proposals which specify greater responsibilities for parties, including:[47]

- the enactment of a set of guiding principles for the conduct of civil disputes;
- greater compliance by government agencies with the Model Litigant Policy; and
- the ability of courts to take into account parties' attempts to engage in ADR when making costs orders.

2.2.2 *Duty to Participate In Mediation In Good Faith*

Duties to participate in mediation oblige parties to engage in the process in varying degrees but they do not require parties to compromise or reach settlement. Participation duties usually take one of two forms. An obligation to attend mediation – at least the first session – is found in the rules of various courts, tribunals and mediation organisations and has been considered in Chapter 3.[48] Some of these rules specify that the party must attend in person and

44 See the Australian case, *Automasters Australia Pty Ltd v Bruness Pty Ltd* [1999] WASC 39 (21 May 1999).

45 Proposals in relation to the federal *Inquiry into Alternative Dispute Resolution in the Civil Justice System* are due late 2009 and expected to include recommendations on party obligations in mediation.

46 See VLRC, *Proposed Standards of Conduct for Parties to Disputes (including Pre-action Protocols)*, clause 1.

47 See *ADR Blueprint Discussion Paper: Framework for the delivery of alternative dispute resolution ADR Services in NSW* and the *ADR Blueprint Draft Recommendations Report 1* (Sydney: NSW Attorney-General's Department 2009).

48 See the Comparative Table of International Mediation Rules in Appendix B, especially Article 18 of the WIPO Mediation Rules which allows parties to terminate mediation only after having attended the first session, Article 6(1) of the Netherlands

not through a representative.[49] The more onerous obligation, namely to participate in the mediation process in good faith, can be found as a standard term in many agreements to mediate and in institutional rules such as Article 11 of the UNCITRAL Conciliation Rules (UCR). Besides *good faith* other terms used in relation to this participation duty include *meaningful*, *reasonable, conscionable* and *genuine*.[50] Article 3(d) of the CPR Mediation Procedure requires that the parties *co-operate fully with the mediator*.

Despite initial judicial reluctance in some jurisdictions to enforce contractual obligations to mediate in good faith on the basis that they were too vague, uncertain and subjective to be legally enforceable, these types of obligations have increasingly attracted judicial recognition and enforcement.[51] Good faith obligations are also found in numerous statutes and court rules. In the United States, for example, at least 22 states have statutes requiring good faith and 21 federal district courts and 17 state courts have good faith requirements in their rules.[52] In Australia positive duties to participate in negotiation and mediation in good faith can be found in s 11 of the Farm Debt Mediation Act 1994 (NSW) and s 31(1)(b) of the Native Title Act 1993 (Cth).

In France Article 1134 of the Civil Code requires good faith in the performance of contracts. While the jurisprudence in relation to this provision is said to be underdeveloped, one interpretation is that the provision offers 'a reserve obligation of honest conduct where the duties of the parties are not laid down by their contract or by law'.[53] In other words, where parties are not caught by provisions relating to fraud, duress, misrepresentation or other specified bad faith conduct, Article 1134 might come into play. Another view is that the

Mediation Institute (NMI) Mediation Rules, Article 9 of the ICDR International Mediation Rules. In Australia Peden identified more than 55 statutes requiring good faith negotiation or mediation: E Peden, *Good Faith in the Performance of Contracts* (Butterworths: Sydney 2003) at 193 et seq.

49 See, for example, New South Wales Law Society Mediation Rules ss 8 and 9. In the United States see the case of *Segui v Margrill* 844 So 2d 820 at 821 (Fla Dist Ct App 2003) where sanctions were applied against a party who sent his legal representative to the mediation and was himself available by phone. The court found that the presence of the parties was required at mediation.

50 See the comments of J Priestly in *Renard Constructions (ME) Pty Ltd v Minister for Public Works* (1992) 26 NSWLR 234 at 265 in relation to the overlap among some of these terms.

51 See, for example, the Australian cases, *United Group Rail Services Ltd v Rail Corporation NSW* [2008] NSWSC 1364 and *Aiton Australia Pty Ltd v Transfield Pty Ltd* [1999] NSWSC 996 at para 156.

52 See J Lande, 'Why a Good-Faith Requirement is a Bad Idea for Mediation' (2005) 23 *Alternatives to the High Cost of Litigation* 7.

53 R Zimmermann and S Whittaker, 'Good Faith in European Contract Law: Surveying the Legal Landscape' in R Zimmermann and S Whittaker (eds), *Good Faith in European Contract Law* (Cambridge: Cambridge University Press 2000) at 48.

provision simply means that parties must keep to their agreements as evidenced by their intentions.[54] Whether Article 1134 of the Civil Code applies to mediation participation remains to be seen. However the French High Court has held that disputing parties acted in bad faith in breach of Article 1134 of the Code where they failed to comply with their mediation clause and proceeded directly to court.[55]

The German Civil Code contains a requirement of good faith performance in § 242 which has enjoyed wide application.[56] German courts have been known to imply § 242 terms into contracts,[57] although there has been no application to mediation practice to date. Most agreements to mediate contain a duty on the part of the parties to cooperate (*Mitwirkungspflicht*) to resolve the dispute in a mediation procedure[58] and good faith could be implied here. Moreover German courts have appeared willing to imply a duty to act in good faith in relation to mediation clauses.[59]

In the absence of a positive duty to mediate in good faith the duty may effectively be introduced through the imposition of costs sanctions. In the United States r 16 of the Federal Rules of Civil Procedure provides that a court may order a pre-trial conference for the purposes, *inter alia*, of facilitating settlement. Under r 16(F)(1)(b) the court can impose sanctions on a party for not participating in good faith at the conference. This is a negative way of achieving the same objective as a positive good faith obligation.

On the other side of the Atlantic the English case of *Earl of Malmesbury v Strutt and Parker*[60] considered the application of cost sanctions in relation to a party's unreasonable behaviour in mediation. The case dealt with a dispute in which the Earl ultimately prevailed in court, but the financial quantum awarded was significantly less than both his claim and his final offer at mediation. Jack J made the following comments:

54 See Zimmermann and Whittaker (2000), above note 53 at 34.

55 See Cour Cass 1e civ 08.04.2009 N° 08–10866.

56 See H Kötz and H Leser, *German Private and Commercial Law: An Introduction* (New York: Oxford University Press 1982).

57 See I Forrester, S Goren and H Ilgen, *The German Civil Code* (Amsterdam: North-Holland Publishing Co 1975).

58 See H Prütting, 'Haftung' in F Haft and K von Schlieffen (eds), *Handbuch Mediation* (2nd ed, München: C H Beck 2009) 1135 at 1136 et seq.

59 See the decision of the Bundesgerichtshof (German Federal Court) of November 18, 1998 (VIII ZR 344/97), cons. 3. b. The decision is reproduced in (1999) *Neue Juristische Wochenzeitschrift*, 647, (1999) *Zeitschrift für Wirtschafts- und Bankrecht*, 651 and (1999) *Der Betrieb*, 215. See also the judgment of the Regional Court Köln dated 29 October 2002, file number 89 0 46/02.

60 *Earl of Malmesbury v Strutt and Parker* [2008] EWHC 424 (QB). In this case both parties waived privilege so that evidence from the mediation could be considered in relation to the award of costs.

> [T]he claimant's position at the mediation was plainly unrealistic and unreasonable. Had they made an offer which better reflected their true position, the mediation might have succeeded.[61]

The judge equated the behaviour of a party who had agreed to mediate and then acted unreasonably with that of a party who unreasonably refused to mediate. As the latter behaviour could, under the CPR, be taken into account in costs determinations, his Honour considered it appropriate to take the former category of behaviour into account.

The concept of good faith creates definitional difficulties to the extent that most statutes that require it avoid defining the term. As suggested previously, good faith can be seen as a subjective concept that lends itself to different views as to both the type of behaviour necessary to constitute good faith and the type which falls below the standard. Various academic commentators distinguish between the objective and subjective elements of good faith and focus attention on the establishment of an objective framework or test for legal purposes.[62] However case law suggests that the subjective component of good faith going to the parties' actual state of mind is a necessary, even if not a sufficient, requirement for establishing good faith in concrete circumstances.[63]

The *excluder* theory of good faith as articulated by Summers is another approach to defining the concept which has provided the doctrinal basis for some judicial determinations on the topic.[64] It maintains that good faith is best, or at least more easily, described and applied in terms of the various forms of bad faith that it excludes.[65] As the following table shows examples of bad faith are more concrete and tangible to grasp than examples of good faith. Positive requirements of good faith are therefore often given meaning in practice by reference to the negative attributes which preclude it. Table 5 sets out possible meanings of good faith and bad faith with illustrative references from mediation

61 See the *Earl of Malmesbury v Strutt and Parker*, above note 60 at para 72.

62 See, for example, E Farnsworth, 'Good Faith Performance and Commercial Reasonableness under the Uniform Commercial Code' (1963) 30 *University of Chicago Law Review* 666 at 671 and R Zimmermann and S Whittaker (eds), *Good Faith in European Contract Law* (Cambridge: Cambridge University Press 2000).

63 See the Australian cases of *Marjorie May Strickland and Ors v Minister for Land and Anor* [1998] FCA 868 and *Western Australia v Taylor (Njamal People)* (1996) 134 FLR 211 which consider good faith to have objective (reasonable behaviour in the circumstances) and subjective (state of mind of parties regarding intention) elements.

64 R Summers, '"Good Faith" in General Contract Law and the Sales Provisions of the Uniform Commercial Code' (1968) 54 *Virginia Law Review* 195. The excluder theory was approved by J Priestly in *Renard Constructions (ME) Pty Ltd v Minister for Public Works* (1992) 26 NSWLR 234 at 266–267 and used by Member Sumner in *Western Australia v Taylor (Njamal People)* (1996) 134 FLR 211.

65 See Summers (1968), above note 64 at 196 and 203.

cases in Australia, England and the United States.[66] It shows that the excluder theory is alive and well in mediation case law, though ultimately the practical meaning and application of good faith requirements depend on the particular wording of obligations, as well as on the canons of interpretation applied by courts in given jurisdictions.

Table 5
Good Faith Participation as Absence of Bad Faith Conduct

Form of bad faith conduct	Meaning of good faith
– Refusing to participate in contractually prescribed ADR process.[67]	– Performing contractual obligations as agreed.
– Not attending a court-referred ADR process.[68]	– Willingness to be involved in the process.
– Unreasonable refusal to consider or engage in mediation.[69]	– Reasonable and proportionate approach to using dispute resolution options.
– Obstructive attitude towards attempts to narrow the issues.[70]	– Constructively contributing to the definition of dispute issues

66 Table 5 was first published as N Alexander, 'Good Faith in Mediation' (2009) 11 *ADR Bulletin* 68 and is reproduced with the kind permission of the Bond University Dispute Resolution Centre. Table 5 is adapted from Summers (1968), above note 64 at 203. The cases are drawn from common law jurisdictions due to the paucity of decisions on this topic in civil law jurisprudence.

67 See the cases on enforcement of mediation clauses in Chapter 4 such as *Cable and Wireless Plc v IBM United Kingdom Ltd* [2002] EWHC 2059 (Comm Ct).

68 See *Segui v Margrill* 844 So 2d 820 at 821 (Fla Dist Ct App 2003), above note 49.

69 In the 2006 English case of *P4 Ltd v Unite Integrated Solutions plc* [2006] EWHC 2924 (TCC), the court awarded losing party P4 some costs after the winning party refused mediation and as a result denied P4 an opportunity to settle the case at minimum cost. In *Dunnett v Railtrack plc* [2002] 2 All ER 850, Railtrack won the initial case and appeal, but the English Court of Appeal declined to order the defeated claimant to pay Railtrack's costs because Railtrack refused to consider an earlier court suggestion to attempt mediation. For an illustration from the US see: *People's Mortgage Corporation v Kansas Bankers Surety Co* 62 F App'x 232 (10th Cir 2003) where lawyer's fees were awarded against a party partly on the basis of an unreasonable refusal to participate in mediation.

70 See *Capolingua v Phylum Pty Ltd (as trustee for the Gennoe Family Trust)* 1991 5 WAR at 337 where the court refused to award costs to the successful defendant for several reasons including the defendant's unreasonable conduct during mediation. Ipp J held that where it was later shown that issues would have been narrowed at mediation but for a defendant's behaviour, this was a relevant factor in awarding costs in respect of a later trial that had been unnecessarily extended.

Form of bad faith conduct	Meaning of good faith
– Lack of authority to settle.[71]	– Having authority to settle at mediation table.
– Not responding to initial settlement offer and requiring other party to accept own offer within unreasonable time-frame.[72]	– Setting aside reasonable time for mediation and preparedness to consider further offers where first offer not acceptable.
– Not allowing mediator to explain offers from other party.[73]	– Giving mediator opportunity to reframe and translate offers.
– Not engaging in dialogue with mediator and other party to address perceived inadequacies in process.[74]	– Being prepared to negotiate the mediation process as well as the substance of dispute.
– Refusal to consider reasonable options for settlement.[75]	– Preparedness to seriously consider other side's offers.
– Failing to offer options for settlement.[76]	– Making reasonable offers in the negotiation phase of mediation.
– Being unresponsive during an ADR process.[77]	– Acting collaboratively and responsively.
– Unilaterally terminating or abandoning the mediation process without reason.[78]	– Acting conscionably and with persistence in the face of negotiation difficulties.

71 See, for example, the US case *Reliance Nat'l Ins Co v B Von Paris and Sons Inc* 153 F Supp 2d 808 (D Md 2001).

72 See *Brooks v Lincoln Nat'l Life Ins Co* (D Neb Aug 25, 2006).

73 See *Brooks v Lincoln Nat'l Life Ins Co* (D Neb Aug 25, 2006).

74 See *Brooks v Lincoln Nat'l Life Ins Co* (D Neb Aug 25, 2006).

75 See *Malmesbury v Strutt and Parker* [2008] EWHC 424 (QB).

76 See, for example, the American case of *Ferrero v Henderson* N° C –3–00–462, 2003 WL 21796381 at 5–6 (SD Ohio).

77 See the US case of *Gilling v Eastern Airlines Inc* 680 F Supp 169 (DNJ 1988) where a court upheld sanctions against a party for merely 'going through the motions' in mediation. See also the Australian case of *Aiton Australia Pty Ltd v Transfield* [1999] NSWSC 996 where the court indicated that good faith connotes something more than mere attendance in the process.

78 See *Brooks v Lincoln Nat'l Life Ins Co* (D Neb Aug 25, 2006) and *Hoffer v Moyer* (Minn Ct App Sept 12, 2006). In the latter case the court concluded that a trial court did not abuse its discretion in refusing to grant the husband's request that all future custody and parenting disputes be mediated, where it had been the husband who previously 'walked out of the mediation sessions on all occasions' and the husband's

Form of bad faith conduct	Meaning of good faith
– Entering a settlement for unconscionable reasons or reneging on an agreed settlement without justification.[79]	– Acting with integrity and honest intention in relation to settlement and its implementation.

2.3 Lawyers' Duties in Mediation

The lawyer's role in mediation is a multi-faceted one. Lawyers can assist clients to understand the opportunities offered by mediation and the realistic alternatives if no settlement is reached at mediation. They can assist parties with their preparations for mediation and advise them on their obligations in relation to the process. Lawyers can provide advice in relation to the legal appropriateness of settlement options and can review and draft settlement agreements or other documented outcomes of mediation. Power imbalances can in some circumstances be mitigated by the presence of lawyers – a factor which explains why many statutes regulating lawyer participation in mediation relate to disputes involving children, vulnerable adults, such as those afflicted with serious health disorders, and divorcing couples.

In some jurisdictions the law is silent on the role of participants other than mediating parties, leaving the regulation of this aspect of mediation largely to contract law. In France Article 131-8 of the Civil Procedure Code provides

counsel conceded that the parties had mediated in the past and that it had not been 'terribly successful'. In contrast an Australian tribunal held there were no costs implications for abandoning a mediation for health reasons where the party vacating maintained good faith and attended mediation with full intentions of attempting to settle and did not necessarily disadvantage the other party: *Sharp v the Canonical Administrators of St Monica's College Ltd* [2003] VCAT 42 (Unreported, Deputy President McKenzie, 22 January 2003) at para 8.

79 See, for example, the Australian case *Spalla v St George Motor Finance* (2004) 209 ALR 703 which involved a party entering into a mediated settlement in bad faith. See also the US case *Peoples Mortgage Corp v Kansas Bankers Surety Trust Co* 176 F Supp 2d 1199, 1206 (D Kan 2001) in which the court had to determine whether a mediated settlement agreement entered into by an insured person was made in good faith so that the insured could recover indemnification against the insurer. See also *Herrin v The Medical Protective Co* (2007) TX App (6th) 303, where the Tennessee Court of Appeals reversed a grant of summary judgment for the defendant insurer, concluding there were genuine issues of material fact precluding dismissal of claims for breach of contract, fraud, breach of fiduciary duty and breach of duty of good faith and fair dealing based on the insurer's decision not to renew a policy after allegedly telling the insured that his consent to mediated settlement of a tort claim would not affect renewal. For other insurance cases where this issue emerges see Coben and Thompson (2006), above note 2 at 134–135.

that third parties may participate in mediation only with the consent of the disputants. In the United States s 10 of the UMA expressly considers the role of lawyers and other participants in mediation, placing the ongoing decision about their participation with the parties, which includes the right to rescind any previous waivers of participation. The UMA provision reinforces the centrality of party autonomy in mediation, but it also reflects the important role lawyers can play in mediation in the United States and other common law countries. In many civil law jurisdictions there is a less welcoming attitude to lawyers in mediation. However policies and regulations on this point are by no means uniform.

Some sector-specific statutes do not permit lawyer involvement in mediation at all, or express a strong preference that lawyers not attend; others allow mediators to exclude lawyers.[80] In these situations lawyers may still advise parties before mediation, by telephone during the mediation, or at any time outside the mediation room. In addition lawyers may be responsible for drafting and reviewing agreements emanating from mediations. Conversely certain statutes authorise the mediation attendance of lawyers[81] and others disallow their exclusion.[82] Where lawyers are present in mediation, the parties' duty to attend remains and is not affected by the presence of their legal representatives.[83]

In this section three sets of lawyer duties are considered: the duty to disclose, pre-litigation obligations and the duty both to represent the best interests of the client and to engage in mediation in good faith. Finally researchers have noted an increase since the mid-2000s in American judicial decisions relating to ethics and malpractice involving lawyers and some of these are considered in relation to mediation involvement.[84]

80 In the United States see s 3182 of the Cal Fam Code (West 1993) and in Australia see s 57 of the Retail Shop Leases Act 1994 (Qld).

81 In the United States see s 42–810 of the Neb Rev Stat (1997) on domestic relations and in Australia see r 20.6(1)(b) of the Uniform Civil Procedure Rules 2005 (NSW) and r 48.13(7) of the Supreme Court Rules (NT).

82 See, for example, Or Rev Stat s 107.785 (2007) in the United States.

83 See, for example, the case of *Doorstep Beverages of Longwood, Inc v Collier* 928 So 2d 482 (Fla Dist Ct App 2006). On this topic generally see K Kovach, 'Lawyer Ethics Must Keep Pace With Practice: Plurality in Lawyering' (2003) 39 *Idaho Law Review* 399.

84 See J Coben and P Thompson 'Mediation Litigation Trends 1999–2007' (2007) 1 *World Arbitration and Mediation Report* 395 at 413 referring, inter alia, to the case of *Attorney Grievance Com'n of Maryland v Steinberg*, 910 A2d.

2.3.1 *The Duty of Disclosure*

As with mediators, lawyers have a duty of disclosure in relation to (potential) conflicts of interest. In Germany the duty is underpinned by a duty of professional independence and is one of the core duties of lawyers.[85]

Conflicts of interest may include situations in which a person has previously acted in the same matter either as legal adviser or mediator. In the American case of *Peggy K Pappas v Waggoner's Heating and Air, Inc; John Brumfield, Pamela B Long and Catherine M Webb*[86] the plaintiff's lawyers and entire law firm had been disqualified from representing her on the basis that a firm member had earlier acted as mediator in the case. The appeal court reversed the disqualification on the basis that the firm had anticipated potential conflict situations and put in place a screening process among legal staff to prevent actual conflicts occurring. In other jurisdictions lawyers are required by their professional codes of ethics and rules of court to make necessary conflict of interest disclosures which might preclude their involvement in mediation or in post-mediation representation of clients.

2.3.2 *Pre-Litigation Duties*

Legal representatives can play an advisory and supportive role in relation to mediation, with advice-giving beginning well before the first mediation meeting. As indicated previously policies encouraging model conduct in civil proceedings affect both parties and lawyers and make it incumbent on lawyers to advise clients as to appropriate dispute resolution options and to engage in the selected dispute resolution process in good faith. As regards the duty to consider options and act reasonably in relation to ADR in England,[87] Allen comments that,

> [b]efore the CPR reforms, there was a degree of worry that an expression of being willing to engage in mediation was in itself evidence of weakness, signalling a wish to compromise which would give comfort to opponents and stiffen their resolve to fight on. The combination of the CPR and significant court decisions since then has effectively abolished that fear, as there is a generalised duty to consider ADR without any duty to settle.[88]

85 See § 43a Legal Professional Rules for Lawyers the Bundesrechtsanwaltordnung (BRAO) Grundpflichten des Rechtsanwalts.

86 *Peggy K Pappas v Waggoner's Heating and Air, Inc; John Brumfield, Pamela B Long and Catherine M Webb* 2005 OK CIV APP 11. In Australia see the case of *Williamson v Schmidt* [1998] 2 Qd R discussed in Chapter 6.

87 See previous discussion on the duty of parties to act reasonably in relation to mediation and ADR.

88 T Allen, *Implementing the EU Directive on Mediation: A Draft Consultation Paper* (London: 2009) at 28. At the time of writing, the paper was in draft form. For updates

The new reality affords lawyers wide scope to advise on appropriate options in that jurisdiction without concerns over weakening their bargaining position. Similarly in Australia the Advocacy Rules of the NSW Law Society stipulate that practitioners,

> must inform the client or the instructing practitioner about the alternatives to fully contested adjudication of the case which are reasonably available to the client.

Preparing clients for mediation includes advising them on their role in mediation. In *Doorstep Beverages of Longwood, Inc v Collier*[89] the court imposed sanctions on counsel (at counsel's request) for the failure of the client to appear at the appellate mediation where counsel admitted to the court that he failed to advise his client that this attendance was required. Some organisations provide codes of conduct for lawyers in mediation. By way of example, The Law Council of Australia's Guidelines for Lawyers in Mediations offers a set of ethical principles for all stages of mediation supplemented by practical comments with examples.[90]

2.3.3 Duty to Represent Client Interests and Participate in Mediation in Good Faith

Lawyers have a duty to represent the interests of clients, not only in court but in all dispute resolution processes including mediation.[91] At the same time they are obliged to participate in the process in good faith and, in some cases, to comply with reasonable requests of mediators.[92] Much has been written about potential inconsistencies between traditional adversarial approaches to trial advocacy and the collaborative spirit of mediation and how duties relating to the former may be compromised by obligations relating to the latter.[93] However even as advocates, lawyers have long been subject to strict ethical obligations such as the duty not to mislead a court and in some circumstances to correct misleading

consult the Centre for Effective Dispute Resolution (CEDR) website: www.cedr.co.uk.

89 *Doorstep Beverages of Longwood, Inc v Collier* 928 So 2d 482 (Fla Dist Ct App 2006).

90 See The Law Council of Australia, *Guidelines for Lawyers in Mediations* (Canberra: March 2007) available at www.lawcouncil.asn.au.

91 See, for example, § 9(1) of the Lawyers' Professional Rules, (Rechtsanwaltsordnung RAO) in Austria.

92 See, for example, Article 5(5) of the ADR Rules of the International Chamber of Commerce (ICC), Article 11 PCA Optional Conciliation Rules, Article 11 UCR, Article 10 WIPO Mediation Rules referred to in Appendix B.

93 See C Caputo, 'Lawyers' Participation in Mediation' (2007) 18 *Australasian Dispute Resolution Journal* 84.

statements.[94] In addition considerable ground has been covered since the introduction of contemporary mediation, and the emergence of practices and policies drawing on collaborative and preventative law principles signals a shift in legal dispute resolution culture. A duty to represent the client's best interests is not inconsistent with engaging in collaborative processes such as mediation. Once in mediation there is a good faith obligation to explore settlement possibilities but there is no duty to recommend compromise. On the contrary, clients have been known to bring legal actions to set aside mediated settlements on grounds of negligent legal advice and proceedings against their lawyers for professional negligence and misconduct, as the following cases illustrate.

In the Australian case *Studer v Boettcher*[95] the court considered the question of whether or not a solicitor had been negligent in preparing the client's case for mediation and representing the client in the mediation. The dispute, which involved the sale of real property, was settled at mediation. Subsequent to the mediation, the appellant took action against his solicitor (the respondent), claiming:

1. that his solicitor had unduly pressured him into accepting the mediated settlement by negligent advice, and/or improper pressure; and
2. that if the original action had proceeded to judgment the appellant would have obtained a better financial outcome.

With respect to the issue of coercion, the court stated that it is never the function of a legal adviser to coerce the client. A solicitor is entitled to seek to persuade a client to accept and act on the solicitor's advice on the basis that it is in the client's interest. Any persuasion undertaken by the lawyer must be devoid of self-interest. Ultimately, however, the decision lies with the client. It is the lawyer's job to ensure that the client's decision is an informed one.

On the issue of negligence the court pointed out that it is often impossible to predict the outcome of litigation with a high degree of certainty. Therefore advice is not necessarily negligent merely because the court ultimately takes a different view than one party's legal representative.

Finally the court found that the solicitor had adequately prepared for the mediation and had given sound advice to his client, the appellant. In reaching this conclusion it considered the following matters:

[94] See, for example, rr 23 and 24 of the Barristers Rules Qld (Australia) 2007 which provide not only that barristers must not knowingly mislead the court but also that they must take all necessary steps to correct any misleading statement they make once they become aware of its misleading nature. See also § 43 especially § 43a(III) of the German Lawyers Rules (Bundesrechtsanwaltsordnung BRAO) which deals with lawyers' professional conduct generally.

[95] *Studer v Boettcher* [2000] NSWCA 263.

1. Based on the law and the documentary evidence, the appellant had a very difficult case.
2. The appellant faced difficulty in terms of producing certain witnesses at trial.
3. Although the respondent originally had hoped to settle at the mediation for considerably less than the sum finally agreed upon, the nature of the evidence changed immediately prior to, and during, the mediation. The solicitor's response to these changes was reflected in his advice to his client to settle.

In its deliberations the court referred to the solicitor's discussions with his client about the costs of defending the claim and also the amount of costs for which the client could be liable if he failed in his claim. Again the court found the lawyer's advice in this regard to be reasonable. The mediation literature refers to this practice as reality testing and it is an important component in the role of the legal representative in mediation.[96]

In *Louis v Galbally and O'Bryan (legal practice)*,[97] the court held that the mediation party 'had to have shown that [its lawyer's] negligence caused the loss of the opportunity to settle [its] case for a greater amount than the amount offered' and that in this case 'no such lost opportunity was made out on the facts'. In dismissing the claims against the lawyer, the court was influenced by two factors: first that the lawyer was not in possession of, or could reasonably have been expected to gain possession of, any other information which would have enabled him to better comply with his client's instructions or induce the other party to make a higher offer, and second that the court accepted that there was no real prospect of the matter settling at mediation regardless of the lawyer's efforts.

A similar claim by a mediation party against its lawyer was made in the English case of *Cumbria Waste Management Ltd and Lakeland Waste Management Ltd v Baines Wilson.*[98] Here a party to a mediation claimed that its lawyer provided negligent advice in relation to negotiating, drafting and advising on terms of the settlement agreement, and sought to recover damages based on the shortfall between the amount of the mediated settlement and the amount the party considered it would have received but for the negligent legal advice provided in mediation. However, as discussed in the next chapter, the court did not rule directly on the issue of lawyer negligence but decided on the release and admissibility of certain mediation documentation in relation to the dispute.

[96] On reality testing, see M Schonewille, *Toolkit Generating Outcomes* (The Hague: Sdu Uitgevers 2009) at III–11.

[97] *Louis v Galbally and O'Bryan (legal practice)* [2008] VCAT 2186.

[98] See *Cumbria Waste Management Ltd and Lakeland Waste Management Ltd v Baines Wilson* [2008] EWHC 786 (QB), discussed in Chapter 6.

While it may be difficult for clients to establish negligence on the part of their legal advisers, it is possible. In an American case, *Attorney Grievance Com'n of Maryland v Steinberg,*[99] the court held that a lawyer who failed to appear at a client meeting, as well as arrived late and unprepared at the mediation session, had breached professional conduct rules. Other examples of conduct that may fall foul of professional standards for lawyers representing clients in mediation include:

- failing to communicate with clients about a settlement offer put forward by the other party's lawyer;
- breaching confidentiality provisions by, for example, disclosing confidential information from private sessions in subsequent arbitral or court proceedings;
- failing to schedule required mediations;
- seeking to enforce a mediated settlement without a client's consent;
- failing to pay mediation fees and associated administrative costs;
- failing to pay the sum agreed to in a mediated settlement in a timely way;
- misleading a client about what happened at mediation where the client has not attended or left early; and
- refusing the request of the mediator to bring the client to the mediation.[100]

Finally codes of conduct may contain very specific duties for lawyers in mediation. For example the New South Wales (Australia) Law Society Guidelines for Legal Representatives in a Mediation provide that where lawyers are of the view that opposing parties are not negotiating in good faith they should inform their clients and the mediators (s 4.2.3).

2.4 Experts, Witnesses, Interpreters and Others

Consistent with principles of party autonomy and choice in mediation, the roles of additional participants are usually established by mediators in consultation with the parties and set out in the agreement to mediate.[101] In relation to experts, court procedures such as the provision of concurrent evidence are increasingly being integrated into mediation and other dispute resolution processes. Here

[99] *Attorney Grievance Com'n of Maryland v Steinberg* 910 A 2d 429 (Md 2006).

[100] This list is adapted from Coben and Thompson (2006), above note 2 at 93–94. The authors refer to American case law in relation to the various forms of misconduct.

[101] B Ahmed, *The Role of Experts in ADR – How to Play the Part* (2007), available at www.cedr.com.

experts are requested to meet together, submit a joint report and answer questions from the mediating parties.

In terms of obligations, additional participants in mediation may be subject to duties of confidentiality[102] and good faith participation. Experts may be subject to additional professional duties such as a duty of care and appropriate disclosure in relation to potential conflicts of interest. Similar principles pertain to other participants in mediation such as witnesses and interpreters. Interpreters in mediation have a primary duty to the process and not to one or more parties. They are subject to duties of disclosure, neutrality, good faith, confidentiality, competency and accuracy, to name a few. They must refrain from giving advice to, or advocating on behalf of, one or more parties.[103]

3. Liability and Remedies

This section deals with the consequences of a breach of the various duties of mediators and participants, with the main focus on mediators. As regards the liability of mediators, Steffek suggests that from an international comparative perspective legal principles relating to mediator liability are far and few between and that courts have been slow to develop the jurisprudence in this area.[104] This situation reflects the fact that most actions against mediators are either unsuccessful or are settled out of court.[105]

Mediation is considered to be a low risk activity and, although professional indemnity insurance is required for accredited mediators in Australia and Austria, views have been expressed in relation to civil law jurisdictions that such protection in relation to mediator liability is unnecessary.[106] However mediation service providers may require their

[102] See, for example, the case of *Ryan Nominees Pty Ltd v Western Australian Planning Commission* [2002] WASC 45 (21 March 2002) which held that expert reports prepared for mediation were provided on a confidential basis.

[103] See, for example, K Laster and V Taylor, *Interpreters and the Legal System* (Sydney: Federation Press 1994).

[104] F Steffek, 'Mediation in Europa und die Welt' (2009) *Zeitschrift für Konfliktmanagement* 21 at 24.

[105] Research on case law confirms this view. See also the oft-cited Australian case of *Tapoohi v Lewenberg* (N° 2) [2003] VSC 410 which was ultimately settled out-of-court.

[106] This statement refers to comments by G Hopt, in relation to Austria and G Nettersheim, in relation to Germany at the *Jahrestreffen der Freunde des Max Planck Instituts für ausländisches und internationales Privatrecht* (Hamburg, 13 June 2009). While Austria already has compulsory professional indemnity insurance, Germany seems unlikely to introduce it with the planned legislative reforms required by the European Directive on Mediation.

members to be insured, as is the case with the French *Chambre professionnelle de la médiation et de la négociation.*

From an English perspective Allen notes that 'there is no recorded claim against mediators in the UK and their professional indemnity premiums remain low'.[107] He goes on to question the ability of claimants to establish a breach of a mediator's duty, such as a breach of confidence or negligence, in addition to establishing that damage has been caused by a mediator, especially when operating in a broadly facilitative model. The limited case law that does exist in relation to mediation seems to support this view, as mediators who face allegations by parties that they breached their professional duties tend to operate outside of a facilitative practice model.

In general terms mediator liability may be regulated by contract, common law, tort and equity. As explained in Chapter 4, agreements to mediate usually set out the duties of the mediator. They may also contain provisions limiting a mediator's liability for breach of those duties. The extent to which the limitations will be enforceable will depend on relevant legislation and judicial and public policy.[108] It is likely that such clauses will be interpreted *contra proferentem* and in favour of clients, and they would not be effective to protect mediators from deliberate misconduct such as fraud or criminal conduct. However clauses limiting the amount of damages recoverable from a mediator may be enforceable. Moreover restrictive liability clauses, and the agreements in which they are contained, may also be avoided where the mediators can be said to be acting beyond the scope of their mediation mandate. This argument may apply where third party neutrals are acting more like advisers than facilitative mediators, as was the case in *Hadid v Lenfest Communication Inc.*[109] Here the court judged the third party according to the standards of an adviser rather than a mediator. Therefore there was no need to interpret the liability clause in the agreement to mediate as it would only have offered protection for acts and omissions by a third party acting as mediator. Finally limited liability clauses would not be effective against non-signatories to the agreement to mediate.

Tortious actions against mediators might be based in breach of confidence, defamation, misleading and deceptive conduct, undue influence,

[107] See Allen (2009), above note 88 at 19.

[108] In Australia, for example, mediators cannot exclude liability for misleading and deceptive conduct under s 52 of the Trade Practices Act 1974 (Cth).

[109] *Hadid v Lenfest Communication Inc* [1999] FCA 1798. See also the New Zealand case of *McCosh v Williams* [2003] NCZA 192 where the court held that the mediator had exceeded his jurisdiction according to the terms of the agreement to mediate by making a determination as to rectification of the settlement contract, rather than restricting himself to the interpretation of settlement terms, which was permitted by the agreement to mediate.

unconscionability or negligence.[110] References to the excessively directive mediator have been made elsewhere.[111] In litigation cultures it is not difficult to imagine a mediator providing legal advice, making settlement suggestions, or even exaggerating or overstating the other side's position as part of their reality testing role. Each of these techniques could conceivably lead to an action against the mediator by a party disgruntled with the outcome of the mediation and seeking redress of some kind. Negligence actions against mediators generally require breach of a duty of care owed by the mediator to a party, who as a result of the mediator's negligence, sustains actual damage. Where a mediator encourages parties to seek independent legal advice, a causal link between the mediator's acts and omissions and the damage suffered by the party will be more difficult to prove. Courts will also look to see if the plaintiff has either contributed to the damage or has failed to mitigate it.

In terms of legislative provisions regulating damages, the French Civil Procedure Code states that mediators are liable for damages caused to mediation parties in the execution of their duties.[112] Thus, mediators in breach of their duty of disclosure or impartiality may be liable to pay damages. Damages based on a party's expenditures, such as the mediator's fees, lawyers' costs, fees for preparation and participation, disbursements and other expenses are easy to calculate. However speculative damages, such as loss suffered as a result of entering a settlement because of mediator coercion, as alleged in the *Tapoohi* case,[113] may be more difficult to prove.[114]

In relation to equitable principles, courts and commentators in some jurisdictions have suggested that mediators stand in a fiduciary relationship towards the parties.[115] In the context of mediation a fiduciary relationship might exist between the mediator and respective parties whereby the parties place their trust in the mediator to exercise his or her power to influence their affairs in a manner that will benefit each of them. Boulle points out that law of fiduciary duties imposes a strict liability and therefore may be attractive to some plaintiffs

110 On claims in tort, see D Baker, S Blay, L Corbin and A Gibson, *Torts Law in Principle* (3rd ed, Pyrmont: LawBook Co 2002) 8.9–8.10.

111 See Chapters 3 and 7.

112 See Article 131-10 C pr civ.

113 See the discussion of *Tapoohi v Lewenberg* (N° 2) [2003] VSC 410 discussed in Chapters 3 and 7.

114 On the challenges of proving damages see L Cadiet, 'L'Effet processuel des clauses de médiation' (2003) *Recueil des Cours de l'Academie de Droit International* 182 and X Lagarde, 'L'Efficacité des clauses de médiation ou de conciliation' (2000) *Rev Arbitrage* 376.

115 See the Australian case of *Hadid v Lenfest Communication Inc* [1999] FCA 1798 and the American case of *Lehrer v Zwernemann* 14 SW 3d 775 where the point was raised but not decided by the court. See also A Chaykin, 'Mediator Liability: A New Role for Fiduciary Duties?' (1984) 53 *University of Cincinnati Law Review* 731 at 733.

contemplating litigation, as they do not need to establish causation and loss as is the case with tortious claims. [116] However there may be difficulties with the application of the principle, such as the fact that a fiduciary cannot act for two beneficiaries at the same time. Moreover the facilitative model of mediation seems at odds with the notion that mediators exercise power to influence parties' interests and rights.

An interesting and intelligent sanction for breach of a specific mediator duty is found in s 9(2)(d) of the UMA. It provides for the forfeiture of mediator privilege in the event of non-disclosure.[117] Thus the mediator can be required to testify and cannot claim privilege in relation to non-disclosure actions, such as those involving conflicts of interest. The loss of such a privilege is said to provide some measure of accountability from the mediator.

In addition to mediator liability in terms of civil wrongs, parties may seek redress through complaints handling, disciplinary and accreditation systems. In some cases these avenues may be easier to access for parties, although they may not offer the remedies such as damages and enforcement that they seek. Here potential remedies include disqualification or removal from a mediation, and disciplining or de-accreditation of the mediator by a professional or accreditation body.[118]

A continuing debate among mediators and mediation policy-makers relates to the extent that mediators enjoy immunity from legal action in a similar fashion to judges and arbitrators. Generally judicial mediators enjoy judicial immunity when mediating, and arbitral immunity may extend to arbitrators mediating within the framework of an arbitration. However immunity may not extend to mediating judges and arbitrators once they move out of their primary roles as judges and arbitrators respectively. This was the situation in the case of *Morgan Phillips Inc v JAMS/Endispute*[119] in which a dispute resolution practitioner who withdrew from his arbitral role at an early stage and then proceeded to mediate the dispute was found not to have the benefit of arbitral immunity, as there was not a sufficient nexus between the two roles.

In many court-related mediation programs mediators are granted statutory immunity, whether they are employees of the court, such as registrars, or external mediators. Whereas judicial immunity is usually unqualified, statutory immunity afforded to mediators may be qualified. Qualified mediator immunity operates where mediators can satisfy certain conditions, for example that they have acted in good faith or without fraud or deceit.[120] Alternatively,

[116] See L Boulle, *Mediation: Principles, Process, Practice* (Sydney: Lexis Nexis 2005) at 513.

[117] Note that the loss of privilege does not apply to judicial mediators: s 9(e) UMA.

[118] See, for example, complaints handling procedures of the International Mediation Institute at www.imimediation.org.

[119] *Morgan Phillips Inc v JAMS/Endispute* LLC 44 Cal Rptr 3d 782 (Cal Ct App 2006).

[120] See, for example, s 12 of the Mediation Act (ACT) in Australia.

qualified immunity may only extend to certain actions against mediators, such as negligence, or it may be limited to the mediation session and not extend to preliminary meetings and initial and subsequent phone calls and emails. Mediators must be mindful about the extent to which they are covered by statutory immunity. In the case of *Tapoohi*,[121] for example, the mediator failed to complete the necessary formalities in relation to a litigation matter that he was to mediate. As a result he was not covered by the statutory immunity of the court-annexed mediation program. The case is discussed elsewhere in the book.[122] Parties and their legal advisers also need to be clear about the level of accountability of the mediator. This matter can be discussed in preliminary meetings and should be spelled out in the agreement to mediate.

Apart from mediators, other mediation participants may also face sanctions for breach of their mediation duties. Lawyers face potential striking off or suspension if they fall below their professional standard of care in mediation, as the case of *In re Fletcher*[123] shows. Here a court affirmed a lawyer's suspension from practice for three years for repeated abusive behaviour while participating in mediations, including use of profanity in one mediation and, in another, the threat to publicise confidential information illicitly copied by his client. Other potential remedies against legal representatives include costs sanctions[124] and damages. As indicated previously, damages may be claimed for loss incurred in terms of the value of the actual settlement compared to what it could reasonably have been anticipated to be, but for the negligent legal advice.

Other professionals such as experts and interpreters found liable for professional negligence in mediation risk sanctions from their professional bodies, as well as civil claims by parties who can demonstrate that they have suffered damages as a result of a negligent expert assessment or translation, as the case may be.

Finally where parties in mediation breach a duty in relation to mediation, potential remedies usually take the form of cost sanctions. These are examined in Chapter 7.

121 See *Tapoohi v Lewenberg* (N° 2) [2003] VSC 410

122 See Chapters 3 and 7.

123 See *In re Fletcher* 424 F 3d 783 (8th Cir 2005) and also *Brooks v Lincoln Nat'l Life Ins Co* (D Neb Aug 25, 2006).

124 See, for example, *Doorstep Beverages of Longwood, Inc v Collier* 928 So 2d 482 (Fla Dist Ct App 2006).

Chapter 6
Confidentiality

1. Overview

This chapter examines mediation confidentiality from a number of perspectives. First the rationale for confidentiality is considered, followed by the identification of three types of confidentiality and an exploration of these with reference to international literature and legal regulation. Regulatory sources of confidentiality are critically assessed in light of the relevant case law, followed by an extensive examination of the concept of legal privilege. The analysis of confidentiality concludes with a consideration of its exceptions.

2 The Rationale Behind and Parameters of Mediation Confidentiality

Confidentiality is said to be an essential quality of mediation as it ensures the integrity of the process and protects the interests of all mediation participants.[1] Sekolec and Getty refer to it as a safeguard which is 'the centrepiece of the conciliation [mediation] regime'.[2]

It is widely contended that confidentiality encourages parties to speak freely and openly in mediation. In the absence of rules of evidence and other legal safeguards, communications in mediation may extend to matters beyond those considered relevant for arbitral, judicial or tribunal proceedings to include personal, commercial and non-legal issues. Parties do not generally expect what

1 For American literature, see K Brown, 'Comment, Confidentiality in Mediation: Status and Implications' (1991) 2 *Journal of Dispute Resolution* 307, L Freedman and M Prigoff, 'Confidentiality in Mediation: The Need for Protection' (1986) 2 *Ohio State Journal on Dispute Resolution* 37 at 37–38. On Germany see C Hartmann, 'Sicherung der Vertraulichkeit' in F Haft and K von Schlieffen (eds), *Handbuch Mediation* (2nd ed, München: C H Beck 2009) 1087 et seq and K Hopt and F Steffek, 'Rechtsvergleich, Regelungsmodelle, Grundsatzprobleme' in K Hopt and F Steffek (eds), *Mediation-Rechtstatsachen, Rechtsvergleich, Regelungen* (Tübingen: Mohr Siebeck 2008) at 39–41. On France see K Deckert, 'Mediation in Frankreich – Rechtlicher Rahmen und praktische Erfahrungen' in K Hopt and F Steffek (eds), *Mediation – Rechtstatsachen, Rechtsvergleich, Regelungen* (Tübingen: Mohr Siebeck 2008) 183 at 207–210.

2 J Sekolec and M Getty, 'The UMA and the UNCITRAL Model Rule: An Emerging Consensus on Mediation and Conciliation' (2003) *Journal of Dispute Resolution* 175 at 189.

they say and do in mediation to have the same consequences as if they occurred in a courtroom.

Without the confidentiality protection lawyers and clients might be reluctant to disclose certain information potentially useful for settlement discussions on the basis that they risk it being used against them in later proceedings. This could inhibit their negotiation conduct. In this regard the English Court of Appeal, in supporting the significance of confidentiality, has indicated that parties may adopt any position they wish in mediation and subsequently change their position without detriment should the matter proceed to arbitration or litigation.[3] Moreover mediation conducted without comprehensive confidentiality protection can invite fishing expeditions with good catches to be made by opportunistic negotiators at the expense of vulnerable parties such as those that are unrepresented.

It is also contended that the ability of mediators to maintain perceived impartiality in a process based on open and full communications is derived largely from the confidentiality obligation which binds all participants, including mediators, and the fact that mediators are *prima facie* not permitted to give court testimony in relation to events which occurred in their mediations.[4]

Another attribute of confidentiality is the contribution it is said to make to efficiency in the mediation system. As a confidential process, mediation avoids much of the time and cost that would be involved in formal documentation, responding to inquiries from outsiders and reporting or testifying to what occurred in mediations. Finally confidentiality of the mediation process is said to limit the grounds for judicial review and therefore afford it a considerable level of procedural finality, even if no settlement is reached.[5]

The majority of views in the literature, as well as contemporary mediation practice, endorse the confidentiality principle. However confidentiality is not universally considered to be an essential ingredient of mediation and it also has limitations. Reich comments that, 'the value of confidentiality presupposes that people will reveal information if they believe that the information will be kept in confidence.'[6] Challenging popular thought, he argues that people do not necessarily act in accordance with this principle. He claims support from the absence of empirical evidence indicating that confidentiality is necessary for the success of the mediation process.[7] Finally he

3 See *Halsey v Milton Keynes General NHS Trust and Steel v Joy and Halliday* [2004] 4 All ER 920.

4 See Hartmann (2009), above note 1 at 1087 et seq and 1108 et seq and see Hopt and Steffek (2008), above note 1 at 13 et seq.

5 On review of mediation by courts see Chapter 7.

6 J Reich, 'A Call for Intellectual Honesty: a Response to the Uniform Mediation Act's Privilege Against Disclosure' (2001) *Journal of Dispute Resolution* 197 at 217–218.

7 Reich (2001), above note 6 at 209.

suggests that statutory provisions on confidentiality do not significantly influence parties' communications in mediation as they are rarely aware of the implications of such provisions. Here reference is made to an empirical study showing that clients do not necessarily confide all relevant information to their lawyers despite the existence of lawyer-client privilege, although lawyers may believe that they do.[8]

Moreover there are limitations to the scope of confidentiality and there are risks associated with mediator assurances that everything said by parties in mediation will remain confidential. Mediation cannot be used to hide information that would otherwise be legally discoverable. Once information has been put on the mediation table and becomes known to the other party the acquired knowledge cannot be negated and parties are free to use it in strategic ways. For example, in the course of mediation one party may gain information about the credibility of the other party's case and their settlement bottom-line. Such information may be useful in planning litigation strategies and in deciding subsequent to the mediation whether or not to make an offer of settlement just below the other party's bottom line *without prejudice except as to costs*.[9] It is conceivable that the making of such an offer may later prove advantageous to the offeror in relation to costs awards.

A false sense of confidentiality may not only cause damage to a party, it may impair the credibility of the mediation system in general. In certain circumstances a promise of confidentiality may encourage unethical, improper or even illegal behaviour such as misleading or deceptive conduct. Case law indicates a willingness by courts to provide exceptions to the principle of confidentiality so that it does not protect such behaviour.[10]

From an inter-cultural perspective, confidentiality in mediation has been referred to as a western construct which takes on heightened significance in a litigation context. Antaki refers to ethno-cultural contexts in which confidentiality is not the norm and mediations take place in a group forum with elements of public symbolism.[11] Here community members are considered stakeholders in the conflict and mediations may be conducted in front of and with the participation of members of the group. In some legal systems such cultural factors may influence the development of legal policy on mediation confidentiality.

8 Reich (2001), above note 6 at 228.

9 In England such offers are known as Part 36 offers. They may be admitted in court proceedings in relation to costs determinations as evidence of good faith attempts to resolve disputes.

10 On this point see Chapter 5.

11 See N Antaki, 'Cultural Diversity and ADR Practices in the World' in J Goldsmith, A Ingen-Housz and G Pointon (eds), *ADR in Business: Practice and Issues across Countries and Cultures* (Alphen aan den Rijn: Kluwer Law International 2006) chapter 1.

3. The Dimensions of Confidentiality

Confidentiality attaches to the mediation process. Agreements to mediate initiating mediation and mediated settlement agreements at its conclusion are generally not considered part of the mediation process. Subject to party arrangements to the contrary[12] these agreements fall outside the scope of confidentiality; the fact that a party contracted to mediate and the written terms of a mediated settlement are *prima facie* not protected by the confidentiality attaching to the mediation process. Parties may therefore produce as evidence before court an agreement to mediate in order to establish the terms of the mediation, including the nature of the agreed confidentiality provisions. Similarly parties may submit a written settlement agreement in evidence before court in order to enforce its terms.[13] In the event of a disputed oral settlement agreement, the extent to which confidential mediation communications may be relied upon in evidence to prove or disprove the existence of the agreement is a topic of debate in regulatory and judicial circles, as considered further below and in Chapter 7.

Confidentiality may extend to various aspects of the mediation process including, *inter alia*:[14]

- information created or shared in a mediation joint session, such as the mediator's notes, and documents and visual material prepared for the purposes of mediation;
- information provided to the mediator in a private session or in a phone call or email with one of the parties;
- observations on the behaviour and conduct of participants in mediation; and
- the reasons for failure to reach agreement at mediation.

These situations lend themselves to the following tripartite classification of confidentiality, namely insider/outsider, insider/insider and insider/court confidentiality.

[12] See Article 14 of the Optional Conciliation Rules, Permanent Court of Arbitration, for an example of an institutional rule which provides that all matters relating to the conciliation process, including the settlement agreement, shall be kept confidential unless disclosure is necessary for enforcement.

[13] See, for example, *Fair v Bakhtari* (2006) 40 Cal 4th 189, 51 Cal Rptr 3d 871.

[14] The list is adapted from K Reichert, 'Confidentiality in International Mediation' (2005) 59 *Dispute Resolution Journal* 62.

3.1 Insider/Outsider Confidentiality

Insider/outsider confidentiality refers to a general duty of confidentiality *vis-à-vis* outside parties. It entails that parties to a mediation cannot make prohibited disclosures to outside parties. The duty can apply to the various participants in mediation such as parties, advisers, experts, interpreters, witnesses, the mediator and relevant support staff. It prohibits these various participants from disclosing information from the mediation to outsiders or non-participants. Broadly-worded statutory duties generally take the form of insider/outsider confidentiality. For example § 18 of the Austrian Law on Mediation in Civil Cases 2001 provides: [15]

> The mediator is obliged to secrecy about the facts which he has become aware of in the course of the mediation or which have otherwise become known. He shall deal with documents provided or delivered to him in the course of the mediation confidentially. The same applies to the supporting staff of the mediator as well as to persons who act for a mediator, under his direction in the course of a practical training.

As discussed later this provision has been interpreted widely to extend to insider/court confidentiality.

3.2 Insider/Insider Confidentiality

Insider/insider confidentiality regulates flows of information within mediation, especially in relation to private sessions, which are also known as caucus sessions in some jurisdictions. Many institutional mediation rules do not deal with this aspect of confidentiality as it is considered a matter of procedure best left to the mediator and parties. The rules that do exist in relation to insider/insider confidentiality generally take the form of default laws.

Mediators manage insider/insider confidentiality in one of two ways, the open communication approach or the in-confidence approach. In the former information passed to mediators in private sessions is not treated as confidential unless specifically requested by relevant parties. It is based on the principle that a free flow of information in mediation is essential for building trust and rapport and encouraging full and frank negotiations among the parties. At the same time this approach recognises that parties may wish to be able to communicate with the mediator on a confidential basis. The open communication approach puts the

[15] Translation from the German Original by Maria Theresa Trofaier MA (KCL) DipICArb, Solicitor (England and Wales), Registered with the Vienna Rechtsanwaltskammer, Accredited Mediators in Austria (Ministry of Justice List). Duties of confidentiality can also be found in Article 9 MLICC, Article 4 European Code of Conduct for Mediators and Article 24 of the Law of 1995 in France.

onus on parties and their representatives to identify specific pieces of information they wish to keep confidential. Mediators may pass on information provided to them by either party unless specifically requested not to do so. This practice has been criticised on the basis that putting the onus on parties to identify confidential information is likely to limit the extent to which they will be prepared to be candid and confide in mediators.[16] The open communication approach has been adopted by the JAMS International ADR Center, the Model Law on International Commercial Conciliation (MLICC), the UNCITRAL Conciliation Rules[17] and the Optional Conciliation Rules of the Permanent Court of Arbitration (1996).[18] In practice it is used in a variety of commercial contexts and also in some family mediation practices and transformative mediation programmes.

The other approach, the in-confidence model, operates conversely by treating all information disclosed privately as confidential unless indicated otherwise by the disclosing party. This means the mediator is unable to disclose such information without the express consent of the party providing it. The in-confidence approach is based on a belief that participants are more likely to feel comfortable disclosing information to the mediator if they know that it is disclosed on a confidential basis. Critics of this practice argue that it is more difficult for mediators to continuously manage the distinction between information imparted to them in private sessions and in joint sessions (the in-confidence approach) than to remember the specific items they cannot reveal to the other party (the open communication approach). In addition this model is said to promote distrust among parties as they may view the mediator as the keeper of secrets. This argument has more force in situations where parties know that certain information is being withheld from them than in situations where they do not have such knowledge but can only speculate.

The in-confidence approach is widely adopted in many situations. It is the preferred practice in the following sets of rules: the MEDAL International Mediation Rules 2005, the London Court of International Arbitration (LCIA) Mediation Procedure 1999, the Rules of the Mediation Institute of the Stockholm Chamber of Commerce 1999, the Netherlands Mediation Institute (NMI) Mediation Rules 2008, the World Intellectual Property Organisation (WIPO) Mediation Rules 2002 and the International Centre for Dispute Resolution (ICDR) International Mediation Rules 2008.[19]

16 See, for example, Reichert (2005), above note 14 at 65.

17 The UNCITRAL Conciliation Rules (1980) are referred to as the UCR.

18 The Permanent Court of Arbitration is referred to as the PCA.

19 See the Comparative Table of International Mediation Rules in Appendix B. See also comments by Reichert (2005), above note 14 at 64.

3.3 Insider/Court Confidentiality

One of the major concerns for mediation parties, or at least for their lawyers,[20] is the possibility that something said or done in, or for the purposes of, mediation might be used to their disadvantage in subsequent civil or criminal proceedings. The behaviours and communications relevant here are wide-ranging. They include information, documents, recordings or other communications created or shared in joint or private mediation sessions, observations about party behaviour and reasons for inability to settle and the fact that a party has made an offer to settle. Insider/court confidentiality involves the rights and obligations associated with protecting these mediation communications from being legally discovered or admitted in evidence in subsequent court and arbitral proceedings. It is a specific form of insider/outsider confidentiality. Insider/court confidentiality is the only aspect of confidentiality to be dealt with by the European Directive on Mediation; it is the primary focus of the Uniform Mediation Act (2001) (UMA) and it is addressed in Article 10 of the MLICC.

Not surprisingly this aspect of confidentiality has created the most controversy and litigation. It traverses the space between the mediation process and the court system and as such generates a host of potentially complex legal evidential issues, the most important of which are dealt with below.

4. Challenging Confidentiality

There are many cases, mainly from common law jurisdictions, in which the confidentiality of the mediation process has been challenged. Mediation participants may seek to admit evidence from a mediation in any one of the following circumstances:

- one party taking action against another for disclosing commercially confidential information to outsiders;
- the mediator seeking to recover fees from parties;
- one party seeking to set aside the mediated settlement or to enforce it;
- one party suing the mediator for improperly disclosing private session information to the other party;
- one party alleging breach of a legal duty to mediate;
- claims for costs or other sanctions for failure by one party to participate in good faith in mediation;

[20] Compare the view of Reich who argues that statutory-based insider/court confidentiality protections do not affect significantly the behaviour of parties: Reich (2001), above note 6.

- legal representative seeking access to documents produced at mediation for the purposes of litigation against them for negligent legal advice in the course of mediation;
- one party suing the mediator for professional misconduct;
- mediator responding to claim of professional misconduct;
- one or both parties suing mediator for breaching confidentiality in a way that caused damage;
- third party seeking access to documents produced at mediation for the purposes of litigation involving the same fact situation addressed in mediation;
- third party seeking access to documents produced at mediation under freedom of information (also known as open records) legislation;
- court order for a mediator or other mediation participant to testify or produce notes or documents in proceedings after mediation;
- party seeking to set aside arbitral award on basis of bias in a situation where arbitrator also acted as mediator; or
- party seeking disqualification of judge for bias in JDR context.[21]

The confidentiality principle in mediation, and its restrictions, reflects the tension between the integrity of this system and that of the due administration of justice. In one case the court considered public confidence in the impartiality of mediators so important that it outweighed the public interest in compelling mediator testimony which could result in the mediator losing trust in relation to similar future cases.[22] In terms of access to justice there are competing public interests, on one hand, of supporting out-of-court settlements through confidential mediation processes and, on the other hand, of the desirability of relevant evidence being made available to courts. The UMA, for example, links insider/court confidentiality to upholding, throughout the mediation, principles of procedural fairness, process integrity and informed party consent.[23] Therefore where mediators breach a professional duty under the Act they may lose the confidentiality privilege. In this way the UMA adopts a regulatory approach to confidentiality which attempts to balance competing interests.

The complexity of the legal issues raised by confidentiality is reflected in an extensive literature, the extent and range of regulation and the significant number of sometimes conflicting judgments on the topic. As this chapter shows,

21 On JDR (judicial dispute resolution), see Chapter 3.

22 See *NLRB v Macaluso* 618 F 2d 51 (9th Cir 1980).

23 See the Uniform Mediation Act (2001) with Prefatory Notes and Comments, available at www.nccusl.org. The provisions include mediator disclosure requirements to parties (s 9), limitations on mediators reporting to judges and others who may rule on the case (s 7), permission for parties to bring lawyers or support persons to mediation (s 10) and exceptions to the privilege (s 6).

courts have taken different approaches to insider/court confidentiality[24] deepening uncertainty in this emerging field of jurisprudence.

5. COURTS AND CONFIDENTIALITY

Human nature dictates that people tend talk to others despite obligations of confidentiality. More often than not breaches of confidentiality do not have significant consequences. However when they do litigation may follow. Some court decisions relating to insider/insider and insider/outsider confidentiality have dealt with the consequences of its breach.[25] Most litigation about confidentiality, however, relates to insider/court confidentiality and raises questions about admissibility of evidence in court and arbitral proceedings. There have also been a number of decisions concerning judicial disqualification where, for example, a judge has been privy to confidential information from an earlier mediation.[26]

Judicial approaches to confidentiality differ widely, partly because the field is relatively new and also because of the diverse sources of law that regulate mediation's three categories of confidentiality. In some jurisdictions courts have shown reluctance to forfeit their ability to admit and assess evidence relating to mediations. In the United States, for example, few courts have held mediation discussions to be privileged in the absence of protective legislation and generally such legislation is interpreted narrowly.[27] Reuben highlights court trends in two ADR-progressive states, California and Texas, where courts have

24 See, for example, *Brown v Rice and Patel* [2007] EWHC 625 (Ch) in England. See also the approach of the Californian Supreme Court in *Rojas v Superior Court* 33 Cal 4th 407 (Cal 2004). In the *Rojas* case it is interesting – and perhaps unsettling – to note the different approaches to confidentiality evident in the sequence of decisions from the court of first instance to the Court of Appeal and then to the Supreme Court.

25 In the United States see *Toon v Wackenhut Corrs Corp* 250 F 3d 950 (5th Cir 2001), *Moore v Kaufman* N° 13154357, 2003 WL 1930322 (Cal Ct App Apr 24 2003) cert denied (July 9 2003) referred to in See J Coben and P Thompson 'Disputing Irony: A Systematic Look at Litigation About Mediation' (2006) 11 *Harvard Negotiation Law Review* 43 at 58 et seq.

26 See Chapter 3 for a discussion of case law and legislation on this point. See, for example, the Australian case of *Ruffles v Chilman* [1999] WASCA 112. In the United States see *Metz v Metz* 61 P 3d 383 (Wyo 2003) and *Enterprise Leasing Co v Jones* 789 So 2d 964 (Fla 2001) referred to in Coben and Thompson (2006) above note 25 at 58.

27 See the discussion on securing confidentiality and the role of contract later in this chapter.

continued to develop exceptions to statutory privilege despite their not being expressly contained in the legislation.[28] As the author explains,

> Courts have generally refused to categorically exclude mediation communications from admissibility. Rather, courts have viewed such "mediation is confidential" statutes as requiring them to balance the mediation confidentiality interests against the parties' interest in the evidence in the case before them – frequently deciding in favor of admissibility.

In the US case of *Olam*, for example, the court ordered a mediator to testify about whether a mediated settlement agreement was the product of duress or not and stated that mediation privilege was subordinate to the 'orderly administration of justice' regardless of whether or not the mediator objected.[29] Similarly the court in *Rinaker* concluded that mediation confidentiality was subordinate to the 'constitutional right to effective impeachment'.[30]

Conversely courts have been prepared to refuse admission of mediation evidence even in cases where such an approach has caused hardship to the party seeking admission of the evidence, as the case of *Rojas v Superior Court* demonstrates.[31] Here the issue related to the production of materials and reports from an earlier mediation between a building owner and construction company; they were for the benefit of a group of former tenants of the building not party to the dispute between the owner and construction company and not participants in the mediation. Three years after the mediation Rojas and other tenants, many of whom were children, sued the building owner and others, alleging *inter alia* defective construction causing serious health problems. They sought production of all files, photographs and reports, including those from the previous mediation.

In relation to the photographs of the building defects which had been prepared for mediation, the tenants alleged that as the defects had since been repaired they had no other evidential avenue available to prove defects. The tenants advanced two main arguments. First they contended that the need to be able to present to a court evidence not otherwise available was in the interests of justice and outweighed the policy objective of protecting the confidentiality of the mediation and the benefits associated with it. The second part of the argument related to the nature of the photographs as pure evidence, raw data or non-derivative evidentiary material. It was argued that the confidentiality (in this

[28] R Reuben, 'The Sound of Dust Settling: A Response to Criticisms of the UMA' (2003) 1 *Journal of Dispute Resolution* 99 at 114–116.

[29] *Olam v Congress Mortgage Co* 68 F Supp 2d 1110 (ND Cal 1999) at 1132.

[30] *Rinaker v Superior Court* 62 Cal App 4th 155 (Cal 1998) at 164.

[31] *Rojas v Superior Court* 33 Cal 4th 407 (Cal 2004). See also the earlier case of *Foxgate Homeowners' Association v Bramalea California Inc* 26 Cal 4th 1 (Cal 2001), 25 P3d 1117, 108 Cal Rpter 2d 642, also referred to in Chapters 3 and 7.

case privilege and evidence) laws protected only 'the substance of the mediation', such as communications, negotiations and admissions and other derivative evidentiary material, and *not* raw data such as photographs, for to do so would permit parties to quarantine evidence by introducing it into mediation. This argument persuaded the Court of Appeal which ordered production of the photographs and associated non-derivative material. However in a final appeal the Supreme Court overturned this decision and held that the legislature's intention in ss 1119 and 1120 of the California Evidence Code was to extend privilege to all information forming part of mediation and that in this case the court management order and the mediated settlement signalled similar intentions. As a result the materials including reports and photographs were protected from disclosure, despite the hardship and injustice that this decision caused the tenants. The final outcome illustrates a judicial policy of granting mediation communications a high level of confidentiality protection and thereby generating greater certainty around the use of the process.

At first glance the comments of Dyson LJ in the case of *Halsey* suggest that English courts will also be reluctant to lift the cloak of confidentiality:[32]

> We make it clear that it was common ground before us (and we accept) that parties are entitled in an ADR to adopt whatever position they wish, and if as a result the dispute is not settled, that is not a matter for the court... if the integrity and confidentiality of the process is to be respected, the court should not know, and therefore should not investigate, why the process did not result in agreement.

However, as in the United States, there have been numerous cases where English courts have found exceptions to confidentiality rules.[33] In the case of *Farm Assist N° 2*[34] the court, after examining applicable law on confidentiality and privilege, refused an application to dismiss a witness summons for a mediator despite contractual confidentiality provisions prohibiting the parties from calling the mediator as witness.

Coben and Thompson express a degree of alarm over the large number of cases in which courts appear to have ignored confidentiality provisions. Referring to cases from the United States the authors go so far as to suggest that parties' behaviour and attitude in mediation have influenced courts' decisions on

32 *Halsey v Milton Keynes General NHS Trust and Steel v Joy and Halliday* [2004] 4 All ER 920 at para 14.

33 For examples of where English courts have lifted the veil of confidentiality, see *Chantrey Vellacott v The Convergence Group PLC and others* [2007] EWHC 1774 (Ch) and *Brown v Rice and Patel* [2007] EWHC 625 (Ch). These cases are discussed later in this chapter.

34 See *Farm Assist Limited (in liquidation) v The Secretary of State for the Environment, Food and Rural Affairs (N° 2)* [2009] EWHC 1102 (TCC).

the merits.[35] Moreover in numerous cases there have been no objections to mediation disclosures by mediators, by parties and others about mediators' statements and actions, or by parties and lawyers about their own mediation communications and conduct.[36] Uncontested mediation disclosures occurred in approximately 30 per cent of litigated mediation cases between 1999 and 2003. This trend continued in subsequent years, although a decrease in evidence from mediation participants, other than mediators, was noted in cases during 2004–2005.[37]

The UMA in s 6 provides for *in camera* determination of issues relating to confidentiality so that the benefits of confidentiality protection are not jeopardised the moment confidentiality is challenged in open court. The English Civil Procedure Rules in Part 39.2(3)(c) and (g) also provide for *in camera* determinations of certain types of confidential information where the court considers it necessary in the interests of justice. However the court in *Cumbria Waste Management*[38] rejected an application for an *in camera* hearing in relation to the admissibility of mediation evidence on the basis that, in the circumstances, it was more important for justice to be seen to be done. A similar provision is being considered in law reform discussions in Australia.

In civil law jurisdictions there has not been the same level of litigation on confidentiality issues. French decisions have notably demonstrated strong support for upholding confidentiality in mediation. In the SNECMA case[39] the parties engaged in mediation pursuant to an agreement to mediate containing a confidentiality clause, but they did not reach a settlement agreement. At the close of the mediation the parties instructed the mediator to prepare a report on the mediation on the basis that they would then decide if and how the report was to be used. In subsequent litigation proceedings in the Commercial Court the

35 See J Coben and P Thompson 'Mediation Litigation Trends 1999–2007' (2007) 1 *World Arbitration and Mediation Report* 395 at 408.

36 See Coben and Thompson (2006), above note 25 at 58–60. In Australia see *Commonwealth Development Bank of Australia Pty Ltd and Anor v Cassegrain* [2002] NSWSC 965 where a mediator's report was admitted into evidence without objection.

37 See Coben and Thompson (2007), above note 35 at 401–402. At the time of writing more up to date statistics were not available. Readers are encouraged to check the Mediation Law Project Website at Hamline University for updates: www.law.hamline.edu/adr/mediation-case-law-project.html.

38 *Cumbria Waste Management Ltd and Lakeland Waste Management Ltd v Baines Wilson* [2008] EWHC 786 (QB) at para 32.

39 See, for example, Cass crim, 28.02.2001 N° 00–83365, Bull crim N° 54, 186 and Paris Court of Large Claims (Paris Trib gr inst, TGI Paris), 18.01.1999 *SNECMA v P Ségui et autres*, *La Gazette du Palais* (29 April–3 May 2001) 45 referred to in Deckert (2008), above note 1 at 208 and A Mourre, *ADR – International Application. Special Supplement to the ICC International Court of Arbitration Bulletin* (Paris: ICC Publication N° 640, 2001 Edition 2001) 68 at 70–71.

plaintiff referred in the writ to the contents of the mediator's report, including to offers of compromise that had been made and to the mediator's views and findings. The defendant applied to the Paris Tribunal de Grande Instance seeking a summary order that the plaintiff withdraw the writ and serve a new one without any reference to the mediation, hand over all confidential documents in connection with the mediation to a sequestrator and withdraw all the said documents from evidence submitted in the Commercial Court. In his decision the Chief Judge of the Paris Tribunal de Grande Instance emphasised confidentiality as a fundamental aspect of the mediation, as enshrined in Article 131-14 of the C pr civ[40] and reinforced in the parties' agreement to mediate. He held that confidentiality extended to offers made by the parties and in this case included the mediator's report, except to the extent that the parties *and mediator* decided otherwise. The Chief Judge found the plaintiff in breach of the obligation of confidentiality incumbent on all those involved in mediation and concluded that such behaviour amounted to 'a manifestly unlawful disturbance' within the terms of Articles 809(1) and 873(1) of the Civil Procedure Code.

Thus courts have taken different approaches to confidentiality protection in mediation. As indicated previously one of the reasons for this relates to the way in which mediation confidentiality is regulated in a given jurisdiction. The next section examines the different regulatory approaches to mediation confidentiality.

6. Approaches to Confidentiality

There are different regulatory approaches to confidentiality in mediation.[41] Confidentiality can be regulated by institutional rules, codes of conduct, agreement, statute or a combination of these.[42]

At the adoption of the UMA in 2001 there were more than 300 state statutes throughout the United States providing some form of protection of

[40] See also the following cases which dealt with confidentiality issues related to Article 24 du loi de 1995: CA Paris 11.10.2007 N° 05/04126 and Cass crim 28.02.2001 N° 00–83365.

[41] On the different regulatory approaches to confidentiality, see Uniform Mediation Act (2001) with Prefatory Notes and Reporter's Notes for § 5(5)(a)–(c) at www.pon.harvard.edu/guests/uma/NovUMAWP.html.

[42] In United States the Alternative Dispute Resolution Act 1998 requires all federal courts to develop local rules in relation to mediation confidentiality. The European Directive on Mediation requires the EU member states to transpose the Directive into national law and Article 7 deals with confidentiality. See Directive 2008/52/EC on Certain Aspects of Mediation in Civil and Commercial Matters, proposal as adopted by the European Parliament and the Council of the European Union on 21 May 2008, L 136/3, 24/05/2008.

insider/court confidentiality.[43] While the high number of laws indicated strong policy support for confidentiality in the United States, varied approaches to the topic lead to uncertainty in interstate mediations. Furthermore local court rules on confidentiality can affect the interpretation and application of mediation confidentiality provisions. In some jurisdictions court orders can direct parties to mediation in specific cases and set out the parameters of the referral in relation to issues such as confidentiality for the case in question. The UMA is an attempt to create uniformity in this area.

As indicated in Chapter 3 mediator backgrounds are varied and span different disciplines and professions. Mediators with more than one professional membership are likely to be bound by multiple sets of professional ethical guidelines. Lawyer–mediators, for example, are likely to be members of bar associations as well as mediation associations. Confidentiality obligations to clients and related issues are frequently included in professional rules and form part of the regulatory mix relevant to confidentiality.

In terms of legal constructs, confidentiality can be addressed in a number of ways. These include a general duty of confidentiality, privilege, prohibition on calling a witness, right of refusal to testify and evidentiary exclusion. In relation to insider/court confidentiality the following discussion highlights the different approaches to mediation evidence in subsequent civil and criminal proceedings. By way of example, Article 7 of the European Directive focuses solely on civil proceedings, thereby *prima facie* permitting the admission of mediation evidence in criminal proceedings, whereas Austrian law sets out separate regulations for mediator confidentiality in relation to civil and criminal proceedings.

6.1 Duty of Confidentiality

Duties of confidentiality, also known as duties of silence (*Verschwiegenheitspflicht*)[44] and secrecy (*le médiateur est tenu au secret*),[45] are generally positively-framed obligations to keep certain information confidential. They deal with insider/outsider confidentiality in its extended sense to include insider/court confidentiality. Where specified in institutional rules and

[43] See J Reichert, 'Bar Organisations Urge Uniformity in Mediation Law' (1999) 35 *Trial* 104 at 105 quoting N Rogers, the reporter for the National Conference of Commissioners on Uniform State Laws (NCCUSL).

[44] See, for example, § 18 of the Austrian Law on Mediation in Civil Cases discussed below.

[45] See the Centre de Mediation et d'Arbitrage de Paris (CMAP) Rules of Mediation (Règlement de Médiation) available at www.cmap.fr. CMAP is a leading French dispute resolution organisation.

agreements to mediate, duties of confidentiality may apply to insider/insider confidentiality.[46]

Duties of confidentiality in mediation usually take the form of contractual or legislative obligations.[47] In some jurisdictions there may also be implied or equitable duties of confidentiality – independent of express contractual commitments and legislative obligations – which arise when a person receives information which he knows or should know is confidential. Ramsay J in *Farm Assist N° 2* has suggested that this duty would apply to a mediator in the course of a mediation.[48] In common law jurisdictions it has been said that a duty of confidentiality is unlikely of itself to be,

> a bar to disclosure of documents or information in the process of litigation, but the court will only compel such disclosure if it considers it necessary for the fair disposal of the case.[49]

However duties of confidentiality in civil law jurisdictions are more likely to be interpreted broadly. The Austrian Law on Mediation in Civil Cases 2001 in § 18 sets out a duty of confidentiality for accredited mediators in respect of information entrusted to them or of which they otherwise become aware.[50] This provision covers information made available to mediators in the plenary sessions of mediation, that is insider/outsider confidentiality. In addition it would seem to extend to information entrusted to mediators in a private session by one party only, that is insider/insider confidentiality. Although not framed as an evidentiary exclusion, § 18 will likely be interpreted broadly so that mediators will not be permitted to give evidence from the mediation in civil or criminal court proceedings. The notes to the bill introducing the Austrian Law (*Regierungsvorlage*) point out that a prohibition on the introduction of mediation evidence from the mediator in subsequent court proceedings would flow from an interplay of § 18 of the Law and other legal procedural protections

46 See, for example, JAMS International ADR Center, clause 1.

47 In relation to contractual obligations see, for example, the CMAP Rules of Mediation Article 3 (Règlement de Médiation) at www.cmap.fr.

48 See *Farm Assist N° 2*, above note 34, at paras 23–29 referring inter alia to C Phipps and R Toulson, *Confidentiality* (2nd ed, UK: Sweet and Maxwell 2006) at para 15–016.

49 See Phipps and Toulson (2006), above note 48 at para 17–001 referring to *British Steel Corporation v Granada Television Ltd* [1981] AC 1096.

50 The Act only applies to accredited mediators according to § 3(1)(N° 2) of the Austrian Law on Mediation in Civil Cases. See also A Likar and K Krommer, 'Mediation und Recht – Das Recht in der Mediation' (2005) *Österreichisches Anwaltsblatt* 60 at 62 et seq who argue that the duty should extend to all mediators and M Roth and D Gherdane, 'Mediation in Österreich' in K Hopt and F Steffek (eds), *Mediation – Rechtstatsachen, Rechtsvergleich, Regelungen* (Tübingen: Mohr Siebeck 2008) 105 at 139 who reject this argument.

in Austrian law.[51] However the ability of parties and other mediation participants to introduce mediation evidence in subsequent judicial proceedings does not seem to be directly regulated by the Austrian Law on Mediation in Civil Cases. As a point of comparison, § 5 of the Slovakian mediation law[52] sets out similar obligations of confidentiality to those found in § 18 of the Austrian law, but it extends the obligation beyond mediators to 'parties to mediation and other natural persons invited by the mediator or by the party to mediation'.

Leading French academic opinion and court decisions[53] support a duty of confidentiality in relation to all mediation participants even though the statutory duty of confidentiality in Article 24 of the Law of 1995 is expressed only in relation to mediators. The extension of the duty to other mediation participants is encouraged through its inclusion in institutional rules and agreements to mediate.[54] It has been said to encompass all aspects of insider/outsider and insider/court confidentiality in relation to mediators, administrative assistants, parties, lawyers, experts, referring judges and others.

As foreshadowed previously, the nature of confidentiality obligations can vary according to the professional affiliation of mediators. In Austria lawyer–mediators must comply with confidentiality rules pursuant to the Austrian Rules for Lawyers,[55] in addition to their obligations under the Austrian Law on Mediation in Civil Cases. They are said to have a general duty of confidentiality acting as lawyers[56] and a special duty of confidentiality when acting as mediators.[57] Other professional examples include notary–mediators[58] and psychologist–mediators.[59]

51 See Government bill (Regierungsvorlage) ZivMediatG at 30. See also N Pitkowitz, 'Die neuen Mediationsregeln der EU – Ist Österreich noch Wegbereiter' (2005) *Zeitschrift für Schiedsverfahren* 81 at 86.

52 Slovakian Act of 25 June 2004 on Mediation and Amendment of Certain Acts at www.mediationworld.net.

53 See CA Paris, 24.09.1999: CA Paris 24.09.1999, *La Gazette du Palais* 16–17.02.2000, 17 with comments by Lacabarats and Cass. Civ. 3e. 29.02.2002 N° 00–19422, *La Gazette du Palais* 13.06.2002 at 26 referred to in Deckert (2008) above note 1 at 208–209.

54 See, for example, Article 3 CMAP Rules of Mediation (Règlement de médiation) at www.cmap.fr. See also Cass crim, 28.02.2001 N° 00–83365, Bull crim N° 54, 186, *La Gazette du Palais* 17.11.2001, 26, *La Gazette du Palais* 29.4–3.05.2001, 45, Paris Trib gr inst (TGI Paris) 18.01.1999 and Séverin, (2003) *Revue trim de droit civ* 229 at 232. These are referred to in Deckert (2008) above note 1 at 208.

55 See §§ 8(5) and 9(2) of the Austrian Rules for Lawyers (Rechtsanwaltsordnung, RAO).

56 See the RAO, above note 55.

57 See § 65 of the Professional Standards for Lawyers (Richtlinien für die Ausübung des Rechtsanwaltsberufes für die Überwachung der Pflichten des Rechtsanwaltes und für die Ausbildung der Rechtsanwaltsanwärter 1977, RL–BA) and W Steinacher, 'Die Mediationsrichtlinie' (2000) *Österreichisches Anwaltsblatt* 124 at 127 et seq.

In the absence of legislative provisions on confidentiality directly applicable to mediation, German mediators must look to the laws that govern their professional affiliation. For example, § 18 of the National Rules of Professional Practice for Lawyers[60] provides that lawyers may practice as mediators and in doing so are subject to applicable professional laws,[61] including a broad obligation of confidentiality. Legal representatives in mediation remain subject to their general duty of confidentiality as lawyers. However this duty is for the benefit of their clients and, subject to the terms of the agreement to mediate,[62] there is nothing to prevent lawyers and parties presenting mediation evidence in subsequent proceedings.[63]

In the absence of laws dealing with rights and obligations of parties in relation to confidentiality, reference is generally made to confidentiality provisions in express or implied agreements to mediate. In Germany leading academic opinion suggests that by entering the mediation process parties agree to accept its fundamental principles including confidentiality and thus enter an implied agreement in relation to confidentiality in the mediation.[64] In determining the existence and scope of an implied contractual duty of confidentiality the court, in accordance with §§ 133 and 157 of the German Civil Code,[65] will take into account the attendant circumstances and the intention of the parties.[66]

In short, depending on the scope of the obligation and the jurisdiction in which it applies, a duty of confidentiality may extend to insider/outsider, insider/insider and insider/court situations. It may be found in agreements to mediate, whether express or implied, in legislation and in codes of conduct.

58 See §§ 5(4b) and 37 of the Austrian Notary Code (Notariatsordnung, NO) and §§ 32 et seq of the Standesrichtlinien der Notare (STR 2000).

59 See § 15 of the Law on Psychotherapy (Psychotherapiegesetz).

60 See the Berufsordnung (BORA).

61 Such as § 43a(2) of the National Lawyers' Rules (Bundesrechtsanwaltsordnung, BRAO) discussed below.

62 In Germany the use of procedural contracts (Prozess- und Beweismittelvertrag) within the framework of an agreement to mediate could effectively commit the signatories to the agreement to obligations of confidentiality including insider/court confidentiality. Such contracts are recognised by the courts.

63 G Wagner and C Thole, 'Die Europäische Mediations-Richtlinie – Inhalt, Probleme und Umsetzungsperspektiven' in D Baegte, J Hein and M Hinden (eds), *Die richtige Ordnung, Festschrift für Jan Kropholler zum 70 Geburtstag* (Tübingen: Mohr-Siebeck 2008) at 937–938.

64 See Hartmann (2009), above note 1 at 1099.

65 See O Palandt et al (eds), *Bürgerliches Gesetzbuch* (68th ed, Munich: Beck Juristischer Verlag 2009) at § 133 and § 157 BGB.

66 See Hartmann (2009), above note 1 at 1099.

6.2 Evidentiary Exclusion

Evidentiary exclusions refer to rules designed to exclude from arbitral or court proceedings evidence considered unreliable or, for policy reasons, inappropriate, regardless of its source. As indicated previously policy reasons in relation to mediation include encouraging genuine and frank settlement negotiations so that parties need not fear that what they say or do during negotiations could be used against them, for example as evidence of admission of liability in subsequent litigation. The scope of evidentiary exclusion is generally limited, traditionally extending only to evidence offered to prove the validity or the amount of a claim.[67] Unlike privilege and rights of refusal to testify, evidentiary exclusions do not attach to mediation participants and therefore cannot be waived.

In relation to mediation, evidentiary exclusions take the form of either a list of specific information or communications that are subject to confidentiality, such as in Article 10 of the MLICC,[68] or a general rule of exclusion according to which all evidence from a mediation or from a mediator and/or identified mediation participants is *prima facie* inadmissible, subject to specified exceptions.

The French Civil Procedure Code, Article 131-14, illustrates the evidentiary exclusion approach. It provides that in subsequent proceedings no evidence can be adduced, relied upon or referred to in relation to statements, explanations, observations or findings of mediators without the parties' consent. The principle has been confirmed by the courts.[69] However, unlike in other jurisdictions such as Austria, mediation confidentiality, while well-protected in French law, is not mandatory and parties may contract out of the relevant provisions of the Code if they wish.[70]

The Californian Evidence Code (§ 1119) and the Evidence Act 1995 in Australia (s 131) provide further examples of the evidentiary exclusion approach. The *US Federal Rule of Evidence, r 408, takes the form of an evidentiary exclusion. It is considered below in the context of protection of settlement negotiations.* In England there is no statutory evidentiary exclusion for mediation, but r 32.1(2) of the Civil Procedure Rules (CPR) gives judges the right to exclude evidence otherwise admissible and it remains to be seen if and how this might be applied in relation to mediation.

Where evidentiary exclusions are framed in absolute terms they may significantly limit judicial review surrounding mediation events, as illustrated by

67 See, for example, in the United States r 408 of the *Federal Rules of Evidence.*

68 On Article 10 MLICC, see Chapter 9.

69 See Cass Crim, 28.02.2001, N° 00–83365, Bull N° 54, 186.

70 See Deckert (2008), above note 1 at 208. See also *La Gazette du Palais* 16–17.02.2000, 1776 and *La Gazette du Palais* 20.06.2004, 2.

the Australian case of *Gain v Commonwealth Bank of Australia.*[71] This case involved the NSW Farm Debt Mediation Act 1994, s 15(1) which provides that,

> [e]vidence of anything said or admitted during a mediation session and a document prepared for the purposes of, in the course of or pursuant to, a mediation session are not admissible in any proceedings in a court or before a person or body authorised to hear and receive evidence.

The court held that a decision to issue a pre-litigation certificate stating that the parties had attempted to mediate the matter in good faith was not amenable to judicial review because s 15 of the Act rendered inadmissible the very evidence upon which any such review would need to be conducted.

6.3 Prohibition on Calling a Mediator to Testify

In addition to the duty of confidentiality placed on mediators by the Austrian Law on Mediation in Civil Cases (see above), the Austrian Code of Civil Procedure[72] prohibits accredited mediators[73] being called to testify in civil court proceedings in relation to mediations they have conducted. As a result mediators are classified as incapable of testimony[74] and the law precludes the presentation of mediation evidence by them.[75] Exceptions to the general prohibition include evidence in relation to the commencement, continuation and termination of the mediation process as this may be crucial in determining the possible suspension of litigation limitation periods.[76] Furthermore the parties cannot release

[71] *Gain and another v Commonwealth Bank of Australia* (1997) 42 NSWLR 252. However in *Hurworth Nominees Pty Ltd v ANZ Banking Group Ltd* [2006] NSWSC 1278 the court, while acknowledging the decision in *Gain,* found that there was limited scope for judicial review of a decision to issue a pre-litigation certificate.

[72] See § 320 N° 4 of the Austrian Zivilprozessordnung, ZPO.

[73] G Falk and G Koren (eds), *Zivilrechts-Mediations-Gesetz, Kommentar* (Wien: Verlag Österreich 2005) at § 18 RN 1.17. M Pruckner (ed), *Recht der Mediation* (Wien: Linde 2003) at 33. Note that in contrast to § 18 of the Law, this provision does not extend to mediator assistants or trainees: W Rechberger (ed), *Kommentar zur Zivilprozessordnung* (3rd ed, Wien: Springer 2006) at § 320 RN 7. However some commentators suggest that assistants and trainees may be covered by analogy: P Oberhammer and T Domej, 'Ein rechtlicher Rahmen für die Mediation in Österreich – Zum neuen Zivilrechts-Mediations-Gesetz' (2003) *Zeitschrift für Konfliktmanagement* 144 at 147.

[74] A similar approach is used in Minnesota, United States where the mediator in deemed incompetent to testify in subsequent proceedings.

[75] Regierungsvorlage ZivMediaG at 37 and C Fuchshuber (ed), *Mediation im Zivilrecht* (Wien: LexisNexis 2004) at 17.

[76] On limitation periods generally see Chapter 7 and in Austria see § 22 of the Austrian Law on Mediation and Pitkowitz (2005), above note 51 at 86. Falk and Koren argue that, by extension, details of the identity of parties and subject-matter of mediation

mediators from this prohibition[77] and, unlike some forms of mediator privilege discussed below, it seems that Austrian mediators cannot block testimony or evidence of other mediation participants. Finally this arrangement may restrict mediators in defending themselves against claims of misconduct or professional negligence.

Austrian law thus seeks to secure high level protection for mediator confidentiality with minimal exceptions.[78] The intention is confirmed by the fact that a suggestion in the draft mediation law to allow parties to waive the prohibition (similar to a right of refusal to testify or a privilege) was rejected for the final version.[79]

6.4 Right of Refusal to Testify

The right of refusal to testify in court is an exception to the general public duty to testify. It relates to insider/court confidentiality. It is similar to privilege, dealt with below, in that it attaches to the holder of the right and as a right it must be asserted but can also be waived.

The right of refusal to testify is to be distinguished from a prohibition on being called as a witness according to which the person subject to the prohibition has no choice in relation to testifying.[80] As indicated in the previous section, Austrian mediators are subject to a prohibition on being called as witnesses in civil proceedings. However this is not the case in relation to criminal proceedings where accredited mediators and their assistants and trainees are afforded the right to refuse to give evidence, placing them on equal footing with lawyers, notaries and defence counsel who also have the right to refuse to give evidence[81] in relation to matters in which they practise as professionals.[82] In other words mediators have the option of offering evidence and testimony in subsequent criminal proceedings if they wish. The

would also fall within the exception as these facts may be necessary to apply the statue of limitations provisions: Falk and Koren (2005), above note 73 at § 18 RN 1.19. Pruckner (2003), above note 73 at 36.

77 Hopt and Steffek take a critical stance on this point. See Hopt and Steffek (2008), above note 1 at 41 referring inter alia to Article 1(1) of the European Directive on Mediation which refers to the need to ensure 'a balanced relationship between mediation and judicial proceedings'.

78 See Regierungsvorlage ZivMediaG at 37.

79 G Hopf, 'Auf dem Weg zu einer gesetzlichen Regelung der Mediation in Österreich', in Simotta (ed), *Der Zivilprozess zu Beginn des 21. Jahrhunderts*, Festschrift für Wolfgang Jelinek (Wien: LexisNexis 2002) 69 at 78 et seq. Roth and Gherdane (2008), above note 154 at 141.

80 Hopf (2002), above note 79 at 80 et seq.

81 See § 152(1) N° 4 of the Austrian Code of Criminal Procedure (Strafprozessordnung, StPO).

82 Hopf (2002), above note 79 at 80 et seq.

differentiated treatment between a prohibition in civil proceedings and a discretion in criminal proceedings reflects the higher importance placed upon access to evidence where a person's liberty may be at stake.

In Germany a right of refusal to testify may apply to mediators despite the absence of relevant legislative provisions expressly including mediators.[83] In relation to civil proceedings the right of refusal to testify[84] is an exception to the general duty to testify.[85] § 383(1) N° 6 of the German Code of Civil Procedure provides a right of refusal to testify for persons who, on the basis of their profession or business, are entrusted with confidential information.[86] Thus mediators offering mediation services as part of a profession listed in the legislation, such as lawyers, notaries, psychologists, social workers and counsellors, may possess a right of refusal to testify by virtue of that profession.[87] Mediators acting in an honorary capacity have no refusal right because of the lack of the element 'profession or business'.[88]

Mediators subject to statutory duties of confidentiality such as lawyer–mediators and notary–mediators may be *obliged* to make use of the right of refusal to testify in order to uphold their obligations of confidentiality,[89] unless the disputing parties release them from this obligation.[90] Where mediators are not subject to statutory duties of confidentiality but to one claimed on the basis of contract or common usage, the situation is less clear. However some commentators argue that, on the basis of contractual confidentiality provisions

83 At the time of writing this topic had been identified as in need of reform by German commentators and members of the Mediation Expert Consultant Group to the Federal Ministry of Justice in Germany.

84 See §§ 383 to 385 of the German Code of Civil Procedure (Zivilprozessordnung, ZPO) and F Stein and M Jonas (eds), *Kommentar zur Zivilprozessordnung, Band 5* (22nd ed, Tübingen: Mohr Siebeck 2006) at § 383 RN 1. See also the related provisions §§ 142 and 144 of the Code of Civil Procedure.

85 In Germany every person has a general public duty to testify. This encompasses the obligation to appear (§§ 380, 382 of the German Code of Civil Procedure Zivilprozessordnung, ZPO) and to tell the truth (§§ 393 et seq, 376, 390 of the German Civil Procedure Rules). See Stein and Jonas (2006), above note 84 at § 373 RN 18.

86 In relation to mediators see Hartmann (2009), above note 1 at 1112 and Wagner and Thole (2008), above note 63 at 936–937.

87 For lawyers and notaries see § 59b(2)(N° 5a) and § 43a(2) of the National Lawyers' Rules and § 24(1) of the National Notary Rules, which explicitly state that mediation is part of their respective professions.

88 Hartmann (2009), above note 1, 1087 at 1109.

89 Hartmann (2009), above note 1, 1087 at 1109.

90 See § 385(2) ZPO and Wagner and Thole (2008), above note 63.

and the centrality of confidentiality to the mediation process, mediators have the right of refusal to testify irrespective of profession.[91]

Due to the public interest element of this right, the categories of persons entitled to refuse to testify cannot be extended by contract and a provision in an agreement to mediate conferring such a right on a mediator is unlikely to be enforced by a court.[92] Parties may waive their individual right of refusal to testify and jointly they may override a mediator's right of refusal to testify.[93]

The right of refusal to testify operates in a similar manner in relation to criminal proceedings, although not all professions offering mediation services are recognised by the Criminal Procedure Code.[94]

6.5 Protection of Settlement Negotiations

Traditionally many jurisdictions have excluded evidence of settlement negotiations on the basis that that there is an implied agreement to this effect between parties offering or agreeing to negotiate to settle out of court and that it is good policy to encourage settlement without court proceedings.[95] Protection of settlement negotiations can involve evidentiary exclusion and without prejudice privilege. This section looks at the application of settlement negotiation protections to mediation.

In English[96] and Australian[97] law this principle takes the form of without prejudice privilege – a legal privilege attaching to parties in settlement negotiations.[98] The concept of privilege derives from common law systems. Although there are many variations in relation to privilege the following general comments can be made. Privilege is based on the idea of a 'private law applied

91 See Wagner and Thole (2008), above note 63 and Stein and Jonas (2006), above note 84 at § 383 RN 59 and 85. See also Hartmann (2009), above note 1, 1087 at 1110.

92 R Zöller (ed), *Zivilprozessordnung* (26th ed, Köln: Dr Otto Schmidt 2007) at § 383 RN 3.

93 See § 383(2) of the Code of Civil Procedure (Zivilprozessordnung, ZPO).

94 See § 53(1)(N° 3) German Code of Criminal Procedure (Strafprozessordnung, StPO). See also Hartmann (2009) above note 1 at 1110 and 1113 and R Eckardt and B Dendorfer, 'Der Mediator zwischen Vertraulichkeit und Zeugnispflicht-Schutz durch Prozessvertrag' (2001) *Monatsschrift für Deutsches Recht* 786 at 788.

95 See *Cumbria Waste Management Ltd and Lakeland Waste Management Ltd v Baines Wilson* [2008] EWHC 786 (QB) at para 18, quoting Walker LJ in *Muller v Linsley and Mortimer* [1996] PNLR 74 (CA).

96 See, for example, *Hall and another v Pertemps Group Ltd and another* [2005] All ER (D) 15 (Nov).

97 See s 131 of the Evidence Act 1995 (Cth).

98 There is some argument that the without prejudice rule is not a privilege, but the majority academic view and case law treat it as a privilege: see Reich (2001), above note 6 and the discussion below.

to a small group of persons as a special prerogative'.[99] Essentially privilege provides a right to refuse to reveal information and in some circumstances to prevent others from revealing information, for the purposes of discovery or evidence, providing an exemption to the fundamental maxim that the public has a right to every person's evidence. It refers to rules which exclude evidence on the basis that it would be adverse to a fundamental principle or relationship.[100] Depending on jurisdiction, privilege can include without prejudice privilege, legal professional privilege, privilege against self-incrimination, marital privilege, public interest privilege and mediation privilege.

Where without prejudice privilege is asserted, written and verbal communications made during the course of genuine negotiations conducted with a view to settling an existing dispute are protected from being disclosed to the detriment of the disclosing party's rights.[101] In Australia the without prejudice privilege will apply where the communication is made or documentation prepared 'in connection with an attempt to negotiate a settlement of the dispute'.[102] However in other jurisdictions the privilege may require that documents are prepared for the sole or dominant purpose of settlement. The privilege is designed to protect disputing parties and extends to determinations on costs liabilities, unless the parties expressly agree otherwise or there is a statutory exception to this effect.[103] There is a number of exceptions to the without prejudice rule and they include the following:[104]

- There is no existing dispute – this is unlikely to arise in a formal mediation setting.
- There is unambiguous impropriety, including threats made to induce settlement.[105]

[99] See Reich (2001), above note 6 at 202.

[100] See *Australian Legal Dictionary* (Sydney: Butterworths 1998).

[101] See D Spencer and M Brogan, *Mediation Law and Practice* (Cambridge: Cambridge University Press 2006). See also See D Foskett, *The Law and Practice of Compromise* (6th ed, London: Sweet and Maxwell 2005) and the cases *Field v Commissioner for Railways* NSW (1957) 99 CLR 285 (Australia) and *Rush and Tompkins Ltd v Greater London Council* (1989) 1 AC 1280 (England).

[102] In Australia see s 131(2) of the Evidence Act 1995 (Cth), which removes the bar to admissibility otherwise imposed by s 131(1) in relation to questions of liability for costs, and see the case *Azzi and Ors v Volvo Car Australia Pty Ltd (Costs)* [2007] NSWSC 375 on this point.

[103] See *Cutts v Head* [1884] 1 All ER 697 (CA).

[104] In relation to exceptions, see also s 131(2), (3) and (4) of the Evidence Act 1995 (Cth).

[105] Allen refers to the case of *Unilever v Proctor and Gamble* [2001] 1 All ER 783 to highlight the restrictive approach of English courts to this exception: T Allen, *Implementing the EU Directive on Mediation: A Draft Consultation Paper* (London: 2009) at 11–12. At the time of writing, the paper was in draft form. For updates

- Communications are made in furtherance of an abuse of power or fraud.[106]
- The evidence is merely that certain statements were made and does not go to proof of admission against interest.[107] This exception may be relied on by third parties to mediation such as sub-contractors who were not party to the original dispute but who want access to information from a mediation to justify their own settlement proposals.
- A party is estopped from asserting privilege where another relies to its detriment on a misleading without prejudice statement. Further the privilege must not be abused for the purposes of misleading the court.[108]
- There is waiver of privilege which can be express or implied.
- There is a settlement of the dispute and one party is seeking to enforce it or set it aside.

Without prejudice privilege has been applied to mediation in a number of jurisdictions including Australia[109] and England.[110] In the English case of *Brown v Rice and Patel,*[111] a court held that mediation takes the form of assisted without prejudice negotiation to which, by implication, the privilege applies.[112] Allen notes that this is not an uncontroversial view as mediation differs in many respects from unassisted negotiation.[113] Indeed the Australian case of *Rajski v Tectran Corp* suggests that where there is specific legislation relating to mediation confidentiality, it will override general provisions on evidence

consult the Centre for Effective Dispute Resolution (CEDR) website: www.cedr.co.uk.

106 In Australia see s 131(2) of the Evidence Act 1995 (Cth).

107 This exception has been subject to different interpretations by the courts. See, for example, *Cattley v Pollard* [2007] Ch 353 and *Muller v Linsley and Mortimer* [1996] PNLR 74 (CA) where third party access to mediation was granted. Compare the following cases where it was refused: *Rush and Tompkins v GLC* (HL) [1989] 1 AC 1280 and *Cumbria Waste Management Ltd and Lakeland Waste Management Ltd v Baines Wilson* [2008] EWHC 786 (QB). However in *Ofulue and Anor v Bossert* [2009] UKHL 16 at para 26, the House of Lords directly referred to *Rush* and held that the 'without prejudice' rule cannot extend to cover a statement of fact that is common to the pleaded cases of both parties, whether or not it can sensibly be regarded as an admission and against interest.

108 See *McFadden v Snow* (1952) 69 WN (NSW) 8.

109 See, for example, *AWA v Daniels* (1992) 7 ACSR 436.

110 See, for example, *Cumbria Waste Management Ltd and Lakeland Waste Management Ltd v Baines Wilson* [2008] EWHC 786 (QB).

111 See Stuart Isaacs QC in *Brown v Rice and Patel* [2007] EWHC 625 (Ch).

112 See also May LJ in *Aird v Prime Meridian* [2006] EWCA Civ 1866 and *Farm Assist N° 2*, above note 34.

113 Allen (2009), above note 105 at 9.

because mediation is a 'special process of settlement'.[114] However in the absence of specific statutory provisions dealing with mediation privilege and confidentiality the without prejudice privilege has found its way into mediation case law. The Australian case of *Lukies v Ripley* is authority for the proposition that mediations conducted for the purposes of resolving only part of a dispute or narrowing the issues in dispute will also attract the without prejudice privilege.[115]

In terms of the scope of the privilege applied to mediation, the following cases provide useful insights. *Cumbria Waste Management Ltd and Lakeland Waste Management Ltd v Baines Wilson*[116] concerned a party to a mediation who sued its legal representatives, claiming negligent advice and seeking to recover damages based on the shortfall between the amount of the mediated settlement and the amount the party considered it would have received but for the negligent legal advice provided in mediation. The defendant lawyers sought wide disclosure of mediation documents and the plaintiffs claimed that they were privileged and confidential. They relied on the without prejudice privilege at common law and as incorporated into the agreement to mediate along with other confidentiality provisions. The court refused to order disclosure on the basis of the without prejudice privilege. Kirkham J went on to consider the agreement to mediate, again finding no basis for disclosure and adding judicial support for the enforceability of contractual confidentiality.

The case of *Aird and Aird v Prime Meridian Ltd*[117] held that the without prejudice rule will not protect source documents from discovery when they are referred to in mediation, although reference cannot be made to actual statements made at mediation. In this case directions were given for a stay for purposes of a meeting of architectural experts to define areas of agreement and disagreement and a subsequent mediation. The order for the meeting and joint summary of experts did not clarify that it was for the purpose of the mediation only. The matter did not settle at mediation and in the subsequent litigation one party argued, *inter alia*, that the documents from the experts' meeting could be disclosed as they were not covered by without prejudice privilege. The Court of Appeal, reversing the first instance decision, held that the documents were not privileged and as such could be used in court proceedings, explaining that just because the documents in question were produced for the first time at the mediation did not clothe them with privilege. In other words, otherwise

114 See *Rajski v Tectran Corp Pty Ltd* [2003] NSW 476 (unreported, Palmer J, 26 May 2003).
115 *Lukies v Ripley* (N° 2) (1994) 35 NSWLR 283.
116 *Cumbria Waste Management Ltd and Lakeland Waste Management Ltd v Baines Wilson* [2008] EWHC 786 (QB) at paras 24–27 and 30.
117 See *Aird and Aird v Prime Meridian Ltd* [2006] EWHC (TCC) 2338.

discoverable documents should not be assumed to be subject to the without prejudice privilege just because they have been produced at mediation.[118]

In relation to mediated settlements *Rush and Tompkins Ltd v Greater London Council*[119] held that, unlike statements and documents relating to the course of the mediation, documents setting out terms of a mediated agreement are not subject to without prejudice privilege and therefore may be produced in evidence.[120]

The Australian case of *Quad Consulting Pty Ltd v David R Bleakley and Associates Pty Ltd*[121] illustrates an exception to without prejudice, namely that a party to mediation cannot rely on the privilege to escape liability for unlawful conduct. This case concerned a subpoena for the production of notes made at a settlement meeting. The Court held that the notes were discoverable to the extent that they touched upon allegations of deceptive and misleading conduct on the part of the party claiming the privilege. *Quad Consulting* highlights the competing public interests which can emerge in the application of without prejudice privilege.

Situations in which Australian courts have found exceptions to the without prejudice rule as it applies to mediation[122] include proving that a settlement was reached,[123] costs determinations,[124] seeking to set a settlement aside on grounds of misleading conduct,[125] misrepresentation,[126] unconscionable conduct,[127] and where a party sues their solicitor in relation to professional misconduct or where those solicitors join counsel and the mediator seeking contributions as joint tortfeasors.[128]

118 See also the leading Australian case of *AWA Ltd v Daniels* (1992) 7 ASCR 436 and the US case of *Wimsatt et al v Superior Court of California* 152 Cal App 4th 137, 61 Cal Rpter 3d 200 (2007).

119 See *Rush and Tompkins Ltd v Greater London Council* [1989] 1 AC 1280.

120 For another example, see *Austotel Management Pty Limited v Jamieson* (1995) 57 FCR 411 where *Rush and Tompkins Ltd* was applied with a different result.

121 See *Quad Consulting Pty Ltd v David R Bleakley and Associates Pty Ltd* (1990–1991) 98 ALR 659.

122 As outlined by Limbury, citing the cases which appear in footnotes 123–128 below: A Limbury, 'Should there be a distinct 'Mediation Privilege'?' (2007) *LEADR Update* available at www.leadr.com.au/update/update14sept07.htm, at 3.

123 *Barry v City West Water Ltd* [2002] FCA 1214.

124 *Capolingua v Phylum Pty Ltd* (1991) 5 WAR 137. Contrast the English approach referred to above and the case of *Reed Executive v Reed Business Systems* [2004] 4 All ER 942 (CA).

125 See *Quad Consulting Pty Ltd v David R Bleakley and Associates Pty Ltd* (1990 – 1991) 98 ALR 659.

126 *Williams v Commonwealth Bank* [1999] NSWCA 345.

127 *Abriel v Australian Guarantee Corporation Ltd* [2000] FCA 1198.

128 *Tapoohi v Lewenberg and Ors* (N° 2) [2003] VSC 410 (21 October 2003). Contrast the approach of the English court in *Cumbria Waste Management* referred to above.

Finally the case of the *Earl of Malmesbury v Strutt and Parker*[129] confirms that privilege, by its nature, can be waived by each party to mediation, and mediators have no veto in this regard.[130] This case was discussed earlier in relation to good faith participation duties in mediation and is referred to below in the context of mediation privilege.

As indicated earlier the US Federal Rule of Evidence r 408 – known as the settlement negotiation rule – takes the form of an evidentiary exclusion and has been applied to mediations.[131] The Rule admits evidence of settlement negotiations except when the evidence is offered to:

- prove liability for, invalidity of, or amount of a claim that was disputed as to validity or amount; or
- impeach through a prior inconsistent statement or contradiction.

In other words evidence is admitted for all other purposes including, but not limited to, evidence to determine when the statute of limitations begins to run[132] or to prove witness bias, professional negligence, undue influence or other process-related allegations.[133] Thus it is formulated more narrowly than privilege which can be claimed in the discretion of the privilege holder for any purpose.

6.6 Protection of Lawyer–Client Communications and Related Material

Protection of lawyer–client communications may take the form of legal professional privilege (also known as attorney-client privilege) in common law jurisdictions, the work-product doctrine in the United States, or positive duties of confidentiality in civil law jurisdictions.

Legal professional privilege applies to confidential discussions between legal advisers and clients for the purpose of providing legal advice regarding pending or contemplated litigation. It includes documents used in mediation

[129] *Earl of Malmesbury v Strutt and Parker* [2008] EWHC 424 (QB).

[130] See also *Nicholson v Knox Ukiwa* [2008] EWHC 1222 (QB).

[131] See, for example, *Smith v Genstar Capital*, LLC, N° C–01–3936 MMC, 2001 WL 1658315 (ND Cal Dec 20, 2001).

[132] See, for example, *Kraft v St John's Lutheran Church* 414 F 3d 943 (8th cir 2005).

[133] See G Collins and A Halaby, 'Of "Purposes not Prohibited": New Federal Rule of Evidence 408(b)' (2007) 40 *Creighton Law Review* 679. For an analysis of the different approaches to interpreting r 408 (pre–2006 amendment) see V Alabanza, 'When are Settlement Communications Protected as "Offers to Compromise" under Rule 408?' (2000) 40 *Santa Clara Law Review* 547. See also the case of *Johnson v Land O'Lakes Inc* 181 FRD 388 (ND Iowa 1998) where the court examined the different circuit approaches to r 408.

which have come into existence for the purposes of legal advice or for use in judicial or quasi-judicial proceedings.[134] The privilege can be claimed by lawyers and their clients only and has been successfully used in relation to mediation of litigation and pre-litigation matters. The English case of *Farm Assist (in liquidation) v DEFRA*[135] concerned an allegation of economic duress in mediation. The party seeking to prove this allegation, DEFRA, sought disclosure of all advice provided to the other, FAL, by its lawyers, which had led to their decision to settle at the mediation. FAL objected to disclosure on grounds of legal professional privilege.[136] DEFRA argued that FAL had waived privilege by bringing proceedings against it in a way which made material the state of mind of FAL before and at mediation. The court held that legal professional privilege was not implicitly waived by the production of privileged documents at mediation. The court went on to comment that waiver would only be implied in a situation where a client sued their lawyer.

In the United States federal law regulates attorney-client privilege and the closely-related work-product doctrine in r 502 of the Federal Rules of Evidence. The work-product doctrine protects materials prepared in anticipation of litigation from discovery by opposing counsel. Although broader than attorney-client privilege in some regards, it is not a privilege and therefore may be overcome by a showing of necessity as set out in the Federal Rules of Civil Procedure r 26(b)(3).[137]

The civil law counterparts to lawyer–client privilege such as the *secret professionnel* (professional secret) in France and the *Verschwiegenheitspflichten* (duty of silence) in Germany[138] and Austria[139] generally take the form of a

[134] See, for example, *Esso Australia Resources v FCT* (1999) 201 CLR 49. This principle is referred to in Australian evidence legislation as 'client legal privilege': Evidence Act 1995 (Cth) ss 117–119.

[135] *Farm Assist Ltd v Secretary of State for Environment Food and Rural Affairs (N°1)* [2008] EWHC 3079 (TCC) at paras 11–12 and 49–58. DEFRA is the acronym for Department for Environment, Food and Rural Affairs.

[136] In England there are two types of legal professional privilege: legal advice privilege and litigation privilege.

[137] On the history of the relationship between attorney-client privilege and the work-product doctrine, see R Kirst, 'A Third Option; Regulating Discovery of Transaction Work Product Without Distorting the Attorney-Client Privilege' (2000) 31 *Secton Hall Law Review* 229. On the work-product doctrine generally see T Wilson, 'The Work Product Doctrine: Why Have an Ordinary Course of Business Exception?' (1988) *Columbia Business Law Review* 587.

[138] In Germany § 43a(2) of the National Lawyers' Rules provides that a lawyer when practicing as a lawyer is subject to confidentiality (or a duty of silence) and is obliged to keep confidential all information and insights derived in connection with the mediation. See W Hartung and T Holl (eds), *Anwaltliche Berufsordnung – Fachanwaltsordning, Europäische Standesregeln* (München: C H Beck 2001) at § 18 BerufsO, RN 34.

positive duty extending to courts, tribunals and other bodies. In France lawyers' duty of confidentiality (*secret professionnel* or *confidentialité*) is found in Article 66-5 of the Law of 1971 and Article 4 of the Decree of 12 July 2005.[140] French law does not distinguish between information and knowledge that lawyers acquire as litigators and that which comes to them in an advisory role. The duty is general in its application and not limited by time. Exceptions include situations where lawyers find themselves defending claims against them by current or former clients. Breaches of the duty may result in criminal proceedings and disciplinary proceedings by the bar (*ordre des avocats*). Furthermore written exchanges between lawyers are protected by confidentiality. This aspect of confidentiality has a long tradition in France and is based on ideas of collegiality (*confraternité*) and loyalty (*loyauté*) among members of the legal profession.[141]

6.7 Mediation Privilege

As indicated above, legal professional privilege and without prejudice privilege may apply in the mediation context but these forms of privilege do not extend to mediators specifically and mediation generally. However the issue is a matter of debate and this section considers the concept of mediation privilege – first at common law and then in statutory form – and its potential application to mediators and other mediation participants.

Kentra argues that courts are likely to extend the application of privilege to mediation and therefore to mediators, but this view is not universally shared.[142] The approach to courts recognising new privileges in many common law jurisdictions is based on Wigmore's four-part test.[143]

139 In Austria the lawyer's duty of confidence (silence) extends to matters entrusted to lawyers by their clients and to other information and material that comes to their knowledge in the exercise of their profession where it is in the interest of the client to keep such matters confidential. The provision expressly refers to a lawyer's right of refusal to testify on the basis of his/her duty of confidence. See § 9(2) of the Austrian Lawyers' Code (Rechtsanwaltsordnung RAO). On the right of refusal to testify see above.

140 Article 66.5 of the Law of 1971 provides that consultations and correspondence between lawyer and client are covered by professional secrecy; Article 4 of Decree N° 2005–790 of 12 July 2005 provides that a lawyer cannot divulge anything contravening the professional secrecy.

141 On the lawyer's duty of confidentiality in France see generally Deckert (2008), above note 1 at 209.

142 P Kentra, 'Hear No Evil, See No Evil, Speak No Evil: The Intolerable Conflict for Attorney-Mediators Between the Duty to Maintain Mediation Confidentiality and the Duty to Report Fellow Attorney Misconduct' (1997) *Brigham Young University Law Review* 715 at 728. See also J Engelbart, 'Federal Mediation Privilege: Should Mediation Communications be Protected from Subsequent Civil and Criminal

The first part of Wigmore's test is that communications must originate in the confidence that they will not be disclosed. In most western models of mediation the process occurs in a private and confidential forum. Many jurisdictions have legislation ensuring the confidentiality of mediation and standard agreements to mediate include confidentiality provisions.[144] Previous elucidation of its rationale has demonstrated judicial and academic support for confidentiality as an essential safeguard of mediation communications. The first part of Wigmore's test appears easily satisfied.

Next confidentiality must be essential to the full and satisfactory maintenance of the relationship between the parties. It has been pointed out that an ongoing relationship between disputing parties is not always important in mediation.[145] However their relationship during the mediation and for the period of implementation of settlement is of the utmost importance. Here a parallel can be drawn with the without prejudice privilege. Arguably this aspect of the relationship is sufficient to fulfil the second part of Wigmore's test.

The third part of the test is a requirement that the relationship be one which, in the opinion of the community, ought to be fostered. Here commentators point to different types of relationships in mediation. In addition to the relationship between the parties attempting to settle their dispute, discussed above, the relationship of trust and confidence that is said to develop between mediators and parties is relevant here. In many countries mediation has become a recognised and valued dispute resolution process in the community and mediation is supported by public and judicial policy. Moreover many Australian and US states have established statutory mediation privileges, an indication of a positive societal acceptance of the importance of protecting the various relationships in mediation.

The final part of the Wigmore test requires that the injury that would result from disclosure of the communications must be greater than the benefit gained for the due process conduct of the litigation. This criterion requires a cost/benefit analysis. The effectiveness of the mediation process is said to be largely dependent on the protection of communication that occurs as part of the

Proceedings' (1999) *Journal of Dispute Resolution* 73 at 78. Compare Reich's comments that privilege has not traditionally been applied to relationships of competing or adversarial needs but rather to relationships of support and trust such as lawyer–client, doctor–patient and priest–penitent: see Reich (2001), above note 6 at 221–230 and 252.

143 Wigmore, *Evidence* §§ 2191–92, 2285 (McNaughton Rev 1961). Wigmore provides a utilitarian analysis for the creation or application of privilege.

144 Compare Reich's view that the lack of uniformity in the practice of confidentiality in mediation coupled with the lack of empirical evidence that parties rely on mediator promises of confidentiality leads to non-fulfilment of the first of Wigmore's criteria: Reich (2001), above note 6.

145 See Reich (2001), above note 6 at 223.

process. At the same time a mediation privilege could result in the loss of certain evidence to the justice system, thereby infringing the public interest in access to all material evidence. Courts in common law jurisdictions have indicated a willingness to interpret insider/court confidentiality provisions in relation to mediation narrowly in order to minimise abuse of confidentiality protection and the potential loss of evidence associated with it.[146] Such an approach can be described as qualified privilege, as distinct from absolute privilege, and it appears to sit well with the fourth element in Wigmore's test.

The above analysis suggests that a mediation privilege could develop at common law.[147] The English High Court in *Brown v Rice and Patel*[148] has suggested the need for future consideration of a mediation privilege for the security of both the process and those who take part in it. However to date courts have failed to endorse a common law mediation privilege, although it would be consistent with Article 7 of the European Directive on Mediation requiring regulation of insider/court confidentiality. The presence of statutory mediation privileges in Australia and the US may explain the lack of judicial development on this point in these jurisdictions.

In so far as mediation privilege exists it takes the form of a statutory privilege and is well-represented in the United States[149] and Australia.[150] Statutory mediation privilege is explored here with reference to the UMA as an example, with some reference to other statutes. Specifically the following aspects of statutory mediation privilege are considered: scope of the privilege, parts of the mediation covered by the privilege, the nature of communications and information subject to the privilege, holders of the privilege and the subsequent proceedings at which the privilege can be asserted.

[146] See cases discussed earlier in relation to without prejudice privilege.

[147] In support of this view see M Briggs, 'Mediation Privilege?' – Parts 1 and 2 (2009) *New Law Journal*, available at www.newlawjournal.co.uk. For a different view see N Andrews, *The Modern Civil Process: Judicial and Alternative Forms of Dispute Resolution in England* (Tübingen: Mohr Siebeck 2008) at 11.54–11.57. In the context of family conciliation involving children the common law in England has recognised a distinct privilege: see *Re D (Minors) (Conciliation: Disclosure of Information)* [1993] Fam 231 at 238.

[148] See *Brown v Rice and Patel* [2007] EWHC 625 (Ch) and the discussion of this point in A Limbury, 'Should there be a distinct 'Mediation Privilege'?' (2007) *LEADR Update* available at www.leadr.com.au/update/update14sept07.htm.

[149] See, for example, New Jersey Rules of Evidence r 519 and the Texas Civil Practice and Remedies Code s 154.053 (1991) (b) and (c).

[150] See, for example, Mediation Act 1997 (ACT) s 11; Alternative Dispute Resolution Act 2001 (TAS) s 10(2). See also *Sharjade Pty Ltd v RAAF (Landings) Ex-Servicemen Charitable Fund Pty Ltd* [2008] NSWSC 1347 in relation to statutory mediation privilege.

The confidentiality provisions of the UMA[151] are broad in scope. The privilege applies to court-ordered mediations, to mediations to which the parties agree and which are intended to be subject to privilege and to any mediation conducted by persons holding themselves out as mediators (§ 4(a)). In other words it applies *prima facie* to all mediations irrespective of the path taken to get to mediation. Exceptions relate to collective bargaining, for which there are long-standing and specific regulations, school mediation, mediation in which parties are residents of a youth correctional centre and mediations conducted by judges who will rule on the case (§ 4(b)).[152] In addition parties may opt out of privilege protection in relation to all or part of a mediation provided they do so in writing and in advance of the mediation (§ 3(c)). An even broader privilege in terms of scope can be found in Texas. Here the mediation privilege attaches to that part of the mediation relating to the subject-matter of any civil or criminal dispute.[153]

Many statutes adopt significantly narrower approaches and extend privilege only to mediations conducted under the auspices of a particular court, mediation program, dispute resolution procedure or agreement, or only to mediators with specific qualifications or training.[154] Sector-specific privilege statutes make it easier to distinguish mediation activities that fall within the privilege from those that do not, but there are also potential pitfalls as mediations warranting protection may not be covered by narrowly framed privilege statutes. Private mediations of litigation matters, for example, may not fall within a privilege statute only relating to court-annexed mediation and a mediation in which the mediator is discovered not to have the requisite mediator qualifications may also not attract the privilege. These situations could appear to be arbitrary. Moreover confusion is likely to emerge in jurisdictions with several narrowly drawn sector-specific privilege statutes as lawyers seek to advise clients on their level of confidentiality protection and shop around for the most appropriate form.

151 See ss 4–7 UMA.

152 On judicial settlement and mediation, see Chapter 3.

153 See §§ 154.073 a-c and 154.053 of the Texas Civil Practice and Remedies Code available at www.law.onecle.com/texas/civil/index.html. The Texas provisions 'set out a broad confidentiality rule applicable to Texas mediations and other non-binding procedures and include a form of evidentiary privilege that applies to both participants and neutrals.' B Shannon, 'Dancing with the One that "Brung Us" – Why the Texas ADR Community Has Declined to Embrace the UMA' (2003) *Journal of Dispute Resolution* 197 at 203.

154 See, for example, the following sector-specific privilege provisions from Australia: Supreme Court Act 1935 (WA) applies privilege and confidentiality only to 'mediation under direction', the NSW Civil Procedure Act 2005 applies the privilege provisions only to civil proceedings of the kind referred to in Schedule 1 and the Community Justice Centres Act 1983 (NSW) attaches privilege to community justice centre mediations.

Other variations in the scope of mediation privilege include the requirement of a special formulation of words and other written forms of agreement to activate the privilege. This may be difficult in relation to mediations conducted with the use of telecommunications and careless parties may unwittingly find themselves outside the net of privilege.

Mediation privilege must specify not only the category of mediation, but also the aspects of the mediation to which it applies, such as intake sessions, preliminary meetings, telephone conversations, emails, private meetings and follow-up sessions. The extent to which initial communications between mediator and parties before an agreement to mediate has been signed are covered by privilege may become a crucial legal point should litigation follow the mediation. In Australia the NSW Civil Procedure Act 2005 s 30(1) illustrates a sensibly broad approach to this issue, defining a mediation session for the purposes of privilege as including 'any steps taken in the course of making arrangements for the session or in the course of the follow-up of a session'. The case of *Sharjade v RAAF*[155] illustrates the importance of identifying when the mediation commences and concludes for the purpose of applying privilege. The Texas Civil Practice and Remedies Code expressly extends privilege to insider/insider confidentiality, that is private sessions.

Related to the aspects of mediation to which the privilege attaches is the question of the nature of the information and communications covered by the privilege. Again privilege statutes differ in their approaches to this issue, some providing broad definitions followed by specific exclusions and others with narrower circumscriptions of what is included. The broad definition of communication in the UMA includes statements that are made orally, through conduct, in writing or through other recorded activity.[156] Johnson notes that the level of protection here is similar to that of attorney-client privilege in that mediators' observations, impressions and work product fall within the privilege (§ 3(3)).[157] However in some jurisdictions documents, proposals or reports prepared as a result of mediation may not be protected by privilege.[158]

[155] See *Sharjade Pty Ltd v RAAF (Landings) Ex-Servicemen Charitable Fund Pty Ltd* [2008] NSWSC 1347.

[156] Section 4 of the Uniform Mediation Act 2001 provides that a mediation communication is privileged. Section 2 of the UMA defines 'mediation communication' as a statement, whether oral, or in a record, verbal/non verbal, that occurs during a mediation or is made for purposes of considering, conducting, participating in, initiating, continuing, or reconvening a mediation or retaining a mediator.

[157] P Johnson Jr, 'Confidentiality In Mediation: What Can Florida Glean From The Uniform Mediation Act?' (2003) 30 *Florida State University Law Review* 487 at 492.

[158] See *Ridgecity Holdings Pty Ltd v City of Albany* [2006] WASAT 97 where an amended development proposal which followed a mediation between the local council and the applicant developer was not subject to confidentiality provisions.

Privilege applies to subsequent proceedings, but the exact nature of the proceedings may vary depending on the statute. Section 154.073 of the Texas Civil Practice and Remedies Code, for example, extends the coverage to 'any judicial or administrative proceeding' and s 4 of the Uniform Mediation Act extends coverage to 'a proceeding' which s 2(7) defines as a legislative hearing or similar process, a judicial, arbitral, or other adjudicative process, including related pre-hearing and post-hearing motions, conferences and discovery. Other statutes limit the application of the privilege to civil proceedings thereby excluding mediation communications which might be relevant to criminal proceedings.

A critical function of privilege statutes is the designation of who holds the right to claim or waive the privilege and otherwise exercise it in the future. As discussed previously, mediation parties and their representatives have an interest in knowing that information disclosed will be kept in confidence and that what transpires in mediation is not admissible in any court or arbitral proceedings that may follow. The ability of mediators to build trust and rapport with parties and to be seen as impartial is linked to the privacy and confidentiality of the process. Accordingly mediators have a strong interest in maintaining confidentiality. Mediators are generally reluctant to provide evidence about what occurred in mediation unless responding to negligence, malpractice or similar claims against them.

In order for mediation privilege to offer substantial confidentiality protection, everyone with access to mediation information should hold the privilege to some extent. Section 4 of the Uniform Mediation Act provides differentiated privileges for mediation participants. Mediation parties may refuse to disclose, and may prevent other persons from disclosing, any mediation communication. A mediator may refuse to disclose, and may prevent any other person from disclosing, a mediation communication of the mediator. Finally a non-party participant may refuse to disclose, and may prevent any other person from disclosing, a mediation communication of the non-party participant. Parties have the broadest privilege and the ability to prevent disclosures by any mediation participant including the mediator, while the mediator and other participants possess a privilege limited to their own communications.

There are other approaches to statutory mediation privilege that are not as inclusive in relation to holders of the privilege. Statutes may make parties exclusive holders of the mediation privilege, leaving mediators open to being subpoenaed to testify in subsequent proceedings. Alternatively privilege may avail only mediators. Article 7 of the European Directive on Mediation, for example, directs its confidentiality provisions to mediators, requiring member-states to ensure that mediators and those involved in mediation administration cannot be compelled to give evidence from the mediation in subsequent proceedings unless the parties otherwise agree. While there may be other protections for parties and lawyers, such as without prejudice and lawyer-client privilege, these differ in nature to the mediator's privilege, creating potential gaps in, and the opportunity for challenges to, confidentiality. In certain privilege statutes mediators have a veto over party disclosures. These laws, known as joint-holder statutes, are said to balance the power to assert or waive the privilege, but they also have the potential for producing stalemates.

In relation to waiver of privilege, s 5 of the UMA requires an express waiver, formal and on the record, and not a waiver implied or by conduct. The intent of this provision is to protect the unintentional waiver of privilege, especially by non-lawyers. However a person who has made representations about a mediation communication that prejudices another person in the proceeding is precluded from claiming privilege to the extent necessary for the person prejudiced to respond. Anyone intentionally using a mediation for criminal activity is also precluded from asserting the privilege.

7. Remedies

The nature of remedies for breach of confidentiality rules depends on the legal approach to confidentiality and may involve civil and/ or criminal consequences. Remedies may include:

- Fine and/or imprisonment for breach of confidence, also referred to as violation of private secrets.[159]
- Damages for breach of confidentiality insofar as these can be proved.[160]
- Damages for breach of confidence, for example where a mediation participant profits from knowledge of a trade secret.
- Injunction to restrain breach of confidence.

[159] See, for example, the Austrian Law on Mediation in Civil Cases (Zivilrechts-Mediations-Gesetz, ZivMediatG) according to which accredited mediators who breach confidentiality under § 18 of the Law on Mediation may incur criminal liability if their actions harmed a legitimate interest of a person (§ 31(1) of the Law on Mediation) and this person files a private criminal action (§ 31 (3) of the Law on Mediation and § 2(2) of the Criminal Procedure Code. Penalties include imprisonment and a fine. See also § 203(1) [Violation of Private Secrets] of the German Criminal Code (Strafgesetzbuch, StGB). In France see Article 226-13 and Article 226-14 of the Penal Code (Code Pénal) to the effect that professionals revealing secret information obtained by them in their professional capacity may be punishable by one year's imprisonment and a fine.

[160] See, for example, civil damages claims in Germany, § 280 of the German Civil Code and in France, Article 1150 of the French Civil Code (Code Civil). In relation to Germany see Hartmann (2009), above note 1 at 1116. See also H Eidenmüller, *Vertrags- und Verfahrensrecht in der Wirtschaftsmediation* (Köln: Dr Otto Schmidt 2001) at 28.

- Inadmissibility of evidence submitted.[161]
- Disciplinary proceedings against lawyers or other professionals by their professional associations.
- Direct or indirect procedural sanctions including the forced withdrawal of a claim.[162]
- Invocation of penalty clauses for breach of contract.[163]
- Costs sanctions for subpoenaing a mediator whose testimony is inadmissible at law.[164]

There is limited jurisprudence on remedies for breach of confidentiality, but the few cases available indicate a reluctance on the part of common law courts to impose sanctions for breach of confidentiality in the absence of evidence of bad faith,[165] or an adverse impact on the dispute or the mediated settlement.[166]

8. Exceptions to Confidentiality

As indicated previously, the public interest in ensuring mediation confidentiality needs to be balanced against the principle of availability of evidence in court processes.[167] The integrity of the mediation process requires that confidentiality provisions do not provide safe-havens for participant wrongdoing or injustice.[168] Despite statutory or contractually based confidentiality provisions, interlocutory injunctions may be sought from courts to guarantee certain fundamental rights and abuse of the mediation process will not be condoned because of confidentiality provisions.

161 Rechberger (2006), above note 73 at § 266 RN 24, Pitkowitz (2005), above note 51 at 86.

162 See, for example, § 1128 of the California Evidence Code according to which inappropriate references to a mediation during a subsequent trial may be grounds for vacating or modifying a decision in that matter. In France a claimant may be forced to withdraw its claim according to Articles 809(1) and 873(1) C pr civ (*trouble manifestement illicite*); see also Paris trib gr inst (TGI Paris) 18.01.1999, *La Gazette du Palais* 29.4 – 03.5.2001, 45 and *La Gazette du Palais* 16 – 17.02.2000 at 17.

163 In Germany these are called Vertragsstrafen and are agreements in the contract which need to comply with the provisions of the German Civil Code.

164 See California Evidence Code § 1127.

165 See *Lawson v Brown's Day Care Centre Inc* 776 A 2d 390, 394 (Vt 2001).

166 See the American cases *Concerned Citizens of Belle Haven v Belle Haven Club* N° civ 3:99 CV1467, 2002 WL 32124959 (D Conn 2002) and *In re Anonymous* 283 F 3d 627 (4th Cir 2002).

167 See the American case of *Folb v Motion Picture Industry Pension and Health Plans,* 16 F Supp 2d 1164, 1174 (CD Cal 1998) where the court endorsed this principle.

168 Hence the German phrase *Keine Flucht in die Mediation* (No escape in mediation).

In many jurisdictions the general principle seems to be that mediation disclosure is not ordered unless a court finds a competing public interest need of sufficient magnitude to outweigh maintaining the integrity of the mediation for participants and public confidence that mediation communications will be kept confidential. This principle is expressed in s 6(b) of the UMA which provides an exception to confidentiality protection where, in relation to evidence sought to be admitted in criminal proceedings or in relation to a claim to set aside the mediated settlement, evidence is not otherwise available and the need for the evidence outweighs the interest in protecting confidentiality.[169] This provision signals a qualified approach to privilege and the intention of balancing competing public policy needs.[170] Similarly the European Directive on Mediation provides in Article 7 that confidentiality is to be subject, *inter alia,* to public policy requirements and the need to establish the existence or otherwise of a settlement agreement.

Generally exceptions to confidentiality are construed narrowly so that disclosure is proportional to the exception. Therefore disclosures are permitted strictly for the purposes underlying the exception and only that part of a mediation communication necessary for applying the exception is disclosed or admitted as evidence. The principle of proportionality is enshrined in s 6(d) of the UMA.

As indicated previously s 6(b) of the UMA provides for *in camera* hearings before a judge for a party to establish the basis for certain exceptions. This approach attempts to preserve confidentiality in the first instance, while preventing parties from hiding under its cloak.

In European civil law countries the law on exceptions to mediation confidentiality appears less developed. The Austrian Law on Mediation in Civil Cases in § 31(2) provides that if public or legitimate private interests justify disclosure then accredited mediators will not be criminally penalised for breaching confidentiality. However this exception does not appear to apply to insider/court confidentiality.[171] Austrian academic opinion is divided as to whether the exception should be extended or whether the mediator's duty of confidentiality is best represented by a right of refusal to testify, while leaving

[169] Note limitations to this exception to confidentiality insofar as mediators cannot be compelled to give evidence about a mediation in relation, *inter alia,* to claims to set aside mediated settlements (s 6(c)).

[170] By way of contrast the confidentiality provisions of the Californian Evidence Code are drafted and interpreted in fairly absolute terms: see, for example, the case of *Rojas v Superior Court* 33 Cal 4th 407 (Cal 2004) and *Wimsatt et al v Superior Court of California* 152 Cal App 4th 137, 61 Cal Rptr 3d 200 (2007).

[171] Here insider/court confidentiality refers to the prohibition on calling the mediator as a witness in civil proceedings and the mediator's right of refusal to testify in criminal proceedings.

mediators free to disclose information for the evidence gathering process only.[172]

In Germany confidentiality obligations of lawyers and notaries acting as mediators are limited by the German Criminal Code, which obliges them to inform relevant authorities when they become aware that a mediation participant is planning a serious criminal offence.[173] In addition the right of refusal to testify is subject to public interest and policy exceptions.[174] However there is little academic opinion or jurisprudence on the extent to which other exceptions to confidentiality exist, for example in situations where one party is seeking to set aside a mediated settlement on the basis of contractual defences such as fraud, duress and unconscionability. In relation to this last point, Wagner and Thole suggest that legal reform is required in order to bring German law into line with the European Directive on Mediation.[175] In relation to France, Deckert surmises that the limits of confidentiality are still uncertain.[176]

An international comparative overview of confidentiality laws reveals the following main categories of exceptions:

- *Pre-existing information* otherwise subject to discovery or equivalent procedures. The principle behind this exception is that evidence otherwise admissible does not become inadmissible just because it is disclosed in mediation.[177] In other words, parties should not be able to use mediation to conceal otherwise discoverable information as this would amount to an abuse of mediation process.[178]
- *Information open to the public.* This exception refers to information generally available, or accessible under freedom of information[179] and

172 B Knoetzel and E Zach, 'Taking the Best from Mediation Regulations – The EC Mediation Directive and the Austrian Mediation Act' (2007) 23 *Arbitration International* 663.

173 See § 138 StGB Strafgesetzbuch and Hartmann (2009), above note 1 at 1092.

174 See Wagner and Thole (2008), above note 63 at 937 referring to the Entscheidung des Reichsgerichts in Zivilsachen (RGZ) 89.

175 See Wagner and Thole (2008), above note 63 at 937 and Article 7 of the EU Directive on Mediation.

176 See Deckert (2008), above note 1 at 210.

177 See, for example, s 5 of the UMA, Article 10(5) of the MLICC and the cases *AWA v Daniels* (1992) 7 ASCR 436 and *Aird and Aird v Prime Meridian* [2006] EWCA Civ 1886.

178 S Hughes, 'The Uniform Mediation Act: To the Spoiled Go the Privileges' (2001) 85 *Marquette Law Review* 9.

179 See s 7(a)(2) of the UMA. At the US Federal level see the Freedom of Information Act 1966 and at state level the various Open Records Acts or Open Public Records Acts such as Washington's Open Records Act (Revised Code of Washington (RCW) s 42.56) and California Public Records Act (California Government Code §§ 6250 – 6276.48). In England see the Freedom of Information Act 2000 and in Australia the

privacy laws.[180] It also applies to information created during a phase of the mediation that the parties agreed would be public or was required by law to be public.

- *Breach of duty/professional misconduct.* An exception is also appropriate to allow disclosure of mediation information if a dispute arises between the mediator and any of the parties, or the professional conduct of the mediator or other participants in mediation such as legal representatives is challenged. These exceptions are illustrated by ss 6(a)(5) and 6(a)(6) of the UMA. Similarly under Florida's Mediation Confidentiality and Privilege Act disclosure is permitted for the defence or assertion of mediator misconduct[181] and the Slovakian mediation legislation provides that mediators are not bound by the obligation of confidentiality to the extent required for the assessment of breach of their professional obligations.[182] Issues relating to mediator liability are considered in the next chapter. However despite making provision for the exception, the UMA specifically prevents mediators from being called to give evidence in relation to professional misconduct claims against representatives or others in mediation (s 6(c)).
- *Threat of future violence or harm to others and communications to plan or attempt crimes or to conceal ongoing criminal activity.* Provisions to this effect can be found in s 5(c) and s 6(a)(3) and (4) of the UMA, Article 7(1)(a) of the European Directive and the German Criminal Code, as indicated previously. However many statutes are silent on this point, leaving it to courts to rely on general principles to imply the exception on public interest and policy grounds. As with other exceptions the aim of such provisions is to protect the integrity of the mediation process and not leave it open to abuse by those contemplating or involved in criminal activity. The prevention of physical or psychological harm to a person is also an important public interest here. However the approach taken to this issue will depend very much on national legal culture and public policy. It is sometimes thought that where a mediating party admits to criminal offences this should not provide an exception to privilege because it may discourage parties to engage in the process. However there are provisions in some

Freedom of Information Act 1982 (Cth) at federal level and various FOI Acts at state levels.

180 See, for example, the Privacy Act 1988 (Cth) in Australia.

181 Mediation Confidentiality and Privilege Act [FS 44.405]. Contrast the Californian confidentiality provisions which contain no such exception as discussed in *Morgan Phillips v JAMS/Endispute* LLC (2006) Cal App 4th 795, 44 Cal Rptr 3d 782.

182 See § 6 of the Slovakian Act of 25 June 2004 on Mediation and Amendment of Certain Acts.

jurisdictions that might require mediators to report certain types of crimes to police upon becoming aware of them.[183]

- *Abuse of a child or vulnerable party.* Protection of children and other vulnerable members of society has long been a public policy exception to confidential communications in many situations such as those between doctor and patient. Similarly mediation communications that go to show the abuse, neglect or abandonment of a child or vulnerable party may not be subject to confidentiality provisions. Examples can be found in s 6(a)(7) of the UMA and Article 7(1)(a) of the European Directive on Mediation.
- *To prove the existence of a settlement agreement.* Exceptions to confidentiality are often invoked by post-mediation actions seeking to prove or set aside mediated settlements, or make a case for sanctions against another party (see below). For example Article 10(3) of the MLICC provides for disclosure and admission of evidence 'for the purposes of implementation or enforcement of a settlement agreement.' The European Directive on Mediation contains a similar exception, more narrowly worded. Article 7(1)(b) of the Directive provides an exception to the prohibition on mediator testimony 'where disclosure of the *content of the agreement* resulting from mediation is necessary in order to implement or enforce that agreement' [*emphasis added*]. In the United States this exception is expressly included in the public interest provision, s 6(b) of the UMA. However the UMA does not go so far as to permit courts to compel mediators to provide evidence of mediation communications in relation to such claims (s 6(c)). In other words, mediators cannot be required to provide testimony about the conduct of parties or other participants in relation to enforcing settlement agreements, but evidence from other sources may be adduced. Thus the terms of this particular UMA exception are distinctly narrower than equivalent exceptions in other legal instruments granting mediators greater – albeit not absolute – security in relation to their confidentiality obligations. Cases dealing with these situations are considered in detail in the next chapter on post-mediation issues. However the English case of *Brown v Rice and Patel*[184] is mentioned here because it shows how

[183] See, for example, s 316 of the Crimes Act in Australia which provides that a person who becomes aware that a serious indictable offence has been committed must inform the police or face a jail sentence. At the time of writing mediators were not included in the occupations – such as doctor and solicitor – excepted from this provision.

[184] *Brown v Rice and Patel* [2007] EWHC 625 (Ch). In contrast see the Californian Supreme Court in *Simmons v Ghaderi* (2008) 44 Cal 4th 570, 2008 WL 2789224. Here, in an action to determine whether a valid oral mediated settlement existed, the

broadly this exception can be interpreted. In this case the agreement to mediate provided that a mediated settlement would not be binding until and unless it was recorded in writing and signed, which had not occurred. Nonetheless the party seeking to enforce the settlement sought to admit evidence of mediation communications to prove the existence of an agreement between the parties to settle. Despite opposition from the mediation provider (ADR Group) and the other party, the court admitted evidence from the mediation on the basis that it fell within an exception to the without prejudice rule, namely to prove the existence of a concluded settlement. In justification for his view the judge reasoned that it was conceivable that parties might vary, waive or even be estopped from asserting the writing requirement in the agreement to mediate. However in situations where parties agree that only a written and signed agreement is to be recognised as legally binding, they send a signal that they do not wish a court to delve into confidential mediation communications to establish the existence of a settlement not meeting these criteria. The wide interpretation of this exception by the court in *Brown v Rice and Patel* does not encourage confidence in the protection and privacy that confidentiality is said to offer parties and other participants.

- *Costs determinations.* In certain jurisdictions courts have been willing to admit limited evidence from mediations in applications for costs of the mediation or proceedings to which the mediation relates. Here evidence may be adduced relating to participants' behaviour to show lack of good faith or unreasonable behaviour in relation to the mediation.[185] These provisions and cases are considered in Chapter 7 under the heading, *Costs sanctions*.

9. SECURING CONFIDENTIALITY AND THE ROLE OF CONTRACT

In a cross-border context it is imperative to ensure that confidentiality provisions are effective in the relevant jurisdiction. The above examination of the law of confidentiality has shown that there are different types of confidentiality that can be regulated in different ways, depending on jurisdiction. One of these regulatory forms is private contract. Drafting contracts containing confidentiality provisions – particularly contracts which traverse national borders and legal cultures – requires an analysis of the applicable law on

court allowed a party to rely on confidentiality to prevent mediation evidence being admitted.

185 See the section on duties of parties in Chapter 5.

mediation confidentiality and the extent to which the relevant courts recognise contractual undertakings of this nature.

Contractual instruments such as agreements to mediate containing confidentiality provisions are limited in relation to their ability to bind non-signatories to the contract and to address public policy concerns. Nevertheless the use of contractual terms can be a desirable form of regulating confidentiality and, as indicated earlier, is often used in addition to other forms of regulation.[186] Parties and their legal representatives should consider how incorporating confidentiality provisions into mediation clauses, agreements to mediate and other relevant contractual instruments can help to secure the type of confidentiality protection they desire.

Contract as a form of mediation regulation highlights the opportunities and risks of party autonomy in the process. The attraction of contract lies in the ability of parties to tailor confidentiality provisions to suit their circumstances. Different levels of confidentiality obligation may apply to different people with varied consequences for breach and there may be specific exceptions parties wish to include in the contract.[187]

Contractual provisions will not override mandatory forms of regulation and they may be subject to exercises of judicial discretion. They can, however, be useful in clarifying the existing law and parties' intentions, especially with regard to discretionary law and any gaps in existing regulation. By way of example, neither the UMA nor the European Directive on Mediation provide for a positive duty of confidentiality. In other words they do not extend to insider/insider and insider/outsider confidentiality and only regulate insider/court confidentiality. In relation to the UMA, the Commissioners considered it unnecessary to subject insider/insider and insider/outsider obligations of confidentiality to uniform legislative application. In the spirit of party autonomy it was felt that parties could choose to regulate confidentiality for themselves in relation to non-proceeding disclosures. In this regard institutional mediation rules routinely include confidentiality provisions and these can be incorporated into agreements to mediate. However some institutional rules do not set a standard for insider/insider confidentiality, leaving

186 On the advantages of contractual regulation of confidentiality in mediation, see Reich (2001), above note 6. For a critique of the use of contract to safeguard confidentiality, see A Kirtley, 'The Mediation Privilege's Transition From Theory To Implementation: Designing A Mediation Privilege Standard To Protect Mediation Participants, The Process and The Public Interest' (1995) *Journal of Dispute Resol*ution 1 at 10–11.

187 For example, the Centre for Effective Dispute Resolution (CEDR) model agreement to mediate provides an absolute bar on calling the mediator as witness: see clause 7 CEDR Model Mediation Agreement in Appendix A.

this internal process aspect of mediation to the parties and mediator to negotiate.[188]

In France the Law of 1995 permits parties to agree to contractually exclude the application of confidentiality provisions.[189] According to German law parties can enter into a so-called procedural agreement (*Prozessvertrag*)[190] to regulate confidentiality as they wish, for example that certain witnesses or evidence are not to be called in subsequent civil proceedings.[191] Provided the agreements comply with mandatory laws and do not offend public policy they are valid and recognised by German courts.[192]

As indicated in the previous chapter there are many situations where comprehensive confidentiality provisions are neither warranted nor desired. Cultural traditions may dictate different degrees of permissible disclosure.[193] The human condition demands opportunities to reflect and talk through conflict situations. The use of contract gives parties the opportunity to consider and select the extent to which confidentiality will play a role in their mediation. Conventional wisdom suggests that parties are more likely to be aware of, and therefore comply with, an agreement they have had explained to them by professional advisers and then signed, than a statutory law the existence of which they are blissfully unaware. With the benefit of legal advice on the terms of the contract it is also probable that parties will be aware that confidentiality has its limitations and is not absolute. They are then in an informed position to be able to participate in the mediation as they deem appropriate. Conversely ill-advised clients may have unrealistic expectations of the effectiveness of confidentiality provisions included in agreements to mediate. As most people are not aware of their *prima facie* duty to testify in court, contractual confidentiality provisions may lead to a false sense of security, which in turn may encourage unintended disclosures at the mediation table.

188 See, for example, the following provisions referred to in the Comparative Table of International Mediation Rules in Appendix B: MEDAL International Mediation Rules 2005, Mediation Rules of the Mediation Institute of the Stockholm Chamber of Commerce 1999, ADR Rules of the International Chamber of Commerce, and the International Centre for Dispute Resolution (ICDR) International Dispute Resolution Procedures – International Mediation Rules 2008.

189 See the Law of 8 February 1995 and Decree of 22 July1996.

190 G Wagner, 'Sicherung der Vertraulichkeit von Mediationsverfahren durch Vertrag' (2001) *Neue Juristische Wochenzeitschrift* 1398 at 1399, F Stein and M Jonas (eds), *Kommentar zur Zivilprozessordnung, Band 3* (22nd ed, Tübingen: Mohr Siebeck 2005) at § 128 RN 303.

191 Hartmann (2009), above note 1, 1087 at 1104 et seq.

192 Note that procedural agreements allow parties to rely on certain pleas (*Einreden*): Stein and Jonas (2005), above note 190 at § 128 RN 306, 314 and 315. See also Eidenmüller (2001), above note 160 at 27.

193 Reuben (2003), above note 28 at 124–125.

Agreements about confidentiality may be implied. In Germany academic opinion suggests that where parties consent to mediation they implicitly agree to enter a process with certain fundamental characteristics including confidentiality and the rights and obligations associated with it. Alternatively when mediators introduce the mediation process and inform parties about confidentiality and other aspects of the system, parties have the opportunity to agree expressly, albeit it orally, to be bound by confidentiality.[194]

Contracts only bind the parties to them and insofar as a contract seeks to confer duties or rights in relation to non-parties it is not effective. This could arise, for example, in relation to a mediator's staff or administrative assistants or others present who have not signed the terms of an agreement to mediate. Non-parties would therefore be free to discuss the mediation and could also appear as witnesses in subsequent determinative proceedings. As a matter of practice, mediation participants who are not parties to the agreement to mediate can be asked to sign a separate undertaking, obliging them to keep the events of the mediation private and confidential.

The limitations to the scope of contractual liability to maintain confidentiality in mediation were highlighted in the Australian case of *Williamson v Schmidt*.[195] Here the question to be decided was whether a solicitor could be prevented from acting against a former opponent. In this case the defendant solicitor had taken part in a mediation representing the plaintiff's opponent and four years later was working for a different firm acting against the plaintiff in a similar matter. The plaintiff brought an action to restrain the solicitor from acting against it in the later proceedings. The court held that as the mediation agreement purported to bind only the parties and the mediator, the solicitor, although a signatory to the agreement, was *not* under an obligation to keep confidential information and documents concerning the dispute which had been disclosed during mediation. At the same time the court indicated that it would have power to restrain a legal adviser from acting for a client in circumstances where a real possibility of misuse of information obtained in the earlier proceedings could be demonstrated; however it was not satisfied that such a possibility existed in this case.[196]

In interpreting contractual confidentiality provisions, courts generally address the competing tensions relating to confidentiality outlined above. If they construe them as attempts to suppress otherwise admissible or discoverable evidence courts may refuse to enforce contractual confidentiality provisions on

194 See Hartmann (2009), above note 1, 1087 at 1099 and §§ 133, 157 of the German Civil Code (Bürgerliches Gesetzbuch, BGB). See also Palandt et al (2009), above note 65 at § 133 and § 157. In interpreting the agreement the court will consider the attendant circumstances and the implied intention of the parties.

195 *Williamson v Schmidt* [1998] 2 Qd R 317.

196 *Williamson v Schmidt* [1998] 2 Qd R 317 at 337. See also duties of lawyers discussed in Chapter 5.

the basis that they infringe public policy.[197] It has been said that, '[t]he mere fact that information may be regarded as confidential by reason of a contractual, professional or moral obligation does not of itself create a right or privilege to withhold it in legal proceedings.'[198] Therefore there may be limitations on the extent to which contract can ensure insider/court confidentiality. Ultimately this is an area in which guidance is required from legislative bodies.

Courts have, however, also supported provisions clearly intended to encourage candid communication through confidentiality protections.[199] In these situations well-drafted contractual provisions can place parties' intentions and interests clearly on the agenda for courts in their deliberations on the competing policy considerations. In England the Civil Mediation Council has issued a Guidance Note[200] in relation to mediation confidentiality. As the preamble to the Note indicates, it was drafted in response to the inconsistent attitude of the English courts towards mediation confidentiality and in particular as a result of the judgement in *Farm Assist N° 2* which adopted a restrictive approach to confidentiality.[201] In this case it was held that a court may override a claim to contractual confidentiality if it considers it necessary to do so in the interests of justice. Accordingly, in the absence of a statutory or common law mediation privilege in England, the Guidance Note encourages the drafting of comprehensive contractual confidentiality provisions which have broad application and are subject to minimal or no exceptions.[202] The Note also contains the following advice:

[197] See, for example, in the United States, *Soc'y of Lloyds v Ward* N° 1:05–CV–32, 2006 WL 13221, and in England, *Farm Assist N° 2*, above note 34. See also P Johnson, 'Confidentiality In Mediation: What Can Florida Glean From The Uniform Mediation Act?' (2003) 30 *Florida State University Law Review* 487 at 490.

[198] See H Brown and A Marriott, *ADR Principles and Practice* (2nd ed, London: Sweet and Maxwell 1999) at para 22–043.

[199] For cases where courts have upheld contractual confidentiality provisions see, for example, the US cases: *Parazino v Barnett Bank of South Florida* 690 So2d 725 (Fla Dist Ct App 1997), *US v Kentucky Utilities Co 124 FRD* 146 (E D *Ky* 1989) at 147. See also the English case of *Cumbria Waste Management Ltd and Lakeland Waste Management Ltd v Baines Wilson,* which seemed to suggest that courts might find a special mediation privilege where the parties had included appropriate confidentiality obligations in their agreement to mediate: [2008] EWHC 786 (QB).

[200] See *Civil Mediation Council Guidance Note* N° 1, 'Mediation Confidentiality' (8th July 2009).

[201] See *Farm Assist Limited (in liquidation) v The Secretary of State for the Environment, Food and Rural Affairs (N° 2)* [2009] EWHC 1102 (TCC), referred to previously in this chapter.

[202] See Chapter 4 in relation to the drafting of contractual mediation provisions in mediation clauses and agreements to mediate.

> In reviewing their mediation agreements mediators and mediation providers may wish to consider a term requiring a party who seeks to call a mediator to give evidence to indemnify the mediator in respect of any costs he or she incurs in dealing with the application and even to provide for mediators to be paid at their hourly rate for the time spent dealing with such applications or giving evidence.

The message in England and elsewhere is therefore that parties should clearly state their intentions in relation to confidentiality and to this end may choose to incorporate suitable institutional mediation rules into agreements.[203]

10. Closing Comments

Laws about the confidentiality in mediation deal with the rights and obligations of mediation participants and traverse the interface between mediation and the legal system. As explained in Chapter 2, these types of legal rules are suitable for legislative intervention and there is a high level of interest in their uniformity, especially in cross-border situations. The European Directive on Mediation and model laws such as the MLICC and the UMA each address the issue of mediation confidentiality in slightly different ways. In terms of the European Directive member states will be examining their current laws in order to attain compliance by 2011.[204]

In analysing confidentiality rules in relation to choice of law, lawyers and parties will find the following questions useful:

1. *What is the scope of the confidentiality provision?* Here the tripartite classification of insider/outsider, insider/insider and insider/court mediation is helpful in analysing the extent and nature of the confidentiality protection. There may, for example, be a strict prohibition on admitting material from mediation as court evidence (insider/court), but no prohibition on informing outsiders about what transpired in the mediation (insider/outsider).
2. *Who holds obligations or rights in relation to confidentiality?* Article 7 of the European Directive requires member states to introduce regulations which ensure insider/court confidentiality for mediators and

[203] L Harman, 'Confidentiality in Mediation' in G Raftesath and S Thaler (eds), *Cases for Mediation* (Sydney: LBC Information Services 1999) at 29.

[204] For a discussion of the Austrian legal situation regarding confidentiality in commercial mediation in the light of the European Directive on Mediation see Pitkowitz (2005), above note 51 at 81 et seq. In relation to Germany see *Beschlüsse des 67. Deutscher Juristentag* (Erfurt, 2008) at 23 and F Becker and C Horn, 'Notwendige Regelungen eines deutschen Mediationsgesetzes' (2006) 5 *Zeitschrift für Schiedsverfahren* 270 at 272 et seq.

those involved in the administration of the mediation process, but the Directive encourages member states to enact even stricter and broader rules on confidentiality.

3. *What is protected by confidentiality?* The protection of confidentiality can extend to verbal and non-verbal communications and to documents prepared for, and created in, the mediation. It has been shown above that the definition of mediation communication in the UMA is very broad.
4. *To which parts of the mediation do the various obligations of confidentiality attach?* For the purposes of confidentiality, it is important to be clear about whether the mediation includes preliminary contact between parties and mediator, separate sessions and interim and follow up contact.
5. *Are there any exceptions to the confidentiality provisions*? In jurisdictions with legislation dedicated to mediation it can be relatively easy to identify the exceptions to confidentiality, but in others they may not be obvious and one may need to search through various criminal and civil procedural codes and other laws to find them. Moreover as shown above courts have taken inconsistent approaches to confidentiality exceptions.

Parties and lawyers assessing the suitability of a particular regulatory regime in relation to confidentiality in mediation need to consider the issues raised in the above questions and their impact on management of their dispute. The relevant law is likely to be that of the jurisdiction where the litigation may take place, not where the mediation occurs. Consideration needs to be given to the most suitable regulatory mechanisms in relation to parties' confidentiality needs. Generally broad-based protection for mediation communications with clearly-worded exceptions is preferable as it is more straightforward to apply and explain to parties. Where litigation in relation to mediation confidentiality exists, court judgments provide valuable insights into the attitudes of judges in relation to the parameters and limits of confidentiality.

[illegible]

3. [illegible] the extent of [illegible] in the mediation? It has been [illegible] (for [illegible]) mediation communications [illegible] broad.
4. *The mediation process: the exception, for the whole range of* [illegible]. For the purposes of confidentiality, it is important to be clear about whether the mediation includes preliminary contact between parties and mediator, separate sessions and interim and follow-up contact.
5. *Are there any exceptions to the confidentiality provisions?* In jurisdictions with legislation dedicated to mediation it can be relatively easy to identify the exceptions to confidentiality, but in others they may not be obvious and one may need to search through various criminal and civil procedural codes and other laws to find them. Moreover, as shown above, courts have taken inconsistent approaches to confidentiality exceptions.

Parties and lawyers assessing the suitability of a particular regulatory regime in relation to confidentiality in mediation need to consider the issues raised in the above questions and their impact on management of their dispute. The relevant law is likely to be that of the jurisdiction where the litigation may take place, not where the mediation occurs. Consideration needs to be given to the most suitable regulatory mechanisms in relation to parties' confidentiality needs. Generally, broad-based protection of mediation communications with clearly worded exceptions is preferable, as it is more straightforward to apply and explain to parties. Where there is a challenge in relation to mediation confidentiality, court judgments provide valuable insight into the attitudes of judges in relation to the parameters and limits of confidentiality.

Chapter 7
Post-Mediation Issues

1. Introduction

Many legal issues in relation to mediation emerge only after mediation proceedings have finished. Questions about the legal status and enforceability of mediated settlements may arise at this stage, and together with them issues relating to the admissibility of information from the mediation as evidence in subsequent proceedings. The potential role of mediators in these proceedings, that is whether mediators can act as arbitrators or professional party representatives in arbitration or litigation following the mediation, may also be relevant in a post-mediation context. In certain situations, mediators will have reporting duties to referring bodies such as courts after the mediation.

Issues relating to admissibility of evidence from mediation in subsequent legal proceedings have been dealt with in the previous chapter under the topic of confidentiality and will not be re-examined here.

2. Mediation and Parties' Legal Rights and Remedies

This section deals with the relationship between the procedures and outcomes of mediation and parties' legal rights and remedies flowing from the original dispute. The discussion commences with an examination of how entering the mediation process – even where a settlement is not reached – can affect parties' legal rights and their potential remedies available post-mediation. It then considers the situation where a mediated settlement of a dispute has been reached.

It is said that parties do not forfeit their legal rights by entering into the mediation process.[1] Undertakings of this kind are frequently made to litigation parties to encourage them to engage in mediation. As explained in Chapter 4 a contractual obligation to mediate typically takes the form of a condition precedent to litigation and as such parties do not lose their right to access the courts. In addition numerous statutes and institutional rules expressly recognise that parties may need to initiate legal proceedings, while mediation is on foot, in

[1] See, for example, the US case of *Scaffidi v Fiserv Inc* which held that a party did not waive its right to arbitration by participating in mediation: N° 05–C–1046, 2006 WL 2038348 (ED Wis, July 20, 2006) and affirmed, 2007 WL 648178 (7th Cir Feb 28, 2007).

order to preserve their legal rights.[2] However there is a number of situations, short of reaching a mediated settlement, where parties' rights may be affected.

The first relates to admissibility of evidence in subsequent legal proceedings. Despite mediation being promoted as a confidential process, Chapter 6 has outlined the circumstances in which disclosures made at mediation may be used as evidence in subsequent proceedings in situations where no mediated settlement was reached.

Another important question that arises is the extent to which laws on limitation periods for causes of action are affected by the initiation of pre-litigation mediation.[3] In this chapter what are variously known as litigation limitation periods, prescription periods or statute of limitations provisions, are referred to generically as limitation periods.

2.1 Limitation Periods

Mediation is often recommended to parties on the basis that they have nothing to lose in terms of their legal rights and remedies – aggrieved parties can always pursue their rights in court should mediation not result in resolution. Such promises assume, *inter alia,* that permitted time periods for parties to lodge their claims do not expire during the course of the mediation with the result that the claim cannot be heard in post-mediation proceedings.[4] In addition where parties are compelled to comply with mediation clauses, there is a strong argument that this compliance should not prejudice them in terms of the time available to prepare and lodge documents to initiate legal proceedings and comply with other relevant time periods.[5] Finally allowing limitation periods to run during mediation could have the effect of encouraging respondent parties to participate in, or even initiate, mediation for the primary purpose of delaying initiation of court proceedings in the hope that the limitation period expires before the mediation does. For these reasons the European Directive on Mediation specifies in Article 8(1) that mediation parties are not to suffer any detriment

[2] See, for example, Article 13 of the UNCITRAL Model Law on International Commercial Conciliation (2002) (MLICC) and the commentary on this provision in Chapter 8 and the institutional rules in Appendix B.

[3] In relation to post-filing court-related mediation the issue of limitation periods does not arise as the court proceedings have already been commenced.

[4] S Grünberger, 'Die Regelung der Mediation im EheRÄG 1999' (2000) *Östereichische Juristen-Zeitung* 50 at 55. H Eidenmüller, 'Establishing a Legal Framework for Mediation in Europe: The Proposal for an EC Mediation Directive' (2005) *Zeitschrift für Schiedsverfahren* 124 at 127.

[5] See L Cadiet, 'L'Effet processuel des clauses de médiation' (2003) *Recueil des Cours de l'Academie de Droit International* 182 at 189.

with respect to any limitation periods that apply to their claim.[6] Similarly the regulation of limitation periods in the Austrian Law on Mediation in Civil Cases was seen as an essential condition for the promotion and legal legitimisation of mediation in that country.[7]

The primary approach to regulating the impact of pre-litigation mediation on limitation periods seems to be suspension,[8] although interruption of the limitation period is also a legal option. In this context *interruption* of limitation periods during mediation signifies that the limitation period is to run again from the beginning once the interruption is over. This appears to be the case in Hungary and Poland. In Poland, for example, the Civil Code states that the running of the limitation period ceases entirely when mediation commences. Once mediation has formally ended the full limitation period restarts from the beginning.[9] In Hungary the commencement of the mediation process interrupts the limitation period, provided that the parties have jointly initiated mediation in writing.[10] Once the mediation is terminated then the five year limitation period will recommence, that is there will be a full five years during which legal proceedings relating to any claims considered in the mediation can be brought.[11] Presumably the writing requirement facilitates determination of the date of commencement of mediation and the date from which the interruption runs. Moreover the requirement that both parties sign off on the initiation of mediation would appear to minimise the risk of one party initiating mediation for the sole purpose of interrupting the limitation period and winning another five years to contemplate bringing a claim.

Conversely the effect of *suspension*, as understood in this context, is that the limitation period does not run for the duration of the mediation and resumes where it left off once the mediation process has been terminated. Jurisdictions such as Austria and Germany provide for the suspension of

6 Directive 2008/52/EC on Certain Aspects of Mediation in Civil and Commercial Matters, proposal as adopted by the European Parliament and the Council of the European Union on 21 May 2008, L 136/3, 24.05.2008.

7 Stellungnahme 56/SN–283/ME (XXI GP) der Vereinigung der österreichischen Richter at 2.

8 Countries which provide for suspension of limitation periods include Austria, Germany, France, Belgium and Afghanistan.

9 See Articles 123 and 124 of the Polish Civil Code and E Niedzwiedzka, 'Mediation in Polen' in K Hopt and F Steffek (eds), *Mediation – Rechtstatsachen, Rechtsvergleich, Regelungen* (Tübingen: Mohr Siebeck 2008) 788 at 790.

10 See s 31(2) of the Hungarian Mediation Act (2002), Act LV of 2002 on Mediation Activity.

11 See C Jessel-Holst, 'Mediation in Ungarn' in K Hopt and F Steffek (eds) (2008), above note 9, 905 at 908. The English translation of the relevant legislation refers to the 'successful completion of the mediation' as being the trigger for recommencement of the limitation period. This has been understood to mean the successful termination of the mediation without a full settlement of the dispute.

limitations periods. It has been said that the Austrian provision provides a best practice example of how to regulate the impact of mediation on limitation periods.[12] The Austrian Law on Mediation in Civil Cases[13] provides for the suspension of limitation periods which apply to any claims and rights dealt with in a mediation conducted by an accredited mediator.[14] An exception is provided in family law where, subject to the parties agreeing otherwise,[15] the suspension applies not only to claims and rights the subject of the mediation process, but also *ex lege* to any other claims and rights arising out of family law.[16] The suspension is continuous (*Fortlaufhemmung*)[17] which means that the running of the relevant limitation periods are suspended during mediation and continue to run again once the mediation ends.[18] The ability to identify the commencement and termination of mediation can be of critical importance especially where limitation periods are about to expire or may have already expired.[19] The Austrian Law identifies the beginning of the mediation as the point of time at which the parties agree to resolve their dispute by mediation and the end of the mediation as the point in time at which a party to the mediation or the mediator declares that the mediation should be discontinued or when the dispute is resolved.[20]

In Germany the preponderance of academic opinion suggests that the current provisions of the German Civil Code on the suspension of litigation

12 See K Hopt and F Steffek, 'Mediation – Rechtsvergleich, Regelungsmodelle, Grundsatzprobleme' in K Hopt and F Steffek (eds), *Mediation – Rechtstatsachen, Rechtsvergleich, Regelungen* (Tübingen: Mohr Siebeck 2008) 3 at 30.

13 See § 22 of the Zivilrechtsmediationsgesetz, ZivMediaG.

14 The parties can, however, contractually agree to suspend a limitation or any other time period including those pertaining to other claims between them that are not subject to mediation: § 22(2) ZivMediaG and M Roth and D Gherdane, 'Mediation in Österreich - Zivilrechts-Mediations-Gesetz: Rechtlicher Rahmen und praktische Erfahrungen' in K Hopt and F Steffek (eds) (2008), above note 9, 105 at 123.

15 On the ability of parties to limit or bar limitation provisions in Austria see Roth and Gherdane (2008), above note 14 at 125.

16 See § 22 ZivMediatG.

17 Note that § 22 applies to material limitation periods (*materiell-rechtliche Fristen*), for example §§ 57, 95 Matrimonial Law (Ehegesetz), but not to procedural limitation periods (*verfahrensrechtliche Fristen*). On suspension of limitation periods see Roth and Gherdane (2008), above note 14 at 123 et seq.

18 C Fuchshuber and R Fucik, *Mediation im Zivilrecht* (Vienna: LexisNexis 2004) at 8.

19 See comments of the court in the Australian case of *Sharjade* highlighting the importance of the mediator informing the court of the date of the termination of mediation in accordance with the relevant procedure rules so that the court can determine the scope of application of confidentiality: *Sharjade Pty Ltd v RAAF (Landings) Ex-Servicemen Charitable Fund Pty Ltd* [2008] NSWSC 1347.

20 See § 17(1) Zivilrechtsmediationsgesetz, ZivMediaG.

limitation periods[21] apply in relation to mediation despite only referring to negotiations.[22] The effect of these provisions is to suspend limitation periods during settlement negotiations including mediation.[23] Importantly the Civil Code provisions provide that claims relevant to settlement negotiations cannot be barred for three months after the mediation has ended. This grace period guarantees parties a window of opportunity to follow up on the mediation, take further advice and reconsider their position before finally initiating litigation. Anecdotal evidence suggests that many mediations settle after the formal mediation has ended and so the post-mediation period may be of practical use to disputing parties. However doubt remains as to whether the German provisions apply to all mediations or only those conducted by recognised institutions.[24] In addition, unlike in the Austrian law, the beginning and end of negotiations are not clearly defined as the view was taken that this may inhibit the diversity of formal and informal approaches to dispute resolution.[25] This may cause some uncertainty in relation to mediation, although commencement and termination of mediation in Germany is likely to be approached and interpreted in a similar manner to that of the Austrian provisions discussed previously.[26] For these reasons some commentators suggest that legislative reform to clarify these aspects of the application of the suspension of limitation periods to mediation, while perhaps not strictly necessary to comply with the European Directive, is warranted.[27]

21 See §§ 203 and 204(I) N° 4 Bürgerliches Gesetzbuch, BGB. § 203 deals with the suspension of limitation periods during settlement negotiations between debtor and creditor: see O Palandt et al (eds), *Bürgerliches Gesetzbuch* (68th ed, Munich: Beck Juristischer Verlag 2009) at § 203 BGB. § 204(I) N° 4 provides that suspension is activated by the lodgement of a notice of application for conciliation at a recognised conciliation body and in certain circumstances any other conciliation body: see Palandt et al (2009) referred to in this note at § 204 BGB.

22 See, for example, G Wagner and C Thole, 'Die Europäische Mediations -Richtlinie – Inhalt, Probleme und Umsetzungsperspektiven' in D Bägte, J Hein and M Hinden (eds), *Die richtige Ordnung, Festschrift für Jan Kropholler zum 70 Geburtstag* (Tübingen: Mohr Siebeck 2008) at 940 and B Hess, 'Rechtsgrundlagen der Mediation' in F Haft and K von Schlieffen (eds), *Handbuch Mediation* (2nd ed, München: C H Beck 2009) 1053 at 1080.

23 See H Eidenmüller, 'Die Auswirkung der Einleitung eines ADR-Verfahrens auf die Verjährung' (2003) *Zeitschrift für Schiedsverfahren* 163 and Wagner and Thole (2008), above note 22 at 940.

24 See, for example, Wagner and Thole (2008), above note 22 at 940. On the recognised conciliation bodies see also § 15a(1), (5) and (6) of the Introductory Law of the German Civil Procedure Code (Gesetz betreffend die Einführung der Zivilprozessordnung, EGZPO) which regulates them.

25 Hess (2009), above note 22 at 1081.

26 Hess (2009), above note 22 at 1081.

27 See Wagner and Thole (2008), above note 22 at 940–941 who put forward a specific reform recommendation. See also the statement of the German Federal Ministry of

French legislation does not expressly regulate the impact of pre-litigation mediation on limitation periods.[28] However the Supreme Court (*Cour de Cassation*) has developed jurisprudence on the issue, holding that the commencement of a mediation process suspends but does not interrupt the limitation period.[29] The dates of commencement and termination of the mediation for the purposes of defining the suspension period have not been clarified by the courts and there are different academic views on the topic.[30]

Furthermore it is unclear if the suspension principle enunciated by the French Supreme Court also applies to mediation conducted where there is no contractual obligation to do so. Pre-2003 French jurisprudence would suggest that it does not.[31] However there has been significant change in mediation usage and law since that time and government policy encouraging the use of mediation is consistent with the suspension of limitation periods for all mediations. At the time of writing the French Parliament is deliberating on a bill to regulate limitation periods generally. If passed, good faith negotiations, which include non-contractual mediation, will initiate the suspension of relevant limitation periods.

Justice that the legislature should expressly include mediation in § 204 of the German Civil Code: Bundesministerium der Justiz, *Mediation als Verfahren konsensualer Streitbeilegung –Regelungsbedarf im Verfahrens – und Berufsrecht* (Berlin: BMJ September 2008) at 2 and see comments by Graf-Schicker that such a reform would enhance the status of mediation: M-L Graf-Schlicker, 'Die EU-Richtlinie zur Mediation – zum Stand der Umsetzung' Vortrag der Leiterin der Abteilung Rechtspflege im Bundesministerium der Justiz (Berlin: 13th Mediations-Kongress 2009) 1 at 7. For a different view see A Becker and C Horn, 'Notwendige Regelungen eines deutschen Mediationsgesetzes' (2006) *Zeitschrift für Schiedsverfahren* 270 at 273.

28 There is, however, a specific law regarding bank mediations. According to L 312-1-3 of the French Monetary and Financial Code bank mediations attract the suspension of limitation periods during the two month mediation process.

29 See Cass (ch mixte) 14.02.2003 N° 00–19423 00–19424, (25.02.2003) *Gazette du Palais* 23 at 37, X Lagarde, 'Esquisse d'un régime juridique des clauses de conciliation' (2003) *Recueil des Cours de l'Acadèmie de Droit International* 189 at 194.

30 For example, Cadiet suggests that commencement is the moment when one party initiates mediation and communicates this to the other: Cadiet (2003), above note 5 at 189. Conversely Jarrossson favours the moment when both parties are agreed to go to mediation: C Jarrosson, *Statement in the Public Hearing on the Preparation of the Floch Report (Rapport d'information Floch)* Annexe 2: Compte-rendu de l'audition publique de 1 février 2007 at 81, available at www.assemblee-nationale.fr/12/europe/rap-info/i3696.asp.

31 See, for example, Cass civ 2ième 08.06.1988 N° 86–14736, *Bull civ* 1988 II N° 137 at 73, *Rev trim de droit civ* (1989) 751, Cass civ 2ième 05.10.1988 N° 87–16371, (1989) *Dalloz* 209 with comments by Choppin de Janvry, Cass Civ 3ième 18.02.1998 N° 96–14525, *Bull civ* 1989 III N° 38 at 27.

Where national laws permit it, parties may contractually agree to suspend limitation periods. In Germany, for example, parties can suspend the period of limitation by way of a special form of contract called *Vereinbarung über die Verjährung*. This operates in addition to the existing law on limitation periods and may vary certain aspects of it such as the duration of the suspension. Here institutional mediation rules may be useful as many contain provisions on the suspension of limitation periods. For example, the mediation rules of the Handelskammer Hamburg (Germany) recommend suspension of the limitation period up until two months after the mediation has been completed.[32] In another example, the World Intellectual Property Organisation (WIPO) Mediation Rules suspend limitation periods for the duration of the mediation, to the extent permitted by the applicable law.[33]

In some jurisdictions an agreement by the parties is necessary to trigger the suspension of limitation periods during mediation. In Croatia, for example, commencing mediation does not suspend the applicable limitation periods unless the parties agree to a suspension in writing.[34] In the United States the practice of *tolling agreements* is used to waive a right to claim that an action should be dismissed on the basis of an applicable statute of limitations.[35]

A third arrangement is found in jurisdictions such as England which have thus far omitted to regulate the matter and so the limitation period for a cause of action continues to run for the duration of mediative attempts to settle the dispute.[36] If the limitation period is near expiry when mediation procedures are envisaged, it is essential either for the parties to agree that time should stop running[37] or for the claimant to start court proceedings and then seek the court's consent to a suspension of its place in the court schedule whilst the mediation is conducted.[38] It seems likely that England will reform the law on this topic in order to conform with the European Directive on Mediation.

[32] See 'Mediationsvereinbarung zwischen den Parteien und dem/der Mediator(in)' available at www.hk24.de.

[33] See Article 27 WIPO Mediation Rules and other institutional rules in Appendix B.

[34] See Article 14 of the Croatian Law on Mediation (2003).

[35] See T Allen, *Implementing the EU Directive on Mediation: A Draft Consultation Paper* (London: 2009) at 7. At the time of writing, the paper was in draft form. For updates consult the Centre for Effective Dispute Resolution (CEDR) website: www.cedr.co.uk.

[36] See Clifford Chance, *The EU Directive on Mediation 2008 – Will mediation finally establish itself in Europe?* (Frankfurt am Main 2008), available at www.cliffordchance.com.

[37] The ability of parties to enter into an agreement regarding limitation periods is not regulated in England. However academics have interpreted this non-regulation to mean that such an agreement is not impossible. See T Prime and G Scanlan, *The Law of Limitation* (2nd ed, Oxford: Oxford University Press 2001) at 35.

[38] See, for example, Pre-Action Protocol for Construction and Engineering Disputes, r 6 of the Civil Procedure Rules (1998) (CPR).

This discussion has highlighted the importance of parties being aware of the implications for their legal rights of participating in mediation.

2.2 The Impact of Settlements on Parties' Rights and Remedies

Where mediated agreements are achieved in full or partial resolution of a dispute, they may affect the parties' original legal rights and remedies. The extent to which this occurs will depend on factors such as the legal status of the agreement and the intention of the parties, in particular the extent to which they intended all relevant legal rights and remedies to be forfeited by signing the mediated settlement. Where, for example, parties reach an agreement which falls short of a legally binding outcome, such as a memorandum of understanding or statement of intention, their purpose may be to convert this into a final and binding agreement pending approval by outside parties or compliance with specified conditions. However until such time as a legally recognised resolution is reached, they may be able to seek an outcome in relation to the dispute through other mechanisms such as arbitration or litigation. In relation to partial settlements, issues may arise around which rights and remedies remain and which have been forfeited under the agreement.

In some jurisdictions the signing of a mediated agreement may not automatically terminate the associated legal proceedings. For this reason lawyers frequently insert into mediated settlements clauses reciprocally releasing the parties from legal obligations to, and extinguishing their claims against, one another in relation to the original dispute. In France there is a requirement that all parties must submit a notice of withdrawal of action (*désistement d'action)* [39] in addition to finalising the terms of their agreement, unless the mediated agreement takes the form of a settlement deed or settlement by compromise (*transaction*).[40] Legal proceedings are then formally terminated by the responsible judge (*décision de dessaisissement*). The *désistement d'action* can be submitted with the mediator's report or with an application to the court for an execution of the settlement (see below).

Finally where the terms or existence of the mediated settlement are disputed, there is potential for litigation which may involve revisiting aspects of the mediation and calling mediators or others as witnesses. In these circumstances an interesting question arises as to whether or not aggrieved parties can initiate legal action in the court or tribunal from which they would have sought relief had the mediation not resulted in settlement. In other words, can an alleged mediated settlement agreement result in a potential forfeiture of jurisdiction because the original cause of action has been extinguished? From a

[39] The notice of withdrawal of action is similar to the common law notice of discontinuance.

[40] See Article 384 C pr civ.

legal perspective a dispute about a mediated settlement, while dealing with the same or similar subject-matter, is technically a different dispute from the original and as such involves a completely new litigation matter, and in some cases a different court or tribunal may have jurisdiction. This point was considered in the Australian anti-discrimination case of *Sebastian v Rail Infrastructure Corp*[41] with the tribunal of original jurisdiction concluding that it did have authority to hear a dispute relating to a mediated settlement. Similarly in *Spencer v Spencer*[42] the Tribunal which had original jurisdiction in a dispute that had settled at mediation was asked to determine the applicability of its own jurisdiction in relation to a breach of the mediated settlement. Here the tribunal held that although the dispute did not involve the original application, it had jurisdiction in relation to the alleged breach of settlement on the basis that the latter claim was still 'a domestic building dispute' within the tribunal's jurisdiction.

3. Enforceability of Mediated Agreements

As indicated in Chapter 4 the term *mediated agreement* is used interchangeably with *(mediated) settlement* and refers to agreements between parties arising out of mediation that resolve some or all of the issues in dispute. Issues relating to the validity and enforceability of mediated agreements can arise where one party defaults on its obligations and the other seeks remedies for breach or where one party seeks to have the agreement set aside.

As shown later mediated settlements can be enforced as contracts, deeds of settlement, court orders and arbitral awards. However this issue is not always addressed directly in regulatory instruments. For this and other reasons the enforcement of mediated settlements in the United States is the most litigated mediation issue. Between 1999 and 2003, it accounted for 46 per cent of mediation litigation cases[43] and has continued to be a major source of case law on mediation. In the majority of these cases, courts enforced the mediated settlements and dismissed the challenges made in relation to them,[44] indicating a recognition of the integrity of the mediation process and its outcomes.

The two primary international legal instruments on mediation, the European Directive and the UNCITRAL Model Law on International Commercial Conciliation (2002) (MLICC), both fall short of establishing uniform standards in relation to the enforceability of mediated agreements. The

41 See *Sebastian v Rail Infrastructure Corp* [2005] NSWADT 281.

42 See *Spencer v Spencer* [2003] QBT 183.

43 See J Coben and P Thompson, 'Disputing Irony: A Systematic Look at Litigation About Mediation' (2006) 11 *Harvard Negotiation Law Review* 43 at 73.

44 See J Coben and P Thompson, 'Mediation Litigation Trends: 1999–2007' (2007) 1 *World Arbitration and Mediation Report* 395 at 403.

MLICC leaves the manner of dealing with the question of enforceability of mediated agreements open to nation-states to regulate as they wish.[45] Similarly, Article 6 of the European Directive on Mediation[46] requires member states to provide mechanisms through which mediated settlements can, with the consent of both parties, be made enforceable. The Directive envisages enforceability through courts, other competent authorities and specific types of legal instruments such as deeds. However ultimately the precise legal mode of enforceability is left to member states and the potential exceptions to Article 6 seem very broad. Article 6 does not apply where the content of the mediated agreement is either contrary to law of the member state in which the agreement is sought to be enforced or where that law does not provide for its enforceability. Thus the diversity in regulation of the enforceability of mediated agreements is likely to continue within the frameworks of both the EU and UNCITRAL legal instruments on the topic. In relation to England, Allen ponders the meaning of the term *enforceable* in the Directive and whether it requires immediate access to enforcement or whether the ability to sue on a mediated settlement according to general contract law principles would suffice. In relation to cross-border enforcement of mediated settlements the former option is likely to be more attractive for disputants and would put mediation on an enforceability par with arbitration.

Finally the Uniform Mediation Act (2001) (UMA) deals with mediated settlements, but only in relation to admissibility of evidence.[47] Implicit in this provision, however, is an acknowledgement of the potential legal validity and enforceability of settlements.

With little cross-border guidance on this issue, the approach of different jurisdictions to the enforceability of mediated settlements takes on heightened significance, especially in relation to matters concerning choice of court and applicable law.[48] Legal comparativists, Hopt and Steffek, refer to the tradition of the *Vergleich* (settlement) as a popular legal mechanism to implement settlement agreements, as explained later. At the same time they recognise the practice in many countries of giving expression to mediation's flexibility and party autonomy by encouraging choice and flexibility in relation to the legal form of mediated outcomes.[49]

45 See Article 14 of the MLICC and the examination of this provision in Chapter 9.

46 See the European Directive on Mediation, above note 6.

47 See ss 6(a)(1) and 6(b)(2) of the UMA.

48 On these issues and private international law and mediation see Chapter 2.

49 See Hopt and Steffek (2008), above note 12 at 36–37.

3.1 Mediated Outcomes and Legal Form

Mediated outcomes can take different forms, including non-binding agreements such as memoranda of understanding, standard legal contracts, various categories of settlement deeds, court orders and arbitral awards.[50] In relation to non-binding outcomes, some community justice mediations are legislatively declared to be unenforceable in a court of law.[51]

As indicated in Chapter 4, agreements to mediate may contain provisions relating to the legal form required for binding settlements. For example, there may be a requirement that a mediated settlement is not binding until it is reduced to a specific form of writing and signed by the parties, and in some cases witnessed. In this situation heads of agreement summarised by the mediator or legal representatives may not suffice to lend the outcome a legally binding status. These type of requirements aim to avoid confusion about those aspects of the mediation process that form part of the settlement agreement and those that do not. Other agreements to mediate require that heads of agreement form the basis for a formal contract which is to be drafted and executed within a specified time-frame.

There may also be legislative provisions and rules of court that dictate the legal form and status of mediated outcomes. The Slovakian Law on Mediation expressly recognises different legal forms for mediated settlements.[52] It provides that mediated settlements must be in writing in order to be binding on the parties.[53] In addition where the agreement is executed in the form of a notarial deed and has been 'approved as conciliation before a court [or] arbitration body' then a party may apply to the court for judicial execution of the settlement.[54] In the Netherlands mediated settlements are statutorily accommodated by the legal mechanism of the declaratory settlement deed *(Vaststellingsovereenkomst)*.[55]

By way of contrast in France and Austria the relevant laws on mediation in civil matters are silent on the legal form of mediated settlements,

50 In relation to Austria see W Steinacher, 'Die Mediationsrichtlinie' (2000) *Östereichisches Anwaltsblatt* 124 at 129.

51 In Australia see, for example, ss 23(3) and (4) of the Community Justice Centres Act 1983 (NSW).

52 See § 15 of the Slovakian Act of 25 June 2004 on Mediation and Amendment of Certain Acts.

53 See § 15(1) of the Slovakian Act on Mediation, above note 52.

54 See § 15(2) of the Slovakian Act on Mediation, above note 52.

55 For a discussion of the declaratory settlement deed (author's translation from the German, Feststellungsvertrag) see L Schmiedel, 'Mediation in den Niederlanden – Entwicklung und Praxis zwischen staatlicher Forderung und privater Regulierung' in K Hopt and F Steffek (eds), *Mediation – Rechtstatsachen, Rechtsvergleich, Regelungen* (Tübingen: Mohr Siebeck 2008) 329 at 363.

implicitly acknowledging parties' autonomy to choose one of a number of legal forms to enforce agreements resulting from mediation.[56] However in Austria this contractual liberty is accompanied by a duty on mediators to advise parties on the available legal mechanisms to implement the mediation outcome.[57] In many jurisdictions, particularly those in the common law tradition, legislative provisions relating to the legal status and enforceability of mediated settlements frequently take the form of sector-specific regulation and are not uniform throughout the jurisdiction. In Australia and certain US states, for example, the status of mediated agreements may depend on whether or not the mediations took place under the aegis of a court or tribunal.[58]

The following paragraphs examine the main legal forms relating to mediated settlements. The analysis shows that there are different levels of enforceability and that in many cases mediated settlements are not directly enforceable and require some form of review or ratification, for example by a notary, (arbitral) tribunal or court. In some jurisdictions parties may have different procedural paths to enforceability open to them.

3.1.1 Mediated Settlements as Contracts

In most jurisdictions mediated settlements may take the form of standard contracts. At common law this means that the basic elements of contract formation – offer, consideration, acceptance and intention to create legal relations – must be present.[59] In addition any legislative requirements applicable to the relevant type of contract must be satisfied, for example de facto property settlements in some Australian states must include financial statements from each of the parties.[60] Similarly in civil law jurisdictions there must be compliance with the general law on contracts and any additional legal requirements applicable to the category of contract being established. In many jurisdictions mediated settlement agreements, like standard contracts, can *prima facie* be made orally and free from formal requirements.[61] However formal

[56] In Austria see The Law on Mediation in Civil Cases 2001 (ZivMediatG) and in France see the Civil Procedure Code (C pr civ).

[57] See § 16(3) ZivMediatG and S Ferz and E Filler, *Mediation – Gesetzestext und Kommentar* (Wien: WUV Universitätsverlag 2003) at § 17 RN 4.

[58] On the United States see R Kulms, 'Alternative Streitbeteiligung durch Mediation in den USA' in K Hopt and F Steffek (eds) (2008), above note 9, 403 at 443 and on Australia see D Spencer and M Brogan, *Mediation Law and Practice* (Melbourne: CUP 2006) at 356 et seq.

[59] See D Spencer and M Brogan (2006), above note 58 at 356–357.

[60] See, for example, s 266 of the Property Law Act 1974 (Qld).

[61] On the enforcement of an oral mediated settlement which was confirmed by a letter from the mediator see the case of *Joseph v Edison Control Corp* N° A–3856–04T1 2006 WL 2033666 (NJ Super Ct App Div 2006).

written requirements for contract formation can be found in numerous categories of contract such as transfer of land, collateral agreements, time-sharing and consumer credit contracts. Contract formation issues in relation to mediated settlement contracts have been the subject of litigation in jurisdictions such as Australia, the United States and the Netherlands and these are discussed below.

Where the contents of the mediated settlement are disputed, this may lead to litigation requiring a review of what occurred in the mediation. Here tensions arise between the accountability of the mediation participants and the confidentiality of the mediation process. Different jurisdictional approaches to this issue are discussed below.

3.1.2 Contracts Subject to Ratification and Review

Some mediated agreements require ratification by an external body to which a negotiating party is accountable, such as a board, council or cabinet. In other situations it may be decided or understood that agreements will be reviewed by lawyers, accountants or other professional advisers after the mediation meeting. Where there are cooling-off clauses in settlement agreements mediating parties have the benefit of reviewing their commitments during the allocated time. This practice is encountered in areas where a power imbalance between parties is assumed, for example in consumer situations.[62]

Ratification and review provide safeguards for mediating parties. They also provide an opportunity for persons not privy to the dynamics of a mediation and the efforts of the negotiating parties to undermine significant decisions that have been made in the mediation. Other settlement forms which contain a ratification and/or review mechanism include settlement deeds, court orders and consent awards. These are examined below.

3.1.3 Special Forms of Settlement and Deeds

Settlement deeds and other special forms of settlement are agreements that have particular form requirements and a special legal status in terms of enforceability. They are a popular legal form for mediated settlements in civil law jurisdictions and in this section are referred to collectively as settlement deeds, although the forms and legal natures of the various categories of *Vergleich* (Germany), *transaction* (France) and other settlement deeds are different.

While the legal peculiarities of settlement deeds vary according to jurisdiction, they share a number of features. Generally speaking settlement

[62] Generally on this topic see L Boulle, *Mediation: Principles Process Practice* (Sydney: LexisNexis 2005) at 450 et seq. In Australia see, for example, s 11A(2) of the Farm Debt Mediation Act 1994 (NSW) which imposes a 14-day cooling-off period during which the farmer as client of the bank can rescind the settlement agreement.

deeds must be in writing and signed by the parties.[63] Depending on jurisdiction they may also need to be signed by witnesses,[64] lawyers,[65] notaries,[66] judges[67] or any combination of these parties.[68] The involvement of other parties in the finalisation of a settlement deed serves to highlight to the parties the seriousness of the commitment they are making by entering the deed. Where lawyers and notaries sign the deed, they will have associated duties to advise parties in relation to the contents of the agreement and review its terms before signing. The advisory and review elements of settlement deeds offer an extra level of quality assurance in relation to the enforceability of mediated agreements.

In France, Austria[69] and Germany[70] there is a requirement that parties make mutual concessions for settlement deeds to be valid. It is sometimes referred to as settlement by compromise.[71] This differs from the declaratory

63 However in German law, settlement by compromise does not require a particular form (§ 793 BGB) unless expedited enforcement is sought: see, for example, § 794 Abs. 1 N° 5 German Code of Civil Procedure (Zivilprozessordnung, ZPO) (notarised settlement deed).

64 See, for example, Spencer and Brogan (2006), above note 58 at 356–357, in relation to common law practice in Australia.

65 In Germany see §§ 796a and 794(I) N° 4b ZPO which deal with the lawyers' settlement deed (*Anwaltsvergleich*). In Austria the lawyers' settlement deed (*Anwaltsvergleich*) does not have the same level of enforceability as its German counterpart, see N Pitkowitz 'Die neuen Mediationsregeln der EU – Ist Österreich noch Wegbereiter?' (2005) *SchiedsVZ* 81 at 85.

66 See the various references to notarised settlements in the chapters of K Hopt and F Steffek (eds), *Mediation – Rechtstatsachen, Rechtsvergleich, Regelungen* (Tübingen: Mohr Siebeck 2008): for Austria see M Roth and D Gherdane, 'Mediation in Österreich – Zivilrechts-Mediations-Gesetz: Rechtlicher Rahmen und praktische Erfahrung ' 105 at 136 and see also § 3 of the Austrian Notaries Act (Notariatsordnung) and § 1 N° 17 of the Austrian Enforcement Code (Exekutionsordnung); for the Netherlands see Article 430(1) Wetboek van Burgerlijke Rechtsverordnung (Rv) referred to in L Schmiedel, 'Mediation in den Niederlanden – Entwicklung und Praxis zwischen staatlicher Förderung und privater Regulierung' 329 at 346; for Japan see H Baum and E Schwittek, 'Mediation in Japan – Entwicklung und Praxis der aussergerichtlichen Streitbeilegung' 483 at 521; and for Hungary see C Jessel-Holst, 'Mediation in Ungarn' 905 at 911–912. In relation to Germany see § 794(I) N° 5 ZPO.

67 On judicial settlements see Chapter 3.

68 See § 15 of the Slovakian Act on Mediation, above note 52.

69 See §§ 1380(1) and (2) and 1381 of the Austrian Civil Code (Allgemeines Bürgerliches Gesetzbuch ABGB).

70 On the use of the settlement deed (Vergleich) for mediated agreements in Germany see H Eidenmüller, *Vertrags- und Verfahrensrecht der Wirtschaftsmediation* (Köln: Dr Otto Schmidt 2001) at 43–44.

71 See A Mourre, 'Mediation and French Law: Recent Landmarks in Legislation and Case Law' (2001) *ICC International Court of Arbitration Bulletin (Special Supplement)* 63 at 71.

settlement deed *(Vaststellingsovereenkomst)*,[72] which is widely used for mediated settlements in the Netherlands. Here there is no requirement for both parties to make concessions and the deed can clarify and regulate the parties' legal relationship as a means of resolving and finalising the dispute. Institutional mediation rules may require mediators to ensure that what is agreed between the parties is correctly recorded in the declaratory settlement deed.[73] This is a significant and potentially onerous duty as the declaratory settlement deed is likely to be the primary, if not the only, admissible evidence of the agreement between the parties.[74]

At common law settlement deeds require neither mutual concessions by the parties nor the contractual element of consideration.[75] The English tradition is to have recitals at the commencement of deeds of agreement setting out the history of the dispute and the background to the agreement. Recitals, when read in conjunction with the operative parts of the document, can be useful in relation to the interpretation of the agreement's provisions.[76]

In terms of enforceability, settlement deeds usually afford expedited enforcement by courts provided there has been compliance with the relevant form requirements and the deed does not embody an illegal agreement.[77] Challenges to settlement deeds may be restricted, as is discussed below.

3.1.4 Court or Tribunal Ratification

In certain situations the ratification of a court or other external authority is available to validate mediated agreements. In France, for example, parties may apply to court for a ruling that mediated settlements by compromise (*transaction*) – as defined in Article 2044 of the Civil Code – are immediately

72 See § 7:900 et seq of the Dutch Civil Code (Burgerlijk Wetboek, BW).

73 See, for example, Article 14 of the Netherlands Mediation Institute (NMI) Mediation Rules in the Netherlands.

74 See Schmiedel (2008), above note 55 at 354, 364 and the references to Dutch case law.

75 See Spencer and Brogan (2006), above note 58. Deeds may also permit third party beneficiaries to enforce an undertaking in the deed, thereby overcoming the doctrine of privity: A Griffiths, *Contracting With Companies* (London: Hart Publishing 2005) at 7.

76 See Spencer and Brogan (2006), above note 58.

77 See, for example, the following French case where the court has refused to execute a settlement deed: CA Versailles, 18.06.2003, G Huchet, 'Retour sur l'article 1441-4 du NCPC' (2007) *Gazette du Palais* 6 at 8 and J-B Racine 'Les incertitudes de la transaction dite "homologuée" (à propos de l'article 1441-4 du Nouveau Code de procédure civile, in: P Chevalier, Y Desdevises and P Milburn (eds), *Les mondes de règlement des litiges: les voies nouvelles d'une autre justice* (Paris: La Documentation française 2003) 15 at 16.

enforceable.[78] In England litigation parties, upon reaching a mediated settlement, may use a Tomlin Order which provides expedited court enforcement of the terms of settlement as if they were embodied in a judgment.[79]

In some jurisdictions it is a requirement that all parties to a mediated settlement apply to court to ratify the settlement. This leads to a potential risk that one party may refuse to make the application. Where this occurs the party seeking to enforce the settlement may still do so by suing for breach of the contractual settlement. Here the contract will not be subject to expedited enforcement as it would have been had it been sanctioned by the court. In the American case of *Envtl Abatement Inc v Astrum*[80] the judge refused to enter a consent decree on the grounds that one party had withdrawn consent prior to the order and the agreement was neither in written form nor had it been presented in open court. Coben and Thompson suggest that although in this case the consent decree was refused, the agreement may still be enforceable as a contract,[81] although the confidentiality principle may create evidential difficulties in this regard.

In terms of the powers of review by the ratifying body, these vary according to jurisdiction and are generally restricted to a few areas. For example in France if all the parties to a pre-litigation (non-contentious) mediated settlement agree, the court may review and confirm the agreement.[82] Here the review of the mediated settlement is typically limited to factors such as the *bona fides* of the agreement, the informed consent of the parties, clarity in relation to the interpretation of the agreement, the ability of the agreement to be performed, the legality of the terms of the agreement, and whether it injures third party rights.[83]

78 See Article 1441-4 of the New Code of Civil Procedure, Decree 98–1231 of 28 December 1998. However the Court of Cassation decided in 2001 that this provision could not be used to enforce an eviction: see (2001) *Rev trim dr civ* 384.

79 For a Tomlin Order precedent see the CEDR model mediation settlement at www.cedr.co.uk/library/documents/settlement_agreement.pdf. There may also be the possibility of summary enforcement according to r 24 of the CPR, but this is not a rule expressly directed at mediated settlements.

80 See *Envtl Abatement Inc v Astrum RE Corp* 27 SW 3d 530 (Tenn Ct App 2000) at 541–542.

81 See Coben and Thompson (2006), above note 43 at 78. However in the case of *JN Intern Inc v MS Transgene Biotek Ltd* Nos 8:05CV67, 8:05CV158, 2006 WL 1559709 (D Neb 2006) the court refused to consider the enforceability of a mediated settlement as the parties had not submitted it to the court for approval before asking the court to enforce it.

82 See Article 131-12 C pr civ.

83 These are summarised by K Deckert 'Mediation in Frankreich – Rechtlicher Rahmen und praktische Erfahrungen' in K Hopt and F Steffek (eds) (2008), above note 9, 183 at 205–206.

In Australia, where mediation is attached to certain tribunals, tribunal members can make consent determinations only after establishing that mediated agreements are consistent with a tribunal's jurisdiction and relevant policy requirements.[84] By way of example, the Administrative Decisions Tribunal (NSW) may refer matters arising in proceedings before it to mediation if it considers the circumstances appropriate and if the parties consent. The Tribunal has the power to make orders giving effect to agreements arising out of mediations, but its powers are limited by the requirement that the Tribunal is satisfied that it would have had the power to make a decision in the terms of the agreement.[85]

In relation to family matters mandatory court review of mediated settlements is found in some jurisdictions. By way of example, French courts review the terms of family agreements to ensure that the contents reflect the best interests of the children.[86] Similar arrangements can be found in Australia.[87]

Settlements sanctioned by courts which take the form of court orders may fall within the scope of cross-border legal instruments dealing with recognition and enforcement of court judgments. Chapter 57 of the Brussels I Regulation is entitled *Authentic Instruments and Court Settlements* and provides that mediated settlements sanctioned by the court in the original country may be recognised as 'authentic foreign instruments' throughout the European Union.[88]

84 See, for example, the Commonwealth Administrative Appeals Tribunal, the NSW Administrative Decisions Tribunal, the NSW Consumer, Trader and Tenancy Tribunal and the following provisions: ss 34A and 42C(1)(c) Administrative Appeals Tribunal Act 1975 (Cth) and s 61 Consumer, Trader and Tenancy Tribunal Act 2001 (NSW).

85 See Administrative Decisions Tribunal Act 1997 (NSW) ss 102(1), 105(1) and 86(1).

86 See Article 268 C pr civ; see also Deckert (2008), above note 83 at 223.

87 See Family Law Rules 2004, r 1.06.

88 Article 57 considers a document formally drawn up or registered as an authentic instrument enforceable in other member states if the procedures provided for in Article 38 et seq are adhered to. An appeal may be lodged under Article 43 or Article 44 against enforceability, but a declaration of enforceability can only be refused or revoked if the instrument is manifestly contrary to public policy in the member state. A settlement is considered enforceable under the same conditions as authentic instruments under Article 58. There is a standard form in Annex V of the Regulation which the court/competent authority of the member state in which settlement was approved must issue at the request of an interested party. Enforcement of the settlement must be applied for (Article 38), except in the UK where registration suffices. The proper court to apply to is listed in Annex II, with jurisdiction applicable according to place of enforcement, or place of domicile of party (Article 39). Procedure is to be that of the law of the member state of enforcement (Article 40) with enforceability declared upon completion of the formalities in Article 53 (Article 41), and the declaration of enforceability is to brought to the notice or served on the applicant forthwith (Article 42). The Brussels II Regulation provides exceptions concerning the recognition and enforcement of judgements in matrimonial

In addition the European Regulation on Enforcement Order for uncontested claims would seem to include mediated settlements of disputes which have not been the subject of litigation.[89]

The Hague Choice of Court Convention establishes rules for enforcement of choice of court agreements in international commercial transactions and certain international civil matters and its terms were introduced in Chapter 2.[90] Under the Convention contracting states may declare that their courts will recognise and enforce judgments given by courts of other contracting states designated in a non-exclusive choice of court agreement (Article 22). Judicial settlements resulting from an exclusive choice of court agreement approved by the court of a contracting state shall be enforced under the Convention in the same manner as judgments (Article 12). It remains to be seen to what extent court sanctioned mediated settlements will be enforceable under the Convention.[91]

3.1.5 Settlement in the Form of an Arbitral Award

Yet another form of expedited enforcement is found where settlements take the form and legal force of an arbitral award. Such awards are called *consent awards* and are also known as *awards on consent* or *awards on agreed terms*.[92] Wiwen-Nilsson points out that while the New York Convention does not expressly address consent awards, the predominant view is that such awards are covered by the Convention.[93] Generally arbitral tribunals have the power to review a mediated settlement agreement and even to refuse to record it in the form of an award.[94]

Consent awards can occur in three primary ways, namely (1) as a settlement in the course of an arbitral process, (2) as a settlement between parties to an arbitral agreement prior to arbitration or (3) where the law provides

matters and matters involving parental responsibility: Preamble, N° 22 Council Regulation EC N° 2201/2003 of 27.11.2003.

89 See Articles 3(1)(a) and (d), 24 and 25 of Regulation EC N° 805/2004 of the European Parliament and of the Council of 21.04.2004 creating a European Enforcement Order for uncontested claims.

90 On the Brussels 1 Regulation and the Hague Convention see Chapter 2.

91 Compare the distinction made between judicial settlements and mediation in the European Directive on Mediation Article 3(a), discussed in Chapter 3.

92 See T Wiwen-Nilsson, 'Commercial dispute Settlement: issues for the future' in *Modern Law for Global Commerce: Congress to celebrate the 40th annual session of UNCITRAL* (Vienna: UNCITRAL 2007) at 3, available at www.uncitral.org. Article 31 of the MLICA recognises consent awards and sets out the requirements as to form.

93 See Wiwen-Nilsson (2007), above note 92 at 4 and G Lörcher, 'Enforceability of Agreed Awards in Foreign Jurisdictions' (2001) 17 *Arbitration International* 275.

94 See, for example, Articles 30 and 31 of the MLICA and Article 51(2) of the Arbitration Act 1996 in England.

that a mediated settlement can be treated as an award, provided there is compliance with certain conditions.

By way of example, arbitration laws in Germany, Austria and England provide that an amicable settlement of a dispute within an arbitration procedure shall be recorded by the tribunal as an award on agreed terms if so requested by the parties.[95] Such awards have the same effect as any other award with respect to the merits of the case. In China Article 51 of the Arbitration Law of the People's Republic of China provides that conciliation may be conducted by an arbitral tribunal and if settlement occurs the tribunal may document it as either a written conciliation statement or an arbitration award in accordance with the settlement agreement.

In Bermuda parties to an arbitration agreement can appoint a conciliator to assist them settle their dispute with the advantage that any resulting settlement is treated as an award on an arbitration agreement and, with the leave of the court, may be enforced in the same manner as a judgment to the same effect. Moreover, with leave of the court, judgment may be entered in terms of the agreement. Here the disputants must be parties to an arbitration agreement, but it is not essential that an arbitration process has been initiated before the appointment of a conciliator.[96]

In jurisdictions such as France, Croatia[97] and Korea[98] mediated settlements can still take the form of arbitral awards in the absence of an arbitration agreement or arbitration process. In France, for example, this is referred to as the *sentence d'accord-parties*. Here the award can be issued at any time by either the mediator turned arbitrator or by another arbitrator brought in for that purpose.[99]

Consent awards are an attractive option for parties in an international dispute as they promise the high level of enforceability associated with cross-border arbitral awards.[100] However there is a number of uncertainties and

[95] See § 1053 of the German Code of Civil Procedure (ZPO), § 605 N° 1 of the Austrian Arbitration Law Amendment of 2006 and Article 52 of the English Arbitration Act 1996.

[96] See Bermuda International Conciliation and Arbitration Act (1993) ss 20 and 48. Similar provisions operate in Hong Kong: see Hong Kong Special Administrative Region of China, s 2C of the Arbitration Ordinance (Cap 341) 1997 as amended. Order 73 r 10 of the Rules of the High Court applies the procedure for enforcing arbitral awards to the enforcement of settlement agreements.

[97] See Article 10(2) of the Law on Conciliation in Croatia.

[98] See Article 18(3) of the Commercial Arbitration Rules of the Korean Commercial Arbitration Board.

[99] See Deckert (2008), above note 83 at 206.

[100] Note the view of Steele, that consent awards are a 'trick of legal fiction'. The US commentator does not deny that there are benefits to consent awards, but argues that they are not arbitral awards *per se*, they are just treated as such. See B Steele,

potential difficulties with mediated settlements adopting the legal form of consent awards. These have been examined by Wiwen-Nilsson and are summarised here:[101]

- Should the consent award contain the entirety of the terms of the mediated settlement or should the terms of the agreement be reframed as orders and written into the award by the parties' representatives or the arbitrator? Wiwen-Nilsson suggests that the terms of the consent award should be sufficiently certain so as not to require reformulation for inclusion into the award.
- Where the mediated settlement deals with matters not covered by the arbitration agreement or the submission to arbitration, then it is unlikely that the tribunal has jurisdiction to render the award, unless an agreement between the parties and arbitrators is made to extend the terms of the arbitration agreement or to introduce the matters covered in the settlement into the arbitration submission.
- It seems that where part of a consent award lies outside the jurisdiction of the arbitral tribunal, it may be possible to sever that part from the rest of the consent award that has been validly issued, thereby saving the latter part of the award.[102]
- Mediated settlements may be conditional upon certain events occurring or may contain other terms – for example conferring rights on a third party – which cannot be transformed into consent awards.
- Whereas most settlements contain dispute resolution clauses, consent awards do not. Wiwen-Nilssen asks whether such a provision would be inconsistent with the notion of a final and binding award.
- Are parties entitled to settle their dispute and then commence arbitration for the purpose of converting the settlement contract into a consent award? Article 30 of the MLICA applies where the dispute is settled during – and not after – arbitral proceedings and therefore would not extend to this type of situation. As indicated previously, Germany and England take a similar approach.

3.2 Mediated Settlements: Challenges and Remedies

When a party realises the negative or otherwise untenable consequences of a settlement to which it has (allegedly) agreed, it may seek redress. This may take

'Enforcing International Commercial Mediation Agreements as Arbitral Awards under the New York Convention' (2006–2007) 54 *UCLA Law Review* 1397.

101 These are examined by Wiwen-Nilsson (2007), above note 92 at 5–7.

102 See the New York Convention on the Recognition and Enforcement of Foreign Arbitral Awards 1958, Article V(c).

the form of challenging the existence of a binding settlement or seeking to set it aside on recognised contractual grounds of review. An indirect challenge to the mediated agreement may occur where a party takes legal action against the mediator or their own legal adviser/s.

The nature and extent of review available for mediated settlements depends largely on the legal form and status of the instrument containing the settlement agreement. The grounds for challenging mediated settlements are generally more extensive in relation to standard contracts than settlement forms which involve review and ratification by professional dispute resolution practitioners such as lawyers, notaries, mediators, arbitrators and judges. This type of regulatory policy recognises that parties who seek a mediated outcome with an expedited enforcement mechanism waive the right to challenge the agreement as if it were an ordinary contract. Moreover such settlement forms are typically subject to review before they are ratified and it is arguably at this point that potential problems with, or potential challenges to, the mediated agreement should be addressed. In the absence of statutory provisions requiring a cooling-off period or ratification by a third party, contract law will *prima facie* recognise and enforce such settlement agreements.

Another aspect of mediated settlements adding a layer of complexity to the question of review is the confidential nature of the mediation process. This topic and the associated tension between encouraging participation and open communication in mediation through confidentiality, on one hand, and keeping mediators and mediation participants accountable, on the other, has been examined extensively in Chapter 6. The extent to which courts are prepared to consider mediation evidence in relation to establishing the enforceability or otherwise of mediated settlements depends largely on how they interpret and apply the relevant law on confidentiality. Where statutes are worded in terms of absolute confidentiality, it may be difficult for courts to find exceptions to permit consideration of mediation evidence. The Californian case of *Simmons v Ghaderi,*[103] for example, concerned an action to determine whether a valid oral mediated settlement existed. Here the Supreme Court permitted a party to rely on the strictly worded confidentiality provisions of the Californian Evidence Code to prevent mediation evidence being admitted even though that party had voluntarily declared the facts to be true, stipulated that it did not dispute them, submitted evidence of them and litigated their effect, and only invoked mediation confidentiality for the first time at trial. However as Chapter 6 indicates, there are numerous confidentiality rules, both legislative and at

[103] See *Simmons v Ghaderi* (2008) 44 Cal 4th 570, 2008, Cal Lexis 907, 2008 WL 2789224.

common law, which effectively permit mediation evidence in relation to enforceability issues.[104]

Assuming that scope for admission of mediation evidence exists, the next section outlines the main grounds for challenging mediated settlements. Given the scarcity of relevant court decisions from civil law jurisdictions, the discussion will focus on common law cases with brief reference to applicable laws from civil law countries.

3.2.1 Challenges Based on Traditional Contract Principles

Enforceability cases often deal with traditional contract defences available at common law and in legislation. These defences, which have developed around negotiated agreements, are *prima facie* applicable to mediated settlements. However the roles of mediators and legal representatives may affect the manner in which contractual defence principles play out in a supervised negotiation process such as mediation. Contract defences which have been used in mediation enforceability cases include issues around formation of contract and grounds for setting aside agreements such as mistake, duress, undue influence, fraud, unconscionability, and misleading and deceptive conduct. As indicated earlier there has been litigation on contract formation in various jurisdictions with the following issues raised:[105]

- authority to settle;[106]
- legal capacity;[107]
- meeting of the parties' minds;[108]
- intention to be legally bound;[109]
- agreement to agree;[110] and

104 See, for example, s 6(b)(2) of the UMA and Article 7(1)(b) of the European Directive on Mediation and the English cases relating to without prejudice privilege referred to in Chapter 6.

105 See Coben and Thompson (2007), above note 44 at 404 in relation to relevant US cases.

106 See, for example, the US case of *McKown v US Dept of Agric* 276 F Supp 2d 1201 (D N M 2003) at 1210.

107 See, for example, *Domanque v Domanque* 2005 WL1828553 (Tex App Aug 3 2005) where the court found that a party was competent to enter into a mediated agreement despite illness (Hepatitis C) and use of medication that was alleged to cause depression and memory loss.

108 See, for example, *Esser v Esser* 586 SE 2d 627 (Ga 2003) at 628.

109 See, for example, the cases on heads of agreement discussed below.

110 See, for example, the New Zealand case of *Fletcher Challenge Energy Ltd v Electricity Corporation of New Zealand Ltd* [2001] 2 NZLR 219. Although not strictly speaking a mediation case, it has been applied to mediation scenarios as discussed in Chapter 4.

– lack of required formality.[111]

In cases where mediated settlements are challenged on the basis of a formality or technicality, they have on occasion been held to be unenforceable as the next two American cases demonstrate. In an oft-cited case, *Vernon v Acton*,[112] the court refused to enforce an oral mediation agreement on a number of grounds including that oral communications in the mediation were confidential and therefore evidence to prove the existence of the settlement could not be admitted. In another case, *Haghighi v Russian-American Broadcasting Co*,[113] a court refused to enforce a written mediated agreement which included a clause to the effect that it was a 'full and final mutual release of all claims' because the agreement did not contain the precise wording required by statute. Coben and Thompson suggest that such cases represent an exception to the practice of US courts and that seldom do 'courts refuse to enforce an agreement based on purely technical defences'.[114] Mediated settlements which fall short of final form have been upheld in jurisdictions such as the United States, Australia and the Netherlands as the following discussion shows.[115]

Disputes about lack of formality may arise in the context of settlements taking the form of *interim agreements* or *heads of agreement*. Here important considerations for courts include the purpose of relevant legislation and the extent to which parties intended the *interim* agreement to be the final and binding arrangement between them, which would then be executed in a formal manner.[116] Such agreements are more likely to be enforced than those which amount to no more than agreements in principle or agreements to agree, as such arrangements leave essential aspects of the agreement, such as the terms of releases,[117] to be sorted out at a later date.[118]

111 See, for example, *Haghighi v Russian-American Broadcasting Co* 173 F 3d 1086 (8th Cir 1999) at 1088–89 and *Cincinnati Ins Co v Barber Insulation Inc* 2006 WL 1577847 (Ala 2006).

112 See *Vernon v Acton* 732 NE 2d 805 (8th Cir 1999) at 806.

113 See *Haghighi v Russian-American Broadcasting Co* 173 F 3d 1086 (8th Cir 1999) at 1088–89.

114 See Coben and Thompson (2006), above note 43 at 87.

115 In relation to the Netherlands see Schmiedel (2008), above note 55 at 365, referring to the relevant case law, including the decisions of the Amsterdam Appellate Court (Gerechtshof Amsterdam) of 10.12.2003, LJN AR 5521 and the Arnheim District Court (Rechtbank Arnhem) of 13.11.2002, LJN AQ 2634.

116 See, for example, the parties' memorandum of agreement in *Chesney v Hypertension Diagnostics Inc* N° A05–2210, 2006 WL 2256590 (Minn Ct App 2006), which included terms to the effect that the memorandum was binding on, and enforceable against, each of the signatories and that it was not dependent on the execution of formal documents containing the detail of the agreement.

117 See the following cases where the final release had not yet been included in the terms of settlement, and the settlement was held to be unenforceable: *Chappell and Roth*

In the American case of *Delyanis*[119] the court found that a handwritten agreement drafted by the mediator and signed by the parties and lawyers was not enforceable because the agreement specifically stated that it was not intended to be legally enforceable in this form. However subsequent emails by the parties indicating an intention to be bound by those terms constituted an enforceable agreement.

In another example, the applicant in the Australian case of *The Intercon v Nakajima*[120] denied the existence of the settlement, arguing that it was conditional upon satisfactory terms and appropriate releases being signed by the parties. He further submitted that his representative at mediation was suffering from bipolar disorder and had failed to take his medication on the morning of the mediation with the result that his decision-making was impaired. The Tribunal held that there was sufficient intention and certainty in the settlement to require the parties to comply with their mediated bargain. The medical evidence presented was accepted by tribunal, but was held to be insufficient to show special disadvantage or incapacity to make decisions.[121]

Another basis for enforcing mediated outcomes that do not comply with required formalities is equitable estoppel. Thus a party may be estopped from avoiding compliance with heads of agreement or similar documentation intended to form the basis for a full and final agreement. This was the situation in the US case of *Affordable Erecting Inc v Neosho Trompler Inc.*[122] Here the court concluded that the mediated settlement did not comply with the statutory requirements of writing and signature as the lawyer had signed but noted that the settlement was contingent on the client's approval. Nevertheless the court

548 SE 2d 499 (NC 2001) at 500 and *Am Network Leasing Corp v Corp Funding Houston Inc* N° 01–00–00789–CV 2002 WL 31266230 (Tex App Oct 10, 2002). Conversely see *Coulter v Carewell Corp of Okla* 21 P3d 1078 (Okla Civ App 2001) at 1082–1084.

118 On incomplete agreements which leave essential elements outstanding, see the discussion on contractual certainty in Chapter 4 and the case of *Fletcher Challenge Energy Ltd v Electrical Corporation of New Zealand Ltd* [2001] 2 NZLR 219. For examples of cases where the mediated agreement was held not to be final and binding see *Catamount State Prods Inc v Sheldon* 845 A2d 324 (Vt 2003) at 331 and *Riner v Newbraugh* 563 SE2d 802 (W Va 2002) at 805–806. In the latter case the mediator testified to the effect that the parties had reached a final agreement at mediation. However one party had subsequently prepared the written settlement and the other party refused to sign it, claiming that it contained provisions that had never been addressed during mediation. The court refused to enforce the settlement.

119 See *Delyanis v Dyna-Empire Inc* 465 F Supp 2d 170 (EDNY 2006).

120 See *Intercon v Nakajima* [2005] VCAT 1703.

121 See also *Sebastian v Rail Infrastructure Corp* [2005] NSWADT 281 where the settlement document was entitled 'Principles of Agreement' and was held to be enforceable.

122 See *Affordable Erecting Inc v Neosho Trompler Inc* 715 NW 2d 620 (Wis 2006).

reasoned that the client was estopped from avoiding the settlement as its actions, including assurances that the mediated settlement would be signed, induced reliance on them. Thus the agreement was held to be enforceable on the basis of equitable estoppel.

However the English case of *Brown v Rice and Patel*[123] shows that, although courts may endeavour to uphold settlements falling short on form, they must ultimately adhere to the parties' intentions. In this case the court went beyond the stipulated writing requirements of settlement contained in an agreement to mediate in order to examine whether or not there was an enforceable settlement. Despite the terms of the agreement to mediate, the court took the view that it was conceivable for a party to be estopped from asserting the writing requirement, and that the parties might have varied or waived formal settlement requirements or even entered into a binding oral collateral agreement not subject to the formalities. In the final analysis, however, the court held that there was no binding agreement as the writing requirement, which continued to represent the parties' intention, had not been fulfilled. The case raises questions about the extent to which parties can render enforceability of settlements conditional on formal writing requirements and simultaneously be confident that mediation confidentiality will be upheld.

In addition to challenges to the formation of mediated settlements, other grounds for setting aside mediated settlements may include mistake, duress, undue influence, fraud, unconscionability, and misleading and deceptive conduct. As with the contract defences relating to formation issues, these defences are often bundled together as grounds to set aside mediated settlements. For example, claims of unconscionability may be coupled with allegations of undue influence, coercion, duress and evidence demonstrating the vulnerability of the claimant. In the case of successful defences it may not always be clear from the court's judgment the precise grounds upon which the settlement has been set aside.

Mediation cases dealing with mistake have involved allegations of mutual or unilateral mistake relating to a material fact which goes to the essence of the settlement agreement.[124] As is the case with many of these defences, mistake has been rarely successful as a defence, especially unilateral mistake which requires that the other party should have reasonably been aware of the mistake or even caused it.[125]

[123] See *Brown v Rice and Patel* [2007] EWHC 625 (Ch) also discussed in Chapter 6.

[124] See *Sheng v Starkey Labs Inc* 117 F 3d 1081 (8th Cir 1997) at 1084.

[125] See the data collated by Coben and Thompson on mistake and other contractual defences in mediation enforceability cases in the United States. In 2004 and 2005 there were seven unilateral mistake cases, none of which were successful. Of the 16 mutual mistake cases, only three were successful: Coben and Thompson (2007), above note 44 at 405–406.

Fraud, misleading and deceptive conduct may arise as a contract defence in enforcement cases where, for example, one party becomes aware of certain information after the mediation settlement has been finalised. If a party can show that, in agreeing to the settlement, it relied to its detriment on such conduct then it may be possible to set aside the mediated settlement agreement.[126] However the standards applied by courts in determining whether fraudulent, misleading or deceptive conduct is established may vary according to legal culture and bargaining expectations. In their review of the American case law on the topic Coben and Thompson suggest that US judges are prepared to accommodate a wide range of adversarial and position tactics in mediation. They conclude that 'parties must retain their adversarial viligance'[127] even in a process such as mediation that is described as collaborative and interest-based. Thus in *In re Patterson*[128] a party who relied on an incorrect representation of income by the other side was unable to set the settlement aside. The court took the view that the aggrieved party should not expect to be able to rely on the other party's income appraisal especially when it could have arranged for its own valuation of the same.

Allegations of duress, undue influence, coercion and unconscionability in mediation have formed the basis for a number of American and Australian decisions. Unconscionability cases often involve a structural or perceived power imbalance between the parties, such as may exist in Business to Consumer (B2C) disputes and family conflicts involving dependent children.[129] In farm debt mediations there have been applications for review alleging duress, unconscionability and misleading and deceptive conduct on the part of banks. By way of example, the Australian case of *Cassegrain v Commonwealth Development Bank of Australia Ltd*[130] concerned a farm debt mediation with allegations of unconscionability and bank misconduct. The court found, however, that on the evidence unconscionability had not been established and the settlement was held to be enforceable.

Duress and undue influence claims may involve allegations of threats made, or inappropriate pressure applied, to one party by another party, the mediator, a legal representative, or a combination of mediation participants. Moreover it is not uncommon to find plaintiffs described as vulnerable or

126 See *Hargraves Secured Investments Ltd v Ryan* [2007] NSWSC 404 where a claim of misleading and deceptive conduct in relation to a settlement by a farmer against a bank was not upheld.

127 See Coben and Thompson (2006), above note 43 at 81.

128 *In re Patterson* 969 P 2d 1106 (Wash Ct App 1999) at 1110–1111.

129 In the United States enforcement cases alleging unconscionability often involve child support and custody arrangement which involve the rights of children: Coben and Thompson (2006), above note 43 at 86.

130 *Cassegrain v Commonwealth Development Bank of Australia* Ltd [2003] NSWCA 260.

suffering from illness in the case law. These claims have also shown themselves to be difficult to prove in the context of mediation. In the Australian decision of *Pittorino v Meynert,* for example,[131] the applicant argued that the other parties took advantage of her discomfort during the mediation. She alleged that the mediator tried to influence her, that the mediation was excessively lengthy, that she was suffering from an injury and that her requests to have the mediation adjourned were ignored. The court held that the allegations were not established on the evidence.

Similarly in the American case of *Olam v Congress Mortgage Co*[132] the 65 year old plaintiff suffered from a number of medical conditions and submitted in evidence that she was weak, dizzy and experiencing pain during the mediation. She further alleged that her lawyer, the defendants and their lawyers pressured her into reaching settlement at 1 am in the morning in a mediation that continued for 15 hours. After a detailed and considered judgement the court held that there was insufficient evidence of undue influence to justify setting aside the contract.

In the case of *Deville*[133] claims of duress were also dismissed. Here the plaintiff who was suffering from severe post-surgery knee pain argued that his lawyer prevented him from leaving the mediation session and pressured him into settlement. However his evidence was contradicted by the mediator and the plaintiff's lawyer.

However in *Ryles v Palace Hotel*[134] the court did not enforce the settlement, finding that there was a coercive atmosphere around the execution of the mediated settlement and that the,

> plaintiff was misled [by her lawyer and others] about whether she would be given a fair hearing […], threatened with the loss of her home and other serious financial consequences.

Sometimes actions challenging the enforceability of mediated settlements may involve allegations of professional negligence or misconduct in addition to contractual defences.[135] This was the case in *Tapoohi v Lewenberg* where claims that the mediator had exceeded his authority by being excessively directive were coupled with allegations of undue pressure. In holding that there was a case to

131 See *Pittorino v Meynert (as Executrix of the Wills of Guiseppe Pittorino (dec) and Guiseppina Pittorino (dec)and Ors* [2002] WASC 76.

132 See *Olam v Congress Mortgage* Co 68 F Supp 2d 1110 (ND Cal 1999) at 1139–51.

133 See *Deville v US ex rel Dept of Veteran Affairs* 202 F App'x 761 (5th Cir 2006).

134 See *Ryles v Palace Hotel* N° C 04–5326 SBA, 2006 WL 3093678 (ND Cal 2006).

135 See, for example, the American cases of *Gelfand v Gabriel* N° SCO61373, 2002 WL 1397037 (Cal Ct App 2002) and *Kendrick v Barker* 2001 15 p 3d 734 (Wyo 2001) at 741. Both cases involved allegations of pressure to settle by the party's own lawyers and in both cases the mediated settlements were enforced.

answer, The Victorian Supreme Court suggested that the mediator's excessively directive behaviour could conceivably amount to a breach of his duty of care to the disputants. The case has been considered elsewhere in this book.[136] However the observation has been made that allegations of excessive pressure, coercion and duress by the mediator may sometimes amount to what mediators refer to as the technique of *reality testing.*[137] In the case of *Estate of Skalka v Skalka*[138] the judicial mediator highlighted the burdensome costs to the parties of continuing to litigate and strongly suggested that the financing of further litigation would cost them the property which was the subject of dispute. After the mediation one of the parties sought to set aside the settlement based *inter alia* on mediator coercion. The court dismissed the claim.

Finally the US case of *Cabellero v Wikse*[139] involved a claim for specific performance of a mediated settlement of an employment dispute. The defendant employee left the mediation before settlement was reached, with words to the effect of 'Jim, I'm leaving. You handle it.' The defendant argued that while these words may have given his lawyer authority to make counter-proposals, they did not authorise him to bind the defendant to the terms upon which settlement was made, and that therefore the lawyer had exceeded his authority in agreeing to settlement terms. The settlement terms included a provision that the defendant would not be re-instated by his employer, whereas the defendant subsequently asserted that he did wish to be re-instated. The court held that even if the defendant's lawyer lacked actual authority to settle on the defendant's behalf, in the circumstances the lawyer was vested with apparent authority. The court ordered specific performance of the settlement.

As indicated previously there is a paucity of jurisprudence from civil law jurisdictions on enforceability of mediated settlements. However academic opinion indicates that in the absence of specific legislation on the topic, the general laws applicable to contract will apply to mediated settlements.

In Austria, for example, the comprehensive Austrian Law on Mediation in Civil Cases does not regulate review of mediated settlements; rather it is left to the general provisions of the Austrian Civil Code.[140] Similarly in Germany general contract law is applicable to mediated settlements and parties may contest settlements based upon mistake,[141] incorrect communication of intent,[142]

[136] See *Tapoohi v Lewenberg* [2003] VSC 410, also discussed in Chapter 3.

[137] See Coben and Thompson (2006), above note 43 at 96.

[138] See *Estate of Skalka v Skalka* 751 NE 2d 769 (Ind Ct App 2001) at 772.

[139] See *Cabellero v Wikse* N° 27995, 2004 WL 858710 (Idaho 2004).

[140] See, for example §§ 1385 (mistake) of the Austrian Civil Code (Allgemeines Bürgerliches Zivilgesetzbuch, ABGB). See also Roth and Gherdane (2008), above note 14 at137.

[141] See § 119 of the German Civil Code (Bürgerliches Gesetzbuch, BGB) and Palandt et al (2009), above note 21 at § 119.

[142] See § 120 of the German Civil Code.

or on the grounds of deceit and duress.[143] Thus if one party uses deceit or unlawful duress in the mediation process and so induces the other to enter into a settlement, the latter party can contest the agreement.[144] Similarly if the mediator exercises undue pressure on the parties to persuade them to settle, the settlement contract may be contested according to another provision of the Civil Code.[145]

This examination of the jurisprudence on enforceability cases in mediation has shown that while contractual defences can be successful, they seem to more frequently fail. Some commentators have suggested that the increased use of cooling-off periods in settlement agreements might reduce the number of cases of post-settlement remorse.[146] In addition parties might consider subjecting their freshly mediated agreement to review by a notary, court or other body. However as the following discussion shows, once the review is done and the settlement is ratified, there may be limited avenues available to set it aside.

3.2.2 Challenges to Other Forms of Settlement

The previous discussion examined challenges to mediated settlements on the basis of defences available in contract law. However as explained above not all mediated settlements take the legal form of a conventional contract. Where settlements involve review, ratification or confirmation by courts, tribunals, arbitrators or legal professionals such as lawyers and notaries, the grounds for challenging them on the merits may be restricted. This is likely to be the case where the agreement between the parties has undergone some element of review before being formalised.[147]

In relation to settlement deeds the grounds of review vary according to jurisdiction. At common law deeds of settlement will not cure illegalities and can be challenged, although equitable remedies such as specific performance are not available in some jurisdictions.[148] In Germany challenges to settlement deeds (*Vergleich*) must be grounded in the general rules of the Civil Code.[149] However in Austria the ability to challenge settlement deeds on various grounds including certain legal defects,[150] mistake and *Verletzung über die Hälfte*[151] may be

143 See § 123 of the German Civil Code and Palandt et al (2009), above note 21 at § 123.
144 See § 123(1) of the German Civil Code and Eidenmüller (2001) above note 70 at 44.
145 See § 123(2) of the Civil Code and Hess (2009), above note 22 at 1076 et seq.
146 See Coben and Thompson (2006), above note 43 at 136.
147 See the previous discussion on mediated settlements and legal form in this chapter.
148 See Spencer and Brogan (2006), above note 58 at 73.
149 See §§ 119 et seq of the German Civil Code (BGB). § 779(I) BGB regulates the legal consequences if there is a mistake as to the basis of the settlement.
150 See § 1387 of the Austrian Civil Code (ABGB).
151 Literally, *breach of the half*, referring to a party's right to rescind a *mutual contract* where the party seeking to rescind has not received half of the value that it has, in

restricted.[152] More generally settlement deeds may contain provisions that deal with cancellation and termination of the deed, and these may be relevant if and when the deed is challenged.

As indicated in Chapter 1, the review of arbitral awards is usually restricted to procedural review, although review on the merits is available in some jurisdictions. According to the terms of the Model Law on International Commercial Arbitration (1985) (MLICA), review may involve assessments of excess of jurisdiction, procedural error, invalidity of an arbitral agreement, the award's subject-matter not being capable of settlement by arbitration, and violation of the *ordre public*.[153] However there are questions about the extent to which the grounds on which an arbitral award can be challenged apply to a consent award and whether, by agreeing on terms and applying for a consent award, the parties have waived their rights to challenge an award on some of these grounds.[154]

In relation to mediated settlements ratified by courts and tribunals, the previous discussion shows that these are directly enforceable in a summary manner. Generally review is limited to procedural irregularities in the ratification process, such as the failure of the court to consider a relevant factor when reviewing the parties' agreement.[155] However an interesting dilemma emerges in relation to French law. Reflecting on the nature of judicially confirmed settlements and consent awards in France, Mourre refers to their hybrid nature and queries whether they can be subject to judicial appeal as is the case with court judgments on contentious matters.[156] He concedes that on a

accordance with the terms of the contract, passed to the other party: see §§ 934 and 1386 of the Austrian Civil Code (ABGB).

152 See, for example, the limited grounds for challenge in Austria: §§ 1385, 1386, 1387 and 1388 ABGB. See also Roth and Gherdane (2008), above note 14 at137.

153 See Articles 33 and 34 MLICA. Wiwen-Nilsson (2007), above note 92 at 7, cites § 1053 of the Code of Civil Procedure in Germany as an example of limited review of consent awards.

154 Suggestions were made during the UNCITRAL Working Group sessions on Arbitration and Conciliation to reduce the grounds on which the recognition and enforcement of mediated settlements in the form of consent awards could be refused to: (1) incapacity of a party, (2) violation of public policy and (3) non-arbitrability of the dispute: see *Report of the Working Group on Arbitration and Conciliation on the work of its thirty-second session* (Vienna: 20–31 March 2000) A/CN.9/468, s 4. Enforceability of settlement agreements reached in conciliation proceedings.

155 See, for example, the US case of *DR Lakes Inc v Brandsmart USA* 819 So 2d 971 (Fla Dist Ct App 2002) at 974–975 where the issue was whether or not the mediated agreement had been correctly recorded in the court order. See also *Hanson v Hanson* N° C2–98–1427, 1999 WL 31174 (Minn Ct App 1999).

156 See Mourre (2001), above note 71 at 72. Article 131-12 of the French Code of Civil Procedure provides that judicial confirmation of settlements is considered a non-

reading of the relevant French legislation, judicially confirmed settlements seem to be regarded as judicial acts and therefore potentially subject to appeal. In other words there may be contentious appeal proceedings in relation to a judge's confirmation of a non-contentious mediated settlement as if it were a judicial decision. However he goes on to indicate the flaws in the legislation, concluding that mediated settlements, whether judicially confirmed or not, should be subject to the laws governing arbitration awards and not those governing judicial acts.

In light of conflicting approaches in different jurisdictions, a number of writers have called for a uniform set of rules applicable to all agreements rendered enforceable by courts. As indicated previously, the Brussels I Regulation, the European Regulation creating a European Enforcement Order for uncontested claims, and the Hague Choice of Court Convention may apply to court-sanctioned mediated settlements. However the extent to which these instruments affect the reviewability of court-ratified mediated settlements remains unclear.

3.2.3 Judicial Review of Administrative Decisions Relevant to Mediation

Where mediation programs and systems involve decision-making by a public or administrative body there may be scope for judicial review of the decision. This may occur, for example, in the context of mandatory referral to mediation by a tribunal[157] or public agency. Here it is the decision to refer to mediation which may, in certain circumstances, be subject to review.

As a general principle, judicial review of decisions of administrative bodies and public officials can be sought by those whose rights or legitimate expectations have been affected by them. Judicial review is designed to ensure the accountability of public bodies, including agencies, officials and tribunals, whose powers derive from statute and have to be exercised in terms of legislative objectives and the public interest. While a merits review may be possible in some circumstances, judicial review generally involves an assessment of the process of decision-making and whether it was unlawful, improper or irregular. Thus, taking up the earlier example of mandatory referrals to mediation, judicial review of the decision to refer a matter to mediation could conceivably find that the decision-maker, namely the referring court or judge:

- exceeded lawful authority;[158]

contentious matter and Article 543 provides that non-contentious matters can be subject to appeal (see also Article 60).

157 Here *tribunals* refer to the court-like institutions in common law jurisdictions, in which cases are presided over by non-judicial members rather than judges. The laws relating to the judiciary and its institutions do not per se apply to tribunals, thereby permitting them greater procedural flexibility.

158 On the authority of courts to make mandatory mediation referrals, see Chapter 3.

- considered referral factors that were not relevant to the decision;[159]
- failed to consider relevant referral factors;[160]
- acted for an improper purpose; or
- did not comply with relevant procedural fairness requirements.

In any of these circumstances judicial review may result in the setting aside of a referral decision or the remittal of the matter to the original decision-maker, the referrer, with instructions to exercise the decision-making process again in a lawful and regular manner. In the latter situation it is possible for the referral body to reach the same conclusion as previously and this will be unimpeachable if it has conducted its decision-making according to the appropriate and proper procedures.

Other potential examples of mediation-related decisions that may be susceptible to judicial review include decisions made in intake sessions about a dispute's suitability for mediation, decisions of tribunals and other administrative bodies to ratify mediated settlements and decisions made by mediators during the course of the mediation. The types of mediator decisions that could be characterised as administrative decisions that may have an impact on parties' rights or legitimate expectations include:

- deciding whether to continue or terminate the mediation; and
- deciding whether or not certain admissions, statements or conduct of the parties must be reported to an appropriate public agency as an exception to the principle of mediation confidentiality.[161]

The case of *Teamsters Local 808 v National Mediation Board*[162] provides an example of the limited application of judicial review to mediation decisions. In this case the court reviewed a decision of the US National Mediation Board (NMB) to continue mediation of the dispute in question. The court effectively substituted its decision for that of the NMD, namely to terminate mediation and move directly to arbitration. On appeal the decision at first instance was reversed, the appeal court emphasising that judicial review of NMB decisions in relation to mediation is only available in 'extraordinary situation[s] bordering on patent official bad faith.'[163]

159 On factors relevant to court referral to mediation, see Chapter 3.

160 See previous note.

161 On exceptions to confidentiality and the associated reporting obligations of mediators, for example, where the welfare and safety of children is being threatened, see Chapter 6.

162 See *Teamsters Local 808 v National Mediation Board 888* F2d 1434.

163 See above note 162 at para 21.

Given its public law nature, judicial review is not applicable to private sector mediations. Thus its application is likely to be restricted to decisions made in relation to mediation provided by the administrative arm of the state, such as government departments and tribunals. In practice, however, there is little evidence of judicial review of mediation-related decisions of public bodies.

4. MEDIATOR REPORTING

Mediators undertake documenting and reporting functions in an increasing number of dispute resolution programs, courts, and industry and corporate contexts. This development raises questions about the relationship between mediators' confidentiality obligations and their reporting functions. Mediator reporting varies according to the level of discretion the mediator has in relation to reporting, the contents of reports, to whom they are made available and for what purposes reports are made. In this section reference to mediator reporting includes documenting functions.

In terms of cross-border legal instruments, both the MLICC and the European Directive on Mediation are silent on mediators' reporting functions. However UMA contains a provision headed *Prohibited Mediator Reports* which is discussed below.

4.1 Obligatory and Discretionary Documentation and Reporting

Obligatory reporting and documenting provisions can be found in general mediation legislation in a number of jurisdictions, including Austria and France. In Austria, for example, mediators are required to document the beginning and the end of the mediation, as well as the circumstances that justify continuation of the process over multiple sessions.[164] The documentation may serve as evidence of when and how the mediation was conducted in any subsequent court proceedings.[165] Upon request of the parties, mediators must additionally record the terms of the mediated outcome and the required formalities for implementation. This is regarded as a form of legal information as opposed to legal advice and it is a duty of the mediator.[166] Mediators must keep their documentation on file for at least seven years. Within this time period they may be requested to provide the parties with a copy of such documentation including their contemporaneous notes of the mediation sessions.[167]

164 See § 17(1) ZivMediatG.
165 Ferz and Filler (2003), above note 57 at § 17 RN 1.
166 See § 17(2) ZivMediatG.
167 See § 17(3) ZivMediatG and Ferz and Filler (2003), above note 57 at § 17 RN 5.

In the absence of general legislative reporting duties, court mediation programs often require reports from mediators upon termination of the process,[168] an arrangement referred to further below. In addition industry groups and large organisations that are repeat users and funders of mediation services may request mediator reports as a matter of practice.

In addition to reporting on intrinsic aspects of a mediation, there may be reporting duties to public agencies on matters of sexual abuse or risk to children and other vulnerable people required by statute, regulations, codes of conduct or contract.[169] In some circumstances mediators will have duties to report serious threats to injure others to law enforcement bodies such as the police. These matters have been considered in Chapter 6.

Mediators have also been known to submit reports on mediations on their own initiative. Courts have been reluctant to accept these as evidence in subsequent proceedings on the basis that it is not part of the function of a mediator and is a *prima facie* breach of confidentiality principles. In the American case of *VJL Red and DDD*,[170] the Wyoming Supreme Court explained,

> [T]he function of a mediator is to be a conciliator, to bring parties together in an effort to reconcile their differences. Interjecting oneself into court proceedings after the fact of the mediation as basically a witness to discredit the truthfulness and character of a party to the mediation would not seem to comport with the functions of a mediator.

In contrast to the above laws, programs and practices there is a general prohibition on mediator reporting in the UMA. Section 7(a) expressly prohibits 'reports and other listed communications to those who may rule on the dispute being mediated',[171] such as courts, administrative and arbitral tribunals and other decision-making bodies. This provision aims to uphold mediation principles such as mediator impartiality, fair process and confidentiality. It also seeks to prevent potential conflicts of interests in situations where judges may find themselves privy to information from the mediation not otherwise admissible in court. Exceptions to the general prohibition are couched in discretionary language and embody a minimalist reporting approach as described below.

168 See, for example, the reporting duties of court mediators in the Western Australian Supreme Court discussed below in the case of *Streeter*.

169 See, for example, s 7(b)(3) UMA.

170 See *VJL v Red and DDD* 39 P 3d 1110 (Wyo 2002) at 1113 and In re *RH Macy and Co, Inc*, 236 BR 583 (Bankr SDNY 1999) at 587, aff'd, 283 BR 140 (Bankr SDNY 2002).

171 See Reporter's Notes to the UMA in National Conference of Commissioners on Uniform State Laws, *Uniform Mediation Act with Prefatory Note and Comments* (Chicago: NCCUSL 2001) in relation to s 7 at 37.

4.2 Minimalist and Evaluative Reporting

Some courts, tribunals and statutory agencies oblige mediators to provide the referring body with certificates relating to the completion of mediations and indicating whether or not settlements were reached, but without commenting on the extent to which parties participated or refused to participate in the process.[172] This type of reporting is described as minimalist as it does involve any assessment of the process or the participants conduct within it. The UMA adopts this approach, permitting reports to courts and other adjudicative bodies only in relation to 'whether the mediation occurred or has terminated, whether a settlement was reached, and attendance'.[173] Reports that go beyond these parameters cannot be considered by the body or person ruling on the dispute.[174] In France Article 131-11 of the Civil Procedure Code imposes a duty on mediators to report to court on the outcome of the mediation and in particular whether or not there was an agreement. The report must respect the principles of confidentiality set out in the Civil Procedure Code[175] and in contract. These minimalist reporting requirements aim to protect the integrity of the mediation process and its associated principle of confidentiality, while at the same time fulfilling administrative tasks required in relation to the mediation.

Other laws and policies require mediators to evaluate the behaviour and *bona fides* of parties in mediation, to report on mediation outcomes and to include copies of agreements reached. These more evaluative functions effectively suspend confidentiality for reporting purposes. The reports can be useful for courts and other bodies which have review and ratification functions in relation to mediated settlements. The reports are also used in determining the extent to which there has been compliance with good faith and similar requirements and whether or not costs or other sanctions are appropriate.[176] In the Australian case of *Rajski v Tectran Corp Pty Ltd*[177] the court considered the interpretation of a statute, which permitted mediators to disclose information to the court in connection with the administration of the legislation. It held that a mediator's report, including an opinion on whether the mediation should continue, was admissible and assisted the court in administering the legislation. It also held that the confidentiality and privilege sections of the Act did not

[172] In Australia see, for example, rr 331(2) and 335 of the Queensland Uniform Civil Procedure Rules (1999). Here the mediator can report that a party failed to attend but not on how they performed in the mediation. See also the Supreme Court of Queensland Act 1991, s 108. Contrast the Farm Debt Mediation Act 1994 (NSW) s 18A.

[173] See s 7(a) and (b)(1) of the UMA (2001).

[174] See s 7(c) of the UMA (2001).

[175] See Article 131-14 C pr civ.

[176] See discussion later in this chapter on costs sanctions.

[177] See *Rajski v Tectran Corp Pty Ltd* [2003] NSWSC 476 (unreported, 27 May 2003).

apply to the mediator's report and that such reports generally ought to be admissible.

The case of *Western Areas Exploration Pty Ltd v Streeter* dealt with mediator reporting in the Western Australian court system. According to the relevant legislation, mediator reports may include the mediator's view about any failure by a party to cooperate in a mediation conference. However the report may only be disclosed to the trial judge for the purposes of determining questions as to legal costs. This case confirmed mediator reports to be the only evidence admissible in relation to costs sanctions and therefore refused to allow affidavit evidence as to costs.[178]

In some jurisdictions, particularly those with legal requirements to make good faith attempts to settle disputes through mediation, there are signs of increasing pressure on mediators to provide evaluative reports to courts or agencies, a practice which generates some tension in relation to the confidentiality principle.[179]

5. Mediator Debriefing

In some situations a post-mediation debriefing and feedback session is conducted between co-mediators or between mediators and external supervisors. By way of example, the International Mediation Institute requires certified mediators to prepare and maintain a *feedback digest* based on feedback from participants in at least five mediations and the comments and advice of a senior professional in the mediation field called a reviewer.[180] In some community justice and legal aid programs there may be a reporting requirement in the form of a debriefing report which is completed by mediators and submitted to the director of the program.

Mediation debriefing serves certain functions such as encouraging mediators to develop self-awareness as a basis for their continuing professional development. It also assists with quality assurance by providing information to supervisors within a mediation service. It constitutes a form of mediator accountability and provides a basis for responding to complaints. Finally it provides information on mediation in the form of data on success rates,

[178] *Western Areas Exploration Pty Ltd v Streeter* [2009] WASCA 15.

[179] See, for example, Proposal 15 of the NSW ADR Blueprint to the effect that courts should take into account parties' attempts to engage in ADR when making orders as to costs, see *NSW ADR Blueprint Discussion Paper: Framework for the delivery of alternative dispute resolution ADR Services in NSW* (Sydney: NSW Attorney-General's Department 2009) at 27. See also J Scherpe and B Vollers, 'Mediation in England – Rechtlicher Rahmen und praktische Erfahrungen' in K Hopt and F Steffek (eds) (2008), above note 9, 259 at 318.

[180] See the website of the International Mediation Institute: www.imimediation.org.

customer views and continuing training requirements, subject to the normal confidentiality constraints.[181]

6. OTHER POST-MEDIATION ACTIVITIES

Mediators are sometimes involved in providing information about the mediation to outsiders affected by the mediated outcome. In parenting disputes mediators may have to communicate with children and respond to their queries about the settlement and its consequences for them. Some mediators monitor mediated settlements and supervise their implementation to maintain the parties' momentum and help avoid non-compliance.[182] In certain circumstances a follow-up meeting can offer the parties a chance to reflect on the effectiveness of the mediation and the outcome reached. Parties are able to discuss what has worked well and, in relation to challenges that may have presented themselves since the termination of the mediation, to explore whether any aspects of the mediated settlement might warrant variation. This approach is helpful not only in family contexts but also where corporate and business relationships are ongoing.

Where mediated settlements are subject to ratification or formalisation by others such as notaries, arbitrators or courts, mediators may accompany parties until the ratification process is complete. Where a cooling-off period is imposed by law[183] or inserted by the parties, mediators might be involved in discussions where one party attempts to activate it. Mediators, service-providers, tribunals or courts may also hold funds or documents pending compliance with an obligation in the mediated settlement. As indicated previously, accredited mediators in Austria are obliged to keep mediation documentation on file for seven years and to provide it to the parties upon request.[184]

7. MEDIATORS AS SUBSEQUENT ARBITRATORS

The tensions in the dual role of mediator and arbitrator, and practical strategies to deal with potential breaches of procedural fairness and other possible problems, have been considered elsewhere in this book.[185] However it is usually after a mediation that has not resolved a dispute that parties may need to

[181] See Boulle (2005), above note 62 at 199 and T Sourdin, *Alternative Dispute Resolution* (2nd ed, Pyrmont: Lawbook 2005) at 74.

[182] See Boulle (2005), above note 62 at 200.

[183] See for example the farm debt mediation legislation referred to in above note 62.

[184] See Ferz and Filler (2003), above note 57 at 52 et seq.

[185] See Chapters 3 and 9 on the dual role of mediators and arbitrators.

consider whether or not to move into another dispute resolution process such as arbitration. In situations where the parties have an existing agreement to engage in an MDR process such as med-arb, they may not have pre-determined all aspects of hybrid procedure such as whether the mediator will also be involved in a subsequent arbitration. Most legal rules on this point are default in nature, leaving the ultimate decision to the parties.[186] The dual role of mediator and arbitrator carries particular responsibilities related to disclosure, decision-making and accountability as the following cases exemplify.

Appropriate disclosure in situations where mediation and arbitration functions fall to the same person has been a theme in US cases.[187] In the absence of adequate disclosure third party neutrals may be removed[188] and arbitral awards set aside. However courts will recognise the integrity of these dispute resolution processes and their outcomes where the defendant can establish that the plaintiff was already aware of the potential conflict of interest[189] or the previous mediation process was insufficiently related to the subsequent arbitration.[190]

In relation to decision-making functions, MDR practitioners must comply with the relevant rules of natural justice as they apply to mediation and arbitration.[191] This may mean that information revealed to MDR practitioners in private sessions during the mediation phase cannot be taken into account in making decisions in terms of the arbitration. However the principle of party autonomy also permits parties to structure their own arrangements in this regard, as the case of *US Steel Mining Co, LLC v Wilson Downhole Services* shows.[192] Here the court considered an MDR process involving mediation and final-offer arbitration.[193] The arbitral award was challenged on the basis that the arbitrator, in choosing between the parties' last offers, improperly relied on information conveyed during confidential private sessions in mediation. The court dismissed the argument and enforced the award, noting that the parties' amended arbitration agreement stated that the arbitrator 'may rely on information which he deems relevant, whether obtained in *ex parte* communication or otherwise'.

Finally legal questions may arise where an MDR practitioner is subject to different standards of accountability. In the case of *Morgan Phillips Inc v*

186 See, for example, Article 13 MLICC and the relevant rules in Appendix B.
187 On the duty of disclosure generally, see Chapter 5.
188 See, for example, *Rodrigue v LaFourche Parish Sch Bd* 928 So 2d 533 (La 2006).
189 See, for example, *Fininen v Barlow* 47 Cal Rptr 3d 687 (Cal Ct App 2006).
190 See, for example, *Guseinov v Burns* (2006) 145 Cal App 4th 944.
191 See also Chapter 3 on this point.
192 *US Steel Mining Co, LLC v Wilson Downhole Services* N° 02:00CV1758, 2006 WL 2869535 (WD Pa 2006).
193 Final offer arbitration involves the arbitrator choosing from the parties' last offers as the basis for the arbitral decision.

JAMS/Endispute[194] a breach of contract action was brought against an MDR practitioner who first acted as an arbitrator and, without stated reasons, withdrew from the arbitration, before proceeding to mediate the dispute. In his role as mediator, the MDR practitioner claimed immunity on the basis of arbitration legislation, but the court held that the role of the third party neutral was not sufficiently associated with the determinative phase of arbitration to justify arbitral immunity.[195]

8. Costs Sanctions

The traditional approach towards mediation costs has been for parties to share equally the costs of mediation and pay their own associated legal expenses. Parties may also agree for mediation costs to be shared in a different ratio or, as in some jurisdictions such as England and Australia, to be calculated by a court as costs in the case.[196]

As explained in Chapter 5, parties' compliance or otherwise with obligations relating to mediation may be reflected in costs awards as a form of sanction. It is believed that costs sanctions not only encourage compliance with duties related to mediation,[197] but that they may also promote a sense of proportionality in the conduct of mediation by discouraging the usually unnecessary use of large legal teams in some areas of mediation practice.[198]

In the United States there are numerous cases dealing with the fees and charges associated with mediation, including mediator and lawyer fees, and how these expenses are to be apportioned among the parties in light of their conduct in mediation and in the absence of an agreement regarding costs. The cases include both disputes settled at mediation and disputes which did not settle and continued to trial.[199] Courts have taken different approaches to the issue, reflecting the diversity in relevant statutory rules and contractual obligations and the fact that in many cases there is simply no statutory or rule authority available.[200]

194 *Morgan Phillips Inc v JAMS/Endispute* LLC 44 Cal Rptr 3d 782 (Cal Ct App 2006).

195 On the accountability and liability of mediators generally see Chapter 5.

196 See, for example, the CEDR agreement to mediate, clause 11. It provides that the parties will share mediation fees and carry their own legal and associated costs, subject to the discretionary power of courts to treat these outgoings as costs in the case.

197 On parties' duties in relation to mediation see Chapter 5.

198 See Allen (2009), above note 35 at 30.

199 Research suggests that these cases accounted for 20 per cent of mediation cases from 1999 until the end of 2006: Coben and Thompson (2007), above note 44 at 410.

200 See Coben and Thompson (2006), above note 43 at 112–119 and the cases referred to there.

In France the commercial chamber of the Supreme Court has taken the view that a party who delays in relation to mediation or otherwise shows an absence of good faith may be ordered to pay the costs incurred as a result of the delay.[201]

In England and Australia costs sanctions may involve a reapportionment of costs in the case, for example, between parties where one side has either unreasonably refused to mediate or is in breach of a duty to mediate in good faith. In *Capolingua v Phylum*[202] the Supreme Court of Western Australia refused to award costs to the successful defendant for several reasons, including its unreasonable conduct during mediation, which meant that a trial that should have taken only two days in fact took four days.

In some Australian court-related mediation schemes once the power of referral is invoked, costs are entirely at the discretion of the court, irrespective of the parties' wishes.[203] In Queensland, for example, the legislation requires parties to act 'reasonably and genuinely' and allows the imposition of sanctions against parties who fail to attend mediation or who impede mediators during the process.[204] Sanctions include taking the parties' actions into account when awarding costs, or ordering a stay of any claim for relief by the defaulting party.[205]

In other Australian jurisdictions, and subject to a costs agreement between the parties, mediation fees and associated legal costs may also be taken into account by courts when awarding the costs of the case.[206] In *Newcastle City Council v Paul Wieland,*[207] for example, the NSW Court of Appeal included mediation costs as *costs of the proceedings*. The court reasoned that mediation was part of the proceedings, for the purposes of the Civil Procedure Act 2005, as it was court-ordered and undertaken by a judicial officer on the court's premises. As there was no express costs agreement between the parties preventing such award, the court had the power to award the costs of the mediation at its discretion.

201 Cass com, 28.11.1995 N° 94–12285.

202 *Capolingua v Phylum Pty Ltd (as trustee for the Gennoe Family Trust)* 1991 5 WAR at 337. See also *Deepsilver Pty Ltd v Aquatherm Australia Pty Ltd* [2007] WADC 160 which applied *Capolingua.*

203 See the Uniform Civil Procedure Rules 1999 (Qld) s 323 and Supreme Court (General Civil Procedure) Rules 2005 (Vic) r 50.07(8).

204 See Supreme Court Act 1991 (Qld) s 103. *Impede* is further defined as failing to attend, participate or pay an amount the party is required to pay under a referring order: Uniform Civil Procedure Rules 1999 (Qld) s 322.

205 Supreme Court Act 1991 (Qld) s 103(2).

206 In Australia see the following legislation and rules which grants courts discretion in relation to mediation costs: Court Procedure Rules 2006 (ACT) r 1181, Civil Procedure Act 2005 (NSW) s 28 and Supreme Court Rules 2000 (Tas) r 522.

207 *Newcastle City Council v Paul Wieland* [2009] NSWCA 113.

In England case law confirms the presumption that mediation costs are costs in the case. In *National Westminster Bank Plc v Thomas Feeney and Linda Feeney,* [208] the court stated that,

> as a matter of general principle, costs incurred in a mediation would form part of the costs of the action just as any reasonable costs of negotiation would.

However in this case the successful party was not awarded costs because the parties had expressly agreed to bear their own mediation costs and associated legal expenses. The Tomlin Order executed to expedite enforcement did not expressly contradict the costs arrangement between the parties and so it remained intact. As a result the presumption that mediation costs be calculated as costs in the case was rebutted. This principle was upheld in *Lobster Group Ltd v Heidelberg Graphic Equipment Ltd,*[209] but here the court held that the presumption relating to mediation costs did not apply to pre-proceedings mediations. Coulson J made the following comments:

> [U]nlike the costs incurred in a pre-action protocol, I do not believe that the costs of a separate pre-action mediation can ordinarily be described as "costs of and incidental to the proceedings". On the contrary, it seems to me clear that they are not. They are the costs incurred in pursuing a valid method of alternative dispute resolution. Those costs were incurred in a form of dispute resolution which had no connection to these proceedings.

There are several implications flowing from these judgments. First in pre-action proceedings mediation costs will follow the case unless parties include other arrangements in their agreements to mediate. Contractual arrangements as to costs are not overridden by Tomlin Orders, unless the latter contain an express provision to this effect. Parties engaging in mediation independently of pre-action protocols or other rules must make costs arrangements themselves as the courts appear reluctant to do so.

However parties must remain alert to sector-specific legislative rules which diverge from the principle of mediation costs being calculated as costs in the case as *Dowell v Caruso*[210] demonstrates. According to the applicable legislation in this case, 'parties pay their own costs unless the interests of justice require otherwise.'[211] Further the legislation provided that a party is not entitled

[208] *National Westminster Bank Plc v Thomas Feeney and Linda Feeney* [2006] EWHC90066 (Costs) and [2007] (Costs Appeal). See also *Eagleson v Liddell* [2001] EWCA Civ 155 and *Chantrey Vellacott v The Convergence Group plc, Convergence Group International SA and Mr and Mrs Robinson* [2007] EWHC 1774 (Ch).

[209] *Lobster Group Ltd v Heidelberg Graphic Equipment Ltd* [2008] EWHC 413 (TCC).

[210] See *Dowell v Caruso* [2007] QCCTB 164 (13 November 2007). See also *Tamawood Ltd and Anorr v Paans* [2005] QCA 111.

[211] See the Commercial and Consumer Tribunal Act 2003 (Qld) s 70.

to costs merely because that party was the beneficiary of an order of the Tribunal, or the party was legally represented at the hearing.[212] Here an applicant successfully enforced a mediated settlement for building rectifications, but was not awarded costs. The court indicated that although the applicant, through no fault of her own, had the inconvenience of coming to the tribunal in order to enforce the settlement she had, in the light of the legislation, no automatic rights as to costs.

As indicated previously, parties' conduct in mediation may have an impact on costs awards. To this end, mediator reports in certain jurisdictions contain an evaluation of the conduct of the mediation participants sufficient for a costs determination.[213] In the absence of such reports the admissibility of evidence relevant to costs is largely dependent on rule-based exceptions to confidentiality principles. These may be expressly set out in legislation such as in the Evidence Act in Australia[214] and the Civil Procedure Rules in England. The Civil Procedure Rules provide that courts may take into account the behaviour of the parties *before* and *during* the proceedings, including their attempts to resolve the dispute and whether or not they have followed pre-action protocols.[215] In other words the parties' conduct in relation to mediation can rebut the presumption referred to previously that mediation costs follow the case. The Civil Procedure Rules go further than the law in most other jurisdictions insofar as they provide for potential sanctioning of the refusal to engage in mediation. In *Dunnett v Railtrack plc*[216] the successful party was required to pay the costs of the case due to refusing an offer to mediate from the unsuccessful party. Similarly in *P4 Ltd v United Integrated Solutions plc*[217] the court awarded losing party P4 some of their costs after the successful party refused mediation and as a result denied P4 an opportunity to settle at minimum cost. These cases provide a useful example of courts reversing the normal costs rules. Australian proposals for legal reform include an increased use of costs sanctions along the lines of the English CPR and pre-action protocols.[218]

212 See the Commercial and Consumer Tribunal Act 2003 (Qld) s 71(5).

213 See the Australian case of *Western Areas Exploration Pty Ltd v Streeter* [N° 2] [2009] WASCA 15 discussed previously.

214 See s 131(2) of the Evidence Act 1995 (Cth) which removes the bar to admissibility otherwise imposed by s 131(1) in relation to questions of liability for costs. See also *The Silver Fox Co Pty Ltd as Trustee for the Baker Family Trust v Lenard's Pty Ltd* [2004] FCA 1570 referring to the policy behind the confidentiality provisions of the Evidence Act, namely to prevent disclosures affecting the primary matters in issue, not merely the outcome as to costs.

215 See Civil Procedure Rules r 44.3(5).

216 *Dunnett v Railtrack plc* [2002] EWCA Civ 303.

217 *P4 Ltd v United Integrated Solutions plc* [2006] EWHC 2924 (TCC).

218 See, for example, Proposal 15 of the NSW ADR Blueprint to the effect that courts should take into account parties' attempts to engage in ADR when making orders as to costs in *NSW ADR Blueprint Discussion Paper* (2009), above note 179 at 27.

In the absence of legislative rules permitting courts to sanction parties for their conduct in relation to mediation, courts will play an interpretative role in balancing confidentiality protections with the ability to sanction abuse of the mediation process. For example, in the costs application, *Azzi and Ors v Volvo Car Australia Pty Ltd (Costs),*[219] the court rejected as inadmissible evidence of communications and offers made at mediation by reason of the confidentiality provisions of the Civil Procedure Act.[220] The court stated that the plaintiff's failure to accept the offer made at the mediation, in a context in which it was not apparent that it could or would be relied on in connection with costs, was not so unreasonable as to justify an indemnity costs order. Conversely, in the American case of *Foxgate*[221] the mediator filed a report with the court to the effect that one of the parties had acted in bad faith and should be sanctioned. On appeal the California Supreme Court held that the report could not be admitted in evidence and that, even in relation to possible sanctions, confidentiality within the terms of the Californian Evidence Act must be upheld.

9. CLOSE

This chapter has covered some of the legal issues which may arise *after* the mediation has been terminated. However as with many aspects of life, it is helpful to be prepared. Contemplating limitation periods, enforceability of possible outcomes and costs arrangements ahead of a mediation provides parties with opportunities to consider what sort of impact these matters may have on them. In relation to MDR processes a discussion about the potential involvement of the mediator in subsequent proceedings is useful at an early stage. Once parties have made informed decisions about these various issues, they may wish to include them in their agreement to mediate.

219 *Azzi and Ors v Volvo Car Australia Pty Ltd (Costs)* [2007] NSWSC 375.

220 See the Civil Procedure Act 2005 (NSW) s 30(4)(a).

221 *Foxgate Homeowners' Association v Bramalea California Inc* (2001) 26 Cal 4th 1.

Chapter 8
UNCITRAL and International Mediation

1. Introduction

This chapter commences with an explanation of the role of the United Nations Commission on International Trade Law (UNCITRAL) and the background to the development of the Model Law on International Commercial Conciliation (2002) (MLICC). It then provides an overview of the MLICC, which is also referred to in this chapter as the Model Law. The chapter concludes with an interview between the author and the former Secretary of UNCITRAL on the workings and themes of the Model Law.

As explained in Chapter 1 there is not a consistent approach to the terms *mediation* and *conciliation*. This chapter will principally follow the Model Law's term conciliation although both words will be used interchangeably.

2. Background to UNCITRAL[1]

UNCITRAL is a subsidiary body of the General Assembly of the United Nations.[2] The Secretariat of UNCITRAL is the International Trade Law division of the Office of Legal Affairs of the United Nations. Whereas the General Assembly comprises representatives of all 192 member states,[3] the Commission comprises a smaller number of elected member states representing different geographical regions, namely Africa, Asia, Eastern Europe, Latin America and the Caribbean, and Western European and other states.[4]

UNCITRAL was established in 1966 and has a mandate to progress and modernise the regulation of international trade, *inter alia,* through the harmonisation and unification of relevant national laws on the subject. Harmonisation refers to attempts to ensure that different legal systems generate transactions with similar effects across the jurisdictions. Unification goes further and involves the adoption of the same laws in different legal systems, a process

1 The information for this section is drawn primarily from the UNCITRAL website: www.uncitral.org.

2 For more information on the General Assembly of the United Nations, see www.un.org under the heading *Main Bodies*.

3 For a list of the member states of the UN and the dates on which they joined the organisation see www.un.org/Overview/unmember.html.

4 For a list of the member states representing each regional group, see the UNCITRAL website at www.uncitral.org or www.uncitral.org/uncitral/en/about/origin.html.

which typically requires countries to repeal their existing laws on the topic and replace them with the unified version. UNCITRAL's mandate reflects the belief that increased international trade, leading to increased interdependence among countries and interaction among people from different jurisdictions, contributes to world peace – an integral part of the UN's mission.[5] In this context UNCITRAL has the specific brief to ensure that the voices and interests of developing countries are considered. It does this by preparing and promoting the adoption of new international conventions, model laws and uniform laws.[6]

In fulfilling its mandate, UNCITRAL has debated, drafted and adopted a range of legislative instruments relating to commercial and trade law, including model laws and conventions, which impact on international trade and cross-border commercial transactions.[7] These texts are intended for voluntary enactment by domestic legislatures of nation states, irrespective of their membership of the United Nations.[8] Decisions at UNCITRAL are typically taken by consensus, reflecting the desire of the Commission to produce texts that are acceptable to, and therefore likely to be adopted by, the maximum number of participating countries, whether or not they are members. Moreover, participation in preparing legislative texts is not limited to member states. In addition to member states, other states, interested inter-governmental organisations (IGOs) and non-governmental organisations (NGOs) may participate in the proceedings of the Commission and its working groups as observers.[9] In this capacity they may participate actively in the discussion and drafting of legislative texts and other instruments. The rationale behind this practice is found in UNCITRAL's international mandate and the potential worldwide application of UNCITRAL instruments.[10]

5 See comments by J Wah-Teck Chan, 'Process and methods of international rule-making: Allocation of work among formulating agencies' in *Modern Law for Global Commerce: Congress to celebrate the 40th annual session for UNCITRAL, Studies, Proposals and Backgrounds Papers* (Vienna 2007) 1 at 12.

6 *General Assembly Resolution on the Establishment of the United Nations Commission on International Trade Law*, GA Res 2205, UN GAOR, 21st Sess, UN Doc A/Res/2205 (1966).

7 See the UNCITRAL website: www.uncitral.org.

8 The only 'independent' country that is not a member of the United Nations is the Vatican. However, the number of non-members is largely dependent on whether or not a political entity is recognised as independent or not. At the time of writing the following countries are political entities but not United Nations members: Kosovo, Palestine and Taiwan.

9 Working groups are organisational groups within UNCITRAL designated to work on particular topics such as conciliation.

10 A list of non-member states, IGOs, NGOs and other entities with observer status can be found in a Note by the Secretariat of the 59th session of the UN General Assembly: *List of non-member states, entities and organisations having received a*

3. THE NATURE OF UNCITRAL MODEL LAWS AND RULES

UNCITRAL model laws are legislative texts which have been adopted by resolution of the UN General Assembly as a model for members and other states to adopt as part of domestic legislation. Model laws may be adopted without amendment by enacting states. Alternatively, enacting states may elect to amend parts of a model law so that it better suits local substantive and procedural legal requirements. Because of the ability of domestic legislatures to amend their provisions, UN model laws are flexible instruments and complete uniformity among national provisions, while desirable, is not expected. Where amendments are made, however, enacting states are encouraged to maintain the basic principles of the law and to make as few changes as possible to the provisions. National laws are more likely to be interpreted consistently in different jurisdictions where similar terms are used. From disputing parties' perspectives, consistent interpretation of national laws on conciliation potentially increases clarity and certainty with respect to their meaning, application and implementation. At the same time the flexible nature of the MLICC allows states to make adjustments to comply with national public policy and procedural law.[11]

While the Commission operates in different areas in the field of dispute resolution, the UNCITRAL Model Law on International Commercial Arbitration (1985) (MLICA) and its Model Law on International Commercial Conciliation (2002) (MLICC) are the relevant model laws for present purposes.

UNCITRAL also drafts non-legislative texts, such as its Arbitration Rules (1976) (UAR) and its Conciliation Rules (1980) (UCR), which are directed at parties, rather than states, to use as part of their dispute resolution procedures. The UNCITRAL arbitration and conciliation rules can be incorporated into dispute resolution clauses in commercial contracts or as part of an agreement to mediate or arbitrate. They may also be adopted by dispute resolution organisations as part of their recommended procedural rules for dispute resolution processes. As an illustration, the Australian Centre for International Commercial Arbitration (ACICA) and the Hong Kong International Arbitration Centre include provisions from the UAR as part of their recommended procedures for international arbitration.

In relation to conciliation numerous institutions have adopted the wording of the UNCITRAL Conciliation Rules for their own institutional rules.

standing invitation to participate as observers in the sessions and the work of the General Assembly (UN Doc A/INF/59/4/Add.1, 14 December 2004.)

11 However see the restrictions on amendments (reservations) to UN conventions: *UNCITRAL Model Law on International Commercial Conciliation with Guide to Enactment and Use 2002* (New York: United Nations 2004) referred to as the *Guide to Enactment* at para 14 at www.uncitral.org/pdf/english/texts/arbitration/ml-conc/ml-conc-e.pdf.

By way of example, ACICA recommends using the UCR to parties engaging in mediation and conciliation. The Optional Conciliation Rules of the Permanent Court of Arbitration (PCA) are closely modelled upon the UCR Rules and other institutional rules draw upon the UCR, including the Netherlands Mediation Institute (NMI) Mediation Rules. In addition Article 10 UCR, which provides that conciliators must disclose the substance of all actual information received from one party to the other party unless expressly requested not to do so by the informing party, has been adopted by the Indian Council of Arbitration (ICA) in Article 10 of its Rules of Conciliation and the PCA in Article 10 of its Optional Conciliation Rules. As another example, Article 9 of the UCR which states that the conciliator may meet or communicate with each of the parties separately can be found in Article 11 of the Mediation Rules of the World Intellectual Property Organisation (WIPO) 2002, Article 9 of the Rules of Conciliation of the ICA, and Article 3(d) of the Model Mediation Procedure Rules 1998 of the International Institute for Conflict Prevention and Resolution (CPR).

UNCITRAL rules may be used by public entities or private parties whether they are nationals of member states or not. While the MLICC is designed to dovetail with the UNCITRAL Conciliation Rules, both texts operate independently of each other and they can interact with different dispute resolution laws and rules. While the UCR can operate as a set of *ad hoc* procedural guidelines or as the basis for institutional rules, the Model Law is designed as a template for the design and incorporation of international commercial conciliation into national laws.

4. THE MLICC: BACKGROUND AND DEVELOPMENT

Although the MLICC was first adopted in 2002, conciliation had been visible on the international agenda of UNCITRAL since its first session in 1968.[12] During the early years of the Commission conciliation was viewed primarily as a complement to arbitration rather than a dispute resolution process in its own right. It was in this context that the UNCITRAL Conciliation Rules were adopted by the Commission in 1980, shortly after the adoption of the UNCITRAL Arbitration Rules in 1976 and before the adoption of the Model Law on International Commercial Arbitration in 1985.

In 1998 the Commission reviewed the generally positive response to the three texts referred to in the previous paragraph and requested the Secretariat

[12] See, for example, UNCITRAL, *Report of the Commission on the work of its first session* (Official Records of the General Assembly, 23rd session, Supplement N° 16 (A/72/16), 1968) at 80 and UNCITRAL, *Report of the Commission on the work of its eleventh session* (Official Records of the General Assembly, 33rd session, Supplement N° 17, 1978) at 25.

to prepare a Note entitled 'Possible future work in the area of international commercial arbitration'. This was to be used as a basis for evaluating the impact of UNCITRAL's work in arbitration and for considering and assessing new ideas and proposals for improving 'arbitration laws, rules and practices'.[13] Conciliation was specified in the Note as a possible work item for the Commission, and was subsequently identified as a priority item.[14]

The Commission referred the task to the Working Group on Arbitration, later renamed the Working Group on Arbitration and Conciliation. The group comprised representatives from all member states of UNCITRAL, observer states and international organisations – more than 50 representatives with diverse backgrounds, views and positions.[15] Participating states such as the US, Canada and the UK had existing sophisticated systems of mediation and conciliation in their jurisdictions and their representatives were keen to develop a model law that was, as far as possible, consistent with these systems. Countries such as India and Indonesia had virtually no systems of institutionalised ADR and some continued to use customary traditions in consensus-based dispute resolution processes. Additional perspectives were provided by observers from the following international organisations: Economic Commission for Europe, NAFTA Article 2022 Advisory Committee on Private Commercial Disputes, Permanent Court of Arbitration, Cairo Regional Centre for International Commercial Arbitration, Chartered Institute of Arbitrators, International Chamber of Commerce (ICC) and International Federation of Commercial Arbitration Institutions.

As the Working Group deliberations developed it became clear that conciliation or mediation, depending on one's definitional view, was emerging as a preferred method of dispute resolution in many domestic jurisdictions, both as an independent process and in combination with arbitration. As a response to this practice preference, the Working Group turned its attention to the development of a model law on conciliation.

13 UNCITRAL, *Report of the Working Group on Arbitration on the Work of its 32nd Session* (32nd session, UN doc A/CN.9/468 2000), hereafter referred to as *Working Group Report* 468, paras 4 and 5.

14 The other priority items were the requirement of a written form for the arbitration agreements, the enforceability of interim measures of protection and the possible enforceability of an award that had been set aside in the state of origin: UNCITRAL, *Report of the United Nations Commission on International Trade Law on the work of its thirty-second session* (Official Records of the General Assembly, 54th Session, Supplement N° 17 (A/54/17) 1999) paras 340–343 (regarding conciliation), paras 344–350 (on written form requirement), paras 371–373 (on enforceability of interim measures) and paras 374–375 (enforceability of award set aside in state of origin).

15 A list of the participants in the Working Group at its 32nd session can be found in *Working Group Report* 468, above note 13, paragraphs 11–13.

The Working Group first met to discuss how to progress the use of conciliation in cross-border disputes during its 32nd session in Vienna in March 2000. The drafting process occurred over four sessions of the Working Group from 2000 to 2002,[16] during which it met every six months. During and between these meetings the Secretariat of UNCITRAL collated, summarised and documented the official deliberations (as distinct from the corridor deliberations) of the Working Group and the various drafts of the Model Law. At the end of the fourth drafting session the Working Group circulated the draft Model Law to UN member states for comment. Sekolec and Getty refer to the 90 states, 12 intergovernmental organisations and 22 international non-governmental organisations, which either participated at the Working Group level or commented on the draft as members of the United Nations.[17]

In 2002 the Model Law was adopted by the General Assembly of the United Nations by general resolution.[18] The annex to the resolution contains the final version of the Model Law. The remarkably short period between the identification of conciliation as a possible work topic at UNCITRAL and the adoption of the Model Law reflects the perceived urgency of responding to the rapid growth of ADR in many parts of the world at that time.

During the period of the final drafting of the Model Law, the Commission Secretariat prepared the Guide to Enactment and Use of the UNCITRAL Model Law on International Commercial Conciliation (2002). In this chapter it will be referred to as the Guide to Enactment. Largely based on the *travaux préparatoires* of the Model Law, it is directed at enacting states, particularly executive governments and legislators, to aid in their discussions and deliberations pertaining to the enactment of the Model Law in their respective jurisdictions.[19] It is also valuable for commercial parties, practitioners, academics and judges. The Guide to Enactment provides background information to the provisions of the Model Law, explaining the rationale behind them and the choice of terminology and wording. However the Guide is not the text itself, and its influence is likely to vary according to the

16 Working Group sessions 32 to 35 inclusive, see UN documents A/CN.9/468 on session 32, A/CN.9/485 on session 33, A/CN.9/487 on session 34 and A/CN.9/506 on session 35, published on the UNCITRAL website: www.uncitral.org.

17 J Sekolec and M Getty, 'The UMA and the UNCITRAL Model Rule: An Emerging Consensus on Mediation and Conciliation' (2003) *Journal of Dispute Resolution* 175 at 183.

18 *General Assembly Resolution on the Model Law on International Commercial Conciliation of the United Nations Commission on International Trade Law,* GA Res 10102, UN GAOR, 75th session, UN Doc A/RES/57/18. R Dobbins, 'UNCITRAL Model Law on International Commercial Conciliation: From a Topic of Possible Discussion to Approval by the General Assembly' (2003) 3 *Pepperdine Dispute Resolution Law Journal* 529.

19 See the Guide to Enactment at para 1.

jurisdiction applying the Model Law and what it considers to be acceptable methods of interpretation.

Numerous jurisdictions have adopted mediation legislation based on the model law or have expressed an interest in doing so. As countries do not always inform UNCITRAL of changes in their laws, it is not possible to follow these systematically. The following outline attempts to summarise the situation in 2009.

Countries which have passed or proposed laws based closely on the Model Law include Afghanistan, Canada, Croatia, Kosovo, Russia and the United States. In the United States the MLICC was inserted into the Uniform Mediation Act (2001) (UMA) by way of amendment in relation to international disputes. A number of changes were made to the text of the MLICC relating to confidentiality and they are discussed in Chapter 9. Thus the amended version of the MLICC has been enacted – as part of the UMA – in the States of Illinois, Iowa, Nebraska, New Jersey, Ohio, South Dakota, Utah, Vermont and Washington, and in the District of Columbia.[20]

Countries which have enacted mediation legislation more loosely based on the MLICC include Ecuador, Nicaragua, Norway, Romania, Serbia, Slovakia and Turkey. In other countries the Model Law has been used as a starting-point for the preparation and drafting of legislation on mediation; however the end-product does not necessarily reflect the provisions of the Model Law. By way of example, Bulgaria and Hungary have introduced laws which do not appear to be influenced greatly by the Model Law, though they may have been prompted, at least in part, by it.

5. An Overview of the MLICC

This section provides a structural and substantive overview of the MLICC. It begins with an explanation of the goals of the Model Law and how these fit within the overall framework of mediation objectives and principles depicted in Chapter 2 before considering its other important features.

5.1 How the Objectives of the MLICC Relate to the Objectives of Mediation

The objectives of the MLICC fall within the overall mandate of UNCITRAL to facilitate and encourage international trade and commerce. In this context UN General Assembly Resolution 57/18 acknowledges the increase in the use of conciliation, mediation and other ADR processes in domestic jurisdictions. The

20 See the Comparative Table of Laws Adopting the MLICC in Appendix C to this book.

Resolution emphasises the aspiration of the MLICC to encourage the use of international commercial conciliation and the need to increase the integrity of the conciliation process by providing greater predictability and certainty in its use. The Resolution responds to the numerous *ad hoc* developments in ADR in different jurisdictions and the emergence of e-commerce and the disputes associated with it, which together have heightened the need for consistency in international dispute resolution procedures.

The Resolution specifically refers to the application of international commercial conciliation to reduce the costs of justice administration and to repair commercial and trading relationships between disputants. It draws on both quantitative mediation goals, such as improved service-delivery and access to justice through reduced disputing costs, and the qualitative goals of party autonomy and relationship restoration in dispute management. These articulated goals are consistent with those of many court-related mediation programs and private commercial mediation services around the world.[21]

5.2 How the MLICC is Structured

The MLICC can be considered in three parts.[22] The first part, comprising Articles 1 to 3, establishes the scope of the law. It provides definitions of important terms (Article 1), guidelines on interpretation (Article 2), and establishes the majority of the Model Law as default provisions, rather than mandatory ones (Article 3).

The second part of the MLICC consists of Articles 4 to 11 and deals with the period during the conciliation proper. This covers procedural aspects of conciliation, namely, the commencement and termination of the conciliation (Articles 4 and 11), the appointment of conciliators (Article 5) and issues of conduct (Article 6), communication (Article 7) and confidentiality (Articles 8, 9 and 10) in the conciliation. It also addresses the suspension of legal proceedings (optional Article X).

The third and final part of the Model Law, Articles 12 to 14, addresses post-conciliation issues such as the role of the conciliator in subsequent processes (Article 12) and enforcement issues relating to mediation clauses, agreements to mediate (Article 13) and mediated settlements (Article 14).

The Model Law regulates different aspects of mediation and includes provisions that set out the scope of the Law (Article 1), procedural laws (Articles 4 to 7 and 11 generally), rules serving as standards of conduct for conciliators (Articles 5(3) and 6(3)) and rules about rights and obligations, referred to in this book as beneficial laws (Articles 10, 12 to 14 and optional

21 On the goals of mediation programs, see Chapter 1.

22 This structure is echoed in the Guide to Enactment at paras 23–24.

Article X).[23] As shown in Chapter 2 these are typical aspects of mediation, which can be subject to regulation. While the Model Law covers a broad range of matters, it does not cover aspects of mediation such as the triggering or initiation of the mediation process and accreditation issues.

The brevity of the Model Law, with only 14 provisions, disguises the potential complexity of issues that it covers. The judicious use of succinct yet broadly-framed default provisions renders the Model Law open to diverse interpretations and variations by the parties.

5.3 Five Themes of the MLICC

An analysis of the Model Law reveals five main themes that characterise its approach to mediation and conciliation and provide a useful orientation for users of the Law. The themes are introduced here and considered in more detail in the commentary below.

The first theme relates to how conciliation is defined. The Model Law defines the concept broadly and seems to encompass all facilitative and advisory – in other words, non-determinative – dispute resolution processes. It provides a descriptive definition which appears sufficiently wide to include processes such as neutral evaluation (Article 1(3)). As indicated in Chapter 2, broad descriptive definitions encourage diversity in practice, which in turn offer challenges in terms of establishing consistent standards of conduct.

The second theme is the principle of party autonomy – a core characteristic of mediation and conciliation processes and a pillar of the Model Law. Article 1(7) provides that the parties may elect to opt out of the Model Law as a whole. In other words the entire Law is optional and parties can choose a different set of rules to apply to their mediation should they so desire. Conversely, parties can voluntarily opt into the Law where there is doubt as to its applicability (Article 1(6)). Where the Model Law applies, there remains much scope for party autonomy. The principle of party autonomy can apply to decisions to enter into and participate in the conciliation process, to choices made in relation to the outcome of a conciliation and, in the event that an agreement is reached, to the legal form of the agreement. There are only two mandatory provisions in the entire Model Law – Articles 2 and 6(3). Article 2 deals with interpretation of the Law while Article 6(3) creates one of the exceptions to the principle of party autonomy in the mandatory requirement that mediators treat the parties fairly.

The principle of fair treatment in this article is the third defining characteristic of the Model Law. It sets a standard of procedural fairness which must be maintained by mediators. Failure to do so may leave the process and the practitioner open to criticism and provide a basis for judicial review of the

[23] On different types of regulations, see Chapter 2.

mediated outcome. The principle of fair treatment attempts to set outer parameters for the otherwise ubiquitous concept of party autonomy by providing a non-negotiable quality standard for the conduct of the process.

Confidentiality is one of the hallmarks of contemporary mediation processes and is the next major aspect of the Model Law. As indicated in the commentary that follows, the Model Law provides for three types of confidentiality – insider/outsider, insider/insider and insider/court. Like most other aspects of the Law, the confidentiality provisions are subject to the overarching objective of enhancing party autonomy, which means that parties can vary the level of confidentiality protection by mutual agreement.

The fifth and final feature of the Model Law relates to the enforceability of settlements. Contrary to the expectations of a number of commentators, Article 14 of the Model Law provides neither a mandatory nor a default standard enforcement procedure for mediated settlements. Rather the provision requires enacting states to import their preferred enforcement procedures into their domestic version of the Model Law. In doing so, Article 14 effectively entertains the adoption of diverse national enforcement procedures for international mediated settlements. As evidenced by the provisions of national laws that have enacted the Model Law, such an approach will result in some lack of consistency and certainty in relation to enforcement issues.

The five themes of the Model Law provide a sense of UNCITRAL's approach to regulation in this field and, in particular, how the diversity–consistency dilemma of mediation regulation is likely to be played out.[24] While the mandatory Article 6(3) of the Model Law, relating to procedural fairness, offers some consistency in the form of a standard of conduct, other provisions such as those on confidentiality, enforceability and limitation periods can be overridden by agreement of the parties. The dominant principle is party autonomy and it is subject only to the mandatory requirement of fair treatment. On balance, the diversity–consistency tension appears to be tipped in favour of diversity.

6. Critique of the MLICC

The MLICC has been successful in creating a unified document acceptable to many legal jurisdictions and cultural traditions, and in focusing on some of the key issues pertaining to contemporary mediation and conciliation. It has been in itself a 'mediative' exercise in finding compromises among competing legal rules and world-views and in disseminating it for transnational usage. While the legislative take-up by domestic jurisdictions has been much slower than in the case of the extensively integrated MLICA, this is partly explicable in terms of

[24] On the diversity–consistency dilemma, see Chapter 2.

the short duration of its existence, the less normative domain of conciliation and the creative ambiguities that any Model Law must contain. As domestic legislation preceded the Model Law on arbitration, different jurisdictions tended to coalesce around common principles in this field. This led to less variation once this Model Law had been drafted. It can be assumed that the Model Law on Arbitration drew on settled principles across jurisdictions. By comparison the MLICC had less settled doctrine on which to draw, and when introduced into the relative regulatory vacuum of domestic systems, has been adapted – sometimes with significant changes – to suit local circumstances. These factors have led to inevitable criticisms of the MLICC. However as explained in the interview later in the chapter, the Model Law has provided an important starting point for an ongoing international conversation on reconciling different approaches to mediation and conciliation and working towards a common standard in the regulation of the field.

The primary criticism of the Model Law relates to the dominance it affords to the principle of party autonomy. The Law fails to differentiate between the importance of party autonomy and procedural flexibility, on one hand and the need, on the other, to set clear international standards for regulating interactions between conciliation and the legal system in which it operates. In offering default, as opposed to mandatory, standards the Model Law arguably fails to provide a robust legal framework for international disputes and disputants in its deference to party autonomy and procedural flexibility. Some commentators are critical of the Model Law's lowest common denominator approach to standards, a function of its complex negotiation dynamics, and express disappointment that UNCITRAL did not take the opportunity to set best practice standards to which the international community could aspire.[25]

Another criticism relates to the breadth of matters that are regulated by the Model Law. The regulatory principles of the mediation mix introduced in Chapter 2 suggest that not all aspects of mediation are best regulated by legislation. Different regulatory approaches, such as market, industry or framework regulation, may be preferable depending on the aspect of mediation being regulated. Many provisions in the Model Law are drawn from the UCR and deal with procedural aspects of mediation that are generally covered by industry rules, such as those of the ICC. Ginkel argues that the inclusion of procedural and standard-setting rules in the Model Law is potentially confusing both for policy-makers and for lawyers advising mediation parties.[26] He argues that the Model Law should have restricted itself to rules dealing with rights and obligations that require legislative enforcement, namely beneficial and interface provisions as defined in Chapter 2.

[25] See, for example, See E Ginkel, 'The UNCITRAL Model Law on International Commercial Conciliation: A Critical Appraisal' (2004) 21 *Journal of International Arbitration* 1 at 7–8 and the references to Ginkel in Chapter 2.

[26] Ginkel (2004), above note 25 at 8–9.

Finally an amendment of the UCR to bring it into line with current thinking may have provided a more up-to-date companion for the MLICC. Adopted in 1980, the UCR does not have the benefit of the wealth of contemporary mediation experience, knowledge and know-how that has since emerged. By way of example, as indicated earlier, Article 10 of the UCR regulates the confidentiality aspects of private sessions in mediation by requiring the conciliator to disclose information received from one party to another party, except where it is given with the specific condition that it be kept confidential. This approach to confidentiality in private sessions is referred to in Chapter 6 as the open communication approach. It is distinguished from the more widely accepted in-confidence approach whereby private sessions are treated as confidential unless the party to the private session specifically requests that particular information be passed on to others outside the session.[27] Similarly provisions in the UCR expressly permitting conciliators to make settlement proposals (Article 7(4)) and to draft or assist in the drafting of settlement agreements (Article 13(2)) are more controversial today than they were in 1980 and are not in line with legislation and case law in some countries.[28]

From the perspective of UNCITRAL, however, the approach taken has been a considered one and reflects as much the political reality of creating internationally acceptable legal instruments as the deliberate choice of certain principles of mediation, such as party autonomy. Two aspects of UNCITRAL's decision-making practice are important in understanding the reasons behind the final form and content of the Model Law. The first is the consensus-based approach to decision-making in UNCITRAL and the United Nations and the second is the role of the UCR.

With regard to the first point, UNCITRAL decision-making processes, as discussed above, are based on participant consensus. Consequently the Commission tends to work towards the lowest common denominator approach with a view to encouraging as many countries as possible to accept and subsequently enact a legislative text. To this end participants in drafting processes work assiduously to find terminology that is suitable across legal systems. In practice, such an approach leads to broadly formulated provisions, which are amenable to diverse interpretations and applications – in a sense difficult policy decisions are deferred for future resolution. Sekolec explains that

27 On these different approaches to confidentiality, see Chapter 6. For examples of the in-confidence approach see Article 5 of the Mediation Procedure of the London Court of International Arbitration 1999, Article 7(5) of the NMI Mediation Rules 2008 in the Netherlands and Article 11 of Mediation Rules 2002 of the World Intellectual Property Organisation (WIPO).

28 See, for example, the Australian National Practice Standards, which prima facie do not permit mediators to make settlement proposals and the case of *Tapoohi v Lewenberg* [2003] VSC 410, which takes a similar view. Both are discussed in Chapter 3.

the MLICC as adopted in 2002 is a first step in working towards international standards for the practice of mediation in cross-border disputes.[29]

The case of the United States provides a useful illustration of the consensus-based approach to decision-making. One year prior to the MLICC being adopted, the United States had promulgated its own model law, the Uniform Mediation Act (2001) (UMA). As a national Model Law the UMA focused on American legal practice issues in the field of mediation. It is no surprise therefore that the provisions and, in particular, the drafting language of the UMA differed considerably from that of the MLICC. Rather than amend the provisions of the UMA to incorporate the MLICC and risk causing confusion, it was decided to incorporate the provisions of the UNCITRAL Model Law for the purposes of international commercial conciliations only. The amendment of the UMA reflects the view that common legal language and regulation is a high priority in an international context.

The second aspect of UNCITRAL's decision-making practice referred to above is the role of the UCR. The wording of the Model Law is substantially drawn from the UNCITRAL Conciliation Rules. The Conciliation Rules were drafted and adopted more than 20 years prior to the Model Law and as explained earlier were intended primarily for use within an arbitration-focused framework. The Rules have formed the basis and inspiration for many industry sets of conciliation rules in different jurisdictions.

As previously indicated, mediation has now developed as a major form of dispute resolution in its own right. Theoretical and practical developments have taken the form of case law, jurisprudence, legislation, codes of conduct, conciliation clauses, training and accreditation schemes, and court-related conciliation programs. As a result thinking on mediation processes and issues has changed significantly. Yet the Working Group and the Commission were reluctant to depart from the ideas and the wording in the Conciliation Rules. Many long-term members of UNCITRAL who had debated, developed and then adopted the Model Law on International Commercial Arbitration and made use of the Conciliation and Arbitration Rules continued to be heavily influenced by these texts. Moreover some members felt that the Model Law would be more attractive to countries if it was consistent with the familiar and tried and tested Conciliation Rules.

In relation to this second point, the Commission, as explained previously, ultimately considered it appropriate to include procedural rules in the Model Law as default provisions. The inclusion of process rules as default provisions in the Model Law has enabled the practical application of contemporary mediation processes, while at the same time allowing jurisdictions with process preferences for the system to opt out of certain parts of the Model

[29] See the interview with Jernej Sekolec, former Secretary of UNCITRAL, later in this chapter.

Law. In addition, the Commission considered a broad legislative text containing default process rules useful to deal with situations where parties had elected to mediate but had not agreed on procedural rules. The use of mandatory and default rules in the Model Law is considered in the following chapter.

The result is a model law on conciliation that offers choice and flexibility to informed users who have the time and negotiating power to adapt the provisions of the MLICC to suit their needs. For others the Model Law offers a starting point for managing their international mediation. It may also harbour some unexpected risks.

The next section in this chapter presents an interview with the former Secretary of UNCITRAL, Jernej Sekolec. It was during Sekolec's term and under his leadership that the Model Law was prepared and debated and ultimately adopted by the United Nations.

7. THE UNCITRAL MODEL LAW ON INTERNATIONAL COMMERCIAL CONCILIATION (2002)

An Interview with Mr Jernej Sekolec, Former Secretary of UNCITRAL, July 2009[30]	**Themes and key words**
Alexander *When people talk about conciliation and mediation in a global context there is a tension between diversity and consistency. On one hand, there is the desire to experiment, develop mediation as a flexible process with a diversity of styles; on the other hand there is the aim of ensuring consistent quality by regulating mediation. How has UNCITRAL dealt with this tension?*	Diversity versus consistency in mediation practice
Sekolec UNCITRAL treaded lightly on this issue. The general philosophy of UNCITRAL is to avoid over-regulation and rigid procedural recommendations. We are dealing with international mediation. It is referred to by various terms, including conciliation, but there is no difference in the essential concept, at least from the legislative point of view. The Intergovernmental Working Group that prepared the Model Law on Conciliation (Model Law) was conscious	Meaning of mediation and conciliation

[30] Reprinted with the permission of Juris Publishing, Inc., Huntington, New York, USA, www.jurispub.com from the original interview (with updates) that was published in (2004) 15 *World Arbitration and Mediation Report* 105.

that the Model Law would need to be grafted onto an existing legal system in any given country. There are, in fact, numerous legislative rules in existing legal systems that will complement the body of the Model Law. So we were aware at UNCITRAL that we did not have to regulate everything. We regulated the primary pillars of mediation only. The reasons for this were, firstly, that the Model Law is part of a larger picture of international dispute resolution and, secondly, most Working Group members believed that at this stage in the development of mediation procedural regulation would not be beneficial. Personally, I believe that the development of quality in mediation should come from education and promotion rather than through procedural safeguards.

Regulation of primary pillars of mediation

Quality in mediation

Alexander
You are suggesting that at 'this stage of the development of mediation' too much regulation is inappropriate. At what stage do you think we find ourselves now?

Sekolec
One cannot give a uniform answer that covers all countries. I think we are at the stage where mediation is very fashionable. This may result in people tending to expect too much from it. But there are core aspects, which I think are very useful and here to stay. One does not want to create controversy or stifle development by hasty regulation.

Mediation as fashion

Alexander
So you are really trying to encourage experimentation within a particular framework?

Sekolec
Yes. For example, consider where the initiatives for mediation come from: the courts, arbitrators, lawyers and even the parties themselves? Who acts as the mediator? Will it be the senior personalities in the trade concerned, village chiefs, the community mediation centres, the big law firms or arbitration centres? All these aspects of international dispute resolution need to develop. If one regulates the process too early then one restricts the options available – and one may be left with commercial mediations between sophisticated parties only. The huge spectrum of mediation

Diversity of mediation initiatives

needs to be left alone to enable it to expand and thrive.

Alexander
You mention mediation by village chiefs and arbitration centres. One current theme in the literature focuses on the differences between western mediation and some of the traditional forms of mediation-like processes in first nation cultures such as indigenous Australians and Americans where, for example, notions of neutrality and confidentiality have very different meanings, if they exist at all.

Traditional mediation versus western mediation

Sekolec
Yes, the world of dispute resolution comprises much more than western notions of mediation. The Model Law is drafted in such a way as to accommodate as many cultural concepts of mediation as possible, which have the ability to operate within the legal system of a given country.

Alexander
In the Model Law are processes such as neutral evaluation or mini-trial also included in the definition of conciliation?

Sekolec
Yes they are. Article 1 defines conciliation. It provides that conciliation is a process where two parties in a dispute engage a third person to help them settle it. Article 1 also provides that conciliation can also be referred to by terms such as mediation and other words with a similar meaning. Therefore mini-trial and neutral evaluation are also covered by Article 1.

Definition of conciliation

The Working Group was conscious of the fact that in practice there may be some real differences between conciliation, mediation and mini-trial in terms of techniques and approaches. For example, there may be variations regarding the role of the mediator, whether the mediator has a more active or passive role, whether the mediator proposes solutions to a settlement and variations in the type of persons representing the parties (for example, a mini-trial typically involves the most senior management unlike other forms of dispute resolution). From a legislative point of view, however, these differences do not matter because the legislative rule must be flexible enough to incorporate all non-determinative dispute resolution processes.

Conciliation in practice

Flexibility as a feature of dispute resolution

Another point is that in practice one will find elements of mediation, conciliation, neutral evaluation and even mini-trial in a single case. *Pure cases* where the mediator does not offer his or her opinion in a direct or indirect manner are rare in international commercial dispute resolution.

So the short answer to your question is yes. All these processes fit into the broad definition of conciliation whereby parties engage a third person to assist them in resolving their differences.

Alexander
So in essence it comes back to the tension between flexibility and regulation. If the Working Group had been clearer about definitions, it would have lost some of the flexibility of conciliation.

Sekolec
Yes. Flexibility is one of the core features of mediation and a feature which makes it a very attractive process for disputants because they can adjust the precise nature of the process to suit their needs.

Alexander
You spoke earlier about the need for quality processes and that in your view quality comes from education. If we link that idea to the different sorts of processes that might arise under the definition of conciliation – mini-trial, neutral evaluation, conciliation and mediation – it seems that a need emerges to educate clients and lawyers about the distinctions between these processes. Clients need to be in a position to give informed consent to the process in which they participate.

Quality of the mediation processes

Sekolec
My reaction to your question is that the environment itself would define the need for process differentiation. In a particular country a party may well be familiar with the kind of processes that would work well for it in that jurisdiction and would select from that range. In commercial disputes one would require a particular type of process and in neighbourhood disputes a very different one. The issues related to quality are diverse across cultures and

Process differentiation

environments.

Continuing education should be a requirement so that one does not attend a one-week course and become a mediator for life. A mediator needs to develop and learn new things and evaluate their own experiences. Only in this way will mediators be able to keep abreast of current techniques and continually improve their skills.

Training, education and continuous improvement

Alexander

The Model Law provides a broad definition of conciliation, which includes interest-based facilitative processes, on one hand and directive, more evaluative processes, on the other. Do you think there is a danger in the international commercial field that mediation practice will become more directive and evaluative because many lawyers and arbitrators trained in directive and determinative processes are moving into international commercial conciliation roles?

Definition of conciliation; interest-based and evaluative mediation models

Sekolec

I think this danger exists. However, the danger does not come from the Model Law or from the legislature of the enacting state. Rather, it comes from the procedural rules that the lawyers draft in contracts. If the lawyers shoot themselves in the foot by making the process more complex and expensive, then one cannot protect them from it. In some cases a highly structured mediation is not appropriate, while in other cases it is. If the parties and their representatives organise the dispute resolution process poorly, then they have to live with the consequences. They will learn from these lessons and do it differently next time.

Risk of international commercial conciliation becoming directive and evaluative

Alexander

So in other words, there is a responsibility on the parties themselves and on the dispute resolution service-providers to take responsibility for the management of disputes.

In your opinion what is likely to happen in sophisticated international business-to-business (B2B) transactions in terms of the use of this law? Do you think that international business will embrace mediation or will they rather take a multi-tiered approach and engage in conciliation followed by arbitration or some other dispute resolution process?

Responsibility and party autonomy

Sekolec
We are seeing again and again that the best thing to do is to leave the practice to the parties and their lawyers. The parties can adopt iron-clad, structured sets of procedural obligations if they so choose. One sees this in some construction contracts and it suits the industry. No doubt in five years they will have invented new process solutions.

Multi-tiered dispute resolution processes

Then there are hybrids or blended processes that contain elements of arbitration and mediation within the one procedure. For example, in some forms of neutral evaluation, the dispute resolution provider proposes a settlement to the parties. If they do not object to it within 30 days, the settlement becomes binding and enforceable as a judgment. So there are elements of advisory and determinative processes at work.

Alexander
Would this situation fall within the Model Law – after all there is a potentially binding outcome proposed by the dispute resolution provider?

Sekolec

Role of neutral third party

That is an interesting question. The Model Law specifically states that the conciliator has no power to impose a binding decision on the parties. It is really a matter of interpretation. Has the third party imposed a decision indirectly and by default; or has s/he made a suggestion that the parties have, after 30 days reflection, chosen to adopt in a binding and enforceable form? My own sense is that, as such a process aims at formulating a recommendation to which the parties are invited to agree, the process will be conducted as a conciliation. After all, the parties are free to reject the proposal within 30 days of it being made. Therefore it should fall within the Model Law.

Alexander
Earlier you mentioned the pillars of the Model Law. What are the main pillars of the Model Law?

Sekolec
The pillars of the Model Law are confidentiality, party autonomy and fair treatment. The single most important pillar, which I think requires legislative action, is the issue

of confidentiality or the evidentiary privilege relating to admissions, proposals and views expressed during the mediation process.

Confidentiality Admissibility of evidence in subsequent proceedings *In Chapter 6 this is referred to as insider/insider confidentiality*

One aspect of confidentiality relates to the admissibility of evidence in subsequent proceedings. In order to succeed, parties in mediation must be able show their cards and have open and frank discussions. The parties do not want to make admissions if these admissions are likely to come back to haunt them. This may occur if in the event of an unsuccessful mediation, the case then goes to arbitration or other determinative proceedings. If, for example, during the mediation one party admits that its engineer made a technical error with the expectation of a similar admission from the other party, it is crucial that a legislative guarantee exists to the effect that such a statement is inadmissible as evidence in court or other subsequent proceedings.

Even where the parties commit themselves contractually not to offer what is said during mediation as evidence in subsequent proceedings, there are many legal systems in which such an agreement may not be binding on the court or an arbitral tribunal. This would be the case in a number of central European states. In these and other jurisdictions, a judge may insist on hearing the evidence where it is considered crucial to the case. Accordingly, rules of conciliation procedure agreed upon by the parties, such as the UNCITRAL conciliation rules and rules of other conciliation institutions, cannot guarantee the inadmissibility of admissions, proposals and statements made during the mediation as evidence in subsequent proceedings. This is the reason why a legislative regulation on mediation is necessary.

Prohibition on mediator to act in another role in subsequent proceedings

Another aspect of confidentiality is the prohibition on the mediator from acting as an arbitrator or advisor in subsequent proceedings. It is good to enshrine this point in legislation and make the prohibition clear so as to give the parties security on this matter.

Specific duty of confidentiality *In Chapter 6 this is referred to as insider/court confidentiality*

A further aspect of confidentiality arises in the context of information received by the mediator from one party on the condition that it is kept confidential. In these circumstances, the conciliator has a duty to keep the information confidential.

General duty of confidentiality. In Chapter 6 this is referred to as insider/outsider confidentiality

The final aspect of confidentiality is that the parties are bound by a general duty of confidentiality not to disclose to anyone what happened during the mediation. They are not at liberty to publish or, for example, have a press conference about what happened during the mediation.

The statutory duty of confidentiality is a useful disciplinary measure. But it would not be recommended to have a law of mediation about confidentiality alone. That is why the Working Group began with a definition of mediation (conciliation), which is the subject of the regulation. It was considered useful to offer something like a starter kit for mediation proceedings. So, for example, the Model Law regulates the appointment of mediators and expresses a few general and universally acceptable procedural principles. While it was not essential to do so, it is valuable to include some general procedural regulation in the form of default provisions to give more context to the Model Law. Parties can always regulate these aspects differently by contract. This allows mediation to maintain its flexibility.

Default procedural provisions

Alexander
What would you say to people who criticise the confidentiality provisions as having so many exceptions as to render the objective of mediation facilitating a full and frank discussion meaningless?

Sekolec
I would regard this criticism as unfounded. It is perhaps even dangerous from the viewpoint of public policy. If I am in a mediation and I make an admission or a proposal, of course I want this to be confidential. But if I have an invoice in my hand before I even become aware of the mediation and I show it to the other party in an effort to convince him/her to pay, then I should not lose the opportunity to use this piece of evidence in subsequent court proceedings. If the law provided that I would lose this piece of evidence, I would be in a quandary. I would want to use the invoice in the mediation, but would scarcely be able to do so because if the mediation failed I would need the invoice as evidence to prove my case in court. Perfectly admissible evidence that existed before the mediation takes place does not become inadmissible solely by virtue of the fact that it has

Criticism of the confidentiality provisions

been used in mediation. Admissions, proposals, statements and views, the fact that one party indicated its willingness to accept a proposal – all these matters that actually arise during the mediation process are inadmissible. Everything else is potentially admissible.

Exceptions to confidentiality

In addition, for reasons of public policy, the duty of confidentiality must be subject to further overriding exceptions. For example, if a mediation would reveal an imminent threat to public health, an intent to harm the environment, a terrorist threat or similar, the duty of confidentiality must yield to other principles of law.

Additional duty of confidentiality

There is of course the additional general duty of confidentiality in Article 9. Certain information, which does not fall under Article 10, may be caught by Article 9. For example, while certain information may be admissible in evidence in other proceedings, the conciliator and participants are forbidden from passing on that information to other persons or the public.

A balanced approach

I think the articles on confidentiality were drafted very carefully and provide a balanced solution. Such an approach manages potential misuse of the mediation process. For example, it does not attach inadmissibility to something which should be admissible for reasons of public policy. At the same time it provides a commercially reasonable solution to safeguard the legitimate interests of parties.

Alexander

Related issues are the enforceability of agreements to mediate and the enforceability of settlements. Could you make some comments about those?

Sekolec

Enforceability of mediated settlements

First let us discuss the enforceability of settlements. Everybody agrees that the settlement agreement is a contract and therefore enforceable as a contract. If parties participating in the mediation are properly advised, they will draft a settlement agreement that is legally binding as a contract and will be able to obtain a judgment to enforce it. So my first observation is that the problem is not as severe as it seems. There is no compelling need to change the nature of an instrument, which is, in essence, a contract. Why do we want to give the settlement agreement the force of a judgment?

Alexander
Or an award?

Sekolec
Indeed. Settlement agreements are the result of the parties taking control of the management of their own dispute with the help of a mediator. They often contain elements that are unique to the parties and not easily enforceable as judgments or awards. Settlement agreements may include revisions of existing contracts, promises to negotiate contractual obligations in the future, or *best efforts* clauses. There may also be clear-cut obligations in settlement agreements: for example, to pay an amount of money.

Enforceability of mediated settlements

It is a potential source of problems to give a settlement agreement the force of a judgment or an award because it is not formulated by a judge or an arbitrator as the result of an adversarial process. By declaring the settlement agreement an award or a judgment, one may lose the opportunity of addressing potential issues of fraud and duress that may have occurred during the mediation process. Addressing those issues for the purposes of converting a settlement agreement into an award or judgment is complicated and, in the view of many, not worth the trouble.

Therefore, if a settlement were to be regarded as a judgment or an award, there would also be a need for a system of setting aside a settlement obtained as a result of duress or mistake. A court judgment typically cannot be challenged on such grounds because the parties are not responsible for the terms of the judgment. Such additions would introduce technical difficulties in the mediation system.

But these are not the only reasons. If one goes to court with a settlement agreement, the amount of proving one has to do is very limited. It is limited to the existence of the settlement agreement. One does not have to prove liability or fault stemming from the underlying conflict. Everything is crystallised in the settlement agreement. So the process of getting a judgment or an award is much more straightforward than going to court to prove a case.

Alexander

Where there is a settlement agreement and one party is trying to prove that misleading and deceptive conduct or even fraud occurred during the mediation, it will need to refer to events that occurred during the mediation and may want to subpoena the mediator? Doesn't this sort of situation open up a Pandora's box of conflicting domestic laws?

Sekolec

Illegal activity, fraud, misleading and deceptive conduct and duress during the mediation

Yes, it would open up a Pandora's box indeed. There has been a small percentage of cases in which duress, cheating or other illegal activity occurs in the negotiating phase. I doubt that any legislature would want to forgo the tools that exist in the various domestic legal systems to control and manage these rare instances in the context of mediation.

Giving a settlement agreement the strength of an arbitral award, or a court judgment, in my opinion, means bowing to fashion. Mediation is now a big deal and people are so eager to promote it that they feel it should be institutionalised in order to give it more legal effect. But in my view we should not go overboard.

It is a different matter if one allows the parties to appoint an arbitrator with the specific purpose of incorporating the settlement agreement into an arbitral award or to approach a judge to confer expedited enforceability on the settlement in a standardised process. This may work in a number of jurisdictions and may add a welcome new quality to the mediation. The flexibility of the Model Law allows the parties to make a conscious decision to incorporate processes which involve transforming a settlement agreement into an award or court order. However, the parties will need to ensure they select a jurisdiction, the laws of which will facilitate their dispute processing needs.

Alexander

Enforceability of mediated settlements

At this point in time could I ask if it is fair to say that there are the following two views on the enforceability of settlements? First, giving settlement agreements the strength of a judgment or an award would encourage parties to mediate transnational disputes. In particular, there would be more certainty and finality about the enforceability of a mediated agreement. Second, the alternate view (and your view) is that a contract is a very different creature to an award or a judgment. One cannot always include in an award matters that one would include in a settlement agreement. Items such as apologies, acknowledgements of past behaviour or acts, statements of intention of future behaviour and agreements to negotiate in the future are not typically enforceable and therefore would not be suitable for the terms of an award or judgment in most jurisdictions. Moreover, institutionalising settlement agreements by turning them into awards or judgments goes against the principles of voluntariness, party autonomy and responsibility in mediation. The idea that parties take responsibility for their dispute, agree on a way forward and remain responsible for the implementation of what they have agreed is abandoned the moment settlement agreements are institutionalised. At this point the parties are relying on the international justice system to guarantee an end to their dispute.

Sekolec
Yes that is a fair summary. However, having said that, it is perhaps useful to provide expedited enforceability to certain settlements. Here we come across different domestic procedural traditions and these traditions do not lend themselves to a uniform rule. I would encourage states which adopt the Model Law to use procedures for the enforceability of settlement agreements with which they are familiar and comfortable in their particular legal tradition. For example, in a number of countries if a notary co-signs a settlement agreement then it becomes enforceable in the same way as an award or a judgment. In other countries a similar effect may be achieved if the parties' attorneys co-sign the settlement. These solutions, which are known, for example, in Germany and Austria, work well in some systems but may not work as well in others.

Alexander
Would the German approach have been an option that might have worked well in the Model Law?

Sekolec
We did not include it in the Model Law *not* because we did

not believe in this form of notarised settlement, but because we wanted countries to consider the law from their own perspective and include it if they so chose. For example, considering the function of US notaries, I doubt that the US legislature would be ready to permit notarised settlements to have such far-reaching legal consequences.

The Model Law only offers limited harmonised rules upon which the UNCITRAL Working Group could agree on a global level. The enforceability issue is left to each country to deal with in the context of the enacting state.

If the parties really want enforceability they can appoint an arbitrator; they can even appoint a mediator as an arbitrator if it is done with the agreement of both parties. There is, of course, a prohibition in the Model Law on mediators also acting as arbitrators. However, as it is a default provision, both parties can agree to override it.

Alexander

This last point of yours takes us back to one of the pillars of the Model Law: party autonomy.

Sekolec

Appointing mediator as arbitrator to convert settlement into award

Exactly. Consider the possibility that the parties, after they have reached a settlement agreement, appoint the mediator to be an arbitrator for five minutes. During those five minutes the mediator/arbitrator could issue an arbitral award on the agreed terms, which is recognised by Article 31 of the UNCITRAL Model Law on Arbitration.

When we discussed this possibility in the inter-governmental Working Group, some people said that it would work well on the basis of the experience in their countries. Others from legal systems such as the US indicated that while it was an attractive idea, technically it would not work because in order to have an arbitration one needs to have a dispute. By definition once a settlement has been reached, there is no longer a dispute. So from their perspective, it would not work. I would venture to suggest that common law legal systems are particularly susceptible to this argumentation. While some may dispute the validity of this argument, it was considered important enough to exclude this form of med–arb[31] from the Model Law.

Alexander
Why would the idea of the mediator being appointed as an arbitrator to transform the settlement agreement into an award be less of a problem in civil law jurisdictions?

Sekolec
In civil law jurisdictions, the notion of dispute as a condition precedent to arbitration is broader than in common law jurisdictions. Where debtors agree that they are liable but maintain that they do not have the money to pay, then there is no dispute in common law jurisdictions. However, in civil law jurisdictions there may still be a dispute. But this does not apply to all civil law countries. So one may need more than a clearly drafted settlement clause in order to convert it into an arbitral award or make it otherwise directly enforceable.

Enforceability of settlement as arbitral award

Alexander
So from what you are saying, the process for enforceability of mediated settlements needs to be developed with practice. I imagine it would be very important at the preliminary meetings before a mediation to look at the level of enforceability desired by the parties and to be very clear about this.

Sekolec
Yes. This leads to the related issues about the applicable law, negotiating the process of enforceability upfront and committing it all to writing.

Alexander
Some people would say that this sort of system would encourage forum shopping. Where one party decides it no longer wishes to abide by the terms of a settlement agreement, that party may forum shop to find the domestic law least likely to enforce the settlement. What are your thoughts on this point?

Forum shopping

[31] For an explanation of med–arb, see Chapter 1.

Sekolec

In a voluntary process in which each party can pull the plug at any moment, there is no harm in forum shopping. People can choose the mediator, the place and the applicable law. If they cannot agree on these views then the mediation will terminate anyway. In most cases these issues will be sorted out before a settlement is reached.

Appointment of conciliators

Alexander

Article 5 deals with the appointment of conciliators. Under the provision it is quite possible that the parties may not be able to agree on the conciliator(s). There is no fallback or default provision if the parties cannot agree. If this provision was a contractual clause in Australia, there is a good chance that a court would hold it to be unenforceable due to lack of certainty of terms. What was UNCITRAL's reasoning for providing such an open-ended appointment process?

Sekolec

The idea was that the parties should be able to successfully negotiate the appointment of conciliators themselves if they are serious about participating in the conciliation. There is therefore no compelling need for a complete fall-back procedure.

Of course often the parties will agree to refer to standard rules of an institution or procedural traditions in order to appoint a mediator. In court-annexed mediation the court may appoint a mediator. The Model Law will yield to these specific situations because of the default nature of Article 5. Again UNCITRAL's texts aim to be workable in all countries of the world, so a non-intrusive default provision is more likely to be acceptable across the board.

Enforceability of agreements to mediate

Alexander

We have spoken about the enforceability of settlements. What about the enforceability of agreements to conciliate? What happens when one party initiates conciliation on the basis of an agreement to conciliate in a commercial contract and the other party argues that this clause is not enforceable?

Sekolec

Well, in that case it will depend on how the clause was drafted. There may be contractual liability for costs if a party does not live up to what it has agreed. If the case was referred to mediation by a court, whether or not there was an agreement to mediate, then there may be further consequences – even contempt of court depending on what the local law provides. The Working Group elected not to legislate on such matters because it would interfere to an unnecessary extent with well-established principles of domestic contract law and procedural law.

It is left to the national laws to determine whether an agreement to conciliate is enforceable and to determine the consequences of the violation of such agreements. Whether an agreement to conciliate is enforceable pursuant to the national law depends on the origin of the mediation process – whether it be an existing clause in a commercial contract or an *ad hoc* agreement by the parties. The enforceability of such an agreement also depends on the drafting of the clause. If, for example, one has an elaborate clause saying that the parties commit themselves not to commence arbitration proceedings until they have had five meetings with mediators and explored all options, it would be reasonable to have some contractual consequences for violating this clause. On the other hand, one could have a more generally worded clause saying that the parties will try to settle their dispute amicably and, if not, go to arbitration. What does this clause mean? Must the parties engage (and pay) a third party neutral mediator before they can go to arbitration? The answer depends on the interpretation of the clause. One cannot determine whether an agreement to conciliate is enforceable, without considering the law of the applicable jurisdiction. Professor Alexander, you mentioned that under Australian law certain conciliation agreements are not enforceable because their terms are not sufficiently clear and certain. Hence the enforceability of a duty to mediate or conciliate is left to a contractual agreement and the applicable contract law of national jurisdictions. It may be that at some time in the future harmonised rules on the enforceability of agreements to mediate will be prepared, but at this stage I think the international community is not ready for it. Such an agreement would then be enforced either by a court under international private law or by an international arbitral tribunal where conciliation was specified as a pre-condition to arbitration.

Alexander

Article 13 deals with the possibility of staying arbitral and judicial proceedings as a way to enforce agreements to conciliate in which the commitment to refrain from arbitrating or litigating until certain pre-conditions are met is clearly set out. The proviso 'except to the extent necessary for a party, in its opinion, to preserve its rights' has been criticised for being so wide as to strip the provision of its effectiveness. What are your views on this?

Stay of proceedings to enforce agreement to conciliate

Sekolec

It is true that the provision opens a wide door to instituting arbitral or court proceedings. At the same time, it gives comfort to parties. They will be more likely to agree to mediate because they will not be subject to restrictions regarding their process options.

Alexander

You have spoken about the voluntary nature of mediation and the fact that the parties may pull the plug or withdraw from the mediation at any time. In fact, under the terms of the Model Law the parties are not compelled to attend a first mediation session. Many institutionalised rules of courts or chambers of commerce such as the ICC require disputing parties to attend the first meeting. Beyond this point, the parties are free to withdraw at any time. The theory is that in the context of a global disputing culture in rapid change, such mandatory attendance rules establish a minimum certainty of participation and, importantly, may enable parties from cultures where negotiating is a sign of weakness to save face. Where parties have engaged a skilled conciliator, they may see an opportunity in the first meeting to settle. If they don't, they have lost nothing. Why did UNCITRAL not go down this path?

Voluntary nature of mediation – no requirement of first meeting

Sekolec

There were indeed suggestions that UNCITRAL should draft a rule stipulating that the parties must have at least one meeting. There were several reasons why we did not go down this path. One reason was that, unlike the ICC which is operating with a specific dispute resolution clause and a set of rules providing a certain predictability of procedure, UNCITRAL is dealing with the broadest spectrum of international situations including 'dinner party mediations'.

Alexander
What is a 'dinner party mediation'?

'Dinner party' mediations

Sekolec
When two people have a dispute and they call a third person that they trust and say, 'Let's go for a beer. Can you help us solve our dispute?' No one may have uttered the word *mediation.* These people do what comes naturally and makes common sense. They ask a business elder to help them solve their problem. Now, according to the Model Law this is a mediation. These parties and the mediator may therefore be covered by the Model Law.

What does it mean 'to meet'? Would this count as a first meeting or would it be classified as a preliminary pre-mediation meeting?

Meaning of meeting in e-mediation

Let's use electronic commerce as another example. If you are in Australia and I am in Austria, we can meet in cyberspace; we could exchange emails. But where are we technically meeting and are we meeting at all in the first place?

Utility of requiring first mediation meeting

It is true that requiring the parties to meet can be very useful in many cases. However, if one applies it to cover the whole spectrum of mediation situations, it is too rigid. This is why we left any obligation to meet to the agreed procedural rules. UNCITRAL wants to encourage as many countries as possible to enact the Model Law and not to discourage them by being overly prescriptive about procedural elements of mediation.

Alexander
Why is the article on suspension of limitation periods optional rather than one which operates by default?

Suspension of limitation periods

Sekolec
There were strong arguments in favour of making it a default article. But again, let's put ourselves in the situation where two disputing parties on either side of a European border enlist the assistance of the third person to help them

solve their dispute. They do not use the word mediation or conciliation. They just ask the third person over to dinner or for a drink at a bar – a 'dinner party mediation'. Would this conversation officially signify the commencement of conciliation proceedings? Would the limitation period regarding a legal claim be suspended at this point? Here we are in a grey area: what is the point at which a conversation behind a bar becomes a mediation? Are you mediating or are you just engaging in a normal conversation? Technical legal consequences flowing from the commencement of conciliation proceedings function well if linked to structured mediation rules of an institution or a court-directed process. However, if one is involved in a spontaneous mediation, the parties may be totally unaware that they are interrupting something called a limitation period. I think one of the principles governing the interruption of limitation periods is that the party with the claim must be reasonably capable of knowing that it has lost the benefit of the limitation period.

Perhaps the more forceful argument is that in many countries the parties are free to agree on how they will manage the limitation periods linked to related legal claims. For example, the parties may agree to extend the limitation period. In those countries where parties are not free to do so, I would say that the legislature should empower them to manage the limitation period themselves so that when they start a mediation they can agree on the suspension of the running of the limitation period. I see no rational reason why commercial parties should not be able to enter into agreements relating to limitation periods. I regard limitations to this freedom as outdated.

Alexander

Confidentiality provisions as default provisions

You point out that one of the reasons for making the suspension of limitation period provisions optional rather than default was that as a default provision parties may not be aware of the implications of beginning a mediation process. Can't you apply the same reasoning to the confidentiality provisions? Parties might begin a dinner party mediation and not be aware of the confidentiality provisions of the Model Law that apply as a default measure.

Sekolec
Yes, but then one would also have to interpret that particular situation to determine the extent to which the parties have waived the obligation of confidentiality by talking about the mediation in front of other people. This involves interpreting the will of the parties. It may well be that if one party speaks to a friend about the mediation, it will not have violated any statutory duty.

Alexander
Did the UNCITRAL Working Group draw inspiration from the Model Law on Arbitration?

Sekolec
The Model Law on Arbitration deals with a different animal. Arbitration involves an adversarial process to which the parties have committed themselves. In arbitration, there is a binding decision at the end, whether the parties like it or not. For my part, I do not think we drew any direct inspiration from the Model Arbitration Law when drafting the substance of the Model Law on Conciliation. More generally, however, the context in which the Arbitration Model Law was drafted was not dissimilar to the context in which the Model Law on Conciliation was drafted. In both cases we worked against the backdrop of widely-used influential sets of contractual rules such as the UNCITRAL Arbitration Rules from 1976 and the UNCITRAL Conciliation Rules from 1980. We also studied the contractual rules of many mediation and conciliation institutions as we had studied the procedural and contractual provisions of arbitration institutions previously. The model rules from these institutions have rendered tremendous service to the world of arbitration and now to the world of mediation. However we came to realise first with arbitration and then with conciliation that, in addition to a contractual regime, a statute was needed. If the general law thwarts the parties' contractual agreement, they will experience tensions and uncertainty. That is why UNCITRAL prepared the highly successful Model Law on Arbitration and later we decided it would be good to prepare a Model Law on Conciliation. We prepared the Model Law with a view to dealing with those few points which are necessary to be addressed by statute.

UNCITRAL Model Law on Arbitration; Arbitration and conciliation in context

Alexander

So in other words, the philosophy was to keep it simple and focus on the main features or the pillars that require legislative action, leaving the rest to enacting states.

Sekolec

When we drafted the Model Law, we not only had to take into account the governments and industries but also the mediation and arbitration community in order to arrive at a text that was practice-friendly.

NGOs

If you consult the documentation of the sessions of the UNCITRAL Working Group on Conciliation in which we discuss the provisions of the Model Law you will see the active role of non-governmental organisations. Over the years 90 states have participated in the sessions and 20 non-governmental organisations.

Alexander

UNCITRAL Conciliation Rules (1980)

Could you comment on the relationship between the Model Law (2002) and the Conciliation Rules (1980)?

Sekolec

UNCITRAL is flexible in terms of the procedural rules that parties choose to use. Where current rules of mediation institutions function well, UNCITRAL does not wish to interfere with them. Over the past 23 years the UNCITRAL conciliation rules have actually radiated a lot of influence. When I look at the mediation rules used in Argentina, Australia or Germany, for example, I notice formulations based on the UNCITRAL Conciliation Rules.

For example, the general Magna Carta of the UNCITRAL Conciliation rules is that the conciliator will respect the will of the parties and will conduct the process as he or she considers appropriate. One sees these principles reflected in many sets of rules.

Alexander
Mr Sekolec, you and Michael Getty[32] *have written an article about the UNCITRAL Model Law on Conciliation and the Model Uniform Mediation Act of the United States (UMA). Could you make some comments about the relationship between these two pieces of model legislation?*

Uniform Mediation Act (UMA) in the United States

Sekolec
The draft Uniform Mediation Act was being discussed at the National Conference of Commissioners for Uniform State Laws while we were getting together the ideas for the Model Law. It was always interesting to read reports of the NCCUSL. Let me give you an example of how we were inspired by those discussions. America, like many other countries, decided to do something about enforceability. Many said, 'Let's declare that a settlement agreement is as enforceable as a judgment because this would promote the use of mediation'. However, there were some interesting comments from the drafters of the UMA who gave an example of a case in Texas. In this case a woman maintained that she was cheated and coerced in the mediation process. She claimed the other side had acted fraudulently. The drafters considered what to do in the case of fraud. If they were to declare a settlement agreement enforceable as a judgment then they would need to provide a safety net for fraudulent cases. At UNCITRAL we were able to learn from the deliberations of the NCCUSL, which in turn escalated the pace of our own deliberations.

UMA; Enforceability of mediated settlements

Alexander
So both the UNCITRAL Working Group on Conciliation and the NCCUSL considered similar issues, but these bodies reached different conclusions on how to regulate certain aspects of mediation?

Sekolec
Yes. Although the issues we were facing were quite similar, the NCCUSL were dealing with mediation in a national context. For example, the right to be represented by an

32 The Hon Michael B Getty, a former chancery court judge and legislator in Illinois, served as Chair of the Uniform Mediation Act Drafting Committee of the National Conference of Commissioners on Uniform State Laws as a US Advisor to the Drafting Committee of the UNCITRAL Model Law for Commercial Conciliation.

attorney is so sacred in US practice that an attorney or another individual designated to represent a party may accompany the party in a mediation. In circumstances in which a waiver of legal participation has been given before the mediation, such a waiver may be rescinded by the party wanting representation. Furthermore, the definition of mediation in the UMA is narrower than the UNCITRAL definition, but equally legitimate. For instance, the US Uniform Mediation Act only covers mediations by mediators who hold themselves out as providing mediation. At UNCITRAL we were also looking at the interests and experience of other countries in mediation, for example Kenya, India, Argentina, Peru and Australia. We were gathering materials from these countries and were also inspired by them. As you know, in August 2003 the NCCUSL included a new provision in the UMA, subjecting international cases to the UNCITRAL Model Law.

UMA and Model Law

Alexander
So in other words the UMA applies only to domestic cases in the United States?

Sekolec
Yes. If there is an international case, then according to the provisions of the Uniform Mediation Act, the case is governed by a slightly modified version of the UNCITRAL Model Law. Therefore there is a direct incorporation of the UNCITRAL Model Law into the Uniform Mediation Act.

Alexander
What feedback do you have from other countries regarding their interest in enacting the Model Law?

Enacting states

Sekolec
In addition to the United States a number of countries have based their mediation legislation on the Model Law or have expressed an interest in doing so. Countries which have introduced or proposed laws based on the Model Law include Slovenia, Afghanistan, Canada, Croatia, Kosovo and Russia. Other countries such as Ecuador, Nicaragua, Norway, Romania, Serbia, Slovakia and Turkey have introduced laws, which have varying degrees of similarity to the Model Law. In yet other cases, countries have

Deviations from the Model Law; Regulatory approaches

introduced mediation laws, but it is not clear to what extent they have been influenced by the Model Law. As countries do not always inform UNCITRAL of changes in their laws, it is not possible to follow these systematically. In some instances English translations are not available on the internet. Nations such as Bulgaria and Hungary have introduced laws which do not appear to be influenced greatly by the Model Law, although I understand that they were inspired and prompted by it.

Alexander
There certainly seems to be a lot of regulatory activity in relation to mediation.

Sekolec
Judging by the interest expressed in the Model Law at the sixth (Legal) Committee of the United Nations General Assembly, as well as elsewhere, many countries are looking at mediation as a promising form of dispute resolution. Countries are also realising that it is necessary to have minimum statutory regulation as a foundation to support the development of international mediation practice.

Alexander
My sense is that many countries wanting to enact a domestic mediation law from scratch are looking to the Model Law as a starting point. However with impulses from the European Union Directive and other regulatory requirements, these proposed mediation laws go through so many variations that at the end some of them only loosely resemble the Model Law if at all. I think Hungary is a case in point. Does that not pose a challenge for the harmonisation objectives of UNCITRAL?

Sekolec
Difference between mediation and arbitration

There are a number of points that I would like to make here. The first relates to the fundamental difference between arbitration and mediation. UNCITRAL model legislation on arbitration seeks to ensure contract discipline worldwide and this calls for predictable and tested solutions. Conversely the Model Law on Conciliation seeks in the first place to encourage parties to trust and feel comfortable negotiating within a conciliation process, the form of which depends largely on social, cultural, commercial, institutional and legal factors. The flexibility and adaptability of conciliation does not lend itself to a high level of unification. At the same time – and this is the second point – I have the feeling that departures from the Model Law are not always justified by such local particularities; rather they seem to be a result of the interplay of the economic and professional interests of associations of mediators, attorneys and judges, on one hand and the desire by policy- and law-makers to systematically and centrally regulate mediation on the other. This desire for governmental regulatory control of mediation is typical of civil law thinking. Here laws are generally drafted by ministry officials and others with no mediation practice experience. I think laws benefit greatly from input from a variety of interest groups including practitioners.[33]

Deviations from the Model Law; local policy and politics

In any event, mediation has proven to be useful in cross-border and intercultural disputes and there is a need for harmonised regulatory solutions in these matters. One way to manage the situation is the somewhat complex solution of separate regulation for domestic and international mediation. This would reduce local pressure to deviate from internationally negotiated solutions for cross-border cases, while still allowing home-grown or -adapted solutions for domestic conciliation.

Alexander

Earlier we were speaking about the approach of the American UMA. Australia has taken a different approach. I would be interested to hear your views on it. There is an interdisciplinary body in Australia, called NADRAC (National Alternative Dispute Resolution Advisory Council), which was set up in 1995 to advise the government on issues relating to ADR. In the year 2001 NADRAC released a report on ADR standards. The report recommended a framework approach rather than uniform mediation standards.

NADRAC, framework approach

A framework approach provides a model for balancing the desire for diversity and flexibility in practice on one hand and the need for quality assurance and consistency in practice on the other. It involves

33 On regulatory approaches to mediation, see Chapter 2.

organisations and industries committing to address specific criteria relating to training and service delivery standards. However, the precise manner in which industries and organisations deal with these issues is left to them.

Sekolec

UNCITRAL approach

What you are describing is very interesting and is compatible with UNCITRAL's approach. As a body proposing model legislation, UNCITRAL has taken the path of minimum regulation of the foundations of mediation (primarily confidentiality) and has encouraged mediation institutions throughout the world to provide rules of procedure suitable to their contexts, taking into account cultural, political, legal and industry factors.

In my view an assurance of the fundamental features of mediation can only credibly be given by the law and not by the agreement of the parties. I think it is a sign of good progress to provide minimum standards.

Beyond the minimum standards, there will be diversity. For example, how does one deal with the issue of the duties of the mediator when s/he caucuses with a party? Must s/he keep that information confidential upfront unless the party provides the mediator with special dispensation? Or is it the other way around, so that the mediator can inform the other party of everything unless the first party specifically requests the mediator not to do so on these issues? Life is beautiful because of these differences and the consequences and merits of each approach will unfold as mediation practice increases. Perhaps one approach will emerge as the better, or maybe both will co-exist. It may depend on the atmosphere and the dynamics of the particular case. We will wait and see.

Alexander

Good faith and natural justice

I would like to discuss the roles that good faith and natural justice play in the Model Law and in international dispute resolution generally.

Sekolec

This is an important question. Good faith, natural justice, fairness, equity and all related concepts have a different meaning if one moves from legal system to legal system. In arbitration very rigorous adherence to due process of law (natural justice) is required. Without due process, the award will be vitiated. However, mediation is a voluntary process and either party can terminate the process at any moment. Therefore one does not need a rigorous adherence to due process in the arbitral sense of the term. In arbitration one is dealing with past issues and liabilities, whereas mediation goes beyond this and deals with how to set aside a dispute and restructure the relationship for the future. In mediation one is dealing with the (re)-creation of a contractual relationship, not a statutory-based award. There is no judge or arbitrator who evaluates whether a mediated settlement agreement meets the criteria of good faith. What is fair is ultimately up to the parties. I think it would be a disservice to mediation if UNCITRAL would include in the Rules, or worse in the Law, that a mediated settlement must meet some criteria of substantive equity, fairness or justice.

Fair process

It is the *process* that must be fair – the procedure rather than the settlement. For example, parties must be able to negotiate without suffering duress from the other side; they must feel confident that the *process* is kept confidential, that the other side is not engaging in misleading, deceptive or fraudulent conduct. One party must not take advantage of the other. The process must be rigorous and fair but the outcome is like any other contract. It is a business relationship and it is for the parties to decide what is good for them. In mediation the law protects the parties from the same risks as in the normal run of contractual negotiations.

We should not invent special concepts of fairness and natural justice for mediation because mediation is nothing more than a sophisticated, third-party assisted contractual negotiation. We already have the appropriate mechanisms and concepts in contract law.

Fair treatment

Article 6(3) of the Model Law uses the words 'fair treatment'. It has been drafted very carefully to indicate that the test of fair treatment applies to the conduct of the parties during the proceedings and not to the outcome or to the substance of the agreement. So the issues of good faith and equity play out differently in mediation compared with arbitration.

Alexander
So when you say that we have the mechanisms already in place, you are referring to the enacting states.

Sekolec
Each enacting state has contract law that already deals with how far a judge should go in ensuring fairness and natural justice in pre-contractual dealings.

Law of enacting states; Fairness

Alexander
I can imagine there might be some criticism of the word fairness. Fairness is a wonderfully all-encompassing term. However the law of contract and statute law in many jurisdictions would not be able to enforce a contractual clause requiring fairness.

Sekolec
That is true and that is also the beauty of the Model Law. If a concept does not fit a particular national system, the enacting state can change it.

Fairness and equity

The word *fairness* has an interesting linguistic meaning. When fairness is translated into Latin-based languages such as French and Spanish it becomes *equité* and *equidad.* These terms are related to the concept of equity. The common law countries were nervous when they saw the word *equity*, because it also has a technical meaning and because the meaning could spill over into the equity of the settlement. We did not want to subject a settlement agreement to the test of equity. Nobody should look over the shoulders of the parties and determine whether the settlement agreement is equitable or not. The Guide to Enactment clarifies that the term *fairness* refers to the procedural aspects of the conciliation and not to the outcome.

Alexander
The concept of good faith in contractual relationships has had a very different history in common law jurisdictions compared with civil law jurisdictions. Could you comment on this in light of the Model Law?

Good faith

Sekolec
While there were historical differences, it is nowadays too

simplistic to refer to how the common law deals with these issues versus how the civil law does. Common law countries consist of over 40 different jurisdictions. Interventionist judges exist in both systems. So called civil law judges are becoming more and more reluctant to intervene in a legitimate contractual relationship on the basis of the lack of good faith. And in common law jurisdictions recent developments in case law and in legislation have, in certain circumstances, required parties to act in good faith in pre-contractual dealings especially in consumer legislation.

Alexander
So, in your experience, the two systems are effectively moving towards each other?

Sekolec
Yes. So it is becoming increasingly difficult to make generalisations about legal systems and traditions as we did in the past.

Alexander
The provisions in the Model Law take the form of default provisions so the parties can contract out of them. Are there any exceptions to this?

Nature of provisions of Model Law

Sekolec
There are two exceptions: Articles 2 and 6(3). Article 2 is the interpretation provision. I do not think that it is technically necessary to make this provision mandatory but there is no harm. Article 2(1) provides that: 'In the interpretation of this Law, regard is to be had to its international origin and to the need to promote uniformity in its application and the observance of good faith.'

Mandatory provision – Article 2

The article is a reminder to the judge and it is a guideline for interpretation, which favours harmony in an international context. Article 2(2) provides that where the answer to an issue governed by the Model Law is not expressly settled in the Law, one should look to the general principles on which the Model Law is based. So when there is a technical point that falls within the ambit of the provisions of the Model Law, one should first look for an answer in the philosophy of the Model Law rather than the

Interpretation of the Model Law

(national) law outside the Model Law. Article 2 encourages national courts to look to the international character and origin of the Model law, which may include how other countries have understood and interpreted their enactment of the Model Law.

Alexander
Just on that point, won't countries be tempted first to look to what their national law says either in the field of mediation or conciliation or in a parallel field such as arbitration?

Sekolec
If the issue is not governed by the Model Law then judges will look at their national laws to solve the problem and would be justified in doing so. If, however, an issue is governed by the Model Law but not expressly settled by it, then the user of the law must look to the Model Law for interpretation. This is the same principle that has been adopted in other pieces of legislation such as the United Nations Convention on Contracts for the International Sale of Goods. It promotes predictability and I have the feeling it is increasingly accepted and understood by practitioners and judges around the world.

Alexander
Was that principle adopted in the Model Law on Arbitration also?

Sekolec
We did not use it in the original 1985 version of the Model Law on Arbitration. At that time it was somewhat conservatively thought that while the principle had its place in an international treaty, it was out of place in a Model Law because deviations from the Model Law could be significant and a UNCITRAL Model Law should not be telling a national judge what to do. So we focused on the quality of the provisions rather than the issue of uniformity. However times have changed. The Model Law on Arbitration has received much uniform enactment and therefore such a provision plays a useful role and is no longer controversial. As a result the principle was included in the 2006 revision of the Model Law on Arbitration as it had been in the 2002 Model Law on Conciliation.

This time we gave more emphasis to the fact that the Model Law is an instrument of harmonisation of national laws and that it should be interpreted uniformly (that is, taking into account the international character and origin of the law and the need to promote uniformity in its application). The message to all national courts of enacting states dealing with an issue governed by the Model Law is to think globally and look at the philosophy underlying this law.

Alexander
You mentioned Article 6 as the other mandatory provision?

Sekolec
The other mandatory provision is Article 6(3): 'In any case, in conducting the proceedings, the conciliator shall seek to maintain fair treatment of the parties and, in so doing, shall take into account the circumstances of the case.'

Mandatory provision – Article 6(3)

It is the 'shall seek fair treatment of the parties' part of the article, which is important. I think public policy is the big hand watching over the well-being of the parties. The obligation of procedural fair treatment is something that should always be there for the parties. If it is not, then the form of dispute resolution loses the character of mediation or conciliation and becomes something else.

Hopefully this fair treatment will not be translated into something which will require the substance of mediated agreements to meet equitable criteria.

Fair treatment

Alexander
Why did you choose fair treatment to be a mandatory provision but not confidentiality?

Sekolec
Confidentiality is for the benefit of the parties and they can always dispense with it. There may be some situations in which parties do not require all or part of the mediation to be confidential. Indeed, the parties may agree to go public with some or all aspects of their dispute and the legislator should have no reason to prevent them from doing so. Also, as we discussed earlier, there may be certain cultures and dispute resolution traditions where confidentiality does not play such a significant role as in western mediation.

Confidentiality as a default provision

Alexander

The Model Law is envisaged for business-to-business (B2B) disputes in an international context. It can also be used by enacting states as a model for commercial domestic disputes. What about business-to-consumer (B2C) disputes, particularly in the context of electronic commerce such as eBay? Often consumers commit themselves to mediation in the event of a dispute through a consumer contract. Bearing in mind the power imbalance that exists between an individual consumer and a large corporation, might there not be scope for an argument that more of the Model Law should be mandatory, rather than default – for example the confidentiality provisions?

Sekolec

Definition of commercial - B2B disputes and B2C disputes

My reply would simply be that the Model Law is indeed meant for commercial (B2B) cases only. Although what is commercial is subject to a somewhat flexible definition referred to in a footnote of the Model Law. It provides that: 'the term 'commercial' should be given a wide interpretation so as to cover matters arising from all relationships of a commercial nature, whether contractual or not' and it gives examples of relationships of a commercial nature. Therefore an eBay relationship may in some cases be regarded as commercial and not in others. It is a question of interpretation.

We were confident that this text was suitable for commercial cases; however, we also thought that most of the text, if not all of it, would be suitable for non-commercial cases such as consumer cases. With respect to non-commercial cases there may be scope to amend parts of the Model Law and the nature of the provisions in order to protect the weaker party. Again, UNCITRAL has restricted the application of the Model Law to B2B disputes only and left any extension of the law to B2C disputes and other non-commercial cases to the enacting states. Why? Because the approaches of the legislatures in countries like Australia, some European countries and the United States concerning consumer protection are different from the approach of developing countries. And there are differences among developing countries as well.

Applicability of Model Law to consumer disputes

An interesting possibility is for states to provide that the Model Law applies to B2B and B2C disputes, subject to consumer protection legislation. Such an approach is relatively easy to achieve from a legislative perspective, although it is not very transparent. However, with the rapid increase in cross-border e-commerce, this is an issue that national jurisdictions will have to consider carefully.

Alexander
Earlier you explained the minimum legislative approach of UNCITRAL, which aims to encourage flexibility and diversity in national and international mediation practice. You also spoke of the need for quality assurance in mediation practice. Which bodies do you think should be establishing quality assurance systems such as benchmarks, trust mark systems, standards for conduct in mediation, ethical codes and so on? It seems that to leave this only to nation states would encourage a proliferation of different quality assurance systems and methods. This, in turn, could lead to an unnecessarily complex conflict of laws issues, for example, with respect to mediator liability issues. So, who do you think should be regulating these matters?

Quality assurance

Sekolec
I agree with you that a national institution – public or private – is not the ideal body to establish quality assurance schemes for international disputes. At the same time, it would be much too bold, too precipitous, for UNCITRAL as an intergovernmental body to start setting up frameworks for standards of mediation practice.

My reaction is that cross-border private institutions such as the International Chamber of Commerce would be appropriate to manage quality issues. The advantage of such organisations is that they operate on an international or regional basis already and in many cases provide the procedural rules within which international mediations occur. Further, regulations of private institutions can be amended more easily than the regulations created by governments. When governments start regulating, the rules become difficult to change and in some circumstances can become an impediment to trade.

Alexander
After the publication of the Model Law, what steps is UNCITRAL proposing to encourage uniformity of application of the Model Law?

Uniformity of application of the Model Law

Sekolec
One way in which UNCITRAL works on promoting unification is though the CLOUT system, which stands for 'Case Law and UNCITRAL texts'. After the Model Law on Arbitration was published, UNCITRAL gathered court decisions and arbitral decisions dealing with the Law. The published results are available in the six languages of the United Nations and show how judges and other interpreters of different jurisdictions have applied the law. This system has worked very successfully with the Model Law on Arbitration. UNCITRAL has published a large number of cases and now a digest of case law is about to be launched. The CLOUT system reaches many people – lawyers, arbitrators, dispute resolution providers, policy makers and law-makers. It influences the future development of international arbitration and I have every reason to believe it will extend similar guidance to the development of international commercial conciliation.

CLOUT System

The UNCITRAL approach is a step-by-step approach to the development of a harmonised system of international dispute resolution. It starts with a minimal interference approach and then works with nation-states, NGOs and international service-providers to further improve the rules and to increase harmonisation, whilst still maintaining flexibility in the future.

Jernej Sekolec **is the former Secretary of the United Nations Commission on International Trade Law (UNCITRAL) and former Director of the International Trade Law Division of the United Nations Office of Legal Affairs in Vienna, Austria. He now lives and works in Vienna as an independent arbitrator and mediator. He is also regularly engaged as a consultant in law reform projects, particularly in the area of commercial disputes. Jernej Sekolec is a member of numerous international law and dispute resolution bodies and sits on the London Court of International Arbitration. The views expressed in this interview are his own and do not purport to represent those of UNCITRAL. The legal instruments referred to in this interview are listed below.**

- **UNCITRAL Arbitration Rules 1976;**
- **UNCITRAL Conciliation Rules 1980;**
- **United Nations Convention on Contracts for the International Sale of Goods 1980;**
- **UNCITRAL Model Law on International Commercial Arbitration 1985;**
- **UNCITRAL Model Law on International Commercial Conciliation 2002.**

Chapter 9
The UNCITRAL Model Law on International Commercial Conciliation (2002)

1. Overview

In the commentary that follows the UNCITRAL[1] Model Law on International Commercial Conciliation (2002) (MLICC) is considered article by article. Each article is introduced by its text followed by an analysis and commentary.

States contemplating enacting the Model Law are advised to review their existing dispute resolution and related laws that may have an impact upon conciliation with a view to making them compatible with the Model Law. For example Article 6 of the Model Law permits conciliators to adopt an advisory style of mediation – an approach which may conflict with mediator accreditation and practice codes in some jurisdictions.[2] Chapter 2 provides a model for policy and law-makers to follow in this regard.

This commentary on the MLICC is placed at the end of the book so that reference can be made to the international comparative analysis in previous chapters. Readers who have not read the previous chapters are encouraged to consult specific parts of the book referenced in the footnotes to this chapter.

The meanings of, and relationships between, the terms *mediation* and *conciliation* have been explored in Chapter 1. In this chapter the terminology of the MLICC, conciliation, is used interchangeably with mediation.

2. Article 1

Article 1: Scope of application and definitions

1. This Law applies to international[1] commercial[2] conciliation.
2. For the purposes of this Law, "conciliator" means a sole conciliator or two or more conciliators, as the case may be.
3. For the purposes of this Law, "conciliation" means a process, whether referred to by the expression conciliation, mediation or an expression of similar import, whereby parties request a third person or persons ("the

1 UNCITRAL is the United Nations Commission on International Trade Law and is also referred to as the Commission from time to time in this chapter. For a background to UNCITRAL, see Chapter 8. The text of the Model Law on International Commercial Conciliation (2002) is reproduced throughout this chapter with the kind permission of UNCITRAL.

2 See, for example, ss 3(4)(g)(i) and 10(3) and (5)) of the Australian National Mediator Standards.

conciliator") to assist them in their attempt to reach an amicable settlement of their dispute arising out of or relating to a contractual or other legal relationship. The conciliator does not have the authority to impose upon the parties a solution to the dispute.

4. A conciliation is international if:
   a. The parties to an agreement to conciliate have, at the time of the conclusion of that agreement, their places of business in different States; or
   b. The State in which the parties have their places of business is different from either:
      i. The State in which a substantial part of the obligations of the commercial relationship is to be performed; or
      ii. The State with which the subject matter of the dispute is most closely connected.
5. For the purposes of this article:
   a. If a party has more than one place of business, the place of business is that which has the closest relationship to the agreement to conciliate;
   b. If a party does not have a place of business, reference is to be made to the party's habitual residence.
6. This Law also applies to a commercial conciliation when the parties agree that the conciliation is international or agree to the applicability of this Law.
7. The parties are free to agree to exclude the applicability of this Law.
8. Subject to the provisions of paragraph 9 of this article, this Law applies irrespective of the basis upon which the conciliation is carried out, including agreement between the parties whether reached before or after a dispute has arisen, an obligation established by law, or a direction or suggestion of a court, arbitral tribunal or competent governmental entity.
9. This Law does not apply to:
   a. Cases where a judge or an arbitrator, in the course of judicial or arbitral proceedings, attempts to facilitate a settlement; and
   b. [. . .]

[Footnotes to Article 1]

[1] States wishing to enact this Model Law to apply to domestic as well as international conciliation may wish to consider the following changes to the text:

- Delete the word "international" in paragraph 1 of Article 1; and
- Delete paragraphs 4, 5 and 6 of Article 1.

[2] The term "commercial" should be given a wide interpretation so as to cover matters arising from all relationships of a commercial nature, whether contractual or not. Relationships of a commercial nature include, but are not limited to, the following transactions: any trade transaction for the supply or exchange of goods or services; distribution agreement; commercial representation or agency; factoring; leasing; construction of works; consulting; engineering; licensing; investment; financing; banking; insurance; exploitation agreement or concession; joint venture and other forms of industrial or business cooperation; carriage of goods or passengers by air, sea, rail or road.

Article 1 contains nine paragraphs dealing with a range of issues relating to definitions and scope of the Model Law. They are considered here under the following headings: the scope of application of the Model Law and its limits, the meaning of the terms *international*, *commercial*, *conciliator* and *conciliation*, and finally, how the Model Law is triggered.

2.1 Scope of Application of the Model Law and Its Limits

The Model Law applies to international commercial conciliation (Article 1(1)) irrespective of its origin (Article 1(8)). In other words, the Model Law applies *prima facie* to all variations of voluntary and mandatory conciliation. These include situations where parties have agreed to conciliation, whether before or after the dispute has arisen, and referrals to conciliation by a court, tribunal or other body. In practice commercial parties are becoming exposed to the inclusion of conciliation clauses in international commercial contracts and courts in many jurisdictions now recognise and enforce these. The growing trend in some countries to mandate mediation through court referral means that, looking to the future, disputing parties are increasingly likely to find themselves at conciliation whether they like it or not. In such cases Article 1(8)) is a significant and useful provision to clarify issues relating to the applicability of the Law.

As indicated in Chapter 8, party autonomy is a major theme in the Model Law. Parties may opt in to the Model Law even where their conciliation does not meet the criteria of *international* and *commercial* (Article 1(6)). They may do this by simply agreeing that the conciliation is international or that the Model Law is applicable. This option may be useful where, for example, the international character of the conciliation as defined in Article 1(4) and (5) is uncertain. However Binder argues that the ability to agree to the applicability of the law covers all relevant scenarios and that therefore the reference to the parties' ability to agree on the international character of the conciliation is superfluous.[3]

In addition to opting in to the Model Law, parties may also opt out of it (Article 1(7)). This provision allows parties to exclude the application of the Model Law, confirming the non-mandatory or default nature of the Law. It envisages a situation where parties may wish to have their disputes settled according to a particular domestic law regulating conciliation even though the conciliation would otherwise be characterised as *international* and *commercial* and fall within the scope of the Model Law. Consider the following illustration. The businesses of the disputing parties are in the same state but the commercial obligations are incurred in a variety of jurisdictions, including that of the parties'

3 See P Binder, *International Commercial Arbitration and Conciliation in UNCITRAL Model Law Jurisdictions* (London: Sweet and Maxwell 2005) at para 10-018-019.

places of business, and conciliation takes place in yet another state. In such a situation all parties may feel safer knowing a domestic law will be applied, particularly where it provides a higher level of certainty and enforceability than the Model Law. Criticisms of this provision emphasise the need to balance party autonomy with the need for predictability in the law and suggest that the Model Law has gone too far by favouring party autonomy and, by extension, diversity at the expense of certainty and consistency.[4]

The Model Law covers all varieties of conciliation including mandatory referrals by domestic courts and contractually-initiated mediation (Article 1(8)). This provision has been criticised by Sanders who contends that the Model Law should only deal with conciliation based on an agreement of the parties, leaving individual governments to regulate court-ordered proceedings and other situations where an obligation to conciliate is established by law. He argues that court-ordered conciliation is not founded on consensus and thereby differs from contractually-based conciliation.[5] Sanders' distinctions between court-related and consensus-based conciliation may appear at first glance to be useful, but the dichotomy is misleading. Court-ordered mediation is not limited to mandatory programs. As explained in Chapter 3, it varies greatly in terms of the nature of participation of disputing parties, blurring the distinction between voluntary and mandatory participation. Pre-litigation duties of lawyers and parties outlined in Chapter 5 further complicate the nature of obligation in the mediation landscape. Sanders' distinction is therefore difficult to sustain. The approach of the MLICC to target a wide mediation audience and apply to mediation irrespective of the identity of the gatekeeper – court, tribunal, legislation or contract – parallels that of the UMA in the United States.[6]

Further, as discussed below in relation to Article 4, the scope of the Model Law is restricted to regulating the conciliation process as it occurs between parties. In other words the Model Law does not interfere with domestic law obligations to participate in conciliation. Therefore the regulation and enforcement of obligations to attend conciliation or to participate according to a good faith standard are left to the relevant domestic law.

On a point of drafting in Article 1(8), the proviso subjecting Article 1(8) to the provisions of Article 1(9) seems misplaced. Article 1(9) provides

4 Comments by the Government of Hungary: see *Draft Model Law on International Commercial Conciliation, Compilation of Comments by Governments and International Organisations* UN Doc N° A/CN.9/513 (2002) 6. See also E van Ginkel, 'The UNCITRAL Model Law on International Commercial Conciliation: A Critical Appraisal' (2004) 21 *Journal of International Arbitration* 1 at 7–8. See also the commentary to Article 3.

5 See P Sanders, *The Work of UNCITRAL on Arbitration and Conciliation* (2nd ed, The Hague: Kluwer Law International 2004) at 207.

6 See s 3 of the UMA and Chapter 2 on the scope of mediation laws. See also the commentary in relation to Article 4 below.

exceptions to the Model Law as a whole, that is, to all of its provisions. Therefore it seems unnecessary to specify that a certain provision of the MLICC is subject to the exceptions to the Law. Other provisions in the Model Law are also subject to Article 1(9) but contain no such proviso. The resulting inconsistency in drafting is confusing and enacting states may consider remedying this situation when drafting the Model Law into their national legislation.[7]

As indicated above Article 1(9) provides an exception to the application of the Model Law and offers an opportunity for enacting states to add further exceptions. The one exception relates to settlement attempts in determinative dispute resolution processes so that the Model Law does not apply to judges or arbitrators facilitating settlement in the course of judicial or arbitral proceedings. It is the intention of the Model Law to interfere neither with domestic civil procedure law nor with arbitration processes.[8]

Chapter 3 examined four models of judicial dispute resolution including judicial settlement. While judicial settlement falls outside the scope of the Model Law, this may not be the case with other forms of judicial dispute resolution (JDR) such as judicial mediation. Where applicable, enacting states are advised to address the applicability of the Model Law in relation to different JDR processes. The Guide to Enactment suggests that states specify in legislation enacting the Model Law whether its provisions govern court-related dispute resolution processes – including judicial mediation – or not.

By providing that attempts to settle disputes in the course of arbitration are not covered by the MLICC, Article 1(9)(a) implicitly acknowledges different cultural understandings of, and practices in, arbitration around the world. In some legal cultures arbitrators are expected or even required to engage in settlement attempts as part of the arbitration process.[9] As in the case of judicial settlement, arbitration practice is rarely as neatly compartmentalised as legislative definitions might suggest. Enacting states must be able to distinguish between mediation as part of multi-tiered dispute resolution processes (MDR), on one hand, and settlements within the course of arbitration, on the other.

There may be other areas of commercial mediation practice that enacting states wish to subject to domestic policies and legislation and therefore regulate separately from the Model Law. The exceptions can be listed in Article 1(9). Franchising, retail tenancy and farm debt[10] mediation laws deal with

7 See Ginkel (2004), above note 4 at 20.

8 See the *Guide to Enactment and Use of the UNCITRAL Model Law on International Commercial Conciliation* (2002) (referred to in this chapter as the Guide to Enactment) at paras 34 and 38, available at www.uncitral.org/pdf/english/texts/arbitration/ml-conc/ml-conc-e.pdf.

9 On the culture of arbitration, see Chapter 1.

10 On mediation between farmers and financial institutions, see Chapter 2. For an example of a specific legislative policy see s 11A(3) of the Farm Debt Mediation Act

commercial disputes where parties are not engaged in dealings 'at arms' length' and where a power imbalance may exist between parties. Specific policies and legislation to address power imbalances in a dispute resolution context are not uncommon. Enacting states will need to consider the extent to which the provisions of the Model Law – a law drafted to address the needs of commercial parties transacting on a more or less equal playing field – are to apply to commercial situations involving a potential power imbalance.

2.2 Meaning of Commercial

The restriction of the application of the Model Law to commercial disputes is the result of two factors, namely that commercial matters have been the traditional mandate of UNCITRAL, and that non-commercial matters are more likely to clash with public policies specific to legal cultures and national circumstances.[11]

As an example of a non-commercial matter, the Guide to Enactment refers to collective bargaining and suggests that where states have well-developed collective bargaining laws providing for mediation they are likely to be based on policy considerations that differ from the Model Law principles.[12] Where the domestic law approaches to commercial matters are sufficiently broad to encompass areas normally subject to different legal principles, such as collective bargaining, consumer protection, environmental policy and other areas, enacting states are advised to consider the Model Law's appropriateness to these practice fields and adjust their drafting accordingly.

The Model Law itself does not provide a definitive definition of commercial. Rather a broad explanation of the term, together with an illustrative list of examples, can be found in the second footnote to Article 1. It is identical to the definition of commercial in the second footnote of Article 1 to the MLICA.[13] Placing the definition of commercial in a footnote to the text suggests the Working Group was unable to agree on a definition to locate in the text of the Model Law but nevertheless thought it important to provide guidance on the meaning of commercial in footnote form. This definition may be useful for countries without a discrete body of commercial law and it is expected to have a

1994 (NSW), which requires mediated settlements to include a cooling-off period within which parties may withdraw from agreements.

11 J Sekolec and M Getty, 'The UMA and the UNCITRAL Model Rule: An Emerging Consensus on Mediation and Conciliation' (2003) *Journal of Dispute Resolution* 175 at 184.

12 See the Guide to Enactment at para 38.

13 References to the MLICA throughout this chapter are to the UNCITRAL Model Law on International Commercial Arbitration (1985).

harmonising effect among those countries with discrete and well-developed areas of commercial law.[14]

2.3 Meaning of Conciliator and Conciliation

Article 1 does not define *conciliator*; it merely states in Article 1(2) that the singular includes the plural, thereby referring to the possibility of panels of two or more conciliators acting in one conciliation.

The definition of conciliator, however, can be drawn from the definition of *conciliation* in Article 1(3). Conciliation is defined as a process whereby the parties request a third party – or parties – to assist them in reaching an amicable settlement of their dispute. The paragraph goes on to explain that conciliators have no authority to impose a solution to the dispute on the parties. As such it covers both facilitative and advisory dispute resolution processes, but not determinative systems such as arbitration. Article 1(3) specifically refers, but does not limit its application, to processes known as conciliation and mediation. The Guide to Enactment goes further and identifies the processes of neutral evaluation and mini-trial as falling within the definition of conciliation. Accordingly the provision looks to the nature of the dispute resolution process rather than the label, so that parties need not refer to the term *conciliation* for the Model Law to apply. As indicated in Chapter 1, broadly worded descriptive definitions of mediation and conciliation such as found in Article 1(3) encourage diversity in practice.[15] The only hint of a conceptual definition is found not in the Model Law but in the Guide to Enactment which describes conciliation as an interest-based dispute resolution process where,

> the conciliator assists the parties in negotiating a settlement that is designed to meet the needs and interests of the parties in dispute.[16]

Conciliation under the MLICC therefore includes institutionalised and *ad hoc* conciliations.[17] Institutionalised conciliations typically include reference to a set of procedural rules such as the UNCITRAL Conciliation Rules (UCR), the MEDAL Rules or one of many others,[18] which clarify the parties' intentions on the nature and characteristics of the process in which they are engaging. The intention of the parties may be much less clear in *ad hoc* conciliations. Parties may, for example, engage in a dispute resolution process with very different understandings of its purpose. This was the case in *Acorn Farms Ltd v*

14 See the Guide to Enactment at para 29.
15 On the diversity–consistency debate, see Chapter 2.
16 See the Guide to Enactment at para 6.
17 On institutionalised and ad hoc mediation and arbitration, see Chapter 1.
18 For these and other examples see the Comparative Table of International Mediation Rules in Appendix B.

Schnuriger[19] where the plaintiff thought it was engaged in a mediation process and not, as was found to be the case, arbitration. Alternatively parties may engage in a conciliation-like process without being aware that they potentially fall within the scope of the Model Law. This situation has been referred to in the interview in Chapter 8 and may conceivably occur where questions relating to the applicable law arise, for example in relation to enforcing a mediated settlement.

In these situations Sekolec and Getty suggest that, when determining the applicability of the Model Law, national courts take into account case circumstances and the understanding and expectations of the parties regarding the nature of the process they have entered.[20] This approach echoes that taken by a New Zealand court in *Acorn Farms* cited above. By way of comparison, the UMA in the United States provides a set of criteria – which also include reference to parties' expectations – to assist in determination of whether or not a process can be defined as mediation for the purposes of the Act.[21] International policy differences and intercultural considerations steered UNCITRAL away from such an approach.

Legal questions arise as to the Model Law's applicability to multi-tiered dispute resolution arrangements involving a determinative process such as med–arb.[22] Chapter 4 highlights challenges involved in determining whether or not a particular MDR process falls within the terms of mediation laws or clauses. For example, is a med–arb clause to be interpreted as a determinative process because there is the potential for arbitration, even though this might not eventuate and the med–arb process may effectively operate as a mediation? Alternatively is it possible that the mediation phase of med–arb may be covered by mediation legislation such as the MLICC and the arbitration phase by arbitration legislation? Ultimately answers to these questions will depend on the wording of the specific MDR clause and the applicable law.[23]

The reference to a 'dispute arising out of or relating to a contractual or other legal relationship' in Article 1(3) clarifies that the Model Law does not only apply to the mediation of contractual claims. However it does seem to suggest that the conciliator's jurisdiction is only invoked if there is a legal dispute. In other words, conciliators appear to have no pre-emptive or declaratory jurisdiction in relation to disputes, and transactional mediation may also fall outside the scope of the Model Law.[24]

19 See *Acorn Farms Ltd v Schnuriger* [2003] 3 NZLR 121.

20 Sekolec and Getty (2003), above note 11 at 185.

21 See s 3 of the UMA 2001.

22 See comments by Sekolec in the interview in Chapter 8.

23 For a discussion of these issues, see Chapter 4.

24 Transactional mediation is also known as deal mediation and is referred to in Chapter 1. It is interesting to consider the applicability of the law to pre-contractual disputes where claims of promissory estoppel are made.

The Commission noted the suitability of conciliation and the provisions of the Model Law for multi-party disputes. It debated the possibility of including a reference to multi-party disputes, corporate insolvency and other matters in a footnote to the law.[25] However the view was taken that such an inclusion might be seen as limiting the application of the Model Law. Instead a reference to multi-party disputes in the context of corporate insolvency matters can be found in the Guide to Enactment.[26]

2.4 Meaning of International

The application of the Model Law is limited to commercial conciliations with an international character. Articles 1(4) and (5) explain the meaning of the term *international*. The language of these paragraphs is drawn from the MLICA.[27] Essentially a conciliation is international if at least two states are involved. The connection to a state may be to:

- the place of business of one or both parties;
- the place where a substantial part of the commercial obligation is to be performed; or
- the place with which the subject-matter of the dispute is most closely connected.

Article 1(5) goes on to provide a test to determine the 'place of business' in situations where a party may have either no place of business or several. Where a party has no place of business, reference is made to the party's habitual place of residence; where a party has several places of business the place which has the closest relationship to the agreement to conciliate is the relevant place of business. The Guide to Enactment indicates a number of factors relevant to establishing the closest relationship which include the second and third dot points in the previous paragraph.[28]

Whereas there have not yet been any reported cases in CLOUT (Case Law on UNCITRAL Texts database) on the meaning of international with respect to the MLICC, there have been a number of decisions on the almost identically worded provision of the MLICA, Article 1(3)(b)(ii). The following arbitration cases illustrate the principle's operation.

In *Fung Sang Trading Limited v Kai Sun Sea Products and Food Company Limited* the High Court of Hong Kong had to determine whether the arbitration was international for the purposes of Article 1(3)(b)(ii) of the

[25] *Official Records of the General Assembly Fifty-seventh Session,* Supplement N° 17 (A/57/17) at paras 173–177.

[26] See the Guide to Enactment at para 39.

[27] See Articles 1(3) and 1(4) of the MLICA (1985).

[28] See the Guide to Enactment at para 33.

MLICA. The case concerned a contract for the supply of soybean into China between two Hong Kong companies. The court found that although both parties were based in the same state (Hong Kong) the contract was still international because delivery, which was to take place outside of Hong Kong, was a 'substantial part of the obligations of the commercial relationship' and the contract was international for the purposes of the article.[29]

This case was affirmed by the High Court of Hong Kong is 1995 in *D Heung and Associates, Architects and Engineers v Pacific Enterprises (Holdings) Company Limite*d, another case concerning a contract between two Hong Kong companies. The plaintiff had been appointed by the defendant to design a project in Dongshan Island, China. The issue was whether the MLICA applied, despite the fact that both companies were from Hong Kong and the contract was to be partly performed there. The High Court held that it was an international agreement for the purposes of Article 1(3)(b)(ii) because the subject-matter of the dispute was most closely connected with the project in China and because a substantial part of the defendant's duties were related to the design and supervision of that project.[30]

The restriction of the Model Law to international conciliation is due to a number of factors. UNCITRAL's mandate has a cross-border focus and the Commission has repeatedly expressed a desire *not* to interfere in the domestic law of enacting states.[31] In addition states with existing domestic laws on conciliation may be reluctant to amend them, especially where they represent the culmination of substantial processes of consultation, debate, consensus and drafting, as was the case with the UMA in the United States. Accordingly by restricting the Model Law to international conciliations UNCITRAL intended to increase its attractiveness and utility among states. In the United States case the approach seems to have worked. The UMA was adopted in 2001 – one year before the MLICC was passed by the UN General Assembly. There was little motivation to adopt the MLICC as a basis for American domestic law but the view was taken that it could still be used as a basis for international mediation law. Accordingly an amendment was drafted and approved, the new 11 UMA, incorporating the MLICC into the UMA with three limitations: first the MLICC provision is optional, second it only applies to international conciliations and third the confidentiality provision (Article 10) of the MLICC is excluded.[32] The

29 *Fung Sang Trading Limited v Kai Sun Sea Products and Food Company Limited* [1991] HKCFI 93.

30 *D Heung and Associates, Architects and Engineers v Pacific Enterprises (Holdings) Company Limited. High Court of Hong Kong*, 04.05.1995, CLOUT case N° 108.

31 *Report of the Working Group on Arbitration on the Work of its Thirty-Third Session* (2000) UN Doc N° A/CN.9/485 paras 117–120, at www.uncitral.org/uncitral/en/commission/working_groups/2Arbitration.htm.

32 See National Conference of Commissioners on Uniform State Laws, *Amendment to the Uniform Mediation Act to Add an Article Regarding International Commercial*

amendment gives US states adopting the UMA the option of also adopting the provisions of the MLICC (apart from the confidentiality provisions) in relation to mediation of international disputes. Insofar as US states choose this option they will be creating a dual system for domestic and international mediation. In relation to confidentiality the UMA provisions (ss 4, 5 and 6), which impose a higher level of confidentiality, will apply to both domestic and international conciliations.[33]

The challenges inherent in separate sets of rules for international and domestic conciliation include the risk of litigation on the question of whether or not a conciliation is international.[34] Distinguishing international commerce from domestic can be especially difficult in federal States with substantial decentralised law-making such as the United States, Canada, Germany and Australia.[35] Where multiple parties are entangled in different disputes, both domestic and international, emanating from the same set of facts, it may be unnecessarily complex and contrived for conciliation of these disputes to be dealt with under different laws. Where one conciliation process is commenced with a view to dealing with the interrelated disputes, a conflict of applicable conciliation laws may emerge.

The Working Group was aware of potential confusion that could arise out of a dual system with different rules for domestic and international conciliation and envisaged that states may wish to use the Model Law as a basis for domestic and international regulation. As a result footnote 1 to Article 1(1) MLICC makes suggestions for adapting the MLICC for domestic application. To date a number of countries that have enacted the Model Law, in whole or in part, have used it as a basis for their domestic mediation laws, which in some cases were not well-developed prior to enactment. These countries include Albania, Afghanistan, Bosnia-Herzegovina, Canada, Croatia, Kosovo, Nicaragua, Russia, Serbia, Slovakia, Slovenia, Turkey, and in the United States, Washington DC, South Dakota, and Utah.[36]

Conciliation (2003) at www.law.upenn.edu/library/ulc/mediaticca/am03.pdf and www.law.upenn.edu/bll/archives/ulc/mediat/2003finaldraft.htm for the final version of the UMA.

33 See the discussion on confidentiality below. Note that the application of ss 4, 5 and 6 of the UMA is subject to s 3(c) according to which parties may agree that the mediation is not privileged at all.

34 The same issues arise in the case of international arbitration. On this point see E Ginkel, 'Reframing the Dilemma of Expanded Judicial Review: Arbitral Appeal Vacatur' (2003) 3 *Pepperdine Dispute Resolution Law Journal* 157 at 205–206.

35 See the Guide to Enactment at para 29 and the American mediation case of *Olam v Congress Mortgage Company* 68 F Supp 2d 1110, 1115 (ND Cal 1999) in which the underlying claims were a mix of federal and state law issues.

36 See Appendix C for details on the extent to which these countries have enacted the Model Law.

In the absence of uniform domestic and international regulation, Article 1(6) of the Model Law provides an opt-in provision whereby parties may deem the conciliation to be *international* in order to attract applicability of the Law. On a practical level the opt-in provision provides a mechanism to overcome potential difficulties associated with managing disputes involving domestic and cross-border elements – for example, complex multi-party disputes where domestic law may apply to one set of parties and the Model Law to a second set of parties.

As indicated previously, however, if parties can simply agree to the applicability of the Model Law it seems unnecessary to provide the option that they can also agree on the international nature of the conciliation. Ginkel suggests that the current drafting is a result of the historical fact that Article 1(3)(c) MLICA – a provision which creates a fiction about the location of the subject-matter of the dispute in relation to the definition of international – was the original model for Article 1(6).[37] Although the Working Group considered applying this concept to the MLICC early in their deliberations, its view changed in favour of creating a separate opt-in provision in the form of Article 1(6).[38] However not all changes in the conceptual framework of Article 1(6) were accompanied by changes in the language of the provision. Accordingly enacting states may wish to vary the wording of this provision by deleting the reference to the international nature of the conciliation, so that the section simply reads,

> This Law also applies to a commercial conciliation when the parties agree to the applicability of this Law.

Determining the internationality of a dispute resolution process can be challenging and complex. Many laws offer a positive definition of international, requiring criteria to be met before a conciliation can be recognised as such. As shown above, the MLICC takes this approach in Article 1(4) and (5). Ginkel favours a different approach, namely to define the term international negatively, that is an arbitration is international if it is not domestic.[39] Extending this

37 See Ginkel (2004), above note 4 at 18. See also Binder's criticism of parties' ability to agree that the conciliation is international in Article 1(6): Binder (2005), above note 3. On the interpretation of Article 1(3)(c) of the MLICA see *Explanatory Note by the UNCITRAL Secretariat on the Model Law on International Commercial Arbitration* at para 11.

38 For the Working Group's comments on this, see the *Settlement of commercial disputes, Model legislative provisions on international commercial conciliation: Note by the Secretariat* (19–30 November 2001) UN Doc N° A/CN.9/WG.II/WP.115 at 7, remark 13.

39 See Ginkel (2004), above note 4 at 18 referring to the English Arbitration Act 1996 as an example.

concept to the MLICC would not remove the duality problem but would arguably reduce the confusion about whether a particular conciliation was domestic or international in nature.

2.5 How is the Model Law Triggered?

The principle of party autonomy is the ultimate determining factor in relation to triggering the Model Law's application. In essence, the Model Law applies if the parties opt-in to the Law or once an international commercial conciliation has commenced.[40] Read as a whole, the Model Law treats the conciliation process as entirely voluntary with no duty to participate. Therefore if parties cannot agree on a time and place to conciliate, the application of the Model Law is not triggered. In such cases reference is made to the rules of private international law,[41] which may be of use where applicable domestic laws require attendance at, or consideration of, mediation. Potential litigation about mediation obligations in domestic law may prompt a reluctant party to commence conciliation, at which point the Model Law may be triggered.

The contentious nature of this aspect of the Model Law is reflected in the documentation of the Working Group sessions on the topic. Earlier drafts of the Model Law identified the *place of conciliation* as one of the main elements triggering its application.[42] In other words, if the place of international commercial conciliation was in the enacting state, then the Model Law would be *prima facie* applicable. Known as the *territorial factor*, this concept is based on Article 1(2) MLICA. Designed to increase certainty as to when the Model Law would apply, the territorial factor would have followed the parties' agreement in relation to the place of conciliation in the first instance. Failing the existence or enforceability of such agreement it would be left to conciliators to assist the parties in determining the place of conciliation. Subsequent drafts of the MLICC reflect the rise and fall of the territorial factor as a trigger for the operation of the Model Law and simultaneously the rise and rise of the principle of party autonomy.

In dismissing the need for the territoriality factor, the Commission highlighted fundamental differences between consensus-based and determinative dispute resolution processes. In contrast to arbitration, it considered that the flexibility of the conciliation process lent itself to process innovation and experimentation. Moreover the ubiquitous principle of party autonomy in the MLICC granted parties the freedom to participate in conciliation at will. Accordingly it was considered of no practical value to impose concepts linking the place of the conciliation to the applicable law.

40 Note also the opt-in provision of the Model Law discussed above.

41 On private international law, see Chapter 2.

42 See the *Draft Guide to Enactment and Use of the UNCITRAL Model Law on International Commercial Conciliation (2002)* UN Doc N° A/CN.9/WG.II/WP.116.

Finally Sekolec and Getty point out that an international conciliation is increasingly likely to take place in a number of different locations and/or electronically, making the place of conciliation an increasingly difficult factor to identify.[43]

However others argue that the absence of the territorial factor is a major weakness in the Model Law.[44] Their arguments centre on the complex relationships that exist among mediation, arbitration and domestic legal systems and the overriding need for certainty in applicable law rules. In numerous domestic jurisdictions, courts are frequently requested to make mediation referrals, to interpret mediation clauses and mediated outcomes and to consider the extent to which conciliation is protected by confidentiality and privilege. In all these situations it is vital to be able to determine the applicable law. In an MDR context, conciliation may be followed by determinative proceedings such as arbitration. Here clarity about the law that applies to a particular conciliation would help predict the place of a subsequent arbitration. With the growing practice of med–arb and other multi-tiered procedures a similar system for determining how the relevant conciliation and arbitration laws are triggered would likely increase clarity and certainty. Ginkel suggests that the MLICC should have provided that certain of its beneficial provisions – such as Articles 10, 12, 13 and 14 – apply to conciliations held abroad in order to enhance cross-border uniformity.[45] This approach has been successfully used in Article 1(2) MLICA with respect to arbitration. As a harmonising and unifying legal text it seems the MLICC may have missed an opportunity to set a standard in relation to applicable law.

3. ARTICLE 2

Article 2: Interpretation

1. In the interpretation of this Law, regard is to be had to its international origin and to the need to promote uniformity in its application and the observance of good faith.

43 Sekolec and Getty (2003), above note 11 at 187–188. See also *Report of the Working Group on Arbitration on the work of its thirty-fifth session,* (19-30 November 2001) UN Doc N° A/CN.9/506 at 18–21.

44 For a critical examination of the factors that led to the deletion of the territorial factor from the MLICC see Ginkel (2004), above note 4 at 13–15. Binder discusses these issues at 10–017–10–018: Binder (2005), above note 3. See also Deason's analysis of the applicable law dilemma in the United States: E Deason, 'Reply: The Quest For Uniformity In Mediation Confidentiality: Foolish Consistency Or Crucial Predictability?' (2001) 85 *Marquette Law Review* 79 at 95–101.

45 See Ginkel (2004), above note 4 at 14 and the Guide to Enactment at para 6.

2. Questions concerning matters governed by this Law which are not expressly settled in it are to be settled in conformity with the general principles on which this Law is based.

The aim of the MLICC is not only to achieve uniform legal provisions across borders; it also aspires to uniform meaning. This task becomes increasingly challenging as regulation of mediation at local, national and regional levels accelerates and overlapping spheres of regulation create potentially conflicting norms.

Article 2, which has many comparable provisions in UNCITRAL legislative texts, provides guidance to courts and other national or local authorities in their interpretation of the Model Law so that they give due regard to its international origin and limit the extent to which a uniform text would be interpreted by reference to local law.[46] The provision is also a signal to policy-makers and legislative drafters when enacting the Model Law to provide sufficient guidance, clarity and, if necessary, authority to those who will interpret the law as enacted domestically.

Article 2(2) deals with matters that the Model Law governs but which it does not clearly settle. The provision states that these matters are to be determined without resorting to domestic law, but rather in conformity with general principles of the Model Law itself; only if no relevant general principles can be identified should resort be made to local law. General principles underpinning the MLICC have been discussed in Chapter 8 and are also noted in the Guide to Enactment. They include desire for uniform law, harmonised solutions, party autonomy, active party involvement, process integrity, good faith, fair treatment, confidentiality, and diversity in terms of both process and outcome.[47]

Good faith has been identified as one of the general principles of the MLICC and also of the United Nations Convention on Contracts for the International Sale of Goods (CISG). A consideration of relevant case law relating to CISG may provide insights into its potential application to the MLICC. In a French case the court justified an order to one party to pay damages on the basis that that party's conduct was 'contrary to the principle of good faith in international trade laid down in Article 7 CISG'.[48] The court stated that abuse of process violates the good faith principle. In another case the *Bundesgerichtshof* (Federal Court) in Germany[49] held that the principle of good faith requires parties to cooperate with each other and exchange information

[46] See the Guide to Enactment at para 40.

[47] See the Guide to Enactment at para 41.

[48] See Cour d'appel Grenoble, France, 22 February 1995, CLOUT case N° 154.

[49] See the decision of the Federal Court (Bundesgerichtshof) VIII ZR 60/01 dated 31 October 2001 at III 3. Other cases on this point can be located on the CLOUT database accessible on the UNCITRAL website.

relevant for performance of their respective obligations. These judicial statements are consistent with fundamental mediation principles and dispute resolution objectives. The cases may be indicative of the direction of courts in relation to the Model Law.

The stated desire for uniform law and harmonised solutions, and the international origin of Article 2, support the use of case law from other jurisdictions to interpret comparable provisions. As is the case with arbitration, the CLOUT database containing case law and arbitral awards from around the world on UNCITRAL uniform texts, will assist nations to work towards a uniform interpretation and meaning with respect to the MLICC. Domestic courts of enacting states are encouraged to apply case law from around the world as a guideline, a type of non-binding precedent, to disputes involving the MLICC. As indicated previously, such an approach attempts to restrict the extent to which the enacted Model Law is interpreted according to local law.[50] At the time of writing, no case law on the MLICC is available on CLOUT, reflecting the still early days in the life of the Model Law.

4. Article 3

> **Article 3: Variation by agreement**
> Except for the provisions of Article 2 and Article 6, paragraph 3, the parties may agree to exclude or vary any of the provisions of this Law.

Article 3 addresses the diversity–consistency issue, seeking to strike a balance between, on one hand, encouraging flexibility and diversity by preserving party autonomy and, on the other, protecting the integrity of the conciliation process by anchoring the fair treatment principle in all conciliations. The following commentary considers the principle of party autonomy, the nature of default and mandatory provisions and a number of drafting points.

4.1 Party Autonomy

By enacting the principle of party autonomy in a separate provision the Model Law drafters highlight its importance for the overall interpretation of the Law. As indicated in Chapter 8, Article 3 states that the parties may agree to vary any of the provisions of the Model Law subject to two exceptions, which are discussed below. It therefore asserts the principle of party autonomy and recognises conciliation as a process based on the central value of the will of the parties. In doing so Article 3 establishes the *default* nature of the Model Law. Articles 1(6) and 1(7) further contribute to the prominent role of party autonomy

[50] See the Guide to Enactment at para 40.

in the Model Law.[51] Criticisms of the overriding role of party autonomy have been addressed previously.[52]

4.2 The Exceptions

The two exceptions to the party autonomy principle relate to the interpretation of the Model Law (Article 2) and the principle of fair treatment in the conciliation process (Article 6(3)). These provisions take on a mandatory nature.

The first exception in Article 2 is directed to enacting states and in particular their courts and tribunals. It sets out guidelines for the interpretation of the Model Law and has been examined previously. The mandatory nature of this provision aims to ensure that courts do not vary the interpretation of the Model Law according to local laws and policies as such an approach would defeat the very purpose of a uniform legislative text.

The second exception relates to fair treatment of the parties. Article 6(3) sets a mandatory minimum standard for fair process in conciliation, which may have implications for professional standards and duties of conciliators and the enforceability of settlements reached through conciliation. Article 6(3) is examined later in the chapter.

4.3 Mandatory and Default Provisions

The distinction between default and mandatory provisions and its implications has been canvassed in Chapter 2 and is not repeated here. As indicated in that chapter there is a correlation between the function of regulatory provisions and the mandatory–default distinction that may provide guidance for enacting states drafting policy and legislation.[53]

The Model Law has been criticised for its failure to set mandatory requirements in relation to the beneficial rules it contains, that is rules relating to legal rights and obligations of conciliation participants.[54] Laws relating to confidentiality provide a typical example of beneficial rules which can provide consistent evidentiary protection with respect to disclosures made during conciliation only if imbued with a mandatory character.[55] Further examples in relation to the Model Law and other regulatory instruments are provided in Chapter 2. Enacting states are advised to consider the implications of mandatory

51 On party autonomy generally, see Chapters 1 and 8.

52 On Articles 1(6) and 1(7) see the commentary on Article 1. For a critique of the Model Law, see Chapter 8.

53 For an explanation of the relationship of function to the mandatory–default distinction, see Diagram 1 in Chapter 2 and the related discussion.

54 For a definition of beneficial and other types of rules, see Chapter 2.

55 See the criticisms of the Model Law outlined in Chapter 8 and Ginkel (2004), above note 4 at 8 et seq. On this point, see also the section on confidentiality in Chapter 6.

and default regulation in relation to all aspects of mediation subject to legislation. The mediation mix introduced in Chapter 2 provides both a methodology and a tool for policy makers and drafters to do so.

4.4 Drafting Points

Two drafting points arise in relation to the wording of Article 3. The phrase 'unless otherwise agreed', which highlights the party autonomy principle, is found in various but not all provisions of the Model Law. The result is potential confusion in relation to the distinction between mandatory and default provisions. Questions may arise as to whether Article 3 still applies to provisions in which the phrase does not appear. The wording of Article 3 referring to the parties' power to 'exclude or vary *any* provisions of this Law'[56] suggests an affirmative answer to this question, as does the commentary in the Guide to Enactment.[57] In other words, subject to the two express exceptions, Article 3 applies to the entire Model Law whether or not the phrase 'unless otherwise agreed' is present. Enacting states may consider redrafting these provisions for consistency either by removing the phrase 'unless otherwise agreed' or else applying it consistently throughout the Model Law text.

In the context of multi-party disputes a question may arise as to whether or not all parties must agree in order to exclude or vary a provision of the Model Law. The current wording in Article 3 that 'the parties may agree' contrasts with an equivalent provision in Article 1 International Chamber of Commerce (ICC) ADR Rules, which refers to 'all of the parties'. However the general principles of party autonomy and fair treatment in the Model Law suggest that the agreement of all parties is required. Enacting states may consider using the formulation in the ICC ADR Rules should there be any concern about ambiguity.

5. ARTICLE 4

Article 4: Commencement of conciliation proceedings[3]

1. Conciliation proceedings in respect of a dispute that has arisen commence on the day on which the parties to that dispute agree to engage in conciliation proceedings.
2. If a party that invited another party to conciliate does not receive an acceptance of the invitation within thirty days from the day on which the invitation was sent, or within such other period of time as specified in the

56 Emphasis added to quote.

57 See the Guide to Enactment at para 42. See a similar discussion in relation to Article 1(8) above.

invitation, the party may elect to treat this as a rejection of the invitation to conciliate.

[Footnote to Article 4]

[3] The following text is suggested for States that might wish to adopt a provision on the suspension of the limitation period:

Article X: Suspension of limitation period

(1) When the conciliation proceedings commence, the running of the limitation period regarding the claim that is the subject matter of the conciliation is suspended.
(2) Where the conciliation proceedings have terminated without a settlement agreement, the limitation period resumes running from the time the conciliation ended without a settlement agreement.

Article 4 provides guidance as to when a conciliation process can be understood to have commenced.[58] This is important for a number of reasons. It determines at which point provisions relating to confidentiality and evidentiary protection of information disclosed in mediation begin to run. It also determines, where applicable, the point at which the suspension of the limitation period for legal claims would operate. After some general comments about Article 4, the commentary outlines the different paths to conciliation that are covered by the law, and how the article deals with obligations to conciliate, timeframes for acceptance of offers to conciliate and withdrawal of such offers.

5.1 There are Many Paths to Conciliation

Article 4(1) is to be read and understood in connection with Article 1(8). As explained previously the latter provision provides for application of the Model Law irrespective of how the conciliation is initiated, that is, by agreement or by direction of a court, arbitral or other tribunal or government authority. The Guide to Enactment highlights two common examples of how mediations covered by the Model Law may be initiated: first, when a party extends a verbal or written offer to the other which is subsequently accepted, and secondly, where the parties accept or implement a direction or recommendation by a court, tribunal or other body to conciliate their dispute. The offer and acceptance scenario manifests itself in two primary ways: a pre-existing agreement to conciliate, typically in the form of a dispute resolution clause in a commercial contract, and a post-dispute agreement to conciliate.[59]

The absence of a writing requirement reflects a broad understanding of contract law and accommodates the diversity of domestic legal systems around

[58] See the Guide to Enactment at para 43.

[59] The question as to if and when the parties agreed to conciliate is a question of evidence to be decided according to domestic law.

the world in relation to the validity and enforceability of agreements to mediate.[60] It also means that cross-border parties verbally entering into an *ad hoc* and informal conciliation may technically find themselves subject to the Model Law.[61]

5.2 The Effect of Article 4 on Obligations to Conciliate

As explained previously, while the Model Law acknowledges that parties may have legal obligations to mediate, it does not seek not enforce such obligations.[62] Rather, it leaves issues relating to parties' failure to fulfil statutory, contractual or other obligations to conciliate and the enforcement of such to applicable domestic law and provides that conciliation proceedings – under the Model Law – do not commence until the parties agree *to engage* in conciliation proceedings. This interpretation highlights the overarching importance of the party autonomy principle and is consistent with a whole text reading of the Model Law including Article 11, which permits parties to terminate mediation at any time.

Article 4 contrasts with institutional ADR rules that honour the premise of party autonomy while requiring parties to attend at least one mediation session. Examples can be found in Article 3(b) CPR Mediation Procedure, Article 18 WIPO Rules and Articles 5(1) and 6(1)(b) of the ICC ADR Rules. Here the notion of party autonomy acknowledges that parties have contractually bound themselves to attend mediation by agreeing to the application of relevant institutional rules. The Model Law may have benefited from a *one meeting requirement*.[63]

5.3 Time-Frame for Acceptance of Offer to Conciliate

Article 4(2) deals with situations where one party extends an invitation to the other to engage in conciliation in an attempt to settle their dispute and seems to refer to post-dispute offers of conciliation only. Drawing on Article 2 UNCITRAL Conciliation Rules it provides that a receiving party has 30 days from the date of sending an invitation to conciliate to accept, after which the invitation is taken to have been refused. Consistent with the principle of party autonomy and the default nature of Article 4, the provision specifically states

60 On writing requirements in agreements to mediate, see Chapter 4.

61 See the reference to dinner party mediation in the interview with the former Secretary of UNCITRAL in Chapter 8.

62 In relation to this point, see also the commentary on Article 1(8) above. On mandatory referrals to mediation, see Chapter 3 and on the enforceability of mediation clauses, see Chapter 4.

63 Ginkel points out that inserting the one meeting requirement would also require Articles 5 and 11 of the MLICC to be modified: Ginkel (2004), above note 4 at 27.

that the inviting party may specify a different time-frame – presumably to accommodate particular procedural needs of the parties.

Where prior to a dispute arising parties had concluded a general agreement to conciliate in respect of future disputes and upon a dispute arising one party no longer wishes to conciliate, Article 4(2) cannot to be used to allow that party an opportunity to disregard contractual obligations under applicable domestic law simply by not responding to the invitation to conciliate within 30 days. The domestic obligation remains and can be pursued through appropriate channels where remedies may vary considerably.

Nevertheless this provision remains susceptible to abuse of power by parties attempting to take advantage of the party autonomy focus in Article 4(2) to avoid conciliation. The default nature of the article means that parties maintain the option of contracting out of it. However doing so presupposes that they have put their minds to the issues potentially arising out of Article 4 in advance of the conciliation and the dispute and agreed to deal with initiation of conciliation in a different manner.

5.4 Withdrawal of Offer

Article 4 does not deal specifically with a party's ability to withdraw an offer to conciliate. In light of the fact that either party may terminate conciliation at any time (Article 11(d)) it would be superfluous. In addition UNCITRAL took the view that to include such a provision in the Model Law could unduly interfere with the domestic law of offer and acceptance in some countries.[64]

6. ARTICLE X

[Footnote to Article 4]

[3] The following text is suggested for States that might wish to adopt a provision on the suspension of the limitation period:

Article X: Suspension of limitation period

(1) When the conciliation proceedings commence, the running of the limitation period regarding the claim that is the subject matter of the conciliation is suspended.

(2) Where the conciliation proceedings have terminated without a settlement agreement, the limitation period resumes running from the time the conciliation ended without a settlement agreement.

The footnote to Article 4 sets out an optional Article X which provides for suspension of limitation periods for legal claims related to the subject-matter of

64 See the Guide to Enactment at para 47.

the conciliation for the duration of the conciliation.[65] The designation of the article as optional and the decision to include it as a footnote to the Model Law represents a compromise of differing opinions and reflects the strong debates surrounding the status of its inclusion in the Model Law.

The effect of conciliation proceedings on the running of litigation and arbitral limitation periods has been addressed in Chapter 7. While the Commission recognised that the main advantage to including such a provision in the Model Law would be the preservation of parties' legal rights during conciliation,[66] the inclusion of such a provision in the main text of the Model Law was controversial for the following reasons.

First the Model Law provisions relating to commencement and termination leave much scope for variation by parties and for different approaches to interpretation by domestic courts. Therefore the view was taken by some members of the Working Group that it might be difficult to determine with any certainty precise dates for the start and completion of conciliations during which the limitation period would be suspended. Thus a more precise definition of commencement and cessation in relation to conciliation may have swayed certain Working Group members to include Article X in the main body of the Model Law.[67]

Moreover it was considered that litigation limitation provisions might require changes to domestic civil procedural rules, which could give rise to 'complex technical issues'[68] and discourage enacting states from adopting the Model Law. For example a distinction is made between jurisdictions that provide for the interruption[69] of limitation periods, those that provide for their suspension and those that have no regulations in this regard. The different legal implications of these approaches could conceivably cause more confusion than certainty in cross-border mediations.

Finally the view was articulated that Article X was unnecessary because it many jurisdictions it was open to the parties to preserve their legal rights through other means such as:

65 On the suspension of limitation periods generally, see Chapter 7.

66 See also Article 13 on the preservation of parties' rights. For a critical perspective see Sanders who suggests that the placement of Article X in the text rather than in a footnote would have enhanced the utility of the Model Law and the attractiveness of conciliation for potential participants: Sanders (2004), above note 5 at 212.

67 See *Report of the Working Group on Arbitration on the work of its thirty-fifth session* (19-30 November 2001) UN Doc N° A/CN.9/506 at para 93.

68 See the Guide to Enactment at para 48.

69 As indicated in Chapter 7, interruption refers to the situation where once the limitation period has been interrupted by conciliation, the limitation period would run again from the beginning once the conciliation had ended.

- special forms of contract, by which parties agree to extend the limitation period for a claim; and
- the commencement of arbitral or court proceedings with the aim of suspending the running of the limitation period.[70]

In this regard Article 13 of the Model Law specifically provides that parties may initiate arbitral or judicial proceedings to the extent that it is necessary to preserve their legal rights and this will not affect their agreement to conciliate. However the initiation of formal determinative proceedings for the sole purpose of extending the limitation period may involve unnecessary expense and effort that potentially steers parties away from collaborative attempts to resolve their differences and encourages them to focus on legal positions and adversarial claims.

7. ARTICLE 5

Article 5: Number and appointment of conciliators

1. There shall be one conciliator, unless the parties agree that there shall be two or more conciliators.
2. The parties shall endeavour to reach agreement on a conciliator or conciliators, unless a different procedure for their appointment has been agreed upon.
3. Parties may seek the assistance of an institution or person in connection with the appointment of conciliators. In particular:
   a. A party may request such an institution or person to recommend suitable persons to act as conciliator; or
   b. The parties may agree that the appointment of one or more conciliators be made directly by such an institution or person.
4. In recommending or appointing individuals to act as conciliator, the institution or person shall have regard to such considerations as are likely to secure the appointment of an independent and impartial conciliator and, where appropriate, shall take into account the advisability of appointing a conciliator of a nationality other than the nationalities of the parties.
5. When a person is approached in connection with his or her possible appointment as conciliator, he or she shall disclose any circumstances likely to give rise to justifiable doubts as to his or her impartiality or independence. A conciliator, from the time of his or her appointment and throughout the conciliation proceedings, shall without delay disclose any such circumstances to the parties unless they have already been informed of them by him or her.

70 Guide to Enactment at para 48.

Article 5 provides procedural guidelines for the appointment of conciliators. It deals with the number of conciliators and their appointment, including criteria for selection. The provision also deals with disclosure of potential conflicts of interest by conciliators.

7.1 Appointment and Number of Conciliators

Article 5(1) recognises the default practice of appointing one conciliator only, while allowing parties to agree on a different number. This differs from the practice in international commercial arbitration where, in the absence of parties agreeing on one or three arbitrators, the default arrangement involves three arbitrators.[71]

Article 5(2) requires parties to negotiate the terms of the process such as number and selection of the conciliator/s before engaging with the substantive aspects of the conciliation. In this way the concepts of collaboration and consensus in conciliation are encouraged before its commencement. Negotiating the process prior to negotiating the substance of a dispute is a well-known interest-based strategy used in mediation. As parties develop confidence in bargaining with each other on matters not at the core of their dispute, they can begin to create a constructive working atmosphere and a climate of collaboration. There is, however, no fall-back procedure should parties not reach consensus on conciliator selection.[72] Here reference to institutional rules discussed below may be useful.

Despite the terms of Article 5(2) it is possible, and even likely, that parties familiar with international arbitration will continue to adopt appointment methods typically used for arbitration, such as joint appointment of one independent arbitrator followed by party appointments of second and third arbitrators. Surprisingly the Guide to Enactment encourages this type of appointment procedure for conciliation, suggesting that it may be efficient and that party-appointed conciliators would be well-placed to 'clarify the positions of the parties and thereby enhance the likelihood of settlement'.[73] However conciliators appointed in this manner are more likely to adopt partisan positions in conciliation and promote these to the third conciliator, thereby creating a process akin to neutral evaluation[74] rather than a facilitative process. While facilitative and advisory dispute resolution processes fall within the Model

[71] See Article 10(2) of the MLICA and Article 5 of the UNCITRAL Arbitration Rules (1976) (UAR).

[72] See Sander's comments in relation to this provision on what he sees as a gap in the Model Law. Given the lack of a requirement for a first meeting in conciliation, he views the risk of conciliations falling apart as significant: Sanders (2004), above note 5 at 215 et seq.

[73] See the Guide to Enactment at para 50.

[74] For an explanation of neutral evaluation, see Chapter 1.

Law's scope, a significant theme underpinning the Law is the promotion of conciliation as a facilitative process which seeks outcomes based on interests rather than purely on rights.[75] The use of a typical arbitration appointment procedure for conciliators reflects an over-reliance on familiar arbitration procedures and a flawed understanding of interest-based approaches to conciliation.[76] At the very least it is incomplete and misleading as it promotes advisory forms of dispute resolution over facilitative processes.

Preferable procedures for conciliator appointments can be found in mediation rules of various dispute resolution organisations such as the ICC, London Court of International Arbitration (LCIA), Stockholm Chamber of Commerce, World Intellectual Property Organisation (WIPO) and others represented in the Comparative Table of International Mediation Rules in Appendix B. Generally they involve mediators being appointed in the first place by the agreement of all parties and, if no such agreement is forthcoming, then on the advice or nomination of the selected dispute resolution institution. This approach ensures that a conciliator will be appointed in any event and covers the gap left by the Model Law in Article 5(2) where parties cannot agree on a single conciliator or a panel. Sometimes the dispute resolution institution submits a list of potential conciliators to parties from which they may select their preferences and these form the basis for initial discussions between them.

Procedural matters such as appointment of conciliators deal with the internal process aspects of conciliation and are adequately regulated by institutional rules and contract law.[77] Therefore it is no surprise that virtually all international mediation rules contain provisions on appointment procedure.

Article 5(3) provides that parties may seek assistance from an 'institution or person'. This may take the form of a request to a dispute resolution institution to recommend potential conciliators (Article 5(3)(a)) or to appoint them directly (Article 5(3)(b)). As explained in Chapter 1 dispute resolution institutions offer services in relation to the management and co-ordination of conciliation. In addition they offer to supply conciliators with a track record of independent and impartial performance – a key criterion in conciliator selection.

Article 5(4) sets out a number of considerations to be taken into account when appointing conciliators. Here the emphasis is on promoting conciliators who are, and are perceived to be, impartial and independent. To this end, one suggestion contained in the provision is the appointment of conciliators of nationalities other than those of the parties. The requirement of impartiality

75 See the Guide to Enactment at para 6.

76 On the fundamental differences between arbitration and mediation, see Chapter 1.

77 One may question the necessity of regulating these matters in the Model Law itself. On the regulation of procedural aspects of mediation, see Chapter 2 and See F Steffek, 'Mediation in Europa und der Welt' (2009) 1 *Zeitschrift für Konfliktmanagement* 21 at 23.

and independence on the part of a mediator is consistent with the requirement of fair treatment in Article 6(3).

The Model Law does not require conciliators to possess formal qualifications, but as explained in Chapter 3 this aspect of conciliation is increasingly regulated through domestic legislation and other standards. Local, national and international mediator accreditation initiatives play an important role here. Typically the administering dispute resolution body will require that conciliators meet certain accreditation and conduct standards. It is essential to ensure that any institutional standards are consistent with mandatory national law on the topic.

Finally the 'institution or person' that is the appointing authority in Article 5(3) and 5(4) is not defined in the MLICC. It is left to the enacting state to regulate the recognition of such bodies if it desires. Parties will need to ensure that their dispute resolution administering body meets any requirements set by national law. In a time of rapid expansion and regulation of the field, it may not always be a straightforward matter to determine the law applicable to the conciliation and therefore to the appointment of conciliators from recognised dispute resolution bodies.

7.2 Duty of Disclosure

Article 5(5) imposes an obligation on a conciliator to disclose 'any circumstances likely to give rise to justifiable doubts as to his or her impartiality or independence'. As with most contemporary mediation standards the duty begins before commencement of conciliation and continues throughout it.[78]

The principle of *justifiable doubts* in relation to impartiality does not have an equivalent in contemporary ethical standards for mediators. Rather the concept seems to have entered the MLICC from the world of arbitration and the MLICA. However, unlike in UNCITRAL's Model Law on Arbitration and Arbitration Rules,[79] there is no specific MLICC provision that allows the appointment of conciliators to be challenged on the basis of justifiable doubts as to independence and impartiality. This may not be of practical significance in a process which the parties can abandon at any time.

Article 5(5) contains no definition of justifiable doubts. As Chapter 5 shows, other mediation standards use language such as '[matters that] a reasonable individual would consider likely to affect the impartiality of the mediator'[80] and 'potential conflicts of interest that are reasonably known to the

[78] See, for example, Article 2.1 of the European Code of Conduct and the disclosure provisions in the Comparative Table of International Mediation Rules in Appendix B. On the duty of disclosure, see Chapter 5.
[79] See Article 10(2) of the MLICA and Article 10 of the UAR.
[80] See s 9(a)(1) of the UMA.

mediator'.[81] In the final analysis there may be considerable overlap among the different terminologies in terms of impact.

Ginkel asserts that there is little difference between ethical standards as they apply to conciliators and arbitrators.[82] This view is supported by the fact that case law examples of situations that may create justifiable doubt of arbitrator impartiality are similar to legislative illustrations of matters potentially affecting mediator impartiality and requiring disclosure. The European Code of Conduct for Mediators provides the following examples in Article 2.1: any personal or business relationship with one of the parties, any financial or other interest in the outcome of the mediation, and the mediator or a member of his or her firm having acted in any capacity other than mediator for one of the parties.

Unlike many equivalent regulatory provisions,[83] Article 5(5) places no duty on conciliators to withdraw from conciliation or obtain permission from parties to continue where there is justifiable doubt as to their impartiality or independence. This void is arguably addressed by the mandatory requirement of fair treatment in Article 6(3) MLICC. It is difficult to see how a conciliator, having disclosed sufficiently serious matters as to raise a justifiable doubt as to his or her impartiality or independence, could treat parties fairly in mediation. The party autonomy principle provides yet another safeguard, allowing parties to leave the process if not satisfied with the mediator.

Finally Article 5(5) makes no statement about consequences that might flow from failure to make appropriate disclosure, for example, whether non-disclosures might have an impact on mediated settlements or remove mediators' claims to privilege as in s 9(2)(d) of the UMA. This is left to applicable domestic law.

8. ARTICLE 6

Article 6: Conduct of conciliation

1. The parties are free to agree, by reference to a set of rules or otherwise, on the manner in which the conciliation is to be conducted.
2. Failing agreement on the manner in which the conciliation is to be conducted, the conciliator may conduct the conciliation proceedings in such a manner as the conciliator considers appropriate, taking into account the circumstances of the case, any wishes that the parties may express and the need for a speedy settlement of the dispute.

[81] See Standard III(C) Model Standards of Conduct for Mediators (US, AAA, ABA and ACR) at www.mediate.com/pdf/ModelStandardsofConductforMediatorsfinal05.pdf.

[82] See Ginkel (2004), above note 4 at 33.

[83] See, for example, Article 2.1 of the European Code of Conduct for Mediators, s 9 of the UMA as discussed in Chapter 5 on disclosure.

3. In any case, in conducting the proceedings, the conciliator shall seek to maintain fair treatment of the parties and, in so doing, shall take into account the circumstances of the case.
4. The conciliator may, at any stage of the conciliation proceedings, make proposals for a settlement of the dispute.

Article 6 deals with the conciliation process and the roles of the conciliator and the parties in this regard. It also contains the mandatory requirement relating to fair treatment of the parties.

8.1 Conduct of Conciliation Process

Article 6(1) states that the parties are free to agree on the manner in which the conciliation will be conducted, confirming the principle of party autonomy and the flexible nature of the process. Thus the parties may negotiate the procedure themselves or with the assistance of their lawyers, the conciliator or others. Alternatively they may agree on procedural details by reference to an existing set of rules or code of conduct.[84] The important role of the conciliator in shaping the conciliation process is recognised in Article 6(2). To the extent that parties do not agree on how the process will be conducted, these decisions are left to the conciliators who must take into account parties' wishes, their professional judgment of what is appropriate in the circumstances and the 'need for a speedy settlement'. The last factor highlights the service-delivery objective of mediation, which is frequently present in commercial and court-related dispute resolution programs.[85] Thus conciliators are given potentially high levels of discretion in relation to process decisions, an approach which promotes diversity in practice. Similar provisions can be found in many institutional rules, as the Comparative Table in Appendix B shows.

Articles 6(1) and (2) – unlike Article 6(3) below – take the form of default provisions. However Ginkel suggests that these two paragraphs are, by their very nature, mandatory. He argues that as the primary principle underpinning the Model Law is party autonomy then, subject to Article 1(7) allowing parties to opt out of the entire law, Article 6(1) establishing party autonomy in relation to the manner in which the process is to be conducted should be read as mandatory, as should the default rule in Article 6(2). As a matter of practice, party autonomy under terms of the Model Law means that parties may abandon the process at will and are not bound to attend even an initial meeting. Therefore arguments about the precise nature of these provisions in their current form may prove to be without practical impact.

84 See the Comparative Table of International Mediation Rules in Appendix B.
85 On the objectives of mediation, see Chapter 1.

8.2 Fair Treatment

Article 6(3) sets out the mandatory obligation on the part of conciliators to treat parties fairly, taking into account the circumstances of the case. This is an important provision for a number of reasons. It sets a minimum standard and basic obligation for conciliators, namely to conduct the process fairly.[86] Further, in so far as the parties do not exclude the applicability of the entire Model Law as permitted by Article 1(7), they cannot contract out of this provision.

The requirement of fair treatment flows from the notions of independence and impartiality in Article 5 MLICC.[87] In conjunction with Article 5(5) this provision demands a high level of transparency on the part of conciliators, which should encourage participants to develop trust in conciliators to conduct a fair and impartial process. As a practical illustration, the Guide to Enactment states that the duty of fair treatment does *not* require that conciliators spend exactly the same amount of time with the various parties in separate meetings, rather it requires that the manner in which separate sessions are conducted affects neither conciliators' impartiality nor parties' perception thereof.

Furthermore the Guide to Enactment emphasises that fair treatment refers to the process and not to the outcome of the dispute.[88] This approach is consistent with western mediation theory, according to which mediators control the process and parties the outcome of the dispute. Sekolec and Getty explain that there is neither a standard for measuring the fairness of outcomes in the Model Law nor in general contract law.[89] Fairness in procedure, however, is a principle with a long legal history. In other contexts it takes the form of due process,[90] procedural fairness and integrity, natural justice or good faith.

86 See the Guide to Enactment at para 55.

87 While Article 1(3) does not specify that dispute resolution practitioners must be neutral, independent or impartial, the Guide to Enactment refers to an 'impartial and independent third party'. On the deletion of references to 'independent' and 'impartial' in the earlier drafts of the Model Law, see the *Settlement of commercial disputes, Model legislative provisions on international commercial conciliation: Note by the Secretariat* (19–30 November 2001) UN Doc N° A/CN.9/WG.II/WP.115 at para 10 and the *Report of the Working Group* UN Doc N° A/CN.9/506 at para 29.

88 See Guide to Enactment at para 55. See also *Official Records of the General Assembly Fifty-seventh Session*, Supplement N° 17 (A/57/17) para 158.

89 See Sekolec and Getty (2003), above note 11 at 186.

90 Natural justice is known in the US as due process: F Dutile, 'Law and Governance Affecting the Resolution of Academic and Disciplinary Disputes at Scottish Universities: An American Perspective' (1997) 8 *Indiana International and Comparative Law Review* 1 at 54.

Consequences of breach are not spelled out in the MLICC and therefore reference will need to be made to applicable domestic law in this regard.[91]

8.3 Conciliators May Make Settlement Proposals

Article 6(4) states that conciliators may make proposals for the settlement of disputes in the course of a conciliation. Although criticised by facilitative mediators, this provision is consistent with the broad definition of conciliation in Article 1(3) MLICC which extends to facilitative and advisory dispute resolution processes. It confirms that conciliators are entitled to use a variety of interventions, including advisory techniques.[92] Parties are able to vary the terms of this default provision if they wish, for example to require mediators to comply with a facilitative standard. As indicated in Chapter 3, institutional rules and domestic legislation vary on this point with some provisions[93] reflecting the approach of the MLICC and others prohibiting mediators from making proposals for settlement or giving advice on the merits of a case.[94] In addition numerous rules and legislation are silent on the point, leaving the matter to the relevant codes of conduct or to the discretion of the mediator.[95]

8.4 Code of Mediator Ethics

During the planning and drafting of the Model Law, UNCITRAL referred to the Working Group the idea of a code of mediation ethics, the aim of which would be to build confidence in the conciliation process by distilling principles and precedents from the best traditions and openly enunciating standards of practice.[96] The Working Group considered the matter and ultimately decided that, apart from the mandatory core standard of fair treatment in Article 6(3) and a small number of default provisions such as Article 6(4), standards would generally be better dealt with in the form of a regulatory code of conduct on a

91 On the mediator's duty to be impartial and consequences for breach thereof, see Chapter 5.

92 On different mediation models, see Chapter 1.

93 See, for example, Article 7(4) UCR.

94 See, for example, r 20 of the Chicago International Dispute Resolution Association (CIDRA) Mediation Rules. The Australian National Mediator Practice Standards provide that mediators can provide neither legal advice nor assistance of a counselling nature. However advice may be provided in blended processes if certain conditions are met: see ss 3(4)(g)(i) and 10(3) and (5)) of the Standards.

95 See, for example, Netherlands Mediation Institute (NMI) Mediation Rules (2008).

96 See *Report of the United Nations Commission on International Trade Law on its thirty-second session* (20-31 March 2000) UN Doc N° A/CN.9/468 paras 56-59.

national or regional basis such as the European Code of Conduct for Mediators.[97]

9. ARTICLE 7

Article 7: Communication between conciliator and parties
The conciliator may meet or communicate with the parties together or with each of them separately.

Article 7 establishes the presumption that conciliators are free to employ the common conciliation technique of meeting with parties either together or separately. This is usual practice in most models of commercial mediation practice and is included in numerous institutional rules.[98] In American nomenclature this technique is called caucusing; in jurisdictions such as Australia it referred to as conducting private sessions or separate meetings. Private sessions may occur before, and at any time during, the mediation.

Private sessions highlight a critical distinction between mediation and arbitration, namely the nature of decision-making. As discussed in Chapter 1 arbitration is a determinative process with arbitrators making final and binding decisions which affect parties' rights, while mediation is a consensus-based system with mediators facilitating the process and possessing no decision-making power in relation to the substantive outcome of a dispute. Procedural guarantees in arbitration, such as the prohibition of private sessions with one party, the right of parties to respond to all evidence provided by the other party and the corresponding duty of arbitrators to disclose all information received by one party to the other, do not necessarily apply to non-determinative processes such as mediation.[99] As mediators do not possess decision-making power, the use of private sessions of itself does not infringe the principle of fair treatment enshrined in Article 6(3) of the Model Law.[100]

9.1 Procedure and Practice

As discussed earlier in relation to Article 5, the Model Law recognises the general practice of appointing one mediator only but makes provision for parties to appoint a different number. Where more than one mediator is conducting the process there may be different practices in relation to mediator attendance at private sessions. One approach requires all mediators to attend all mediation

[97] On different regulatory forms, see Chapter 2.

[98] See the Comparative Table of International Mediation Rules in Appendix B.

[99] See the Guide to Enactment at para 9.

[100] There are however concerns about med–arb practitioners who conduct private sessions. See the discussion in Chapter 3.

sessions whether joint or private. This practice seeks to assist the mediators build rapport and trust with all parties and prevents perceptions of impartiality emerging. In relation to MDR procedures such as med–arb, Chapter 3 shows that complex issues of procedural fairness may arise with respect to private sessions. Here a number of creative approaches have developed including identifying those med–arb practitioners from the panel who will conduct the arbitration phase of the process should it eventuate and prohibiting them from taking part in private sessions during the mediation phase. Thus in a med–arb situation with a panel of three med–arb practitioners, one may conduct private sessions during the mediation while the other two take a break. In the event that no agreement is reached during mediation, the two med–arb practitioners who did not take part in the private mediation sessions may continue and conduct the arbitration and the third panel member who conducted the private sessions retires from the process. Another approach is *med–arb simultanés*,[101] which involves parallel mediation and arbitration processes with different dispute resolution practitioners. Yet another possibility for parties is to contract out of Article 7 and only permit joint sessions in the mediation phase of an MDR process.[102]

9.2 Three Articles on Confidentiality

Three kinds of confidentiality in relation to mediation have been previously identified in this book: insider/insider, insider/outsider and insider/court confidentiality.[103] Articles 8, 9 and 10 regulate each of these in turn. The Model Law provisions relating to confidentiality are all default in nature so that parties are free to vary their terms. Given the significant role of confidentiality in mediation and the need to offer parties a certain level of regulatory certainty in cross-border mediation, this aspect of the Model Law has been the subject of criticism, explored in Chapter 8. The commentaries on Articles 8, 9 and 10 assume an understanding of the principles of confidentiality.

10. ARTICLE 8

> **Article 8: Disclosure of information**
> When the conciliator receives information concerning the dispute from a party, the conciliator may disclose the substance of that information to any other party to the conciliation. However, when a party gives any information to the

[101] In relation to this process, see the website of the French dispute resolution organisation, CMAP: www.cmap.fr.

[102] See also Articles 6(1) and 6(2) of the MLICC which deal with decisions about the conduct of the process.

[103] See Chapter 6 on the three kinds of confidentiality in mediation.

> conciliator, subject to a specific condition that it be kept confidential, that information shall not be disclosed to any other party to the conciliation.

Article 8 deals with insider/ insider confidentiality. It concerns the flow of information within conciliation, particularly as it relates to private sessions with the conciliator (see Article 7). Specifically the article provides that any information a party gives to a conciliator may be disclosed to the other party, unless the party providing the information specifically requests otherwise. This approach draws on Article 10 UCR and is called the open communication model. It is to be distinguished from the in-confidence model according to which all information is treated as confidential unless the relevant party decides otherwise.[104]

As with other provisions of the Model Law (such as Article 6(2)), Article 8 provides another example of the broad discretion granted to conciliators. As a matter of practice conciliators may disclose information from private sessions to other mediation participants where they believe it will assist the parties in reaching settlement. They have, however, no duty to disclose such information. By contrast Article 10 UCR uses the word 'must', as opposed to the MLICC 'may', thereby requiring the conciliator to disclose information revealed by one party to the other. The UCR wording appears to derive from natural justice principles applicable to determinative process in which parties must be given the opportunity to respond to submissions made by the other side. As discussed earlier, a different set of natural justice standards is more appropriate for facilitative and advisory dispute resolution processes.

In the Working Group discussions certain countries viewed the open-communication model of Article 8 as outdated and inconsistent with their own approach. They considered a requirement that the conciliator maintain strict confidentiality in relation to private session information, the in-confidence approach, as the better way of ensuring frankness and openness in mediation communications in the conciliation process.[105]

Managing the disclosure of information from private sessions is an internal mediation process issue and therefore usually left to the discretion of mediators or covered in procedural rules rather than in legislation. One may question the wisdom of including such a provision in the Model Law, particularly where very different approaches are apparent in practice. However, given the strong tradition of arbitration in UNCITRAL and in international dispute resolution generally, and the absence of private sessions in determinative

[104] For an examination of these two approaches, see Chapter 6. Notably the only formal comment submitted by Australia's National Alternative Dispute Resolution Advisory Council (NADRAC) in relation to a draft of the Model Law argued for the adoption of the in-confidence model: *Letter from NADRAC to UNCITRAL* (2000).

[105] See *Report of the United Nations Commission on International Trade Law on its thirty-fourth session* (21 June – 1 May 2001) UN Doc N° A/CN.9/487, para 131.

processes, the Working Group considered it useful to include provisions on private sessions in order to clarify their applicability to, and appropriateness in, conciliation. As Article 8 is a default provision, parties may agree to deal with private sessions differently, for example by adopting the in-confidence model described above.

The term *information* is not defined in Article 8. The Guide to Enactment suggests that it refers to information received in a variety of forms, including verbally in face-to-face private sessions or by tele-conference and in written form by email or letters addressed to the conciliator. Importantly Article 8 refers to the 'the substance of that information', highlighting the fact that conciliators do not always communicate the literal content of information received from the parties; rather they use the information in different ways to help parties move towards settlement.[106] It was suggested during drafting that the phrase 'substance of that information' be replaced with 'that information'. However the Commission noted in its Report that the current text,

> was preferable to avoid burdening the conciliator with an obligation to communicate the literal content of any information received from the parties.[107]

It would seem therefore that information in Article 8 MLICC is to be interpreted broadly.[108] Enacting states desirous of removing any doubt about its meaning would be wise follow other legal instruments such as the UMA which define equivalent terms. As indicated in Chapter 6, s 2(2) UMA contains a broad definition of *mediation communication* which includes verbal and written statements, conduct and actions undertaken during, and for purposes of, mediation.

Finally the application of Article 8 is limited to disclosures to the other party, presumably including their legal representative.[109] However it is conceivable that mediators may wish to disclose certain information from private sessions to other mediation participants such as experts and administrative staff. Enacting states may wish to amend Article 8 in relation to this point.

[106] See *Official Records of the General Assembly fifty-seventh Session,* Supplement N° 17 (A/57/17) at para 36 and the Guide to Enactment at para 60.

[107] *Report of the Working Group on Arbitration on the Work of its Thirty-fifth Session* (19-30 November 2001) UN Doc N° A/CN.9/506 at para 81.

[108] See the Guide to Enactment at para 60.

[109] Note that Article 10 includes a reference to administrative staff of the conciliator in relation to exceptions to insider/court confidentiality.

11. ARTICLE 9

> **Article 9: Confidentiality**
> Unless otherwise agreed by the parties, all information relating to the conciliation proceedings shall be kept confidential, except where disclosure is required under the law or for the purposes of implementation or enforcement of a settlement agreement.

Article 9 of the Model Law recognises a general duty of insider/outsider confidentiality, namely that information revealed in mediation remains confidential in relation to outsiders.[110] The duty of confidentiality is subject to a number of exceptions which are examined below. It attaches to 'all information relating to the conciliation', irrespective of who has the information and may wish to disclose it.[111]Article 9 reflects a broad understanding of information and is said to include information relating to the conciliation disclosed prior to the proceedings, such as the decision to conciliate and choice of conciliators, the terms of the agreement to conciliate and information disclosed during conciliation proceedings. In addition the Guide to Enactment suggests that Article 9 would cover the result of a conciliation,[112] but this is by no means clear. While Article 14 UCR specifically extends confidentiality to the settlement agreement, Article 9 does not, raising the question whether the Model Law provision covers:

- the settlement agreement;
- the substance of the result of conciliation proceedings; and/or
- the fact of whether or not there was a settlement.

The seemingly broad confidentiality protection afforded by Article 9 of the Model Law is subject to two exceptions. The first relates to the situation where disclosure is required by law and the second permits disclosure where it is

[110] For an explanation of insider/outsider confidentiality, see Chapter 6.

[111] Note Binder's criticism of the fact that Article 9 of the MLICC, unlike Article 14 of the UCR upon which it is based, does not have an express addressee. He notes the concern voiced in the Working Group that mediation participants and mediators could conceivably take part in a conciliation, and unaware that it is covered by the Model Law, inadvertently violate Article 9. He suggests that it might have been worth clarifying that the provision applies to those in possession of information who are also aware that they are in a conciliation to which the Model Law applies: Binder (2005), above note 3 at para 10-065. However it is unclear why ignorance of the application of the Model Law would exclude application of the provision. See Chapter 6 for a discussion of insider/outsider confidentiality provisions, some of which, like Article 9 of the MLICC, do not have an express addressee.

[112] See the Guide to Enactment at para 61.

required for the purposes of implementation or enforcement of a settlement agreement.

In relation to the first exception the Working Group refrained from listing examples of disclosures required by law out of concern that they might be interpreted as an exhaustive list. Instead UNCITRAL provides a list of examples in the Guide to Enactment.[113] They include:

- an obligation to disclose evidence of a criminal offence, for example, fraud;
- where there is a threat that a person will suffer death or substantial bodily harm if the information is not disclosed; and
- where laws require disclosure in the public interest, for example to prevent a safety, health or environmental threat.

As explained in Chapter 6, identifying exceptions to confidentiality involves balancing various interests related to maintaining the integrity of the mediation process, encouraging out of court settlements and addressing policy interests such as access to, and the administration of, justice. As public policy differs according to legal system and culture, this is a challenging area for unification and standardisation initiatives. However a non-exhaustive list of exceptions may have served as a useful indicator of the drafters' intention in relation to how extensively they wished the exception to be interpreted.

The second exception ensures that parties seeking to enforce or set aside a mediated agreement are not prevented from disclosing information from the mediation in order to enforce their claim. The exception is found in numerous laws and institutional rules[114] and is considered in Chapters 6 and 7.

In relation to establishing a breach of Article 9, the Guide to Enactment refers to the drafters' intention, namely that regard is to be had to the intention of the conciliating parties, their understanding of the nature of the process in which they are involved and their expectations regarding confidentiality.[115] Enacting states seeking to establish guidelines in this regard may consider incorporating these factors into their legislation. Furthermore the consequences of breaching the confidentiality duty contained in Article 9 are not addressed in the provision itself or elsewhere in the Model Law. Accordingly these matters fall to be regulated by the law of the enacting state.

The default nature of Article 9 allows the parties to agree to another arrangement as regards insider/outsider confidentiality. This aspect of Article 9

113 See the Guide to Enactment at para 63.

114 See, for example, s 6(b) of the UMA and Article 7(1)(b) of the European Directive on Mediation as discussed in Chapter 6 and Article 7(1) of the ADR Rules of the ICC.

115 See the Guide to Enactment at para 63 and also the New Zealand case of *Acorn Farms Ltd v Schnuriger* [2003] 3 NZLR 121 at 128–129 in relation to parties' understandings of the process in which they are engaged.

is comparable with provision 1122 of the Californian Evidence Code, save that in the latter provision the conciliator must agree with the parties to deviations from the default duty of confidentiality.[116] As with the majority of provisions in the Model Law, this provision is not mandatory by virtue of Article 3. Therefore the express proviso in Article 9, 'unless otherwise agreed by the parties' seems unnecessary and potentially confusing.

The foregoing discussion has shown that Article 9 is a complex provision due to the broad nature of its exceptions and the uncertainty it raises regarding consequences of breach. Enacting states may therefore consider the following suggestions in relation to Article 9 Model Law:

- inclusion in the legislative text of a non-exhaustive list of examples of the first exception;
- inclusion in the legislative text of consequences of breach, for example whether it provides a ground for challenging the mediated agreement; and
- clarification in the legislative text of the intention of the drafters regarding interpretation of this article.

12. ARTICLE 10

Article 10: Admissibility of evidence in other proceedings

1. A party to the conciliation proceedings, the conciliator and any third person, including those involved in the administration of the conciliation proceedings, shall not in arbitral, judicial or similar proceedings rely on, introduce as evidence or give testimony or evidence regarding any of the following:
   a. An invitation by a party to engage in conciliation proceedings or the fact that a party was willing to participate in conciliation proceedings;
   b. Views expressed or suggestions made by a party in the conciliation in respect of a possible settlement of the dispute;
   c. Statements or admissions made by a party in the course of the conciliation proceedings;
   d. Proposals made by the conciliator;
   e. The fact that a party had indicated its willingness to accept a proposal for settlement made by the conciliator;
   f. A document prepared solely for purposes of the conciliation proceedings.
2. Paragraph 1 of this Article applies irrespective of the form of the information or evidence referred to therein.
3. The disclosure of the information referred to in paragraph 1 of this article shall not be ordered by an arbitral tribunal, court or other competent

[116] See ss 1122(a)(1) and 1122 (b) of the Californian Evidence Code.

governmental authority and, if such information is offered as evidence in contravention of paragraph 1 of this article, that evidence shall be treated as inadmissible. Nevertheless, such information may be disclosed or admitted in evidence to the extent required under the law or for the purposes of implementation or enforcement of a settlement agreement.

4. The provisions of paragraphs 1, 2 and 3 of this article apply whether or not the arbitral, judicial or similar proceedings relate to the dispute that is or was the subject matter of the conciliation proceedings.
5. Subject to the limitations of paragraph 1 of this article, evidence that is otherwise admissible in arbitral or judicial or similar proceedings does not become inadmissible as a consequence of having been used in a conciliation.

Article 10 regulates confidentiality in relation to the use of information in discovery or evidence in subsequent proceedings of a judicial, arbitral or administrative nature. It is, at least in part, based on Article 20 of the UCR and reference will be made to this provision in the following commentary as appropriate. Generally Article 10 of the MLICC is broader in scope than Article 20 UCR. For example, Article 10(1) applies not only to the parties but also to the conciliator and other mediation participants. In addition Article 10(1) extends the notion of arbitral or judicial proceedings in Article 20 UCR to include other 'similar proceedings'. The impact of these changes is discussed below.

The different regulatory forms used in relation to mediation have been introduced in Chapter 2 and reference has been made to these in Chapter 8 in relation to the MLICC. UNCITRAL considered that Article 10 of the Model Law would be more useful to parties as a default legislative provision than as a UCR rule incorporated into an agreement to mediate for a number of reasons. First, in some jurisdictions confidentiality provisions in contracts are difficult to enforce. The interpretation of contracts is subject to domestic legal interpretation and policy which heightens unpredictability and uncertainty in an international context. Courts in some jurisdictions may not give full effect to agreements concerning the admissibility of evidence in court with the result that those agreements may be subject to court directions to hear evidence. By way of example, judges have been known to bypass such provisions and permit mediators to be called as witnesses in judicial proceedings.[117] Conversely the interpretation of legislative provisions enacting the Model Law would be subject to the principles of interpretation enshrined in Article 2 MLICC – harmonisation and uniformity. Moreover Article 10 imposes a prohibition not only on participants in subsequent proceedings wanting to use the type of information listed in Article 10(1), it also obliges courts to treat such evidence as

[117] See, for example, the view of the court *Farm Assist Limited (in liquidation) v The Secretary of State for the Environment, Food and Rural Affairs* (N° 2) [2009] EWHC 1102 (TCC) referred to in Chapter 6.

inadmissible. Finally contractual obligations of confidentiality only bind signatories to the agreement and not necessarily all participants in the conciliation. Therefore experts, witnesses, interpreters and others not signing the agreement would not be bound by it. By contrast Article 10 applies to all participants in the conciliation, including those involved in its administration, irrespective of who has signed the agreement to conciliate.

12.1 Insider/Court Confidentiality

Article 10 aims to encourage full and frank discussions and disclosures in conciliation in two ways. First it prohibits the use of information or evidence listed in Article 10(1) in subsequent arbitral, judicial or similar proceedings. Second it imposes an obligation on courts, tribunals and other government bodies not to order disclosure of the types of information referred to in Article 10(1), and insofar as any such information is tendered as evidence, to treat it as inadmissible (Article 10(3)). The court's obligation is limited by an exception found in the final sentence of Article 10(3), which is addressed below. Thus courts may deal with breaches of insider/court confidentiality by ordering that such evidence is inadmissible or applying any sanctions provided by applicable law. Section 5(b) of the UMA provides an example of a domestic law sanction, namely that the person prejudiced by the wrongful disclosure can respond to it and the person who has made the wrongful reference is precluded from claiming privilege under s 4 UMA to the extent necessary for such response.

Confidentiality obligations attach to conciliators, parties and any third person 'including those involved in the administration of the conciliation proceedings'. Thus Article 10(1) is broadly framed to maximise confidentiality protection, extending to all conciliation participants including parties, legal representatives and others who may be present in the conciliation such as experts, translators and witnesses. It specifically extends to those involved in the organisation and administration of the conciliation process such as the conciliator's staff.

In addition Article 10(1) specifies the type of mediation communications and information subject to the confidentiality obligations. Article 10(2) indicates that Article 10(1) is intended to apply broadly, irrespective of the form of information or evidence, and the Guide to Enactment states that the provision extends to written, verbal and electronic forms. Given the broad wording of Article 10(2) non-verbal conduct may also be included as in s 2(2) of the UMA. Some comments follow in relation to the list of items in Article 10(1).

Article 10(1)(a) refers to invitations 'by a party to engage in conciliation proceedings or the fact that a party was willing to participate in conciliation proceedings'. In some legal cultures such invitations may be unjustifiably interpreted as an acknowledgment of a weak case and a willingness to compromise. However such attitudes are changing, as discussed in Chapter 4. Sanders is critical of this exception arguing that it should be removed.[118] He points out that the corollary of this provision is that a party's unwillingness to participate in conciliation proceedings is not covered by the confidentiality protection of Article 10(1)(a) and may be introduced as evidence in subsequent proceedings. This is consistent with the practice in a number of jurisdictions where parties' behaviour in relation to mediation may be taken into account by courts in relation to awarding costs.[119]

Article 10(1)(b) focuses on the expression of settlement options during conciliation. A proposed amendment to this paragraph to extend its application to include views or suggestions made in respect of 'matters in dispute' in addition to 'a possible settlement of the dispute' was rejected by the Working Group.[120] However the wording of the following paragraph (c) seems to be wide enough to catch views or suggestions made about 'matters in dispute' that fall short of being categorised as suggestions for settlement.

Article 10(1)(c) refers to '[s]tatements or admissions made by a party in the course of the conciliation proceedings'. The wording is an extension of Article 20 UCR which refers only to admissions and seems to catch those statements that fall outside the scope of Article 10(1)(b), that is statements made in a conciliation which are not made directly in relation to a possible settlement. The provision also seems to capture statements that do not amount to admissions in addition to statements and admissions contained in documents which have not been prepared solely for the purposes of conciliation and which therefore fall short of Article 10(1)(f) below.

Article 10(1)(d) refers to '[p]roposals made by the conciliator'. These need not necessarily be proposals for settlement but they must be made by the conciliator and not another participant. In addition to settlement proposals, proposals may be made in relation to the merits of the parties' respective legal cases and dispute resolution strategies.

In Article 10(1)(e) '[t]he fact that a party had indicated its willingness to accept a proposal for settlement made by the conciliator' could been seen as a sign of admission or fault and therefore will not be admissible as evidence in subsequent proceedings. It is not clear why Article 10(1)(e) is limited to proposals made by conciliators. However it is possible that all responses to a proposal made by a participant other than in response to the conciliator are

118 See Sanders (2004), above note 5 at 223.

119 On costs sanctions for unreasonable refusal to consider or participate in mediation, see Chapter 7.

120 See the discussion of the Working Group on this point: *Report of the Working Group on Arbitration on the work of its thirty-fourth session* (21 June – 1 May 2001) UN Doc N° A/CN.9/487 at 38–39 para 141, see para 139 for draft text of proposed amendment.

captured by Article 10(1)(b) above. Unwillingness to accept an offer made in the context of conciliation is not excluded from evidence under Article 10(1)(e).[121]

Article 10(1)(f) excludes from evidence and testimony in other proceedings documents 'prepared solely for purposes of the conciliation proceedings'. These may include statements of the parties, witness statements and expert opinions. The sole purpose test identified in this provision reflects the strictest approach to the issue. According to this approach documents prepared primarily but not only for mediation are not covered by confidentiality protection and are thus admissible as evidence in subsequent proceedings. However in jurisdictions such as Australia[122] where a dominant purpose test is used, such documents fall within the insider/outsider confidentiality protection and are therefore not admissible as evidence in court or arbitration.

Neither the Guide nor the published records of the Working Group offer an explanation of the reasons behind the choice of the above list of items. However an indication may be found in the explanatory notes to the draft version of Article 20 UCR[123] from which the list is drawn. Here reference is made to the public policy tension discussed in relation to Article 9 MLICC above – the attempt to balance two potentially conflicting needs: on one hand, the need for evidentiary protection in order to encourage parties to engage in full and frank settlement discussions and, on the other, the need to acknowledge public policy interests that might outweigh the reasons behind Article 10 protection. The explanatory notes to the draft UCR provision highlight that it is the potentially prejudicial nature of the listed items to one or other party that justified their exclusion from subsequent proceedings. This may be a useful standard for courts to apply in determining whether a potential item of evidence falls within the scope of Article 10(1) MLICC.

121 For an example where refusal to accept an offer in mediation was taken into account by a court in awarding costs see *Earl of Malmesbury v Strutt and Parker* [2008] EWHC 424 (QB) referred to in Chapter 5.

122 See Evidence Act 1995 (Cth) ss 118–120 in relation to the dominant purpose test. Section 118 provides that '[e]vidence is not to be adduced if, on objection by a client, the court finds that adducing the evidence would result in disclosure of: (c) the contents of a confidential document (whether delivered or not) prepared by the client, lawyer or another person; for the dominant purpose of the lawyer, or one or more of the lawyers, providing legal advice to the client'. Section 120 contains a virtually identical provision in relation to unrepresented parties. See also s 131(1)(b) which states that '[e]vidence is not to be adduced of [...] (b) a document (whether delivered or not) that has been prepared *in connection with* an attempt to negotiate a settlement of a dispute.' [Emphasis added].

123 In its draft form, Article 20 UCR was Article 27 Draft Conciliation Rules, 10 *Yearbook of the United Nations Commission on Trade Law* (1979) 89 at 93 and 100, paras 73–77 at www.uncitral.org/pdf/english/yearbooks/yb-1979-e/yb_1979_e.pdf.

12.2 Implications of the Default Nature of Article 10

By virtue of the fact that Article 10 is a default provision,[124] parties have the ability to opt out of the provision and, if they wish, to enter different contractual arrangements as to admissibility of evidence in other proceedings. They do not require the consent of the mediator or any other participants such as witnesses or experts. As such parties have the ability to affect others' rights in relation to admissible evidence and testimony in subsequent proceedings. It is therefore imperative that conciliators and other participants are aware of what arrangements parties have made in relation to this important evidential issue so they can prepare themselves accordingly.

As discussed previously there appears to be a presumption in relation to multi-party disputes that all parties must agree in order to exclude or vary any provisions of the Model Law. This raises a potentially complex practice issue where some parties wish to opt out of or vary Article 10 as to the extent to which differentiated arrangements may be negotiated in relation to confidentiality and evidential matters. Future practice arrangements will provide resolution to this issue.

12.3 Exceptions to the Confidentiality Provisions of Article 10

As indicated above Article 10(3) prohibits courts from ordering disclosure of information and admitting evidence and testimony identified in Article 10(1). The final sentence of Article 10(3) provides two exceptions to the prohibition: first 'such information may be disclosed or admitted in evidence to the extent required under the law' and secondly disclosure or admission is permitted for the 'purposes of implementation or enforcement of a settlement agreement.' Both exceptions are couched in similar terms to Article 9 of the Model Law.

In relation to the first exception Sekolec and Getty point out that the reasoning behind such a generally-worded exception is to accommodate differences in national public policy and culture.[125] However as indicated in relation to Article 9 it can also pose challenges for uniformity and harmonisation of laws and practice. The competing interests relevant to identifying exceptions to confidentiality have been examined in various parts of this book and referred to in relation to Article 9.[126]

124 The Working Group's consideration of the question as to whether Article 10 should be mandatory or not can be found in the *Report of the Working Group on Arbitration on the Work of its Thirty-fifth Session* (19-30 November 2001) UN Doc N° A/CN.9/506 at 29 para 102.

125 See Sekolec and Getty (2003), above note 11 at 189.

126 See Chapter 6 on this point.

The Guide to Enactment emphasises the need for compelling reasons of public policy to override the otherwise inadmissible nature of the evidence identified in Article 10(1) and provides the following examples:[127]

1. the need to disclose threats made by a participant to inflict bodily harm or unlawful loss or damage;
2. where a participant attempts to use the conciliation to plan or commit a crime;
3. where evidence is needed to establish or disprove an allegation of professional misconduct based on the conduct occurring during a conciliation;
4. where evidence is needed in a proceeding in which fraud or duress is in issue regarding the validity or enforceability of an agreement reached by the parties; or
5. where statements made during a conciliation show a significant threat to *public* health or safety.

These items are similar to those found in the UMA.[128] There are, however, a number of differences. Generally the Guide to Enactment suggestions are framed more broadly, and items 4 and 5 above do not appear in the UMA. However the UMA includes other exceptions, namely a settlement agreement signed by the parties, mediation communications made during an open mediation session and information that is available to non-participants under freedom of information or similar legislation. Enacting states may consider including in their legislative text a list of items such as that found in the Guide to Enactment or the UMA.[129]

The Guide to Enactment states that the term *law* in the phrase 'to the extent required under the law' is intended to refer to statute law and does not include court orders for disclosure on the basis that they form part of case law. However certain types of court orders derive from legislation and arguably fall into the definition of legislatively-based law. Court orders based on legislative policy imperatives such as protecting public safety and orders based on the law of criminal procedure and accompanied by criminal sanctions for non-compliance may fall into a legislative category. The extent to which enacting states implement the inferred intentions of the drafter remains to be seen and will depend on their legal tradition, understandings of law and canons of interpretation.

[127] See the Guide to Enactment at para 71.

[128] See the discussion of ss 5(c), 6(a) and 6(b)(2) of the UMA discussed in Chapter 6.

[129] See, for example, Ginkel's redrafting of the Model Law which identifies a non-exhaustive list of situations where disclosure is required by law: Ginkel (2004), above note 4 at 62 (recommended Article 15).

The second exception is well-recognised in other legal instruments such as s 6(b)(2) of the UMA and has been examined with reference to case law in Chapter 7. As discussed previously most litigation about mediation involves enforcement issues.

12.4 Evidence Otherwise Admissible

Article 10(5) aims to prevent abuse of the conciliation process by preventing parties using the system to hide information or evidence that would otherwise be admissible.

The general principle is that use of existing admissible evidence in the context of a conciliation does not result in its prohibition from use or make it otherwise inadmissible in subsequent proceedings. As explained in Chapter 6, where a document was admissible in court proceedings before conciliation it is still admissible post conciliation and producing the document in the conciliation does not make it inadmissible. Similarly information that forms the basis for a suggestion made or view expressed in mediation and which was admissible before the mediation remains admissible after the process is completed, even though the views expressed in mediation may be inadmissible in subsequent proceedings under the terms of Article 10(1) MLICC.[130]

In terms of drafting, the previous paragraph Article 10(4), which defines *dispute* broadly for the purposes of confidentiality protection, expressly extends to the first three paragraphs of Article 10 but not to 10(5). However the latter provision seems to have the benefit of Article 10(4) by virtue of its being 'subject to the limitations of paragraph 1 of this article'. In order to remove any doubt on the matter, enacting states may wish to amend the wording of Article 10(4) so that is expressly extends to Article 10(5).

12.5 Documents Already Privileged

Whereas the previous section dealt with the admissibility of otherwise admissible evidence, this paragraph deals with the status of otherwise privileged documents. Where documents are privileged independently of the conciliation, the question may arise as to how their use in conciliation proceedings affects the privileged nature of the information. The types of documents under consideration could include legal opinions on the merits of a party's case produced before mediation was contemplated and covered by legal professional privilege.[131] Generally parties do not waive their rights to privilege simply by using privileged information in conciliation. To do otherwise would discourage engagement in the process. However where there is uncertainty on this point in

[130] See the Guide to Enactment at para 73.
[131] On legal professional privilege, see Chapter 6.

domestic law, enacting states may consider inserting a provision to preserve the privileged nature of such information when used in conciliation.[132]

12.6 Subsequent Proceedings

The phrase 'similar proceedings' in Article 10(1) suggests that in addition to court and arbitration, other proceedings such as administrative proceedings, discovery and depositions belong to the types of proceedings in which mediation evidence or testimony is inadmissible. This point may be significant in jurisdictions such as the United States where evidence gathering procedures may not be covered by the term judicial proceedings.[133] Consider the following example: A mediation between Nicaraguan and American parties takes place in Nicaragua. The law of Nicaragua is applicable to the conciliation. The matter does not settle at mediation whereupon the American party institutes proceedings in the United States, a country well-known for pre-trial discovery mechanisms. According to the applicable Nicaraguan law (Article 10(5) of the Model Law) evidence otherwise admissible in arbitral, judicial or similar proceedings does not become inadmissible because it was introduced in conciliation. However Article 10(5) does not mention discovery proceedings explicitly. Unless discovery proceedings can be said to fall within the definition of 'similar proceedings' in Article 10(5), evidence that is otherwise discoverable could conceivably become 'undiscoverable' by virtue of the fact that it has been introduced into mediation. Enacting states concerned about the interpretation of Article 10(5) in this regard may wish to expressly include discovery proceedings in the provision.

Article 10(4) provides that paragraphs 1, 2 and 3 apply irrespective of whether or not the arbitral, judicial or similar proceedings apply to the 'dispute that is or was the subject matter of the conciliation proceedings'. This paragraph was introduced to prevent parties circumventing the operation of Article 10 by arguing that the dispute subject of judicial, arbitral or similar proceedings involves different primary legal issues from that in the conciliation. This type of argumentation has found favour in a limited number of court decisions. However it is not consistent with leading judicial and academic opinion which suggests that insider/court confidentiality should extend to subsequent proceedings related to the mediated dispute.[134] In addition the use of present and past tense – 'the dispute that *is* or *was* the subject matter of the conciliation proceedings'[135]– leaves no doubt that concurrent and subsequent proceedings fall within the scope of Article 10(4). Thus if mediation has been suspended

[132] See the Guide to Enactment at para 74.

[133] See the Guide to Enactment at para 64.

[134] See, for example, L Boulle, *Mediation: Principles, Process, Practice* (Sydney: Lexis Nexis 2005) at 543.

[135] Emphasis added to quote.

rather than terminated or if, as in the French *med–arb simultanés* referred to previously, the arbitration or part of it runs parallel to the mediation process, the provisions of Article 10 still apply.[136]

13. ARTICLE 11

Article 11: Termination of conciliation proceedings

The conciliation proceedings are terminated:

a. By the conclusion of a settlement agreement by the parties, on the date of the agreement;
b. By a declaration of the conciliator, after consultation with the parties, to the effect that further efforts at conciliation are no longer justified, on the date of the declaration;
c. By a declaration of the parties addressed to the conciliator to the effect that the conciliation proceedings are terminated, on the date of the declaration; or
d. By a declaration of a party to the other party or parties and the conciliator, if appointed, to the effect that the conciliation proceedings are terminated, on the date of the declaration.

Article 11 provides for termination of a conciliation. It outlines how conciliations can be terminated and identifies the date on which termination is effective. The provision is important for a number of reasons. Where, for example, the relevant litigation limitation period has been suspended for the duration of a mediation, the date of termination of the mediation is necessary to determine the date of recommencement of the limitation period.[137] The date of termination is also necessary to identify the end of the period during which the confidentiality protection of Articles 8 to 10 apply.[138]

Mediations can end in several ways and these are outlined in Article 11 MLICC. The paragraphs in Article 11 are similar to those in many institutional rules found in Appendix B.[139] Article 11(a) refers to a situation where the conciliation results in a settlement of the dispute. It uses the term *conclusion,* rather than *signing,* of a settlement agreement[140] in order to accommodate electronic and other forms of settlement which may not involve signatures. Here the date of the agreement is identified as the date of termination of a mediation.

136 See also Article 11 on this point.

137 On litigation limitation periods, see Chapter 7 and the discussion on optional Article X above.

138 Note however that on some views confidentiality provisions may apply prior to commencement of conciliation.

139 See, for example, the ADR Rules of the ICC Articles 6(1) and 6(2) and the LCIA Mediation Procedure Articles 6 and 19.

140 Emphasis added.

Article 11(b) deals with termination by the conciliator in consultation with the parties where further conciliation efforts are not justified, presumably on the basis that there is no reasonable likelihood of settlement. It seems that the Working Group intended that Article 11(b) would also cover abandonment of the mediation implied by the parties' conduct where a conciliator attempts to contact parties to consult about the future of the conciliation proceedings and receives no response.[141] Articles 11(c) and 11(d) deal with termination by both parties or one party. In the absence of an agreement by parties to the contrary, Article 11(d) permits a party no longer wishing to comply with a dispute resolution clause to avoid participation by addressing a declaration to the other party and conciliator to the effect that the conciliation proceedings are terminated. It seems that if the enforceability of a mediation clause is ever questioned the party disputing enforceability needs only invoke Article 11(d) by issuing a declaration. As indicated earlier in relation to Article 6 MLICC the primary principle of party autonomy in the Model Law effectively means that parties are not required to attend an initial mediation meeting.

In Articles 11(b) to 11(d) the date of the relevant termination is the date of the declaration. Article 11 does not deal specifically with circumstances in which there is only partial settlement of the dispute, although this may be covered by Article 11(b) with respect to outstanding issues.[142]

There is no formal writing requirement for a declaration of termination referred to in Article 11. However it would seem preferable to put the declaration in writing, especially where it affects the running of litigation limitation periods. Accordingly enacting states may wish to specify a written form for termination in Article 11.

14. ARTICLE 12

> **Article 12: Conciliator acting as arbitrator**
> Unless otherwise agreed by the parties, the conciliator shall not act as an arbitrator in respect of a dispute that was or is the subject of the conciliation proceedings or in respect of another dispute that has arisen from the same contract or legal relationship or any related contract or legal relationship.

[141] See the Guide to Enactment at para 75 and *Official Records of the General Assembly fifty-seventh Session,* Supplement N° 17 (A/57/17) at para 169. Compare s 1125(5) of the California Evidence Code which deals inter alia with the situation where '[f]or 10 calendar days, there is no communication between the mediator and any of the parties to the mediation relating to the dispute.' However the section does not specifically mention mediator attempts to contact parties.

[142] See s 1125(5) of the California Evidence Code which deals with the situation where there is a partial settlement of the dispute.

Article 12 deals with situations where mediation does not result in full settlement of disputes and a question arises as to whether a mediator can or should move into the arbitrator's role. This may include MDR procedures such as med–arb as well as decisions to arbitrate made during mediation as it becomes clear that parties are unlikely to reach agreement on all issues. Essentially Article 12 prohibits conciliators from acting as arbitrators in relation to the mediated dispute or related ones, unless parties agree otherwise.

The tension of dual conciliator and arbitrator roles has been canvassed elsewhere in the book and can be summarised as follows.[143] The nature of information passed to arbitrators is generally more restricted than that to which mediators are privy especially where private mediation sessions are held. As a result parties may be less likely to engage in open and constructive settlement discussions where they know their conciliator may subsequently act as arbitrator. In addition questions of natural justice may arise where arbitrators have been privy to one party's confidential information during the private sessions of the mediation.

The scope of Article 12 is very broad and there are two aspects to it. First, consistent with Article 10(4) MLICC discussed previously, the provision applies to past and ongoing conciliations. This point is clear from the wording of Article 12 which states that: 'a conciliator shall not act as an arbitrator in respect of a dispute that *was* or *is* the subject of the conciliation proceedings […]'[144]

Second, again consistent with Article 10(4) MLICC, the prohibition in Article 12 on a conciliator subsequently acting as arbitrator is not limited to the same dispute. It extends to other disputes arising from the same or a related contract or legal relationship. In other words disputes legally distinct but closely related in a factual or commercial sense fall within the scope of Article 12. The Guide to Enactment points out that the reference to 'another dispute' was intended by the Commission to include parties other than those in the conciliation proceedings.

The broad scope of Article 12 aims to give parties a sense of certainty and security when participating in conciliation, so they feel free to engage in full and frank discussions without fear that a conciliator will subsequently assume an arbitrator role and impose a decision on the parties in the form of an award. In addition Article 12 reinforces the principles of insider/court confidentiality articulated in Article 10. Even though Article 10 creates an inadmissibility bar for certain types of mediation communications and information, what is said and done in mediation remains in the mind of the conciliator turned arbitrator and no legal rule can remove it. As indicated previously, this situation can contribute to parties feeling anxious about what and how they contribute to the conciliation. In addition, the presumption against the dual conciliator–arbitrator role in

143 On the dual role of mediator and arbitrator, see Chapters 1 and 3.
144 Emphasis added to quote.

Article 10 gives conciliation a better chance because it is less tempting to move directly into arbitration in circumstances where the conciliation is proving difficult.

As pointed out in relation to Article 9, the express provision in Article 12 that parties may agree to allow conciliators to arbitrate is strictly speaking unnecessary as Article 12 is a default provision by virtue of Article 3. However this wording may reflect the fact that the Working Group wished to expressly recognise a diversity of practice in relation to the issue and the ability of parties to appoint the same person as mediator and arbitrator.[145] Some parties may see the prior knowledge of a conciliator as a distinct advantage when arbitrating and it may cut down the length and possibly the formality of arbitration proceedings and increase its efficiency.[146]

As indicated in Chapter 1 the practice of arbitrators attempting to facilitate settlement before delivering an award is not uncommon in certain jurisdictions, such as the People's Republic of China. During the Working Group's deliberations it was suggested it would be useful to clarify that such practices are *prima facie* consistent with MLICC provisions.[147] Ultimately it was considered inappropriate to regulate the role of an arbitrator in a model law on conciliation and the MLICA was viewed as a more appropriate text to regulate this aspect of an arbitrator's role.[148] In any event Article 1(9) excludes application of the Model Law from cases where *inter alia* an arbitrator engages in conciliation in the course of arbitral proceedings.

Finally the Guide to Enactment indicates that an earlier draft of Article 12 also precluded conciliators from acting as party representatives, subject to the parties agreeing otherwise.[149] This was removed out of concern about its impact on the ethical professional rules of lawyers in enacting states.[150] However Article 19 of the UCR includes such a provision and some commentators are critical of this omission in the Model Law, especially given the default nature of Article 12.[151]

145 See, however, the practice note for arbitrators to exercise caution before suggesting or taking part in a conciliation relating to the dispute: *The UNCITRAL Notes on Organising Arbitral Proceedings* (Vienna: United Nations 1996) at para 47.

146 See the Guide to Enactment at para 79.

147 See the *Settlement of commercial disputes, Model legislative provisions on international commercial conciliation: Note by the Secretariat* (19–30 November 2001) UN Doc N° A/CN.9/WG.II/WP.115 at para 44.

148 See *Report of the United Nations Commission on International Trade Law on its thirty-fifth session* (19-30 November 2001) UN Doc N° A/CN.9/506 at para 132 and UN Doc N° A/CN.9/514 at para 73.

149 See the Guide to Enactment at para 82.

150 See *Report of the United Nations Commission on International Trade Law on its thirty-fifth session* (19-30 November 2001) UN Doc N° A/CN.9/506 at para 117 and UN Doc N° A/CN.9/514 at para 74.

151 See, for example, Sanders (2004), above note 5 at 228–229.

15. ARTICLE 13

> **Article 13: Resort to arbitral or judicial proceedings**
> Where the parties have agreed to conciliate and have expressly undertaken not to initiate during a specified period of time or until a specified event has occurred arbitral or judicial proceedings with respect to an existing or future dispute, such an undertaking shall be given effect by the arbitral tribunal or the court until the terms of the undertaking have been complied with, except to the extent necessary for a party, in its opinion, to preserve its rights. Initiation of such proceedings is not of itself to be regarded as a waiver of the agreement to conciliate or as a termination of the conciliation proceedings.

Article 13 deals with parties' ability to initiate arbitral or court proceedings in respect of a dispute, the subject of conciliation proceedings. *Prima facie* parties have the right to institute arbitral or judicial proceedings at any time they desire, irrespective of current or future conciliation proceedings relating to the same dispute. Article 13 refers to a situation where parties have agreed not to initiate arbitral or court proceedings pending conciliation. These agreements have been referred to in the book as mediation clauses and agreements to mediate.[152] They provide that a court must give effect to parties' agreements by staying arbitral or court proceedings 'except to the extent necessary for a party, in its opinion, to preserve its rights.'

In addition to recognising the *prima facie* enforceability of parties' agreements regarding mediation, the rationale of Article 13 supports the notion that initiation of arbitral or judicial proceedings may have negative impacts on conciliation proceedings in terms of parties' willingness to engage in good faith and in a collaborative spirit. Where the spectre of imminent determinative proceedings looms, parties may be more reluctant to disclose information about their interests, needs and goals than where such proceedings have not yet been initiated. Referring to this last point, Sanders compares Article 13 MLICC with the equivalent provision in the UCR which prohibits the institution of proceedings 'during the conciliation proceedings'.[153] He queries the necessity of the requirement in Article 13 for an agreement to mediate and an express undertaking by the parties not to initiate arbitral or judicial proceedings according to the terms of Article 13, arguing that all conciliations would benefit from a prohibition on the initiation of arbitration or litigation.[154] However given the broad nature of the exception to Article 13 outlined below, Sander's suggestion may have little practical impact.

[152] See Chapter 4 for an examination of the law relating to mediation clauses and agreements to mediate.
[153] See Article 16 UCR.
[154] See Sanders (2004), above note 5 at 230.

To fall within the scope of Article 13 parties' agreements must meet the following criteria. First they must specify conciliation as the dispute resolution method to be used prior to initiation of arbitral or judicial proceedings in respect of existing or future disputes. In many dispute resolution clauses conciliation is identified as the initial dispute resolution process in parties' agreement. However it is conceivable that an agreement may require parties to first attempt to negotiate a settlement in good faith before moving into structured dispute resolution procedures such as conciliation followed by arbitration.[155] The reference to existing or future disputes indicates that the provision includes in its scope both pre-dispute and post-dispute agreements to conciliate.

Second, the parties' agreement must expressly undertake not to initiate arbitral or court proceedings either (1) during a specified period of time, or (2) until a specified event has occurred. An example of the specification of a particular event to trigger the ability to initiate arbitral or judicial proceedings is found in ICC ADR Rules where a mediation must have commenced and all parties must have attended at least one meeting with a mediator.

The exception in Article 13 permits parties to bring relevant actions when they consider it necessary to preserve their rights. For example, a party may seek interim measures such as an injunction pending the outcome of a conciliation or to avoid expiration of a limitation period.[156] Article 12 makes clear that bringing an arbitral or court action does not in itself amount to a waiver of parties' agreement to mediate or a termination of mediation. Here the assumption is that parties are acting in good faith. However where one party is of the view that the other is stalling or not adequately participating in conciliation proceedings they may terminate the mediation in accordance with Article 11 and arbitral or judicial proceedings could then be initiated.

The exception in Article 13 has been criticised as being too broad and subjective and being open to misuse by parties not genuinely seeking to preserve rights they feel would otherwise be jeopardised. Ginkel suggests that an exception based on a more objective test such as 'to the extent [...] reasonably necessary to preserve its rights' would have injected Article 13 with greater rigour and provided parties to conciliation proceedings with more predictability and certainty.[157]

It is important to note the relationship between Article 13 and the optional Article X contained in the footnote to Article 4.[158] If Article X is incorporated into a Model Law text by an enacting state the operation of the applicable limitation statute would automatically be suspended on commencement of conciliation proceedings. This would go some way towards

[155] See Appendix A for samples of dispute resolution clauses and Chapter 4 on dispute resolution clauses generally.

[156] See the Guide to Enactment at para 85.

[157] See Ginkel (2004) above note 4 at 55.

[158] See the previous discussion in this chapter on the optional Article X.

preserving parties' rights, but it would not remove the need for Article 13. There would continue to be situations where parties might want to preserve rights in ways not covered by the operation of limitations statutes, for example in relation to placement of a caveat or lien on property or assets the subject of the dispute.

As discussed previously in relation to other Model Law provisions that regulate the interface between the legal system and the mediation process,[159] Article 13 would benefit from a mandatory rather than default regulatory form.[160] Enacting states may wish to amend the provision accordingly.

16. ARTICLE 14

Article 14: Enforceability of settlement agreement[4]
If the parties conclude an agreement settling a dispute, that settlement agreement is binding and enforceable ... [*the enacting State may insert a description of the method of enforcing settlement agreements or refer to provisions governing such enforcement*].

[Footnote to Article 14]
[4] When implementing the procedure for enforcement of settlement agreements, an enacting State may consider the possibility of such a procedure being mandatory.

Article 14 deals with enforceability of mediated settlement agreements and leaves it to states to decide on legal mechanisms by which settlement agreements become binding and enforceable.[161]

Although the Working Group recognised a strong interest in a uniform approach to legal requirements for binding and enforceable settlements, it was unable to agree on a common approach and, as a matter of policy, was reluctant to interfere with the enacting states' domestic procedural law.[162] In relation to the last point, many countries, in particular civil law jurisdictions, provide mechanisms for enforceability of settlement agreements as an integral part of domestic civil procedure and the Working Group took the view that requiring such laws to be amended might discourage take-up of the Model Law.

Moreover the Working Group acknowledged the diversity of enforcement requirements and mechanisms for expedited enforcement of settlement agreements. These include agreements signed by parties and their

[159] See Articles 9, 10, 14 and optional Article X.

[160] For an explanation of the relationship of function to the mandatory–default distinction see Diagram 1 in Chapter 2 and the related discussion. See also the discussion on this point in relation to Article 3 above and in Chapter 7.

[161] On the various legal requirements for binding and enforceable mediated settlement agreements, see Chapter 7.

[162] See the Guide to Enactment at para 88.

legal advisers (deeds), agreements formalised by a notary (notarised deeds), agreements taking the form of awards and those sanctioned by a judge.[163] The various approaches of national legal jurisdictions to enforceability of settlement agreements have been explained in Chapter 7.

In an earlier draft of Article 14 four variations to the enforceability issue were considered and it is useful to address these briefly:[164]

A. The current version of the Model Law, namely that a signed settlement agreement is enforceable, leaving it to enacting states to select how enforceability is achieved.
B. That a settlement agreement is enforceable as a contract irrespective of form. Here specific form requirements are not necessary for settlement agreements to be enforceable as contracts. In terms of enforceability the contract is subject to the contract law of enacting states.
C. That parties have the option to appoint an arbitrator to convert the terms of settlement into an award. This variant is based on Article 30 of MLICA. Article 30 in conjunction with Article 31 MLICA provides a procedural framework for converting terms of settlement into awards.[165]
D. That signed settlement agreements are immediately binding and enforceable as arbitral awards. Here parties need do nothing more than sign an agreement and have the conciliator sign it also.[166]

In the case of the first two variants (called variants A and B in the draft provision) the terms of the settlement are not directly enforceable and non-compliance may result in litigation in order to achieve a directly enforceable claim.

The last two variants (variants C and D in the draft provision) reflect a practice established by Article 30 MLICA in the arbitration context. Given UNCITRAL's familiarity and experience with arbitration and the existence of an international legal framework for enforceability of arbitral awards, it is not

[163] See *UNCITRAL Working Group II (Arbitration and Conciliation) Thirty-fifth session, Note by the Secretariat* (2001) UN Doc N° A/CN.9/WG.II/WP.116 at 22 para 71. See Chapter 7 for different procedures for expedited enforcement of settlement agreements.

[164] See *UNCITRAL Working Group II (Arbitration and Conciliation) Thirty-fifth session, Note by the Secretariat* (2001) UN Doc N° A.CN.9/WG.II/WP.116 at paras 66–70.

[165] See *UNCITRAL Working Group II (Arbitration and Conciliation) Thirty-fifth session, Note by the Secretariat* (2001) UN Doc N° A.CN.9/WG.II/WP.116 at para 69.

[166] The Working Group refers to arts 30, 35 and 36 of the MLICA for guidance on the meaning of the words 'enforceable as an arbitral award': UNCITRAL, *Report of the Working Group on Arbitration on the work of its thirty-fifth session,* (19-30 November 2001) UN Doc N° A/CN.9/506 at para 43.

surprising that variants C and D focus on enforceability of settlement agreements through the mechanism of arbitral awards. These two variants provide parties to conciliated settlement agreements with higher levels of enforceability and greater uniformity than variants A and B in the sense that enforcement is procedurally unified and expedited. Once a settlement agreement takes the form of an arbitral award, the provisions of international commercial arbitration law apply.[167]

Critics of Article 14 argue that variant C or D should have been adopted so that settlement agreements could be enforceable as awards and have the benefit of the international legislative framework available to arbitration.[168] However the following challenges emerge with this option. In terms of enforcing arbitral awards one of the advantages is that the grounds for setting aside an award are more restrictive than those for setting aside a settlement agreement. As explained in Chapter 7, once a settlement has the force of an award it is no longer open to one or other party to attempt to set aside the settlement using traditional contractual defences.[169] Determinative proceedings are subject to certain legal checks and balances such as rules of evidence, natural justice and a legally-based decision from a qualified expert. This means that the process has undergone a certain level of quality assurance which justifies the limited grounds of appeal on arbitral awards and the expedited enforceability associated with them. Mediated outcomes are not subject to substantive scrutiny by an independent expert and there are no equivalent quality assurance mechanisms as in the case of arbitration.

Another potential issue concerns the applicability of the New York Convention on Arbitral Awards to settlement awards. As indicated in Chapter 7, while leading opinion affirms the Convention's applicability, this view is not universally shared. Another challenge is that certain settlement provisions may not fit well into the form of an award, for example dispute resolution clauses and matters that would not have fallen within the scope of arbitration.[170]

167 On international arbitration law, see Chapter 1.

168 See, for example, Sanders (2004), above note 5 at 234. Binder (2005), above note 3 makes a similar point at para 10–100 and Ginkel (2004), above note 4 discusses these issues at 57.

169 For the limited grounds on which awards can be set aside see Article 34 of the MLICA.

170 In the discussions of the Working Group on this issue one of the proposals was to 'adapt Article 36 of the Model Law to the characteristics of settlements reached in a conciliation. [T]he proposal was to reduce the grounds on which the recognition or enforcement of a settlement may be refused to: incapacity of a party, and violation of public policy. Non-arbitrability of a dispute was mentioned as a further possible ground for refusal to recognize or enforce a settlement.' See the *Report on the Working Group on Arbitration on the work of its thirty-second session* (20-31 March 2000) UN Doc N° A.CN9/468 at para 40.

Finally some jurisdictions require the existence of a dispute for the initiation of arbitral proceedings. Once a settlement agreement has been reached there is no longer a formal dispute and it is not possible to initiate arbitration proceedings.[171] Ginkel suggests this formalistic interpretation has not been a bar to the interpretation of Article 30(2) MLICA from which it is drawn and therefore should not be a bar to enforcing settlement agreements as awards.[172] These difficulties with variants C and D contributed significantly to the Working Group's ultimate reluctance to adopt either of them.

Therefore Article 14 places the burden of addressing the enforceability issue on enacting states, with the Model Law itself providing no guidance. While it seems likely that future amendments of the Model Law will move towards harmonisation in this area, diversity continues to dominate the current arrangements and the resulting uncertainty may discourage cross-border parties to use mediation as their dispute resolution system of choice.

Finally the footnote to Article 14 suggests that enacting states may consider making Article 14 mandatory on the basis that certainty and predictability in relation to cross-border enforcement issues is of paramount importance. As discussed previously Article 14 gives enacting states a mandate to establish legal requirements regarding this issue, which means that as between states there will be different approaches to enforceability of settlement agreements. To allow parties to vary the state-endorsed approach to enforceability in a cross-border context where there is already substantial variety seems inappropriate and could create additional confusion among parties in relation to the legal implications of their mediated outcome.[173]

171 See J Sekolec, 'International Dispute Resolution: Areas Where Further Research may be Useful' (2003) 20 *Journal of International Arbitration* 35 at 36–37.

172 See Ginkel (2004), above note 4 at 57.

173 See generally *UNCITRAL Working Group on Arbitration Thirty-third* (20 November – 1 December 2000) UN Doc N° A/CN.9/WG.II/WP.110 at paras 105–112 and *UNCITRAL Working Group on Arbitration Thirty-second session* (20 – 31 March 2000) UN Doc N° A/CN.9/WG.II/WP.108 paras 34–42.

Appendix A
Model Clauses and Agreements

The selected clauses and agreements to mediate offer a sampling of mediation precedents available through different organisations in a variety of jurisdictions. Together with other precedents they have been referred to throughout this book. No assurances are made in relation to the suitability or legal validity of the following clauses.

1. Model Mediation Clause (NADRAC)[1]

1. If a dispute arises from or in connection with this contract, a party to the contract must not commence court or arbitration proceedings relating to the dispute unless that party has participated in a mediation in accordance with paragraphs 2, 3 and 4 of this clause. This paragraph does not apply to an application for urgent interlocutory relief.
2. A party to this contract claiming that a dispute has arisen from the contract ("*the Dispute*") must give a written notice specifying the nature of the Dispute ("*the Notice*") to the other party or parties to the contract. The parties must then participate in mediation in accordance with this clause.
3. If the parties do not agree, within seven days of receipt of the Notice (or within a longer period agreed in writing by them) on:
   a. the procedures to be adopted in a mediation of the Dispute; and
   b. the timetable for all the steps in those procedures; and
   c. the identity and fees of the mediator; then, the [independent appointment body or person][2] will appoint a mediator accredited under the National Mediator Accreditation System, determine the mediator's fees and the parties will pay those fees equally.
4. If the mediator is appointed by [independent appointment body or person] in accordance with paragraph 3, the parties must mediate the Dispute:
   a. in good faith; and
   b. in accordance with the Practice Standards articulated in the National Mediator Accreditation System
5. If a party commences proceedings relating to the Dispute other than for urgent interlocutory relief, that party must consent to orders by the Court in which the proceedings are commenced that:

1 National Alternative Dispute Resolution Advisory Board (NADRAC), 'Model ADR Clauses for Contracts' in 46th Council Meeting (Sydney: Attorney-General's Department, 2009) 37–41 at 40, Copyright Commonwealth of Australia, reproduced with permission. At the time of writing this clause is under discussion at NADRAC and it may be subject to amendment. NADRAC acknowledges the assistance of the Law Society of NSW in the drafting of this clause. The clause is based on the precedent clause prepared for the Law Society of NSW and published on their web site www.lawsociety.com.au.

2 Note the independent appointment body could be a Recognised Mediator Accreditation Body. For a list of such bodies see www.nadrac.gov.au.

a. the proceedings relating to the Dispute be referred to mediation by a mediator; and
b. if the parties do not agree on a mediator within seven days of the order referred to in paragraph 4.1, the mediator appointed by the [independent appointment body or person] will be deemed to have been appointed by the Court.

6. If a party:
   a. refuses to participate in a mediation of the Dispute to which it earlier agreed; or
   b. refuses to comply with paragraph 5 of this clause, a notice having been served in accordance with paragraph 2; then,
      i. that party shall not take any steps to recover its costs whether by way of obtaining or enforcing any order for costs, and,
      ii. that party shall consent to an order of a Court of competent jurisdiction that it will specifically perform and carry into execution paragraph 3 and 4 of this clause.

2. Mediation Agreement (JAMS International ADR Center)[3]

I. Participants and Procedure

The parties and if they desire, their representatives are invited to attend mediation sessions. No one else may attend without the permission of the parties and the consent of the mediator.

During the session, the mediator may have joint and separate meetings with the parties and their counsel. If a party informs the mediator that information is being conveyed to the mediator in confidence, the mediator will not disclose the information. The parties agree that the mediator is not acting as an attorney or providing legal advice on behalf of any party.

If a party wishes to terminate its participation for any reason, it may do so by giving notice to the mediator and the other parties. The parties will continue to be bound by the confidentiality provisions of this agreement and will also continue to be bound by their agreement to pay for those services rendered up to the point of that party's withdrawal.

[3] Reprinted with permission. Copyright 2009 JAMS International ADR Center (United States and Europe). All rights reserved. Mediation agreements are referred to as agreements to mediate in Chapter 4.

II. Disclosure

The mediator, each party and counsel confirm that they have disclosed any past or present relationship or other information that a reasonable person would believe could influence the mediator's impartiality and that no conflict of interest or appearance of a conflict of interest exists.

In addition, the mediator practices in association with JAMS International ADR Center. From time to time, JAMS International ADR Center may enter into arrangements with corporations (including insurance companies), government entities and other organizations to make available dispute resolution professionals in a particular locale, for a specific type of matter or training, or for a particular period of time. Also, because of the nature and size of JAMS International ADR Center, the parties should assume that one or more of the other neutrals who practice with JAMS International ADR Center may have participated in an arbitration, mediation or other dispute resolution proceeding with the parties, counsel or insurers in this case and may do so in the future. Furthermore, the parties should be aware that each JAMS International ADR Center neutral, including the neutral in this case, has an economic interest in the overall financial success of JAMS International ADR Center. The mediator is not aware of any aspect of these relationships that would create a conflict or interfere with his/her acting as a mediator in this matter. The parties acknowledge that these factors do not constitute a conflict of interest or the appearance of a conflict of interest.

III. Confidentiality

In order to promote communication among the parties, counsel and the mediator and to facilitate settlement of the dispute, each of the undersigned agrees that the entire mediation process is confidential. All statements made during the course of the mediation are privileged settlement discussions and are made without prejudice to any party's legal position and are inadmissible for any purpose in any legal proceeding. These offers, promises, conduct and statements (a) will not be disclosed to third parties except persons associated with the participants in the process and (b) are privileged and inadmissible for any purposes.

IV. Disqualification of Mediator and Exclusion of Liability

Each party agrees to make no attempt to compel the mediator's or any JAMS International ADR Center employee's testimony, nor to compel the mediator or any JAMS International ADR Center employee to produce any document provided by the other party to the mediator or to JAMS International ADR Center. The parties agree that neither the mediator nor JAMS International ADR Center is a necessary party in any arbitral or judicial proceeding relating to the mediation or to the subject matter of the mediation. Neither JAMS International ADR Center nor its employees or agents, including the mediator, shall be liable to any party for any act or omission in connection with any mediation conducted under this Agreement.

V. Records

Any documents provided to the mediator by the parties will be destroyed by JAMS International ADR Center 60 days after the conclusion of the mediation, unless JAMS International ADR Center is otherwise instructed by the parties.

VI. Fees

The parties and their attorneys agree to pay JAMS International ADR Center as set forth in the attached Fee Schedule, which is incorporated in this Agreement.

BY: ____________________ BY: ____________________

FOR: ____________________ FOR: ____________________

DATED: ____________________ DATED: ____________________

BY: ____________________ BY: ____________________

FOR: ____________________ FOR: ____________________

DATED: ____________________ DATED: ____________________

DATED: ____________________
JAMS [Mediator]

3. MODEL MEDIATION AGREEMENT (CEDR)[4]

This Agreement dated ______________ is made between

Party A

____________________________ of ____________________________

Party B

____________________________ of ____________________________

(together referred to as 'the Parties')

The Mediator

____________________________ of ____________________________

(a term which includes any agreed Assistant Mediator)

and

CEDR Solve of IDCR, 70 Fleet Street, London EC4Y 1EU

in relation to a mediation to be held

on ____

at ____

('the Mediation')

concerning a dispute between the Parties in relation to

____

____

____

____

('the Dispute')

It is agreed by those signing this Agreement that:

The Mediation

1. The Parties agree to attempt in good faith to settle the Dispute at the Mediation. All signing this Agreement agree that the Mediation will be conducted in accordance with its terms and consistent with the CEDR

[4] Centre for Effective Dispute Resolution (CEDR), England. The 10th edition of this model mediation agreement is reprinted with permission from CEDR. Updates available at www.cedr.com. Mediation agreements are referred to as agreements to mediate in Chapter 4.

Solve Model Mediation Procedure and the CEDR Code of Conduct for Mediators current at the date of this Agreement.

Authority and Status

2. The person signing this Agreement on behalf of each Party warrants having authority to bind that Party and all other persons present on that Party's behalf at the Mediation to observe the terms of this Agreement and also having authority to bind that Party to the terms of any settlement.
3. The Mediator is an independent contractor and not an agent of CEDR Solve and neither the Mediator nor CEDR Solve is an agent for any of the Parties in relation to the Dispute or this Agreement.
4. Neither the Mediator nor CEDR Solve shall be liable to the Parties for any act or omission in relation to the Mediation unless the act or omission is proved to have been fraudulent or involved wilful misconduct.

Confidentiality and Without Prejudice Status

5. Every person involved in the Mediation:
   5.1 will keep confidential all information arising out of or in connection with the Mediation, including the fact and terms of any settlement, but not including the fact that the Mediation is to take place or has taken place or where disclosure is required by law to implement or to enforce terms of settlement; and
   5.2 acknowledges that all such information passing between the Parties, the Mediator and CEDR Solve, however communicated, is agreed to be without prejudice to any Party's legal position and may not be produced as evidence or disclosed to any judge, arbitrator or other decision-maker in any legal or other formal process, except where otherwise disclosable in law.
6. Where a Party privately discloses to the Mediator any information in confidence before, during or after the Mediation, the Mediator will not disclose that information to any other Party or person without the consent of the Party disclosing it, unless required by law to make disclosure.
7. The Parties will not call the Mediator or any employee or consultant of CEDR Solve as a witness, nor require them to produce in evidence any records or notes relating to the Mediation, in any litigation, arbitration or other formal process arising from or in connection with the Dispute

and the Mediation; nor will the Mediator nor any CEDR Solve employee or consultant act or agree to act as a witness, expert, arbitrator or consultant in any such process.

8. No verbatim recording or transcript of the mediation will be made in any form.

Settlement Formalities

9. No terms of settlement reached at the Mediation will be legally binding until set out in writing and signed by or on behalf of each of the Parties.

Fees and Costs of the Mediation

10. The Parties will be responsible for the fees and expenses of CEDR Solve and the Mediator ("the Mediation Fees") in accordance with CEDR Solve's Terms and Conditions of Business current at the date of this Agreement.
11. Unless otherwise agreed by the Parties and CEDR Solve in writing, each Party agrees to share the Mediation Fees equally and also to bear its own legal and other costs and expenses of preparing for and attending the Mediation ("each Party's Legal Costs") prior to the Mediation. However, each Party further agrees that any court or tribunal may treat both the Mediation Fees and each Party's Legal Costs as costs in the case in relation to any litigation or arbitration where that court or tribunal has power to assess or make orders as to costs, whether or not the Mediation results in settlement of the Dispute.

Legal Status and Effect of the Mediation

12. Any contemplated or existing litigation or arbitration in relation to the Dispute may be started or continued despite the Mediation, unless the Parties agree or a Court orders otherwise.
13. This Agreement is governed by the law of [England and Wales] and the courts of [England and Wales] shall have exclusive jurisdiction to decide any matters arising out of or in connection with this Agreement and the Mediation.
14. The referral of the dispute to the Mediation does not affect any rights that exist under Article 6 of the European Convention of Human Rights and if the Dispute does not settle through the Mediation, the Parties' right to a fair trial remains unaffected.

Changes to this Agreement

15. All agreed changes to this Agreement and/or the Model Procedure are set out as follows:

Signed

Party A: ____

Party B: ____

Mediator: ____

CEDR Solve: ____

4. Med-Arb Clause (LCIA)[5]

In the event of a dispute arising out of or relating to this contract, including any question regarding its existence, validity or termination, the parties shall first seek settlement of that dispute by mediation in accordance with the LCIA Mediation Procedure, which Procedure is deemed to be incorporated by reference into this clause.

If the dispute is not settled by mediation within [...] days of the appointment of the mediator, or such further period as the parties shall agree in writing, the dispute shall be referred to and finally resolved by arbitration under the LCIA Rules, which Rules are deemed to be incorporated by reference into this clause.

The language to be used in the mediation and in the arbitration shall be [...].

The governing law of the contract shall be the substantive law of [...].

In any arbitration commenced pursuant to this clause,

i. the number of arbitrators shall be [one/three]; and
ii. the seat, or legal place, of arbitration shall be [City and/or Country].

5 London Court of International Arbitration, England. The clause is reproduced with permission from the LCIA. Updates are available at www.lcia.org.

Appendix B
Comparative Table of International Mediation Rules

This Table compares ten sets of international mediation and ADR rules from diverse sources including a chamber of commerce, an international trade law body, and mediation and arbitration organisations. The terms mediation and conciliation follow the usage in the rules. The rules are presented in a comparative perspective using the regulatory classification model introduced in Chapter 2. As with most conceptual models, there is the potential for overlap among categories. Here the provisions are defined according to their scope and *primary* function. Thus where rules have more than one function, they are placed in their primary function category. As indicated in Chapter 2, there are four categories of functions.

1. Triggering rules have the primary function of triggering or initiating a mediation process.
2. Procedural rules deal with internal matters of an administrative nature such as commencement, termination, appointment of mediators, costs and similar procedures.
3. Standard-setting rules set out the role of the mediator, mediator accreditation requirements and standards relating to the nature and conduct of the mediation process.
4. Beneficial rules traverse the interface between the mediation process and the legal system in which it operates. Beneficial rules have a primary function to benefit or protect those with a connection to the mediation process. As such they deal with rights and obligations and include themes such as disclosure, confidentiality, liability and enforcement.

The provisions in the Comparative Table that follow are not reproduced verbatim from the relevant rules, rather they have been summarised for inclusion in the Table. The phrase 'unless otherwise agreed' and similar phrases, which appear in a number of provisions, have been omitted for the sake of brevity. As institutional rules may form the basis of parties' contractual arrangements, parties are generally free to vary them to suit their particular needs.

International Mediation Rules **Page**

1 MEDAL Member Organisations include ACB Mediation (Netherlands), ADR Center (Italy), CEDR Solve (UK), CMAP (France) and JAMS (United States).

Institutional Rule and Scope	Function			
	Triggering	Procedural	Standards	Beneficial
ADR Rules of the International Chamber of Commerce (ICC) (1.7.2001) All national or international business disputes may be referred (Art 1)	Written request to the registrar including brief statement of nature and value of dispute, copy of prior agreement, all relevant personal information and registration fee (Art 1) Where request for mediation not made jointly, party requesting mediation must send request for mediation to other party/parties (Art 1(2))	**Pre-Mediation** Where no prior agreement to use Rules, party receiving request shall advise ICC whether it agrees or declines to participate. If no response within 15 days, ADR deemed declined (Art 2B) Parties filing a request for ADR to include a non-refundable registration fee (Art 4(1)) In absence of party agreement, neutral will determine language and place of proceedings (Art 5(4)) **Appointment of Mediator** If parties jointly designate neutrals, ADR procedure shall commence. If no designation, ICC appoints neutral (Art 3(1)) Party to notify ICC of objection, with reasons, to appointed neutral within 15 days. If party raises objection, ICC to appoint another neutral (Art 3(3))	**Conduct of the Process** Parties may agree to modify Rules subject to ICC approval (Art 1) Neutral to reach agreement with parties on settlement technique to apply and ADR process to follow, with mediation to be used failing agreement (Art 5(1) and 5(2)) **Nature of the Process** Amicable settlement is desirable (Preamble) Neutral shall be guided by the principles of fairness and impartiality and by the wishes of the parties (Art 5(3))	**Good faith** Each party shall cooperate in good faith with the Neutral (Art 5(5)) **Confidentiality** Proceedings and outcome are private and confidential. Settlement agreement confidential unless law requires disclosure or disclosure necessary for enforcement (Art 7(1)) Unless legally required no documents, statements or communications on ADR proceedings shall be produced as evidence in any judicial, arbitration or other proceedings nor shall any views, admissions or indications for settlement be disclosed in subsequent proceedings (Art 7(2)) Unless required by law neutrals shall not give testimony in subsequent proceedings concerning any aspects of the ADR proceedings (Art 7(4))

Institutional Rule and Scope	Function			
	Triggering	**Procedural**	**Standards**	**Beneficial**
		Upon agreement of all parties more than one neutral may be appointed (Art 3(4))		**Disclosure** Neutral must provide ICC with CV, a statement of independence and disclose to ICC facts which may impact on impartiality. ICC is to inform parties (Art 3(2))
		Termination ADR proceedings terminated where: – parties sign settlement agreement; – neutrals notify parties that dispute will not be resolved by ADR; – after at least one meeting, one or more parties notify neutral that ADR proceedings are no longer to be pursued; – the time limit set for ADR proceedings expires without any extension; – parties notify ICC not less than 15 days after due date that payments have not been made; – ICC notifies the parties that there has been a failure to designate neutrals (Art 6(1))		**Liability** No liability for the neutral or ICC (Art 7(5)) **Other proceedings** Neutral not to act in any judicial, arbitration or similar proceedings relating to the dispute whether as a judge, arbitrator, expert, representative or advisor of a party (Art 7(3))
		Neutral to immediately notify ICC of termination and ICC to confirm in writing (Art 6(2))		

Institutional Rule and Scope	Function			
	Triggering	Procedural	Standards	Beneficial
		Costs of Mediation Costs include administrative expenses and fees, covered with deposit (Art 4(2), subject to readjustment where necessary (4(3)) and borne equally by all parties (4(5)). Excess payment to be reimbursed to parties upon termination (4(4)		
London Court of International Arbitration (LCIA) Mediation Procedure (1.10.1999) Any agreement providing for mediation of existing or future disputes under the rules of the LCIA (Preamble)	Written request to the registrar including brief statement of nature and value of dispute, copy of prior agreement, all relevant personal information and registration fee (Art 1) Where request for mediation not made jointly, party requesting mediation must	**Pre-Mediation** Where no prior agreement to mediate under LCIA procedure, party receiving request shall advise Registrar within 14 days of agreement or refusal to mediate. If no response, mediation will not proceed (Art 2(3) and 2(4)) Parties to provide background of dispute and issues to be resolved in writing to mediator at least 7 days prior to mediation. Parties shall attach relevant documentation and copies of documents shall be submitted to the other parties (Art 4) **Appointment of Mediators** LCIA appoints mediators after receipt of request, with regard to nominations	**Conduct of the Process** Mediators to conduct mediation in a manner they see fit considering the circumstances and wishes of the parties (Art 5(1)) Mediator may meet parties jointly or individually and determine venue of meetings (Art 5(2)) Mediator to decide language in which mediation to be conducted (Art 5(6))	**Confidentiality** Process, statements and documents shall be confidential and covered by without prejudice or negotiation privilege (Art 10(2)) Unless required by law no disclosure to outside parties will be made regarding the mediation, any settlement terms or the outcome (Art 10(3)) Parties shall not present as evidence in any arbitral/judicial proceedings, any documents or other information produced for or arising in relation to the mediation, unless that information would otherwise be admissible (Art 10(4))

Institutional Rule and Scope	Function			
	Triggering	**Procedural**	**Standards**	**Beneficial**
	send request for mediation to other party/parties (Art 1(2))	or selection criteria suggested by parties (Art 1(4) and Art 2(5))	Parties to notify mediators of the number and identity of persons who will attend meetings (Art 5(4)) and those who have authority to settle dispute (Art 5(5))	No formal record of mediation (Art 10(5))
		Parties may object where doubts of mediator's impartiality or independence exists. LCIA shall appoint a new mediator (Art 3(2))		Express consent of party making a communication to mediator in private session is required for mediator to repeat to other party (Art 5(3))
		Commencement Where prior agreement to mediate, date of commencement is date registrar receives request (Art 1(5)) Where no prior agreement, date of commencement is date registrar receives an agreement from other party (Art 2(6))	**Nature of the Process** Mediation sessions shall be private and only to be attended by mediators, the parties and explicitly authorised persons (Art 10(1))	No party may seek to make the LCIA, the LCIA Court, the registrar, any deputy registrar, or the mediator a witness in any legal or other proceedings arising out of the mediation (Art 11(2))
		Termination Mediation ends where – Parties sign settlement agreement; – Parties advise mediator settlement cannot be reached and that they wish to terminate mediation; – Mediator advises parties that mediation will not resolve the dispute;	**Role of the Mediator** At the request of the parties the mediator can assist with drawing up of the settlement agreement (Art 7(1))	**Disclosure** Mediators furnish the registrar with a written résumé of past and present professional positions and sign a declaration of independence and impartiality. Copies provided to the parties (Art 3(1))

Institutional Rule and Scope	Function			
	Triggering	**Procedural**	**Standards**	**Beneficial**
		– Time limit for mediation has expired and there has been no extension agreed to (Art 6) **Costs of Mediation** The costs include the mediator's fees/ expenses and LCIA administrative charges and are paid equally by the parties (Art 8(1) and 8(2)). Parties are to file a deposit after commencement to be paid in equal shares (Art 8(3)) At conclusion of mediation costs to be fixed. Where deposit exceeds costs, parties to be reimbursed (Art 8(5) and 8(6))		**Liability** No liability for LCIA, the LCIA Court, the Registrar and mediators except for conscious and deliberate wrong doing (Art 11(1)) **Legally binding settlement** Agreed terms of settlement to be set out in settlement agreement and signed by parties (Art 7(1)) By doing so, the parties agree to be bound by its terms (Art 7(2)) **Other proceedings** Parties may continue or initiate arbitration or other judicial proceedings (Art 9)
MEDAL (The International Mediation Services Alliance) International Mediation Rules	Filing of submission or written request for mediation with a MEDAL Member Organisation	**Pre-Mediation** Where no prior agreement to mediate, party receiving invite from MMO at other party's request must reply within 30 days (Art 3) Parties can request to refer mediation to another MEDAL member country (Art 17)	**Conduct of the Process** Parties may agree to vary rules in writing (Art 1) Mediator may conduct mediation as considers appropriate having regard to circumstances	**Confidentiality** All information, admissions made, proposals, views, records, reports or other documents provided to any MMO in connection with the initiation of the mediation or produced in the mediation will be confidential and will not be introduced as

Institutional Rule and Scope	Function			
	Triggering	Procedural	Standards	Beneficial
(06.11.2005) **MEDAL Member Organisations include ACB Mediation (Netherlands) ADR Center (Italy) CEDR Solve (UK) CMAP (France) JAMS (United States)** Any dispute where the parties have agreed that the rules shall apply (Art 1)	(MMO) (Art 2) Request for mediation should contain brief statement of nature of the dispute, contact information of all parties and the counsel, if any, who will represent them in the mediation (Art 4)	Mediator to fix time and date of mediation (Art 8) **Appointment of Mediator** If parties have not jointly notified MMO of their choice MMO will provide parties with list of ≥3 persons considered appropriate for the mediation. Parties then choose 1 mediator from list (Art 5) MMO to have regard of the following when considering appropriateness of mediators; nationalities of parties, language of mediation, place of mediation, substantive expertise of mediators, availability and any known conflict of interests (Art 5) Where mediator for any reason unable to act MMO may in consultation with parties appoint alternative mediator from list previously provided (Art 6) **Termination** Mediation will terminate when a Party withdraws from the mediation and	of case, wishes of parties and need for speedy settlement (Art 9) Party can select representatives if they have authority to settle (Art 7) Party may withdraw from the mediation at any time and must inform mediator and other representatives in writing (Art 19) **Nature of the Process** Mediation sessions are private (Art 10) **Mediators Role** Mediator does not have power to impose settlement (Art 9)	evidence in any arbitral/judicial proceeding (Art 11) Mediator cannot be forced to testify in regard to mediation in any adversarial proceedings or judicial forum (Art 11) The parties and everyone present at the mediation -including counsel and experts- will maintain the confidentiality of the mediation (Art 11) Exceptions to confidentiality requirements include consent of the parties to disclosure, mediator required to disclose under law or mediator reasonably considers there is a serious risk of significant harm to life or safety of any person, or serious risk of being subject to criminal proceedings, unless information in question is disclosed (Art 11)

Institutional Rule and Scope	Function			
	Triggering	Procedural	Standards	Beneficial
		informs mediator and others in writing, mediator withdraws from mediation, or a written settlement agreement is concluded (Art 19) **Costs of Mediation** Costs of mediation divided equally among/between parties (Art 14)	Mediator is authorised to conduct joint/separate meetings, and where requested by all parties in writing may make oral and written recom-mendations concerning resolution of the dispute (Art 9) The mediator may adjourn the mediation to allow parties to consider specific proposals, to get further information or for any other reason, which the mediator considers helpful in furthering the mediation process. The mediation will then reconvene with the agreement of the parties (Art 19) Mediator to interpret and apply rules which relate	**Disclosure** Mediators must disclose any financial or personal interest in the outcome of the mediation in addition to any conflict of interest (apparent/potential/actual) in mediation (Art 6) **Liability** Neither mediator, MMO, employee or consultant will be liable for any act or omission in connection with any mediation (Art 12) **Legally-binding settlement** Settlement will not be legally binding until reduced to writing and signed by parties (Art 20) **Other proceedings** Mediator cannot act as arbitrator or representative of party in any arbitral or judicial proceedings relat-ing to dispute which is the subject of mediation without consent of parties (Art 15)

Institutional Rule and Scope	Function			
	Triggering	**Procedural**	**Standards**	**Beneficial**
			to mediator's rules and responsibilities. All other procedure interpreted and applied by MMO administering mediation (Art 13)	Parties undertake not to initiate during mediation any arbitral or judicial proceedings in respect of dispute except where necessary to comply with limitations periods or to preserve rights in event mediation is unsuccessful (Art 16) **Applicable law** Mediation governed by laws of MMO administering mediation. Courts of that MMO have exclusive jurisdiction to settle claim (Art 18)
Netherlands Mediation Institute (NMI) Mediation Rules (2008) The Rules shall apply to the mediation to which the parties have	Parties wanting assistance of NMI in selecting a mediator must make a written request detailing names of parties, representatives and issues to be dealt with (Art 2(2))	**Pre-Mediation** Mediation will commence as soon as the mediation agreement has been signed by the parties (Art 3) **Appointment of mediator** Parties shall appoint mediator (Art 2(1)) If parties cannot agree, parties may then choose mediator from NMI list of mediators sent to them and upon acceptance of instruction by mediator sign a mediation	**Conduct of Process** Mediator is to decide after consulting with parties of how mediation is to be conducted (Art 4(2)) Parties may deviate from NMI rules provided there is agreement in writing and explicit consent of mediator (Art 14)	**Confidentiality** Parties are not to disclose to any third party (including courts and arbitrators) any information concerning the progress of the mediation (Art 7(1)) or documents revealed, shown, quoted from, or paraphrased by, any party involved in mediation (unless party had documents at its disposal independently of mediation) (Art 7(2). Applies to mediation *mutatis mutandis* (Art 7(3))

Institutional Rule and Scope	Function			
	Triggering	**Procedural**	**Standards**	**Beneficial**
committed themselves by the signing of the mediation agreement (Art 3 together with Art 1(c) that provides the definition of mediation)	Mediator will draw up Mediation Agreement once accepts instructions (Art 2(6))	agreement (Art 2) **Termination** Parties and mediator can terminate mediation at any time (Art 5) by: – signing settlement agreement; – written statement from mediator to parties stating mediation has ended; – written statement from either party withdrawing from the mediation (Art 8)	**Nature of Process** Parties and mediator shall ensure mediation proceeds in expeditious manner (Art 4(4)) Mediation is voluntary (Art 5(1)) **Mediators Role** Mediator may communicate with parties separately and confidentially (Art 4(3)) Mediator bound by Rules of Conduct for NMI registered mediators and subject to complaints scheme and disciplinary rules in accordance with the Rules (Art 12)	Parties waive right to use anything which transpired during mediation in evidence and cannot cause mediator or others to act as witnesses for any information supplied/recorded or agreement made during mediation (Art 7(4)) Information supplied to mediator during separate talks with parties shall be treated by the mediator as confidential (Art 7(5)) Provisions 7(1) – 7(5) will not apply where there is information regarding a criminal act (where there is statutory obligation to report), a threat of a crime or complaints/disciplinary proceedings against mediator (Art 7(6)) Parties may lodge a complaint within 12 months of termination of mediation (Art 12)

Institutional Rule and Scope	Function			
	Triggering	**Procedural**	**Standards**	**Beneficial**
				The content of the written agreement may be submitted in court if necessary in order to claim compliance with agreement (Art 10(3)) **Liability** Mediator not liable for contents of the recorded mediation agreement (Art 10(2)) Parties to indemnify mediator from third party claims, except in cases of international act or gross negligence. Mediator liability limited according to professional indemnity insurance (Art 11) **Legally binding settlement** Parties bound only by terms of an agreement set down in writing and signed by both parties, and are responsible for these terms. (Art 5(2) & Art 10(1)). Parties not bound by positions adopted or proposals made during mediation. Interim agreements only binding if written and signed. (Art 5(2)

Institutional Rule and Scope	Function			
	Triggering	**Procedural**	**Standards**	**Beneficial**
				Other proceedings Parties cannot institute proceedings regarding mediation issues for duration of mediation and any legal proceedings already commenced shall be stayed (except if necessary to safeguard rights) (Art 9) **Applicable law** The rules shall be governed by Dutch Law
Permanent Court of Arbitration **(PCA) Optional Conciliation Rules (1.7.1996)** Disputes arising out of contractual legal relationships	Party initiating conciliation sends written invitation to other party to conciliate under PCA Rules (Art 2(1))	**Pre-Conciliation** Proceedings commence where party accepts an invitation to conciliate (Art 2(2)) Where no response received to conciliation invitation within 30 days, party initiating proceedings may elect to treat as a rejection (Art 2(4)) Parties to submit to conciliator and other party written statement describing dispute and issues. Mediator can request further clarification (Art 5)	**Conduct of Process** Parties may agree to exclude or vary any of the rules at any time (Art 1(2)) Conciliator to conduct conciliation in such a manner as considered appropriate having regard to circumstances of case, wishes of parties and special need for speedy settlement of dispute (Art 7(3))	**Good faith** Parties to participate in good faith (Art 11) **Confidentiality** Conciliator must disclose substance of factual information received from one party to another party except where information given with specific condition that it be kept confidential (Art 10) All matters relating to the conciliation procedure including the settlement agreement shall be

Institutional Rule and Scope	Function			
	Triggering	Procedural	Standards	Beneficial
or other circumstances where parties have agreed PCA Rules apply (Art 1)		**Appointment of conciliator** 1 conciliator – parties agree 2 conciliators – parties select one each 3 conciliators – parties select one each and then agree on 3rd (Art 4(1)) Parties may seek assistance of institution/person or Secretary General of PCA in recommending or appointing conciliators (Art 4(2) and Art 4(3)) In recommending or appointing conciliators such considerations as are likely to secure an independent and impartial conciliator are to be had (including nationality of conciliator v parties) (Art 4) **Termination** Mediation is terminated by: – signing of a settlement agreement by parties; – written declaration of the conciliators after consultation with parties that conciliation efforts are no longer justified;	Parties may be represented by persons of their choice and are to be communicated to conciliator and other party. Must clarify whether there for purpose of representation or assistance (Art 6) Each party may submit to conciliator suggestions for settlement of dispute (Art 12) Any settlement agreement reached is to be reduced to writing and signed by both parties. Conciliator can assist in drawing up the written settlement agreement (Art 13(2)) Parties/conciliator may request administrative assistance of suitable institution/person or	kept confidential unless disclosure is necessary for purposes of implementation and enforcement (Art 14) Parties cannot use proposals, admissions, views or suggestions made during conciliation as evidence in judicial or arbitral proceedings (Art 20) **Legally binding settlement** Parties by signing settlement agreement are bound by the contents (Art 13(3)) **Other proceedings** Parties undertake not to initiate any arbitral or judicial proceedings in respect of a dispute that is subject to conciliation except where necessary to preserve legal rights (Art 16) Conciliator cannot act as arbitrator, representative, witness or counsel of a party in any arbitral or judicial

Institutional Rule and Scope	Function			
	Triggering	Procedural	Standards	Beneficial
		– written declaration of the parties to the conciliator that proceedings are terminated; – written declaration of one party to the other and conciliators that the proceedings are terminated (Art 15) **Costs of Conciliation** Upon termination of conciliation the conciliator fixes costs and gives notice to parties. Costs to be borne equally by parties (Art 17) Costs include conciliator fee and travel expenses, witness travel expenses, costs of expert advice required by conciliator, cost of assistance provided (Art 17) Conciliator may request each party pay equal deposit (Art 18)	International Bureau of PCA (Art 8) **Role of Conciliator** Conciliator to assist parties in an independent and impartial manner (Art 7(1)) Conciliator to be guided by principles of objectivity, fairness and justice (Art 7(2)) Conciliator may make proposals for settlement (Art 7(4)) Conciliator may communicate with parties jointly or separately (Art 9) **Nature of Process** Voluntary process with flexible procedures, integrated dispute resolution system (Introduction)	proceedings in respect of dispute (Art 19)

Institutional Rule and Scope	Function			
	Triggering	**Procedural**	**Standards**	**Beneficial**
Mediation Rules of the Mediation Institute of the Stockholm Chamber of Commerce (1.4.1999) Domestic and international disputes may be referred (Foreword, Art 15)	Written request for mediation including a summary of the dispute, contact information and a statement whether parties have agreed to mediate the dispute as well as upfront payment of the registration fee (Art 4 and Art 5)	**Pre-Mediation** Where one party submits request, agreement by other party shall be communicated to the Institute (Art 4(2) **Appointment of Mediator** Mediator appointed by the Institute in consultation with parties (Art 6) Where mediator unable to fulfil duties and functions new mediator is appointed (Art 7) **Termination** Mediation to be finished within 2 months of the date of referral, period may be extended (Art 11(1)) Mediation is terminated where there is a: – settlement agreement between the parties; – a declaration of mediators that further efforts are unlikely to lead to resolution; – written request by a party to terminate proceedings (Art 11)	**Conduct of Process** Mediator shall determine conduct of mediation, with view for reaching an expeditious and efficient resolution, giving consideration to parties wishes (Art 10(1)) Each party given sufficient time to present case (Art 10(2)) Where dispute not likely to be resolved mediator may propose alternative means for resolving dispute (Art 10(3)) **Mediator's Role** Mediator must be impartial and independent (Art 1(1))	**Confidentiality** Mediators, the Institute, the parties and any other persons involved in the mediation shall respect the confidentiality of the mediation (Art 3(1)) Any submissions, documents or other materials supplied during the mediation shall be returned to the party having provided it without any copy being retained (Art 3(2)), and notes taken during the mediation shall be destroyed (Art 3(3)) Party cannot introduce as evidence in any judicial/arbitration proceeding any views, statements made during mediation. Mediator and any experts involved in mediation cannot be called as witnesses (Art 3(4)) **Disclosure** Mediator must disclose in writing to the parties any circumstances which give rise to justifiable doubts regarding impartiality and independence (Art 2)

Institutional Rule and Scope	Function			
	Triggering	**Procedural**	**Standards**	**Beneficial**
		Costs of Mediation SCC Mediation shall fix Advance of Costs (Deposit) to be paid in equal shares by parties (Art 8). If no payment is made, dispute to be dismissed (Art 8(5)) Costs include mediator's fee, administrative fee of Institute and compensation due to cover expenses incurred in course of mediation (Art 13) Parties jointly and severally liable for mediation costs and bear mediation costs in equal shares (Art 14)		**Legally Binding Settlement** Upon reaching a settlement agreement the parties may, subject to the approval of the mediator, agree to appoint the mediator as an arbitrator and request him to confirm the settlement agreement in an arbitral award (Art 12) **Other proceedings** Mediator cannot act as arbitrator in any future arbitration relating to the dispute (Art 1(2))
UNCITRAL Conciliation Rules (UCR) (23.7.1980) Disputes arising out of contractual legal relationships	Initiating party sends other party written invitation to conciliate under the rules briefly identifying subject of the dispute (Art 2(1))	**Pre-Conciliation** Proceedings commence where party accepts an invitation to conciliate (Art 2(2)) Where no response received to conciliation invitation within 30 days, party initiating proceedings may elect to treat as a rejection (Art 2(4))	**Conduct of Process** Parties may agree to vary or exclude rules at any time (Art 1(2)) Conciliator to conduct conciliation having regard to circumstances of case, wishes of parties and special need for	**Good faith** Parties to participate in good faith (Art 11) **Confidentiality** Conciliator must disclose substance of factual information received from one party to another party except where information given with specific condition that it be kept

Institutional Rule and Scope	Function			
	Triggering	Procedural	Standards	Beneficial
or other circumstances where parties have agreed that the Rules apply (Art 1)		Parties to submit to conciliator and other party written statement describing dispute and issues. Mediator can request further clarification (Art 5) **Appointment of Conciliator** 1 conciliator – parties agree 2 conciliators – parties select one each 3 conciliators – parties select one each and then agree on 3rd (Art 4(1)) Parties may seek assistance of institution/person in recommending or appointing conciliators (Art 4(2)) In recommending or appointing conciliators such considerations as are likely to secure an independent and impartial conciliator are to be had (including nationality of conciliator v parties) (Art 4) Termination – signing of a settlement agreement by parties; – written declaration of the conciliators after consultation with parties that conciliation efforts are no longer justified;	speedy settlement of dispute (Art 7(3)) Parties may be represented by persons of their choice and this must be communicated to conciliator and other party. Must clarify whether there for purpose of representation or assistance (Art 6) Each party may submit to conciliator suggestions for settlement of dispute (Art 12) Any settlement agreement reached is to be written and signed by both parties. Conciliator can assist in drawing up this written settlement agreement (Art 13(2)) Parties/conciliator may request administrative	confidential (Art 10) All matters relating to the conciliation procedure including the settlement agreement shall be kept confidential unless disclosure is necessary for purposes of implementation and enforcement (Art 14) Parties cannot use proposals, admissions, views or suggestions made during conciliation as evidence in judicial or arbitral proceedings (Art 20) **Legally binding settlement** Parties by signing settlement agreement are bound by the contents (Art 13(3)) **Other proceedings** Parties undertake not to initiate any arbitral or judicial proceedings in respect of a dispute that is subject to conciliation except where necessary to preserve legal rights (Art 16)

Institutional Rule and Scope	Function			
	Triggering	Procedural	Standards	Beneficial
		– written declaration of the parties to conciliators that proceedings are terminated; – written declaration of one party to the other and conciliators that the proceedings are terminated (Art 15) **Costs of Conciliation** Upon termination the conciliator fixes costs and gives notice to parties. Costs are to be borne equally by parties (Art 17) Costs include conciliator fee and travel expenses, witness travel expenses, costs of expert advice required by conciliator, cost of assistance provided (Art 17) Conciliator may request each party pay equal deposit upon appointment as advance for costs (Art 18)	assistance of suitable institution/person (Art 8) **Role of Conciliator** Conciliator to assist parties in an independent and impartial manner (Art 7(1)) Conciliator to be guided by principles of objectivity, fairness and justice (Art 7(2)) Conciliator may make proposals for settlement (Art 7(4)) Conciliator may communicate with parties jointly or separately (Art 9)	Conciliator cannot act as arbitrator, representative, witness or counsel of a party in any arbitral of judicial proceedings in respect of dispute (Art 19)

Institutional Rule and Scope	Function			
	Triggering	Procedural	Standards	Beneficial
World Intellectual Property Organization (WIPO) Mediation Rules (1.10.2002) Applicable where a mediation agreement provides for mediation under the WIPO mediation rules (Art 2)	Party wishing to commence mediation submits a written request for mediation to the Arbitration and Mediation Center and other party (Art 3(a))	**Pre-Mediation** Request will contain details of the parties, copy of the mediation agreement and statement regarding nature of the dispute (Art 3(b)) Date of commencement of mediation is date request received by Center (Art 4) Center will inform parties of receipt of request and date of commencement (Art 5) Mediator in consultation with parties arrange for the submission by each party summarising background and status of dispute and information/documents necessary for the purpose of mediation (Art 12) **Appointment of Mediator** Mediator is appointed by Center in consultation with parties (Art 6) Center may at appointment of mediator require each party to deposit equal amount (Art 23)	**Conduct of Process** Mediation is to be conducted in manner agreed upon by parties or, in the absence of agreement, in accordance with rules (Art 9) Parties may be represented or assisted in mediations but must provide mediator and other party with names and addresses of persons authorised to represent that party and of persons attending mediation in assistance (Art 8) **Mediators Role** Mediator shall be neutral, impartial and independent (Art 7) Mediator free to meet with parties jointly or separately (Art 11)	**Good faith** Parties to cooperate in good faith to advance the mediation as expeditiously as possible (Art 10) **Confidentiality** Mediators not to disclose confidential information shared in caucus to other party unless by written authorisation (Art 12) Each person involved in mediation to sign confidentiality agreement and not to use or disclose any information obtained during mediation. After termination, documents to be returned to providing party without retaining a copy (Arts 14 to 16) Mediator is not to disclose any information arising from separate meetings with parties (Art 11) Parties/Mediator cannot use proposals, admissions or views made during mediation by the parties in any judicial or arbitral proceedings (Art 17)

Institutional Rule and Scope	Function			
	Triggering	Procedural	Standards	Beneficial
		Termination Mediation may be terminated: – signing of settlement agreement; – by the mediator where he/she considers resolution of dispute is unlikely; – by written declaration of party at any time after attending first meeting and before the signing of any settlement agreement (Art 18); – where party fails to pay deposit 15 days after 2nd reminder notice (Art 23) **Cost of Mediation** Request for mediation is subject to administration fee. Failure to pay will result in the Center not taking action on the Request for Mediation (Art 21) Center to fix fee for mediator after consultation with parties, with mediator's fees to be calculated on hourly basis taking into account complexity of dispute. Parties may be required to pay a deposit as advance for costs of mediation (Art 22(a) and 22(b))	Mediator does not have the power to impose settlement on parties but will attempt to help them reach a satisfactory resolution of their dispute (Art 13) Where dispute not likely to be resolved mediator may propose alternative means for resolving dispute (Art 13(b))	The parties and mediator agree that any statements or comments, whether written or oral, made or used by them or their representatives in preparation for or in the course of the mediation shall not be relied upon to found or maintain any action for defamation, libel, slander or any related complaint and this Article may be pleaded as a bar to any such action (Art 26) **Reporting** Mediators to inform Center on dates and modes of settlement, i.e. full or partial in order to aggregate statistical data without revealing identity of parties and circumstances of dispute (Art 19) **Liability** Except in case of deliberate wrongdoing no liability for WIPO, Center or mediator (Art 25) **Other proceedings** Unless authorised by court or parties, mediator cannot act in any

Institutional Rule and Scope	Function			
	Triggering	Procedural	Standards	Beneficial
		Costs (mediator fees, travel expense, etc) of mediation to be borne in equal shares by parties (Art 24)		capacity other than mediator in other proceedings relating to dispute (Art 20) **Limitation periods** Limitation period shall be suspended in relation to the dispute that is the subject of the mediation from the date of commencement until the date of termination of the mediation (Art 27)
International Centre for Dispute Resolution (ICDR) International Dispute Resolution Procedures – International Mediation Rules (01.03.2008)	Where prior existing agreement to mediate under ICDR, mediation can be initiated by making request for mediation to ICDR and notifying other party (Art 2) Where no prior existing agreement	**Pre-Mediation** Request will contain details of the parties, a copy of the contract, brief statement of nature of the dispute and relief requested and specific qualification the mediator is to possess (Art 2) Names of parties' representatives must be communicated to ICDR (Art 3) **Appointment of Mediator** Parties may appoint own mediator from ICDR's panel of mediators, otherwise if parties cannot agree must list names of mediators in order of preference and	**Conduct of Process** Parties may in mutual agreement vary any part of the Rules (Art 1) Parties to choose their representatives (Art 3) Mediation conducted according to principle of self-determination (Art 7(a)) Mediation conferences and related communication	**Good Faith** Parties and their representatives shall exercise their best efforts to prepare for and engage in meaningful and productive mediation (Art 8) **Confidentiality** Mediator shall maintain confidentiality of all information/documents obtained in the mediation (Art 10) Confidential information disclosed during the course of mediation shall not be divulged by mediator

Institutional Rule and Scope	Function			
	Triggering	Procedural	Standards	Beneficial
Any dispute whenever parties have agreed in writing to mediate disputes under these International Mediation Rules, or under the auspices of the ICDR, or the AAA without designating particular rules (Art 1)	exists, a party may request ICDR to invite another party to participate in mediation by 'voluntary submission' (Art 2)	ICDR will invite mediator to serve based on those selections (Art 4) Termination – By executed settlement agreement; – By written/verbal declaration of mediator that mediation will not resolve issues in dispute; – Written/verbal declaration of parties that mediation is terminated; – Where there has been no communication between mediator and any party of party's representative for 21 days (Art 12) **Costs of Mediation** Unless otherwise directed by mediator parties must deposit amount to cover costs and expenses prior to mediation. Unexpended balance will be returned to the parties (Art 15) Expenses of mediation (including expenses and charges of mediator) borne equally by parties (Art 16)	are private. Only parties, their representatives and the mediator can attend (Art 9) Parties must authorise representatives to make binding agreements (Art 8) **Role of Mediator** Mediators to abide by Model Standards of Conduct (Art 5) Mediator may hold separate sessions and communications with parties and/or representatives before, during or after mediation (Art 7(b)) Mediator has no power to impose settlement on parties but will attempt	or parties in any judicial forum or proceeding, unless agreed by parties or required by applicable law (Art 10) ICDR and Mediator cannot be compelled to divulge information or testify in regard to mediation (Art 10 and Art 13) **Disclosure** ICDR must disclose to parties any potential conflict of interest of the mediator. Party can then choose to either waive such conflict or replace the mediator (Art 5) Mediators are required to make reasonable inquiry to determine and disclose to the ICDR facts likely to affect the mediator's impartiality or create a potential or actual conflict of interest for the mediator (Art 5)

Institutional Rule and Scope	Function			
	Triggering	Procedural	Standards	Beneficial
		Cost of mediation based on hourly mediation rate published on mediator's ICDR profile. Parties billed equally for costs (Art 17)	to help them reach a satisfactory resolution of their dispute (Art 7(d)) Where complete settlement of dispute is not achieved, mediator may continue to communicate with parties to facilitate settlement (Art 7(e)) Mediator is not a legal representative of the parties and has no fiduciary duties (Art 7(f))	**Liability** ICDR and mediator not liable for any error, act or omission in connection with any mediation conducted under rules (Art 13)
CPR (International Institute for Conflict Prevention and Resolution) Mediation Procedure (01.04.1998)	CPR mediation procedure may be adopted by agreement of the parties, with or without modification, before or after a dispute has	**Pre-Mediation** Written statement to be submitted by each party at least 10 days prior to mediation summarizing background of dispute, dispute's present status, settlement efforts and other useful or mediator requested material Submission to include an analysis of party's real interests and needs and of its litigation risks (Art 5)	**Conduct of Mediation** The mediation process is non binding (Art 3(a)) The mediator shall control process aspects of the mediation (Art 3(d))	**Good Faith** The parties will cooperate fully with the mediator (Art 3(d)) **Confidentiality** The mediator will not transmit information received in confidence from any party to any other party or 3rd party without authorization

Institutional Rule and Scope	Function			
	Triggering	Procedural	Standards	Beneficial
Any agreement between the parties to adopt the CPR Mediation Procedure	arisen through a pre-dispute clause or an existing dispute submission agreement (Art 1)	**Appointment of Mediator** Mediators selected from a CPR panel of neutrals, unless parties agree otherwise. Where parties cannot agree they will notify CPR of any preferences as to mediation style, subject matter expertise and geographic location. CPR will then submit ≥3 candidates for parties to agree upon. Where parties cannot agree on candidate from list, each party within 15 days will send to CPR list of candidates *ranked in descending* order. Candidate with lowest score appointed as mediator (Art 2) Where there is a clear conflict, candidate is not proposed. Other circumstances will be disclosed to parties who may then challenge mediator candidate (Art 2) **Termination** Each party may withdraw at any time before execution of written settlement agreement by written notice to mediator and other parties (Art 3(b))	Formal rules of evidence or procedure will not apply (Art 3(d)(i)) Each party will be represented at mediation by a business executive or other person authorised to negotiate a resolution. Mediator may limit number of persons representing each party (Art 3(e)) Each party will be represented by Counsel to advise it in mediation (Art 3(f)) If any party has substantial need for documents of other party, parties with or without help of mediator shall attempt to agree thereon. Any documents exchanged to	or unless ordered to do so by court (Art 3(h)) There will be no stenographic record of any meeting (Art 3(d)(ii)) Mediator and any persons assisting mediator are disqualified as witness, consultant or expert in any pending or future proceeding relating to the mediation (Art 3(j)) **Mediation process is confidential as required by law. Parties and mediator cannot disclose any information,** documents, settlement terms, offers, promises, conduct, statements (oral/written) made during course of proceedings. Such offers, promises, conduct and statements are privileged (Art 9) Mediator and any documents/information cannot be subpoenaed in any investigation, action or proceeding (Art 9)

Institutional Rule and Scope	Function			
	Triggering	**Procedural**	**Standards**	**Beneficial**
		Mediation terminated where: – written settlement reached; – mediator concludes and informs parties that further efforts not useful; – one of parties/mediator withdraws from process (Art 6) Mediator may withdraw at anytime in writing: – For serious personal reasons; – If mediator believes party not acting in good faith; – Mediator concludes that further mediation efforts not useful (Art 3(n)) If no resolution can be reached the mediator will discuss with parties possibility of advisory/binding arbitration or another form of ADR (Art 8) **Costs of Mediation** Mediator's rate of compensation to be determined before appointment and costs are to be borne equally by the parties (Art 2)	be returned at conclusion of the mediation process (Art 4) Parties shall exchange with each other and mediator names and job titles of individuals who will attend mediation (Art 4) **Nature of the Process** Mediation will be conducted expeditiously (Art 3(g)) **Role of Mediator** The mediator shall be neutral and impartial (Art 3(c)) The mediator is free to meet and communicate separately with each party (Art 3(d)(i) and Art 6)	Mediation is subject to Federal Rule of Evidence 408, all state counterparts and any applicable statute protecting the confidentiality of mediation (Art 9) Exchange of tangible material is without prejudice to an claim that such material is privileged or protected as work-product within meaning of Federal Rule of Civil Procedure 26 and all state and local counterparts (Art 9) Evidence that is otherwise admissible or discoverable shall not be rendered inadmissible or non-discoverable solely as a result of its presentation or use during mediation (Art 9) Settlement agreement may be disclosed for purposes of enforcement (Art 9)

Institutional Rule and Scope	Function			
	Triggering	Procedural	Standards	Beneficial
		If party withdraws from multiparty mediation, withdrawing party is not responsible for any costs incurred after it has notified mediator and other parties of withdrawal (Art 2)	Parties to initiate and convey to mediator proposals for settlement and mediator may facilitate settlement as mediator believes appropriate. Mediator to help parties focus on interests, explore resolution alternatives and settlement options (Art 6) If parties do not reach agreement, mediator may submit a final settlement proposal and, if qualified, offer evaluation of likely outcome if case goes to trial (Art 6) Mediator will decide when to hold joint/ separate meetings with parties and will fix agenda in consultation with parties (Art 3(d)(i))	**Disclosure** Mediator candidate must disclose any circumstances that would cause reasonable doubt regarding candidate's impartiality (Art 2) Any person proposed as an independent expert is required to disclose any circumstances known which would cause reasonable doubt regarding person's impartiality (Art 3(l)) **Liability** No liability for CPR or mediator for any act of omission in connection with mediation except if there has been wilful misconduct (Art 3(m)) **Legally binding settlement** Parties or mediator to reduce any settlement into writing in a written settlement document incorporating all settlement terms. Agreement is to signed and parties may request the court enter the settlement agreement as a consent judgment (Art 7)

Institutional Rule and Scope	Function			
	Triggering	Procedural	Standards	Beneficial
			Mediator may obtain assistance and independent expert advice if parties agree and pay expenses (Art 3(l))	**Other Proceedings** Parties will refrain from pursuing litigation or any administrative or judicial remedies during the mediation process insofar as they do not prejudice their legal rights (Art 3(i)) If dispute goes to arbitration, mediator shall not serve as arbitrator (Art 3(k) and Art 8)

Appendix C
Comparative Table of Laws Based on the UNCITRAL Model Law on International Commercial Conciliation (2002)

The following table compares the national and state laws that have adopted the UNCITRAL Model Law on International Commercial Conciliation of 2002 (MLICC). As the Table shows, some enacting states have used the Model Law as a basis for their domestic and international mediation laws, while others have adopted it only in relation to international mediation. The Table covers those laws which have considerable similarity to the MLICC and excludes those referred to in Chapter 8 which, although possibly inspired by the Model Law, ultimately bear little resemblance to it and at best borrow one or two MLICC provisions. It analyses the selected laws from the following countries and these appear in alphabetical order: Albania, Afghanistan, Bosnia-Herzegovina (Bosnia-Herz), Canada, Croatia, Kosovo, Nicaragua, Russia, Serbia, Slovakia, Slovenia and Turkey.[1] It also examines the laws of three states of the United States, namely Washington DC, South Dakota and Utah. These states have adopted the Uniform Mediation Act of 2001 (UMA) and its amendment which incorporates the MLICC in relation to international mediation.

As indicated throughout this book the terms *mediation* and *conciliation* can be used interchangeably and the Table indicates the terminology adopted by each statute. In addition the Table identifies whether the scope of the law is restricted to commercial mediation as in the MLICC or moves beyond to include other fields of mediation. Finally the Table compares the selected laws with the MLICC by indicating on an article-by-article basis the extent to which the laws adopt the wording of the Model Law. To this end the following Table Key contains symbols used in the Table and explains their meaning. It will assist readers to recognise and understand the contents of each law both individually and from an international comparative perspective. The text of the MLICC can be found in the Chapter 9 commentary and on the UNCITRAL website. The other laws are available at www.mediationworld.net.

[1] The legal texts available in relation to Afghanistan, Russia and Turkey were in draft form at the time of writing.

Table Key to Appendix C

—	No reference to this or a similar UNCITRAL provision	**Int**	Act expressly applies to international disputes
Cls	Close: provision is very close in meaning/content to the UNCITRAL provision	**Med**	The terminology *mediation* is used in the Act
Comm	Act expressly applies to commercial disputes only	**Sim**	Similar to the UNCITRAL provision: some similarities, possibly some differences
Comm+	Act expressly applies to commercial disputes and other types of disputes, such as family law	**Vbtm**	Verbatim: provision is taken verbatim from UNCITRAL
Concil	The terminology *conciliation* is used in the Act	**Cntry**	Provision is directly contradictory to the UNCITRAL provision

	Alba-nia	Afghan-istan	Bosnia/ Herz	Canada	Croatia	Kosovo	Nicar-agua	Russia	Serbia	Slova-kia	Slov-enia	Turkey	UMA[1] (US: Washington DC, South Dakota, Utah)
Article	**Med**	**Med**	**Med**	**Med**	**Concil**	**Med**	**Med**	**Concil**	**Med**	**Med**	**Med**	**Med**	**Med**
1(1)	— Comm+	Cls	—	Cls, Int Comm	Sim, Int Comm+	Sim, Comm+	Sim Int	Int Comm+	Sim Comm+	Sim	Sim Comm+	Sim	Cls Int[2]
1(2)	—	Cls	Cls	—	Cls	Sim	Sim	Cls	Cls	Sim	Cls	Sim	Vbtm
1(3)	—	Cls	Cls	—	Cls	Sim	Vbtm	Cls	Sim	Cls	Cls	Sim	Vbtm
1(4)	—	—	—	Cls	—	—	—	—	—	—	—	—	Vbtm
1(5)	—	—	—	Cls	—	—	—	—	—	—	—	—	Vbtm
1(6)	—	—	—	—	—	—	—	—	—	—	—	—	Vbtm
1(7)	—	Vbtm	—	Cls	Sim	—	—	Cls	Cntry	—	—	—	Vbtm
1(8)	—	—	Sim	—	—	Cls	Sim	Cls	Cls	—	—	Cls	Vbtm
1(9)	—	Sim	—	Sim	Sim	—	Cntry	Cls	—	—	Cls	Sim	Vbtm
2	—	—	—	Cls	—	—	—	—	—	—	Cls	—	Vbtm
3	—	Sim	Cls	Cls	Sim	Cls	Sim	Cls	Cls	—	Cls	—	Vbtm
4(1)	Cls	Vbtm	—	Cls	Sim	Cls	Vbtm	—	Cls	Cls	Cls	Sim	Vbtm
4(2)	Cls (30 days)	Cls	—	—	Sim (15 days)	Sim (15 days)	Cls	Cls (30 days)	Sim (15 days)	Sim (14 days)	Cls	Cls (30 days)	Vbtm
5(1)	Cls	Sim	Cls	Cls	Sim	Cls	Vbtm	Sim	Sim	—	—	—	Vbtm

	Alba-nia	Afghan-istan	Bosnia/Herz	Canada	Croatia	Kosovo	Nicar-agua	Russia	Serbia	Slova-kia	Slov-enia	Turkey	**UMA**[1] (US: Washington DC, South Dakota, Utah)
Article	**Med**	**Med**	**Med**	**Med**	**Concil**	**Med**	**Med**	**Concil**	**Med**	**Med**	**Med**	**Med**	**Med**
5(2)	Cls	—	Cls	Cls	Sim	Sim	Vbtm	Cls	Cls	Cls	Cls	Cls	Vbtm
5(3)	Cls	—	Sim	Cls	Sim	—	Vbtm	Cls	Cls	—	Cls	—	Vbtm
5(4)	Cls	—	Cls	Cls	Cls	—	Vbtm	Cls	Cls	—	Cls	—	Vbtm
5(5)	Cls	Cls	Sim	Cls	Cls	Sim	Vbtm	Cls	Cls	Cls	Cls	Sim	Vbtm
6(1)	Cls	Cls	Sim	Cls	Cls	Cls	Cls	Cls	Cls	Cls	Cls	Cls	Vbtm
6(2)	Cls	Cls	—	Cls	Cls	—	Vbtm	Cls	Cls	—	Cls	Cls	Vbtm
6(3)	Cls	Cls	Cls	Cls	Cls	Cls	Vbtm	Cls	Cls	—	Cls	Sim	Vbtm
6(4)	Cls	Cls	Sim	Cls	Sim	Sim	Vbtm	—	Sim	—	Cls	Cntry	Vbtm
7	Cls	Vbtm	Cls	Cls	Sim	Cls	Vbtm	—	Cls	—	Cls	Cls	Vbtm
8	Sim	Cls	Sim	Cls	—	Sim	Vbtm	Sim	Cls	—	Cls	—	Vbtm
9	Cls	Vbtm	Sim	Cls	Cls	Sim	Vbtm	Cls	Cls	Cls	Vbtm	Sim	Cls
10(1)	Cls	Cls	Cls	Cls	Cls	Sim	Vbtm	Cls	Cls	Sim	Cls	Cls	Sim (see footnote 2)
10(1)(a)	Cls	Vbtm	—	Cls	Cls	—	Cls	Cls	Cls	—	Vbtm	Cls	—
10(1)(b)	Cls	Vbtm	Cls	Cls	Cls	—	Vbtm	Cls	Cls	—	Vbtm	Cls	—

	Alba-nia	Afghan-istan	Bosnia/ Herz	Canada	Croatia	Kosovo	Nicar-agua	Russia	Serbia	Slova-kia	Slov-enia	Turkey	UMA[1] (US: Washington DC, South Dakota, Utah)
Article	**Med**	**Med**	**Med**	**Med**	**Concil**	**Med**	**Med**	**Concil**	**Med**	**Med**	**Med**	**Med**	**Med**
10(1)(c)	Cls	Vbtm	Cls	Cls	Cls	—	Vbtm	Cls	Cls	—	Vbtm	—	—
10(1)(d)	Cls	Vbtm	—	Cls	Cls	—	Vbtm	—	Cls	—	Vbtm	—	—
10(1)(e)	Cls	Vbtm	—	Cls	Cls	—	Vbtm	Cls	Cls	—	Cls	Sim	—
10(1)(f)	Cls	Vbtm	—	Cls	Cls	—	Vbtm	Cls	Sim	—	Vbtm	Cls	—
10(2)	Cls	—	—	—	Cls	—	Vbtm	Cls	—	—	Cls	Cls	—
10(3)	Cls	Cls	—	Cls	Cls	Sim	Vbtm	—	—	—	Cls	Cls	—
10(4)	Cls	—	—	Cls	Cls	—	Vbtm	—	Cls	—	Cls	Cls	—
10(5)	Cls	Cls	—	Cls	Cls	—	Vbtm	—	—	—	Cls	Cls	—
11(a)	Cls	Vbtm	—	Cls	Cls	Cls	Cls	Cls	Cls	Cls	Vbtm	Cls	Vbtm
11(b)	Cls	Vbtm	Cls	Cls	Cls	Cls	Cls	Cls	Cls	Cls	Cls	Cls	Vbtm
11(c)	Cls	Vbtm	—	Cls	Cls	Sim	Cls	Cls	—	Cls	Cls	Cls	Vbtm
11(d)	Cls	Vbtm	Cls	—	Cls	Sim	Cls	Cls	Cls	Cls	Cls	Cls	Vbtm
12	Cls	Cls	—	Cls	Sim	—	Vbtm	Cls	Sim	—	Cls	—	Vbtm
13	Cls	Cls	—	Sim	Cls	—	Vbtm	—	—	—	Cls	—	Vbtm

	Albania	Afghanistan	Bosnia/ Herz	Canada	Croatia	Kosovo	Nicaragua	Russia	Serbia	Slovakia	Slovenia	Turkey	**UMA**[1] (US: Washington DC, South Dakota, Utah)
Article	**Med**	**Med**	**Med**	**Med**	**Concil**	**Med**	**Med**	**Concil**	**Med**	**Med**	**Med**	**Med**	**Med**
14	Cls	Cls	Cls	Cls	—	Cls	Cls	Cls	Sim (binding if filed in court)	Cls	Sim (binding if formulated as award)	Cls	Vbtm
Optional Article X	—	Vbtm	Sim	—	Cntry	—	—	—	Cntry	—	Vbtm	Cntry	—

Notes

1. The UMA entries refer to the UMA in so far as it has enacted the MLICC in relation to international mediation. Note that Illinois, Iowa, Nebraska, New Jersey, Ohio, Vermont and Washington State have adopted the UMA, but not the amendment incorporating s 11 of the MLICC.

2. The UMA incorporates the MLICC, almost verbatim, as Appendix A. Section 11 of the UMA applies the MLICC to all international commercial mediations, except where the parties exclude it in accordance with s 11(d) UMA (s 1(7) of the MLICC). The only major difference arises in s 11(c) of the UMA, which provides that '[u]nless the parties agree in accordance with s 3(c) of this [Act] that all or part of an international commercial mediation is not privileged, sections 4, 5, and 6 and any applicable definitions in section 2 of this [Act] also apply to the mediation and nothing in Article 10 of the MLICC derogates from sections 4, 5 and 6.' In other words the UMA uses its own confidentiality provisions instead of those in Article 10 of the MLICC.

Index

Global Trends in Dispute Resolution

---

1. Nadja Alexander (ed.), *Global Trends in Mediation, Second Edition* (2006 – ISBN 9789041125712).

2. Giuseppe De Palo and Mary B. Trevor (eds), *Arbitration and Mediation in the Southern Mediterranean Countries* (2007 – ISBN 9789041126849).

3. Lars Kirchhoff, *Constructive Interventions – Paradigms, Process and Practice of International Mediation* (2008 – ISBN 9789041126856).

4. Nadja Alexander, *International and Comparative Mediation: Legal Perspectives* (2009 – ISBN 9789041126849)

www.ingramcontent.com/pod-product-compliance
Lightning Source LLC
LaVergne TN
LVHW020647300926
849161LV00004B/850